Developments in Australian Politics

Edited by
Judith Brett
La Trobe University

James Gillespie
Macquarie University

Murray Goot
Macquarie University

M

Copyright © Judith Brett, James A. Gillespie, Murray Goot 1994

All rights reserved.
Except under the conditions described in the
Copyright Act 1968 of Australia and subsequent amendments,
no part of this publication may be reproduced,
stored in a retrieval system, or transmitted in any form or by any means,
electronic, mechanical, photocopying, recording or otherwise,
without the prior permission of the copyright owner.

First published 1994 by
MACMILLAN EDUCATION AUSTRALIA PTY LTD
107 Moray Street, South Melbourne 3205

Associated companies and representatives
throughout the world

National Library of Australia
cataloguing in publication data
Developments in Australian politics.

   Bibliography.
   Includes index.
   ISBN 0 7329 2010 8.
   ISBN 0 7329 2009 4 (pbk.).
   1. Australia — Politics and government — 1976–1990. 2.
   Australia — Politics and government — 1990–. I. Brett, Judith
   Margaret, 1949–. II. Gillespie, James A. (James Andrew).
   III. Goot, Murray.

320.994

Typeset in Times Roman
by Typeset Gallery, Malaysia

Printed in Hong Kong

Cover design by Sergio Fontana
Indexes by Judy Cole and Patricia Holt

Contents

List of Contributors vi
Preface viii

1 Ideology Judith Brett **1**
   Confusions 1
   The Debate about the State 3
   The Debate about Moral and Cultural Values 15
   The Debate about Economic Rationalism 19

PART I

2 Reinterpreting the Constitution A.R. Blackshield **23**
   The 'Free Speech' Cases 23
   Constitutional Foundations 24
   Parliamentary Sovereignty 29
   Appropriate and Proportionate Laws 34
   Judicial Power 42
   Implied Rights 46
   Unanswered Questions 49
   Cases 59

3 New Federalisms James A. Gillespie **60**
   Interpretations of Australian Federalism 62
   A Territorial Basis for Liberty? 69
   Federalism and the Australian State 72
   Whitlam: New Federalism and State Assertiveness 76
   The Fraser Government 79
   The Hawke Government 80
   The New Federalism, Mark III 82

4 Executive Government Geoffrey Hawker **88**
   Managerial Government Now 88
   The Australian Political Executive 89
   Sources of Change 98
   Growth of the Executive 101

iv   *Contents*

    Prime Ministerial Government   102
    Problems of Executive Government   104

5 Parliament   *Rodney Smith*   **106**
    Slow Declines and Golden Ages: Inadequate Approaches
      to Parliament   107
    The Diversity of Australian Parliamentary Politics   109
    Primary Legislation   114
    Enforcing Individual Ministerial Responsibility   119
    Responsibility and Parliamentary Scrutiny of the Bureaucracy   124
    An Aberration in the Senate?   129

6 Political Parties   *Campbell Sharman*   **132**
    The Importance of Parties   132
    The Australian Party System   134
    The Australian Labor Party   136
    The Liberal Party   141
    Smaller Parties and Independents   146

7 Class Voting, Issue Voting and Electoral Volatility
    Murray Goot   **153**
    Old Views and New   153
    Class Voting   156
    Political Issues   167
    Electoral Volatility   173

PART II

8 Aborigines: Citizens and Colonial Subjects   *Tim Rowse*   **182**
    Citizens and Colonial Subjects   182
    Culture and Nation   185
    Theories of Australian Colonialism   187
    History, Theory and Strategic Realism   197

9 Immigration and Immigrants   *Uldis Ozolins*   **202**
    The Origins of Post-war Immigration to Australia   203
    The Politics of Immigration: the 1970s   207
    The Politics of Immigration in Contemporary Australia   209

10 Economic Policy   *Greg Whitwell*   **217**
    Interest Groups and How to Deal With Them   218
    The Economist's Vision   220
    The Political Power of Economic Ideas   224
    The Historical Context of Contemporary Economic Policy   229
    The Hawke/Keating Governments and Economic Rationalism   231

11 Industry Policy   *Winton Higgins*   **234**
    The Politics of Industrialisation   235

Contents v

    The Original Sins of Australian Industrialisation   237
    Policy Networks and Industrial Fortunes   241
    The Search for an Industry Policy   243
    The Empire Strikes Back   247
    Flexible Deckchair Arrangement: A Surrogate Industry Policy   253

12 Unions, the Accord and Economic Restructuring
    Mark Bray   **259**
    The Pre-Accord Period   261
    Unions, the Accord and Economic Restructuring   266

13 Social Policy   *Deborah Brennan*   **277**
    Historical Context   279
    Social Policy Under Labor in the 1980s and 90s   287

14 Foreign Affairs and Trade   *John Ravenhill*   **299**
    Policy Formulation   300
    The New Foreign Policy Agenda   309

15 Media Policy   *Rodney Tiffen*   **322**
    The Characteristics of Media Politics   322
    The Politics of Media Ownership   327
    The Broadcasting Services Act 1992   338
    Making Media Policy   345

16 Environmental Politics   *Peter Christoff*   **348**
    Green Foundations   348
    The Australian Environmental Movement in the 1980s   353
    Electoral Interventions   356
    Environmental Conflict, Corporatism and Changing
        Policy Cultures   360
    Silent Reforms   364
    Greening Australia?   365

17 Censorship, Pornography and Sexual Politics:
    New Issues, New Conflicts   *Barbara Sullivan*   **368**
    Ideology and Sexual Politics   369
    International Trends: Sexuality, Privacy and Decriminalisation   372
    Pornography and Anti-censorship Movements in Australia   373
    Modernising Censorship and Regulating Pornography   374
    New Laws, New Freedoms   376
    New Conflicts   378

Bibliography   383
Subject index   422
Author index   438

List of Contributors

Anthony Blackshield is Professor of Law at Macquarie University and has written extensively on the Australian Constitution.

Mark Bray is Senior Lecturer in the Department of Industrial Relations at Sydney University, author of *Delivering the Goods: A History of the Transport Workers* (Allen and Unwin, 1987), and co-editor of *Economic Restructuring and Industrial Relations in Australia and New Zealand* (ACIRT, 1993).

Deborah Brennan is Senior Lecturer in Government at the University of Sydney. She is the author of *The Politics of Australian Childcare* (Cambridge University Press, 1994).

Judith Brett is Senior Lecturer in Politics at La Trobe University and the author of *Robert Menzies' Forgotten People* (Macmillan, 1992).

Peter Christoff is in the Politics Department of the University of Melbourne and was the Assistant to the Victorian Commissioner for the Environment from 1987 to 1993.

James Gillespie is Senior Lecturer in Politics at Macquarie University and the author of *The Price of Health* (Cambridge University Press, 1991).

Murray Goot is an Associate Professor of Politics at Macquarie University and Visiting Senior Research Fellow at the Australian Centre for Industrial Relations Research and Teaching, Sydney University. He is co-editor of *Australia's Gulf War* (Melbourne University Press, 1992), *Australian Opinion Polls, 1941–1990: An Index* (D.W. Thorpe, 1993) and *Make a Better Offer: The Politics of Mabo* (Pluto, 1994).

Geoffrey Hawker is a Lecturer in Politics at Macquarie University and the author of *Who's Master, Who's Servant? Reforming Bureaucracy* (Allen and Unwin, 1981).

Winton Higgins is Associate Professor of Politics at Macquarie University and co-author of *Unions and the Future of Australian Manufacturing* (Allen and Unwin, 1972).

Uldis Ozolins is Lecturer in Interpreting/Translating at Deakin University and his research interests are in immigration and ethnic policies in both Australia and the Baltic states. He is the author of

The Politics of Language in Australia (Cambridge University Press, 1993).

John Ravenhill is a Senior Fellow in the Department of International Relations, Research School of Pacific Studies, Australian National University. He has written extensively on international political economy and on Australian foreign policy. He is co-editor of *Economic Relations in the Pacific in the 1990s: Cooperation or Conflict?* (Allen and Unwin, 1993).

Tim Rowse works for the Menzies School of Health Research in Alice Springs. He is the author of *Remote Possibilities: The Aboriginal Domain and the Administrative Imagination* (NARU, 1992) and *After Mabo: Interpreting Indigenous Traditions*, Melbourne University Press 1993.

Campbell Sharman is Associate Professor of Politics at the University of Western Australia and has written numerous articles on federalism and political parties.

Rodney Smith is a Senior Lecturer in Politics at the University of New South Wales and editor of *Politics in Australia* (Allen and Unwin, 1993).

Barbara Sullivan is a Lecturer in Government at the University of Queensland.

Rod Tiffen is Senior Lecturer in Government at the University of Sydney and the author of *News and Power* (Allen and Unwin, 1989).

Greg Whitwell is Senior Lecturer in Economic History at the University of Queensland and author of *The Treasury Line* (Allen and Unwin, 1986).

Preface

In June 1992, the High Court of Australia in *Mabo and others* v. *the State of Queensland* found that the law of Australia recognises a form of native title. It found this in relation to the tiny Torres Strait island of Mer, or Murray Island as it is known to Europeans, an island most Australians would find hard to locate on a map. This judgment brought to a head tensions over European occupancy of the land mass of Australia which have been simmering since Aboriginal Australians' demands for land rights began to get some political recognition in the 1970s. These tensions have to do in part with the fear of the economic costs of land claims, through the possibility of loss of access to mining and pastoral leases, but also with the way non-Aboriginal Australians understand their past and their present; with how they explain to themselves why they are living thousands of miles from where their ancestors were born; and with how they understand what it is that links them to the other people who are also living here, on this huge continent and its offshore islands, in the middle of the southern ocean, in the last decade of the twentieth century.

In keeping with the *fin de siècle* mood of other Western nations, the dominant representation of Australia in these last years of the century is that we are at a turning point. Behind us is a relatively secure and prosperous economy, a society based on shared cultural values, and the confidence of Australia's British heritage. Ahead is an uncertain economic future, increasing social and cultural difference, and the task of securing a stable position for Australia in the changing world order. From popular to academic writing, the dominant representation of the 1980s and 90s is as a period of fundamental transition, if not transformation, from one era to another. *The Australian Economy on the Hinge of History*, *The End of Certainty*, *Reinventing Australia* and *Shutdown* are some examples of typical titles.

Some Australians see this transition as both necessary and exciting. It opens up an inward-looking society and a protected economy to the challenges of international economic competition and cosmopolitan culture. Other Australians experience it as destructive of the certainties and values on which their lives have been based, and as offering very little prospect of benefit to them in their lifetimes. This is particularly true of people unemployed as the economy restructures, but it is also true of the securely employed, who worry about the apparent breakdown of sexual morality, apparently increasing levels of violence, and whether their grandchildren will die of skin cancer from increasing levels of ultraviolet radiation. Where some see a bright open future, others fear they are being turned into anachronisms, and are unsure what to teach their children to fit them for their lives.

The closer one gets to political power, the more optimistic are the versions of Australia's future. In the ABC television documentary, *Labor in Power*, both Bob Hawke and Paul Keating talked with pride of the Labor governments' achievements in opening up the economy. Professor Ross Garnaut's extremely influential report, *Australia and the Northeast Asian Ascendancy* opens:

> This is a time of great opportunity for Australia. It is a time when Australians have a chance to grasp the prosperity, self-confidence and independence in an interdependent world...At home, the beginning of internationalisation and liberalisation of economic life in recent years has established an economic, political and intellectual base from which, for the first time this century, it is possible for Australians to seek first best policies and outcomes. (Garnaut 1989: 1)

Paul Kelly, editor-in-chief of the country's leading serious newspaper, the *Australian*, concludes his account of Australian politics in the 1980s and 90s, *The End of Certainty*, on a note of hope:

> The task of leadership now is to create a synthesis between the free market rationalism needed for a stronger economy and the social democracy which inspired the original Australian Settlement ideals of justice and egalitarianism. The end of certainty is not the end of history; it heralds the challenge to create a new history. (Kelly 1991: 686)

In contrast to such optimistic visions of Australia's future from men in power, the media in the 1980s and early 90s were full of stories of economic and social distress: of unemployment, homelessness, family breakdown and sexual violence, as well as stories of the increasing demands of work, role stresses on men and women, and the tensions and pressures of Australia's increasingly racially mixed society. Hugh Mackay's *Reinventing Australia*, subtitled 'The mind and mood of Australia in the 90s', and based on extensive interviewing, is a record of the stresses and anxieties experienced by many Australians during this period:

> Australians have entered a period of anxiety about what it means to be Australian. The redefinition of gender roles by women has

probably had more impact on the *personal* well-being of Australians than any other factor in the Age of Redefinition. The effect of unemployment has been correspondingly severe in its impact on Australians' *economic* wellbeing. But, underlying the personal and individual stresses which Australians suffer as they adapt to life in the Age of Redefinition is a widespread sense of anxiety about our *cultural* identity. (Mackay 1993: 154)

During the 1980s and early 90s Australia's political institutions were widely debated. The post-war consensus on the benefits of the welfare state continued to disintegrate under the combined impact of economic recession and fundamental questioning of the proper role of the state in a liberal democracy. The High Court moved from being regarded as a bastion of conservatism to an instigator of fundamental change, as in its controversial *Mabo* decision. Parliamentary politics became more volatile and more significant, since governments at both state and federal level were unable to rely on comfortable majorities in both houses. Parties were widely attacked as having 'lost touch' with their supporters. And the Public Service went through a series of re-organisations drawn from private sector models, those who hailed the flexibility and efficiency of the new managerialism being matched by critics who pointed to weakening notions of actual public service, as well as ministerial accountability.

This collection of essays surveys recent changes in Australia's political institutions, public policies, and political ideas and values. While it focuses on the changes of the 1980s and early 90s, contributors have placed these in a broader historical context in order to capture long-term structural developments and to isolate what, if anything, is new in recent ones. Contributors also emphasise different, sometimes competing, explanations and frameworks which have been used to make sense of these developments. In some areas, such as the environment, ideological positions have been readily apparent; in others, such as the reform of the Public Service or debates about federalism, technocratic and managerial languages have obscured wider issues of democratic control and accountability.

The collection is primarily intended as a text for tertiary courses in Australian politics and public policy. Its contemporary focus is designed to complement the more structural approach of most existing texts and readers. It is hoped, as well, that in so far as these essays offer illuminating perspectives on political developments in the 1990s, they will be of interest also to a variety of non-student readers.

Judith Brett, James Gillespie, Murray Goot

1
Ideology

JUDITH BRETT

Confusions

Ideology is a word which refers to the complex relationship between ideas, power and political action. In popular usage it is generally applied to very explicit, consciously-held political ideas which can guide action and, as is the case with Marxist-Leninism or fascism, become a basis of state policy. This meaning of ideology is closely linked with dogmatism and zealotry, with the desire to remake social and political reality on the basis of ideas. It is eschewed by those who prefer a more gradualist and pragmatic politics (Bell 1960: Epilogue). The term is always seen as negative, suggesting that 'ideas' have got in the way of 'reality', and will lead to destructive experiments in social engineering. Historically, this meaning of ideology has most often been applied to adherents of Left-wing or reforming political positions, but recently its most frequent application in Australia has been to the adherents of 'economic rationalism'. A typical example is in a comment made by the secretary of the ACTU, Bill Kelty, when launching Carroll and Manne's 1992 book *Shutdown*, which was critical of economic rationalism. Kelty said that the key to progress lay in 'a pragmatic approach' that assessed issues on their merits and particular circumstances rather than 'false ideology' (*Age*, 4 September 1992). The defeat of the Liberal Party at the 1993 election was explained by some commentators as the result of the party having eschewed its traditional pragmatism in favour of the ideology of economic rationalism. Said ex-Liberal Prime Minister Malcolm Fraser: 'The economic rationalist has this ideology and they write down all the rules and then they just apply the rules, regardless of circumstances, regardless of their impact on people' (*Age*, 3 April 1993).

The term 'ideology' can also be used in a wider sense, to refer to less consciously-held ways of thinking about society embedded in people's everyday understandings. For some writers it is a descriptive term, synonymous with political belief systems (Nevitte and Gibbins 1990: 26). For those influenced by Marx's concept of ideology (like Hall 1982), it implies that beliefs are in part based on the need to justify and understand the unequal distribution of life chances in class-divided

2 Ideology

societies. In this wider sense, all political action involves ideology, ways of seeing the world, even when the political actors claim to be acting merely on the basis of common sense.

This chapter will survey the political ideas which have been important in public political debate in Australia over the last two decades. Ideally, such a survey would cover all levels of political thought, from the well-worked-up systems of political intellectuals, through the dominant ideas held by influential bureaucrats, media personalities, businessmen and so on, to the philosophies of the political parties and the political ideas and values of the population at large. The chapter will focus, however, mainly on those ideas which have influenced the political parties and so become the main focus of public debate.

Political debate in Australia over the last two decades has clustered around two main sets of issues: the size and role of the state in regulating the economy and providing a decent life for all its citizens, and the moral and cultural values which should inform individual, family and social life. In both cases there has been a questioning of the consensus seen to hold before the early 1970s. In the first, the regulatory welfare state which developed in the post-war period has been rejected in favour of a greater role for free enterprise and the market. In the second, the moral and social values based on conservative sexual morality, a traditional gender division of labour, and white British superiority have been challenged by arguments about the injustice and oppression to which these values contributed.

Any easy labelling of the positions in these debates is difficult. Individuals can be radical on economic questions and conservative on moral ones or vice versa; they can be radical on both or conservative on both; or they can change their position over time. Compare the journalist P.P. McGuinness, who writes a regular column in the national newspaper, the *Australian*, as does former Liberal Party leader John Howard. On economic matters both could be described as radical Right, radical because they want to change the status quo, and Right because they want to change it in the direction of increasing the role of market forces in the distribution of resources in Australian society. In nineteenth-century Britain, this latter position was described as Right because it was associated with those who held power, as against those who were attempting to change society to make it more just and equal — those described as Left. On questions of social and sexual morality, however, Howard and McGuinness differ sharply. Howard is conservative, wanting to slow down the rate of change and return to the family-centred values which he associates with the 1950s. McGuinness is a libertarian, consistently arguing against government regulation in the areas of private and moral behaviour (Docker 1993).

Australia's adversarial party system adds to the difficulties of mapping the influence of particular ideas on the parties in any given period. Labour and non-labour have been the two poles around which the Australian party system has been organised since it took on its modern shape in the first decade of this century. Then the newly-formed Australian Labor Party forced the Free Traders and Protectionists to bury their differences in the interests of containing the threat of the organised working class in Parliament. In the 1920s the Country Party was formed on the non-Labor side to represent the interests of small farmers. This changed the dynamics of party electoral competition and led to the formation of coalition non-Labor governments. It did not, however, alter the fundamental opposition at the heart of the party system. This oppositional structure has remained constant to the present, and always pulls political debate into the *appearance* of conflict between two systematically opposed groups of political ideas, even when the terrain of political debate is changing rapidly and new ideas are influencing members and supporters on both sides of politics. A degree of discipline is thus imposed on people who try hard to fit their thinking into the mould of two-party conflict, and show the links between new ideas and the parties' traditions. Ideas in politics are used both to attempt to understand reality and guide political action *and* to win political advantage — which includes maintaining a clear sense of difference from opponents. It is as if in viewing the party conflict in this period one is viewing two protagonists who must continue to assert and define their differences, even as the terrain of political debate shifts rapidly beneath their feet and makes many of their old differences irrelevant. Whatever areas of agreement are revealed, the need to assert difference will remain. This is not, of course, to suggest that there may not be significant differences between the parties on particular policies, but rather that the assertion of difference should not be taken for granted.

The remainder of the chapter is structured around the two debates to which I have already referred: the debate about the relationship between the state and the economy, and the debate about social and moral values. In tracing the trajectories of both debates, the election of the Whitlam government in 1972 is a convenient starting point. It marks the end of the post-war consensus on the role of the state. The Whitlam government was the first to be influenced by political demands associated with the social movement politics of the late 1960s and early 1970s, such as the women's movement.

The Debate about the State

Historical Background
The debate about the state in Australia and in other capitalist democracies throughout the 1970s, 1980s and into the 1990s is essentially a debate about the desirable relationship between the state and society.

4 Ideology

For example, how much is the general welfare of citizens the responsibility of the state, and how much is it the responsibility of the individuals themselves? What should be the limits of the state's intervention in the lives of its citizens, and what are individuals' responsibilities to the other members of the society in which they live? What role should the state play in relation to the economy? These are not new questions; they have long been debated.

In Australia the debate about the state has in the main occurred between two traditions which can be described as 'economic liberalism' and 'social liberalism' (Beilharz, Considine and Watts 1992: 13). Both are variants of liberalism, which understands society as based on the individual and gives a paramount place to individual rights and freedoms. The political philosophy of liberalism has its origins in the struggle between the bourgeoisie and the monarchy, as an emerging capitalist economic system pushed against the remnants of feudal restriction. Liberalism's first enemy was the absolute monarchic state, which was deeply involved in the regulation of social and economic life. Thus arguments were developed to support the limitation of the role of the state in the regulation of social and economic life. The proper role of the state was to protect the country against invasion and to maintain a framework of law and order within which economic activity could take place. This minimal state is sometimes described as 'the nightwatchman state'. Economic liberalism favours market mechanisms rather than the state for the distribution of goods and services. It is underpinned by a view of human nature which sees people as naturally competitive, acquisitive and self-interested, and so best motivated by a combination of rewards and sanctions. It believes that continuing material progress will satisfy human wants and desires and so deliver human happiness and the good society (Emy 1991: 13). Economic liberalism is sometimes called *laissez-faire* liberalism, stressing its commitment to minimal state involvement in the economy and is closely associated with the principles of neo-classical political economy.

Social liberalism also begins with the individual — but a different individual from that of economic liberalism, which is motivated by competitive self-interest. It asks how society can be organised so that each of its individual members is able to develop his or her full human potential, and is critical of social arrangements which prevent many people from achieving what they might. Social liberalism was a response to the misery which capitalism's markets, particularly its labour markets, brought to many people, and to the inability of market mechanisms to deal with social problems such as poverty. Social liberalism has a quite different view of the proper role of the state from economic liberalism. It sees the state as a potential agent of reform to eliminate obstacles, such as poverty, poor health or illiteracy, which prevent individuals from developing their full human potential. Thus social liberalism requires a strong state, which is able to reform those institutions and social practices which are impeding individuals' chances of social development. An example is the unequal power relations between employers and employees or, between men and women. Social liberalism is sometimes called developmental liberalism, because of its stress on the rights of each individual to develop their full human capacities and potential (Emy 1991: 14), and sometimes new liberalism, to distinguish it from the 'old' *laissez-faire* economic liberalism (Beilharz, Considine and Watts 1992: 15).

Social liberalism was an important part of political thinking in Australia by the end of the nineteenth century, particularly in Victoria (Macintyre 1991). New settler societies, freed from the class divisions of the Old World, were widely regarded as providing possibilities for a society in which life chances could be more equally distributed (Beilharz, Considine and Watts 1992: 18–21). Such ideas were influential in the emerging labour movement (which led to the formation of the Australian Labor Party in 1901), as well as in parties such as Alfred Deakin's Protectionist Party and his later Liberal Party. They sat easily with the dependence of the new European society in Australia on a strong state to develop the country's economic potential.

During the nineteenth century, Australian colonial governments were heavily involved in assisting immigration, distributing land and developing infrastructure such as port facilities and transport. The social liberalism of Australian settler society was limited, however. In particular it was limited to white people. People of Aboriginal descent were not included; nor were non-Europeans such as Chinese or Pacific Islanders who had come to Australia during the nineteenth century. It was also more concerned with the social rights of men than of women.

Although liberalism provided the broad church within which the major ideas of both labour and non-labour were developed, two other traditions of nineteenth century European thought had some influence. These were conservatism and Marxism.

Conservatism emerges from the response of English conservatives like Edmund Burke to the social experimentation and destruction of the French Revolution. Conservatives argued that social life was so densely complex that it was impossible for any theory to understand it. Any attempt to intervene in society in order to change its basic social and institutional arrangements or its fundamental values was either futile, or risked causing more evil than it cured, since the consequences of actions could never be foreseen (Hirschman 1991: 7). While such arguments were developed to defend a particular social order in which power was held by those who controlled the land, they can be used against any proposals radically to reform society. Australian conservative Ronald Conway sums up the conservative position thus (Conway 1982: 255):

If there is one common mark of those occupying the authoritarian extremes of the political spectrum, it is the belief held by extreme Right and Left alike that social behaviour may by beneficially altered by the raw exercise of political will...The conservative sees it as his more central duty to show the risks to human freedom of all *comprehensive* plans to alter the social contract by political means.

Conservatives were particularly opposed to political action based on explicit and systematic political ideas like Marxism or socialism, but the belief in the likely unintended consequences of all actions gave them a basis from which to oppose any reforming political agenda.

The writings of Karl Marx provided a fundamental critique of the way economic activity was organised under capitalism. Marx argued that capitalist economic relations were not only fundamentally exploitative, but that the inequality of power and resources between those who owned and controlled the means of production (the bourgeoisie) and those who had to sell their labour to live (the proletariat) was such that the proletariat would become more and more pauperised until, having nothing to lose, it would rise up and overthrow the bourgeois social and economic order and usher in Communism. Many of Marx's ideas were taken up by working class political organisations and activists as they struggled against the hardships and injustices caused by an economic system regulated by market forces. In Australia the mainstream of the working class political movement did not commit itself to the revolutionary overthrow of existing social and economic relations. Rather it attempted to harness the power of the state to ameliorate the suffering caused to the working class by existing social and economic relations. The Marxist critique of capitalism did, however, sharpen many of its members' sense of the inherent injustices of capitalism, and contributed to the troublesome socialist objective in the ALP's platform which committed the party to collective ownership where this was necessary to prevent exploitation (O'Meagher 1983). It was also central to the Australian Communist Party, which was formed in the early 1920s and achieved considerable influence in the trade union movement (Davidson 1969). One of the major effects of Marxism on the Australian labour movement was that it provided non-labour with a language with which to oppose labour's political programs, particularly after the 1917 Bolshevik Revolution in Russia. The ALP's programs of reform could be painted as the first step on the road to Communism. Thus the distance between the social liberalism of both labour and non-labour could be exaggerated.

The Post-war Social Liberal Consensus
The debate about the state in Australia has gone through a number of phases during the twentieth century (Beilharz, Considine and Watts:

13–14). During World War II, with the ALP in government, support for social liberalism's view that the state could be a creative agent of the public good strengthened. This was not only because of the obvious role of the state in co-ordinating the war effort, but because of the growing influence of the ideas of the Cambridge economist John Maynard Keynes. Keynes argued that it was possible for national governments to control national economies by regulating demand. So cyclical booms and depressions, hitherto a feature of capitalism, could be avoided. In particular, Keynes argued that national governments could maintain full employment, something which both governments and their populations welcomed after the widespread unemployment and social suffering of the 1930's Depression.

When Robert Menzies formed the Liberal Party in 1944 he explicitly rejected *laissez-faire* notions of the state's role in favour of a commitment to full employment and an expanded provision of welfare (Starr 1980: 93–94, Simms 1982: 14-20, Kemp 1988: 327–29). This represented a substantial shift on the part of non-labour, in which the Victorian branch of the Institute of Public Affairs (a body representing industrial and commercial interests), was crucial. Its pamphlet, *Looking Forward*, argued, that 'full employment, social security and a "new deal" in industrial relations could be achieved within the framework of the traditional business system and without resort to the extreme measures proposed by the socialists' (quoted in Tiver 1978: 32–33). The Liberal government elected in 1949 by and large expanded the role of the state in the provision of services such as health, education and income support developed under ALP governments since 1942. Its coalition partner, the Country Party, continued its support for substantial government assistance to the rural sector. The ALP and the Liberal Party still disagreed as to the degree of state involvement appropriate in various areas, with the Liberal Party having a greater commitment in favour of private enterprise than the ALP. It continued to describe the ALP as socialist.

Two points need to be made about the post-war consensus on the role of the state as it was achieved in Australia. First, the state's role did not expand in Australia to anywhere near the same extent as it did in Western European democracies. No major industries were nationalised, housing and health remained essentially private (although with some subsidies), and most social security benefits were residual, available only to those unable to support themselves, rather than to all citizens as a matter of right (Macintyre 1984: 137). Second, both sides of politics continued to share a commitment to the state having a large role in the development of the country and its resources. Major post-war development projects such as the ambitious post-war immigration scheme and the Snowy Mountain Hydro-electric Scheme, which were begun by the ALP government, were continued by Liberal-Country Party governments after 1949. During the 1950s and 60s, these governments also greatly increased the role of the state in the provision of education. As well, the 1950s saw a continuing commitment to protecting Australian manufacturing industries through tariffs.

The Renewal of Economic Liberalism
The bi-partisan consensus on an increased role for the state depended on stable economic growth. The expansion of the state's activities was underwritten by the expansion and improved productivity of the private sector. When the post-war boom ended, the conditions for this agreement disappeared. From about 1973 onwards, Western economies experienced stagflation — a combination of high inflation and rising unemployment (Emy and Hughes 1988: Chapter 1). Stagflation challenged Keynes' model of how to manage a national economy. According to the Keynesian model, inflation indicated too much demand in the economy, and unemployment too little. The government's task was to bring these into balance by adopting measures to boost or dampen demand as required. According to the model, high unemployment and high inflation should not co-exist. When they did, Keynesianism was thrown into question, and with it the post-war consensus on the role of the state. In Australia the immediate victim was the ambitious reform program of the Whitlam government, which had assumed continuing economic growth.

Since the mid-1970s, the assumptions underlying the welfare state of the post-war boom have been trenchantly attacked by a range of writers and politicians, described as either the New Right or the new conservatives. They have revived the economic liberal view of the state and ushered in a renewed debate on its proper functions and scope. This has been a movement of Anglo-American democracies, and advocates of New Right ideas in Australia have drawn heavily on overseas sources.

The New Right was self-consciously intellectual, looking to models of how society and the economy should work to advocate particular directions for government. It is this that has led to it so often being described as ideological. Some of its seminal texts, several written much earlier, developed both an economic and a moral critique of the regulatory welfare state. They include F.A von Hayek's *The Road to Serfdom* (1944) and *The Constitution of Liberty* (1960), Milton Friedman's *Capitalism and Freedom* (1962), and James Buchanan and Gordon Tullock's *The Calculus of Consent: Logical Foundations of Constitutional Democracy* (1962). Ideas from these were taken up by influential journalists and commentators in the Anglo-American democracies, as well as by some conservative politicians, most notably Margaret Thatcher in the United Kingdom and Ronald Reagan in the United States. Various organisations were formed to publicise New Right ideas and develop alternative policy proposals. Although commentators quickly coined the term New Right, it is important to realise that this did not refer to a coherent political organisation, but rather to a loose alliance of people and organisations. There were many differences amongst them, and many would not have described themselves as members of the New Right. All, however, were engaged in a radical questioning of the assumptions on which the post-war democratic state had been based, as well as in arguing for alternative assumptions and very different public policies.

In Australia the New Right was a similar loose alliance of politicians, journalists, public commentators and academics. It drew much of its inspiration from developments in the United Kingdom and the United States. David Kemp, one of its leading figures, gives a detailed description of the development in Australia of a network of political and intellectual leaders, journalists, commentators and pamphleteers over the decade to 1985 (Kemp 1988). The journals *Quadrant* and *IPA Review* (in a reversal of earlier advocacy of social liberalism during the 1940s), as well as commentators like P.P. McGuinness (1990) in the *Australian Financial Review* and later the *Australian*, Les Hollings in the *Australian* and Terry McCrann in the Melbourne *Herald*, were important publicists for New Right ideas. As well, a number of 'think tanks' were established outside formal party structures, to develop alternative public policies based on a greater role for the market in the provision of goods and services hitherto provided by the state. The Centre for Independent Studies was established in Sydney in 1977 by Greg Lindsay, the Centre for Policy Studies was established at Monash University in 1979 under Michael Porter, and the Australian Institute for Public Policy was established in Perth in 1983 by John Hyde (Moore and Carpenter 1987, Stone 1991: 205).

The New Right argued that the economic problems of Western capitalist democracies were, for the most part, the result of the rapid expansion of the state in the post-war period. The state had taken an increasing share of society's productive resources and had encouraged a dependent and unresourceful population which habitually looked to the state rather than to themselves for solutions to their problems. The expansion of the state had been fuelled both by social liberal and Keynesian ideas held by politicians and bureaucrats, and by the relationship between democratically elected politicians attempting to maximise their support and interest groups attempting to maximise their benefits. This latter argument, developed by public choice theorists, attacked the legitimacy of the responsiveness of democratically elected governments to pressure groups, and concluded that the only way to rein in government spending was through constitutionally imposed limits (Buchanan 1975, Brennan and Buchanan 1980).

The New Right had both a diagnosis of the ills afflicting Western economies and a cure. The public sector needed to be reduced in order to make room for the wealth-creating sectors of society (private enterprise), and enterprise and initiative needed to be encouraged and rewarded in the population. Two main sorts of measures were advocated to reduce the role of the state in the economy. The first were measures designed to reduce government expenditure and economic activity: by eliminating wasteful administration and cutting back on various programs, and by transferring resources from the government to the private sector through the privatisation of various services, such as telecommunications, transport, power and even prisons. The second group of measures involved the deregulation of various areas of activity currently regulated by the state, such as banking, foreign exchange and industrial relations, as well as opposition to any expansion of government regulation, such as the introduction of environmental impact regulations. In both cases the aim was to increase the amount of economic activity controlled by the free play of competitive market forces and to reduce that controlled and regulated by the state.

The regulation of wages through Australia's centralised system of arbitration was a particular target. In the second half of the 1980s several legal challenges to union power were launched by groups associated with the New Right (Coghill 1987a: 131–33). In 1986 a group of New Right activists formed the H.R. Nicholls Society, named after an obscure early twentieth-century Tasmanian newspaper editor who had opposed the minimum wage. The Society's stated aim was 'to help destroy the Arbitration Commission', and its members included people such as Peter Costello, Paul Houlihan, Ian McLachlan and Andrew Hay, who had been involved in various legal actions against unions (Moore and Carpenter 1987: 153–55). More than technical arguments about the economy, attacks on the union movement struck a responsive chord with many people who had always thought the unions had too much power.

The New Right not only mounted economic arguments against the post-war consensus, but moral ones. The more dependent, less resourceful population which, the New Right argued, had been encouraged by the welfare state, was a moral and psychological problem as well as an economic one. In other words, the welfare state had led to people becoming addicted to welfare. The moral dimensions of the New Right's arguments were important to its popular appeal, for they connected technical economic arguments with a much more easily understood appeal to values such as independence and self-reliance. They also attempted to link economic liberal arguments with a conservative social morality.

There were obvious tensions, however, amongst the moral values advocated by the New Right. Sometimes the New Right argued for the individualist market-based values of economic liberalism, such as freedom of choice; at other times it argued for the strengthening of the conservative values of a family-centred morality and a traditional gendered division of labour, as well as for renewed respect for the bearers of social, political and cultural authority. Sometimes both sorts of arguments could be used to support a particular policy direction. For example, as Marian Sawer has pointed out, arguments for strengthening the traditional family, and in particular arguments in support of women staying in the home, served the aim of reducing state expenditure. Women at home would relieve growing demands for the state to provide assistance with child care, as well as for the care of the aged and the handicapped (Sawer 1983). However, there was an obvious tension between the advocacy of conservative social values, which are encouraged by a stable and predictable social world, and radically individualist economics. By the mid-1980s, the Right in Australia had split along this fissure.

With the election of Malcolm Fraser's government in 1975, the ideas of the New Right began to have some influence on government. Fraser saw himself as a politician who took ideas seriously, and he brought into the processes of government several intellectuals of the New Right, such as David Kemp, John Rose and Cliff Walsh (Kemp 1988: 340). Fraser came to government attacking big government and committing himself to shifting resources from the public sector back to the private sector, in line with New Right arguments. By Fraser's third term, however, it was becoming apparent that his rhetoric of small government and deregulation was far in advance of his policies, and that a great deal of dissatisfaction was building within the Liberal Party among more wholehearted adherents of the New Right (O'Brien 1985: 11–37). Fraser's Treasurer, John Howard, has since been very critical of the tardiness with which Fraser's government deregulated the economy (Head and Patience 1989: 488-91).

By the time the Liberals lost government in 1983, sharp divisions about the ideas of the New Right were surfacing in the party. Borrowing from Britain, the main groups were described as the Wets and the Dries. The Wets were generally committed to social liberalism and to the continuation of the policies associated with the post-war welfare state. During the 1980s, the Dries achieved ascendancy in both the parliamentary party and in the party organisation (O'Brien 1985, Kelly 1992: Chapter 2,5).

From 1975 to the end of the 1980s, the two strands of New Right thinking, economic liberalism and social conservatism, maintained an uneasy alliance. The combination of the two can be seen in *Future Directions*, a 109-page policy document launched by John Howard in 1988 when he was leader of the Opposition. In it, arguments for deregulation, including deregulation of the labour market, were combined with arguments for a return to traditional family values and with an affirmation of the priority of national values, under the slogan 'One Australia' (Brett 1989).

With the election of John Hewson as leader in 1990, the economic liberal aspects of the New Right's position came to the fore. In 1992 the Liberal Party published *Fightback!*, a thorough-going program for

12 Ideology

the application of free market principles to managing of the Australian economy. *Fightback!* was based on a view of society as made up of rational individuals acting on self-interest: 'We believe that policies aimed at building incentives, opportunities and rewards for individuals are the most effective way of overcoming the serious economic and social problems which Australia now faces' (Hewson and Fischer 1991: 1).

The Liberal Party fought and lost the 1993 election on the package of economic reforms set out in *Fightback!* Many commentators explained the election defeat as being the result of Labor's successful campaign against the unpopular goods and services tax (GST); (for example, Kemp (*Age*, 30 March 1993). Others, both inside and outside the party, saw the defeat as having deeper causes — for instance, in many voters' hestitation at the competitive social relations projected by *Fightback!* While talk of competition, rewards and incentives is appealing to those who think they are or can be winners, it can also raise deep fears about the costs of competition for the inevitable losers, and about the basis for social integration (Brett 1993).

Labor's Response
The trenchant attack launched by the New Right on the belief that the state had a creative role to play in the production of a more just and equal society, as well as the apparent inability of Keynesian economics to guide government policy in the deteriorating economies of Western democracies, put the ALP, and the Left more generally, on the defensive.

The ALP has always contained people with a range of ideas about the fundamental nature and justice of capitalism, and about the potential of the state to make such a society more just and equal (Jaensch 1989: 84). Within its broad commitment to social liberalism we can distinguish between a labourist and social democratic tradition, with socialism also making some contribution. There is much debate about which of these traditions has had most influence on the party. From the perspective of *socialism*, the party's aim should be to extend collective control over the basic institutions of the economy, by bringing them under the control of the state and by developing various forms of industrial democracy (Emy and Hughes 1988: 70). Most commentators agree that socialist ideas have never been held by the mainstream of the party, and some criticise it or various Labor governments for this (Johnson 1989, Duncan 1978).

From the *labourist* perspective, the party's aim is to improve the conditions of life and work for the working class within the existing framework of social, political and economic institutions. The labourist perspective reflects the ALP's origins as the political wing of the trade union movement, and the unions' large role in its organisation. At its core is the commitment to employment at a sufficient wage for an adult man to provide for himself and his family without recourse to state welfare (Macintyre 1984: 134). It draws on the experiences of male blue collar work and union membership, and on the closeness and interdependence of pre-war working class communities.

The *social democratic* perspective is wider than the labourist, being concerned with injustices and inequalities deriving from bases other than class (such as region, place of residence or, more recently, gender and race). Its high point of influence in the party was the program of reform with which the Whitlam government was elected. Whitlam was deeply committed to the role of the state as a potential agent for reform in all areas of social life, from public transport through education and health to the artistic and cultural life of the country. As he put it (Whitlam 1985: 3):

> The quality of life depends less and less on the things which individuals obtain for themselves and can purchase for themselves from their personal incomes and depends more and more on the things which the community provides for all its members from the combined resources of the community.

This was a vision of the reforming power of the state which went far beyond the limited demands of labourism, and was able to accommodate new political demands emerging from groups such as women and Aborigines. Both labourists and social democrats fit within the tradition described at the beginning of this chapter as social liberalism, stressing the state's positive role in making society more just and equal. The sympathies and concerns of the social democrats are, however, more inclusive.

After the dismissal of the Whitlam government and the ALP's massive rejection by the electorate in 1975 and again in 1977, the ALP was very much on the defensive in the debate on the nature of the state. It was keen to distance itself from the commitment to big spending associated with Whitlam, and to project itself as a party capable of responsible economic management. By the second half of the 1970s, it was starting to become clear that managing the economy in the wake of the post-war boom was going to be tough. The Australian economy, still heavily reliant on the export of commodities, and with a weak and protected manufacturing sector, had particular problems which became increasingly apparent in the 1980s, when a serious deficit problem emerged in Australia's current account (Emy and Hughes 1988: 2–9). Many members of the ALP were alarmed by the edge the New Right seemed to be gaining in public debate. The party responded from both its labourist and social democratic traditions.

The union response developed by the ACTU looked to the social democracies of Western Europe, such as Sweden and West Germany. In these, organised labour had been incorporated into the economic management functions of the state. The central initiative of the Labor government elected in 1983, the Accord, was an outcome of this. The Accord was an agreement negotiated between the ALP and the ACTU for wage restraint and industrial harmony in return for the government's commitment to policies promoting full employment, welfare services and industrial revitalisation (Stilwell 1986). It has been renegotiated a number of times since 1983. The Accord took the union movement beyond immediate concerns with wages and conditions into a central role in economic planning — but it continued the labourist tradition's emphasis on the interests of the organised working class. Non-labour organisations and spokespeople were quick to criticise such a close involvement of organised labour in the government policy making process, seeing the Accord as a way of bypassing the representative institutions of parliamentary democracy, and marginalising the many other interest groups who might expect to have their views heard by government (West 1984: 1–24).

The social-democratic response to the economic liberalism of the New Right was in the main to re-argue for the view of the state as a creative agent for social reform, to stress areas where reform was still urgent, and to point to the increased inequality which would result from increasing the role of market mechanisms in the distribution of goods and services. A very clear statement of the social democratic view of the state directed explicitly against the arguments of the New Right can be found in an essay by Peter Wilenski, 'Can Governments Achieve Fairness? Two Views of Government and Society' (Wilenski 1987, see also Blewett 1982). In contemporary Australian society, Wilenski argues, people are unequal in power, and some organise to dominate others, so limiting their abilities to take full control of their own lives. The role of government is thus 'to emancipate and empower those citizens who would otherwise be subject to coercion'. Wilenski invokes the social liberal ideal of a society in which all members will have a chance to develop their potential, when he argues that: 'In a fairer Australia citizens will be much more equal not only in their economic capacities but also in their freedom and ability to pursue their individual choice.' The concepts of inequality and injustice Wilenski is using here are broad. They include both injustices which flow from class inequalities and those which flow from differences of race, gender, and ethnic background. Since the election of the Whitlam government, there has been a general alliance between the social democratic strand in the ALP and the demands of feminists, ethnic groups and Aborigines which began to be articulated in the early 1970s. This alliance has, however, led to friction within the party, particularly with supporters of the labourist commitment to protecting and improving the wages and conditions of male workers.

The Debate about Moral and Cultural Values

Social Movement Politics

When the Whitlam government was elected in 1972, demands which had been emerging since the mid-1960s began to influence government policy: women's claims for greater social and political equality; Aborigines' demands for land rights; the questioning of assimilation as the goal of non-English-speaking migrants; the danger to the natural environment of continuing development (Horne 1980). These issues went beyond concerns with injustices and inequalities associated with class, to a questioning of other dimensions of oppression, in particular those associated with gender, sexual preference, race and ethnicity (Altman 1988). This questioning by and large took place outside the existing framework of political institutions. The opposition to the Vietnam War among radical students, inspired by the anti-war movement in the United States, had led not only to a widespread challenging of traditional authority, but to a more direct, less institutionally-based form of politics, often described as social movement politics.

Social movement politics can be distinguished from more institutionally dependent politics by three main criteria. First, social movements come into being and operate outside already existing political institutions, and use direct forms of political action such as marches, demonstrations, protests and sit-ins. Second, they do not have an overarching institutional structure, but are loose coalitions of groups, organisations and individuals — although they often lead to the establishment of more conventional pressure groups. Third, they aim to change fundamental social values. In pursuit of this latter aim, social movements are as concerned with changing the consciousness of their members as they are with influencing government policy in the manner of the conventional pressure group. It is this last criterion which brings them into the scope of this chapter, because social movements are intensely concerned with ideas: with challenging accepted values and assumptions, and with developing and arguing for new values and understandings, in particular for new ways of understanding the self and its history (Gusfield 1966, Heberle 1966). Social movements are one important way in which new ideas start to become politically significant.

The politics of the new social movements radically changed the dynamics of political conflict (Altman 1988: 308), popularising radical ideas about sexuality and the family as well as questioning the legitimacy of the domination of Australian society by white men of British descent. The challenge of the social movements to conventional politics can be summed up by the slogan 'the personal is political', which was coined by the women's movement (Altman 1988: 312).

This slogan challenged assumptions about the legitimate scope of politics, and pointed to the operations of power in the private sphere of life, including in the very constitution of a person's sense of self. There is a preoccupation in social movements with the education or consciousness raising of their members: for example, to build a woman's confidence and self-esteem in the face of the damaging experiences of a gender-divided society, was already to start to change social reality.

In consciousness raising groups in the early days of the women's movement, women reworked their personal histories in the light of books such as Simone de Beauvoir's *The Second Sex* (1952), Betty Friedan's *The Feminine Mystique* (1963) and Germaine Greer's *The Female Eunuch* (1970). They worked together to reject the definitions they had accepted of themselves from family, school, church and work, and to construct new definitions giving them greater autonomy and self-respect. Such new definitions were empowering, providing a basis from which women could challenge institutional structures embodying power relations based on definitions of women as inferior in various ways, and less fitted to participate in a public life dominated by men (Curthoys 1988, Burgmann 1993: 77–131). Similar processes of consciousness raising were also engaged in by homosexual men and women, who also formed groups and organisations in which they developed more positive understandings of their sexuality, coining the positive term 'gay' to challenge pejorative descriptions like 'queen' and 'poof' (Johnston and Johnston 1988: 95–98). Aboriginal activists similarly argued for the need for Aborigines to throw off the racist images imposed on them by white society, drawing inspiration from the slogan of the Black Power movement in the United States, whose slogan was 'Black is beautiful'(Miller 1985: 194).

The challenge by women and Aborigines in particular to the supremacy of the values associated with white British men flowed on to a questioning of the expectations of assimilation that had hitherto been made about non-English-speaking migrants. Arguments were put that it was deeply damaging for people to be expected to give up their language and culture, that they had a right to maintain them and to pass them on to their children, and that the state should support this. Migrants began to be described as 'ethnics', which stressed their inherent difference from the mainstream, and the expectation that this would be maintained. Multiculturalism rather than assimilation became the guiding principle of the relationship between non-English-speaking migrants and their children and the dominant British Australian society. Migrant politics was never social movement politics, but it benefited greatly from the general sympathy for minorities and difference in the radical politics of the time.

The other social movement which began to be important at this time was the environmental one. This did not focus on questions of personal identity, but it did challenge fundamental social values: the materialism of Western society and its assumptions about the benefits and the possibilities of continuing material progress.

The ideas and values developed in the social movements of the late 1960s and early 1970s have had a continuing impact on Australian politics. They have been taken into more conventional pressure group politics (for example, feminist ideas into the Women's Electoral Lobby and environmental ideas into the Australian Conservation Foundation) and into the political parties and public bureaucracies, as people influenced by these ideas have achieved senior positions. They have been particularly influential in the ALP, where they have been incorporated into the social democratic tradition of ALP thinking about the potential of the state for reform. As in the labour movement's reliance on the power of the state to intervene to prevent the worst effects of the inequality of capitalist economic relations, so parts of the women's movement looked to the state as the only organisation with sufficient power to intervene in society to reform inequalities between men and women. Equal opportunity legislation, for example, was justified on the grounds that men would never stop discriminating against women in employment unless they were forced by law to do so.

Apart from environmental politics, in which arguments for the rights of natural species and of future generations introduce quite different considerations into the debate about the proper function of the state, social movements can be understood as developments of social or developmental liberalism. They have extended understanding of the impediments to individuals' opportunities to develop their full potential into the areas of gender, sexuality, ethnicity and race. In this they have drawn on another central idea of liberalism — that, except to prevent physical harm to another, the state should not interfere with the ways in which individuals choose to develop their full human potential.

The New Conservatism
During the late 1970s and early 80s, the term New Right was used to refer, as already mentioned, both to radical economic liberalism and to moral conservatism. Even though advocates of one were not always advocates of the other, the tensions between these two sets of values had not become politically apparent. Traditional moral and cultural values and a traditional division of labour were defended against new ideas such as feminism, multiculturalism and gay liberation, developed by the social movements. This defence drew on conservatism rather than liberalism, and in particular on conservatism's deep distrust of attempts to reform social arrangements on the basis of new ideas.

Since the 1970s a group of intellectuals centred on the monthly magazine *Quadrant* have been engaged in a self-conscious effort to make conservative thought more politically significant in Australia.

John Carroll, Robert Manne, Lauchlan Chipman, Frank Knopfelmacher and B.A. Santamaria were and remain particularly prominent. They and others argued that the Left had come to dominate the understanding of both Australian history and contemporary Australian society. The old Left's preoccupation with the inequalities of class, supplemented by the new social movements' preoccupations with the inequalities of gender, race and ethnicity had, they argued, come to dominate the universities during the late 1960s and early 70s, and had been carried by their graduates into the workforce, in particular into teaching, journalism and the Public Service (Manne 1982: xi). These products of the expanded tertiary sector of the 1960s and 70s were referred to by such writers as 'the New Class' (Manne 1982: 65), and demonised as 'antinomians' — people committed to a life of complete self-determination, free from the burdens of traditional obligation and constraints imposed by the law and institutional authority (Shils 1989). Both these terms came from new conservative writers in the United States. Just as the social movements of the late 1960s and early 70s had drawn inspiration from the radical politics of the United States, so did the arguments which were developed against them. The conservatives saw their task as combating the widespread denigration of traditional values and morality. For example, *Quadrant* carried articles criticising multiculturalism in favour of Australia's British political and cultural inheritance (see June 1989 issue), and others defending traditional family life and traditional gender identities, against the attacks of feminists and sexual liberationists.

In its attack on the politics and ideas of the social movements, conservatism was setting itself against one of the implications of social liberalism — that society should be so organised as to give all its members the maximum opportunity to develop their human potential. This had led, argued the conservatives, to a radical relativism which was undermining society's moral foundations. Debate about standards of education and the content of the curriculum was one area in which such arguments surfaced. Conservatives argued, for instance, that advocacy of a plurality of values in educating children was an abdication of education's central role in passing shared core social and cultural values from one generation to the next (see for example, Chipman 1982: 26–30). This argument was repeated regularly by conservative media commentators like Michael Barnard in the *Age*. The need for society to protect its core values was also raised by conservatives in recurring debates about the state's role in regulating violent and pornographic material (see for example, *Quadrant*, August 1989, June 1991).

Conservatism's general suspicion of radical plans to remake society sets it against all programs of radical reform, not just those emanating from social movements. By the late 1980s, tensions had appeared amongst those politicians and writers who were linked together under the label of the New Right during the 1970s and early 80s, as conservatism's central argument about the inherent unpredictability of all attempts to intervene in society's fundamental social and institutional arrangements was turned against the radical reforming plans of the economic liberals. This had led by the early 1990s to an alliance between social liberalism and conservatism in the debate on economic rationalism, as economic liberalism, the theory that the market is the most efficient mechanism for the distribution of goods and services, was by then generally called.

The Debate about Economic Rationalism

In the early 1990s the economic liberalism that had dominated the 1980s began to be more widely questioned. Certain individuals (for example Kenneth Davidson of the *Age*), had continued to argue the case for an interventionist state during the 1980s, but had attracted little support. The publication in 1991 of Michael Pusey's *Economic Rationalism in Canberra*, and in 1992 of two edited collections attacking economic rationalism, Carroll and Manne's *Shutdown* and Donald Horne's *The Trouble with Economic Rationalism*, marked a shift in the climate of public debate. All three books argued for a return to the vision of the role of the state which had dominated Australian political thinking since Federation — that as a new society that was small and geographically isolated Australia needed a strong, interventionist and protective state to ensure a decent way of life for its citizens.

By the beginning of the 1990s, the Australian economy was in deep recession, with the fundamental economic problems of the 1980s unsolved. Governments inspired by economic rationalism had held power for extended periods during the 1980s in the United States, Britain and New Zealand, and had not delivered the solutions promised by free market theories. What is more, inequality increased in these countries during the 1980s. Such societies provided evidence, argued the critics of economic liberalism, that these policies did not work. Their increased inequality drew attention to the potential social costs of the continuing high levels of unemployment.

In Australia, in the context of recession, high levels of unemployment (reaching 11 per cent during 1992) and continuing balance of payments difficulties, debate about economic rationalism focused on the program of tariff reduction being pursued by the Labor government (with the Opposition promising to pursue it even faster if elected). The issue was whether the Australian state should continue to support Australian industry with protective measures such as tariffs and import restrictions, and through the selective support of particular industries, or whether it should dismantle such protective measures in order to allow a greater role to market forces. This question was closely linked with the role of the centralised arbitration system in regulating wages. One of the major arguments for protective measures for Australian industries has always been that they protected the wages and working conditions of Australian workers. The argument against tariffs and other forms of protection thus implied an argument for the deregulation of wages and working conditions, so that Australian businesses would be able to compete with the lower wage cost businesses of Asia.

The 1993 election revealed deep rifts in the non-labour side of politics over economic rationalism. Former Liberal Prime Minister Fraser was unremitting in his attacks on the party's enthusiasm for market mechanisms. It had, he argued, become too ideological since the ascendancy of the economic rationalists. It owed its past electoral success to such pragmatism and common sense, and needed to return to these (*Age*, 3 April 1993; Robert Manne and John Carroll offered similar diagnoses, *Age*, 16 March 1993, *Australian*, 17 March 1993).

Conclusion

The debate about economic rationalism shows the ideological complexity of Australian political life at the end of the twentieth century, in which the terms Left and Right are decreasingly useful as shorthand descriptions of people's political positions. In *The End of Certainty* (1992) Paul Kelly, editor-in-chief of the *Australian*, describes the three positions which had emerged by the 1993 election: first, the free market purists, represented by John Hewson's coalition, who aspired to apply free market principles faster and more extensively than the ALP government; second, the ALP government, led by Prime Minister Paul Keating, who sought a balance between market-orientated reforms and an increased role for government intervention; third a broad group Kelly calls 'the sentimental traditionalists'. This included many members of the Liberal Party, including Malcolm Fraser; many members of the ALP; Independent member for Wills Phil Cleary, who represented a working class constituency alienated by the ALP of the 1980s; virtually the entire formal membership of the National Party; conservative intellectuals based on *Quadrant*; sections of manufacturing industry; a number of powerful unions; and most teachers and Public Service professionals. Kelly comments: 'This was an alliance which defied the established patterns of Australian political conflict...It was a division which cut completely across the existing party system' (Kelly 1992: 661). Kelly does not comment, however, that this alliance reveals a deep rupture between the political values and expectations of government of a wide range of Australians, and the ideas and values of the political élites of both parties, the implications of which are as yet hard to discern (Brett 1992b: 12–13).

Ideological complexity was also apparent in debates about the state's role in relation to personal morality and core cultural values, as issues associated with the new social movements disturbed patterns of support which had developed during the 1970s and 80s. One remarkable alliance was between conservatives and some feminists — on arguments for greater state regulation of pornography, for example.

By the early 1990s, there was a growing awareness of the difficulties facing liberalism generally in providing an adequate and convincing account of the moral basis of communal life. This was apparent both in the economic liberal, and in the social liberal traditions, although for different reasons. In both cases, however, the difficult, unresolved question was the same: how were the shared moral and social values of Australian life to be understood and maintained?

Economic liberalism's problems stem from its ideal of society as made up of individuals in competition with each other, and its reliance on the integrating mechanisms of the market to hold these competing elements together. The trouble with this ideal is that the market is not in itself enough to establish a moral basis for a shared social life. As the 1980s showed, market behaviour untempered by a shared morality does not necessarily benefit society. Following the spectacular bankruptcies of the 1980s, there have been increasing calls for a strengthening of ethics in business, but the logic of the market cannot itself generate such ethical standards. They depend on extra-market, extra-economic considerations such as the desirability of honesty and truth, and on the argument that in the end the market must not only serve the ends of individuals, but of the whole of society.

Historically economic liberalism has been allied with various traditional conservative belief systems, such as religion, patriotism, or family-centred social conservatism, which have provided a firm basis of shared moral values and symbols to express people's experiences of unity, even while the market relations of the economy have put them in competition with each other. However, as religious belief has declined, and as conservative social values have been challenged by the new social movements, these traditional values and unifying symbols have become less convincing to many people. The moral bankruptcy of economic liberalism's view of people's relations with one another in society has thus been starkly exposed. This is clearly seen in the problems facing the Liberal Party in the wake of its 1993 election defeat. It fought that campaign on economic liberal policies, and its lack of success has been partly explained by its inability to link these policies to a convincing social vision. Since then the party has been attempting to rediscover a political language which carries social values as well as economic policies (Brett 1993).

Just as problematic as the moral bankruptcy of economic liberalism, however, is the libertarian heritage of social liberalism. This has pushed the social liberal argument for individual freedom from social constraint (in order to be able to develop one's full human potential in the manner of one's own choosing), to a radically relativist conclusion which also provides little basis for shared community life, and has made it difficult for many modern social liberals to argue for the very values with which social liberalism has historically been identified (Emy 1991). Social liberalism has become better at stressing the importance of pluralism and mutual tolerance, and at discerning the oppressive possibilities of particular value systems, than arguing positively for the values that should guide individual and communal life such as democracy, justice, truth, fairness, honesty, altruism and loyalty.

The problems of both social and economic liberalism in providing a widely-shared understanding of the basis of social unity are becoming apparent in Australia at the same time as the basis of national unity is being widely debated. Since Keating became Prime Minister, and particularly since the 1993 election, issues which raise the relationship of contemporary Australia to its past have come to the fore: in particular the history of Aboriginal and non-Aboriginal Australians, and the debate responding to the High Court's finding in the *Mabo* judgment recognising native common law title (see Chapter 8); and the meaning of Australia's historical relationship with Britain, one of the issues at stake in the debate over whether this country should become a republic. These debates, tinged with the sombre colours of the *fin de siècle*, are increasing the sense of confusion about a viable basis for shared social life to take Australia into the twenty-first century.

2
Reinterpreting the Constitution

A.R. BLACKSHIELD

The 'Free Speech' Cases

In two decisions on 30 September 1992, the High Court of Australia held that legislation enacted by the Commonwealth Parliament was unconstitutional, because it imposed unacceptable restrictions on the democratic freedom of political comment and debate. A guarantee of that freedom was said to be *implied* in the Constitution, as an over-riding limit on Parliament's use of its legislative powers.

In *Nationwide News Pty Ltd* v. *Wills*, the restriction was on public criticisms of the Industrial Relations Commission which might bring it or its members into 'disrepute'. In *Australian Capital Television* v. *The Commonwealth*, the restrictions were on access to radio and television for political broadcasts at election time. In both cases, the Court recognised that *some* restrictions might have been justified, but held that the legislation had failed to strike an appropriate balance. Accordingly, it was invalid.

In *Nationwide News* the result was unanimous — but only four of the seven judges relied on an implied constitutional guarantee. In *Australian Capital Television*, five judges did so. Only Justice Dawson rejected the whole idea. The other dissenter, Justice Brennan, agreed that an implied guarantee exists, but interpreted the political broadcasting scheme as compatible with it (imposing restrictions for legitimate purposes in a legitimate way).

The decisions led to immediate speculation on two main issues. First, what precisely is their effect on freedom of speech in Australia? Second, do the judgments mark a fundamental change in the relationship between Court and Parliament? One question treats the decisions as a bold judicial initiative potentially *enhancing* or *strengthening* Australian democracy; the other treats the same initiative as potentially setting the Court *against* democratic institutions.

The first approach sees the essence of democracy as 'popular sovereignty'. As Justices Deane and Toohey put it, 'the Constitution reserves to the people of the Commonwealth the ultimate power of governmental control'. All of the 'legislative, executive or judicial powers of government' are 'ultimately derived from the people', and a vigorous flow of communication between voters and politicians, and among the voters themselves, is necessary to enable the people 'responsibly to discharge and exercise the powers of governmental control which the Constitution reserves to them'. By protecting this flow of communication against legislative interference, the Court has strengthened Australian democracy.

The second approach sees the essence of democracy as 'parliamentary sovereignty'. It concedes that, in a federal system, this sovereignty is circumscribed by the Constitution itself. The Commonwealth Parliament is one of 'limited' or 'enumerated' powers: it can *only* make laws within those areas which the Constitution assigns to it. But within these areas, the assumption is that Parliament has plenary power. When the constitutional validity of a Commonwealth enactment is challenged, the High Court must determine whether it falls within a relevant Commonwealth power. If not, it is unconstitutional. But once the Court concludes that an enactment *is* 'within power' (or even that it can fairly be described in that way), the judicial function stops there. There is no room for the Court to express its approval or disapproval on the basis of moral, political or social values considered important by it. In a system of responsible government, such issues should be judged by Parliament. If the people do not like the result, that is a matter between them and their elected representatives; an unelected judiciary should not interfere.

Behind this divergence lies the momentous prospect that the High Court itself may be moving from the second approach to the first: that its judgments may signal a paradigm shift in constitutional interpretation from a pervasive assumption of 'parliamentary sovereignty', to one of 'popular sovereignty'.

Constitutional Foundations

The Australian federal polity came into existence at midnight on 1 January 1901, as a product of the Commonwealth of Australia Constitution Act 1900. The Commonwealth as a political entity came into being at that moment, along with its various manifestations of legal and political power. Its *legislative* power was vested primarily in the new Commonwealth Parliament (Constitution, Chapter I); its *executive* power in the Governor-General, advised by a 'Federal Executive Council' consisting of 'Ministers of State' administering government departments (Constitution, Chapter II); its *judicial* power primarily in 'the High Court of Australia, and in such other federal courts as the Parliament creates' (Constitution, Chapter III). This allocation of Commonwealth legislative, executive and judicial powers to three separate chapters of the Constitution has been held to establish at least a partial 'separation of powers'.

The same stroke of midnight which gave life to the Commonwealth also created the federating states. The Commonwealth was created out of nowhere. The states were a political reconceptualisation of what had previously existed as British colonies. Nevertheless, their reconstitution as states was of fundamental importance. The Constitution is sometimes seen as a 'contract' or 'compact' among the states, so that its treatment of Commonwealth powers reflects an agreement among the states on what powers the Commonwealth should have. On that basis, the High Court can be seen as interpreting and enforcing the contractual terms of the states' agreement. But, as Sir Garfield Barwick explained in the *Payroll Tax Case* (1971), the metaphor is misleading. Ours is not a case of pre-existing states coming together in a 'federal compact', but of a federal Constitution coming into operation in a way which *created* the new component state units, simultaneously with the new central Commonwealth. On this view, the states as well as the Commonwealth derive their political and legal existence from the federal Constitution.

In the absence of a compact among the states, the ultimate authority of the Constitution can be explained in three ways (Lindell 1986). One is that the Constitution *did* represent an agreement — not among the colonies as governmental entities, but more directly among their people. Its political legitimacy thus has a popular 'grassroots' democratic base. A second explanation lies in the enactment of the Commonwealth of Australia Constitution Act 1900 by the United Kingdom Parliament. Technically, the Constitution is merely a lengthy recital contained in Section 9 of that Act: 'The Constitution of the Commonwealth shall be as follows...'. Its legal validity thus derives from 'parliamentary sovereignty' ascribed to the Imperial Parliament in respect of the whole British Empire. A third explanation relies on tautological juristic theory: the Constitution is binding simply because it is the Constitution. Its procedural and substantive limits on law making must be observed because to do otherwise is not to act legally. 'The constitutional system of government exists where a constitution is supreme...with the consequence that every act...is carried out in accordance with the law and every such act is authorised by the law' (Cooray 1979: 205). As Sir Owen Dixon put it in *Trethowan's Case* (1931), the ultimate question for a court is 'whether the supreme legislative power in respect of the matter had in truth been exercised in the manner required for its authentic expression and by the elements in which it had come to reside'. The activities of governments, and the lawmaking of parliaments, *must* conform to the legal framework imposed by the Constitution, because outside that framework neither governments nor Parliaments have any legal existence.

The idea that a Constitution is binding simply because it represents 'the legal way of doing things' is an historical abstraction. As between the alternative explanations, relying on the democratic voiceof the Australian people or the authoritative voice of the Imperial Parliament, the historical record is ambiguous. The delegations to the 1891 Convention were *nominated* by the various colonial Parliaments. For the 1897 Convention delegations were *elected* democratically, by direct popular vote, in all colonies except Western Australia (where the delegation was chosen at the last minute by Parliament) and Queensland (which did not attend). The resulting draft Constitution was approved by popular referendum in Victoria, Tasmania and South Australia in June 1898. In New South Wales the people voted 'No', but a second round of referenda in 1899 (on a draft amended by a Premiers' Conference) obtained popular approval in New South Wales and Queensland, and increased majorities in the three colonies already committed. Western Australia voted 'Yes' at a referendum on 31 July 1900, after the Commonwealth of Australia Constitution Act had already been passed.

On the other hand, the Constitution Act had the force of law because it was formally enacted by the United Kingdom Parliament in its imperial capacity. At the time there was probably no real alternative. Each of the Australian colonies was, in British law, an imperial possession. Each had its own self-governing constitution; but these were themselves derived from imperial legislation, and subject to overriding British control. Even if the colonies had tried to federate simply by agreement among themselves, it was doubtful whether their constitutional powers in 1900 could be construed as extending so far. Moreover, when the Australian draft was presented to the British authorities, they did *not* automatically accept it, but sought to impose their own views. In one respect the result was a compromise: the right of appeal from Australian courts to the Privy Council was specifically retained — though with some exceptions in constitutional cases, and with power for the new Australian Parliament to 'limit' appeals *from the High Court*. Successive exercises of this power in 1968 and 1975 had the cumulative effect of *abolishing* appeals to the Privy Council from the High Court, but appeals from Australian state courts remained until the Australia Act 1986. Only then did the compromise of 1900 become obsolete.

As long as Britain's 'parliamentary sovereignty' included a 'paramount' imperial power to alter or override Australian law, the enactment of the Constitution by the Imperial Parliament was inescapably understood as its formal legal source of validity. But progressively through the twentieth century that imperial power has waned. The possibility of British legislation affecting the Australian Commonwealth was extinguished by the Statute of Westminster 1931; the possibility of its affecting the states was extinguished by the Australia Act 1986. With any continued 'sovereignty' of the British Parliament now extinguished, the *present* source of validity of the Constitution must be found within Australia — either in a juristic tautology, or in a 'grassroots' popular base (Lindell 1986, Zines 1991: 27–28).

In this post-1986 context, two features of the Constitution reinforce its claim to a popular base. The original process of enactment in Britain remains in stark contrast with the self-affirmation of the United States Constitution: 'We the People of the United States...do ordain and establish this Constitution...' Ours is not a 'We the People' Constitution. But it gains some of the same rhetorical force from the formula 'Whereas the People'. The Commonwealth of Australia Constitution Act begins:

> Whereas the people of New South Wales, Victoria, South Australia, Queensland, and Tasmania...have agreed to unite in one indissoluble Federal Commonwealth...under the Constitution hereby established.

Notice the *omission* of Western Australia. When the Act received the royal assent on 9 July 1900, the people of that colony had not yet decided whether to federate or not. The Act made it clear that the decision was entirely up to them: the royal proclamation bringing the Commonwealth into existence was to extend to Western Australia only 'if Her Majesty is satisfied that the people of Western Australia have agreed thereto'.

More importantly, as from 1901, the power to *amend* the Constitution was given exclusively to the Australian people. By Section 128, 'This Constitution shall not be altered except in the following manner...' To be sure, the referendum procedure which follows is qualified in several ways. It requires not merely a nationwide majority, but also a majority 'in a majority of the States', and proposed amendments must first be passed by at least one House of the Commonwealth Parliament. The requirement of 'a majority of the States' has usually *not* been a serious obstacle to constitutional change. The requirement that amendments be initiated in the Commonwealth Parliament is more of a problem: the resulting party-political overtones have defeated many worthwhile proposals. Yet, at least in theory, the power of the electorate to control the provisions of the Constitution, and to change any aspect of its workings, makes this Constitution *more* democratic than the 'We the People' model of the United States — where constitutional amendments are normally ratified by state legislatures.

Against this background, the real significance of the 'free speech' cases may lie in an observation by Chief Justice Mason in the *Australian Capital Television Case*. Outlining the basic proposition that sovereignty 'resides in the people' and is exercised 'on their behalf', he concedes that 'one obstacle' to this view was the orthodox legal theory

> that the Constitution owes its legal force to its character as a statute of the Imperial Parliament enacted in the exercise of its legal sovereignty; the Constitution was not a supreme law proceeding from the people's inherent authority to constitute a government.

The point is not merely that 'parliamentary sovereignty' might authorise the Parliament (within its areas of power) to place legislative restrictions on freedom of speech (or other basic values); but that it might leave no room for emphasis on the paramount political role of the people, and hence on the logical necessity for open political debate. Government *of* the people and *for* the people may not really be *by* the people, but government *by* the people requires uninhibited communication *to* the people, *from* the people and *among* the people. To the question whether Parliament can limit that flow of communication, the Chief Justice is conceding that the old assumption of 'parliamentary sovereignty' may have compelled a negative answer. Today, however, he thinks it is possible to take a different view:

> Despite its initial character as a statute of the Imperial Parliament, the Constitution brought into existence a system of representative government for Australia in which the elected representatives exercise sovereign power on behalf of the Australian people... [T]he prescribed procedure for amendment of the Constitution hinges upon a referendum...And, most recently, the Australia Act 1986 (UK) marked the end of the legal sovereignty of the Imperial Parliament and recognized that ultimate sovereignty resided in the Australian people.

In short, the theoretical foundation of the entire Constitution has shifted — and, with it, the assumptions to be made in working out its political meaning.

For most of the judges in the 'free speech' cases the necessity for freedom of political discourse, and hence the implied guarantee of that freedom, followed directly from the basic postulate of 'popular sovereignty'. The reasoning was explained most fully by Justices Deane and Toohey in *Nationwide News*. The idea of representative government is one of 'the general doctrines of government which underlie the Constitution and form part of its structure'. It is clearly reflected in the voting procedures for elections and referenda, since without a sufficient flow of information and opinions there can be no ability to cast an informed and intelligent vote. But the argument extends much further. The 'central thesis' is that the powers of government 'belong to, and are derived from...the people', and are held by politicians, bureaucrats and judges as *representatives* of the people, under a continuing relationship. To make this relationship work there must be a constant exchange of 'information, needs, views, explanations and advice', from people to government and from government to people, as well as continual open discussion among the people themselves.

Most judges took a similar view. Only Justice McHugh tied his decision narrowly to the specific voting provisions in the Constitution — and even he used a broader conception of 'representative government' to explain why the voting provisions must entail wider 'constitutional rights'.

Parliamentary Sovereignty

The theory of 'parliamentary sovereignty' was part of our British heritage. It meant not only that any Parliament constituted on the British model *could* (within its areas of power) override fundamental liberties and moral values if it so chose; but that in particular, if it did so, the courts had no power to resist such a law.

This doctrine had supplanted a much older British tradition. In *Dr Bonham's Case* (1610) Sir Edward Coke, as Chief Justice of the Common Pleas, had proclaimed:

> And it appears in our books, that in many cases, the common law will controul Acts of Parliament, and sometimes adjudge them to be utterly void: for when an Act of Parliament is against common ri... and reason, or repugnant, or impossible to be performed, the com law will controul it and adjudge such Act to be void.

In the American colonies, that aspect of the common law tradition lived on, and became the basis for the modern practice (nowadays based largely on bills of rights) by which the courts can declare legislation to be unconstitutional. In England, the common law claim 'to controul Acts of Parliament' faded away: judges simply stopped making such claims. By the 1880s A.V. Dicey could relegate *Dr Bonham's Case* to a footnote as 'obsolete' (Dicey 1885: 62n). By contrast, what Dicey saw as having evolved from the common law tradition in England was the fundamental principle that Parliament has

> the right to make or unmake any law whatever; and, further, that no person or body is recognised by the law of England as having a right to override or set aside the legislation of Parliament. (Dicey 1885: 40)

In particular, this meant that the courts could not do so: what parliamentary sovereignty really meant was that 'Any Act of Parliament ...will be obeyed by the courts'.

For Dicey and generations of lawyers after him, the crucial test case was one proposed by Leslie Stephen: 'If a legislature decided that all blue-eyed babies should be murdered, the preservation of blue-eyed babies would be illegal' (Stephen 1882: 143). Stephen had added that 'legislators must go mad before they could pass such a law and subjects be idiotic before they could submit to it'. Dicey developed this observation into an elaborate theory of *political* safeguards against the risk of a 'blue-eyed baby' law. But his fundamental doctrine was that there could be no *legal* safeguards.

In a unitary system of government, 'parliamentary sovereignty' on the British model means that Parliament has unlimited power not only as to *how* it will legislate, but as to the *subjects* on which it can legislate. Parliament can do anything. In a federal system, this is obviously not the case: the whole idea is to *distribute* legislative powers between different levels of government by means of a written Constitution. Whether a legislature has exceeded its powers thus becomes a legal question, entrusted by virtually all federations to a constitutional court. But as long as a legislature stays within the limits of its powers, *what it does within those limits* may still be protected by something very like 'parliamentary sovereignty'. So it has been in Australia.

The main areas in which the Commonwealth Parliament can legislate are listed in Section 51 of the Constitution. Most of the High Court's constitutional work has involved the testing of particular laws to determine whether they fall within the appropriate 'heads of power'. There is not (as there is for the Canadian provinces) any corresponding list of state powers: under Sections 106 and 107 the States simply continued *after* 1901 with the powers which they had (as colonies) *before* 1901. A few areas of power are vested *exclusively* in the Commonwealth (notably by Sections 52 and 90); but subject to this and other qualifications, the basic assumptions are as follows.

The states can legislate on *any* subject, with a plenitude of power coming close to that of the Imperial Parliament itself. The Commonwealth can legislate *only* in the areas given to it by the Constitution. Usually the states still have power in these areas, too. The result is 'concurrent' power shared by the Commonwealth and states. But since this creates a possibility of conflict between state and Commonwealth laws, Section 109 provides that in any such conflict the Commonwealth law shall prevail.

The crucial question is always whether the Commonwealth law is valid: if it is, it *automatically* prevails over any inconsistent state law. A good example is the *Franklin Dam Case* (1983), where Commonwealth legislation was used to prevent the building of a Tasmanian dam. Whether the Commonwealth Act was valid involved difficult and controversial questions, on most of which the Court divided 4:3. But once the majority had decided that the Act was (partially) valid, it followed *automatically* that the Act overrode Tasmanian laws authorising the dam.

The first generation of High Court judges tried to temper this potential for Commonwealth supremacy by doctrines of 'balanced federalism'. First, the states and the Commonwealth were each to be treated as 'sovereign' governments, so that neither could be bound by the laws of the other. This reciprocal doctrine of 'implied immunities' extended to the governments and all of their agencies: in particular, it meant that the Commonwealth system of industrial arbitration could not extend to the industrial relations of state agencies, as employers, with Public Service employees. Second, the interpretation of Commonwealth 'heads of power' in Section 51 was tempered by a doctrine of 'reserved State powers'. The Court approached its task of construing the limits of Commonwealth power with an assumption that certain traditional areas were 'reserved' to the states, so that Commonwealth powers must be understood narrowly to avoid any encroachment on these areas.

In 1920, both these doctrines were overruled in the *Engineers' Case*, a landmark judgment by Sir Isaac Isaacs. Joining the Court in 1906, at first as a frequent dissenter, Isaacs had risen by 1920 to commanding intellectual dominance under the ineffectual Chief Justice Sir Adrian Knox. The new directions of the *Engineers' Case* have dominated the Court's work ever since. In 1981, Sir Garfield Barwick's farewell message as Chief Justice was a warning 'to be very wary that the triumph of the *Engineers' Case* is never tarnished' (Barwick 1981: x). The *Engineers' Case* insisted that the states have *no* 'implied immunities': if on its fair interpretation a Commonwealth head of power turns out to extend to laws which bind state governments, so be it. Nor are there any 'reserved State powers': Commonwealth grants of power must be construed *without* preconceptions, and if they turn out to extend into areas previously occupied by the states, this is simply the natural result of the way the Constitution was drafted.

The result was to concentrate the Court's work more closely on the basic task of interpreting what the Commonwealth heads of power mean. In the new approach to that task, 'parliamentary sovereignty' was influential in several ways (Gageler 1987). For one thing: Isaacs' argument depended on reading the Constitution as an Act of the Imperial Parliament, invested with the full 'parliamentary sovereignty' of that Parliament itself. We have seen that after 1986 this approach may no longer be possible. Nowadays we may have to interpret the Constitution simply as the ultimate foundational charter of Australia's framework of laws and governments, with no continuing significance attached to its British origins.

Secondly, it followed that the High Court, in construing Section 51 of the Constitution, was to follow the standard judicial procedures for interpretation of statutes, concentrating on the legal denotation of the actual words. As a British Law Lord had said in *Vacher & Sons* v. *London Society of Compositors* (1913):

> [A] judicial tribunal has nothing to do with the policy of any Act which it may be called upon to interpret...The duty of the court, and its only duty, is to expound the language of the Act in accordance with the settled rules of construction.

Even in the *Engineers' Case*, Isaacs conceded that the Constitution must be read in a wider context — 'in the light of the circumstances in which it was made, with knowledge of the combined fabric of the common law, and the statute law which preceded it'. The emphasis was not *merely* on the actual language, but *also* on the 'recognized principle[s] of the common law of the Constitution'. But this enlarged conception of the relevant legal materials was still limited to legal materials: it did *not* extend (as Isaacs maintained that the earlier cases on 'implied immunities' had done) to

> an interpretation of the Constitution depending on an implication which is formed on a vague, individual conception of the spirit of the compact..., arrived at by the Court on the opinions of Judges as to hopes and expectations respecting vague external conditions.

The sweeping rejection of 'implications' could not be sustained. From 1930 on, it was steadily whittled down by Sir Owen Dixon, who joined the Court in 1929, and by 1952 had become its most influential Chief Justice. In *West's Case* (1937) he wrote:

> Since the *Engineers' Case* a notion seems to have gained currency that in interpreting the Constitution no implications can be made. Such a method of construction would defeat the intention of any instrument, but of all instruments a written constitution seems the last to which it could be applied.

And in *Melbourne Corporation v. The Commonwealth* (1947), Dixon led the Court in deciding that there must be *some* implied limitation on what the Commonwealth can do to the states: its powers cannot be used to enact a law which 'discriminates' against states, or 'places a particular disability or burden' on a state ('more especially upon the execution of its constitutional powers'). To the argument that this implied limitation on Commonwealth powers was founded on 'political rather than legal considerations', Dixon replied that such an objection was 'meaningless':

> The Constitution is a political instrument. It deals with government and governmental powers...It is not a question whether the considerations are political, for nearly every consideration arising from the Constitution can be so described, but whether they are compelling.

Today 'the *Melbourne Corporation* principle' stands as a clear example of a principle judicially found to be *implied* in the Constitution. As the Court explores other 'implied limitations', *Melbourne Corporation* is frequently invoked. In *Leeth* v. *The Commonwealth* (1992), Justices Deane and Toohey used it to argue not only that the Constitution *typically* incorporates 'underlying doctrines or principles' by a process of implication, but that if the Constitution excludes 'arbitrary or discriminatory treatment' of *states*, it must surely exclude discriminatory treatment 'of the people themselves'.

A third impact of British 'parliamentary sovereignty' on the *Engineers' Case* is the idea that once the limits of a Commonwealth 'head of power' are determined, the legislative power within these limits is as plenary as that of the Imperial Parliament itself. In *Hodge* v. *The Queen* (1883) and other nineteenth century cases, the Privy Council had held that grants of colonial self-government gave 'authority as plenary and as ample within the limits prescribed...as the Imperial Parliament in the plenitude of its power possessed and could bestow'. The only limits were those 'of subjects and area'. Thus the grants of power in Section 51 must primarily be understood in terms of subject matter, and the issue for the High Court is whether a particular law can fairly be described as a law 'with respect to' that subject matter. Once a sufficient connection with subject matter is shown, the way Parliament deals with it, its political objectives in doing so, and its harmony or dissonance with social, institutional and moral values, are matters entirely for Parliament.

All this was reinforced in the *Engineers* judgment by yet another aspect of 'parliamentary sovereignty'. One reason why, in Britain, the courts renounced their earlier claims to evaluate and perhaps to invalidate statutes was that this kind of activism would undermine the democratic structure of 'responsible government'. The possibility that Parliament might enact an outrageously unjust or immoral law should be guarded against by political and social restraints, not by judicial intervention. If a Parliament did enact such a law, the remedy was for the electorate to vote the government out. The *Engineers* judgment stressed that the Constitution is 'permeated through and through with the spirit of...responsible government', so that any 'extravagant use of the granted powers' should be 'guarded against by the constituencies and not by the Courts'.

This appeal to 'responsible government' is itself, of course, a political argument. Indeed, the whole issue of how far (and in what sense) judges should be 'political' is itself a political issue (Evans 1976, Galligan 1987). Conceptions of the judicial function are themselves among the political conceptions which influence judicial reasoning. The perception that 'responsible government' no longer *works* is an even more potent factor: if Parliament no longer controls the executive, nor adequately responds to the people, then judges may feel that a greater responsibility for democracy devolves upon them (Zines 1991: 35, Toohey 1993).

Appropriate and Proportionate Laws

A new focus for the judicial review of Commonwealth legislation began to emerge in the *Franklin Dam Case* (1983). The Commonwealth legislation in that case relied in part on the power to legislate with respect to 'external affairs' (Constitution, Section 51(xxix)). The High Court majority accepted an argument that an international treaty or convention (in that case the 1972 UNESCO Convention for the Protection of the World Cultural and Natural Heritage) may impose international *obligations*, and that legislation within Australia to honour these will be valid because this is an aspect of Australia's 'external affairs'. While the basic principle had been established as early as *Roche v. Kronheimer* (1921), its limits (if any) were unclear. Did the principle extend to any treaty obligation whatsoever? Or only to those whose subject matter had some inherently international character or (at the very least) had attracted clear international concern? The *Franklin Dam Case* established that there was no such limitation: *any* treaty obligation might trigger legislation with respect to 'external affairs'. In part this conclusion itself involved deference to 'parliamentary sovereignty'. Thus Justice Mason argued that 'the Court cannot substitute its judgment for that of the executive government and Parliament'. But for those who protested that this would give the Commonwealth unlimited power, the majority judges answered that the validity of any particular law remains open to judicial scrutiny. On this point Justice Mason said:

> I reject the notion that once Australia enters into a treaty Parliament may legislate with respect to the subject-matter of the treaty as if that subject-matter were a new and independent head of Commonwealth legislative power. The law must conform to the treaty and carry its provisions into effect.

This demand for conformity to the treaty was not a new one, but precisely what degree of conformity was necessary had been unclear. The earlier cases allowed *some* degree of divergence from a treaty or selectivity among its provisions: if Parliament can validly implement a treaty, it must have *some* leeway for judgment as to how, and how far, to do so. Yet the conformity must be reasonably close. In the *Franklin Dam Case*, Justices Brennan and Deane took the argument further. What makes the legislation valid in such a case is the *purpose* of implementing the treaty: its connection with 'external affairs' arises only because of that purpose. Accordingly, they said, the law will be valid only if it constitutes an 'appropriate' and 'proportionate' means of achieving that purpose.

In the *Franklin Dam Case* itself, the words 'appropriate' and 'proportionate' were used in an instrumental way. The legislation had sought to protect the 'natural heritage' by prohibiting a list of specific acts: excavations, drilling for minerals, putting up or tearing down buildings, cutting down trees, building roads, or using explosives. But for Justices Brennan and Deane *all* these specific prohibitions were invalid. The UNESCO Convention was not directed to one unique wilderness area, but to general protection for humanity's environmental and cultural heritage — and the Commonwealth legislation was framed in similarly general terms. Yet the need in any specific instance would be for appropriate safeguards of one unique property, perhaps against one unique threat. (How many of the above prohibitions would be appropriate if the Sydney Harbour Bridge had to be preserved?) The solution, said these two judges, was *not* to impose blanket prohibitions on a wide range of acts which in any one case might prove wholly irrelevant, but to devise a protective regime which could be tailored to particular cases: to authorise the government to identify *specific* acts threatening *specific* property, and then to prohibit those acts 'in relation to that property'. Only one paragraph of one sub-section was drafted in these terms. Hence only that paragraph was valid.

In this instance the words 'appropriate' and 'proportionate' called for practical solutions to practical problems. But in other contexts they may involve just the sort of evaluative assessment which the *Engineers' Case* denied. Since 1983 the same criteria have resurfaced in an increasing variety of constitutional contexts, with the Court first reducing the issue of validity to one of 'purpose', and then asking whether legislation is an 'appropriate' and 'proportionate' way of achieving that purpose.

Thus, in *Cole* v. *Whitfield* (1988), the Court undertook a radical reappraisal of over 140 previous decisions on Section 92 of the Constitution, rejecting most of the principles on which the older decisions depended. Traditionally, Section 92 (guaranteeing interstate 'trade, commerce and intercourse' as 'absolutely free') had been read as imposing drastic constraints on the ability of both state and Commonwealth Parliaments to regulate the economy: even laws with no *specific* focus on interstate trade were held invalid in their application to interstate traders. In the *Bank Nationalisation Case* (1948), the Chifley government's nationalisation law was held invalid mainly because of its impact on interstate banking. The unanimous judgment in *Cole* v. *Whitfield* cut back the interpretation of Section 92 to a much narrower scope: henceforth interstate trade will be protected only against 'discriminatory burdens of a protectionist kind'. Ordinary regulatory legislation, not overtly discriminatory, may still be invalid if it is 'discriminatory in effect' and if the effect is 'protectionist': these are 'issues of fact and degree'. A law may pursue a non-protectionist purpose 'in a way or to an extent' that turns out to discriminate against interstate trade in a protectionist way.

The real issue in such a case is 'proportionality', as later cases make clear. In *Castlemaine Tooheys Ltd* v. *South Australia* (1990), South

Australia had regulated the sale of beer by requiring a refundable deposit of 15 cents for a non-refillable bottle (as against 4 cents for a refillable one). The purpose was to encourage the return of non-refillable bottles (thereby reducing litter), but also to limit the manufacture of glass (thereby reducing energy consumption and atmospheric pollution). It was held that these aims could have been achieved by a smaller disparity in refunds. Since non-refillable bottles were used mainly by interstate breweries, the disproportionate differentiation 'discriminated' against interstate brewers, thus protecting their local competitors.

The actual decision is controversial; what is important is the principle. Most judges in *Castlemaine Tooheys* focused on the issue of 'protectionism', asserting that a law with 'a legitimate object' may still infringe Section 92 if its impact on interstate trade is more than merely 'incidental', or is 'disproportionate to the attainment of the legitimate object'. They specifically invoked the *Franklin Dam Case*, explaining that a 'disproportionate' regime will not be considered 'appropriate'. Justices Gaudron and Toohey focused rather on 'discrimination'. For them, a law will be 'discriminatory' if it makes an irrelevant distinction, or if relevant distinctions are not reflected in 'appropriate' differential treatment.

Davis v. The Commonwealth (1988) focused on the 1988 Bicentennial celebrations. The Court agreed that commemoration of the first British settlement in Australia was an appropriate project for the national government. The idea that the Commonwealth can sometimes take action *simply* because it is the national government, with no need to adduce a specific 'head of power', went back to observations by Sir Owen Dixon in the *Pharmaceutical Benefits Case* (1945). In 1988 the whole Court accepted this 'nationhood power'. But Justices Wilson, Dawson and Toohey rejected any notion of 'inherent' power, insisting that *any* Commonwealth power must have a specific basis in the constitutional text. They preferred to think of 'the nationhood power' as an aspect of Commonwealth 'executive power' under Section 61 — with legislation *incidental* to an exercise of this executive power open to Parliament under Section 51(xxxix).

On that basis, the whole Court accepted that the Commonwealth could validly establish a Bicentennial Authority to organise the celebrations, and had validly funded the Authority throughout the 1980s. They further accepted that under the Australian Bicentennial Authority Act 1980, the Authority was validly given some degree of control over bicentennial logos and trademarks. But the Act had extended to a prohibition of any commercial use, without consent, of words like 'Bicentennial', '200 Years', 'First Settlement', 'Sydney' or 'Melbourne'. The Court held that this was 'grossly disproportionate': an 'extraordinary intrusion into freedom of expression', which was not 'reasonably and appropriately adapted' to its purpose.

It is not surprising that *Davis* v. *The Commonwealth* was cited in the 'free speech' cases, nor that as how far the Parliament *could* legitimately regulate or restrict political discussion, the words 'appropriate' and 'proportionate' tended to recur — at least for laws whose effect on political debate is only 'incidental'. For Justice McHugh such a law must be 'designed to protect some competing aspect of the public interest', and any restraint on free communication must not be 'disproportionate to the end sought to be achieved'. Chief Justice Mason also envisaged a weighing of competing public interests. His main criterion was whether the restriction imposed was 'reasonably necessary to achieve the competing public interest'. He, too, reduced this largely to a question of 'proportionality' to the ostensible purpose, since lack of proportion would suggest that the actual 'purpose and effect' was to impair free communication. The analogy with current approaches to Section 92 is obvious.

For laws whose impact is more direct, these judges had a more stringent test. As Justice McHugh put it in *Capital Television*, these are 'laws which restrict the freedom of electoral communications by prohibiting or regulating their contents' (as distinct from 'laws which incidentally limit that freedom by regulating the time, place or manner of communication'). For Chief Justice Mason these are laws 'which target ideas or information' as such. For both judges, such *direct* restrictions will need 'compelling justification'. Even then, the Chief Justice added, 'the restriction must be no more than is reasonably necessary' to protect some 'competing public interest'. Such restrictions will be 'extremely difficult' to justify: in the balance of 'competing public interests', freedom of communication will usually have 'paramount weight'.

For this same class of laws, *directly* interfering with political discourse, Justices Deane and Toohey had a more elaborate test, explained in both cases in almost identical terms. A direct prohibition or control will be valid

> only if, viewed in the context of the standards of our society, it is justified as being in the public interest for the reason that the prohibitions and restrictions on political communications which it imposes are either conducive to the overall availability of the effective means of such communications [in a democratic society] or do not go beyond what is reasonably necessary for the preservation of an ordered and democratic society or for the protection or vindication of the legitimate claims of individuals to live peacefully and with dignity within such a society.

Justice Gaudron drew no distinction between different classes of laws. For her, *any* law impairing freedom of speech must fall within a specific constitutional grant of power, and be 'reasonably and appropriately adapted' to 'some end within the limits of that power'. What is 'reasonable and appropriate' will be determined largely by looking to 'the general law': for example, the existing laws of 'defamation, sedition, blasphemy, obscenity and offensive language'. Justice Brennan did not distinguish different classes of legislation, either. As he put it in *Nationwide News*:

> No law of the Commonwealth can restrict the freedom of the Australian people to discuss governments and political matters unless the law is enacted to fulfil a legitimate purpose and the restriction is appropriate and adapted to the fulfilment of that purpose...The Constitution prohibits any legislative or executive infringement of the freedom...except to the extent necessary to protect other legitimate interests and, in any event, not to an extent which substantially impairs the capacity of, or opportunity for, the Australian people to form the political judgments required for the exercise of their constitutional functions.

He stressed that the judgment is 'a matter of degree' in which 'the material factors include the practicability of protection by a less severe curtailment of the freedom and the extent to which the protection of the other interest itself enhances the ability of the Australian people to enjoy their democratic rights and privileges'.

The differences amongst these formulations are unlikely to be significant. Justice Brennan made it clear that the balancing of interests is primarily a matter for Parliament, with the Court confined to a 'supervisory' role of declaring 'whether a balance struck by the Parliament' falls within 'the range of legitimate legislative choice'. But this, too, is implicit in all the judgments. When Justice Brennan upheld the political broadcasting scheme as valid, it was not because he applied a weaker test than the majority judges, but because, by substantially the same test, he came to a different answer.

What may be more significant is that, in *Nationwide News*, the three judges who did *not* rely on an 'implied guarantee' nonetheless found the law invalid by a very similar test. In particular, Chief Justice Mason gave a powerful reinterpretation of the Court's traditional doctrines. He pointed out that the case depended on 'incidental power': that is, on the settled doctrine that wherever Parliament can legislate 'with respect to' a subject matter, it can also legislate on matters 'incidental to' that subject matter or its 'main purpose'. (This use of 'implied incidental power' has always played an essential part in the broad construction of Commonwealth powers.) To establish the Industrial Relations Commission was obviously an exercise of the *primary* power to legislate with respect to conciliation and arbitration of industrial disputes (Constitution, Section 51(xxxv)). To protect the Commission against public denigration (by analogy with contempt of court) was 'incidental' to the primary power. But the way it was done had left no room for healthy criticism (as we now do when defining contempt of court). In the absence of any such safety valve, the whole Court held that the law went too far.

For Chief Justice Mason this did *not* depend on an 'implied guarantee', but only on a closer analysis of 'incidental power'. What brings such a law within 'incidental power' (he said) is its *purpose*, since this is what establishes the necessary link with the primary subject of power. This element of purpose as a key to questions of 'incidental power' had often been noted in the past. In the 1948 *Bank Nationalisation Case*, for example, Sir Owen Dixon had said:

[I]n all cases where it is sought to connect with a legislative power a measure which lies at the circumference of the subject or can at best be only incidental to it, the end or purpose of the provision, if discernible, will give the key.

But, in any case where the validity of legislation depends on its purpose, it follows (says Chief Justice Mason) that it will only be valid to the extent that it seeks to achieve this by 'appropriate' and 'reasonably proportionate' means. If a law has 'adverse consequences', going beyond 'what is reasonably necessary or conceivably desirable for the achievement of [its] legitimate object', it will be invalid — especially if it entails an 'infringement of fundamental values protected by the common law, such as freedom of expression'. In this case, although *some* protection for the Commission was justified, the law was disproportionate because of its impact on 'such a fundamental freedom as freedom of expression, particularly...in relation to public affairs and freedom to criticise public institutions'.

The older cases had also insisted that questions of 'incidental power' (or of 'reasonable connection' with the subject of power) are only matters of degree. While accepting this description, the Chief Justice added:

[T]he question of degree is not merely a matter for Parliament; although the court will give weight to the view of Parliament, it is a matter for the court in determining whether a reasonable connection exists.

In *Burton* v. *Honan* (1952), Sir Owen Dixon had similarly insisted on *the Court's* concern with 'matters of degree', but added that such issues should *not* be confused with issues of 'justice, fairness, morality and propriety'. In that case the forfeiture provisions in the *Customs Act* 1901 had operated unjustly. The confidence man who fraudulently imported a second-hand Buick had sold it to a dealer, who sold it to an innocent purchaser, from whom it was seized by customs officers once the fraud was detected. What Dixon was saying was that this unfair *result* could not affect his finding that the forfeiture provisions had a 'reasonable connection' with legislative control of imports. Such provisions were a normal feature of laws relating to customs and prohibited imports; there was nothing unusual or extraordinary about them. In *Nationwide News*, the comparable standard of normality was the law of contempt of court. It was measurement against this standard which showed that the law 'went too far'.

In reaching this conclusion, Chief Justice Mason gave explicit weight to 'infringement of fundamental values...such as freedom of expression'. But this, too, was a way of measuring what was unusual or extraordinary about the law. He did not reject the contempt provision *because* it offended the value which we attach to freedom of speech; he weighed up the degree of infringement of that value, and balanced it against the legitimate aim of protecting the Industrial Relations Commission, to conclude that the legitimacy of the objective was 'outweighed by the strength of the public interest in public scrutiny and freedom to criticise'. The weighing of interests and values was undertaken not to determine whether the law was 'good' or 'bad' (which is not a judicial question), but only to determine whether it was 'proportionate' (which is).

Justices Dawson and McHugh agreed with this basic approach, but insisted more anxiously that a judgment of degree (as to whether the incidental power has been stretched too far) is not a judicial value judgment as such (even when 'stretching too far' is measured by adverse effect on accepted values). Justice McHugh was happy to talk of a 'reasonable connection', tested by 'proportionality'; and to find the law disproportionate because of its 'far reaching interference with the common law right of members of the public to make fair comments on matters of public interest'. But he emphasised that if a 'reasonable connection' had been established (on the basis of 'proportionality'), the validity of the law would not thereafter have been open to challenge. At that stage the traditional doctrine of *Burton* v. *Honan* would apply: once a law is fairly within power, its 'justice and wisdom...are matters entirely for the Legislature and not for the Judiciary'.

Justice Dawson made the same point by rejecting altogether the language of 'reasonable connection', since 'it is no part of this court's function...to determine whether in its view the law is reasonable or not'. Instead, he insisted, the question must be merely one of '*sufficient* connection'. He saw the words 'appropriate' and 'proportionate' as similarly misleading:

> No doubt a law which is inappropriate or ill-adapted for the purpose of achieving a legitimate end may fail for want of a power. But it fails not because the court considers the law to be inappropriate or ill adapted but because the very fact that the law is inappropriate or

ill adapted prevents there being a sufficient connection between the law and a relevant head of power. The question is essentially one of connection, not appropriateness or proportionality, and where a sufficient connection is established it is not for the court to judge whether the law is appropriate or disproportionate.

By insisting that this difference 'is more than merely verbal', Justice Dawson was saying simply that one formulation conforms to a traditional orthodox view of the Court's constitutional functions, while the other might carry it into hitherto unacknowledged areas of overt value judgment. But this only highlights, of course, the deeper significance of these three judgments. This is not merely that the current language of 'appropriateness or proportionality', as measured in part by the degree of impact on fundamental values, can now be used to determine whether a law is 'within power' (in any case where the *purpose* of the law is relevant), but that this analysis gives us a clearer understanding of what the Court has always done in such cases.

In particular, in the *Communist Party Case* (1951), all judges except Sir John Latham held that the Communist Party Dissolution Act 1950 was *not* a valid exercise of the 'defence' power (Constitution, Section 51(vi)). In part this was simply a strong reassertion that issues of constitutional power are issues *for the High Court*. The Act began with a long preamble attempting to establish, by recitals of fact, the existence of a sufficient defence emergency to justify its provisions. The Court's rejection of this expedient was memorably summed up by Sir Wilfred Fullagar: 'Parliament cannot recite itself into a field the gates of which are locked against it by superior law.' But the Court then faced a double question of degree — assessing *for itself* the extent to which international hostility or internal subversion might threaten Australia's defence, and balancing this against the degree to which the Act itself subverted traditional liberties and procedural safeguards. (Organisations could be dissolved, and individuals permanently barred from employment by trade unions or the Commonwealth Public Service, on the basis of a determination by the Governor-General, advised by an official security committee but with no adequate means of judicial review.) As the judgments of Sir Wilfred Fullagar and Sir Owen Dixon made clear, a sufficiently grave defence emergency might have justified even this 'derogation of civil and proprietary rights', while even the existing Cold War situation might have justified *some* action against Communists, less drastic in its effect or more open to judicial safeguards. But, as Dixon himself had repeatedly insisted in earlier cases, the test of validity under the 'defence' power is whether a law is conducive to a *purpose* connected with defence. The modern requirement that such a law be 'appropriate' and 'proportionate' to its purpose is an economical explanation of why the Dissolution Act failed.

Alternatively, the Commonwealth had argued that the law was valid as an exercise of what we now call 'the nationhood power'. But both Dixon and Fullagar held that this power could *never* support such a law. As Dixon put it:

> The power is ancillary or incidental to sustaining and carrying on government. Moreover, it is government under the Constitution and that is an instrument framed in accordance with many traditional conceptions, to some of which it gives effect, as, for example, in separating the judicial power from other functions of government, others of which are simply assumed. Among these I think that it may fairly be said that the rule of law forms an assumption.

Judicial Power

These references to 'judicial power' and 'the rule of law' suggest not only that the Court has always felt able to deny the validity of laws with a disproportionate impact on fundamental values, but that, among these values, it will be especially vigilant to defend the 'due process' safeguards traditionally ascribed to the judicial process itself.

In principle, this presupposes that judicial power is constitutionally insulated from legislative or executive encroachments by a strict 'separation of powers'. In the United States this principle extends to the separation of the *executive* government (headed by the President) from the *legislative* power of Congress. By contrast, the British model of 'parliamentary sovereignty' depends on the institutional *integration* of legislative and executive powers. The Ministers who advise the Queen (and head the executive government) must themselves be Members of Parliament, and answerable to it, and much of the day-to-day operation of government depends on *delegation* to the executive of Parliament's *legislative* power (through the power to make regulations and 'statutory rules', albeit under statutory authority and subject to parliamentary review).

Although the Australian Constitution mirrors by its formal division into chapters the American 'separation of powers', the influence of the British parliamentary model has excluded any possibility of a legislative/executive separation in the American sense. Any doubt on this score was finally settled in 1931. A long-running struggle between rival unions for control of the Melbourne waterfront had led to a protracted deadlock between the Labor government and a hostile Senate. In a series of cases culminating in *Dignan's Case* (1931), the High Court refused to interfere. The legal issues involved the government's attempt to give union preference by using regulations which (under an Act of the previous government) could override even Acts of Parliament; but the High Court held that even this extraordinary delegation of legislative power to the executive government was valid.

Owen Dixon explained that 'the time had passed' for any strict separation in Australia of legislative and executive powers. (He based this 'less upon juristic analysis' than 'upon the history and usages of British legislation'.) But he also insisted that for judicial power there *is* a complete separation:

> [B]ecause of the distribution of the functions of government and of the manner in which the Constitution describes the tribunals to be invested with the judicial power of the Commonwealth, and defines the judicial power to be invested in them, the Parliament is restrained both from reposing any power essentially judicial in any other organ or body, and from reposing any other than that judicial power in such tribunals.

Both propositions are important. At the Commonwealth level, judicial power can be exercised only by a court (as defined by Chapter III of the Constitution), and a court cannot be required to exercise anything other than judicial power (as similarly defined).

Twenty-five years after *Dignan's Case*, these arguments came to fruition in the *Boilermakers' Case* (1956). Dixon, as Chief Justice, led the Court in a 4:3 decision. The industrial arbitration power (Constitution, Section 51(xxxv)) had been exercised through the Commonwealth Court of Conciliation and Arbitration since 1904. In *making* industrial awards it functioned as an arbitration tribunal; in *enforcing* these awards it functioned as a court. The *Boilermakers' Case* held that this arrangement was unconstitutional, since it mixed judicial and non-judicial powers in the same tribunal.

In *R.* v. *Joske* (1974), Sir Garfield Barwick criticised this decision as leading to 'excessive subtlety and technicality' without 'any compensating benefit'. In *R.* v. *Joske* (1976) it looked as if *Boilermakers* might be overruled — but the moment passed. Since then the *Boilermakers* principle has been qualified by pragmatic compromises, but not directly challenged. In recent years the view of Chapter III as an exclusive 'code' of Commonwealth judicial power has assumed larger significance.

In *Street* v. *Queensland Bar Association* (1989), Justice Deane set out to refute the idea that the Constitution is not concerned with human rights. He said:

> The Constitution contains a significant number of express or implied guarantees of rights and immunities. The most important of them is the guarantee that the citizen can be subjected to the exercise of Commonwealth judicial power only by the 'courts' designated by Chapter III.

In other words, the vesting of judicial power in 'courts', their insulation in a self-contained chapter of the Constitution, and their guaranteed independence, combine to ensure the effective protection of most of what the Fifth and Fourteenth Amendments to the United States Constitution refer to as 'due process of law'.

Justice Deane has developed this conception in several recent cases — often with significant support, though not as yet with a majority. In *Polyukhovich* v. *The Commonwealth* (1991), the issue was the validity of the War Crimes Amendment Act 1988, aimed at 'persons who committed serious war crimes in Europe during World War II' and later migrated to Australia. The Act provided for such persons to be tried for 'war crimes' in Australian courts. Polyukhovich was the first (and perhaps the last) person so to be tried; on 18 May 1993 he was eventually acquitted. His earlier attack on the validity of the Act had very narrowly failed. The Act had an element of 'retrospectivity', in that it created for the first time a new (and very technical) Australian definition of 'war crimes', applying this retrospectively to events more than forty years earlier. It also had an element of selectivity, in that it made no attempt to cover 'war crimes' in general, but *only* those committed in Europe during World War II. On the initial question of whether the Act was 'within power', a clear majority held it was: it fell within Commonwealth legislative power with respect to 'external affairs' (Constitution, Section 51(xxix)). Justice Brennan dissented because of the law's retrospective operation, and because of the 'oppressive and discriminatory' effect of its very narrow temporal and geographical focus. For him, these defects meant that the law could not be regarded as 'appropriate' or 'proportionate' to any valid legislative purpose.

Justice Deane agreed with the majority view that the law *was* 'within power', but argued that such power could not be used to infringe an implied guarantee against retrospective criminal laws. Not only does Chapter III vest judicial power exclusively in 'courts', but these must be 'courts acting as courts with all that that notion essentially requires'. What it requires in criminal cases is a finding of guilt or innocence *under the law*: that is, an ascertainment of whether in fact the accused contravened a law applicable 'at the time the act was done'. By contrast, the War Crimes Amendment Act

> imposes a legislative enactment of past guilt which it requires the courts, in violation of the basic tenet of our criminal jurisprudence and the doctrine of separation of judicial from legislative and executive powers, to apply and enforce.

In English constitutional history, the extreme example of 'usurpation' of judicial power by Parliament was the use of Bills of Attainder (legislative enactments declaring a specific person to be guilty of a past offence, and imposing punishment). The United States Constitution specifically forbids such a practice; elsewhere it is obsolete. Both Chief

Justice Mason and Justice McHugh rejected the wider implications of Justice Deane's argument, but agreed at least that a Bill of Attainder would be unconstitutional. Justice Dawson also inclined to this view. To that extent, a clear majority recognised an 'implied guarantee'.

Justice Gaudron, moreover, accepted the wider argument in its entirety, and Justice Toohey showed evident sympathy with it, though adding that not *every* retroactive criminal law would offend Chapter III:

> It is only if a law purports to operate in such a way as to require a court to act contrary to accepted notions of judicial power that a contravention of Chapter III may be involved.

Justice Toohey's actual decision was very narrow indeed. The allegations against Polyukhovich were of murder, or of knowingly being concerned in murder. If proved, these acts would have constituted serious crimes, whenever committed. Accordingly, the operation of the Act *in this case* was not 'offensively retroactive': the new definitional elements did not 'alter the nature of the conduct'. He therefore held that, in its application to *this* information against *this* defendant, the Act was 'not retroactive in a way offensive to Chapter III'.

In short, Justices Deane and Gaudron held that the Act was invalid because it infringed an implied guarantee against retroactive criminal laws. Justice Brennan reached the same result by holding (on the basis of similar values) that the Act was not 'within power'. Although the Chief Justice and Justices Dawson and McHugh took a different view, the Act survived constitutional challenge only by virtue of Justice Toohey's holding that it did not operate invalidly in this individual case.

In *Leeth* v. *The Commonwealth* (1992), an 'implied guarantee' was again pressed most strongly by Justice Deane. Under Section 120 of the Constitution, persons convicted under Commonwealth laws are housed in state gaols. Until 1989 this arrangement was regulated by the Commonwealth Prisoners Act 1967, which required that non-parole periods be governed by the laws of the state where the trial took place. Thus state and Commonwealth prisoners within a state had similar parole expectations, but for Commonwealth prisoners in different States, expectations varied widely.

Leeth, who was convicted and sentenced in Queensland, maintained that the 1967 law was unconstitutional — since all Commonwealth prisoners should be treated equally, wherever they were sentenced or imprisoned. The argument depended on an implied constitutional guarantee of equality.

The Chief Justice, and Justices Dawson and McHugh, rejected it. They found *no* 'general implication...[in] the Constitution that Commonwealth laws must not be discriminatory or must operate uniformly throughout the Commonwealth'. They conceded that a law might 'discriminate against particular offenders or classes of offenders in such a way that the legislation travels beyond matters which are incidental to the main power'. But such a law would be invalid *because* it would stretch the 'incidental power' too far — not because of any 'implied prohibition'.

Justices Deane and Toohey held that the Constitution *does* embody a 'general doctrine of legal equality'. Equality is *not* infringed where differential treatment has 'a rational and relevant basis', and it might be appropriate to require a judge 'to take account of' state laws. But to fix parole conditions solely by reference to the place of sentencing involved 'an extraordinary degree of disproportionality'. Justice Gaudron agreed, but (as in *Polyukhovich*), she tied the implied guarantee much more closely to Chapter III of the Constitution. 'An essential feature of judicial power' is its exercise 'in accordance with the judicial process'; and 'the concept of equal justice…is fundamental to the judicial process'.

The deciding vote was that of Justice Brennan. He conceded that discrimination *among offenders* might offend 'the constitutional unity of the Australian people'. Thus 'different maximum penalties for the same offence' might well be invalid. But here the discrimination was among Commonwealth *prisoners*, as to the executive power of parole. As long as Commonwealth prisoners are held in state gaols, adoption of state parole regimes 'is not only a rational ground of discrimination' but 'a necessary ground'.

Polyukhovich was decided in August 1991, and *Leeth* in June 1992. Thus, in the months leading up to the 'free speech' cases, the idea that judicially enforceable guarantees of rights and freedoms are *implied* in the Constitution, though never quite attaining majority acceptance, had been edging steadily closer.

Implied Rights

The American 'Bill of Rights' is embodied in the first ten amendments added to the United States Constitution in 1791. The First Amendment guarantees freedom of religion, freedom of speech and press, the right of assembly and the right of petition. The Fourth Amendment prohibits 'unreasonable searches and seizures'. The Fifth, Sixth and Seventh Amendments guarantee rights of 'due process', including the right to trial by jury. The Eighth Amendment prohibits excessive fines or bail, and 'cruel and unusual punishments'. All of these are judicially enforceable limits on legislative and executive powers at the *federal* level. The Thirteenth and Fourteenth Amendments, added after the Civil War, prohibit slavery or 'involuntary servitude', and extend most of the earlier guarantees to the state level, as well.

Although the Australian Constitution makers deliberately avoided the idea of a systematic Bill of Rights, some fragments of the American language survived. Section 116 adapts the First Amendment language about 'establishment' and 'free exercise' of religion; Section 80 takes from the Sixth Amendment the guarantee of trial by jury in criminal cases. The provision in the Fifth Amendment that property *cannot* be acquired 'without just compensation' becomes, in the Australian Section 51(xxxi), a provision that property *can* be acquired 'on just terms', and the High Court has interpreted this as impliedly *guaranteeing* 'just terms'. But all these guarantees are expressed as limits only on Commonwealth power, not on the powers of the states. At least as to freedom of religion and trial by jury, their practical effect has been minimal.

The idea that additional guarantees might be *implied* in the Constitution was first systematically advocated by Lionel Murphy. In 1973, when Attorney-General, he had tried unsuccessfully to introduce a statutory Bill of Rights. As a High Court judge from 1975 to 1986, he tackled the problem from two other directions.

His first tactic was an attempt to revive the express guarantees that do appear in the text of the Constitution, by arguing against the restrictive construction they had so far received. As to trial by jury, for example, Section 80 provides: 'The trial on indictment of any offence against any law of the Commonwealth shall be by jury...' Clearly this only applies when there is a 'trial on indictment' — but when is that? According to one view, the indictment procedure is used in cases to be tried by a jury. On that basis, Section 80 means only: 'There shall be trial by jury when there is trial by jury.' According to another view, there is a 'trial on indictment' in cases where the relevant legislation prescribes it. On that basis, the Commonwealth Parliament has unlimited discretion to determine whether, for a given offence, the guarantee of trial by jury shall apply or not.

In *Lowenstein's Case* (1938), a joint judgment by Justices Dixon and Evatt had argued that these interpretations must be wrong — that Section 80 must be interpreted as a real guarantee, at least in serious cases. ('The Constitution is not to be mocked.') In *Beckwith* v. *R.* (1976) and *Li Chia Hsing* v. *Rankin* (1978), Justice Murphy revived this argument. It has since been powerfully taken up by Justice Deane in *Kingswell* v. *R.* (1985). He, too, insists that the Court should identify a category of serious cases to which Section 80 *must* apply.

The need to identify such cases has not yet won majority acceptance. But in cases where Section 80 *does* apply, the content of what the guarantee requires is now taken seriously. Under the South Australian Juries Act 1927, as amended in 1984, an accused in a criminal case can waive his right to a jury, electing to be tried by a judge alone. Where trial by jury does proceed, a conviction can be reached by 'majority verdict' (ten out of twelve). But in *Brown* v. *R.* (1986) and *Cheatle* v.

R. (1993), the High Court held that, when a Commonwealth offence is tried in a South Australian court, the guarantee in Section 80 excludes both of these provisions — the waiver provision because 'trial by jury' is not only a personal right but a basic constitutional safeguard, and 'majority verdicts' because unanimity is an essential feature of the conception which Section 80 embodies. (Such strong interpretations of what Section 80 entails in cases *where* it applies have, of course, made it even more anomalous that there still is no judicially enforceable criterion of *when* it applies.)

The second tactic adopted by Justice Murphy was to argue that, beyond the limited *express* guarantees in the Constitution, its overall structure, purpose and history *implied* judicially-enforceable guarantees of basic personal rights. His opening gambit was in *Ex parte Henry* (1975), where he argued that departmental guardianship of migrant children could not validly continue once a child turned eighteen:

> The reason lies in the nature of our Constitution. It is a Constitution for a free society. It would not be constitutionally permissible for the Parliament of Australia or any of the States to...authorize slavery or serfdom. A law which...kept migrants or anyone else in a subordinate role inconsistent with the status of a free person, would be incompatible with a fundamental basis of our Constitution.

In *Buck* v. *Bavone* (1976) and *McGraw-Hinds (Aust.) Pty Ltd* v. *Smith* (1979), he argued for broad implied guarantees of freedom of communication and freedom of movement, a theme which he developed in his final judgment in *Miller* v. *TCN Channel Nine* (1986), handed down on the day of his death. In *Sillery* v. *R.* (1981), he argued for an implied guarantee against 'cruel and unusual punishments', similar to the American guarantee in the Eighth Amendment. And in *Ansett Transport Industries* v. *Wardley* (1980), he argued for a guarantee of gender equality.

His arguments for these implications varied. Sometimes it was simply a matter of underlying values *assumed* by the language or structure of the Constitution. Sometimes, quoting Sir Isaac Isaacs, who in turn was quoting from the Privy Council in *Cooper* v. *Stuart* (1889), he appealed to 'the silent operation of constitutional principles': the unwritten inheritance of ideals and practices on which the operation of the British constitution depends, and which our Constitution tacitly incorporates. Sometimes the argument was that since this is a Constitution 'for a democracy' (or for 'a free society'), it *must* guarantee those elementary personal rights and freedoms which are essential to our conception of 'democracy' or 'a free society' — or at least those on which the successful working of democratic government depends. Sometimes the appeal was to 'the common law tradition' as the background against which the Constitution was written, the supporting framework within which it was enacted, and the interpretive universe of discourse in which it must be construed. Sometimes the appeal was to 'the heritage of the English-speaking peoples' — including the American Bill of Rights.

None of Justice Murphy's specific suggestions was accepted. In *Miller* v. *TCN Nine*, his argument about 'freedom of communication' was expressly rejected by all other judges. But, even while they rejected his specific examples, they took care not to commit themselves on the broader issue of whether, in principle, the Constitution *might* contain 'implied guarantees'. In the New South Wales *Builders' Labourers' Case* (1986), Sir Laurence Street, as Chief Justice of that state, had suggested that an alternative solution might be found in the words 'peace, welfare and good government' (or 'peace, order and good government'), used to confer legislative power in the Commonwealth Constitution and those of most Australian states. The courts, he suggested, might be able to question whether a particular law was *really* conducive to 'peace', or 'welfare', or 'good government'. In *Union Steamship Co. of Australia Ltd* v. *King* (1988), the High Court rejected this suggestion, reasserting that such words were merely the conventional British formula for conferring plenary power. But to this the Court immediately added:

> Whether the exercise of the legislative power is subject to some restraints by reference to rights deeply rooted in our democratic system of government and the common law...[is a question] which we need not explore.

The possibility thus left open, of judicially-enforceable limits on Commonwealth legislative power, moved steadily closer to majority acceptance in cases like *Leeth* and *Polyukhovich*. In the 'free speech' cases, the Court finally took the plunge. Whether it was indeed a plunge, or only a toe in the water, is the fundamental question which will shape the future development of Australian politics and constitutional law.

Unanswered Questions

The limited scope of the 'free speech' decisions left many questions unanswered. First, does the implied guarantee of freedom of speech in political matters extend to free speech in general, or to forms of political participation other than 'speech', such as freedom of assembly? There were indications that these wider implications *might* be involved. Chief Justice Mason noted that similar decisions in Canada had asserted 'an implied freedom of speech and expression' which 'may be more extensive' than what is 'so far' identified for Australia. Justice Gaudron spoke of a guarantee extending 'at the very least' to political discourse, but added:

> The notion of a free society governed in accordance with the principles of representative parliamentary democracy may entail freedom of movement, freedom of association and, perhaps, freedom of speech generally.

Justice McHugh, as we have seen, tied his decision very narrowly to specific electoral provisions. But he added that representative government requires politicians 'to listen to and ascertain' the opinions of their constituents, and that this might imply 'a general right of freedom of communication' in respect of Commonwealth government business. Moreover, even his limited focus on voting rights might involve 'the conceptions of freedom of participation, association and communication' *in respect of elections*.

Behind these questions as to the *scope* of the implied guarantee lies a question about its *sources*. What, precisely, are the logical or argumentative starting points which the Court will now accept as giving rise to constitutional implications? Most of the judgments still insist that any acceptable argument must be confined to rights or freedoms *implied in* the Constitution, as distinct from those which might be *read into* it. Guarantees implied in the Constitution can fairly be spelled out by the judges in the course of their duty to interpret the document, but values not already embodied in the Constitution cannot be read into it simply because the judges think them desirable. The distinction is best illustrated by Justice McHugh's narrow focus on the freedoms actually needed to make sense of the voting provisions; the underlying point is most fully spelled out by Justice Brennan. This focus on rights or freedoms implied in the Constitution still needs further interpretation, however.

The argument which has now been accepted is that because the Constitution establishes a system of government based on democratic political processes, it must at least imply protection for those personal and public freedoms which are necessary to the effective operation of the political processes. At the very least, this would extend beyond freedom of speech to freedom of assembly. But another way of putting it would be simply that this is a Constitution *for a democracy*, and must therefore imply protection of all those individual rights and freedoms which are essential to this concept for us. This would be a much looser and more open-ended approach.

It is widely understood that democracy entails not merely majority rule, but also some protection for minorities and individuals *against* majority rule. The values of individual dignity, liberty, privacy and freedom of choice are all entailed to some extent in our conception of a 'free society'. But although at a platitudinous level this conception might attract widespread consensus, the acceptance of any particular claim to minority or individual 'rights' will often be deeply controversial. The United States Supreme Court is inevitably drawn into such controversies by its responsibility for enforcing a written Bill of Rights. How far should the High Court of Australia go without any such clear textual warrant? Should it venture into such areas at all?

In the *Australian Capital Television Case*, Justice Dawson argued strongly that it should not. The Commonwealth Parliament *did* have power to regulate radio and television broadcasting, and to regulate federal elections; for him it necessarily followed that the political broadcasting scheme was valid. Implied guarantees of constitutional freedoms were in his view entirely unacceptable:

> [T]he Australian Constitution, with few exceptions and in contrast with its American model, does not seek to establish personal liberty by constitutional restrictions upon the exercise of governmental power. The choice was deliberate and based upon a faith in the democratic process to protect Australian citizens against unwarranted incursions upon the freedoms which they enjoy...[T]he guarantee of fundamental freedoms does not lie in any constitutional mandate but in the capacity of a democratic society to preserve for itself its own values...Indeed, those responsible for the drafting of the Constitution saw constitutional guarantees of freedoms as exhibiting a distrust of the democratic process. They preferred to place their trust in Parliament to preserve the nature of our society and regarded as undemocratic guarantees which fettered its powers. Their model in this respect was not the United States Constitution, but the British Parliament, the supremacy of which was by then settled constitutional doctrine.

Yet even Justice Dawson conceded that legislative powers may be limited

> by implications drawn from other provisions of the Constitution or from the terms of the Constitution as a whole. The powers conferred by Section 51 are expressed to be 'subject to this Constitution' and that expression encompasses implied limitations as well as those which are expressed.

What he did *not* accept was Justice Murphy's suggestion, in *Miller* v. *TCN Nine*, that constitutional implications might be drawn 'from the nature of our society'.

Chief Justice Mason's view was not far removed. He, too, thought it important to recall that, when the Constitution was drafted, the American Bill of Rights model was deliberately *rejected*. The 'prevailing sentiment' was that no such safeguard was needed. Thus the 'implication of general guarantees of fundamental rights and freedoms' would be 'difficult, if not impossible'. Justice Brennan made a similar point.

Justice McHugh also treated the rejection of the American model as significant. But for him this led back into the more limited things that the High Court *can* do. The Australian delegates rejected a 'Bill of Rights' as a safeguard against excessive government power because they relied on the British parliamentary system of 'responsible government' to provide such a safeguard. This choice implies a need to protect those mechanisms essential to the working of 'responsible government'.

One reason why a general appeal to the rights or freedoms entailed in 'democracy' may *not* attract widespread judicial support is its lack of precise legal criteria. But there are other starting points which may provide these. One, already partly explored in the *Leeth Case* is the idea that the Constitution implies equality of treatment for all individuals. Another is Dixon's conception of 'The Common Law as an Ultimate Constitutional Foundation' (Dixon 1957), interpreting judge-made common law not only as the framework within which the Constitution was made and must be interpreted, but also as a cultural reservoir of assumptions about the legal and political system which the Constitution established.

The 'free speech' cases left several openings for this idea. In *Nationwide News*, Justices Deane and Toohey said that the powers of the Commonwealth Parliament

> must be read and construed in the context of, and as 'subject to', the Constitution as a whole including the fundamental implications of the doctrines of government upon which the Constitution as a whole is structured and which form part of its fabric. They must also be read and construed in the context of other more particular implications which either are to be discerned in particular provisions of the Constitution or which flow from the fundamental rights and principles recognized by the common law at the time the Constitution was adopted...

In the same case Justice Brennan said:

> In considering whether a particular limitation on a grant of power is implied in the Constitution, the text of the Constitution must be read in the light of the general law...To adopt the words of Sir Owen Dixon, 'constitutional questions should be considered and resolved in the context of the whole law, of which the common law, including in that expression the doctrines of equity, forms not the least essential part'.

In *Capital Television*, Justice Gaudron also quoted Dixon's appeal to 'the general law' and 'the common law', adding for her own part that 'the common law' embraces 'those constitutional principles which have guided the development of democracy and responsible government in the United Kingdom'; that representative democracy 'informs our understanding of the specific provisions of the Constitution' and

> entails consequences, some of which may be obvious and some of which may be revealed by the general law, including the common law.

Moreover, her concept of freedom of speech was explicitly derived from 'the general law' — not only because such a freedom 'depends substantially on the general law' but because 'its limits are also marked out by the general law'. In formulating her test of 'appropriate' and 'proportionate' restrictions, she added:

> [O]f course, what is reasonable and appropriate will, to a large extent, depend on whether the regulation is of a kind that has traditionally been permitted by the general law.

This use of the common law has a double edge. One question immediately arising in the wake of the 'free speech' cases was whether Australian defamation laws should now be modified by the American 'public figure' defence: that is, the idea that 'public figures' (especially politicians) must expect vigorous and sometimes intemperate criticism, and accordingly should *not* be entitled to sue for defamation without some additional element (such as 'malice'). This question may itself, however, illustrate the difference between express and implied guarantees. The American 'public figure' defence arises from the First Amendment's apparently unqualified insistence on 'freedom of speech, or of the press'; if any corresponding Australian freedom is merely to reflect the common law, then the *absence* hitherto of any 'public figure' defence may preclude its introduction. Indeed, in *Capital Television*, Justice Brennan implied as much, using the *existing* law about defamation of public figures as an example of a reasonable limit on freedom of political debate.

This example opens up other unresolved questions. The 1992 cases decided only that a *Commonwealth* law cannot disproportionately restrict discussion of *Commonwealth* political matters. Yet the law of defamation largely depends on *state* legislation. If the constitutional guarantee serves only to limit what the *Commonwealth* Parliament can do, its impact on the law of defamation will be minimal. The same is true of other controversial areas like freedom of assembly. Indeed, most controversial issues about the impact of laws upon personal rights and freedoms are issues arising under state law — so that, unless an implied guarantee applies to the states as well as the Commonwealth, it will have little practical impact.

One question that arises is whether the constitutional guarantee of freedom of speech limits Commonwealth legislative power alone, or state legislative power as well. In *Independent Commission Against Corruption* v. *Cornwall* (1993), a New South Wales judge held that a journalist's refusal to disclose her sources was *not* protected as an aspect of 'political' communication — but also that, in any event, the implied guarantee did *not* extend to state legislative power.

By the time this book went to press, the issue had already been raised in two defamation cases argued before the High Court, but not yet decided. *Theophanous and Herald & Weekly Times* arose under Victorian law. A Commonwealth Member of Parliament had sued for defamation under state law. *Stephens* v. *West Australian Newspapers* was a case arising in Western Australia. State Members of Parliament were suing a state newspaper under state law. Both cases raise the question of a 'public figure' defence, and also the question of whether the 'free speech' principle appplies to state laws or only to Commonwealth ones. The *Stephens* case raises a further question: does the freedom extend to discussion of *state* political matters, or only of *Commonwealth* ones?

This last question may be easier to answer. In *Nationwide News*, Justices Deane and Toohey stressed 'the relationship and interaction' between different levels of government; the organisation of political parties across state and federal lines; and the sheer impossibility of confining 'political ideas' to one artificially delimited level. All this, they argued, meant that any meaningful protection of political debate must affect state and Commonwealth issues alike: the issues are so commingled that no demarcation is possible. In *Capital Television* they repeated these arguments, this time as part of their actual decision (since the political broadcasting scheme applied to state as well as federal elections). Chief Justice Mason took a similar view. Political discussion, he said

> does not lend itself to subdivision. Public affairs and political discussion are indivisible and cannot be subdivided into compartments that correspond with, or relate to, the various tiers of government in Australia...[T]he implied freedom of communication extends to all matters of public affairs and political discussion, notwithstanding that a particular matter at a given time might appear to have a primary or immediate connection with the affairs of a State, a local authority or a Territory.

Justice Gaudron also explored the interaction and overlap of state and federal issues, with emphasis on the referendum procedure for *changing* the Constitution:

> The power of the States to refer matters to the Commonwealth and the power of the people to change the Constitution require that

freedom of political discourse extend to every aspect of the federal arrangements, including the powers of the States and the manner of their exercise...[The freedom] must be seen as extending to matters within the province of the States. The freedom thus involves, at the very least, the free flow of information and ideas bearing on... Commonwealth, State and Territory governments, their agencies and institutions, those persons who are or would be members of their Parliaments and other institutions of government and...political parties or organizations that exist to promote their cause.

Whether in the *Australian Capital Television* case it was necessary to decide this issue may be debatable. But even if the actual decision was only that the *Commonwealth* Parliament cannot unacceptably restrict the discussion of *Commonwealth* political matters, these passages strongly suggest that discussion of *state* political matters is protected as well.

The parallel question is whether the implied guarantee limits only Commonwealth legislative power, or *state* legislative power also. If the areas of protected political debate include both state and Commonwealth matters, a sense of consonance or symmetry may suggest that the protection should prevail against both state and Commonwealth laws. But this need not follow. When the Constitution imposes *express* limits on legislative power (as in Section 80 or Section 116), only *Commonwealth* power is affected. If this is the position for an *express* guarantee, why should it be any different for an *implied* one?

In the *Theophanous Case* there may be an answer, since the relevant political issues concern a *Commonwealth* Member of Parliament. One line of High Court decisions suggests that whenever Commonwealth personnel or activities come within the jurisdictional system of a state, they are subject to the ordinary operation of state laws — just as if no Commonwealth element were involved. The underlying problem is inherent in any federal system: what happens when two legal and political systems coexist and cohabit in the same geographical territory? The first generation of High Court judges answered that each level of government must normally be immune from the other's laws. But that answer was part of the approach abandoned by the *Engineers' Case*. This decision seemed to invite the opposite answer, that each level of government is normally subject to the other's laws — and this remains a possible view. A good example is *Pirrie* v. *McFarlane* (1925), where a Commonwealth air force officer was held to be subject to state traffic laws, including the need for a driver's licence. Another example is *West* v. *Commissioner of Taxation* (1937), where a Commonwealth pension cheque payable in New South Wales was held to be subject to state income tax law. But in later cases Sir Owen Dixon developed an alternative answer: that, at least in some areas, the Commonwealth and its institutions have an inherent immunity from the operation of state laws. This answer received its fullest expression in the *Cigamatic Case* (1962).

One argument sometimes used to support the supposed *Cigamatic* immunity turns on Sections 106 and 107 of the Constitution. When the colonies metamorphosed into states on 1 January 1901, Section 106 required that each former colonial Constitution 'shall...continue'. Similarly (except where the Commonwealth was given *exclusive* power), Section 107 required that the legislative powers of each former colony 'shall...continue'. Thus the legislative powers of the state of Victoria, at midnight on 1 January 1901, were the same as those of the Colony of Victoria one minute earlier. But the Colony of Victoria had *no* legislative power over the Commonwealth, since the Commonwealth did not yet exist. It came into existence as a new political entity, and any state power to control it would have to be new. But the states were given *no* new powers: Sections 106 and 107 say only that their previous colonial powers 'shall...continue'. Hence the Commonwealth must be immune.

If *any* aspect of Commonwealth institutions is 'immune' from state laws, such immunity must at least extend to Commonwealth political institutions, and especially to the Commonwealth Parliament. If democratic freedom of political discussion is entailed in these very institutions, *that freedom* may be within the area which is simply immune from state laws.

According to this reasoning, the implied guarantee spelled out in the 'free speech' cases would operate as a limit on state legislative powers, at least as to Commonwealth political issues. As to state legislative powers in respect of state political issues, here too the answer may depend on Section 106.

The old ambiguity as to the source of validity of the Commonwealth Constitution has been paralleled by a similar ambiguity as to state constitutions. Each of them had its historical source in successive nineteenth-century enactments of the Imperial Parliament; on one view, their legal validity is still derived from the old imperial statutes. But another view is that their validity as state constitutions must now be derived from Section 106 of the Constitution itself. While this is not a novel view, it may be more persuasive after the Australia Act 1986. If all legal and constitutional questions arising within Australia must now be answered in Australian terms, so that the source of validity of the Commonwealth Constitution must now be located within Australia, the same may follow for the state constitutions. On this basis, we may need to read Section 106 not merely as acknowledging the continuing validity of the state constitutions, but as itself conferring validity on them.

Yet Section 106 is expressed to be 'subject to this Constitution'. If those words now govern the validity of the state constitutions, then any fundamental principles embodied in the Commonwealth Constitution may flow on, through Section 106, to the state Constitutions as well.

In *Australian Capital Television* Justice Gaudron did not think it 'necessary to consider whether the implied freedom of political discourse affects the powers of the States'. But, for purposes of argument, she was willing to assume that it does. In *Nationwide News*, Justice Brennan acknowledged that the guarantee

> being implied in the Constitution, may be capable of affecting the laws of a State, at least if those laws purport to impair the exercise by the people of their democratic rights and privileges in federal matters.

He, too, saw no need to decide the issue. But he did draw attention to the possible relevance of Sections 106 and 107. Justices Deane and Toohey went further. They conceded that the 'primary operation' of the guarantee must be upon Commonwealth legislative powers, but added:

> The provisions of the State Constitutions were...preserved under the Federation 'subject to' the Constitution of the Commonwealth and it is strongly arguable that the Constitution's implication of freedom of communication about matters relating to the government of the Commonwealth operates also to confine the scope of State legislative powers.

In short, six High Court judges have held that *Commonwealth* laws cannot unduly restrict discussion of *Commonwealth* political issues. At least four have strongly hinted that *Commonwealth* laws cannot unduly restrict discussion of *state* political issues. At least two find it 'strongly arguable' that *state* laws cannot unduly restrict discussion of *Commonwealth* political issues. And, in so far as that argument depends on a 'flow-on' from the Commonwealth Constitution to the state constitutions, it may follow that *state* laws cannot unduly restrict discussion of state political issues. The strong concept of representative democracy, on which the 'free speech' cases depend, may thus potentially extend to all aspects of Australian political life.

Cases

Ansett Transport Industries (Operations) Pty Ltd v. *Wardley* (1980) 142 CLR 237
Australian Capital Television Pty Ltd v. *The Commonwealth* (1992) 177 CLR 106
Bank Nationalisation Case: Bank of NSW. v. *The Commonwealth* (1948) 76 CLR 1
Beckwith v. *The Queen* (1976) 135 CLR 569
Boilermakers' Case: R. v. *Kirby;* Ex parte *Boilermakers' Society of Australia* (1956) 94 CLR 254

Brown v. *The Queen* (1986) 160 CLR 171
Buck v. *Bavone* (1976) 135 CLR 100
Builders' Labourers' Case: Building Construction Employees and Builders' Labourers' Federation of NSW. v. *Minister for Industrial Relations* (1986) 7 NSWLR 372
Burton v. *Honan* (1952) 86 CLR 169
Castlemaine Tooheys Ltd v. *South Australia* (1990) 169 CLR 436
Cheatle v. *The Queen* (1993) 116 ALR 1
Cigamatic Case: Commonwealth v. *Cigamatic Pty Ltd (in Liquidation)* (1962) 108 CLR 372
Cole v. *Whitfield* (1988) 165 CLR 360
Communist Party Case: Australian Communist Party v. *The Commonwealth* (1951) 83 CLR 1
Cooper v. *Stuart* (1889) 14 App. Cas. 286
Davis v. *The Commonwealth* (1988) 166 CLR 79
Dignan's Case: Victorian Stevedoring & General Contracting Co. Pty Ltd & Meakes v. *Dignan* (1931) 46 CLR 73
Dr Bonham's Case (1610) 8 Coke's Reports 107a, 77 English Reports 646
Engineers' Case: Amalgamated Society of Engineers v. *Adelaide Steamship Co. Ltd* (1920) 28 CLR 129
Franklin Dam Case: Commonwealth v. *Tasmania* (1983) 158 CLR 1
Henry, Ex parte: *R.* v. *Director-General of Social Welfare for Victoria;* Ex parte *Henry* (1975) 133 CLR 369
Hodge v. *The Queen* (1883) 9 App. Cas. 117
Independent Commission Against Corruption v. *Cornwall* (1993) 116 ALR 97
Kingswell v. *The Queen* (1985) 159 CLR 264
Leeth v. *The Commonwealth* (1992) 174 CLR 455
Li Chia Hsing v. *Rankin* (1978) 141 CLR 182
Lowenstein's Case: R. v. *Federal Court of Bankruptcy;* Ex parte *Lowenstein* (1938) 59 CLR 556
McGraw-Hinds (Aust.) Pty Ltd v. *Smith* (1979) 144 CLR 633
Melbourne Corporation v. *The Commonwealth* (1947) 74 CLR 31
Miller v. *TCN Channel Nine Pty Ltd* (1986) 161 CLR 556
Nationwide News Pty Ltd v. *Wills* (1992) 177 CLR 1
Payroll Tax Case: Victoria v. *The Commonwealth* (1971) 122 CLR 353
Pharmaceutical Benefits Case: Attorney-General (Victoria) (ex rel. Dale) v. *The Commonwealth* (1945) 71 CLR 237
Pirrie v. *McFarlane* (1925) 36 CLR 170
Polyukhovich v. *The Commonwealth* (1991) 172 CLR 501
R. v. *Joske;* Ex parte *Australian Building Construction Employees & Builders' Labourers' Federation* (1974) 130 CLR 87
R. v. *Joske;* Ex parte *Shop Distributive and Allied Employees' Association* (1976) 135 CLR 194
Roche v. *Kronheimer* (1921) 29 CLR 329

Sillery v. *The Queen* (1981) 35 ALR 227
Street v. *Queensland Bar Association* (1989) 168 CLR 461
Trethowan's Case: Attorney-General (NSW) v. *Trethowan* (1931) 44 CLR 394
Union Steamship Co. of Australia Ltd v. *King* (1988) 166 CLR 1
Vacher & Sons, Ltd v. *London Society of Compositors* [1913] AC 107
West v. *Commissioner of Taxation (NSW)* (1937) 56 CLR 657

3
New Federalisms

JAMES A. GILLESPIE

Federalism, as the term is usually used, refers to a system of government in which authority is constitutionally divided between central and regional governments. The two levels of government are interdependent: neither can abolish, and each relies on the other in making and implementing policy. Sovereignty, the source of legitimate political power in a society, is divided on a territorial basis. The conflicts that ensue go to the heart of assumptions about the proper role of government in our society, and the capacity of the central state to act. Intergovernmental relations, the system of bargaining, conflict and co-operation, colour most areas of Australian politics.

Since Federation, the vast expansion of central government power, fuelled by the Commonwealth's greater financial resources, has resulted in its dominance of many fields that still remain, constitutionally, state preserves. Faced with this increase in central power, the states have not withered away. Their position as veto points in the political process, controlling the implementation of policy directions decided in Canberra; as representatives of regional economic and social interests; and as power brokers in the party system has, if anything, strengthened along with Commonwealth power. So the federal system of the 1980s and 90s has presented some of the trickiest problems for the survival of federal governments.

The last decade has seen an explosion of academic commentary on problems of federalism and intergovernmental relations. For much of our history federalism has been treated with grudging respect as a restraint on government, or with irritation as a conservative barrier to thorough-going reform. Serious analysis has been dominated by constitutional lawyers, concerned with changes in the formal legal relations between levels of government, and by economists, who have concentrated on 'fiscal federalism', the financial relationships and apportionment of taxing and spending responsibilities between levels of government. Until the 1970s most analysts tended to adopt this constitutional–legal framework, when they took federalism and the states seriously at all.

The original justifications for federalism were cautious and conservative. Since Federation itself was a 'product of convenience rather than conviction', appeals to states' rights have 'typically and realistically been understood as claims to particular shares of the federal pie rather than as articulations of normative principle' (Collins 1985: 152–53). The traditional view was summed up in the Majority Report of the Royal Commission on the Constitution, in 1929. Australia's vast size and its small population made government from a single centre impractical. These conditions had in turn generated marked differences in outlook — although the Commission saw these as mainly urban/ rural rather than specifically along state lines. It also offered two slightly more positive defences. Strong state governments attracted public spirit, local patriotism and local knowledge to public life, and cited Australian loyalty to the British Empire as evidence that local self-government did not detract from higher loyalties. In addition, federalism provided a 'safeguard against disastrous experiment'. Radical change could be quarantined within the borders of one state, and its full implications worked through before it was extended to the nation as a whole. These half-hearted and defensive arguments became the standard repertoire of defences of Australian federalism (Commonwealth of Australia 1929: 240–41).

Such ambivalence about federalism was present in the very design of the Constitution. Contemporaries praised its flexibility. While sentiments of local self-sufficiency were treated with reverence in 1898, the wide range of concurrent powers and financial provisions of the Constitution left wide scope for a steady incremental growth of central power, as loyalty to the Commonwealth superseded old colonial affiliations. Alfred Deakin's 1902 warning that the financial arrangements set up in the Constitution had left the states 'legally free, but bound to the chariot wheels of the central Government' has often been quoted as evidence of unintended centralist effects of federation. But he continued by counselling the defenders of states' rights that as 'the federal domain was carved out of that of the States at the popular behest and against the wishes of their administrations and legislatures', it possessed the greater democratic legitimacy. He predicted that the 'narrow prejudices, the petty jealousies and miserable envies have to be gradually crushed out under the play of the federal forces that were created by union'. The framers could scarcely be surprised at the Commonwealth's financial ascendancy, since they assigned it a monopoly of the main tax bases of the time — customs and excise. The new central government was also granted an array of financial powers and authority to distribute money to the states 'on such terms and conditions as the Parliament sees fit' (Section 96) (Fisher 1911: 26–27, Deakin 1902: 94–98).

The critique of federalism has been most closely identified with the ALP. The states are seen as a negative force, colonial left-overs inhibiting the development of a strong social democracy, a major 'blockage...clogging our democracy', as divided sovereignty sets an insuperable barrier to effective national policies (Maddox 1991:

128–70, 1993: 24). The proposed alternative has not been a simple centralisation of power in Canberra. Calls for abolition of the states have often been justified as the road towards a more effective decentralisation of political power. In 1930 the Labor journalist Warren Denning summed up themes that recurred in Labor thinking about federalism for the next half century (Denning 1930: 13):

> State governments as decentralised units of control are a fallacy. They represent the very essence of centralisation. Arguments against centralising all power in Canberra, however valid they may be, cannot be used as arguments for the retention of the present state system. From one tiny peephole in Sydney the New South Wales Government vainly strives to see the outermost boundaries of a State larger than some of the countries of Europe. From one tiny building in the heart of a great metropolis it strives vainly to understand what each separate district wants.

Australian federalism has been interpreted in three fundamental ways. Each has taken an academic form in learned analyses, but also has provided the political language in which conflicts over the future of government have been expressed.

Interpretations of Australian Federalism

Legal-Constitutional Views: The Problem of Divided Sovereignty
Constitutional law has provided the most powerful discourse through which conflicts over the form of the new Australian state have been fought. The vague wording of the Constitution and the difficulty of obtaining changes by referendum has made the role of the courts crucial. Political conflicts over national goals have been transformed into complex technical legal battles over constitutional powers and jurisdictions of levels of government. Debates over a particular course of action — whether expanding health benefits, the construction of a welfare state or banning the Communist Party — have swiftly shifted from conflicts over ends to questions of legal competence. Does the Constitution give a state or federal government the right to pursue a particular course of action?

The constitutional legal narrative of Australian federalism has been written as a history of decline. The once-sovereign states joined in a federation that aimed to preserve their status, creating a Commonwealth government limited to the minimal powers needed to conduct external relations and handle matters that genuinely spilled over the borders of one state. This dual federalism, preserving the prerogatives of the states, has gradually been undermined by High Court decisions extending the powers of the Commonwealth and allowing it to establish a crushing financial ascendancy. The result has been a federation which is but a pale shadow of its founders' intentions.

The view of constitutional lawyers, then, is that much of the basis of the original federal design has been undermined. Supporters of stronger central powers, like Geoffrey Sawer, invested the march of centralism with an air of inevitability, calling on the courts to facilitate the expansion of Commonwealth powers in the name of keeping 'pace with the integration of the Australian nation' (Sawer 1967: 197). More conservative constitutional lawyers, such as Craven (1992: 55), have asserted that:

> While it is undeniably true that the States still wield considerable power within the Australian federation, it is plain sophistry to suggest that they are anything other than constitutionally beleaguered, that their powers and independence are not gradually being reduced year by year, and that, to the extent that they are now the co-operating partners of the Commonwealth, they are now very junior partners indeed.

These themes come from the British constitutional tradition which, at the time of federation, was very ambivalent about divided sovereignty. The foremost critic of federalism was Dicey. His influential *Introduction to the Study of the Law of the Constitution* argued that, at best, federalism 'has generally been a stage towards unitary government', a poor second best, since 'federalism means weak government', 'conservatism' and 'legalism' (Dicey 1915: 112–16). This negative view of federalism as merely a stage in the march to a unitary state has underpinned much of the legal narrative. This concentrates on changes in the formal distribution of powers between levels of government, as interpreted by the High Court. It starts from a conception of federalism as two levels of government 'complete in themselves'. The drafters of the Constitution wanted a strictly limited central government, impinging as little as possible on the existing functions of the states. Craven notes this: 'Given a choice between a centrally dominated federation and no federation at all, most of the founding fathers would have opted for disunity' (Craven 1992a: 51). In such a view, the history of Australian federalism is a sad tale of the gradual destruction of this ideal. The notion of 'balance', an equilibrium of power between levels of government, is often invoked (Crommelin 1992: 36). From being equal, 'coordinate' partners that retained the bulk of public policy as an exclusive domain, at best the states have become subordinate partners of the Commonwealth, or have been totally pushed aside (Solomon 1992: 133–45, Coper 1988: 150–225).

The key turning points were major decisions by the High Court to extend or, at best, temporarily delay the onward march of Commonwealth power. Since the *Engineers' Case* (1920), there has been a steady shift of power to the Commonwealth government and atrophy of the powers of the states. This has culminated in the High Court's broader reading of powers vested in the Commonwealth in Section 51 (such as the external affairs power), its central control over borrowing and the most lucrative tax revenues, and a gradual encroachment into areas previously the exclusive province of the states (such as education), through grants under Section 96 of the Constitution, which entitles the federal Parliament to 'grant financial assistance to any State on such terms and conditions as the Parliament thinks fit'.

This imbalance has deep consequences for the workings of constitutional doctrines derived from the British tradition. Westminster conventions of responsible government are disturbed where the nexus between responsibility for raising revenue and for expenditure has been severed. The relatively great disparities between the revenue-raising capacities of the states and their growing financial responsibilities, it is argued, undermine government accountability. Dependent on transfers of revenue from Canberra, no-one can be sure who holds final responsibility. Politics becomes an endless game of cost shifting between the Commonwealth and the states, each trying to claim responsibility for the delivery of electorally popular services, while attempting to displace the cost onto the other level of government (Saunders 1992: 120–22). Similarly, the growth of executive federalism, of intergovernmental arrangements, the network of ministerial councils, joint administration of programs, and the use of tied grants, weakens parliamentary authority, as they have by-passed older assumptions about the position of Parliament (Constitutional Centenary Foundation 1993: 38–40).

This view is seriously flawed in historical terms. The notion of federal politics as a 'zero-sum' game in which any advance in the power of one party must cause an equivalent loss to another ignores two main features of the development of Australian government. First, many of the new powers of the federal government were not taken from the states, but represented a move into areas of administration that did not exist at Federation. The significance of the *Engineers' Case* in 1920 was that it enabled the Commonwealth to claim these new domains, such as telecommunications and aviation — although not always with immediate success (Coper 1988: 173–86). Second, there was another level of constitutional power at federation, the Imperial government. It exercised real power for the first decades of federation. Other 'new' areas that the Commonwealth gradually occupied, such as the ability to make treaties with foreign powers, a function denied to it in 1901, were not taken from the states, but from London.

Fiscal Federalism
The financial predominance of the Commonwealth government has also dominated the views of economists. They have focused their

attention on 'fiscal federalism', the distribution of taxing and spending functions between levels of government and intergovernmental transfers of revenues. This means a shift of emphasis from the legal/constitutional approach: formal legal powers are seen as less significant than the independent control of financial resources. The states can have all the legal power in the world, but if they lack financial resources, or depend on transfers from the federal government, legal autonomy is illusory. Economists have taken a far more prescriptive and normative approach than have lawyers in attempting to find more efficient ways to structure federal financial relations.

Again the metaphor of decline from an original state of 'balance' dominates the narrative, following the development of inequalities in fiscal resources. The turning points came with the Commonwealth monopolisation of income tax revenues in 1942 and the steady growth of 'vertical imbalance', the disproportion between the revenues the states raised and controlled themselves and their financial responsibilities. Already stripped of their ability to raise loans independently, the states lost access to the main growth taxes of the post-war decades and were condemned to exploit ingenious but ever-more convoluted and regressive forms of indirect taxes to maintain any financial independence from Canberra.

Economic approaches have followed wider fashions in theory and policy making. The pioneers of Australian public finance took a rather agnostic approach to the developing imbalance in resources and responsibilities. Although conservatives, such as the Country Party leader and federal Treasurer Sir Earle Page, attacked 'the vicious principle of one authority raising taxation for another authority to spend' (Portus 1933: 85), by the late 1920s most had accepted the position of the economist R.C. Mills that: 'by the Constitution, financial inferiority is the lot of the states and after all we are Australians first and members of a State afterwards' (1928: 69–70). Attention focused more on the inefficiencies of federalism, the fragmentation of government authority being seen as an obstacle to development. As Warner 1933: 253) wrote:

> major problems arise from an inadequate distribution of authority; inevitable conflicts; duplication of constitutional machinery; and unco-ordinated activities. The practical result is a chaotic constitutional regime, the costly errors of which are borne by the public at large.

This scepticism about the claims of the states remained strong in the post-war era. Fiscal imbalance was seen as an inevitable and not undesirable companion to Keynesian economic management, a corollary to central control of the main levers of policy making. A comfortable settlement had been reached, and by the 1950s federalism itself had few defenders. The strong critics of Commonwealth financial dominance tended to come from those with an interest in rural settlement and decentralisation, such as the economist Colin Clark. By the 1950s, these voices were an increasingly eccentric minority (Clark 1952: 35, 40, Prest 1963: 236–37).

Only as confidence in Keynesian techniques of economic management waned did consensus among economists disappear. Although some still stress the virtues of Commonwealth financial dominance as a tool of macro-economic policy (Groenewegen 1993), concern over vertical fiscal imbalance has become a central theme with economists who prefer market-based solutions and small government. They have argued that state and federal governments will remain inefficient while they are able to shift the blame for problems to the other level of government. Some have supported a return of income taxation powers to state level, proposing a massive decentralisation of financial power and the withdrawal of the Commonwealth from many of the areas it has occupied since World War II (Walsh 1989: 32–34, 1990: 53–88).

This has been taken even further by economists and political scientists associated with the New Right. They have drawn on American arguments that the unrestrained growth of government provides the main threat to the survival of private property and individual liberty. Much of their work has concentrated on the design of constitutional barriers to increased government spending and revenue raising. Federal government is seen as a further refinement of these restrictions on the power of government. Working with the metaphor of marketplace competition, Ostrom argues that 'the monopoly position of any one government is ameliorated by the availability of alternative governments'. The overlapping jurisdictions and fragmentation of authority of a federal system become major safeguards against mighty central government (Brennan and Buchanan 1980: 174–83, Ostrom 1976: 7, 1987: 26, 104–7, 201–5).

This public choice model starts from the behavioural assumptions of neo-classical economics. Political processes are explained as expressions of the self-interested motivation of individuals. The market performs this function in economic life; in the more artificial world of politics, institutions must be consciously created to steer behaviour. The work of Buchanan, Brennan (the leading Australian exponent), Tullock and other public choice theorists concentrates on these problems of institutional and constitutional design, of constitutional engineering to set rules, and institutional structures that inhibit the growth of government. Starting with the assumption that market forms of allocation of goods are more efficient than centralised control, public choice theorists have been strong advocates of federal forms of dispersed authority, decentralising to introduce 'market-like alternatives into the political process' (Buchanan and Tullock 1962: 114). Popular sovereignty is exercised through individuals shifting jurisdictions in order to find a mix of taxation and service levels that best suit them, 'the more closely political institutions resemble the economic institutions of the competitive market, the more responsive they will be. And the more restricted the scope of a political decision, that is, the more localised the political unit, the more it will approximate that arrangement. Thus, 'the level of government becomes more important than its type' (Osterfield 1989: 155). Where classical models of democratic participation see the vote, or 'voice', as the key moment in citizen participation, these models add 'exit' — voting with the feet (Buchanan and Tullock 1962: 114, Walsh 1990).

There have been problems in applying this approach in Australia. Competition requires a multiplicity of units of governments, and Australia's six states and two territories hardly offer the range of choice expected by American federal theorists. Mobility has also been limited by cost, distance and the structure of Australian labour markets. The one practical example of the widespread use of the exit option to reduce state taxation levels was the abolition of death duties. After Queensland abolished them in 1977, the other states were forced to follow suit (Grossman 1990: 145–59, 1989: 30). More seriously, the Australian experience of competitive federalism has not been a happy one. Bidding between the states for industrial and mining development has often degenerated into a competition in laxity: lowering standards of environmental protection, or scrambling over one another to offer cheap energy resources and other concessions to attract industries, accentuating the fragmented structure and low economies of scale that have inhibited the formation of a national market and stultified Australian industrial development (Butlin, Barnard and Pincus 1982: 86–88, 93, 139).

Politics and Power: State Assertiveness and Institutions
Until the 1970s these two narratives provided the main accounts of federal institutions. Political scientists either adopted the legal constitutional framework or confined themselves to detailed descriptive work on state institutional structures. Searching for an explanation for the stability of federalism, the political scientist P.H. Partridge was perplexed: finding little public affection for the federal system, and arguing that there were none of the linguistic, regional or other cultural differences that sustained federalism in Canada, he could only conclude that the states survived out of 'institutional inertia', and that 'the Constitution tends to perpetuate itself' as few Australians cared enough about the issue to support change (Partridge 1952: 191–93).

More recent defenders of federalism have tried to put their case on a more positive footing. Drawing on the robust traditions of states' rights in the United States they have claimed that divided sovereignty can provide a fundamental guarantee of liberties, limiting the growth of over-powerful central government. With the vogue for market forces, competition between relatively autonomous units of government has been celebrated as the road to efficiency and greater responsiveness to popular preferences. This revived support for federalism has become dominant in Australian political science. Its main proponents now suggest that the older critiques of federalism are victim to 'prejudices' which only survive because of the weakness of existing Australian political theories of federalism. If this ideological gap were filled with a new 'standard repertoire of ideas in Australia that values the regional dispersal of power, the virtues of state autonomy in the solution of local issues, the inherent benefits of diverse solutions to similar problems, and the intrinsic advantages of competition and overlap in the supply of government services', the remaining arguments for stronger central government would swiftly dissolve (Galligan 1989a: 50, 1992, Sharman 1992: 9, 1990b: 211–16).

Some Australian political scientists and economists have moved from a chronicle of decline to a celebration of the continuing vitality of the federal system. There has been a deeper examination of the actual workings of federalism. In contrast with the lawyers' concentration on the formal allocation of powers, greater attention has been paid to the practical mechanics of intergovernmental relations. In the process, the financial predominance of the federal government proves less overpowering than is often assumed. Control of administration — the actual details of implementation of programs — has remained largely in state hands, with great opportunities for local fine tuning or subversion of central government intentions. This new 'realist' approach has built on case studies of particular policy issues. The very chaos and complexity of federal-state relations are revalued: offering scope for 'accommodating multiple values, encouraging bargaining, facilitating participation and adaptability, and imposing constraints on the exercise of power' (Galligan, Hughes and Walsh 1991: 19).

While the growth of Commonwealth power, with its steady intrusion into areas previously the exclusive domain of the states, is undeniable, political scientists have dissented from the lawyers' view that this has been a zero-sum game. One side's gain has not necessarily been the other's loss. Looking at the manner in which federal-state relations are actually played out, rather than the formal rules, shows that the states retain considerable power resources, particularly their control over administration. Even if the Commonwealth sets the guidelines and provides much of the finance, the key to implementation of a policy is frequently in the detail. This is more likely to remain in state hands. Hence the continual tussle between the two levels of government for control and credit for joint programs, with 'informality and *ad hoc*ery' as the key to intergovernmental relations (Nelson 1992a: 181, 185).

The political process, involving relations between different governments, has been moved to the centre, mapping out areas of cooperation and conflict. This has meant a shift from a concentration on Commonwealth intentions to a focus on implementation — how things work out at 'ground level' (Hollander 1992: 342–53). A hierarchical model of Commonwealth-state relations is replaced with one that stresses bargaining and negotiation. At its strongest this can lead to a notion that power is diffused throughout the system: the metaphor of a marble cake is used to stress the non-centralised nature of power in the federal system. However, evidence of sharing and overlapping of functions is hardly evidence of diffusion of power. At its extreme this has led to celebrations of administrative confusion as creating a variety of choice for citizens, a 'non-centralised' system rather than one resting on a hierarchy of levels of government. This is a radical recasting of the usual legal or economists' view of federal relations. Again, it rests heavily on American analogies that are rather weakly based even in their own country (Fletcher 1992: Chapter 2; cf. Scheiber 1980).

A Territorial Basis for Liberty?

Does federalism have the potential to limit the oppressive powers of government? The demand for a more coherent defence of federalism has led to a new interest in divided sovereignty as a limitation on the power of central executive government. One of the oldest arguments for a federal system is based on the belief that the division of powers between levels of government is a guarantee that the state will not become too large or oppressive. The classic statement of this position came in the debates around the adoption of the United States Constitution. *The Federalist*, a series of papers written to win support for a stronger national government in the American federation, reassured opponents who worried about a rebirth of aristocratic tyranny that the limits set by the new Constitution on the powers of the central government would provide a major 'check and balance'. If sovereignty were divided between rival levels of government, each with its own democratic franchise, it would set a major barrier to the concentration of political power in too few hands. First, federalism can limit government power to infringe rights, since it creates the possibility that a legislature wishing to restrict liberties will lack the constitutional power, while the level of government that possesses the power lacks the desire. Second, the tortuous and legalistic decision making processes characteristic of federal systems limit the speed with which governments can act — even if their actions prove to be constitutional. Federalism helps enshrine the principle of 'due process', limiting arbitrary action by the state (Sawer 1967: 195).

The late nineteenth century British liberal tradition, with which the Australian founding fathers were familiar, showed increasing interest in institutional measures to restrict the powers of government. The strength of demands for political democracy — and the potential tyranny of democratic majorities — with the growing size of the imperial state seemed to threaten the liberal traditions of British politics. Divided sovereignty was seen as an important measure of protection of the rights of minorities. Federalism could be a solution to the dilemma of the preservation of liberty in large political units, a bulwark against the majoritarian tide. The British political theorist Harold Laski developed this pluralist defence of federalism, arguing that 'There can be no servility in a State that divides its effective governance. The necessity of balancing interests, the need for combining opinions, results in a wealth of political thought such as no state where the real authority is single can attain' (Laski 1917: 273–74, Burrow 1988: 132–35; for an Australian application see Portus 1948: 14–15).

Galligan, Knopff and Uhr have recently developed similar arguments in the Australian context. They have suggested that the vitality of Australian federalism removes the need for a Bill of Rights to entrench the protection of individual civil liberties in the Constitution. They suggest that 'a federal constitution is itself a bill of rights' as the division of authority between different spheres of government 'guarantees due process in government'; in turn this promotes what they term 'rights-oriented citizenship' (Galligan, Knopff and Uhr 1990: 53–67). The complications, overlapping jurisdictions and administrative inefficiencies of a federal system are transformed into virtues. The citizens of a federal state have more remedies and political resources to draw upon. Equally, in the face of an oppressive state, at least they have the possibility of sheltering from its excesses beneath the sovereign powers of other levels of government. Galligan pushes this further by arguing that the 'enhancement of democratic participation through dual citizenship and multiple governments is undoubtedly federalism's most positive quality that largely explains its strength and resilience in Australia' (Galligan 1989a: 63, 1992). The inefficiencies that the planners of past decades deplored, become a guarantee against government becoming too oppressive, a fragmentation of the 'revenue-maximising Leviathan' state (Brennan and Buchanan 1980: 25–26).

This is more than a revamped theory of competitive federalism — a celebration of the creativity and diversity that can result from maintaining a multiplicity of centres of government. Three major criticisms can be levelled at this attempt to place federal theory on a libertarian basis. First, its authors have been long on general assertions of principle, but rather short on explaining what they mean by 'liberty' and on the presentation of empirical evidence. It is difficult to detect any federal component to the protection of individual rights in Australia. Galligan, Knopff and Uhr manage to present their civil libertarian defence without citing a single case.

Instances of the coincidence of states' rights and individual liberties have been rare. The division of powers between federal and state levels have left many of the key areas affecting minority rights in state hands: the regulation of morals, including medical and mental health, land law and control of indigenous populations, even after the 1967 referendum extended Commonwealth concurrent powers over Aboriginal affairs. The defence of states' rights has hardly provided a theme for those concerned with the rights of Aboriginal communities. Recent discussions of potential statehood for the Northern Territory have been dominated by fears for the future of Aboriginal organisations stripped of the limited protection offered by Canberra. Rowse (1992: 60–63, 72–74) has criticised the Northern Territory's moves to impose the standard model of Australian federalism — a strong state government dominating local government — to eliminate the nascent model of 'dispersed governance' that might enable Aboriginal self-determination.

Second, they confuse the rights of individuals with those of states. In Australia some of the major intergovernmental conflicts in recent decades have been the direct result of federal intervention to secure the rights of minority groups, and required limitations on the powers of state governments. It is also essential to avoid confusion between the constraints set by judicial review, the constitutional power of the courts to overrule Parliament, and federalism itself. The 'parliamentary despotism' of undivided sovereignty has come under strong attack in contemporary Britain. The key problem has been identified as the lack of a written constitution. This could be remedied without introducing federal arrangements — although these are also receiving serious discussion. Finally, their position is based on a very narrow notion of liberty. They see freedom as a negative condition, as the absence of external constraints on action. Government intervention may be a source of freedom — for example by liberating individuals from the crushing dictates of the market by providing social security benefits and health insurance.

A stronger version of this defence of federalism is found in the theory of concurrent majorities, one of the most influential conservative defences of federalism, developed by the American political leader and theorist John C. Calhoun. Calhoun is best known as an apologist for slavery in the pre-Civil War American South. However, in his 'Disquisition on Government' and 'Discourse on the Constitution and Government of the United States' (both completed in 1850, collected in Lence 1992) he developed a broader political justification for the division of powers between federal and state governments. Calhoun argued that unitary political systems, vesting all power in national majorities, led to the oppression of regional minorities. The divided sovereignty of federalism established concurrent majorities, each with its own legitimacy, checking each other's power and preserving liberty. Calhoun's theory has always been tainted by its origins: the regional minority interests that he wished to defend were those of the Southern slaveholders and their plantation economy. A refined version of the theory underpinned the states' rights arguments that excluded black Americans from political participation for most of this century.

However, it has re-emerged in recent years, shorn of its racial politics, as the basis for a defence of Australian federalism (Sharman 1983).

Unsavoury origins are not enough to condemn a theory — although the history of states' rights and resistance to the rights of Australian Aborigines provide one clear parallel over the last quarter of a century. They do, however, suggest a further flaw in the libertarian defence of federalism. Dividing authority on a territorial basis may provide institutions which defend the dominant interests within the region against national majorities. It may also provide the opportunity for these regional majorities to oppress their own minorities. This is not to suggest that enlightenment and true liberalism emanate only from national majorities and central government. Nor does it mean support for a simple majoritarian position which would remove all fetters on the majority party in the House of Representatives.

But placing the defence of freedom on a territorial basis merely raises new questions of power. The beneficiaries of federalism are those regional minorities able to control policy making. These criticisms do not mean that federalism is inherently oppressive nor that the terms of the libertarian argument must be reversed. It does direct our attention to federalism as a set of power relations, with no inherently good or bad qualities. It also suggests that theories of federalism provide a rather shaky foundation for developing a 'rights-based citizenship', or as the justification for rejecting a bill of rights.

Deborah Stone has pointed to the abstract and metaphorical character of most defences of states' rights. She writes that 'underneath the seemingly technical argument that a different structure of authority necessarily produces better outcomes is a vision of competing interests and an effort to limit the power of one. The hope in proposals for structural change is to split up old or potential alliances, establish new ones and so place a favoured interest in a position of dominance' (Stone 1988: 304).

Federalism and the Australian State

The best way to break from this abstract level is to look at the place of federalism in Australian political history, placing current developments in a wider context.

Sharman has stressed the firm historical basis and legitimacy of federal institutions in nineteenth century colonial practice. What are often seen as anomalies or artificial imitations of American models, grafted onto British Westminster practices (a strong upper house, the powers of the Governor-General, etc.), were merely continuations of the practices with which colonial politicians already operated. By adopting the American model of federalism, and with a powerful

Senate, Australia set limits on the powers of a majority in the Commonwealth Parliament. However, the contradiction between the majoritarian principles inherited from the British tradition and the division of powers between levels of government in Australia has inhibited the development of a native-born theory of federalism. Australians have remained rather shamefaced and ambivalent about one of the more creative and libertarian elements of our political system (Sharman 1990a: 1–5, 1990c: 85–104).

In an important reply to Sharman's celebration of the states as the repository of local liberties, Colebatch (1992) has pointed out that Australians have rarely seen government as the protector of liberties, but more as a dispenser of services. Until the 1970s, the characteristic form of state organisation was the independent board or statutory corporation, separate from direct ministerial responsibility and often closely linked to interest groups. Central government agencies were mainly interested in controlling costs, leaving the initiation of policy to the individual agency. The political executive remained weak, with government ministers often part-time or carrying responsibility for a plethora of agencies, with few resources to establish control and 'fragmentation and lack of overall system coherence'. Halligan and Power (1992: Chapter 3) have recently described this mode of public administration as 'protected pluralism' — common throughout Australian government but most deeply entrenched at state level (see also Colebatch 1992: 1–11, Power 1990: 11).

The characteristic response of Australian governments to interest group demands was to establish regulatory systems such as marketing boards and arbitration courts, with strong representation or even direct control by those under their authority. A survey of Victorian government structures in the 1950s noted the 'overwhelmingly administrative character of state government' scattered in a plethora of quasi-autonomous agencies, creating an 'atomised' chain of responsibility in which state agencies were open to capture by producer groups. Hence, the real dispersal of power in the Australian state, of which federalism is a component, has little connection with American notions of concurrent majorities or protection from the Leviathan state. 'Protection all round', the political slogan of the 1920s, is a better description of this Australian tradition of government (Layman 1982–83, Davies 1960: 185, 192).

This pattern has been closely linked to other features of Australia's political economy. In 1930, the historian Keith Hancock noted that the Commonwealth provided a 'ring fence', constructing the institutions of 'domestic defence' which dominated Australian politics until the 1980s. Immigration restriction, industrial protection and arbitration set the main parameters of politics, sheltering Australian industry and labour from the rigours of market forces (Hancock 1930: 64–65, Castles 1989: 30–39). Within this fence the real prizes of political action remained at state level. State governments, both conservative and Labor, were dedicated to policies of development, competing with one another to attract industry and encourage agriculture and mining.

The peculiarities of the Australian state tradition were expressed in two further ways, each with federalism as a central reference point. First, for much of our history sovereignty was shared three ways, not merely between the Commonwealth and the states. Australia was part of the Empire — a Dominion from 1907 — and its foreign and trade policies as well as the powers of its legal system were kept within limits that the British Colonial Office had insisted upon when the Constitution was submitted to the Imperial Parliament. The federal structure of divided power built on familiar patterns. As Robert Garran, one of the drafters of the Constitution, argued, the imperial relationship of shared and often combative authority between different levels of government prepared Australian politicians for federalism itself (Garran 1897: 110–11).

The sovereignty of all Australian governments was limited by the authority of the Privy Council to over-rule decisions of the High Court (in constitutional cases these were abolished in 1968; in all others in 1975) and to take appeals from state Supreme Courts (up to 1986). Similarly, despite occasional independent noises, particularly in the Pacific region, Australian governments accepted that the power to declare war and much of the conduct of foreign policy was a matter for the imperial government in London. In 1931 the Statute of Westminster limited the right of the British Parliament to make laws covering the dominions, unless at their express request, and removed requirements that dominion legislation be consistent with that of Britain. Canberra did not ratify the Statute until 1942 (under the Curtin ALP wartime government) and the states refused to follow suit. As Solomon notes (1992: 131; see also Zines 1992: 87–90) the states

> did not want to shed their colonial ties. They thought that London could protect them from the depredations of Canberra...Australia was therefore in the anomalous position where the national government was independent, while the States were subject to the laws of another (admittedly friendly) country. It was Canberra that was regarded as unfriendly.

It was not until the Australia Act 1986, that these limitations were finally removed. Fiscal federalism provided a framework for settling conflicts over the consequences of 'domestic protection'. The effects of Federation had been faced with some anxiety by the smaller states. South Australia, Western Australia and, to some extent, Queensland, all predominantly agricultural and pastoral producers, felt the effects of rising costs for manufactured goods behind the tariff wall. For the first ten years of Federation their complaints were met by Section 87 of the

Constitution (the Braddon clause), which guaranteed that 75 per cent of the Commonwealth's customs and excise receipts would be returned to the states. When this expired, both Tasmania and Western Australia received special grants, but were not appeased. Similarly, while measures such as the Navigation Act 1913 protected the wages and employment of Australian seamen and shipowners, Tasmanians and West Australians complained that this made transport costs even more onerous. A series of Royal Commissions in the 1920s established that the smaller states had cause for complaint: the tariff and other elements of domestic protection were causing economic problems. The crisis came to a head in 1933, in the depths of the Depression, when Western Australia actually moved to secede from the Commonwealth, citing claims that its citizens would be better off on their own (Melville and Wainwright 1929: 4–5, 11–12, Macintyre 1986: 299–301).

The discontent of the 1920s and 30s introduced a further element to the Australian political system. Protection, arbitration and White Australia were the key elements of 'domestic defence' against the effects of Australia's external vulnerability. Equalisation of resources between states was added as a central principle of the bargains that made up the Australian system of government.

The Commonwealth Grants Commission (CGC) was established in 1933 as a semi-judicial body independently assessing the relative 'disabilities' of each state. This developed into a doctrine that assumed that the government of each state should have the capacity to provide its citizens with a similar array and standard of services as the residents of others. Consequently, the CGC took into account the difficulties faced in raising state taxes. Even if each state made the same 'revenue effort', would the uneven distribution of resources mean that some would be condemned to relative poverty? Problems such as distance, climate and population density were used as indicators of expenditure disabilities. The claimant states, those which were at a disadvantage, were to be compensated through the funding formula used to distribute Commonwealth money to the states (Commonwealth Grants Commission 1936: 75):

> Special grants are justified when a State through financial stress from any cause is unable efficiently to discharge its functions as a member of the federation and should be determined by the amount of help found necessary to make it possible for that State by reasonable effort to function at a standard not appreciably below that of other States.

Equalisation, then, was part of the wider institutional structures of domestic defence, designed to cushion economic competition between the states. States with larger domestic markets and industrial investment (fostered by the tariff wall) would subsidise those less fortunate.

This 'horizontal equity' between states was added to the principle of comparative wage justice between workers (guaranteed by arbitration) to become a central, if little examined and highly technical, aspect of the Australian political system. Not surprisingly, this is anathema to market liberals, since 'it subverts the primary purpose of federalism, which is to create competition between jurisdictions' (Piesse 1935: 73–110, Brennan and Buchanan 1980: 183).

Resentments remained. The larger states claimed bitterly that equalisation worked against their interests. The smaller states, despite benefiting from their mendicant status, continued to assert the stultifying effects of federation on their economic development, arguing, for instance, that Queensland's 'branch office' economy and the stultification of secondary industry continued to be accentuated by the tariff and by the concentration of Commonwealth offices, policy making and employment in the 'iron triangle' of Melbourne, Canberra and Sydney (Stanford 1988).

Whitlam: New Federalism and State Assertiveness

This understanding of the position of the states in the Australian political system is essential to an understanding of the changes of the last quarter century. While garbed with the rhetoric of 'micro-economic reform', or the technical language of 'managerialism', each attempt to shift federal-state relations has been about real political interests. The political institutions of domestic defence have come under particular assault over the last twenty years, as the economy has gradually been opened up to the forces of international competition. The reform of state structures has been part of this process. To use Power and Halligan's categories again, 'protected pluralism' in public administration has been undermined. In all states, and particularly at federal level, it has been superseded by 'strategic political direction', replacing the producer-dominated, decentralised and unco-ordinated structures of government with a public sector more subject to political control, but also more influenced by competitive and 'market'-based models of organisation (Halligan and Power 1992: Chapters 3 and 10).

Although anticipated by some of the measures of the Gorton Liberal Country Party government (1968–71), the Whitlam government made the first attempt since the 1940s to radically shift the boundaries of federalism. While its opponents painted Whitlam as bent on the destruction of the states, his New Federalism had far more pragmatic origins. Administrative reforms to the structure of government were part of wider policy objectives: the modernisation of the Australian economy and the construction of a redistributive welfare state on European lines. The first included dramatic reductions in levels of tariff protection and industry subsidy. The second consisted of increased expenditure on welfare programs and direct involvement in areas previously the exclusive — and increasingly inadequately managed — province of the states, such as urban planning and higher education. Each element involved a departure from the established patterns of Australian economic and political life. It was this that aroused opposition leading to Whitlam's ultimate defeat.

The expansion of Commonwealth power was seen as a recognition of national maturity — even at a symbolic level. Federal government letterheads were changed to read 'Australian Government', to the chagrin of the states, which protested that they were also Australian governments. At the same time, however, the Whitlam government showed a real commitment to administrative decentralisation. While the Commonwealth kept its strategic command, services were to be delivered by local and regional organisations. Some of these innovations were to be achieved through the states, but where they were reluctant, the federal government attempted to go directly to local government, encouraging the development of regional governing bodies, rather on the model foreshadowed by Denning forty years earlier.

The contours of expanded Commonwealth involvement can be seen in Figure 3.1. The weight of federal funding shifted radically towards tied grants; in 1969 these had made up less than 28 per cent of Commonwealth transfers, but by 1975 they comprised almost half federal funding. The offer of tied grant money to the states had two effects: it provided the Commonwealth with the lever to move into

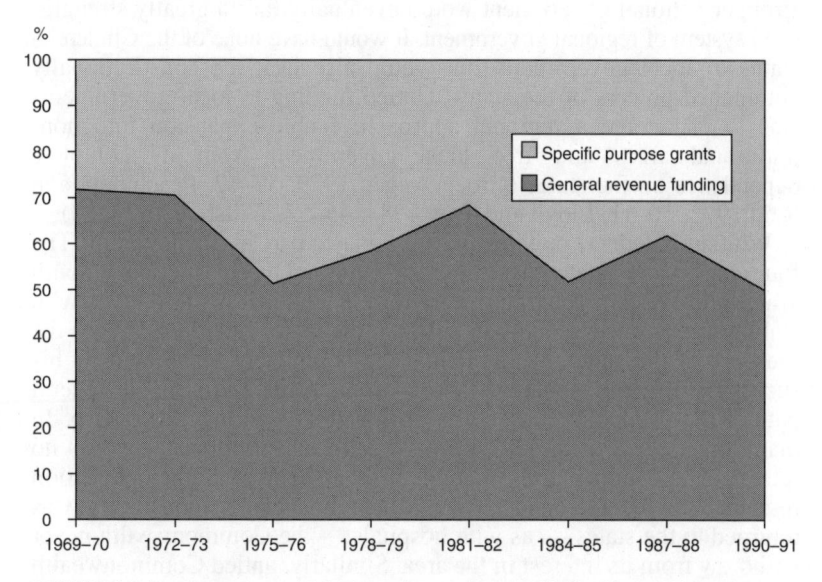

FIGURE 3.1 *Commonwealth Transfers to States, 1969–70 to 1990–91*

areas in which it held no constitutional authority, and the inclusion of matching requirements meant that states had to commit large sections of their own budgets to policies initiated by Canberra.

There was some basis for anti-Labor fears that Whitlam's long-term preference lay with the abolition of the states. He was firmly within Labor's tradition of hostility to state governments. In his 1957 Chifley Lecture he argued that 'there are few functions which the State Parliaments perform which would not be better performed by the Australian Parliament or by regional councils. The states are too large to deal with local matters and too small and weak to deal with national ones' (Whitlam 1977: 33). As we have seen, the traditional Labor view had always been sceptical of the claims of the states as 'closer to the people'. This strand in Labor thinking reached its height with attempts to bypass the states and build a strong link between the Commonwealth and local governments. It was precisely this apparent attempt to support a countervailing set of regional authorities that aroused some of the most bitter antagonism at state level (Troy 1978: 11–37).

Whatever his long-term aspirations, however, in practice Whitlam intended to work with the states, shifting Labor's program from a rather abstract and politically unrealistic commitment to abolition. This did not mean, however, that the aims of 1957 were abandoned. A key to understanding the Whitlam period is that in addition to implementing particular policies, he was committed to a vision of institution building. His urban policies, with their emphasis on regional action by local government, was a step towards a new political landscape in which a stronger national government would eventually face a greatly strengthened system of regional government. It would have none of the Cinderella status of local government, but would also lack the constitutionally entrenched powers of the states. Untied funding to local governments was to encourage a regional approach, enable expansion into non-traditional areas and free local government from its complete dependence on the states (Groenewegen 1979: 57–62, Peachment and Reid 1977: 10–11, Lloyd and Troy 1983: 45–57, Wiltshire 1977: 80).

Whitlam's federal policies played a major part in his downfall. The four conservative state governments (Victoria, Queensland, New South Wales and Western Australia) were hostile, and met his initiatives with stubborn resistance. His urban policies, the major intervention into the preserve of the states, were swiftly and completely repudiated by his successor. But this apparent failure masks some shifts in the federal pattern that Malcolm Fraser was unable (or unwilling) to reverse. In many other areas of direct Commonwealth intervention, there was no retreat. The funding and strategic management of higher education remained in federal hands. Even where financial responsibility was returned to the states — as with hospitals — the Commonwealth never withdrew from its interest in the area. Similarly, untied Commonwealth funding of local government continued, giving the third level of government the resources to show that it was more than the 'creature' of the states. Paradoxically, Whitlam had forced the somnolent state governments to develop policy expertise, even if only to obstruct his intentions more effectively. The partially successfully attempt to increase Commonwealth power did not mean a decline in state influence, but was met by a new state assertiveness which accelerated the reform of the structures of protective pluralism (see the discussion of state assertiveness in Sharman 1992).

The Fraser Government

The fate of Fraser's New Federalism shows the hazards of taking statements of principle more seriously than the actual consequences of policies. His election campaign in 1975 promised to reverse the centralism of the Whitlam years, drawing on the deeply ingrained Liberal belief in states' rights. While using the rhetoric of states' rights and returning financial power and responsibility to state level, Fraser's period of office was marked by conflicts as intense as those under Whitlam. The major study of prime ministerial power under Fraser entitles its chapter on federalism 'Treating with Bandits' (Weller 1989: Chapter 8; see also Starr 1977).

The Fraser government was dominated by an agenda for reducing the size of government. Despite the relatively small size of the Australian public sector by international standards, government rhetoric was dominated by the problem of 'overload' — the managerial problems that had emerged, it was alleged, as strategies of bureaucratic control proved incapable of handling the burden of administrative programs. Advocacy of market-based solutions became fashionable, even if the full panoply of privatisation and deregulation did not emerge until the end of Fraser's regime — and then with dissident groups on the fringes of the Liberal Party.

Fraser's New Federalism had two main objectives: the reduction of the size of government, and the return of power to the states. Vertical fiscal imbalance was to be redressed with revenue sharing, guaranteeing the states and local government a fixed share of 39.87 per cent of personal income tax revenues. The way was also opened for states to levy their own income taxes — an offer none took up. The urban programs of the Whitlam government were abruptly cancelled as tied grants to the states were radically curtailed. By 1981, tied grants were back to one-third of federal funding (see Figure 3.1). It appeared that the autonomy of the states would be restored, while the federal government returned to lines of responsibility familiar from the pre-Whitlam era.

This attempt at constitutional engineering to achieve a permanent reduction in the size of government proved self-defeating. Where the objectives of spending cuts and state autonomy clashed, devolution of power was sacrificed. Spending functions were returned to the states, but at the same time transfers of revenue were reduced. In other words, the states regained control of important services such as hospitals, but in such straightened circumstances that their policy options were reduced to managing closures and funding cuts. Fraser's New Federalism achieved a cut in Commonwealth expenditure, while transferring most of the opprobrium to the states (Groenewegen 1979: 68–69, 1989: 257–59).

The result was continual clashes with the states. From the Commonwealth perspective, the state governments were seen as grasping opportunists, unwilling to make full use of openings to restore financial responsibility — such as state income taxes. The states complained that Fraser was unwilling to match his decentralist aims with real transfers of authority, and that his new deal for the states had become little more than an exercise in cost shifting. As early as 1977, observers noted that 'New Federalism, it appears, lives in democratic rhetoric, not in reality' (Peachment and Reid 1977: 34–37, 53).

Its main tenets were gradually abandoned. Fraser remained a reluctant centralist, determined to defend the prerogatives of the Commonwealth. His clashes with the states were not sparked by attempts to secure a fundamental shift of power and policy initiative to the centre — as were Whitlam's. Instead, they were a series of skirmishes over policy priorities in which Fraser usually pulled back short of outright use of Commonwealth powers to overrule the states. Weller sees him as a well-meaning victim of his adherence to federal principles and his desire to avoid open conflict with the states. He was faced with opponents such as Bjelke–Petersen (Queensland) and Court (Western Australia) whose skills in using their states' political resources had been honed in confrontations with Whitlam, and who possessed few inhibitions in thwarting Fraser's initiatives. By contrast, Fraser was reluctant to test the full potential of Commonwealth powers. In confrontations such as that over the future of the Tasmanian wilderness, he used cajolery and financial incentives to block the construction of the Gordon Dam, and when these failed, was not prepared to test his constitutional powers in the High Court. In this restraint he embodied the recent dilemmas of liberalism (Weller 1989: Chapter 8). As Paul Kelly has noted (1992: 96), by the early 1980s the culture of the Liberal Party had become an obstacle to real change. It was immobilised by its 'respect for private property before a competitive economy, good manners before intellectual combat and states' rights before national imperatives'.

The Hawke Government

The recent debate has been marked by major political realignments. One of the oldest divisions in Australian politics has been between the

Labor view of federalism as an inherently conservative institutional defence of the rights of property from reforming governments and Liberals and Nationals who have generally accepted this image, especially when Labor has been in power in Canberra. It was a momentous event, then, when a Liberal Premier, Nick Greiner, advocated transfer of some powers to central government, and derided the traditional obsession of Australian conservatives with states' rights. At the same time, Bob Hawke — as recently as 1979 an advocate of the abolition of the states (Hawke 1979: 18–19) — argued for a major reorganisation of financial resources to bolster the autonomy of the states, enabling them to match their spending responsibilities with flexible revenue bases under their own control.

In its first three terms (1983–90), the Hawke government showed little interest in the systematic reform of federal-state relations. Wary of any initiative linked to the Whitlam government, Labor quietly shelved platform promises to revive urban policy. The only systematic review of the left-overs of Fraser's New Federalism was an inquiry into Commonwealth grants to local government. This did little more than recommend tidying-up the edges, but proposed that the Fraser scheme continue, making payments through the states. In 1985 the Loan Council endorsed a global approach to state borrowing, relaxing detailed supervision over the purpose of state borrowings, but strengthening limits on the total amount that each state could get (Maskell 1988: 105–7).

By the late 1980s, two major pressures were undermining this *laissez-faire* attitude towards federalism. Australia's worsening international economic position provided the context for an open assault on the main surviving structures of domestic protection. The deregulation of the financial system, rapid reductions in protection and government policies to encourage competition — the 'economic rationalist' agenda of micro-economic reform — did not leave the structures of government unaffected.

First, government expenditure was constrained. Federal budget deficits were transformed into surpluses in the late 1980s, and Paul Keating, as federal Treasurer, repeatedly attacked the states for showing little of the same restraint. The states, Labor and the (rare) non-Liberal governments alike, complained of the same scissors effect as under Fraser. The states were expected to do more as federal programs expanded in areas like health and housing, but with less money, as the resources from the centre were restricted. Unlike the situation under Fraser, state budgets were skewed as tied funding mounted again to, in 1990, just over half (Figure 3.1). Second, the new stress on 'micro-economic reform' brought with it pressures for privatisation and reliance on the market. As these agendas permeated federal and state governments they added to other challenges to the surviving structures of protected pluralism. The 1980s saw a turmoil of

Public Service reorganisation, experiments with new forms of co-ordination, and models of 'strategic political direction', whatever party was in power. The main structures of federalism were not immune from these changes (Halligan and Power 1992).

Pressures from Victoria and New South Wales for a modification of fiscal equalisation received a new impetus. We have seen that the uneven impact of protection provided the political context for the federal crisis of the inter-war years. With the phasing-out of tariffs during the 1980s, the old manufacturing states argued that the basis of equalisation had been undermined. Older justifications for equalisation were also looking weaker. Western Australia and Queensland could no longer claim that their exporters were subsidising inefficient domestic industries in the south-east (Maskell 1988: 105–6, Evatt Research Centre 1989: 417–19, Considine and Costar 1992: 281–84).

The New Federalism, Mark III

These different streams came together in the odd coalition of the New South Wales Liberal Premier Nick Greiner and Prime Minister Bob Hawke. The exact origins of this alliance are murky, but two points stand out. The Hawke government, surprised at its own electoral victory in 1990, was looking for a program to sustain the reformist drive which had kept it in power for three terms. With Keating's leadership ambitions apparent to all, Hawke desperately needed a major policy triumph he could call his own. The Hawke New Federalism was driven, at federal level, by senior bureaucrats, particularly those in the Department of the Prime Minister and Cabinet, centring on its Secretary Mike Codd (*Age*, 29 October 1990). The emphasis in the New South Wales proposals was an extension of 'managerial' reforms to public administration. The efficiency of government was to be enhanced by eliminating areas of overlapping authority, and rationalising administration with 'vacation of fields' of activity, as full responsibility for programs was transferred to the relevant level of government (New South Wales Cabinet Office 1990).

The Greiner/Hawke proposals were phrased in the bland language of managerialism. They presented the issues as technical questions that could be solved in an objective manner if governments, departments and interest groups set aside sectional interests and empire building, and placed the public interest first. But their clear objective was to make government more streamlined, reducing the size of the public sector by rationalising Commonwealth/state functions, and widening moves towards competition throughout state trading enterprises and utilities.

This third New Federalism had three main components. First was a reshaping of federal and state responsibilities, returning to a dual federalist model in which duplication and overlapping functions between levels of government would be reduced, with greater co-ordination of state and federal policy making. States and territories would also accept each other's regulatory standards for goods and occupations. Once an individual gained an occupational qualification or a product had cleared regulatory standards in one state, the principle of mutual recognition would require acceptance by all others. Second, federal state financial relations were to be recast, giving states a broader revenue base, redressing vertical fiscal imbalance. Finally, and at the behest of the larger states, the question of equalisation was reopened. To what extent should the two most populous states continue to subsidise the smaller ones? Since an end to horizontal equalisation would reduce South Australia's revenues by at least 10 per cent, Tasmania 16 per cent and the Northern Territory by over half, Queensland and the smaller states resisted the move intensely (Lane 1992: 265, Parkin and Marshall 1992: 121).

The first of these components, dual federalism, followed two directions. The first was to establish new forms of intergovernmental co-operation to develop a national approach, not by federal fiat, but by joint administration. For example, to end the chaotic and grossly inefficient mismanagement of rail freight services, federal and state governments agreed to combine their rail services into a jointly-owned National Rail Corporation (NRC). Similarly, the new National Food Authority (NFA) worked to develop national standards and to extend the principle of mutual recognition to all the state and federal departments involved with food products. Despite the language of 'overlap' and 'duplication', these ventures involved co-operation with the states, with the Commonwealth being the dominant party. Although the states retain formal constitutional responsibility in this area, the procedures of the NFA treat them as merely one set of corporate bodies among others which must be consulted before setting national standards (National Food Authority 1993: 3, 41–49, Nelson 1992b: 78–91).

A second aspect of these changes proved to be more politically controversial — the transfer of functions between different levels of government. Greiner argued for a major reallocation. Under his proposal the states would refer areas such as industrial relations into the hands of the Commonwealth, which in turn would withdraw gracefully from any involvement in education, health and housing services (*Sydney Morning Herald*, 26 July 1990). Greiner followed this initiative three months later with an attack on his Liberal colleagues, in which he put the managerialist line bluntly: 'Too often we give the impression to the world that we are obsessed with States' rights for their own sake' (*Sydney Morning Herald*, 25 October 1990).

The New Federalism, then, shared none of the aims of decentralisation of power structures and democratisation shared (in radically different ways) by Whitlam and the New Right theorists. This is most marked in the lack of involvement of local government. An odd feature of recent celebrations of federalism is the neglect of this third level of government. Questions of fiscal imbalance are usually presented as a problem of federal-state relations. However, there is an equally serious imbalance within the borders of each state, which the proponents of decentralised government rarely question. State relations with local government replicate the dominance they complain of at federal level: the excessive use of specific-purpose grants as well as limitations on the local tax base. At the same time the problems faced by the capital cities have become less amenable to planning by the characteristic Australian mixture of over-centralised state governments and highly fragmented local governing bodies. The states, however, have been even less willing than the Commonwealth government to contemplate any real devolution of power to the local level (Purdon and Burke 1991: 23–26, 93–96, Jarman and Kouzmin 1993: 155, Jones 1993: Chapter 10).

Whereas Whitlam and Fraser implemented policies that represented a wider ideological position expressed by their parties, often in the face of resistance from key central government departments, Hawke's New Federalism had its origins outside party programs. There have been suggestions that it was the high point of the ALP's long-drawn out 'reconciliation with federalism', a recognition that centralist fantasies of unitary government were at best unrealistic, and that the cause of effective government was best served by improving the existing institutions (Galligan and Mardiste 1992: 71–75). It is argued here that the forces for change came from outside party politics. A strong alliance of state élites, based primarily in the central co-ordinating departments of both levels of government, provided the key ideas and support. Consequently, it is unsurprising that its supporters showed little respect for differences in party regime. Greiner's Liberal National coalition government in New South Wales provided the federal government's most effective ally, but the Labor states, faced with even greater financial problems, were enthusiastic about any measure that might increase their resources (Parkin and Marshall 1992: 120).

The New Federalism proceeded at this level. In late October 1990 a special Premiers' Conference met and arranged for further discussion of the main policy areas. Heads of Governments meetings (HOGS) composed of the Prime Minister, the Premiers and Chief Ministers were instituted to discuss major questions of principle. Working parties of public servants representing the two levels of government would handle the details — at no stage was local government given a serious place in the new scheme of things.

We have already seen that choices in federal politics are rarely purely technical matters. If responsibility for an area of government activity is placed at national level, the opportunities for redistribution are greater than at local level. Similarly, if the objective is to provide equality of treatment or access to services to all sections of the community, this is more likely to be achieved with national involvement than if the initiative is left purely to the states. Hence, deciding which services are best suited to assignment to the federal government is not a neutral activity.

The debate over New Federalism soon acquired a political edge. Supporters of the welfare state saw the moves as an insidious attempt to undermine government intervention by the back door, weakening the financial and administrative mechanisms by which national responsibilities in areas such as housing and health services had developed. From a quite different direction, the more anti-statist libertarians saw the focus on overlapping and duplication as a diversion. With their competitive model of government, such duplication and messiness were to be welcomed. The New Federalism appeared to have acquired the aspect of a cartel, with state and federal officials colluding to divide the areas of government activity.

Resistance soon appeared from two main sources. First, there was strong opposition from the major Commonwealth spending departments and their ministers, in particular in the vulnerable social policy areas of community services, health and social security. There was an immediate suspicion that federal and state finance departments, unable to gain significant cuts in social expenditures by frontal assault on departmental budgets, were attempting the same result by reorganising administrative responsibilities. The existing federal tangle of financial and program responsibilities gave rise not only to buck passing and avoidance of responsibilities, but also made it difficult for a unilateral abandonment of responsibilities from one level. State and federal departments of housing, for example, could use the dense legal jungle of the Commonwealth-State Housing Agreement to protect their programs from marauding Treasury officials. Disentangling these overlaps would make identification and control of expenditure far easier. Lobby groups such as the Australian Council of Social Service (ACOSS) strongly supported the welfare ministers. The Department of Community Services and Health was soon embroiled in a bitter row with the Department of the Prime Minister and Cabinet over the new direction, arguing that those who were complaining of overlapping and duplication had forgotten that the Commonwealth had moved into these areas precisely because of failures on the part of the states (*Sydney Morning Herald*, 11 April 1991).

A commentator in the *Canberra Times* (15 April 1991) put the anti-devolution case, arguing that: 'In social policy terms the shift of responsibility for key community services to the states and territories is a disaster. The historical credentials of the states to perform these functions are woeful. In general, the states have a poor performance record — equity and access to services have rarely been a priority, initiative has been lacking and community-based services have been spurned.' Far from an open attack on the existence of the states, this rejection of the New Federalism laid most stress on the benefits of overlapping administrations. Their chaos was now celebrated as invaluable in holding off the advancing forces of the New Right and small government. Environmentalists also viewed the prospect of devolution of Commonwealth powers with horror. In Aboriginal policy, the shift of responsibility to the state and territory governments was met with dismay. 'In none of the other developed industrial countries has socio-political progress occurred among indigenous people without a persistent and dominant role being played by the national government. Abandonment of that role, either *de facto* or *de jure*, is the road to inaction, heightened racial tensions and social unrest' (Crough 1991: 40).

Even sections of business, otherwise strongly supportive of regulatory reforms, were sceptical of any move of major taxation powers to the states. The Business Council of Australia, which represents the nation's largest corporations, praised the general move towards rationalisation, even calling for the abolition of one (unspecified) level of government by the year 2000. But it expressed misgivings about any weakening of Commonwealth control over national fiscal policy which might follow a major reform of vertical imbalance (Business Council of Australia 1991a, 1991b).

The normal slow progress of any intergovernmental negotiations also took its toll. While all agreed that the National Rail Corporation was a good idea, when it came to the actual financial arrangements this was different. The hazards of reform were displayed when this venture in co-operative federalism almost immediately tottered, as the states haggled over the value and liabilities of their respective rail freight services.

Finally, and most decisively, as doubts grew within Cabinet and the back bench, conflict fed into the growing leadership struggle between Keating and Hawke. From the start Keating took a more sceptical view of the likelihood and desirability of a major reorganisation of the relationships between Canberra and the states. He argued that Hawke's policies would mean that the federal government would abandon essential tools of economic management, encourage a return to 'irresponsible spending' by the states and end the equalisation function that federal control had ensured. When he was Treasurer Keating had shown little sympathy for tax devolution to the states. He now argued that it would be tantamount to 'dismembering the federal government which would inevitably follow from surrendering revenue and other national responsibilities to the States'. There was some support from economists, who argued that the public expenditure cuts of the 1980s would not have been achievable without the centralisation of taxation powers (*Sydney Morning Herald*, 23 October 1991, Groenewegen 1993: 184–89).

Some of these criticisms were fully consistent with Keating's earlier positions. Clearly, however, he saw the issue as a convenient stick with which to attack Hawke's leadership. Few seriously shared the view that New Federalism would mean the end of serious Commonwealth economic management. His victory over Hawke complete, by April 1992 Keating was reviving several of the themes on which he had previously cast scorn. He showed no interest, however, in returning fiscal powers to the states. For the moment this aspect of the agenda was effectively dead.

What, then, remains of this latest stage of New Federalism? Both its principal political sponsors, Hawke and Greiner, had left political life by mid-1992. Discussions at official and head of government level continued, and several of the new authorities — including the NRFC and the NFA — were operational.

In May 1992, the heads of government at their meeting agreed to establish a Council of Australian Governments (COAG). While its second meeting, in June 1993, was dominated by dramatic clashes over the *Mabo* case, elements of the rationalisation agenda have continued. The general areas of agreement give some idea of the limited, but real progress. Under the mutual recognition rubric, the states agreed to proceed with legislation to open up a national market in goods and services, eliminating existing regulatory impediments, to establish a National Road Transport Commission to develop uniform national regulations. They strengthened existing moves to unify rail (the NRC) and the states' electrical grid systems (the National Grid Management Council). Each of these areas fell clearly within market-based moves towards micro-economic reform (Heads of Government Meeting 1992, Department of Primary Industry and Energy 1992: 16–17).

The slow shift from fiscal equalisation has also continued. Both New South Wales and Victoria lose less, but compared with a simple per capita distribution, the Commonwealth still transfers $970 million (New South Wales) and $720 million (Victoria) tax revenues to the other states. Queensland is now on the same basis as the other more populous states (*Intergovernmental News*, Autumn 1993).

The two components of the New Federalist agenda, managerialism and financial devolution, have not fared equally well under the Keating regime. The former was hardly affected by the shift of leadership and the 1993 election. With support from the major parties at both levels of government, the process of rationalisation of functions and the reform of state government economic activities were never under political threat. Obstacles have been the result of hard bargaining over finances rather than over principles. Compared with the open warfare between Canberra and even nominally sympathetic state governments during the Whitlam and Fraser years, the difference is startling.

4
Executive Government

GEOFFREY HAWKER

Managerial Government Now

In 1993 the federal government released a Report reviewing a series of major reforms undertaken over the previous decade 'to increase the efficiency and effectiveness of the administration, and its responsiveness and accountability' (Task Force on Management Improvement). The Report found that 'the direction of the reforms has been correct'. But despite around 600 pages devoted to the 'reforms', only a few sentences discuss ministerial and Cabinet arrangements. Although Australian constitutional doctrine and political rhetoric still stress the central place of Cabinet and individual ministerial responsibility as the link between representative democracy — Parliament — and the bureaucracy, most of the Report is devoted to the discussion of changes within the Public Service. Almost no attention is given to relations with its supposed political masters. This marginalisation of politics and questions of accountability was not a chance omission, but was set in the terms of reference of the Task Force, which was required to concentrate on management issues. This is not an isolated instance. Management practices and Public Service structures have been reformed, restructured and evaluated almost continuously over the last two decades, bringing reforms that have caused fundamental shifts in political arrangements. These transformations in public control and the accountability of executive government have not been untroubled, merely unexamined.

To the extent that recent changes have been reviewed as a whole, observers have seen them as different sides of the one coin: strengthening the political control of the ministry over the Public Service while giving the latter's managers greater authority to carry out their allotted functions. The executive government, that is, Cabinet and the ministry, seems more powerful than ever. Many recent accounts of Australian government have described a fall from grace. A Westminster model of government, taken from Britain, in which ministers were accountable, individually and collectively through Parliament to the wider electorate, has been supplanted by a new managerialism, drawing on private sector organisational models and with little interest in public accountability.

Many writers have seen such changes as natural developments in a system that is still evolving and, on the whole, being improved. Thus

> Australia inherited...the Westminster system...in easy and careful stages, passing through representative and responsible government to full independence. The harmonious way in which Westminster was transplanted and the ease and robustness with which it took root gave an authenticity and persistence to the system in Australia at least equal to the system in the homeland. (Cumes 1988: 1)

This version of administrative and political history makes unwarranted rosy assumptions about the context in which the Australian reforms were launched.

The Australian Political Executive

By the time of Federation the shape of Cabinet and the Public Service was established in forms that have persisted until recently. The federal level of government was well ahead of the states in clarifying political and official responsibilities. Thus the first Commonwealth government of 1901 had a structure within which single ministers were unambiguously responsible for the operations of a single department and a number of associated agencies. Such a situation took many years to achieve in some of the states, and individual state ministers were, and are, often more closely involved in the details of administration than in policy development and oversight. The role of the federal government as a co-ordinator of policy, especially economic policy, emerged only slowly.

The shape of the political executive established by the time of World War I remained substantially unchanged for some sixty years. It was this period that gave rise to the popular images and notions which have governed textbooks on Australian politics. Taken together, these principles were said to constitute 'the Westminster system'. This term was popularised from the late 1930s (Halligan and Power 1992: 9), but did not come into widespread use until the 1960s, paradoxically just when the system it purported to describe began to break down. The Australian model of executive government was instrumental — both government and bureaucracy had legitimate tasks to do — and relational, lines of accountability running from public servants to Ministers, and then to Parliaments and people. Accordingly the authority and roles of Ministers and public servants could be delineated clearly, and detailed mechanisms of accountability and control could be developed.

This Australian system had three key features. First, state and federal Public Services were career-oriented. The normal mode of entry was as a school leaver, and promotion was up the slow ladder of seniority, with 'efficiency' as a vaguely-defined second criterion. Outside recruitment —

of university graduates, for instance — was rare, except in technical departments, such as public health. As a result, most senior public servants had worked their way up through the system. Restrictions on entry by some outsiders were softened after the two world wars. State and federal public services lowered normal entry standards in an 'affirmative action' program for war veterans. Discrimination against married women, however, remained a central part of Public Service personnel practice. Each service had a 'marriage bar', which required female employees to resign when they married.

Critics pointed to the conformity and mediocrity this system appeared to breed. In 1930, W.K. Hancock lamented that 'Democratic sentiment applauds the sound argument that every office boy should have the chance to become a manager, and perverts it into a practical rule that no-one shall become a manager who has not been an office boy' (Hancock 1930: 120). A Westminster-like system need not be conformist; the separation of the bureaucrat from the politician is instead supposed to foster official capacity and independence. But the Australian experience suggests that the danger of conformity can be real. The Public Service was run on departmental lines, with few attempts to staff or manage it as a whole. Promotion was within departments, following the absorption of prevailing departmental policies. There were also clear benefits. Governments found it difficult to interfere in hiring and promotions policies, and the career of a public servant needed to owe little to such outside patronage.

Second, power within the Public Service was dispersed. Australian public administration was marked from an early date by a great reliance on independent boards and commissions, outside the direct control of individual Ministers. This led to a pluralistic system of administrative structure. Co-ordination was not through the collective responsibility of Cabinet, but was far more haphazard, often relying on personal relationships between Ministers. There were variations between states. Victoria, with a reliance on independent authorities, was at one end. This led one analyst to suggest that 'the relation of the central administration to the State utilities suggests the image of a dwarf in control of a troop of giants' (Davies 1960: 184). The Queensland government, on the other hand, made far greater demands on ministerial involvement in the details of departmental administration. All states, however, shared a reliance on statutory corporations and other methods of insulating the political executive, 'diminishing ministerial control to a few strictly defined decision areas' (Wettenhall 1990: 10).

This opened the way to the third distinctive feature of co-ordination in the Australian system. At state level effective administration became dependent on informal alliances between senior public servants and powerful Premiers. Sir John Playford in South Australia and his State Auditor-General, J.W. Wainwright, provide a striking example of this model (Radbone and Robbins 1986: 465–66). Much of the success of resource development in Queensland has been traced to similar links between the state's most powerful politicians (Sir Gordon Chalk, Treasurer from 1965 to 1976 and Sir Joh Bjelke-Petersen, from 1972 to 1987), and a group of able career bureaucrats, most notably Sir Leo Hielscher, the long serving Under-Treasurer (Galligan 1989: 136–37).

The Menzies Era and the Heyday of Westminster
This closed system came under challenge in the post-Depression and war years of the late 1930s and 1940s. The rise of a new group of reforming Keynesian economists and planners in the federal government opened up the prospect of a new sort of public official, no longer the anonymous servant of a government but autonomous and powerful enough to develop and implement policy in partnership with government. The pressures of war helped to undermine, at least temporarily, restrictions on entry to the Commonwealth Public Service. A group of well-educated senior policy advisers, many with post-graduate economics degrees and familiar with Keynesian arguments for wider government intervention to achieve sustained economic growth and full employment, entered Commonwealth employ. Many of these men remained in government employ after the war ended, and developed a new, 'mandarin' style of senior administrator, far removed from the pre-war model. The Department of Post-war Reconstruction, under H.C. Coombs (1943–49), was the focal point of this development. The experience of post-war reconstruction showed that the federal government was moving to a broader policy role, in which it increasingly came to co-ordinate the activities of the state governments, and in which its own apparatus also came increasingly under centralised control.

Soon after the election of 1949, however, the Menzies government set out to reassert 'traditional' norms. For a time Coombs seemed to be facing dismissal (Coombs 1981: 133, 268). He survived and prospered, though others with a similar background suffered periods of eclipse. The doctrine of the anonymous and impartial Public Service was perhaps used in some cases to serve narrow political or even personal ends, but in others it did permit ideas and policy to flow across party lines. Thus Coombs was able to influence Menzies to adopt proposals he had hitherto seemed likely to oppose — including the creation of the central banking system and a continued if diminished emphasis on projects of national development. This suggests that an expert officialdom is likely to be most useful to the executive government when it contains a diversity of values.

Westminster norms of responsible government found their clearest expression in the work of a public servant, Frederick Wheeler, who valued official anonymity as the corollary of ministerial responsibility for policy, however influential officials were in formulating it. As a result his significance is not well known. Wheeler was Chairman of the Public Service Board from 1960 to 71. From this position he promoted the career service in a way unparallelled by any other federal official. His emphasis on graduate recruitment to the Public Service, a notion which an earlier public inquiry had promoted, but which had been rejected by the government (Caiden 1967: 284–87, Halligan and Power 1992: 72–73), was especially important. Promotion on the basis of merit moved gradually away from the earlier combination of basic educational qualifications and seniority towards a concept of merit in which educational qualifications were rated more highly. At the same time, the Commonwealth led the way in removing the marriage bar, in 1966 (Encel and Campbell 1991: 154–57).

By the time of Menzies' retirement at the end of that year, the pattern of executive government in Australia seemed to be strongly established. At the federal level, the 'mandarinate' had been consolidated (Schaffer 1977: 28, Halligan and Power 1992: 70–73). It was capable of operating new systems of financial co-ordination that the Keynesian revolution had wrought within certain norms of administrative behaviour. Paul Hasluck, a long-serving senior minister in Menzies' Cabinets summed up this way of understanding the role of the Public Service:

> [G]ood government requires that the public service should act according to its own lights and in conformity with recognised codes of proper conduct and not with a simple wish to do what the minister wants in the way he wants it. (Hasluck 1986: 13)

These changes had little influence at state level. Systems of control remained dispersed, as individual departments and statutory authorities exercised considerable independence in delivering their services. Co-ordination of departments still owed little to standard Westminster notions of Cabinet government, but depended on the strength of individual Premiers. As late as 1978, the ALP Dunstan government in South Australia faced a major political crisis when the Chief Commissioner of Police, Harold Salisbury, defied Cabinet requests for his resignation after a Royal Commission found that he had misled the government. Salisbury carried the principle of autonomy to the extent of claiming that the Police Commissioner was 'responsible to the Crown — directly to Queen or her representative in Australia [sic]', not to the Minister for Police or to state Cabinet (quoted in Summers 1986: 342).

Change after Menzies
Soon after Menzies' departure, the merits of this degree of Public Service autonomy came under question. Three themes preoccupied reformers over the next twenty years: the capacity of Ministers to control the Public Service; the openness of the Service to the community, and its equity in representing the clients of government; and the capacity of public servants to manage public resources effectively (Campbell and Halligan 1992: 36–39). By the early 1990s,

Ministers had reasserted their control over the Public Service, its openness to the community was no longer a major concern, and the capacity of public servants to manage public resources was still being fiercely debated.

The concern of Prime Ministers and Premiers to increase their control within executive government was manifested in a range of measures: the reorganisation of the work of Cabinets through committees, the strengthening of the Chief Ministers' departments to enhance their capacity to co-ordinate and evaluate policy, and the growth of policy advisers working directly to the Prime Minister or Premier. These changes were not the property of any one party. In some cases, as in South Australia (1965) and Western Australia (1983), the reforms followed a change of government; in others, they were initiated by a new leader who succeeded a long-serving predecessor, only to lose an election to an Opposition that continued the reforms, as in the Commonwealth (1972), New South Wales (1976), Victoria (1982), and Queensland (1989).

These reforms coincided with the breakdown of the established policy order, and the emergence of new issues and preoccupations that gradually saw Australia's protectionist and isolationist orientation become permeated with international, environmental and lifestyle concerns. With the strengthening of the offices of Prime Minister and Premier underway, public services came under scrutiny, chiefly through a range of commissions of inquiry so numerous that the 1970s was called the 'decade of commissions' (Wilenski 1986: 168). These generally favoured the openness and accountability of government, and some progress was made in opening up the Public Service to scrutiny. It was only from the mid-1970s that serious attempts began to be made to open up state services to outsiders. And it was not until the end of that decade that the fragmentation of state administration was tackled, with a move towards 'ministerialisation', replacing independent boards and statutory commissions with departments under the authority of the Minister. Instead of the confused lines of authority under the previous system, responsibility corresponded more (in theory) to notions of collective and individual ministerial responsibility. At the same time, the informal networks and personal authority which Premiers had used to dominate their Cabinets were gradually replaced with more institutionalised lines of co-ordination, stronger Premier's departments and Cabinet offices (Painter 1987: 69–73, 82–93). Again, these changes were uneven, with Queensland retaining older patterns until the fall of Bjelke-Petersen at the end of the 1980s.

At federal level early signs of reform appeared in the late 1960s, during John Gorton's time as Prime Minister (1968–71). Gorton shocked the mandarinate by installing his own head of the Prime Minister's department and carving out a separate Cabinet office, where he installed the previous incumbent. Gorton did not survive long as party leader, but his dissatisfaction with the responsiveness of the senior bureaucracy prefigured the concerns of later governments (Walter 1992: 34–35). Such dissatisfaction had already become apparent in South Australia, where the Labor government, led by Don Dunstan, was experimenting with new methods of enhancing ministerial, and specifically chief ministerial, authority (Painter 1987: 117–23).

These changes concentrated on the workings of Cabinet and the authority of the Prime Minister. Most Australian Cabinets met as a single group, even if often spasmodically, rather than in separate committees concentrating on particular issues or policies. As formal minutes were rarely kept, especially at state level, this gave vast scope to the authority of the Premier and Treasurer (usually the same man), who not only controlled the agenda but was the final authority on decisions reached. At federal level some attempts were made before World War II to depart from this model, by developing specialist Cabinet committees. The most ambitious but short-lived was Lyon's 1938 policy committee of seven senior Ministers, to advise the full Cabinet on general policy. Not until Labor's war and post-war ministries was a full range of committees attempted, but these 'broke down into a disorderly series of *ad hoc* committees'. The Menzies government also used such committees, and in 1956 the ministry was divided into an inner ministry (or Cabinet) and an outer ministry (of junior ministers). However, by the late 1960s, most state Cabinets had 'not even adopted regular or standing Committee systems to lessen the load on full Cabinet...[and the] development of secretarial arrangements [had] also been slow' (Sawer 1968: 70, 58). Rapid change had begun at the federal level by then, with the Prime Minister's department assuming a formal responsibility for arranging Cabinet business and supporting a gradually emerging range of committees (Walter 1992: 31–33). From the 1970s, most state governments also began to adopt formal committee systems and mechanisms of secretarial support by officials.

The Whitlam Government, 1972–75
The Whitlam government marked a watershed in executive government in Australia. In 1973, Whitlam declared his government's need 'to have available machinery and advice to plan for the inevitable and accelerating change now occurring in all modern communities' (*CPD*, 27 February 1973: 11). But the government expected that the system would work for it, and its early changes to the workings of the executive government were few.

The government was also slow to change established systems within Cabinet, but it did abandon the distinction between an inner and outer ministry. The large Cabinet that resulted was unwieldy and uncoordinated (Weller 1991, Gruen and Grattan 1993: 23). Cabinet decisions were referred to Caucus, and on famous occasions disaffected members or Ministers defeated in Cabinet succeeded in reopening and overturning Cabinet decisions (Lloyd and Reid 1974: 153–66). Only in its last year did the government implement a system of Cabinet committees for urgent business (Hawker, Smith and Weller 1979: 74–87).

The range of advice coming to Ministers was broadened by setting up a large number of inquiries into policy issues, expanding their private staffs to include advisers on policy, and creating a new body, the Priorities Review Staff, to offer policy analysis and advice across the whole range of government programs. Whitlam claimed, perhaps disingenuously, that these changes merely 'enhanced' but did not supplant the traditional policy advising role of the senior bureaucracy (Whitlam 1974: 17). In retrospect few of these changes seem radical; succeeding governments adopted and extended them, despite initial claims that they would not do so.

The changes to executive government with the most far-reaching potential were less those concerned with the structure and operations of the Cabinet and upper levels of the bureaucracy than with the composition and responsiveness of the bureaucracy as a whole. The inflexibility and social unrepresentativeness of a Public Service which promoted members in its own image was well recognised by many Ministers and their advisers. An emphasis on graduate recruitment and meritocratic promotion within a service that located an increasing proportion of its senior members in Canberra raised the spectre of a separate administrative class or élite. Women, immigrants from a non-English-speaking background and their descendants, and those without a private school education were absent from senior positions to a striking degree (Wilenski 1978: 33–34). Equal employment opportunity (EEO) programs were introduced in the public sector to provide for the recruitment and training of women, Aborigines, people from non-English-speaking backgrounds and, later, gays and the disabled.

Attempts to devise new mechanisms to redress citizens' grievances with administrative decisions and behaviour generally occurred in the series of programs known as the New Administrative Law. These included mechanisms for review of administrative decisions through the Administrative Appeals Tribunal and elsewhere in the judicial system, and the institution of an Ombudsman, freedom of information legislation, and an Administrative Review Council. 'Equity' attained an equal footing with 'efficiency' and 'effectiveness' as a criterion to judge the performance of the Public Service.

The themes of accountability and responsiveness were crystallised in the Report of the Royal Commission on Australian Government Administration (RCAGA), chaired by Coombs. Established by the government in mid-term as a wide ranging inquiry (Hawker, Smith and Weller 1979: 235–37), the Commission's report emphasised the need for ministerial control within executive government. The Report also endorsed equity and openness as necessary characteristics of a democratically controlled administration and expounded the need for devolved and accountable management within the Public Service.

The Fraser Government 1975–83

The Fraser years were contradictory. During its first term the new government was so concerned to recover basic principles allegedly violated by Labor that the real problems identified by the RCAGA were disregarded. By the end of the Fraser years, many of these lessons — in particular, opening the Public Service to outside entry — had been painfully rediscovered. By 1983, one experienced Canberra journalist noted that 'there seems to be a growing sense of unity between politicians of all colours that the public service is not adequate for the task and that it needs to be changed' (quoted Wilenski 1986: 191).

Part of Fraser's message in his successful election campaigns of 1975 and 1977 was the need to restore the workings of executive government to more traditional lines. He began his period of government by running down or abolishing a number of organisations established by Whitlam and by sidelining some public servants identified too closely with Labor. Hostility towards any measures identified with the Whitlam period was deep-seated. One victim was the limited experiment in the appointment of technically qualified, politically sympathetic senior bureaucrats from outside the Public Service. The RCAGA had recommended an extension of this system. Its proposals were rejected as a threat to the security of tenure of senior officials, and an assault on the Westminster system itself. The First Division Officers Act 1976 limited the ability of governments to appoint non-public servants to senior positions without the approval of the Public Service Board. Other RCAGA suggestions were accepted, EEO survived — although in a somewhat attenuated form — and the new administrative law was maintained.

Fraser was keen to exercise forceful control over his government, something he believed Whitlam had failed to do. Prime ministerial leadership was strengthened by increasing the co-ordinating powers of Cabinet committees and of his own department. These were not new developments, but they did intensify a movement of control to the centre of government and created machinery which was seized upon and extended by his successors: for example, splitting Treasury to create a separate Department of Finance established a base for management oversight in later years. The Parliamentary Secretaries Act 1980, which allowed backbenchers to be appointed as 'parliamentary secretaries' (positions which carried no ministerial authority but allowed promising members to deputise for Ministers), was also taken up by subsequent governments. Fraser also attempted to strengthen ministerial control of the bureaucracy by increasing the size and influence of Ministers' private staffs, despite his earlier hostility to such attempts by Whitlam (Walter 1986: 78–79). Fraser's 'only flattery of Whitlam', noted one of

Selectively interpreted, it influenced later debate about the forms of executive government.

his erstwhile colleagues, 'was imitation of his presidential bureau' (Hasluck 1986: 17).

The attempt to return to a golden age of Westminster principles and a depoliticised Public Service had proved illusory. The problems first posed under Gorton and Whitlam, of asserting ministerial control while improving the technical competence and efficiency of the Public Service, remained. Like Whitlam, the immediate response of the Fraser government was to sponsor yet another round of inquiries. The Parliamentary Joint Committee on Public Accounts recommended the establishment of a mobile and openly recruited group of senior executives which would be responsive to the needs of Ministers. These proposals were given flesh by the government-appointed Review of Commonwealth Government Administration (the Reid Inquiry), which proposed further developments towards what later became the Senior Executive Service (SES), especially the development of 'management skills'.

The Hawke Government: Early Reforms

There were strong lines of continuity between the last Fraser years and the Hawke Labor administration which replaced it. Both governments were obsessed with avoiding the apparent mistakes made by the Whitlam administration. The new government was keen to co-ordinate ministerial activities more effectively than Whitlam had been able to do. The ministry was divided into junior and senior members, the latter constituting the Cabinet. Cabinet committees were set up. The Public Service was reorganised along the lines set out in the 1983 White Paper, *Reforming the Australian Public Service*, in the Public Service Reform Act 1984.

The Act created the Senior Executive Service which had been foreshadowed in earlier reports. This was intended to enhance the responsiveness of senior public servants to elected politicians. The new grouping of officers was to 'undertake higher level policy advice, managerial and professional responsibilities in departments' and could be appointed by open competition from outside the Public Service. Its members were to be a mobile corps of officers moving from job to job, to meet ministerial needs. The Act also formalised a new category, 'ministerial consultants', qualified individuals working under the specific direction of ministers beyond the boundaries of the Public Service. Subsequent appointees swelled the total private staffs of ministers, especially of the Prime Minister. The Liberal Party endorsed this development. In 1983 a committee of review had concluded that future Ministers should 'appoint political staff of demonstrated capacity, rather than apolitical staff' (Liberal Party 1983: 111).

The Act also extended considerations of equity and democracy by requiring departments to adopt EEO guidelines and plans for 'industrial democracy'; the latter involved relatively junior staff in assessing the effectiveness of departmental operations. From the 1980s onwards, however, that prospect faded as the new orthodoxy of economic rationalism placed a renewed emphasis on managerialism within executive government. The third theme of enhancing managerial responsibility was dealt with only briefly in the last section of the 1983 White Paper. It became increasingly important, however, as long-term problems of the Australian economy came to preoccupy the government, and it moved to integrate Australia with world financial markets and to develop a competitive export-oriented industrial base (Emy and Hughes 1991: 10–29). The government's Public Service reforms now emphasised the need to

> enhance medium-term planning and setting of priorities whilst strengthening the management and control of public expenditure; allow public sector managers greater scope and flexibility to respond to change; and make government programs more effective through making managers more accountable for the results achieved with public resources. (House of Representatives Standing Committee 1990: 7)

But accountable to whom? The new stress on 'letting the managers manage', the use of performance-based contracts for senior public servants, and experiments with models borrowed from the private sector caused old problems to re-emerge. To whom should managers owe responsibility? How far should Ministers be answerable for the workings of their departments?

The agenda of managerialism became a counterpart to economic rationalism in the economic sphere. In a political climate increasingly hostile towards public organisations, managerialism has been an approach which sees rationing and limitation of public action as an essential goal. All its main precepts revolve around defining objectives as narrowly as possible, and centralising organisational control in the hands of the managers. As one critic has noted, it is a framework which has concentrated on internal organisational questions, and an apparently endless reshuffling of managerial structures and responsibilities has been one result at federal and state levels. It is inward-looking, and makes 'very few worthwhile changes to the way public organisations seek to learn from and influence their environments' (Considine 1990: 177).

Sources of Change

The ascendancy of the new orthodoxy was established more quickly in the ranks of the senior bureaucrats than in the minds of the Cabinet, as is shown in Michael Pusey's study of the attitudes and values of senior Canberra public servants in the period 1983–85 (Pusey 1991). Pusey interviewed a sample of senior officials in selected departments and found that more than half had qualifications in economics or cognate disciplines, that men from non-government schools were disproportionately represented in their ranks, and that they favoured a diminution in the role of the Australian state in the economy and social life generally. Some commentators disagreed with the connection Pusey implied existed between the values of his respondents and their educational background (Wanna 1992, Davis *et al.* 1993: 121–22), but none doubted their influence in carrying through the agenda of economic rationalism. More telling critiques of Pusey have pointed to the broader context of managerialist and economic rationalist reforms (Hamburger 1991, Schott 1991). The major changes in policy direction of the mid-1980s were not uncontested within the bureaucracy. This applies especially to the ALP/ACTU Accord, initially anathema to the economic Dries of Treasury, but becoming the centrepiece of Labor's wage and social policies. In other words, contrary to Pusey's suggestions, the reform agenda of the Hawke government was not simply imposed by a group of influential economic rationalist bureaucrats. The key Ministers driving government policy picked and chose according to political criteria. The strength of the economic rationalist agenda came from common starting points — particularly agreement on the need for major structural reform of the economy; a sympathy for anti-protectionist arguments that went back to Whitlam's first assaults on Australia's tariff regime; and hostility towards the cushioned business and financial élites (especially the banks) which had profited from a closed economy.

This close alignment of the social and economic values of politicians and officials has important implications for executive government. Ministers and senior bureaucrats worked with a very narrow range of policy options, and were dogmatically hostile towards state intervention. They placed too much faith in the passing intellectual fashions of economic model builders. If Ministers and officials alike find it difficult to think outside contemporary orthodoxies, then the long-term value of the different elements of the executive government to one another must be questioned. In a situation of radical change in the socio-economic environment, a Minister would not be well served by officials who could do no more than reflect a dying orthodoxy — but neither would officials be well served by one that expected no more than the current line.

When compared with overseas models such as Thatcher's Britain or New Zealand's 'Rogernomics', however, the economic rationalist experiment in Australia has been relatively mild. In these other two nations public sector changes have attempted a far more radical divestiture, moving as much activity as possible into the private sector, or into smaller government agencies divorced from ministerial control. The Australian experience, especially at federal level, has been more contradictory. The new managerialism has been accompanied by the rise of the mega-department. A rhetoric which attacks large government and administrative 'overload' has gone hand-in-hand with new forms of administrative centralisation (Hood 1990). This has given older questions of ministerial responsibility a greater political salience in Australia.

The Hawke Government: Second Round of Reform
In 1986 new economies were made in the Public Service in order to set an example to the private sector where 'fundamental restructuring' was required (Hawke 1989: 15). Then, after the election and without Cabinet consultation, the Prime Minister announced a reduction in the previous 27 departments to 18, under a tiered system of ministerial control. Sixteen senior Ministers headed departments and constituted Cabinet, assisted by a varying number of junior Ministers responsible for some parts of their senior's territory. No longer was the ministry merely divided into Cabinet Ministers and junior ones; junior Ministers were now formally subordinate to the senior members of the ministerial executive. With the expanding ranks of parliamentary secretaries (by 1993, there were 10), the ministerial executive now had 3 distinct levels.

These changes were designed to strengthen senior ministerial control over the supervision of policy and the capacity of public service managers to implement policy with maximum autonomy. Hawke said that the new structure would

> reduce overlap and duplication...ensure that all...interests are represented in a Cabinet that is of manageable size...provide the opportunity for improved budgetary and management processes... provide savings from economies of scale; and will introduce broader perspective within portfolios without reducing the necessary impact of particular interests.

These were rather bland and traditional terms to explain a reform the Prime Minister described as 'major', and press commentaries as 'the most dramatic shake-up in the Public Service since Federation'. The themes of accountability and public responsiveness had disappeared entirely, replaced by vague invocations of 'national policy imperatives' (*Canberra Times*, 15 July 1987).

The changes brought strong co-ordination to the centre of government and also a devolution of power to senior officials, through the crucial step of abolishing the Public Service Board. The official statement barely referred to this; the abolition of the Board met with much less comment than the ministerial and departmental reorganisation, but might in the longer term be more significant. Central personnel agencies were also abolished in the states in this period. The effect of the abolitions was to strengthen other central agencies, notably the Department of the Prime Minister and Cabinet, and the Department of Finance and their state government equivalents with new supervisory powers. As would be expected, the public sector unions strongly criticised the changes. The Opposition, however, made few criticisms, the shadow Minister for Public Service Matters noting merely that the government 'was applying the basic reforms outlined in Liberal policy for the past two elections' (*Age*, 15 July 1987). Bipartisan support for changes in executive government was maintained.

Growth of the Executive

The greater status differentiation within the executive and the more complex relations between Ministers and the various sections of the bureaucracy might be seen simply as inevitable characteristics of a greatly expanded executive. The eleven more or less equal federal Cabinet ministers of 1901, with their handful of private advisers and departmental heads, had become by 1993 sixteen Cabinet Ministers, seventeen non-Cabinet Ministers, ten parliamentary secretaries, some 220 ministerial advisers and sixteen departmental heads at the top of organisations containing some hundreds of senior executives running scores of differentiated units (*Government Directory* 1993; 'Members of Parliament: Staff', *CPD, Senate*, 25 May 1993, 1279–81). State governments showed a similar though less marked trend.

Senior public servants now have less certainty of continuity in office (Halligan and Power 1992: 90–91). This has led some critics to fear that the upper levels of the Public Service have become too dependent upon Ministers for their jobs (Hasluck 1986, Weller *et al.* 1993: 20–21). Between 1990 and 1993 three departmental heads were removed from their positions, and after the 1993 elections the head of the Treasury lost his position. The government offered no explanations of these removals. They may have involved no specifically political differences, but rather a loss of confidence between some Ministers and officials on a mixture of policy and personal grounds (Gruen and Grattan 1993: 50–51). It is not surprising in these circumstances that many departmental heads 'now believe that their futures would be more secure if they were actually on contracts' (Waterford 1993: 12).

The tendency to rotate departmental heads, the loss of the Public Service Board, and the principle of increased mobility for other senior officials in the SES seems likely to promote an attitude that officials at the most senior levels are liable to be moved suddenly. So long as broad unity in policy orientation is maintained between Ministers and officials this need not imply the 'politicisation' of the Public Service. However, the procedures now in place would permit such a development if a regime with markedly different policies came to office. Then the long-heralded 'Americanisation' of the bureaucracy (Renouf 1979: 511) might be accomplished.

Prime Ministerial Government?

After an initial period of relative quiescence under Hawke (in comparison with Fraser's period), the influence of the Department of the Prime Minister and Cabinet began to expand again, as shown by the export of its best officers to other departments (Gruen and Grattan 1993: 47–49). In 1972, barely one-fifth of the 27 departmental secretaries had served in the Prime Minister's department; in 1993, nearly one-half of the 35 secretaries and associate secretaries had done so. Those officials transferred and promoted brought to their new locations a sensitivity to the concerns of the centre that was lacking in an older generation of officials whose careers had been restricted to non-central departments. With the abolition of the Public Service Board in 1987, the head of the Prime Minister's department became effectively the head of the Public Service (Walter 1992: 41–42). The private staff of the Prime Minister has also expanded more rapidly than the staffs of other Ministers, growing about 50 per cent between 1986–93, double the rate of the rest of the ministry.

Keating has accentuated these tendencies. After his unexpected electoral triumph of March 1993 he insisted on taking sole responsibility for the selection of the ministry, instead of waiting for the usual deals between Caucus factions to be concluded. He still did not select Ministers himself, as a Liberal leader would have done. He discussed his choices with factional leaders before making a final selection of ministerial appointees, which was then sanctioned by the vote of the full Caucus. Some Ministers, who would almost certainly have been re-elected by Caucus under the old rules, were persuaded to leave the ministry, or to leave Parliament altogether. The customary balancing of factional and ideological interests in Cabinet was largely ignored, with the Prime Minister's Right faction holding 13 of the 19 Cabinet positions. It was even more dominant in committees, occupying all positions or all but one on three of the six. The Prime Minister's post-election statement that he had 'streamline[d] the Cabinet committee system' (Keating 1993: 3) had more than managerial import.

Ministers
So where have these administrative upheavals left the question of ministerial responsibility? The powers and responsibilities of ministerial members of the executive are likely to continue to come into question, for structural reasons. Positioned as they are between a Prime Minister with increasing executive powers and a senior bureaucracy which has substantial management autonomy, the capacity of individual Ministers to fulfil their executive roles is weak.

Once appointed, Ministers have considerable autonomy from the political bodies to which they are supposed to be accountable. It is frequently said that their accountability in any full sense is neither to Parliament nor electorate, but rather to political party. Limitations on accountability to the first two bodies are certainly real enough; there are also severe limitations to their party accountability.

Beyond the party room, in the broad membership of the party, the accountability of Ministers is limited. In principle, Members of Parliament owe preselection to party members in their electorates, or to some mix of these members and other party members selected by the respective head offices or party conferences. But challenges to sitting members are rare, and even more rarely successful, and the preselection defeat of sitting members seems to owe more to contested ideological orientation than to their ability. In part this may reflect deference of party members towards a successful member, but not all Ministers are liked by their rank and file. It is more the case that even moderately competent Ministers have ample resources to shore up their position with the party membership, and make challenges difficult for ideological opponents. The selective recruitment of new members, the patronage of supporting co-operative members into influential but secondary party positions (branch secretary, conference delegate, committee member and so on), the flattery of private conversations, and perhaps the delivery of paid jobs in public employment — all are methods routinely used by members wishing to retain preselection without trouble — and they are used most readily by Ministers. No doubt these methods can be seen as a form of accountability, for they bind the Member or Minister to the party membership. But the relationship is a very unequal one, and the accountability is exiguous when the Member is a Minister who lives within the secrecy of the Cabinet. The problem of Ministers lies precisely in their privileged isolation. Senior Ministers are said to have more authority than ever before, but their collegiality is threatened and the boundaries of their authority are unclear.

The idea of 'Ministerial responsibility' is more difficult than ever to define. Recent events have both clarified and confused matters. According to a Senate committee responding to calls for Senator Collins' resignation after an ineffective tendering process for pay television licences, the

> complexities of modern administration render it not viable for a minister to be compelled to resign for departmental actions for which he or she had at most vicarious responsibility. (Senate Select Committee 1993: 13)

Whether an Opposition with a failing Minister in its sights will abandon the notion of individual responsibility is another matter (Senate Select Committee 1993: Dissenting Report: 34–46). But in any event such a statement does not clarify what activities *would* entail ministerial resignation.

The real sanction against an incompetent Minister still appears to be the fear of the ministry as a whole, and in particular the Prime Minister, that the government's hold on power may be threatened by the a plainly incompetent Minister continuing in office. This sanction may be weak when no election is near, but may also be compelling if a government is approaching an election or is otherwise in difficulties.

Problems of Executive Government

As the executive is presently constituted, Ministers are discouraged from working collectively. Working to the Prime Ministerial centre of power rather than to Cabinet as a whole, there is a risk of Ministers working in isolated fiefdoms supported by their junior Ministers and parliamentary secretaries. The dissolution of Cabinet into committees would strengthen any such tendency. So would the continued enhancement of the capacity of the Prime Minister's office to superintend the work of the government as a whole. Developments such as these may have informed one former Cabinet Minister's gloomy statement that the creation of a ministerial hierarchy over giant departments was 'the biggest mistake we made' (Duffy, quoted Hill 1993: 4).

On coming to office in 1983, the government proposed, as a remedy for the 'overload' on Ministers, 'a regular, at least annual, meeting of Ministers to allow a collegiate examination of national prospects and...priorities' (Commonwealth of Australia 1983: 27). The promise lapsed until revived by Keating in 1993 when addressing an angry Caucus after the failures of consultation during the budgetary process; it would be a means of 'harmonising the directions that caucus wants to take and the directions the executive wants to take' (*Telegraph Mirror*, 8 September 1993). It is unlikely that the renewed promise will come to anything.

The 1993 Task Force on governmental reform assumed that ministerial control over the Public Service was well established. The notable failure of state government Ministers to control or to admit to control over a number of failed commercial activities in the 1980s might suggest that no such assumption could be safely made in regard to the states. Is the federal government different? The Task Force certainly thought so, but its assessment was based on limited surveys of opinion. Parliamentarians were not asked for their views. And the views of the public and clients of government were drawn from a sample which was asked about 'levels of satisfaction with [the] delivery' of services rather than about the reforms themselves, since 'it was not reasonable to expect members of the community to recognise the jargon of the reforms directly or to link their experiences to the effect of reform-driven change' (Task Force on Management Improvement 1993: 586). Those who were asked to evaluate the reforms were the very managers responsible for implementing them; senior officials consistently evaluated them more positively than their juniors.

A Cabinet that is so closely co-ordinated it may surrender collective power to the Prime Minister and his supporting officials in department and private office, is now served by managers who alone are competent to judge their own performance. Such a system will survive as long as its delivery of political and social goods is maintained. Any substantial failure to do so would leave no lingering loyalty to the forms of executive government now dominant. A 'politicised' Public Service and a ministry opened, along American lines, to non-parliamentary members might then win popular support. The rapid pace of recent change, so confidently proclaimed by those who believe they control it, and the evident capacity for a sophisticated system of executive government to fail, should allow us to consider those more radical prospects that may be in store.

5
Parliament

RODNEY SMITH*

The inclusion of a chapter on Parliament in a book devoted to *developments* in Australian politics will seem odd to readers of the literature on Australian parliaments — a literature that is overwhelmingly negative and pessimistic. Regardless of when during the last thirty years an author is writing, the message is the same: Parliament is in decline, it runs, while executive dominance increases. This process is constant and probably irreversible. Parliament is but a 'rubber stamp' or 'sausage machine' irrelevant to the real power processes of Australian politics, because it is subordinate to party discipline, the executive, or ruling class power. *All* aspects of the institution — its legislative and debating functions, question time, the presiding officers, accountability, language and behaviour — are decaying. The Westminster system of responsible government has failed in Australia. Reform is desirable, but — to complete the pessimistic cycle — reform is virtually impossible because of the power of parties and the difficulty of constitutional amendment. According to this dominant view, then, Parliament has not 'developed' in significant ways and is not likely to.

The argument in this chapter is that these views are misleading. There was no 'golden age' from which Australian parliaments have steadily declined throughout this century. Instead, very soon after Federation, they became dominated by disciplined parties, and assumed the features for which they are criticised. Recently, however, parliamentary politics has become more open-ended. Governments have been unable to secure majorities in upper houses, and, in some cases, lower ones. Weakening party loyalties within the electorate mean that this situation is likely to persist. Other recent changes to Parliament — such as changes to its demographic composition, changes to parliamentarians' careers, the move to a new Parliament House and the televising of Parliament — though they have had some effect, have been less important.

This chapter focuses on the three central areas, legislation, individual ministerial responsibility and administrative accountability, in which the executive has been portrayed as omnipotent over Parliament. It

*Thanks to Stuart Crawshaw and Jane Gleeson-White for research assistance

argues that in each area parliamentary politics has increasingly played a stronger part.

Slow Declines and Golden Ages: Inadequate Approaches to Parliament

The view of parliaments as largely moribund became political science orthodoxy from the 1960s. Its entrenchment can be seen clearly in the standard text of the era. From its first edition in 1949 to the early 1960s, Crisp's *The Parliamentary Government of the Commonwealth of Australia* took a reasonably sanguine view of parliamentary politics, arguing that it provided opportunities for government and Opposition alike (see, for example, Crisp 1961: Chapter 5). By the mid-1960s, however, the text — now significantly retitled *Australian National Government* — began its discussion of Parliament thus:

> It is nowadays a commonplace in British countries that Parliament is in eclipse, a pale, even sickly pale, moon reflecting but a little of the shining light of Executive power. Amongst British Parliaments around the world the Australian has perhaps suffered a more substantial eclipse than most. (Crisp 1983: 267)

These sentences open the relevant chapter of every subsequent edition of the book.

Other writers, whether they have taken a Westminster-oriented perspective like Crisp's (see Weller 1979, 1982, Reid 1982: 166, Jaensch 1986, Nelson 1988: 20-21, Emy and Hughes 1991: 359-65, Jaensch 1991: Chapter 7), or a Marxist one (Loney and Playford 1973), have generally taken up this refrain. It is heard even in the most recent texts. Bennett (1992: 71), for example, begins his chapter on state parliaments by arguing that:

> Steadily throughout this century the State legislatures have lost the initiative in policy-making to governments and their agencies, and the traditional view of parliamentary sovereignty has become much diluted. There are important occasions when this is not so, but the overall picture is of institutions whose decline in importance has mirrored a world-wide decline that has been observed in nations with parliaments modelled on Westminster principles.

This view is also dominant among journalists (see, for example, Whitton 1980, Dodd 1988) and in the self-analysis produced by current and former parliamentarians and parliamentary staff (see, for example, Button 1979, McClelland 1986, Department of the Senate 1991).

The idea of a steady decline in the powers and role of Parliament throughout this century — just like the 'golden age' that preceded it — is the stuff of mythology (see McClelland 1986, Hirst 1988, 172-93, Bolton 1991: 471), a mythology which obscures the reasons for fluctuations in power relations within Parliament and between Parliament and other political institutions.

The processes that most contemporary writers identify with the decline of Parliament had in fact largely run their course by the 1920s. By then, party discipline determined parliamentary votes, tactics and procedures at federal and state level (see Hawker 1971: 241-300, Loveday, Martin and Parker 1977, Reid and Forrest 1989: 10, 23, Black 1991). The Commonwealth parliamentary committees that helped determine issues like arbitration, tariffs and welfare in the first decades after Federation had disappeared (Reid and Forrest 1989: 389-92, Aldons 1991, Marsh 1991: 38). Executives had begun relying on party committees and extra-parliamentary bodies to legitimise policy (Reid and Forrest 1989: 25–26). Writing of the 1924 establishment of the Commonwealth Bank Board, Lang (1962: 45) comments: 'That idea [responsible government] was rapidly becoming old-fashioned. Parliament was becoming a rubber stamp for decisions made by boards and experts.' The number of parliamentary sitting hours declined and governments were regularly using Standing Orders to curtail debate (see Table 5.1, Crisp 1983: 284). Green (1969: 54–64), a Clerk of the House of Representatives between 1937 and 1955, claims that the last great parliamentarians disappeared in the 1920s. The parliamentary press gallery shifted its attention to the executive following the 1909 'fusion' of the non-Labor parties and World War I (Reid and Forrest 1989: 450–51). These processes occurred in state parliaments during the same period, with the additional step of abolishing the upper house taken by Queensland in 1922 (see Coaldrake 1985: 220). Rather than steady decline over ninety years, Australian parliaments altered quickly in the first twenty years of the century.

Once the decline of Australian parliaments is properly historically located, its principal causes become clearer. It did not result from an uneven contest between abstract entities called the executive or legislature. Nor was it the inevitable or irreversable outcome of Australia's Westminster system. Rather, it was the result of the existence from around 1910 of an evenly-balanced electoral competition between two disciplined parliamentary party groupings (Labor and non-Labor) that between them shared the loyalties and votes of ninety per cent of Australian citizens (see Aitkin 1982). One of these groupings was thus ensured a majority in the lower house of Parliament following any election. Party discipline promoted the decline of Parliament from within (Rydon 1986: Chapter 13), but it could only do so because the major parties held the support of almost all voters. As soon as the major parties failed to retain this level of support in one or both of the houses of Parliament, and minor groupings took up the balance of power — as has occurred at federal level and in a number of states in recent decades — then Australian parliamentary politics began to lose their 'rubber stamp' character *regardless of the continued operation of highly disciplined parliamentary parties.* Thus while most of Parliament's critics have based their hopes for parliamentary reform on a breakdown of party discipline, seeing this as the root cause of parliamentary decline, the pattern of recent decades suggests that decline and reform rest squarely on the outcome of electoral behaviour and competition.

The Diversity of Australian Parliamentary Politics

If the standard accounts of Australian parliaments misread parliamentary 'decline', they also underplay the diversity of parliamentary politics in Australia. The major element in this is the disposition of parties in parliaments. Figure 5.1 illustrates twenty-eight possible dispositions, many of which have occurred within the parliaments of Australia.

The horizontal axis shows possible dispositions in lower houses. The Westminster requirement that a government maintain the support of a majority of lower house MPs limits these to four: a governing party majority; a governing party minority supported by one or more friendly parties or Independents; a minority governing party supported by neutral parties or Independents; and a government that, in the absence of disciplined parties, must rely on the support of individual MPs. The left of the axis represents the 'rubber stamp' lower houses of dichotomised majoritarian parliaments. Shifts toward the right end of the axis are shifts toward more uncertain, open forms of coalition building parliamentary politics (Sharman, Smith and Moon 1991).

Upper houses create more diversity in Australian parliamentary politics because the governing party, to stay in office, does not require a majority there. Australian political scientists tend to treat upper house as alien to Parliament proper (see, for example, Jaensch 1986: 90, Bennett 1992). This tendency seems to have four sources. The first is a misunderstanding, perpetuated by leading constitutional commentators and sections of the ALP, of the roles of the House of Representatives and the Senate that defines only the former as a popular democratic chamber (see Sharman 1990, Galligan 1991). The second is an objection to the historically élitist composition and means of selection of state upper houses. Complete adult suffrage for upper house elections was granted comparatively recently: 1950 in Victoria, the 1960s in Western Australia and Tasmania, 1974 in South Australia and as late as 1978 in New South Wales. Thus the state upper houses have very short histories as popularly elected houses (Jaensch 1977: 84–85; Page 1990b, Bennett 1992: Chapter 6). The third source, which partly rests on the first two, is objection to specific powers of federal and state upper

FIGURE 5.1 *Possible Dispositions of Parties in Australian Parliaments*

Upper House	Lower House			
	Governing party[a] majority	Governing party and allies[b] majority	Governing party and neutrals[c] majority	Most or all members Independent
No upper house	Closed, one-party majoritarian politics			
Governing party majority				
Opposition party majority				
Opposition party and allies majority				
Governing party and allies majority				
Governing party and neutrals majority				
Most or all members Independent		Open-ended, coalition-building politics		

[a] 'Governing party' includes long-standing coalitions such as that between the Liberal and National parties in the Commonwealth Parliament.
[b] 'Allies' refers to parties or Independents that overwhelmingly align themselves with one of the major parties without necessarily having a formal coalition arrangement with them. Examples of LNP allies have included the Democratic Labor Party (Commonwealth Parliament) and Call to Australia Party (NSW Parliament). ALP allies have included the Green Independents (Tasmanian Parliament).
[c] 'Neutrals' refers to parties or Independents who do not have a record of consistently supporting either of the major parties. The Australian Democrats are the most prominent recent example.

houses to block legislation and thus determine the fate of governments. This argument particularly centres on the Senate's 1975 deferral of Supply Bills which brought down the Whitlam Government (Maddox 1985: 175-88, 409-14). Fourth, these houses provide the clearest evidence of the weaknesses of the 'Parliament as rubber stamp' argument. This holds best if upper houses are presented as not really a part of Parliament at all (compare Jaensch 1986: 44 and 90–99).

In fact, upper houses are integral to the Australian parliaments that have them. Designed to be strong, they have regularly used their powers (Rodan 1983, Sharman 1987: 47–48, Nethercote 1987, Black 1991, Emy and Hughes 1991: 365–70, Galligan 1991). While the government is composed of those MPs who have the support of a majority in the lower house, and the powers of upper houses over money Bills are more limited than those of lower houses, upper houses are as important as lower houses for the vast bulk of parliamentary business. Accounts of Australian parliamentary politics which sideline them are seriously distorted.

Figure 5.1 shows seven possible upper house party dispositions along its vertical axis. Four replicate those in the lower house; the others include the absence of an upper house, an opposition party majority in the upper house, and an upper house majority composed of the opposition party and parties or Independents friendly to it. From top to bottom, the dispositions move from dichotomous majoritarian to coalition-building parliamentary politics.

Combining the two axes, a matrix is constructed. Parliamentary politics in the top-left corner of the matrix is closed and majoritarian, with a single governing party able to push legislation through the legislature. As parliaments move away from this corner, their politics become more open-ended, since the governing party must engage in negotiation and coalition building in one or both houses to pass legislation and remain in office. The far top-left cells conform to the 'rubber stamp' depiction of contemporary Australian parliaments, while the far bottom-right cells represent the parliamentary politics imagined by those who look back to a parliamentary 'Golden Age' (see Crisp 1983: 288–89).

Figure 5.2, based on this matrix, reveals five things about Australian parliaments since 1960 — that is, since they have been overwhelmingly depicted as rubber stamps. First, they have occupied a wide range of positions within this matrix. All but three (Queensland, the Northern Territory and the Australian Capital Territory) have moved from at least one cell to another. Second, parliaments fell into the 'rubber stamp' cells (the far top-left cell and the one immediately beneath it) in just under half (121 years) of the 259 years of parliamentary politics represented in Figure 5.2. For the Commonwealth Parliament, the figure is

FIGURE 5.2 *The Disposition of Parties in Australian Parliaments Since 1960*[a]

Upper House	Lower House			
	Governing party majority	Governing party and allies majority	Governing party and neutrals majority	Most or all MPs Independent
No upper house	Qld 1960– NT 1978–		ACT 1989–	
Governing party majority	Comm. 1975–80 SA 1960–65, 68–70, 79–82 NSW 1973–76, 78–88 Vic. 1970–82, 92– WA 1960–70, 74–83, 93–			
Opposition party majority	SA 1965–68, 70–79 NSW 1960–67, 76–78 WA 1971–74, 83–85	WA 1991–93		
Opposition party and allies majority	Comm. 1972–75 Vic. 1982–92 WA 1985–			
Governing party and allies majority	Comm. 1960–2 NSW 1967–73	NSW 1991	NSW 1991–	
Governing party and neutrals majority	Comm. 1980– SA 1982–89 NSW 1988–91 Vic. 1960–70	SA 1989–		
Most or all MPs Independent	Tas. 1960–69, 72–81, 82–89, 92–	Tas. 1969–72, 1989–91	Tas. 1981–82, 91–92	

[a] Includes genuine parliaments with wide powers of legislation only. This excludes the Northern Territory until 1978 and the Australian Capital Territory until 1989 (see Heatley 1979; Mackerras 1989). Judgements made as to the attribution of 'coalition', 'ally', 'neutral' and 'Independent' status are just that. Some will inevitably be contentious.

Sources: Jaensch 1977; Parker 1978; Holmes 1978; Bennett 1983; Rodan 1983; Turner 1985; Mackerras 1989; Jaensch 1990; Macintyre 1991, Layman 1991, Phillips 1991, Page 1990b, Australian Electoral Commission 1992

just six of 34 years. For roughly half the total parliamentary years since 1960, governing parties have had to engage in coalition building politics to have their legislation passed. Governments in all parliaments except Queensland and the Northern Territory have had to do so at some stage. These first two points sit very awkwardly for those who see Australian parliaments as nothing but rubber stamps and who view their only movement as one of decline.

Third, the parliaments have not moved in similar directions in this period. Roughly half the total years of parliamentary politics in the 1960s were 'rubber stamp' years. This increased to almost two-thirds in the 1970s, but fell back to less than half in the 1980s and early 90s. Some parliaments moved against these trends, or did not move at all, confirming the federal pattern of Australian politics (Holmes and Sharman 1977).

Fourth, most of the movements in the Figure 5.2 are along the vertical axis. This greater movement in upper houses stems partly from the fact that the membership of most such houses is now decided by proportional representation elections, while lower houses — except for Tasmania and the ACT (see Mackerras 1989) — use single member constituency elections. Upper house elections thus give greater opportunities for small parties to win seats. Recent years have seen an increase in voters who, while they support one of the major parties, deliberately direct their upper house vote to minor parties (Chaples 1985: 8-10, 1989: 273–76). They exercise this option knowing that it does not prejudice their party's chances of forming the government, since that issue is determined in the lower house. These voters, combined with minor party supporters, give minor parties a significant vote in upper house elections and look likely to continue to do so. Thus Australian parliamentary politics is unlikely to become more stable in the foreseeable future.

Finally, Figure 5.2 reveals more recent moves away from 'rubber stamp' parliamentary politics in lower houses. In the last few years, the governments of New South Wales, Tasmania, South Australia, Western Australia and the Australian Capital Territory have all had to rely for significant lengths of time on the support of lower house minor parties or Independents. This situation developed partly from parliamentarians defecting from the major parties to sit as Independents, and partly from disaffected electors choosing Independents and minor parties at lower house polls (see Smith 1992a).

Since parliaments have not always been 'rubber stamps', it is worth re-examining the impact of parliaments on key areas in which executives have been depicted as holding complete sway. This examination will focus on the Commonwealth Parliament, but will refer to state developments wherever this is appropriate.

Primary Legislation

Legislation is arguably the central function of parliaments in Westminster-style systems like Australia's (Reid 1982). The contemporary image of Australian parliaments is that they perform this function badly — if at all. Legislation is drawn up by bureaucrats at the behest of the executive. Once the governing party has approved it behind closed doors, it is simply pushed through Parliament. Parliamentary debate on Bills is cut short at government whim by the use of a closure motion (the 'gag') which, if successful, results in the Bill being put to an immediate vote without further debate, or by the 'guillotine' which limits the time allowed for debate on a Bill (see Penguin/Macquarie 1988: 154, 161). As a result, Bills are rushed through Parliament without proper consideration, especially towards the end of parliamentary sessions (Emy and Hughes 1991: 360–61).

Governments have added new weapons to reduce Parliament's legislative function. These include 'legislation by media release', in which the government officially releases details of proposed legislation even before it is introduced into Parliament, and announces that the proposed legislation will take effect immediately rather than on the day of its proclamation following passage through Parliament. An important recent example was the Hawke government's changes to media cross-ownership laws, announced on 25 November 1987 as policy effective from that day. This had crucial repercussions throughout the Australian media industry, before the relevant Bills were even considered by Parliament (see Chapter 15 of this book).

Another weapon is the passage of 'skeletal' Bills that contain broad statements of policy and few legislative details. Determination of these details, which are often the key to the operation and effects of the law, are 'delegated' within the Bill to the executive. The amount and variety of such delegated legislation has increased in recent years.

A third weapon is the increasing use of open-ended proclamation clauses within Bills (Lynch 1988: 7). Legislation comes into effect only when it is proclaimed. Leaving the timing of proclamation in the hands of the executive gives it the power to determine when, if at all, a Bill (or parts of a Bill) will take effect, regardless of the fact that it has been passed by Parliament (Lynch 1988). In 1986, Senator Chris Puplick gave examples of some Bills passed by Parliament up to six years previously, still awaiting proclamation (Lynch 1988, 5, Department of the Senate 1991: 60–61).

The gag, guillotine, legislation by media release, delegation and proclamation are powerful resources for governments. Taken together, they suggest that parliamentary debate and politics indeed play little legislative role. The numbers of sitting days and numbers of Bills passed by Parliament appear to confirm this view of a parliamentary 'sausage machine' that gives small consideration to legislation. Table 5.1

TABLE 5.1 *House of Representatives Sitting Times and Acts passed,. 1990–90*

Period	Sitting days per year	Average sitting hours per year	Acts passed per year	Hours per Act
1901–10	95	577	23	25.1
1911–20	71	449	40	11.2
1921–30	67	425	47	9.0
1931–40	58	382	75	5.1
1941–50	70	452	73	6.2
1951–60	63	461	96	4.8
1961–70	62	483	120	4.0
1971–80	69	543	173	3.1
1981–90	60	535	172	3.1

Source: House of Representatives Standing Committee on Procedure (1986: 64), House of Representatives (1986–90)

shows that while the number of Bills annually passed by the House of Representatives has increased more than sevenfold during this century, the number of hours spent considering each Bill has decreased eightfold. Since the 1970s, the House has dealt with each Bill in an average of three hours.

These figures, often seen as cause for concern, have to be viewed carefully. First, the annual number of House of Representatives sitting hours has not constantly declined since 1901; in fact, it has increased steadily since the 1930s. It is the sheer number of Bills now passed that reduces the hours of parliamentary scrutiny available to each one. If each of the 172 Bills passed annually in the 1980s were to have been debated for the same time as the average for the 23 yearly Bills in the 1900s, the House would have had to sit for 485 days a year! Second, a perusal of *Hansard* suggests that quantity of debate does not equal quality. Where debate is lengthy, even on important Bills, many speakers repeat general points made by their colleagues. This seems to be just as true of the lengthier debates of the distant past. Concerns over reduced parliamentary debate should thus be restricted to other areas: shorter debates may mean more drafting errors remain in legislation; they may mean unacceptable provisions buried within Bills pass unnoticed through the Parliament; and they may mean opportunity for informed community comment on legislation is lost.

Such concerns are valid. The parliamentary politics that has evolved in recent years has, however, increasingly focused on these problems. In particular, developments in the Senate's legislative committee system have reduced the chances of their occurring.

The present Senate committee system began to emerge in 1970, with the establishment of seven Senate legislative and general purpose

TABLE 5.2 *The Senate Legislative and General Purpose Standing Committee System: 1970–71 Committees and Corresponding Committees Since 1987*

1970–71	1987
Health and Welfare	Community Affairs
Education, Science and the Arts	Employment, Education and Training
Social Environment	Environment, Recreation and the Arts
Finance and Government Operations	Finance and Public Administration
Foreign Affairs and Defence	Foreign Affairs, Defence and Trade
Primary and Secondary Industry and Trade	Industry, Science and Technology
Constitutional and Legal Affairs	Legal and Constitutional Affairs
—	Transport, Communications and Infrastructure

Source: Department of the Senate (1990b)

standing committees designed to examine any issues or legislation the Senate might need to investigate (see Table 5.2). Ideas for such a system had been around since the 1950s, but had been resisted by the government (Solomon 1988: 36, Department of the Senate 1990a: 1–5). The success of Senate select committees in the 1960s convinced Coalition Senators to support Labor Senator Lionel Murphy's push for a comprehensive standing committee system. The new committees produced over 300 reports throughout the 1970s and 80s, but their focus was largely on general broad issues rather than legislation. To 1990, only 39 Bills had been referred to them (Miller 1986: 15, Department of the Senate 1991: 4, McNaughton 1991: 35).

Nonetheless, pressures were building for further expansion of the committee system. The Democrats, who have held the Senate balance of power since 1980, learned that sending a Bill to a Senate committee effectively slowed its passage and influenced its content (Department of the Senate 1991: 104). They were able to thus deal with Bills with the co-operation of the government or Opposition. In 1987, the seven standing committees were expanded to eight, and a series of parallel committees established in the House of Representatives (Solomon 1988; Reid and Forrest 1989: 380–81). This meant that, for the first time since 1914, the House could conduct its own specialist committee scrutiny work on legislation (Aldons 1991: 8). Support grew among Senators of all parties for more referral of Bills to committees (Miller 1986: 17). In 1988, the Senate established a select committee on Legislation Procedures to investigate this. Its recommendations were adopted with the support of all parties in 1989, and implemented in August 1991 (Evans 1991: 13–14, McNaughton 1991: 34–36).

A Selection of Bills Committee was established to consider all Bills (except money ones), and to recommend which should be sent to a standing committee. The Senate then either adopts the Selection of Bills Committee's recommendations or amends them. Bills thus chosen by the Senate are sent to the relevant standing committee. These committees have powers to call witnesses and take evidence. They report back to the Senate, suggesting amendments they think appropriate (Evans 1991, McNaughton 1991).

These procedures appear to have had a major impact on parliamentary politics. More Bills have been sent to committees — 17 in the first six months of the new procedures alone (Department of the Senate 1990a: 4; Evans 1991: 15). While the Selection of Bills Committee is supposed to take into account the *general* feeling of Senators about the need to send a Bill to committee (McNaughton 1991: 36–37, Evans 1991: 14), a convention appears to be emerging whereby the request of *any* group of Senators that a committee investigate a Bill will be accepted.

The Democrats, in particular, have used these new procedures to hold up legislation for scrutiny, even when the government considers it urgent. The Broadcasting Services Bill 1992 provides a good example. The Keating government was anxious to pass legislation allowing pay television by 1 October 1992, when a moratorium on pay television lapsed. For different reasons, the Democrats and Coalition objected to the proposed legislation. After sending back one set of amendments to the House, they then further delayed the Bill in June, by sending it to committee for three months (*Sydney Morning Herald*, 24–27 June 1992). The government was powerless to stop this.

Politics within standing committees depends on the interplay between government priorities, the balance of party forces in the Senate, and the independent atmosphere that committee work engenders. Where the government has no firm views on the precise nature of a Bill, or where an issue divides not only Labor and the Coalition but also the Democrats, committee politics is quite flexible and constructive. Where the government has a clear, determined policy and the support of one of the other parties, committee work is less constructive (Weller 1982: 105–6, Miller 1986: 13, Department of the Senate 1991: 32).

Since Bills sent to committee are usually of prior public concern, committee deliberations rarely raise novel amendments (McNaughton 1991: 39), despite the regular calling of witnesses and evidence. Instead, committees calling witnesses force public servants to explain and justify the content of Bills (Evans 1991: 16–17). They also give Senators greater opportunity to judge public reaction to proposed legislation. Evidence to the Community Affairs Committee from the Public Sector Union, for example, clarified Democrat opposition to proposed amendments to the Disability Services Act (*Australian Financial Review*, 16

June 1992). Finally, committees give the government an opportunity to work out which combination of possible amendments will satisfy a majority of Senators once a Bill returns to the Senate. Although the governing party has a majority on each committee, committee reports generally reflect such compromise combinations (McNaughton 1991: 40).

Although the Senate is not bound to accept proposed amendments from the standing committees, it tends to do so. In the period to April 1991, the Senate accepted 233 of 350 amendments (66.6 per cent) resulting from committee consideration of 21 Bills (calculated from Evans 1991: 16–17). These Bills included key government initiatives on banking, health, government data matching, privacy, social security and crime (Evans 1991: 16–17). Committee work produced important amendments to key legislation prior to 1990 (Weller 1982: 104–5, Miller 1986: 10–12, Evans 1991: 13); the new system merely strengthens this role.

The standing committees' work has thus become refocused in the last few years on legislation rather than on general inquiries (compare Missen 1982: 126, Weller 1982: 105–6, Miller 1986: 15). It is clearly no longer true that these committees have no real power, are too general in their focus, and produce reports of no significance (Weller 1979: 62–64, Miller 1986: 6). The problem of slow or non-existent government responses to committee reports, an often-criticised feature of past committee politics (Weller 1982: 105, Aldons 1986: 21–22; Miller 1986: 12–14; Reid and Forrest 1989: 382, Turner 1989: 80–81, Department of the Senate 1990a: 30–31, House of Representatives Standing Committee on Procedure 1990), is largely overcome by the fact that the government wants to get its legislation through the Senate. Without responding to committee reports, it cannot do so. At the same time, the standing committees continue their general inquiry work.

The standing committees have clearly reached some of the 'potential' for changing parliamentary politics seen in them by past commentators (Whitton 1980, Jaensch 1986: 100, Solomon 1986: Chapter 7, 188, 1988, Turner 1989: 75). If governments do not like committee scrutiny, they have had to endure greater and greater discomfort since the 1970s. Most such scrutiny has come from the Senate rather than the House of Representatives, which, despite the 1987 formation of a complete legislative committee system, has continued its tradition of less committee activity than the Senate (Solomon 1979, 1988, Turner 1989: 78–79). Nonetheless, it matters little which house takes on the role of committee scrutiniser, since except for money Bills, the powers of the Senate and the Representatives to amend legislation are equal, and the government must steer its legislation through both houses to have it implemented. The growth of Senate committee politics since the 1960s has been spurred partly by partisan motives (first from Labor, later from the Democrats). Were a governing party to gain control of the

Senate, committee politics would probably decline. The prospects of this in the near future, however, are negligible.

Thus party politics is as much a cause of, as a hindrance to enhanced parliamentary politics. The key issue is the parliamentary disposition of parties. Where the governing party controls the Parliament, committee functions that are retained become internalised within the governing parliamentary party, as occurred most clearly under Joh Bjelke-Petersen in Queensland (Coaldrake 1985). Where the governing party must engage in coalition building to get its legislation passed, as in the Senate, parliamentary committees become more powerful.

Lack of control of the Parliament by the governing party also increases the importance of parliamentary politics outside committees. Bills are regularly amended, supported and defeated in unpredictable ways as the result of conflict and compromise between the parties in the Senate. After eighteen months of negotiation, the Resource Security Bill was defeated in May 1992, ostensibly over disagreements regarding its title! (*Australian Financial Review*, 5 May 1992). More dramatically, as this book went to press the Keating government appeared likely to accept substantial amendments to its 1993 Budget Bills forced on it by opposition in the Senate from the Democrats and the Greens (*Australian Financial Review*, 4 August–15 September 1993).

In response to this loss of control, recent governments have undertaken pre-emptive amendments to legislation before its introduction to Parliament — as, for example, in the Keating government's extensive negotiations and compromises in 1992 with the Democrats, over the proposed Superannuation Guarantee Levy (*Sun Herald*, 21 June 1992).

The government's weapons for ramming legislation through Parliament or circumventing it altogether fail as soon as the governing party loses control of one house of Parliament. Legislation by media release becomes an embarrassment for the government as policy is amended on the floor of Parliament. Vague proclamation dates look more like a defensive weapon for the government, to prevent it having to implement legislation or amendments forced upon it by non-government parties. These can themselves use delegated legislation to reduce government power. As far as legislation is concerned, the Parliament does not resemble a 'rubber stamp'. Instead, it resembles that much more complex piece of office equipment, the word processor, at which a number of authors sit, fighting over the keyboard and struggling to get their thoughts included in the final text.

Enforcing Individual Ministerial Responsibility

Another oft-made criticism of Australian parliaments is their failure to uphold that element of responsible government known as the convention of individual ministerial responsibility. In Australia, this charge has particular weight, since individual and collective ministerial responsibility are generally taken here to encompass the meaning of 'responsible government', rather than to be one of several meanings and measures of an ambigious term (see Lucy 1985: Chapter 1, especially footnote 7, Sharman 1990:1, Emy and Hughes 1991: Chapter 9). The convention of individual ministerial responsibility demands that each minister be responsible to Parliament for three types of activity: the activities of his or her department; the activities of the Minister in his or her official capacity; and his or her activities in various non-ministerial capacities. If the Minister or the department engage in improper activity, or the Minister or department fail to act where they should have, then the Minister takes responsibility, either adequately explaining the problem or, in serious circumstances, resigning (Emy 1978: Chapter 6, Page 1989: 93–94, Emy and Hughes 1991: 350–59).

The Commonwealth Parliament is commonly seen as too weak, too dominated by party considerations, and too uninformed about the activities of ministers and their departments to enforce the convention. Cases where Ministers resign or are dismissed by Prime Ministers following parliamentary action are seen as the exception rather than the rule.

This criticism deserves closer scrutiny. It is often unclear exactly what should be taken as evidence that the convention is operating well or poorly. The number of resignations and dismissals *in itself* cannot be evidence either way. The few cases in which Ministers have stood down or been sacked may not be 'exceptions' at all. They may just as easily be evidence of 'the rule': that is, they may be the only cases in which resignation or dismissal was appropriate. To assert otherwise assumes that a large number of improper ministerial and departmental activities go undetected and unpunished. This assumption is never tested by the critics (although see Emy 1978: 260).

Moreover, the *relative* impacts on Ministers of the punitive sanction and the cultural norm contained in the convention are crucial. If the threat of punishment is all that keeps them in line, then Parliament needs to be much more capable of realising dismissals than it does if Ministers absorb the convention as a positive norm that guides their behaviour. Not surprisingly, Parliament's critics lay stress on its ability to punish. Emy and Hughes (1991: 353), for example, argue: 'Parliament's ability to "call the minister into account" and force a resignation where circumstances warrant, is the sanction on which the convention — and hence the reality of this system of accountability — depends.' Page (1990a: 157), on the other hand, contends that punishment does not exhaust the convention's impact: '...even if ministerial responsibility in Australia were a fiction, it would be an important fiction as long as the protagonists — and the spectators — still see it as part of the rules of the parliamentary game.'

These two issues make any judgment about the efficacy of Parliament in preserving ministerial responsibility much more difficult than many critics assume. The evidence suggests, however, that the convention has been re-asserted in the last two decades and that Parliament has been an active player in this (see Page 1990a: 143).

The first seven decades of the Commonwealth Parliament saw just three ministerial resignations or dismissals on issues of individual ministerial responsibility. They were those of Nationalist Minister for Trade and Customs Jens Jensen in 1918, Labor Treasurer Ted Theodore in 1930, and Nationalist Postmaster-General Alexander McLachlan in 1938. Only McLachlan's resignation was precipitated by parliamentary action (a question placed on notice by the Opposition), the first two cases ensuing from Royal Commissions (see Healy 1989: 4–12).

Since the 1970s, the number of resignations and dismissals has substantially increased under both Labor and Coalition governments. In July 1975, Labor Deputy Prime Minister, Environment Minister and former Treasurer Jim Cairns was sacked by Prime Minister Whitlam following revelations that he had misled Parliament about offering a fee to a businessman seeking overseas loans for the government. Three months later, Minister for Minerals and Energy Rex Connor resigned following revelations that he had misled Parliament over his activities in seeking overseas loans (see Emy 1978: 267–79).

During the Fraser years, five ministers resigned and one was dismissed over individual ministerial responsibility. In 1976, Minister for Post and Telecommunications Vic Garland resigned following allegations (which went to court and were dismissed) that a bribe had been offered to an Independent candidate in Garland's office. In 1977, Treasurer Phillip Lynch resigned upon revelations that a Lynch family trust was linked to unorthodox Victorian land deals. Fraser dismissed Minister for Administrative Services Reg Withers a year later when a Royal Commission found he had acted improperly in suggesting names for two electorates to the Chief Electoral Officer. Minister for Primary Industries Ian Sinclair resigned in 1979 when a New South Wales Corporate Affairs Inquiry reported that he had committed several offences, and he was charged (he was later acquitted). Minister for Health Michael MacKellar and Minister for Business and Consumer Affairs John Moore both resigned in 1982, when MacKellar failed to declare or pay duty on a television set he imported. Moore, as relevant Minister, failed to make sure the matter was dealt with.

Three further cases have occurred under the Hawke-Keating Labor governments. In the first, Special Minister of State Mick Young resigned after he was found to have told a pollster and lobbyist that the government was about to expel a Soviet embassy official in 1983. In 1989, Minister for the Arts, Sport, the Environment, Tourism and Territories John Brown resigned after misleading Parliament over a tender. Finally, in 1992, Minister for Transport and Communications

Graham Richardson resigned following claims that he had misled Parliament over assistance given to a relative.

After three cases in 74 years, the last 13 years have seen 11 instances where individual ministerial responsibility has led to loss of ministerial office. In seven of these cases, parliamentary politics played a significant role in creating a climate for resignation or dismissal.

Question Time has proved a key tool in these parliamentary politics. In the Cairns, Connor, Young, Brown and Richardson cases, the Opposition used parliamentary questions both to force ministers to make statements that were later shown to be questionable or misleading and to generate the production of new material with which to embarrass the government (see Emy 1978: 267–79, Page 1990a: 148–49, *Australian Financial Review*, 29 April–19 May 1992).

Where Question Time does not produce embarrassing ministerial replies, its ability to generate information and media interest has the potential to help cause resignations. In the lead-up to the 1977 federal election, Opposition Leader Whitlam asked a series of parliamentary questions on Lynch's family trust. Labor also used questions in the Victorian Parliament to extract new information on the trust's activities. This threatened to draw media and public attention away from the Coalition government's agenda during the campaign. Fearing this, Fraser forced Lynch to resign (Page 1990a: 150).

Other parliamentary tactics can also prove important. The Opposition built up a climate of controversy around Sinclair by, among other things, moving five censure motions against him in 1978 and 1979 (Page 1990a: 150). It mattered little to Sinclair's reputation that none of these motions passed. In the Senate without a government majority, a wider range of tactics are possible. Non-Labor senators threatened to use their numbers and Standing Orders to prevent Richardson from speaking in the chamber, an extremely difficult (and ironic!) prospect for a communications Minister who was then attempting to guide important legislation through Parliament.

This is not to argue that parliamentary politics have been the only factor in the recent growth of ministerial resignations and dismissals. Between 1976 and 1989 the Prime Minister's view of the situation was critical in every case. The party's view and the Minister's own willingness to leave — traditionally held to be crucial factors — were comparably unimportant (Page 1990a: 141–42, 153–54). The Richardson case fits this pattern. The day before he resigned, Richardson gained 'strong cross-factional support' from his party (*Australian Financial Review*, 18 May 1992). Although he resigned without a request from Keating, the Prime Minister, who was at the time considering Richardson's position, did not try to dissuade him and described his decision as 'admirable' (*Australian Financial Review*, 19 May 1992). The media, both through editorial comment and investigative journalism, played a part in most of the cases discussed above (Emy 1978: 267–79,

Page 1990a: 155). The proximity of elections was important in the Lynch and Richardson cases.

The role of Parliament as one significant element in these cases cannot be denied. They suggest that it is misleading to place too much stress on party loyalty or to see parties and Prime Ministers as immune from political pressures, including the pressures of Parliament. The Richardson case in particular highlights this, since Richardson was a long-time 'mate' of the Prime Minister, and an ALP heavyweight. The claim that 'A minister who retains the support of colleagues and party has little to fear from the Opposition in Parliament' (Emy and Hughes 1991: 348) begs the question, and simply does not stand up against the record of Opposition parliamentary activity as a factor in Ministerial resignations and dismissals throughout the last two decades.

It was argued earlier in this section that the number of resignations alone cannot adequately indicate how well ministerial responsibility is working, both because it gives no suggestion of how many Ministers should have resigned, or of how well the positive norms of the convention are ingrained in parliamentary culture.

These latter issues are difficult, if not impossible, to determine satisfactorily. One yardstick against which the number of resignations could be judged is the number of parliamentary motions of censure, 'no confidence' or condemnation against Ministers. Between 1976 and 1989, Page (1990a: 145) found '41 motions covering 26 separate cases where ministers might be considered liable for censure...' Government majorities in the House of Representatives meant that all such motions there were defeated. Only one of the motions in the Senate was successful, while two others were tied. Since Senate motions cannot bring down individual ministers, these motions did not force ministerial resignations.

In fact, in only five of the 26 cases did Ministers later resign. At first glance this suggests a low success rate. Such a conclusion should, however, be tempered by consideration of three factors. The first is that censure motions on serious issues do not necessarily indicate ministerial guilt. Ian Sinclair, for example, was in 1980 cleared in court of all charges, yet had faced five censure motions prior to his case being heard. Second, in trying to embarrass or distract the government or an individual Minister, the Opposition sometimes resorts to increasing numbers of trivial censure motions. In the past few years, the Coalition Opposition has been guilty of this. This not only blunts the impact of the censure, but expands the base figure against which ministerial resignations are judged.

Finally, the ratio of parliamentary resignation calls to resignations is not the same for all categories of misdemeanour (see Table 5.3). Ministers never resign because of the failings of their departments, yet parliamentary calls for them to do so make up around 40 per cent of all resignation calls. The 'strike rate' is, however, respectable where a

TABLE 5.3 *Parliamentary Calls for Ministerial Resignations[a] and Outcomes in Different Categories of Alleged Misdemeanour, 1976–89*

	Departmental	Alleged misdemeanour Ministerial capacity	Non-ministerial capacity
Calls for resignation	11	12	3
Non-resignation	11	9	1
Resignation[b]	0	4	4

[a] Includes dismissals
[b] Includes resignations not raised in parliamentary motions
Source: Page 1990a: 145, 152

Minister's own actions are involved, especially where these actions do not relate directly to his or her portfolio.

This narrower concentration on actions within a minister's direct control now appears accepted in parliamentary culture. While Ministers do not lose their jobs over departmental actions, even if these actions result in censure motions, they are increasingly seen as responsible for their own actions. A Commonwealth parliamentary working group on ethics began work on a ministerial code of conduct in 1992, in the wake of the Richardson resignation, in order to clarify some of the ethical issues facing Ministers (*Sydney Morning Herald*, 16 June 1992).

Responsibility and Parliamentary Scrutiny of the Bureaucracy

The failure of Parliament to hold Ministers accountable *for their departments* is of greatest concern if Parliament is examined in isolation. When its role is considered in conjunction with other institutions, Parliament's apparent inability to enforce Ministers' responsibility for their departments is less alarming. From the 1970s a range of bodies and practices was established that supplement the traditional single line of accountability through Ministers and Parliament with 'multiple accountability mechanisms'. These allow greater direct public access to, scrutiny of, and redress from, public bureaucracies. At Commonwealth level, they include the Ombudsman, Freedom of Information legislation, and the Administrative Appeals Tribunal (see Whalan 1991: 91–92). Most states have similar mechanisms (see Painter 1986, Thompson and Painter 1986: 14–19, Painter 1987: 64–68). These mechanisms — with their specialist staff, full-time scrutiny and considerable resources — provide much greater possibilities for preventing and rectifying departmental improprieties and inefficiencies than part-time parliaments of generalist MPs. MPs usually play an indirect role in these multiple accountability mechanisms by directing constituents and cases to them and helping publicise their findings.

Nonetheless, sections of the Parliament have retained and developed a role in scrutinising and keeping responsible the bureaucratic arm of the executive. Of particular note here are committees like the Senate estimates committees (SECs), the standing committees, and their older cousin the Senate Standing Committee on Regulations and Ordinances (SSCRO).

Six Senate estimates committees (A-F) were established at the same time as the standing committees to examine projected government expenditure (estimates) in Appropriation Bills. No similar committees exist in the Representatives. Each of the SECs examines budgetary figures for departments and programs, questioning ministers and departmental officials and reporting to the Senate. The criteria and limits of this examination are still matters of controversy among Senators and senior public servants, but they centre on departmental efficiency, program delivery and performance, waste and propriety (Department of the Senate 1990b). Although the work of the SECs has had little effect on specific estimates, it has drawn attention to government inefficiencies, altered some bureaucratic practices within departments and achieved a public explanation of detailed government expenditure (Department of the Senate 1990b, 1991: 16–9).

A move in the 1980s to give the SECs responsibility for examining the annual reports of government departments was abandoned in recognition that this would place too much strain on the SECs. Instead, under a 1989 Senate resolution, the reports are examined by the relevant standing committee (Argument 1991). Thus although the SECs and standing committees do not operate as closely as some Senators would like (Department of the Senate 1990b), between them they now exercise considerable administrative oversight.

The SSCRO was established in 1932 to deal with delegated legislation — that is, detailed rules left unspecified in legislation passed in the Parliament and determined by Ministers and officials of departments or statutory bodies delegated to do so by the legislation (see Pearce 1977, Reid 1982, Whalan 1991: 88, Argument 1992: Chapters 2, 3). Where legislation passed by Parliament leaves room for extensive delegated powers, and where these powers are delegated deep within departments or statutory authorities, the potential for unscrutinised executive power to expand is marked.

While commentators have been concerned about delegated legislation since the 1920s (Argument 1992: Chapters 1–2), delegation has snowballed in recent years as the state has taken on greatly expanded functions (Pearce 1977: Chapter 1, Reid 1982: 149, Administrative Review Council 1992: 5). From 1932 to the 1970s, the annual number of delegated rules and instruments reported by the SSCRO grew slowly, to around 300. Since then this number has accelerated, reaching

1,645 in 1990–91, as Table 5.4 shows (also see O'Keefe 1988: 2, Whalan 1991: 94). The types of delegated legislation have also multiplied, from only 3 in the 1970s to over 100 in the late 1980s. These new types of delegation tend to be less formal than statutory rules, making public knowledge and control of them extremely difficult (Senate Standing Committee on Regulations and Ordinances 1990b, Whalan 1991: 94, Argument 1992: 20–23; Adminstrative Review Council 1992: 88–113).

Parliament has important powers to oversee delegated legislation. Under the Acts Interpretation Act 1901, instruments of delegated legislation have to pass through several hoops before they take effect. They must be published and tabled in both Houses of Parliament within 15 sitting days. If a motion to disallow the instrument is either passed by one house or moved but not resolved within a further 15 sitting days, the instrument is disallowed and cannot be remade within six months (see Reid 1982: 159–60, Whalan 1991: 95).

Commentators disagree about the success of the SSCRO. Some doubt its strength (O'Keefe 1988: 11–12, 35). Others (Whalan 1991: 107) see it as very powerful: 'The Committee has an awesome reputation as a "get-in-first" Committee.' Which view is correct?

As a starting point, neither the Parliament generally nor the SSCRO has prevented the proliferation of delegated legislation. Much of this legislation is not disallowable and thus falls outside parliamentary scrutiny (Argument 1992: 13). If, as Reid (1982) argues, the central function of Parliament is *making* legislation, then it is failing with regard to delegated legislation. Indeed, it is bound to fail.

This does not, however, exhaust the impact of Parliament on such legislation — at least where it is disallowable. Disallowance provides MPs with a strong weapon to *unmake* delegated legislation. Again, care needs to be taken in judging the effectiveness of this. Critics such as O'Keefe (1988: 34–35) argue that disallowance is too rarely used for it be an effective check on the executive. Between 1972 and 1985, for example, only 18 motions of disallowance were moved in the Senate and only 5 were passed. Such an argument ignores several important points. First, majorities in the Senate have on occasions disallowed, or threatened to disallow, regulations that are crucial to key

TABLE 5.4 *Number of Rules and Instruments Reported by the SSCRO,. 1982–83 to 1990–91*

	Year							
	82–83	83–84	84–85	85–86	86–87	87–88	88–90	90–91
Number	703	721	855	657	838	1177	1231	1654

Source: Administrative Review Council 1992: 7

pieces of government legislation. The most famous recent instance was the threatened disallowal of the regulations necessary in 1987 to implement the Hawke government's Australia Card legislation. Without these regulations, the government could not implement a planned national identification system which was to help it determine citizens' eligibility for government benefits and programs (Smith 1989: Chapter 7, Department of the Senate 1990a: 42).

Ministers sometimes attempt to force urgent but suspect instruments past the Senate (Burton 1992). Such confrontational tactics can, however, easily backfire in a house the Minister's party does not control. Moreover, the Democrats have made the government accept disallowable instruments which reduce executive power. The Keating government's plans to proceed with the transfer of veterans' hospitals to the states at ministerial level were brought unstuck by Democrat insistence that every new handover proposed before 1995 be made disallowable by the Senate (*CPD*, Senate, 4 June 1992: 3,572–76).

Second, while the SSCRO cannot itself disallow instruments, the Senate has adopted *every* SSCRO recommendation of disallowal since 1932. Thus the parliamentary body with the closest scrutiny of delegation legislation gets its way whenever it goes to the Senate (Miller 1986: 10, Whalan 1991: 96).

Why, then, are disallowals so rare? The third fact is that, as far as the SSCRO's activity is concerned, recommended disallowals represent the tip of the iceberg. The bulk of its activity lies in discussions with Ministers to get them to amend offending instruments, review or amend covering legislation, or take other action to meet the Committee's concerns. During 1988-89, a fairly typical recent year, 136 of the 1,352 instruments considered by the Committee seemed deficient. The Chair of the Committee wrote to the Ministers concerned and gave 28 notices of motion of disallowance in the Senate to protect against lack of ministerial response. Ministers and departments gave the Committee 25 undertakings to amend legislation and 58 undertakings to make other changes (Senate Standing Committee on Regulations and Ordinances 1990a: Chapter 1). The SSCRO monitors these undertakings and successfully follows up outstanding issues with Ministers (Whalan 1991: 100–11).

Rather than focusing on the few disallowals, then, an adequate examination of the power of the SSCRO must take into account the far larger number of changes agreed to by the executive outside the chambers. Changes have included the elimination of rules which would have:

- reduced a person's right to trial by jury;
- imposed criminal liability on people without proof of guilt;
- extended extreme provision for self-incrimination;
- allowed officials other than judicial officials to issue search warrants;

- enabled officials to enter premises without identification;
- discriminated against non-Christians;
- increased fees under a licence system from a few hundred to $80,000. (see Senate Standing Committee on Regulations and Ordinances 1990a: 4–7, Whalan 1991: 102–3)

The Committee's successful negotiation of improvements to rules of this sort clearly has a significant impact on government.

Finally, the SSCRO's standards have, following periods of conflict with Ministers and administrators, become widely adopted by the latter in drafting delegated legislation (Miller 1986: 9). As 1990 Chair of the Committee, Bob Collins, reported to the Senate (Senate Standing Committee on Regulations and Ordinances 1990a: 9):

> ...it is possible to detect a qualitative change for the better in aspects of concern to the Committee, particularly those affecting the rights and liberties of the individual. Largely as a result of the vigorous insistence of the Committee over the last few years matters of former controversy in delegated legislation are no longer so; safeguards initiated by the Committee in the face of resistance by some administrators are now included in delegated legislation as a matter of course.

The quality of delegated legislation drafting — cause for concern where it produces ambiguities, gaps and contradictions in rules (Argument 1992: 23–25) — has also improved in recent years, following attention from the SSCRO.

The power of the SSCRO is thus seen not just in direct conflicts with the executive on the floor of Parliament, but in changes to executive behaviour designed to pre-empt that conflict, and in changes to the executive culture. Once these facets of the Committee's power are taken into proper account, its impact on delegated legislation must be seen as substantial.

Why are committees like the SECs, standing committees and the SSCRO increasingly powerful? Some commentators suggest that the answer lies in the fact that they are Senate committees. A relaxed and bipartisan atmosphere more often prevails in the Senate than the Representatives (see Reid 1982: 158–59, O'Keefe 1988: 10–17). It is certainly true that the Representatives has not developed anything like the committee work of the Senate. The 1987 system of legislative committees in the Representatives does less work than equivalent committees in the Senate. Nonetheless, the experience of the Senate Scrutiny of Bills Committee, among others, suggests that location of a committee in the Senate does not in itself guarantee success (Weller 1982: 105–6, Miller 1986: 13, Department of the Senate 1991: 32, Whalan 1991: 91, Argument 1992: Chapters 5–6). Nor does a commitment of their members alone explain a committee's success (Whalan 1991: 96), since this begs the question of why ambitious Senators like Bob Collins and Bronwyn Bishop should be committed to such committees in the first place.

Part of the answer seems to be that these committees have convinced themselves and the political parties of the fiction that they deal solely with 'technical' issues, never straying onto questions of ideology or policy. With ideological and policy issues already decided on the floor of Parliament, the partisan friction that the work of these committees might generate is usually averted (O'Keefe 1988: 18, 19, Whalan 1991: 96–97, Argument 1992: 46–47). Committee members are openly disturbed by behaviour that suggests that the committees are being used for partisan advantage (Department of the Senate 1990b). The committees thus take pains to present themselves as the political bodies most acceptable to Australia's utilitarian political culture; as those who weigh facts and make technical judgments about how to satisfy the broadest possible set of interests in society, giving an ideologically-based preference to none.

The self-limiting technical scope of the committees means that they are unlikely to extend their attention into more obvious policy areas. The SSCRO, for example, resists the idea that it should review the merits of delegated legislation, or review the primary legislation providing for delegation, despite calls for it to do so (see Reid 1982: 166–67, O'Keefe 1988: 25–34, Whalan 1991: 92, 106, Administrative Review Council 1992: Chapter 6). Nonetheless, as long as the fiction of their being technical committees holds, they will continue to act as a check on the administrative arm of the executive.

An Aberration in the Senate?

The bulk of the chapter so far has concentrated on developments in the Senate, since it is in this parliamentary arena that most recent developments have taken place. They have taken place there not because the Senate was designed as a 'states' house' or a house of review, or because Senators see their roles differently from Members of the House of Representatives (MHRs), or because of an absence of party discipline. The Senate has almost never operated as a states' house; its review function has only developed when the governing parties have failed to win a majority of seats. Senators habitually pursue the same partisan politics as MHRs, and even Australian Democrat Senators have imposed party discipline in their ranks. What makes the Senate different is that, since the first use of proportional representation elections for Senators in 1949, the major parties have found it difficult to secure Senate majorities. In the Representatives they have not faced such difficulties.

If this argument, that different dispositions of parties have produced the contrasting politics of the Senate and the Representatives, is correct, lower house politics should become more open in cases where the governing party loses its majority status. As Figure 5.2 showed, governing parties have done so recently in several states, with Independent MPs picking up the balance of power. The experiences of lower houses in these states — particularly in Tasmania and New South Wales — appear to confirm the argument.

Between 1989 and 1992 a minority Labor government in Tasmania relied on the support of five Green Independents. This support was initially formalised in an 'Accord'. The Accord collapsed in October 1990, but Labor continued to govern until early 1992 (see Haward and Smith 1990, Smith 1991a, 1991b). After the 1991 New South Wales election, four (and at one point five) Independents have held the balance of power in the Legislative Assembly. One of these, Tony Windsor, supported the Coalition government; the others remain non-aligned (see Smith 1992a, 1992b, 1992c, Chaples 1992).

The impact of these Independents on lower house politics has been considerable (Maddox 1992, Chaples 1992: 29). In Tasmania, the Green Independents determined who would govern following the 1989 election, choosing to support Labor despite the fact that the Liberals held more seats. As relationships between the Green Independents and Labor declined, the former forced the resignation of Labor Education Minister, Peter Patmore, and selectively supported Labor's legislative program, eventually sending Premier Michael Field to the polls in frustration (Smith 1991a, 1991b, Maddox 1992: 21). In New South Wales, the government's legislative program and composition have also been affected by the Independents. Between 1 August 1991 and 1 July 1992, the Legislative Assembly was forced into divisions on 153 occasions. The Government lost 38 of these divisions. It was forced to negotiate with the Independents and make pre-emptive amendments to pass legislation through the lower house. It also opened its legislative research and drafting resources to the Independents and agreed to a program of parliamentary reform. Finally, the non-aligned Independents insisted on the resignation of Premier Nick Greiner and Environment Minister Tim Moore over their involvement in the attempted appointment of former Liberal Minister, Terry Metherell, to a Senior Executive Service job (see Smith 1992a, 1992c).

These examples suggest that the 'rubber stamp' politics of lower houses — like those of upper houses — become more fluid when the disposition of parties moves away from a one-party majority. The developments in Commonwealth parliamentary politics described in this chapter, then, are not *inevitably* limited to the Senate. They would begin to emerge in the Representatives if the election of minor party or Independent MPs prevented any party from achieving a majority, just as they did in the New South Wales and Tasmanian lower houses.

Party disposition is the crucial element determining the politics of both houses.

Conclusion

Those who want to reform the Australian parliaments have traditionally hoped for signs of a breakdown of party discipline *within* the major parliamentary parties. The stimulus for the greater power of Parliament in the last two decades has not, however, come from this source. It has, instead, come from a decline in electoral support for the major parties and an increase in voter support for minor party and Independent candidates. In parliaments where they are no longer assured of a majority in both houses, such as the Commonwealth Parliament, the disciplined major parties have been forced to develop new modes of parliamentary politics. The Independents and small parties, for their part, have been able to use their crucial positions to expand Parliament's role in legislation and executive scrutiny. At national level, these new parliamentary politics have tended to emerge in the Senate, where the governing parties have found it harder to maintain majorities. In the Representatives, party discipline and executive dominance have been less affected, except in the area of individual ministerial responsibility. In the Senate, the executive has encountered a series of strategies which have significantly checked its power and increased public scrutiny. These open-ended Senate politics have taken some twenty years to reach their current form and look set to continue.

New parliamentary politics will also be experienced in lower houses where governing parties fail to achieve majorities, especially if they do so for sustained periods. The parliamentary politics that recently built up around the minority governments of states like New South Wales and Tasmania may well be harbingers of such a development.

6
Political Parties

CAMPBELL SHARMAN

The Importance of Parties

In Australia, as in other liberal democracies, commentators have been almost lyrical in describing the beneficial role that political parties play in providing coherence to the operation of parliaments and elections. Parties aggregate support for the orderly conduct of legislative politics and provide an avenue for the expression of popular opinion (Maddox 1991: 257–65). They are the major agencies for giving effect to popular participatory democracy, and central to the operation of Australian politics (Jaensch 1989b: 1–4). This rosy view of parties is, however, beginning to look decidedly questionable. While parties still play a dominating role in the operation of electoral and parliamentary politics in Australia, neither the nature of their role nor its justification fits the verities of the standard texts.

Many of the virtues seen as attached to the operation of parties have stemmed from collectivist assumptions about the operation of the political process. Power should be concentrated in the hands of the government of the day so it can carry out policies that reflect the wishes of the majority, and so that the government can be held accountable at election time. From this perspective, party is the critical agency in providing stable legislative majorities, in maintaining electoral support for the government, and in producing a rival set of personnel and policies that can act both as Opposition and alternative government. When coupled with a parliamentary system, such views provide a justification for strong party discipline within the legislature, for the subordination of the parliamentary process to the wishes of the executive branch, and for a strongly dichotomous view of the political process.

This perception of the role of party fits squarely within what Lijphart (1989) has called the majoritarian strand of the liberal democratic tradition. This stresses the concentration of governmental power for coherent action in the name of the majority. By contrast, the other strand, sometimes described as consensus democracy (because decisions require consensus across a number of institutions) emphasises the dispersal of power between political institutions. This means that the power of government is checked and governmental action results only after negotiation and compromise between a range of autonomous institutions (Lijphart 1984: 1–36). Consensus democracy sees parties not as agents for the concentration of power, but as mechanisms reflecting social, economic and ideological diversity in representative institutions.

Australian writers have generally favoured the majoritarian view of parties as part of a package that lauded their role in producing effective governmental action (Maddox 1991: 251–54). This view is facing increasing competition both from those who question the desirability of majoritarian democracy, and from a range of evidence showing that existing parties are failing to discharge many of the roles that have traditionally been assigned to them.

The electoral success in recent years of minor party and Independent candidates indicates that there is a substantial section of the community dissatisfied with the existing range of partisan choice, and which can be persuaded to support candidates whose view of their representative role fits the consensus democracy model rather than the majoritarian mould. This is consistent with the growth of public debate over the virtues of parliamentary checks on executive power, bicameralism, federalism and judicial review, all of which work against the majoritarian tradition (Sharman 1990a). Indeed, the concern with the operation of the parliamentary executive demonstrated in the reports of recent state Royal Commissions implies that there are inherent problems of accountability in a party-dominated legislature (Queensland 1989: 123, Western Australia 1992: 5.2).

While traditional views have stressed the centrality of party in shaping debate over public policy, it has also been argued that parties do not produce coherent programs that can be implemented in government, and that, even if electorally successful, parties have only limited success in shaping government policy (e.g. Castles 1982). Not only must party organisations compete with well-placed interest groups and non-governmental organisations to influence policy (Olson 1982: Chapter 3), but the bureaucracy itself is notoriously effective in resisting changes of policy that do not suit its purposes (Peters 1989). Taken together, these arguments represent a powerful attack on the importance of party in the political system, and provide a rival perspective from which parties can be assessed.

The role of party in the electoral process is also being questioned. The image of mass parties as institutions providing the opportunity for popular participation in politics is being undermined by developments occurring within Australia's two largest parties. Both the Labor and Liberal parties have experienced a steady decline in membership, and a corresponding increase in the influence of party élites in these parties. As Ward (1991) points out, the parties are losing their traditional base and becoming 'electoral professional' parties. Many of the traditional functions of party members are being contracted out to polling organisations, management and advertising agencies, and to direct mailing companies. Parties are thus becoming little more than executive-dominated agencies for mobilising electoral opinion and for the recruitment of those who wish to make a career in politics.

The result of all these developments is that the study of parties in Australia must be seen as involving much more than the familiar questions of party structure, ideology and performance. Questions of role and justification are also at stake.

The Australian Party System

How one understands the party system is a key element in understanding both the behaviour of individual parties and the operation of the governmental process. This is not simply because the number and pattern of interaction of the various parties is critically important in describing the character of partisan competition in a political system, but because the analysis of the party system reflects assumptions about the role parties ought to perform.

Party systems can be broadly categorised as being of two kinds: those with two parties and those with more than two. This seemingly innocent, almost trivial distinction has fundamental implications for the style of politics. A two-party system implies a zero sum game where the losses of one party will always be the gains of the other, so that electoral choice is primarily about the selection of government, and parliamentary politics is dominated by the concerns of the executive. This emphasis on dichotomous choices is compatible with class analyses of the party system, assumes a single axis for partisan competition along which the two parties can converge or diverge, and is congruent with majoritarian assumptions about the desirability of concentrating governmental power for effective action.

Where there are more than two parties, voting is not synonymous with the choice of government, and the possibility of coalition and minority governments means that the importance of parliamentary politics is enhanced and the executive weakened. Politics becomes more the expression of diversity than a striving after majorities, a characteristic which is compatible with multiple axes of partisan differences, the dispersal of power in the governmental system, and a consensus style of democracy.

Given these clear differences, it might be expected that the categorisation of a party system as a having two parties or more than two was a simple matter: just count the number of parties. In fact, however, it is a highly contentious issue. There are disagreements over what parties should be counted as relevant, a discussion that is, in turn, often coloured by the preferences of commentators for majoritarian or consensus styles of democracy. Those who favour majoritarian politics tend to find two parties, while those who prefer consensus politics find more than two!

The existence of two parties in Australia which between them account for at least three-quarters of the vote at national elections, the Australian Labor Party and the Liberal Party, coupled with the natural dichotomy between government and Opposition in parliamentary systems, together with majoritarian assumptions about the nature of politics, have led many to view Australia as essentially a two-party system (for example, Crisp 1983, Epstein 1980, Maddox 1991). This has been reinforced by the position of the ALP as the largest single party in most electoral forums for most of the period since 1910, the use of class-derived views of politics, and the development of the notion of the 'two party preferred vote' as a way of treating the votes of those who support minor parties as if they were votes for the biggest two parties.

This last procedure, now widely used in official publications, is a way of presenting electoral contests as though they were no more than a contest between two parties, votes for all other candidates being assigned to one or other of the largest two parties. The use of such a method of assigning voting preferences to create a neat dichotomy has been a topic of controversy (Mayer 1980: 352–53, Jaensch 1989b: 68–72, Sharman 1991: 345–46), on the grounds that it manufactures the illusion of a two-party system, notwithstanding a vote for minor parties and Independents that may exceed 30 per cent. This is a powerful example of the political assumptions of commentators shaping the evidence to suit a preferred outcome.

The problem for those who favour a two party system is that, for the period since 1920, the non-ALP vote has been divided between two parties, the Liberals and the National Party (previously the Country Party), which have needed to form coalitions to gain office nationally, and in some states. For shorter periods, there have also been other parties with a significant share of the vote and representation in one or more parliaments. To illustrate this, Australia has at present four party groupings that qualify under Sartori's (1976) tests of relevance: the ability to form government; to be part of a governing coalition; to have parliamentary representation; or to have a significant affect on the election of candidates from relevant parties. These include the Nationals, the Australian Democrats, Green parties and Independents. These minor parties play a critical role in the pattern of party competition and give the Australian system a significant multi-party component.

There is no neat way out of the apparent contradiction in Australia between the elements of a two-party system and aspects of multipartism. The common description of the system as a two-and-a-half party system is only a partial indication of the mixed nature of partisan competition. Since 1945, most lower house contests in Australia can be accurately described as contests between Labor and non-Labor, government and Opposition. But this general picture masks the fierceness of coalition politics on the non-Labor side, the complexities of preference trading between small and large parties under preferential voting, and the recent spate of minority governments in several states. Nor does it accommodate the multiple axes of partisanship, in which region and religion have supplemented divisions based on economic interest; nor can it easily cope with two additional features of partisan competition in Australia, federalism and bicameralism.

Each of the six states and two territories has its own party system which is not simply a microcosm of the national system (Bennett 1992, Jaensch 1989b: Chapter 6, Sharman 1990b). These party systems vary from a two-party system in South Australia to a three-party system in Queensland, and include systems such as those of Tasmania, the Australian Capital Territory and the Northern Territory, each of which has distinctive features (Bennett 1989, 1992, Jaensch and Loveday 1987, Sharman *et al.* 1991). The federal system itself provides multiple forums for party organisation and competition, and for indicating regional differences in patterns of partisan attachment (Bean and Mughan 1988, Holmes and Sharman 1977: Chapter 4, Jaensch 1989b: Chapter 6)

Similar avenues for diversity can be found in bicameralism (Sharman 1987). Powerful upper houses are a characteristic of all Australian parliaments except those of Queensland, the Australian Capital Territory, and the Northern Territory (Bennett 1992: Chapter 6, Reid 1983). The pattern of partisan competition for upper houses varies significantly from party contests in lower houses, a reflection of different institutional structures, differing electoral laws, and differing patterns of voting between upper and lower chambers. Contests for the Senate, for example, where at least five party groupings have some chance of election, differ significantly from those for the House of Representatives, where three parties dominate.

All this indicates that the analysis of the party system in Australia is contentious both because of the complexities of the details of partisan competition, and because of disagreements over the criteria used to evaluate the system. While the position of the ALP and the nature of a parliamentary executive have provided a powerful drive towards the dynamics of a two-party system, with its majoritarian overtones, the presence of important minor parties and the multiple forums for partisan competition provided by federalism and bicameralism have created a system with several features of a multi-party system. The multi-party aspect has been reinforced by the recent upsurge in support for minor party and Independent candidates, and by changes in the composition and operation of the large parties themselves.

The Australian Labor Party

Until the onset of major economic problems at the end of the decade, the period beginning in the early 1980s was a singularly successful one for the Australian Labor Party. Between 1981 and 1990 it won 17 of the 22 state and federal elections held. It was in office for most of the period in four of the six states, including the two most populous (New South Wales and Victoria). It ended long periods of non-Labor government in Victoria in 1982 (27 years) and Queensland in 1989 (32 years). Only in the smallest political communities — Tasmania, the Northern Territory and the Australian Capital Territory — did it fail to win parliamentary majorities. Its crowning success was winning government in Canberra. Elected in 1983, Labor was returned in 1984, 1987, 1990 and 1993, giving it an unparallelled five terms in office, the longest period of national government in the party's history.

This electoral success can be traced to a variety of factors, not least the disunity and leadership problems of the Liberals. But changes to the ALP itself were also important. Following the bitterness left by events leading to the defeat of the Whitlam government in 1975, the party acquired a new ruthlessness and singlemindedness in the pursuit of office. This was reflected in its eagerness to select leaders who were electorally popular, and in its more pragmatic approach to party policy. The leadership of the ALP had learnt from the economic failures of the Whitlam government that the party must adopt economic policies of wide appeal and must be accepted as broadly responsible by the business community. Only then would it be able to distance itself from its image as a party with little competence in managing the economy. These changes were achieved against considerable internal resistance, and have led to continuing strains. For many, such policies amount to a major reorientation of the party and reinforce the view that there is little rank and file influence over the parliamentary leadership.

A number of other elements can be seen as contributing to the string of ALP electoral successes in the 1980s. The ALP benefited from the party's effective use of increasingly professionalised polling and campaigning strategies (Mills 1986), the exploitation of the natural advantages that accrue to government in the use of the news media (Tiffen 1989, Parker 1990), and changes in electoral laws. Early in its term, the Hawke government moved to implement changes to the electoral system which, while streamlining the administration of electoral law, favoured the established system, in particular the ALP (Rydon 1987, Commonwealth Parliament 1983). Some of these changes were technical, such as those designed to reduce what is arguably a disproportionate loss of ALP support through informal votes (Smith and Hopper 1979); others were broad-ranging, including those to establish public funding of parties and the disclosure of campaign donations (Chaples 1989), and to maximise ALP influence in the Senate (Sharman 1986). But the most important changes were those in the late 1970s to the party's organisation and composition.

Organisational Change and the Rise of Factions
In line with the party's ethos as a mass party of the Left that grew out

of the labour movement around the turn of the century, the ALP has a tradition of stressing rank and file participation in party affairs and the importance of intra-party democracy. A large and active party membership was not just a useful resource for running election campaigns, but provided legitimacy to party policy and the choice of party officials and representatives. This was reflected in the power of the extra-parliamentary organisation over the party's parliamentary representatives. Since the late 1960s the structure of the ALP has been substantially changed.

Such changes have had three broad thrusts. The first has been the increased involvement of the leadership of the parliamentary party in the running of the extra-parliamentary organisations. The parliamentary party or Caucus has always been a powerful element in party affairs, and it alone has the power to choose the party leader. Only in 1967, however, did the parliamentary leadership gain formal representation at the party's National Conference and on its National Executive. This change signalled a greater influence of the pragmatic concerns of the parliamentary wing and the leadership of the party on its direction and policy. These factors, coupled with the massive change that television has introduced over the last twenty years, in personifying the party in its leader (Lloyd 1992), have extended the ability of leaders to shape the direction of party policy.

A second set of changes has greatly increased the size and influence of the national branch of the party. The National Executive and Federal Secretariat have increased their control over the conduct of national campaigns, campaign funding, and the choice of candidates for the national Parliament. This has partly been a consequence of the growth and professionalisation of the ALP's national office, and of structural changes which have altered the federal nature of the party's organisation and reduced, but far from eliminated, the dependence of the national wing of the party on the state branches (Jaensch 1989a: Chapter 6, Lloyd 1983, Rydon 1988, Warhurst 1983).

The most public change to the operation of the ALP during the 1980s, however, was the increasing visibility and formality of its factional groupings (Emy and Hughes 1991: 134–43). Labor has long been host to factional divisions based partly on ideological differences and partly on the struggle to control the party machine (Jaensch 1989a: 137–44, Parkin and Warhurst 1983). In order to reduce the divisive effects of factional hostilities, the party adopted in 1981 the principle of proportional representation for the selection of delegates to the National Conference, a policy that has since been extended to the internal operation of state branches. This policy has entrenched factions as formally organised groups within the party, extending their influence to forums of the party where they had previously been absent, and creating a national system that has reduced the influence of state-based party machines (Lloyd and Swan 1987a, 1987b). The existence of tightly-organised factions has meant that key decisions within the party can be made by a few faction leaders. This simplifies the processes of conflict resolution, but at the expense of other groups within the party.

This stress on pragmatism and managerial effectiveness has not only been a key component of the ALP's electoral success (Gruen and Grattan 1993: Chapter 1), but has coloured its approach to an area that has often caused embarrassment to Labor in the past, its relations with the union movement.

Relations with the Unions
The trade union movement has been an integral part of the ALP since the party's emergence in the 1890s. For those unions affiliated with the party this entails the provision of funds and political support and the formal participation of union representatives in the key decision making forums of the party; unions are affiliated at state level and have around 60 per cent of the representation on state conferences and executive bodies. The incorporation of large sections of the union movement creates a number of tensions within the party, particularly because it attenuates the influence of branch members (Jaensch 1989a: 69–77, Rawson 1966: Chapter 4, 1986).

The relationship between the ALP and the union movement has been influenced both by changes within the party and by changes in the unions, including the decline in the proportion of the workforce with a union affiliation (Peetz 1990). The union movement itself covers a diverse range of organisations with widely varying perspectives on economic, social and political issues. Most unions are members of the Trades and Labor Councils in their states and of the Australian Council of Trade Unions. These bodies offer an alternative means of affecting government policy to that provided by membership of the ALP. The machinery of industrial arbitration represents yet another avenue for the pursuit of union goals, quite apart from those of strike action and direct negotiation with employers.

Differences of perspective, interest and goals have meant that the relationship between unions and the ALP, particularly when in government, has not always been harmonious. There were serious differences between the unions and the Whitlam government, for example, over the direction of economic policy, particularly over the Whitlam government's unilateral decision to cut tariffs by 25 per cent. These difficulties, together with the new stress on economic management, led the ALP and the ACTU to an Accord in 1983.This established a policy of wage restraint on the part of the unions in return for ACTU participation in a broad range of policies affecting employment, plus tax concessions, protection of a 'social wage' (superannuation benefits, Medicare, education and training), and special concern for workers who were poorly paid (see Singleton 1990).

The Accord was hailed by Labor and the ACTU as a major achievement of the Hawke government. In its various renegotiated forms, it has provided a mechanism for maintaining generally harmonious relations between the government and the peak body of the union movement, even though the government has pursued economic policies which have checked the growth of wages, reduced tariffs, changed the pattern of industrial arbitration and employment, and reduced the number of unions. But this accommodation between the ALP and the ACTU in the name of economic responsibility and national productivity has exacerbated tensions both within the unions and between the unions and the ALP. Critics within the union movement have argued that the Accord has forced wage earners to make a disproportionate sacrifice in the process of restructuring the economy and has worked more in the interests of employers than those of the labour movement (see Ewer *et al.* 1991, but compare Singleton 1990). This is part of a broader debate over the direction of ALP policy and the changing nature of the party itself.

The Direction and Composition of the Party
The changes to the ALP's organisation and its re-orientation towards the issues of economic growth, efficiency, and national competitiveness brought electoral success in the 1980s. But this was accompanied by developments that led many commentators, both inside and outside the party, to believe that the ALP had lost much of its tradition as a party of the Left.

For some, the Hawke and Keating governments have presided over a radical change to the whole ethos of the ALP. The concern with electorally popular middle class issues, such as the environment, the responsiveness to business interests, and the attenuation of rank and file control over the party, all amounted to a major shift in the nature of the party. This position is forcefully argued by Jaensch (1989a), who presents a case for the transformation of the ALP from a mass party of the Left, stressing wide popular participation, to a catch- all party dominated by a small élite obsessed with electoral success. Evidence for Jaensch's interpretation is provided by other studies. Shifts in the ideological components of the platforms of the ALP and the Liberal Party have been charted to reveal the convergence of ideological positions in the 1980s (McAllister 1992a: 120–25); and the Labor government's increasing links with business have been documented in some detail (McEachern 1991, Galligan and Singleton 1991). Others (Maddox (1989, Maddox and Battin 1991) stress the Hawke government's betrayal of traditional Labor values and its abandonment of key elements of social democracy (Macintyre 1986a). Some commentators, however, have argued that rather than the Hawke and Keating governments representing a major shift in the party's relationship with its past traditions, they have behaved like any Labor governments in national office: they have tried to make the economic system work effectively and fairly, to bend it to the interests of wage earners, and to humanise the face of capitalism while staying in office. From this perspective, the union movement and the Accord have played a key role in preserving Labor's responsiveness to 'labourist' and social democratic traditions (Manning 1992, Singleton 1990).

Two important studies have analysed the substantial alterations that have taken place in the composition of the party. The first, a careful study by Ward (1989), argues that Labor draws new members disproportionately from people with 'middle class' backgrounds whose interests, political motivation, and loyalties differ significantly from previous traditions of working class solidarity. These new members are more likely to be frustrated with the existing ritual of the branch meetings, with party structures and the role of factions, and with the failure of Labor governments to implement party policy. They are also much more likely to leave the party if their particular political goals are not met. This volatility in party membership, together with an overall decline in numbers, is consistent with the increasing influence of party élites, and with the move of the ALP away from the mass party model towards that of the electoral professional party.

A similar analysis can be found in Scott (1991). He confirms that the membership of the party now reflects the interests of middle class professionals and para-professionals rather than the economically disadvantaged. Unlike Ward, however, Scott argues strongly that the ALP should focus its attention on rebuilding its mass membership, especially among the poor and those alienated from the political system, particularly women and people with non-English-speaking backgrounds.

One of Scott's prescriptions for the renewal of the Party's mass base is the reintroduction of direct membership ballots for a wide range of party offices (Scott 1991: 68). This touches on a wider debate within the ALP over organisational reform. While some, dismayed at the decline in party membership, investigate ways to stabilise or increase it (ALP 1990), others want a future concentration of power at the centre so that the party can respond quickly to the political needs of the parliamentary wing (Burchell and Mathews 1991), thus accentuating the trends that Scott (1991) so trenchantly criticises.

The Liberal Party

The Liberal Party was as unsuccessful in winning government over the last decade as the ALP was successful. By the second half of 1983, the Liberals had lost office nationally and in all five mainland states: only in Tasmania had it seen a realignment of the party system in its favour (see Sharman *et al.* 1991). When the Liberals won office (in coalition with the National Party) in New South Wales in 1988, they did so with only a marginal increase in their electoral support: in 1984 the Liberal vote was 34.2 per cent; in 1988, 35.8 per cent. Even where ALP governments had presided over major financial disasters, as in Victoria and Western Australia, the incoming state coalition governments benefited from only small increases in the Liberal vote (a swing to the Liberals of 3.5 per cent in Victoria in 1992, and 2 per cent in Western Australia in 1993). The growing economic difficulties confronting state and national ALP governments were not being translated into large numbers of votes for the Liberals. Indeed, at the national level, the Liberal vote was virtually unchanged in the four elections from 1983 to 1990: 34.4 per cent of the first preference vote in 1983, 34.4 per cent in 1984, 34.3 per cent in 1987, and 34.8 per cent in 1990 (Macintyre 1991: 11–13). Only in 1993 did the Liberal vote increase, and then only by 2 per cent.

This long period of electoral failure, particularly in national politics, was unprecedented in the party's history. Indeed, since the fusion of the two major non-Labor parties in 1910, the hallmark of non-Labor party politics had been the ability to regroup after defeat at the polls and to recapture national office within, at most, two elections. From 1910 the major non-Labor party was the Liberal Party, until it was reconstituted as the Nationalists in 1917. Another regrouping in 1931 saw it emerge as the United Australia Party. After the disintegration of the UAP in the early 1940s, there was a regrouping in 1944 as the Liberal Party (Tiver 1978, Starr 1978, 1980).

The defeat of the Fraser government in 1983 can be put down to a variety of factors, the most important of which was the steep downturn in economic activity of the early 1980s. After three terms, the Coalition government led by the Liberals was showing signs of lethargy and loss of direction, particularly in comparison with an energetic ALP led by a new and popular leader (Haupt 1983, Kelly 1984, McGregor 1983, Summers 1983). The defeats of 1984, 1987, 1990 and particularly 1993 raise broader questions about problems the Liberals have had in capitalising on the loss of support for ALP governments. Two issues of special relevance to these questions are the debate over ideological issues within the party, and disputes over its leadership and organisation.

The Debate over Ideology

Until the mid-1970s, the Liberals were a highly pragmatic party, and their policies had little ideological content (Turner 1973). Even those who thought that ideology had a role in the operation of the party were circumspect in assessing its nature and importance (Emy 1974: 414–33, Jaensch 1989b, Jupp 1982, Tiver 1978). Although Menzies had stressed at the formation of the Liberal Party in the 1940s that the party was committed to individual freedom and enterprise, the machinery of an interventionist social welfare state was taken for granted. While liberal individualist values represented a major strand in the ethos of the

Liberals (Brett 1992a, Tiver 1978), the promotion of such values was also a rhetorical device to exaggerate the differences between the Liberals and ALP, and to paint Labor as a party committed to socialism and sympathetic to Communism.

The long period in national office from 1949 to 1972 accentuated this pragmatic approach to policy within the Liberal Party. While ideological and factional disputes racked the ALP, the Liberals ran the government. Defeat by Labor in 1972 at first prompted the Liberals to adopt similarly interventionist and nationally-oriented polices, but the growing unpopularity of the Whitlam government and a renewed debate about the role of the state combined to revive an interest in ideological issues.

The decline in post-war optimism about the ability of governments to solve social and economic problems through central planning and regulation corresponded with a rediscovery throughout the Western world of the virtues of the market as a mechanism for expressing collective choices. These ideas were coupled with a view of the state as too often benefiting small sections of the community at the expense of the majority: far from creating equality, government intervention was seen as often exacerbating inequality. The remedy was the reduction of government intervention both as a supplier of goods and services and as a regulator, and the encouragement of policies that made the whole structure of government more open and responsive to citizens as voters and consumers.

These views gained increasing currency in the 1980s (see, generally, Emy and Hughes 1991). Malcolm Fraser had gained the leadership of the Liberals in 1975 in part because he used the language of this new intellectual movement, but his performance in government had more in common with his interventionist predecessors than with the thrust towards deregulation and smaller government (Weller 1989: 403–4). It was left to a group within the party's national parliamentary wing, led by John Hyde, to press for a coherent set of policies based on liberal individualist and market-driven assumptions (Hyde 1982, Kelly 1992: Chapters 5, 13; Kasper *et al.* 1980).

This group, generally described as the Dries, drew much of their intellectual drive from a number of think tanks (Sawer 1982a: 7–9, Stone 1991). Their views not only caused consternation among those on the Left of the political spectrum (Sawer 1982b), but led to tension within the Liberals (O'Brien 1985). There had always been a range of opinion within the party on particular social and economic issues (Tiver 1978), but the existence of a group that challenged the orthodoxy of high tariffs, marketing boards, and the extensive regulation of business and commercial life was a new and unsettling experience. Not only did it call into question the soundness of past Liberal policies, but the adoption of the new ideology disrupted the settled relationships between the party and many powerful interests that had prospered under the previous government, including some of Australia's largest business enterprises (Kelly 1992: Chapter 13). Manufacturing industry in particular, had long assumed that tariff protection for its products (Capling and Galligan 1992: Chapter 3, Tsokhas 1984: Chapter 1), and a centrally directed arbitration system to set wages were immutable aspects of the political landscape. Yet the Dries were willing to attack both as being economically inefficient and socially inequitable.

It would be misleading to see the argument over ideology as the only cause of disunity within the Liberal Party and hence the sole cause of its electoral unpopularity in the 1980s, but the dispute over the philosophical direction of the party highlighted other difficulties among the Liberals. It provided a new cleavage around which factions could be organised. While factions in the Liberal Party do not have the organisational characteristics of those in the Labor Party — they are much looser groupings held together by a mixture of patronage, a common allegiance to set of policies, and the leadership ambitions of particular individuals — the new ideological concerns within the Liberals created division within the party and complicated traditional rivalries.

This was particularly the case with the struggle over the leadership in the 1980s between Peacock (leader from 1983 to 85 and 1989 to 90) and Howard (1985 to 1989). While Howard was more closely identified with the Dries, both leaders had to come to terms with the pressures for new deregulationary and libertarian policies (Kelly 1992: Chapters 2, 10, 12). The choice of Dr Hewson as national leader of the party in 1990 signalled that these ideas had become Liberal Party orthodoxy (Emy and Hughes 1991: Chapter 5).

A commitment to a set of economic policies with intellectual coherence was new to the Liberal Party. Such developments were foreshadowed in Howard's *Future Directions* 1988 policy statement (Kelly 1992: 428–32), and reached their culmination in Hewson's *Fightback!* package in 1992. This amounted to a blueprint for comprehensive change, including a major change to the balance between income and consumption taxes. Whatever their intrinsic merits, these policies cast the Liberals in the unfamiliar role of arguing for more substantial change than the ALP. This change of role exacerbated the organisational difficulties the Party has had in winning office.

Organisation and Leadership
From its formation in 1944, the Liberal Party acquired all the characteristics of a modern mass party with stress on the importance of a large party membership, procedures for intra-party democracy, and consultation at all levels (Starr 1978). This major institutional change was required to accommodate the disparate groups that came together to form the Liberal Party, to counter the influence of the powerful business interests that Menzies felt had been able to manipulate the United Australia Party in the 1930s and early 1940s, and to channel the groundswell of popular support for the new party into electoral advantage (Starr 1978, 1980: Chapter 2).

One of the Liberals' perennial criticisms of the ALP has been the dominance of its extra-parliamentary organisation over its parliamentary representatives. The Liberal Party avoided this situation through a number of organisational features: it did not explicitly bind candidates to the details of its party platform; it gave the responsibility for the framing and articulation of details of policy to the party leader and the parliamentary party; and it preserved the autonomy of each state division of the party (Starr 1978).

All these characteristics worked to give the party great flexibility and resilience in the electoral contests of the 1950s and 60s, but the experience of defeat at the national level since the 1970s has led to strains within the party and pressures for organisational reform. Coupled with the increasing professionalisation of electoral contests, with their reliance on polling and the management of publicity and the news media, there have been calls for the Liberals to emulate Labor and establish greater control in the hands of the party executives at state and national levels (Liberal Party 1983). This was particularly an issue in Victoria after the party's 1987 defeat. The president of the Victorian Liberals, Michael Kroger, campaigned vigorously to get the 'best people' into Parliament by giving the State Executive greater control over the choice of parliamentary candidates. Several bitter preselection contests followed (Warhurst 1990: 10–11). In part, these developments represented a resurgence of pressure for central party control by a cadre of business interests, personified in the late 1980s by the federal president of the party, John Elliot. It was against precisely such interests that Menzies had struggled to establish the Liberals as a mass party in 1944; notwithstanding the pressures for change, modification of the basic structural characteristics of the party was stoutly resisted.

Debates over the reform of the Liberals have highlighted other changes. As with all the established parties in Australia, their party membership has been declining, and there are some indications as well of changes to the nature of their membership. Whereas traditionally Liberal members had links to community groups, service organisations and women's groups, many new members do not have such links. They see the party more as an opportunity for personal advancement than as a part of a settled social network. Women, in particular, are not content to stay within special women's sections of the Party, but want equal access to the main organisation and its offices (Sawer and Simms 1984: 143–52). These changes in the social profile and expectations of the membership may go some way to explaining the divisions that have erupted within the party over preselection. As the choice of candidates is predominantly a matter for the local branch, such contests are not only a struggle for office, but may provide local forums for wider disputes between factions over the control, direction and reform of the party. While factional disputes in the ALP have had a centralising effect on the party, similar disputes in the Liberals have highlighted, and may have reinforced, its decentralised nature.

Although the Liberals' parliamentary leaders have usually been able to distance themselves from disputes within the machine, other problems attend them. The party has had little tolerance for failure: electoral defeat, or the prospect of defeat, has often prompted the parliamentary party to choose a new leader. This willingness to change the leader has been reinforced by the lender's special responsibilities in articulating party policy. In many respects, the leader has been the personification of a particular set of policies, and a change in the direction of policy has implied a change of leader. The fate of *Fightback!*, for example, was very much more closely tied to Hewson as leader than similar policy documents would be to the leader of the ALP — if for no other reason than that there is no mechanism in the Liberal Party for the rank and file to participate formally in the framing of such policy documents. These factors help to explain the rapid turnover of Liberal leaders at state and national levels. There have been four changes of national leader since 1983 — a characteristic that, at best, has had mixed benefits for the party.

In addition to coping with its own problems, the Liberals have the difficulty of relying on the support of the Nationals if they are to gain office in Canberra and in several states. Relations between the Coalition partners are sometimes difficult, especially when the two parties compete for support. On occasions, this has flared into open hostility, as with Premier Bjelke-Petersen's abortive attempt to extend his brand of populist National Party politics from Queensland to Canberra (Costar and Woodward 1985, Kelly 1992: Chapter 15), an attempt which had disastrous effects for the Liberal Party in the 1987 election. Even when parliamentary leaderships agree, rivalries between party machines, particularly over the running of candidates in seats held by the other party, have been a source of friction. Coalition politics both in the electorate and in Parliament has, at the very least, complicated the task of the Liberals in presenting themselves as an alternative government.

Smaller Parties and Independents

The place of parties other than the ALP and the Liberals is both contentious and complicated. The significance and legitimacy of smaller parties and Independents in the political system are matters of dispute (Mayer 1980). The variation in their representation by region and parliamentary forum also makes generalisations about their role difficult.

Writers from the majoritarian perspective have argued that representative democracy operates best when two large parties dominate the system (cf. Maddox 1991: Chapter 9), and that the existence of minor parties impedes the requirement of a clear choice at election time. This view is reinforced by the chauvinism of the large parties, who see small parties at best as an irrelevant nuisance and at worst as a threat to gaining office (Mayer 1980). From the perspective of consensus democracy, however, small parties play a vital role in the political system by increasing the range of choice for electors, by bringing new issues and views of politics into the realm of public debate, and by forcing changes to the operation of parliamentary institutions to make them more responsive to the range of opinion in the community (Lijphart 1989).

Minor parties have been the vehicle for change and flexibility in the Australian party system. This has been as true for the ALP, originally a small party, as it has been for the National Party. It has also been true of parties that have broken away from the ALP, the longest lasting of which, the Democratic Labor Party, had a traumatic impact on Labor politics for twenty years after the 1955 split (see Reynolds 1974) and profoundly changed the operation and significance of the Senate (see Sharman 1986). It is still true of the 1990s, when new issues and new attitudes to politics are challenging the established parties.

The National Party

The National Party is by far the oldest of the smaller parties. Formed about 1920, it began as the Country Party, a response to the particular grievances of farmers and residents of country towns. These communities had little sympathy with the union base of the ALP, distrusted the urban focus of the Nationalists (the major non-Labor party of the time), and had a belief (with strong populist overtones) in the virtues of country life (Graham 1966). These elements have been persistent enough to maintain the party for more than 70 years, gain it around 10 per cent of the conservative vote in national politics since 1945, and more than its share of academic attention (see, generally, Ellis 1963, Graham 1966, Aitkin 1972, Barbalet 1975, Richmond 1978, Costar and Woodward 1985). The Party changed its name to the National-Country Party in 1975, and to the National Party in 1982.

The party's parliamentary representation benefited for many years from malapportioned electorates, but its main strength derives from its geographically concentrated support. With this, the Nationals have been a key component of non-ALP governments in Canberra. The party has been the major conservative party in Queensland for much of the period since the 1950s, and has been an integral part of Coalition governments with the Liberals in New South Wales and Western Australia. While it is a significant player in Victorian politics, it has had little influence in South Australia or the Northern Territory (Jaensch 1985, Jaensch and Loveday 1987), and practically none in Tasmania.

The party's strategy has been to hold enough seats in the lower house of state and Commonwealth parliaments to deny the Liberals the ability to govern alone. The Nationals have used their position as a Coalition partner to demand ministerial positions with portfolios of concern to rural areas, and to shape government policy to favour the same constituency. This strategy has been slowly undermined in recent years by a relative decline in the rural population, the aggressive electoral competition of the Liberal Party in attempting to establish itself as the sole representative of the conservative vote, and the tendency of rural industry to use such organisations as the National Farmers' Federation to lobby governments directly. A recurrent response has been for the party to attempt to broaden its electoral appeal by claiming to represent other primary producers and related industries, and to make a vigorous play for socially conservative voters in suburban areas by stressing the party's commitment to family values. This last aim was the reason for the party's change of name. The policy appeared to be working in Queensland where the Nationals, already the major partner in a long-standing coalition with the Liberals, managed to govern in their own right from 1983. But the maverick behaviour of the Queensland premier Sir Joh Bjelke-Petersen, his ill-fated attempt to enter national politics in 1987, and the revelations of official corruption that led to the Queensland Nationals' defeat in 1989, seriously weakened the party (Coaldrake 1989).

The policy of broadening the party's base, together with the inevitable tensions of Coalition politics, have strained the Nationals' relations with their traditional constituents. The framing of rural policy, the running of candidates in seats held by the Liberals, and negotiations over Coalition arrangements have often been contentious. Three-cornered contests have sometimes plunged the Coalition partners into fierce disputes (Hughes 1986, Woodward and Costar 1988). In Western Australia, in 1978, the Nationals split over relations with the Liberals (Gallop and Layman 1985), rival National parties contesting elections until 1984. The biggest threat to the Nationals, however, is an increase in the Liberal vote sufficient for the Liberals to govern alone. The experience of Victoria shows that this can lead to the party's rapid decline.

Nonetheless, the National Party has maintained an electoral base which ensures that, at least in the immediate future, it will continue to be an important player on the conservative side of politics in the national sphere and in several states. Its formation of a Coalition with the Liberals in Western Australia in 1993 is a case in point. It would be foolish to underestimate the chances of survival of a party that has been able to hang on with such tenacity for more than seventy years.

The Australian Democrats
The Australian Democrats were formed in 1976 by a disillusioned Liberal Senator, Don Chipp. As a new centre party, the Democrats drew support from Labor and Liberal voters, alienated by the strength of the partisan divide which followed the dismissal of the Whitlam government in 1975 (Reynolds 1979, Shamsullah 1990). The party fought its first election in 1977, with considerable success. While the emergence of the Democrats can be attributed to the immediate political circum-

stances, the rise of such a party had been predicted by Kemp (1975), who argued that the increasing number of young technocrats and paraprofessionals in society would produce a party which rejected the divisiveness of class politics and stressed the virtues of social harmony and post-materialist values. These have been precisely the characteristics that have typified Democrat supporters.

The Democrats' initial success in gaining 9.4 per cent of the House of Representatives vote and 11.1 per cent in the Senate suggested that it might produce a realignment of the party system. But its support in the 1980s dropped to less than 7 per cent for the House of Representatives and less than 10 per cent for the Senate. Even in 1990, when the party gained its highest vote at a national election since its creation, questions remained about the nature of its support. The Democrat vote appears to be as much a protest vote against the governing party as a positive attachment to the Democrats (McAllister 1982, 1992: 158–59). The particular policies of the Democrats may have much less significance than the fact that they occupy a policy space between Labor and Liberal, thereby producing a parking space for voters disillusioned with the major parties.

Unlike the Nationals, which have a similar share of the vote, Democrat support is not geographically concentrated. This has generally precluded the party from winning seats in single-member constituencies, although the system of preferential voting permits the Democrats some influence through the flow of second preferences. The party has made its mark in parliamentary chambers that have adopted proportional representation. The Democrats' most important forum has been the Senate, where they have been able to win seats in all states since 1977, notwithstanding attempts by governments to reduce their influence (Sharman 1986). The party has held the balance of power in the Senate since 1980. It has used this position to make a major impact on the legislative programs of all governments, and to reinforce the status of the Senate as a key element in national politics (see Sharman 1986). It has played a similar role in the South Australian upper house and has been an important player in Legislative Council politics in New South Wales.

Apart from their dependence on proportional representation and the skillful use of their pivotal position in Parliament, the other distinguishing feature of the Democrats has been their party organisation. All major decisions on policy and the selection of all key office holders, including the parliamentary leader, are settled by postal ballot of the membership (Shamsullah 1990: 171–73). This feature, combined with an emphasis on the freedom of conscience of the Democrats' parliamentary members, gives concrete expression to the party's commitment to participatory politics and its suspicion of the power of a party machine, but it has led to tensions within the party. What, for example, is the point of a high level of participation in the formulation of Democrat policies if the parliamentary membership is not bound by party policies and is free to exercise freedom of conscience?

The thrust of Democrat ideology has also become less clear. Since the economic downturn, in 1989, the party has maintained its stress on post-materialist values and the environment, but has adopted economic policies more in keeping with those of the traditional Left than of a centre party (Maddox 1991: 310-13, Shamsullah 1990: 173-75). Buffeted by hard economic times, by competitors such as the Greens and the hostility of the major parties, the Democrats face a tough fight to hold their representation. Their attempt to 'keep the bastards honest' through a strong Senate may be the party's strongest claim to the voters' continuing allegiance.

The Green Movement and Environmental Issues
The importance of the Green movement is one of the most contentious issues in any assessment of the Australian party system. Total membership of the various environmental groups far exceeds that of any political party (Ward 1991: 165) and the environment was a major new issue in campaigning for the national election of 1990 (Bean *et al.* 1990). But the significance of Green issues and environmental organisations in affecting the outcome of elections and their potential for shaping party politics in the future are unclear.

In terms of voting support, an assortment of Green candidates (including Nuclear Disarmament ones) mustered only 2.3 per cent of the vote for the 1990 House of Representatives elections, and 3.3 per cent of the aggregate first preference vote for the Senate (calculated from Bean *et al.* 1990: 200-1). Except in a few electorates with high-profile candidates, the Greens made little impact; only in Western Australia did they elect a parliamentary representative, Senator Jo Valentine, an established federal politician (Lloyd 1990: 112-13).

Those who argue for the importance of Green issues contend that they affect the party system indirectly rather than directly. First, to the extent that the Democrats put major stress on the protection of the environment, the Green vote should include the Democrat vote; in 1990, this makes a combined vote of 13.6 per cent (not 2.3 per cent) for the House of Representatives, and 15.9 (not 3.3) per cent for the Senate. Second, if the growing sensitivity to environmental issues signals the importance of post-materialist values and the weakening of traditional ties to the major parties, then the Green movement indicates that a process of partisan dealignment is at work (Papadakis 1990). This growing sensitivity to environmental issues can thus be seen as foreshadowing increased voter volatility, the possibility of increased strains over environmental issues within the major political parties (Bean and McAllister 1990: 90) and, perhaps, a realignment of the party system (Hay and Haward 1988). But the evidence of the 1993 election does not confirm this prediction: while the Green vote did not suffer as much as that of the Democrats, and the Western Australian Greens elected a Senator, there was nothing to suggest that any major change to the party system was in train.

The Rise of Independents
Late in 1991, governments in five of Australia's nine jurisdictions depended on the votes of Independent members: the governments of the Australian Capital Territory, New South Wales, South Australia, Tasmania, and Western Australia. This situation, unprecedented since the 1920s, raised the question of whether the surge in the number and importance of Independent MPs was part of some growing disillusionment with parties, or simply the result of a freak conjunction of events.

The label 'Independent' refers to Members of Parliament with a variety of political backgrounds. Some are elected as Independents because of their status as local notables, or their stand on particular local issues. Although small in number, such candidates have been a perennial feature of some areas of rural Australia and, more recently, in some urban seats. Candidates of this kind have been notable in the New South Wales Legislative Assembly; since 1984, urban independents have won several seats, boosting the number of Independents in that Parliament to a post-war high of seven in 1988. At the national level, Ted Mack (Independent, North Sydney) was elected to the House of Representative in 1990, the first such member since 1966. Phil Cleary won Bob Hawke's old seat of Wills at a by-election in 1992, retaining it in 1993.

Another category are those Independents who have split from a major party before an election on grounds of policy, faction or personality, and taken enough of the local party support with them to get elected as Independents. This has been the case, for example, with the two Independent Labor members elected to the South Australian House of Assembly in 1985 and 1989; each had left the Labor Party after a dispute over their endorsement as ALP candidates.

A third group are those elected as party candidates who subsequently reject their party tie, often resigning from Parliament at the following election. If we add party candidates whose party is little more than a personal vehicle (for example, in New South Wales the Call to Australia Party is heavily dependent on the Reverend Fred Nile) we further increase the variety of 'Independent' MPs.

The recent high visibility of Independents, and their importance in sustaining minority governments is as much a reflection of evenness in the representation of the parties as it is of changes to the voting preferences of the electorate. Yet the rise of Independents of all kinds must be seen as a small but significant indicator of a more general disillusionment with party politics, both on the part of those who vote for Independents and by those members who desert their party to cross the floor of Parliament, or run against it at election time. Even when Independents cease to play a critical role in the support of minority governments, this sign of dissatisfaction with party politics is likely to persist.

Conclusion

This survey of political parties can be read as showing that the Australian party system and its constituent elements are continuing to discharge the traditional role expected of them. Parties continue to be the major factor in structuring electoral choice and in organising coherent majorities in Australian parliaments. In spite of pressures for change, the overall picture appears to be one of stability: the major parties have experienced factional divisions and argue about reform, but the momentum of the party organisations continues; party membership has fallen, but the party élites survive; party identification has weakened, but with little apparent effect on voting (McAllister 1992a: 37–42); the new politics of post-materialism has become important, but has not replaced the old politics of economic issues (Rawson 1991); new parties emerge, but do not threaten to displace the existing large parties; Independents may occasionally hold the balance of power, but the levers of executive power are still held by the major parties.

Yet questions about the role and justification of parties persist. Parties, particularly the major parties, can no longer be seen as major avenues for political participation and influence through the involvement of a mass membership in their affairs. While they retain their critical role in shaping electoral behaviour, recruiting political activists and maintaining discipline in Parliament, it is hard to reconcile the professionalisation of these activities with any theory of broad-based political participation. Parties appear to work much as they have done for the last fifty years, but changes in their structure and operation mean that much of their traditional rationale no longer applies.

As enthusiasm for the interventionist state has waned, so too has the justification for parties as the engines supporting an executive-dominated governmental system. This development is especially significant in Australia where the standard textbook view of parties had been underpinned by a majoritarian view of the political system, one increasingly at odds with both current experience and rival views of how the political system should work. How should we evaluate our parties? This critical question is less about analysing the way parties work, and more about discussing how power should be distributed in a liberal democracy. While there may be doubts about the central role of party in many aspects of the political process, there can be no dispute that parties remain a critical component in the debate over the nature of popular participation in a representative democracy.

7
Class Voting, Issue Voting and Electoral Volatility

MURRAY GOOT*

Old Views and New

A generation ago, Australian political scientists stressed the connection between the country's social structure and the distribution of the vote, the low level of interest in political issues, and the high proportion of voters who could be relied upon to stick to their party preference.

Paramount was the correlation between 'class', whether defined 'subjectively' or 'objectively', and the vote. In the early 1960s, A.F. Davies, for example, made much of a poll in which two-thirds of those who classified themselves as 'working class' (38 per cent of the sample) voted Labor, while two-thirds of those who thought of themselves as 'middle class' (50 per cent of the sample) supported the Coalition. The match was 'close enough', he said, 'to suggest that "class" and party vote...may be largely alternative measures of the same thing — general social stance' (Davies 1961: 17, 1964: 133, 1967: 54–62, 1972: 41, Davies and Encel 1965a: 37, Encel 1970: 96; similarly, Rawson 1961: 2).

At about the same time, Rufus Davis (1960a: 620–24) remarked on the way the 'profile of occupational allegiance', documented by the Gallup Poll between 1946 and 1955, conformed to "the popular view" of the dominant voting habits of each "interest"'. With the possible exception of 'white collar' (clerical) workers, each of the poll's occupational groups 'faithfully peel off, mainly to the "right", or the "left"'. The correlation between occupation and vote was far from perfect; and perhaps as Webb (1954: 109–10, also Sawer 1952b: 32, Miller 1954: 55, Mayer 1955: 93, and Emy 1974: 364) insisted, the fact that most unskilled workers voted Labor was 'less significant' — especially for an understanding of *party* behaviour — than 'the fact that one in five does not'. But for each election since the war the data 'disclosed much the same pattern of occupational support, the minor tidal swings...washing evenly across the board' (Davies 1964: 136).

---

*Much of the critique of Kemp had an earlier airing in Connell and Goot (1979). For comments on a draft of this chapter, I am grateful to David Peetz and Rodney Smith. For word processing, I am grateful to Sue Folwell and Maureen Moseley.

The collective portrait of those swept up by these 'minor tidal swings' was hardly flattering. The idea of a 'responsible group of people...who trim our political course at critical moments', was dismissed by Davies (1964: 138) as 'incurably sentimental and a monument to intellectual laziness'. Fin Crisp (1949: 46–47), concerned that this 'unpolitical section of the electorate' was 'frequently decisive at elections and referenda', railed against the 'dangerous...irresponsibility of the politically ignorant, confused and indifferent "floating vote"' which 'usually surges irresolutely to and fro, in response to irrelevant "issues" or the fleeting excitements of the moment'. Even when he came to acknowledge 'a significant, informed, shrewd and responsible element' in the 'floating vote', there remained a 'distinctly larger proportion' best described as 'politically vacuous and illiterate' (Crisp 1965: 107–8).

Colleagues, starting to use sample surveys to bring the study of electoral behaviour into closer range, found many of Crisp's adjectives applied more widely: 'Most electors have a very limited knowledge of the candidates and their parties; in some respects they are almost incredibly ignorant' (Rawson 1961: 165); in terms of '"competence and affect"', two-thirds of those interviewed could be classified as 'apathetic' (Davies and Encel 1965b: 107); for most, politics was 'simply a vacancy, an unused space' (Davies 1972: 44); merely to interview 'typical voters' during an election campaign 'would be to alter completely the atmosphere of apathy' in which the 'flow of political communications' is 'normally received' (Hughes 1966: 169).

The idea that policies or issues might be vital to the vote was downplayed or dismissed. Dick Spann (1961: 128–129), like Crisp, referred to the electoral salience of 'issues' in inverted commas. Davies and Encel (1965a: 38) relegated evidence of issue voting to a footnote; asked to explain their choices, voters 'rationalised' (Davies 1961: 17, 1972: 41). Don Rawson's (1961: 165) alternative suggestion, that 'people support a party not because it favours a particular policy but because they think it is made up of particular kinds of people — probably people like themselves', had considerable appeal (Rydon 1963: 170, Free University, Sydney 1969: 17, Emy 1974: 365). Trying to point electoral studies in the right direction, Colin Hughes (1966: 167) thought 'the most exciting area of research', and the most neglected, was 'the process of political socialisation whereby children...learn who "their sort of people" are expected to vote for'.

A strong occupational structuring of political allegiance was generally taken to mean that most people never changed their vote. The discovery of widespread apathy reinforced the point. Some, impressed by the relative stability of the parties' aggregate support, succumbed to the 'widely held view' that 40 per cent always vote Labor and 40 per cent always vote non-Labor, leaving precisely 20 per cent — those 'perpetually ready' to change their vote — determining the outcome

(Overacker 1952: 311, Hughes 1966: 166). Even scholars sceptical of a 'stable pool of floating voters' conceded that 'most voters tie themselves to one party or another for years' (Davies 1964: 138, Burns 1961: Chapter 11).

In recent years, each of these claims — about the occupational basis of the vote, about the relevance of issues and about the limited amount of electoral change — has come under challenge.

First, and most direct, has been the challenge to the idea that party preference is explained largely by class self-placement or position on the ladder of occupational prestige. In a major work, organised around two national surveys conducted in 1967 and 1969, and marking the beginning of a full-scale assault on class-based explanations, Don Aitkin (1977, 1982: 119–20, 1973: 303–4 for the first run) dismissed Davies' claim that 'class self-placement and the vote were largely alternative measures of the same thing'; Davies own data, he concluded, gave it 'only faint support'. Occupational prestige also received short shrift. In 1967 it may have been 'the most powerful variable', but it only reduced the unexplained variance in LCP versus Labor voting by 10 per cent; to be really powerful it should have reduced it by about one-third (Aitkin 1982: 114). Even those prepared to defend the significance of class had to acknowledge that more or less uniform electoral swings across all occupational categories posed problems for a theory of voting based on opposing interests (Free University 1969: 16, Goot 1973, Douglas 1978). The biggest blow, however, was delivered by David Kemp's re-analysis of Gallup Poll data from 1946 to 1975. The relationship between people's jobs and their vote, he argued, had become steadily weaker since the 1940s; by the mid-1970s, 'occupational class' had 'almost — though not quite — become useless as a predictor of someone's vote' (Kemp 1977: 4). Other researchers in the behaviourist tradition disagree about when the decline started and how far it has gone, but agree that the end of 'class voting' spells the end of 'class politics'.

In place of voting based on occupation, so the argument runs, it is increasingly based on issues. Voters consider their position on issues (or values) and vote for the party which offers the closest match. Whatever the content of the concern — even if it centres on business power, unions or strikes — votes explained by issues are not votes connected with class.

The electorate is also now said to be 'volatile'. As early as 1969 the British psephologist David Butler (1973: 123) suspected that Australia was 'beginning to be afflicted', as he put it, 'by the electoral volatility which has been such a growing feature of recent British politics'. A sense that Australians have become more willing to change their votes, that the 'stability' of voting patterns has become a thing of the past, and that the party system itself might be on the edge of some sort of transformation, has grown markedly since then.

This chapter provides a fuller account of each of these interconnected and increasingly influential interpretations of post-war electoral change. None, I shall argue, stands close scrutiny; each involves an understanding of electoral politics which is either misconceived or without empirical support.

The argument about 'class voting' exaggerates the continuity of the decline (on the standard measure, there has been no decline since the Whitlam years), misunderstands the nature of the change (the evidence implicating social forces is weak; the evidence that political developments have been crucial is strong), and is hostage to a very crude notion of class. The argument for the growing importance of issues or values is even less persuasive. Those who advocate it have a remarkably poor grasp of what might count as evidence, mishandle whatever evidence there is, and fail to understand how issues or values are often class-related. As for the argument about a rise in electoral volatility, this suffers over the long haul from an extraordinary misreading of political history (the electoral turbulence of the 1980s and early 1990s was not nearly as great as that which characterised electoral politics from the 1910s to the 1940s) and is weakened over the short haul by the use of an unreliable source (voters' recall), by the misreading of evidence (changes in party identification), and by misplaced comparisons (voting for the Senate compared with voting for the House).

Nonetheless, as I stress in the conclusion, to criticise the new is not necessarily to endorse the old. On some points, especially to do with the occupational structuring of the vote and with volatility, there are difficulties for both. On issue voting, we simply lack the evidence to decide.

Class Voting

The New Orthodoxy

The main framework within which changes in the relationship between occupation and vote have come to be defined, argued and measured was established in 1963 with the publication of Robert Alford's *Party and Society*, a young American's study of 'party and class in the Anglo-American democracies'. Like most students of the new survey-based science of electoral behaviour (then and since), Alford thought of class as a category, with membership contingent upon individuals having certain characteristics, and almost everyone fitting into one of two classes: the 'middle class' or the 'working class'. The 'best single indicator' of whether a person was 'working class' or 'middle class' in 'styles of life, education and values', was their occupation; more precisely, this depended on whether their occupation was manual (equated with blue collar work) or non-manual (white collar). Housewives could be assigned (as they were in public opinion polls) to the occupational status of the 'head of household'; others not in the paid workforce, mostly students and retirees, could be omitted altogether (Alford 1963: 74). There was nothing idiosyncratic about any of this; Alford's framework was mainstream American political science, 1950s-style.

The extent to which those in manual and non-manual occupations were divided in their party support could be encapsulated by an 'index of class voting'. This was the innovation. The index, covering those in the non-rural workforce, was computed by subtracting the percentage in non-manual occupations voting for Left parties from the percentage in manual occupations voting for such parties. For Alford (1963: 13, 79–80, 350), the Left in Australia meant the ALP (but not, curiously, the Communist Party) plus, after 1955, the DLP.

To what extent, he asked, had the pattern of 'class voting' changed and what had driven this change? To answer these questions he assembled a series of Gallup polls reporting either intended or recalled vote from 1943 (the earliest available poll data) to 1961, organised by respondents' or 'head of households" occupation. His initial conclusion was that 'class voting' had 'declined fairly consistently'. And it is not difficult to see why. Taking a line through the four polls he selected, from 1943 to 1949, the 'index of class voting' was about 39; from 1951 to the Labor split in 1955 (8 polls) it was 35; between 1958 and 1961 (5 polls), about 32. What appeared to be happening, he suggested, was a 'secular erosion of the class bases of politics under the impact of a period of prosperity and social mobility' (Alford 1963: 178, 350–51). Towards the end of his book, however, he seems to have had second thoughts. This 'slight decline', as he now described it, was 'due largely to the drop in Victoria'. Australian experience did not 'support the hypothesis of a decline of the importance of the class bases of politics' after all (Alford 1963: 291).

Thereafter, as Jones and McAllister (1989: 9) note, those who dipped into the book could carry away whatever conclusion they chose. Hughes (1969: 145) had Alford arguing that 'class voting' had 'declined fairly steadily'; Aitkin (1982: 154, note 15) that Alford's figures showed 'a slow and slight decline'; and Kemp (1978: 59, 66) that while Alford had conceded the possibility of a slight decrease, he had found no evidence of a 'clear long-term decline'. Indeed, by reading Alford as a theory of how industrialisation and urbanisation favoured the 'class polarisation' of the parties, Kemp (1978: 94–95) was certain Alford was arguing against 'substantial longterm decline'.

Kemp's own analysis of the polls (the most succinct statement is Kemp 1975) argued that there had been 'a clear decline'. Using a battery of statistical techniques — phi-square correlation coefficients, linear modelling and ordinary least square regression — Kemp concluded that, from 1946 to 1961, the decline had been a 'slow trend'. Thereafter, from a distinctly lower base, the trend had been faster. In 1946, occupational status had accounted for 14 per cent of the variance in the vote; in 1975, it had accounted for only about 4 per cent (Kemp 1978: 65–67).

The index of 'class voting' had declined, Kemp argued, because among manual workers support for the Left (by which he meant, more correctly than Alford, the ALP) had fallen, while within the non-manual bloc it had increased. But the two groups had not converged at the same rate. The decline among manual workers was considerably greater and steadier — more 'inexorable' — and had fallen across skilled, semi-skilled and unskilled categories alike. On the non-manual side the increase was confined largely to a radicalised 'technocracy' — to tertiary-educated professionals, whose tendency to vote Labor had increased, on average, 'by over 2 per cent every three years'; support among clerical and sales staff had remained steady. In short, the convergence had not been between those in manual and those in non-manual grades (as Rawson 1991: 226 imagines) but between 'upper status non-manuals' and the rest of the population (Kemp 1978: 72–77, 154–58).

The drift from Labor among manual workers was not to be explained by affluence, he said — though what evidence he had of changes in affluence he did not say. Were affluence eroding the class basis of party support, Kemp argued, the drift should have been most obvious among skilled workers. Yet, in the post-1961 period, Labor's largest losses had come from semi-skilled and unskilled workers; among skilled workers the proportion voting Labor changed hardly at all (Kemp 1978: 154–59). Nor was the drift to be explained by the decline in union densities. True, between 1954 and 1969 the proportion of the workforce covered by unions had declined. But among both union and non-unionised workers 'blue collar' support for Labor had declined 'at very similar rates' (Kemp 1978: 171, 175).

What accounted for the drift, Kemp concluded, were 'subjective embourgeoisement' (workers' sense of themselves as 'middle class'), home ownership and suburbanisation — precisely those factors Crisp (1965: 152) had identified as threatening 'the traditional hard core of Labor'. In the mid-1960s, when the party had been in the political wilderness for six terms and looked set to stay there, such views were widely shared. Davies (1964: 136–38), for example, rather hoped that 'a steady evaporation of the manual base of the workforce' and the considerable 'overlap in working and middle class standards and aspirations' might transform the 'old-style bases of political alignment' from one of interest to one of 'political and social ideas'. Rawson (1966: 120–21) noted, among other factors 'hostile' to Labor's continued 'existence and importance', improving standards of living, more people with homes and 'even a few shares or blocks of land'. Louise Overacker (1968: 313, 316), who was sure that 'unlike their parents and grandparents, wage earners thought of themselves as "middle class"', believed 'the old alignment of the major groups dividing along class lines', initially 'broken down' through the DLP, was now in a complete state of 'collapse'.

What was most striking about Kemp's work was not the lack of originality of his thesis but that, at every point, his evidence was vanishingly thin. To establish 'the embourgoisement of a significant portion of the Australian working class', he turned not to any longitudinal data on changing values, aspirations or beliefs, but to a single comparison, from Aitkin's 1967 survey, showing the while 42 per cent of respondents described themselves as 'working class', 60 per cent described their parents this way (Kemp 1978: 118-20; similarly, Broom and Jones 1976: 65–66). A proper comparison, based on a survey of the parents themselves or on a survey conducted a generation earlier, might have enabled a valid inference; this sort of comparison could not. Surveys conducted between 1967 and 1979, in which respondents were asked to which class they belonged, show no trend in the required direction (cf. Aitkin 1982: 366, 379, 389, Graetz 1987: 71). Surveys conducted between 1961 and 1986, when respondents were presented with a list of classes and asked to which one they belonged show no such trend either (cf. Davies 1964: 133, Encel 1970: 88–89, 97–99, Emmison 1991: 267).

Equally unconvincing was the attempt to establish that home ownership had 'encouraged even self-assessed working class voters to become politically conservative' (Kemp 1978: 96, 357). The trouble was three-fold. First, class self-placement questions are very unreliable; Aitkin (1982: 128–29) estimated, on the basis of re-interviews, that 'for perhaps two-thirds' of his sample 'class labels' carried 'little meaning or permanence'. Second, whereas home ownership, on Kemp's own admission, peaked in the mid-to late-1960s, 'class voting', he says, kept on declining. Third, as far as home ownership and voting behaviour are connected it may not be because people who buy homes become more conservative but because people who are conservative are keener to buy their own homes (cf. Heath *et al.* 1985, Chapter 4, for Britain).

As for the evidence of a 'suburban effect', try as he might — by looking at changes in 'subjective class', 'class mixing', and so on — Kemp had the greatest difficulty satisfying himself that there was any. The best he could manage, again from Aitkin's 1967 survey, was to show that 'blue-collar households were significantly more likely to support the major conservative party in the new outer suburbs than in the older inner-city working-class areas'. But there's the rub; the relevant comparison, not with Liberal voting but with Labor voting, shows no statistical relationship at all; the Liberals' apparent gains came at the expense of minor parties, not the ALP (Kemp 1978: 116–17). Ecological correlations, relating aggregate votes to area type, also fail to show a 'suburban effect' of the kind required (cf. Hughes 1969: 147, Scott 1991: 60–61).

Some aspects of Kemp's argument for the decline in the correlation between occupation and vote — his arguments about its timing and extent — have recently been challenged by F.L. Jones and Ian McAllister (1989; for a less technical version, see Jones 1989). They argue that between the late 1940s and 1966 there is 'no evidence of any decline' in the 'structural base' of Australian politics, and that while 'class' declined in importance after the mid-60s, it remained a more important factor than Kemp allows.

In arguing their case, Jones and McAllister examined the polls, and age cohorts within them, at 17-year intervals: in the late 1940s, in 1966, and in 1983. Although they sometimes confuse the two — using evidence about causes to attack those whose concern is with the correlation — their interest was in the extent to which the explanatory power of occupation had changed. The proportion of the variance explained by 'class' in 1966, they conclude, was little different to the proportion explained in 1948–49; and while the proportion explained in 1983 was substantially lower, far from disappearing altogether, 'class' remained the single most important structural determinant of the vote.

More recently, McAllister (1992a: 158–61) has pushed the cohort analysis back to the 1920s (using respondents' recall of their first vote), and forward to the 1990s. 'Class voting' he argues, was strongest in the 1920s and 30s. From the 1940s, its importance declined. But it was the period 1967 to 1990 that saw 'the most substantial', if 'gradual' decline.

Assumptions
Though they disagree on some matters — the extent of the decline in 'class voting' and the point from which this decline set in — the key assumptions of Alford, Kemp and now Jones and McAllister, have a good deal in common.

The first assumption they share is that changes in the level of 'class voting' are determined above all by social change, principally by changing patterns of consumption. Alford (1963: 173) suggested that the level of class voting indicated by the polls 'probably...reflects the actual structural cleavages in as bare a form as possible' — though what such a conclusion meant, or how he arrived at it, he did not stop to say. While Alford did not discount the parties altogether — at one point he thought Australia was reaching a level of 'class voting...not much above the level to be expected from the character of the structural cleavages and class interests still remaining [sic]...and from the differential response to the parties to those interests' (Alford 1963: 178) — the same could not be said of Kemp. 'The perspective adopted in the following analysis', Kemp declared (1978: 20), 'is sociological... differences in electoral behaviour are viewed as expressing...the social situation of the voters'. Changes in the relationship between occupation and vote, over fifteen-year intervals, were represented, in Kemp's analysis, by long straight lines; continuity and simplicity (a 'drift', a 'decay', a 'crumbling', as he describes it) were built into his model. 'Short-term fluctuations do not concern us', wrote Kemp (1978: 64) 'at the moment' — a 'moment' that lasted as long as the book. Hardly surprising, then, that political issues, leaders or ideologies barely rate a mention. That the 'drift' among manual workers away from the ALP, for example, may not have represented their embourgeoisement but their reaction to an 'embourgeoisified ALP' (Douglas 1978: 314) is not even considered. Kemp speculated about possible political *consequences* — Labor's increasingly 'middle class' support 'may well be laying the ground for further fragmentations of the party' (Kemp 1978: 358) — but not about political *causes*.

Similarly for Jones and McAllister. Although each of the three elections to which their data relate, 1949, 1966, 1983, are among the most dramatic of the post-war period, the politics of the various situations seem not to interest them. The Labor split in the 1950s is noted, for instance, only because of the technical difficulties it raises for the calculus of 'class voting' (Jones and McAllister 1989: 11).

The second assumption — or set of assumptions — has to do with class; in particular, the view that the division between 'blue collar' (manual) and 'white collar' (more debatedly, non-manual) is a division by class. Such an assumption hardly does justice to anything that might pass as class theory, whether classical or contemporary. As Western *et al.* (1991: 312) remark, concerning Aitkin (1982: 318), 'the adherence to such simple categorisations' is 'inexcusable'. (Rawson (1991: 226) insists that Aitkin did not use 'class' in this way: 'to his credit', he used the terms "middle class" and "working class" to refer to self-identification'. But this, surely, would be equally inexcusable.

Alford himself glimpsed part of the problem in conceding that 'sales clerks are not in the same "class situation", in Weber's sense, as either professionals or executives of large businesses' (Alford 1963: 78–79). In his work on Australian 'embourgeoisement' — he did not find much evidence of it — Parsler (1970) distinguished between 'blue collar' workers, 'white collar' workers and the 'middle class'. Similarly, when Chaples (1980: 433), came to test Kemp's theory of voting behaviour — and found little support for it — it was those in 'unskilled, skilled or clerical type jobs' he described as 'working class'. Clearly, thinking of class in categorical terms, and stuck with data from the polls, one is safer distinguishing between professionals, executives of large business and small businesspeople, on the one hand, and semi-skilled and unskilled workers, on the other, rather than distinguishing manual from non-manual or blue collars from white.

The larger problem is that class is considerably more than a category — it is a relationship. As Bob Connell and Terry Irving (1992: 4–6) argue, to focus on the characteristics that distinguish 'classes' (here, positions on a scale of occupational prestige) is to overlook the social relations which create these characteristics and to ignore 'the structure of relationships that produces the group'. Above all, it is to deflect attention from the sense in which class is a means of responding to class-structured experiences through vehicles for collective action like companies, unions and political parties.

A third and closely related set of assumptions concern the reliability and meaning of the occupational classifications themselves. A spot check against the Census data (set out in Graetz and McAllister 1988: 183) suggests that in 1949 the 'white collar' element in the polls (46 per cent in the average Morgan sample) was too high, and between 1963 and 1969, too low (41 to 43 per cent of Morgan's non-farm workforce plus non-working spouses). However, since Morgan keeps no detailed records, one cannot say what changed, or when. Certainly, the occupational range has altered enormously since the war, with old jobs disappearing and new ones emerging. There have been massive changes, too, in the nature of many jobs, their prestige, remuneration and skill. And there have been vast changes in labour force composition, especially through casualisation and part-time work, immigration and increased participation among women. There are implications in this for, among other things, the proportion of the electorate registered by the polls under their own occupation rather than that of the 'head of household'. The assumption that we are comparing like with like may be reasonable over the short-term; beyond that, it is fraught with difficulty.

A Re-analysis
To explore how the relationship between occupation and vote might have changed over the last fifty years it is important to think about the ways in which the relationship might be conceptualised and measured; to have a defensible way of periodising the data; and to bring to the task a modicum of political and historical sense.

The relationship between occupation and vote can be thought of, as political scientists usually do, in terms of the manual/non-manual divide. But it can also be thought of in other ways — for example, in terms of the polar categories on the occupational scale, with managers, executives and professionals at one pole and semi-skilled and unskilled workers at the other. This, as we have already suggested, offers a more reasonable rendering of 'middle class' and 'working class' than does the usual distinction. Other sets of pigeonholes open up other possibilities.

Any of these relationships can be measured either in absolute or relative terms (Heath *et al.* 1985: Chapter 3). Absolute 'class voting' is defined as the proportion of the relevant population (those in manual and non-manual grades or those in the polar categories) voting for their 'natural' party — Labor for manual, Liberal for non-manual. Where everyone votes for their 'natural' party the absolute level of 'class voting' is 100; where no-one does, it is 0; where just as many do as don't, and when it therefore has no predictive power, the level is 50.

Interest, however, has never focused on absolute levels of occupational voting but on the distinctiveness of occupational support — the extent to which the parties depend on their 'natural' supporters rather than on pulling support from across the occupational divide. Alford's index is one measure of relative 'class voting'. But it has its weaknesses. Suppose that Labor's support among manual workers during the Vietnam War had dropped from 66 per cent to, say, 27 per cent, while its support within non-manual occupations had dived from 39 per cent to zero. The Alford index would have moved from 27 to 25. But as Heath *et al.* (1985: 41, note 7) suggest, in a situation where Labor drew all its support from manual workers we would probably want to say that this represented a heightening rather than a lowering of 'class' alignment.

A more appropriate measure is the odds ratio. The odds of someone in a non-manual grade voting for the Coalition in 1951 were roughly two to one, while the odds of a manual worker voting for the Coalition were about one to two. The ratio of these odds works out at just over four to one. The larger the odds ratio the stronger the occupational basis of the vote; a ratio of 1:1 would indicate that there was no occupational basis for the vote. As with the Alford index, the odds ratio can be adopted to any set of categories, including the polar ones.

To track the changes we have selected (where possible), the final two polls on voting intention conducted by Morgan (the only regular poll series conducted before 1971) at each federal election from 1943 to 1993, extracted the relevant data and pooled the results. Organising the data around elections and ignoring the soundings taken in between not only makes the task of assembling and analysing the data more manageable, but makes it easier to relate shifts in the pattern of support to changes in the political battle. Looking at voting intentions, and ignoring (as far as possible) polls which report how respondents said they voted reduces the element of unreliability introduced by the use of recalled vote. Pooling the data reduces, though it certainly does not eliminate, the chances that apparent shifts are really due to measurement error.

What do our calculations show? Conceived in terms of a dichotomised model of the occupational structure, the *absolute* level of 'class voting' has clearly declined. In the 1940s and 50s, two-thirds of the electorate appears to have voted for their 'natural' party; today, the proportion is closer to half. But the decline has not been a smooth one. Until the early 1960s there was little sign of it; even Labor's split seems not to have made much difference. The first sign of a decline comes in 1961, when unemployment and a credit squeeze brought the Menzies government close to defeat. A clearer turning point, 1966, coincides with the Vietnam War and an election which Labor not only lost but lost badly; for the first time the absolute figure drops below 60. If the election of the Whitlam government in 1972 saw another decline, it

164 *Class Voting, Issue Voting and Electoral Volatility*

was a decline to a new plateau; the level has hovered at around 55 ever since (see Table 7.1).

Relative levels of 'class voting' have declined more sharply. The Alford index averaged 36 through the 1940s and 50s; in 1993 it stood at only half this. The odds ratio is similar. Between 1943 and 1958, it averaged 4.6; in recent years it, too, has hovered at around half. On both scales the lowest figures recorded in the 1980s were no more than one-third of the size of those recorded in the 1940s.

Again, however, these numbers have a political history — they are

TABLE 7.1 *Party Support, Dichotomised Occupation Structure, 1943–93*

Election	Manual ALP %	Manual LNP %	Non-manual ALP %	Non-manual LNP %	'Class Voting' Absolute %	'Class Voting' Alford %	Odds ratio	n
1943	68	23	31	52	62	37	5.0	(1849)
1946	67	26	34	64	66	33	4.9	(3719)
1949	68	32	29	69	68	39	5.0	(3366)
1951	65	34	31	67	66	34	4.2	(3266)
1954	68	31	32	68	68	36	4.6	(3331)
1955	61	32	27	67	64	34	4.7	(2014)
1958	67	27	31	62	65	36	5.0	(3363)
1961	65	30	34	58	62	31	3.6	(3532)
1963	66	31	39	56	61	27	3.1	(1669)
1966	51	38	25	64	57	26	3.4	n.a.
1969	60	32	35	54	58	25	2.9	n.a.
1972	62	30	41	48	55	21	2.4	n.a
1974	59	35	42	50	55	17	2.0	n.a
1975	51	41	33	60	56	18	2.3	(3582)
1977	55	33	33	54	54	22	2.7	(3720)
1980	59	33	39	51	55	20	2.3	(4618)
1983	63	32	44	48	55	19	2.2	(3487)
1984	60	32	46	44	52	14	1.8	(2273)
1987	59	32	41	49	54	18	2.7	(2972)
1990	54	32	38	45	49	16	2.0	(4343)
1993	57	31	39	49	53	18	2.3	(3704)

Source: Australian Public Opinion Poll (The Gallup Method): No. 18, July 1943; No. 45, September 1946; No. 46, September 1946; No. 68, November 1949; No. 69, December 1949; No. 79, March 1951; No. 80, April 1951; No. 103, November 1954; No. 104, December 1954; No. 114, October 1955; No. 115, November 1955; No. 134, October 1958; No. 135, November 1958; No. 153, November 1961; No. 154, December 1961; No. 164, July 1963; No. 165, October 1963; Nos. 186 and 187, November 1966; Nos 206 and 207, October 1969; Nos 236 and 237, November 1972; Morgan Gallup Poll: No. 29, April-May 1974; No. 30, May 1974; No. 97, November 1975; No. 98, December 1975; No. 190, November 1977; No. 191, December, 1977; Nos 351, 353, October 1980; Nos 491 and 498, February 1983; No. 618, November 1984; No. 625, December 1984; Nos 842 and 847, July 1987; No 1002, February 1990; No. 1020, March-April 1990; No. 1205, February 1993; No. 1209, March 1993.

not just the outcome of some ineluctable force. Only in 1961 and 1963, 1972 and 1974 does the Alford index fall away; before, in between and beyond there are fluctuations, but no real trends. The odds ratios tell a similar, if simpler, story: a clear decline in 1961 and in 1972; for the rest, trendless fluctuation.

The political dynamic of the index is better grasped if we examine its constituent parts. Prior to the split, blue collar support for Labor changed very little; white collar support changed very little either. The split deprived Labor of blue collar and white collar support in almost equal measure; the index was therefore little affected.

The loss of Labor support in 1955, occasioned by the split, was short-lived. From 1958 to 1963, support among blue collar workers grew to be as strong as it had been at any time in the 1940s; among the non-manual workforce, Labor's support eclipsed earlier levels. The sharp decline in the index from 1958 (36 percentage points) to 1963 (26 points) was not the result of any disenchantment with Labor from among manual workers, but a shift to Labor among Kemp's 'middle class'.

The 'Vietnam election' of 1966, and the 1969 election in which Vietnam was still a big issue, reduced the index hardly at all; the collapse and subsequent recovery in Labor's stocks was as evident among manual as it was among non-manual voters. However, whereas Labor's manual support was never to be as great after 1966 as it had been before, its non-manual support was to become even greater.

The surge in support that brought Labor to power in 1972 was more marked among non-manual than among manual workers. This is hardly news: the idea that Whitlam's victory owed much to the 'middle class' is a well-established piece of political lore. And it is this growth in non-manual support, rather than any loss of manual support, that explains the decline in the index in 1972.

Since then, support for Labor among manual and non-manual voters has generally risen or fallen together. There have been two exceptions, 1974 and 1984 — elections at which newly-installed Labor governments sought second terms. On both occasions, Labor appears to have gained ground among non-manual voters (reassured, perhaps, that Labor was not proving to be too radical) and lost it among manual voters (disappointed, perhaps, that after so long a wait more had not been done for them). On each occasion the index contracted: in 1974, to a low of 17; in 1984, to a new low of 14. But in each case, subsequent elections saw the index move up.

The evidence of the polls is confirmed by Aitkin's (1982: 319–20) surveys. These, too, show that 'class voting' declined between 1967 and 1979 and that support for Labor increased among those in non-manual jobs and those in manual jobs. Aitkin, who acknowledges that this differs from Kemp's expectation, is still prepared to take Kemp on trust for the pre-1967 period, and to share his faith in the plausibility of an essentially apolitical account of the charges that took place thereafter.

Compared with the dichotomised model, relative 'class voting' (like absolute 'class voting') has been more marked at the polar extremes. The post-war high was 1949, the year Ben Chifley attempted to nationalise the banks. In the run-up to that election, Labor's support among the professional and managerial class, as registered by the Gallup Poll, was about one-in-eight; among semi-skilled and unskilled workers it rose to nearly eight-in-ten. The (modified) Alford index jumped from 51 to 66, the odds ratio doubling from 12.9 to an extraordinary 26.0 (see Table 7.2).

TABLE 7.2 *Party Support, Polar Occupations, 1943–93*

Election	Semi/unskilled ALP %	Semi/unskilled LNP %	Prof./Managers ALP %	Prof./Managers LNP %	'Class Voting' Absolute %	'Class Voting' Alford %	Odds ratio	n
1943	73	20	21	61	68	52	10.6	(738)
1946	67	27	16	83	71	51	12.9	(1540)
1949	78	22	12	88	82	66	26.0	(1216)
1951	73	27	14	81	76	58	15.6	(1242)
1954	75	25	16	83	78	59	15.7	(1383)
1955	68	26	17	82	75	50	12.8	(1473)
1958	70	27	17	80	74	53	15.7	(1287)
1961	72	22	20	76	74	52	12.4	(1385)
1963	75	23	20	79	76	55	12.9	(613)
1966	59	33	13	79	66	46	10.9	n.a.
1969	64	29	24	68	64	39	5.9	n.a.
1972	66	26	25	64	65	41	6.5	n.a.
1974	60	35	29	62	61	31	3.8	n.a.
1975	58	38	25	70	61	33	4.3	n.a.
1977	60	33	21	64	61	38	6.0	n.a.
1980	63	29	29	66	64	34	4.9	n.a.
1983	63	29	37	59	64	29	3.6	n.a.
1984	60	29	35	51	59	29	3.2	n.a.
1987	59	28	32	60	63	32	4.3	n.a.
1990	58	27	33	51	56	25	3.3	n.a.
1993	56	32	39	48	53	17	2.2	n.a.

Source: Australian Public Opinion Poll (the Gallup Method): No. 18, July 1943; No. 45, September 1946; No. 46, September 1946; No. 68, November 1949; No. 69, December 1949; No. 79, March 1951; No. 80, April 1951; No. 103, November 1954; No. 104, December 1954; No. 114, October 1955; No. 115, November 1955; No. 134, October 1958; No. 135, November 1958; No. 153, November 1961; No. 154, December 1961; No. 164, July 1963; No. 165, October 1963; Nos. 186 and 187, November 1966; Nos 206 and 207, October 1969; Nos.136 and 237, November 1972; Morgan Gallup Poll: No. 29, April-May 1974; No. 30, May 1974; No. 97, November 1975; No. 98, December 1975; No. 190, November 1977; No. 191, December 1977; Nos 351 and 353, October 1980; Nos 491 and 498, February 1983; No. 618, November 1984; No. 625, December 1984; Nos 842 and 847, July 1987; No. 1002, February 1990; No. 1020, March-April 1990; No. 1205, February 1993; No. 1209, March 1993.

There was an inevitable narrowing of the gap in 1951 (the index slipping back to 59); a further narrowing in 1955 (from 59 down to 51, when Labor's working class base was split); and an even clearer decline in 1966 (55 down to 46), when Vietnam again appears to have cost Labor working class support. The decline was also reflected in the odds ratio which fell from 15.6 (1951) to 10.9 (1966).

Under Whitlam as Labor leader the index again declined — first in 1969 (46 to 40) then in 1974 (41 to 31), as middle class voters shifted to Labor (1969) or working class voters shifted away (1974), or both. The shift in the odds ratio was even more dramatic: down by nearly half in 1969 (10.9 to 5.9) and down by nearly one-third again in 1974 (6.5 to 3.8). However, Whitlam's decision to stay on, after 1975, saw the pattern reversed. In 1977 the index rebounded (33 to 39) with the odds ratio, too, moving back to roughly where it was in 1969 (4.3 to 6.0).

It was under Hayden that the middle class came back, and under Hawke that its support surged to levels never previously recorded. This in turn is reflected in the index — down from 39 (1977) to 34 (1980), and then to 26 (1983). The corresponding odds ratios were 6.0, 4.9 and 3.6. In 1993 the fear of Hewson pushed middle class support for Labor even higher: the index dropped from 25 to 17, the odds ratio from 3.3 to 2.2. Had Labor simultaneously lost its semi-skilled and unskilled support, the index would have collapsed. But for the most part Labor's middle class gains over the last twenty years appear to have cost it little by way of working class support. From the re-election of Whitlam in 1974 to the 1993 re-election of the Keating government, the figures for semi-skilled and unskilled support were remarkably steady.

While the figures (for 1963, 1972 and 1993 in particular) generated by the two measures of 'class voting' do not always jell, no-one who has followed Australian politics in the post-war period would find this account altogether puzzling. Anyone, however, looking for some continuing process (like affluence) which has, in Burns' (1964: 6) words, 'bulldozed the class landscape', would be entirely nonplussed.

Political Issues

According to McAllister (1992a: 169), the most prolific and probably most influential of Australian political scientists writing on electoral behaviour today, 'social structure as a whole, not just "class", is declining in electoral importance...with much of the decline being accounted for by the increased importance of political issues in determining how people vote'. McAllister's influence, like Kemp's, owes much to his use of regression techniques, which those who heed him find impressive, but few others who read him understand. In arguing the decline of social structure, and the rise of issues or values as a determinant of the vote, McAllister's mistakes are (as we shall see) strikingly similar to Kemp's.

Social Structure Revisited
McAllister's evidence for the declining importance of social structure derives from the Aitkin surveys, conducted in 1967 and 1979, and the Australian Election Study in 1990. In each, respondents were asked a number of questions about their (or the 'head of household's') life histories, present position and current beliefs. What McAllister calls 'social structure' is fashioned from more than a dozen of these questions. They make a rather strange mix: age, gender, religion (plus church attendance), residence (urban/rural, state) and country of birth; 'occupational class', self-assigned class and trade union membership; and parents' voting behaviour (as reported by respondents). Plugged into the regression equation, 'social structure' is said to have explained 27.8 per cent of the variance in the vote (Labor versus the Coalition) in 1967, 22.2 per cent in 1979 and just 18.8 per cent in 1990 — a precisely measurable, steady decline.

There are, however, grounds for caution. Variables that almost no-one else would think of as social structural (respondents' views of themselves as 'middle class' or 'working class', for example) are included, while variables that anyone familiar with class theory might have wanted to add — variables related to what Weberians call the respondents' market situation (property ownership, income, superannuation, occupational mobility, job security, unemployment experience), work situation (size of enterprise, degree of autonomy, interaction with management) or status situation (most obviously, education) — are not.

Something rather arbitrary seems to be afoot. Indeed, McAllister's view of social structure is in a constant state of flux. Elsewhere, for example, he not only treats subjective class as an attitudinal rather than social structural variable, he treats church attendance this way too. And their inclusion matters: in 1967 they produced 'a sharp rise in the proportion of the variance explained' (McAllister 1992b: 69–71). Education, which McAllister (1990: 168, 173) tells us 'exerted a substantial impact on voting' in the 1990 election is included as a social structural variable in one of his pieces on that election, but dropped from this one. Car and telephone ownership, integral to social class in his analysis of 'class voting' in the late 1940s, mid-1960s and again (for cars) in the early 1980s (Jones and McAllister 1989: 10), in subsequent writings disappear.

Anyone who wants to argue the declining impact of social structure (however defined) must at least have a consistent view of the beast. McAllister does not. As he admits elsewhere, some of the variables (religious affiliation, trade union membership) 'differ in form and context between the surveys making comparisons difficult' (McAllister 1992b: 67–68). Not only do the surveys not specify the variables in the same way, they do not incorporate the same set of variables. Some variables (self-employment, government employment), included in 1979, were not part of the 1967 mix; some (country of birth, urban/rural residence), used in 1979, were omitted in 1990. Other things being equal, this would have produced an underestimate of the decline between 1967 and 1979, but an overestimate of the fall from 1979 to 1990. Indeed, given their contribution in 1979, it is likely that their inclusion in the regression equation in 1990 would have meant no decline, post-1979, showed up at all. Certainly, there is no evidence of a decline in the power of that sub-set of variables labelled 'occupational class' — formerly the division between those in manual and those in non-manual jobs (Jones and McAllister 1989), but now refined to take into account a respondent's employment sector (private/public), employment status (self-employed or not) and managerial status (supervisor or not).

Issue Voting
What, then, of the rise of issues to fill the gap left by 'class'? McAllister's evidence for the growing importance of issue voting derives from responses to a series of seven questions repeated in each of three surveys conducted in 1967, 1979 and 1987. The questions relate to: the power of trade unions and the power of big business; strikes; spending on social services; Asian immigration; capital punishment; and the Queen. These issues, net of the social structural variables, are said to explain 13.3 per cent of the variance in (recalled) vote in 1967, 24.7 per cent in 1979, and 19.0 per cent in 1987. Since both the 1979 and 1987 figures were higher than the 1967 figure there is 'at least suggestive evidence that political issues have become more important in determining electoral behaviour' (McAllister 1992b: 78–81). Elsewhere, arguing for the same conclusion on the basis of nine issues, McAllister (1990: 210–14) dispenses with the regression analysis altogether: the conclusion is plucked out of thin air.

The jump from a grab-bag of issues — including one issue, capital punishment, which has nothing to do with federal politics (let alone party politics) and which could not be taken in any rational sense to explain the vote — to a statement about the explanatory power of issues as such, is breathtaking. (Marks 1993 is even worse.)

The most obvious reason for the apparently low contribution made by issues to the 1967 result is that the main issues of the day were simply overlooked. How one could write about the politics of 1967 without mentioning Vietnam or conscription — though they were covered in the survey (Aitkin 1982: 362) which McAllister uses — beggars belief (cf. Goot and Tiffen 1983: 150–55). McAllister's analysis may tell us something about changes in the explanatory power of a particular set of issues; it says nothing — it cannot say anything — about the contribution of issues overall.

Does the analysis even tell us about the changing contribution of this particular set of issues? Unfortunately, it does not. While attitudes to issues might help shape votes, party preference itself can help shape attitudes to issues. The existence of a correlation tells us nothing about causes; indeed, both issue position and vote may be caused by some third factor. Here McAllister assumes that the causal arrow runs from issues to vote; like Kelley (1988: 70–74), he controls for every 'compounding variable' while overlooking party preference itself. Elsewhere he makes the reverse assumption, arguing that it is 'party identification' that 'provides a filter through which individuals evaluate and interpret the political world' including 'the political issues and attitudes that are the staple of day-to-day political debate' (Graetz and McAllister 1988: 267–68; similarly, Western *et al.* 1991: 321). Forced to choose, most students of electoral behaviour would favour the latter over the former. But there are other possibilities, including interaction effects.

There is an exact parallel to McAllister's mistake about issues in Kemp's treatment of values. In a postscript to his book, and elsewhere, Kemp argues that in place of class location, party preference is better explained by reference to voters' 'cultural location'. This is another recycling from the 1960s and the dispirited Left. It comes not from Crisp, a key source of ideas on embourgeoisement, or from Rawson, on how Labor was responsible for creating a rigid party system based on class, but from Davies, looking forward to the day when the politics of ideas would prevail over the politics of interest. And the evidence Kemp offers for the power of 'cultural location'? A positive correlation between a set of items covering various values, norms and beliefs — 'constructed', he is keen to emphasise, 'without reference to "current leaders" or "current policies" — and party preference or vote (Kemp 1978: 365, 1977: 11). Just as Kemp assumes that the dealignment of occupation and vote tells us about changes among the voters, but not about changes in the parties, so he assumes that the connection between values and votes is a one-way street in which voters (whose values are formed who knows how) seek out the nearest party. The assumed passivity of the parties — a fundamental weakness of 'economic' models of party competition (Downs 1957 is the classic), where parties are treated like firms and voters like consumers whose values are fixed — is nicely illustrated by Kemp's continuing advice to parties about how they should position themselves in the political marketplace. In the late 1980s, Kemp was still warning Labor about the damage they could be doing to 'public support for government authority' by favouring the unions, when surveys showed that the union movement was 'more broadly distrusted than any other significant institution in Australia' (Kemp 1988: 275–76, 426; also Aitkin 1985b: 216).

The connection between support for Labor and attitudes to the unions is worth a closer look. On the basis of survey items which report widespread suspicion of union power and opposition, even among trade unionists, to union affiliation with the ALP (cf. Aitkin 1982: 141–42), Kemp (1977: 5) recommended that Labor break its ties. There was nothing particularly novel about the advice; whenever Labor has been out of office even friends of the party have discussed such moves (cf. Rawson 1961: 30). More interesting was Kemp's failure to see how the root of the problem (from union bashing by governments and the media, to the real hardships caused by industrial strife) might lie in the class situation of unions, or to contemplate the conditions under which the movement's links with Labor might actually work to the party's advantage.

Far from breaking its links with the unions, Labor — led to its 1983 victory by the immediate past president of the ACTU — very publicly strengthened them. Never before had the movement exercised so much power over such a wide area of government activity. Yet the proportion of the electorate concerned about the unions having 'too much power' has not increased during Labor's period in office; on the contrary, after what may have been an initial jump in the polls, the proportion has steadily diminished (*Age*, 23 June 1980, Kelley *et al*. 1984, *Australian*, 10 September 1986, McAllister and Mughan 1987b, 1990, Jones *et al*. 1993). With its sense of partnership between Labor and the unions, and its record of minimising industrial strife, the Accord seems to have taken the heat out of the trade union issue (McAllister and Ascui 1988: 233). Labor continues to be regarded by voters as the best party to handle industrial relations (cf. *Age*, 29 October 1979, *Sydney Morning Herald*, 14 June 1982, Goot 1990: 125, Jones *et al*. 1993).

In arguing for the way 'cultural location' had replaced 'class location' as the touchstone of electoral life, Kemp isolated two 'value dimensions' of particular relevance to the vote. One he described as running from 'acceptance of authority' to 'identification with the underprivileged'; the other ran from 'individualistic isolation' at one end to 'egalitarianism' at the other (Kemp 1978: 365). Classless? Hardly. Both represent classic class issues concerning justice and fairness, freedom and authority. Kemp could hardly have offered clearer proof that despite changes in the occupational structure of the vote, there remained a class structuring in the field of political opinions.

Similarly with McAllister. Many of the issues he chooses to highlight — trade union power, the power of big business, attitudes to strikes — far from being divorced from considerations of class, are intimately connected with them. To say 'there has been a decline in the electoral importance of class' (McAllister 1992b: 81), while arguing that it is issues such as these which are influencing the vote; or to say that 'Australia is an issue-oriented electorate rather than a class-orientated electorate' (Graetz and McAllister 1988: 258), while insisting that the most important aspect of political belief systems 'both overall and in party political terms' concerns 'economic power', is to try to make omelettes without scrambling eggs. One might as well inspect the House of Representatives and the Senate and then ask to be shown the Parliament. This sort of error has a name; it is a 'category-mistake' (Ryle 1949: Chapter 1).

The logic of McAllister's method — a method which, it is important to stress, is not his alone — produces a remarkable paradox: the more that voting is affected by class issues, the less it can be said to be class-related! This is because (in McAllister's lexicon) class politics is synonymous with occupation-based voting; and voting which can be shown to be informed by issues (including class issues) no longer shows up in the regression equation as occupation-based. Indeed, where the regression leaves some connection between occupation and vote, it is always possible that a different set of questions would have whittled it away further. The collapse of class politics is not something to be observed in the world; it is immanent in the method.

If, as McAllister, Kemp and Aitkin argue, occupation-based voting is one thing, and image-based, personality-based or issue-based voting another, then a vote that can (only) be explained in terms of occupation cannot be said to have been rationally cast. Such votes have to be explained in different terms — as acts of habit, as expressions of a political inheritance ('political socialisation' is a term which abounds in these writings), or as a manifestation of 'traditional class loyalties'. This, as McAllister (1992: 78) points out, is not at all like the evaluation of party policies 'according to their social and economic utility'.

The distinction between voting by 'class' and voting by (among other things) issues is captured in the title of McAllister's co-authored book, *Voters Begin to Choose*, subtitled: 'From closed-class to open elections in Britain'. Its argument is that British politics has seen a decline in the extent to which 'social groups determine voting' and a corresponding rise in the number of electors who 'can make a fresh choice at each general election'. No longer can parties 'count on voters being delivered by childhood indoctrination'. Instead, they 'must compete by offering distinctive policies to electors' (Rose and McAllister 1986: 11,13,15).

Not that one has to look overseas for arguments of this sort. 'For many Australians of 1910,' Aitkin (1982: 312) argues, 'a partisan choice hardly presented itself.' As members of 'a kind of tribe (denominational, ethnic, regional, occupational) they chose as the tribe chose. Such tribes are still present, but much reduced in number and importance.' Only in the absence of a 'tribe' is 'some more-or-less conscious choice...forced upon us'.

One small difficulty for these (patronising) accounts of the past — when social structure is said to have explained so much and political issues so little — is the absence of evidence. This is not altogether surprising, since it is difficult to see how theories which assume an entity (group or tribe) which both leads and follows could explain electoral change — or, more to the point, what electoral change there could be to explain.

Electoral Volatility

Given the declining correlation between party and social structure and the ostensible rise of issue voting, should we not expect to find electors increasingly willing to switch their votes, supporting new parties and Independents, even threatening the party system itself? For Rose and McAllister (1986: 11–13), 'open elections' mean just that: 'multiple rather than minimal' parties and voters uncertain about their choices, lacking strong commitments, 'weightless' and likely to float.

Claims

A number of observers have detected such trends. The period 1966 to 1985, is characterised by Jaensch (1989: 81–85), for example, as one in which relative 'electoral stability was replaced by unprecedented swings in patterns of party support'. The 'de-classing' of the party system (for which he sees Kemp's evidence as 'overwhelming') is supported, he says, by the 'concrete evidence of volatility'. The 'marked instability in patterns of electoral support' is part of a process 'where not only is class de-politicised' but the whole electoral party system becomes de-aligned' and replaced by 'issue politics'. For Papadakis (1993: 174–76), too, electoral trends suggest a 'dealignment...may be taking place'. Citing McAllister, he argues that 'class voting' has declined since 1967, the year Whitlam became Labor leader; that voting 'has become more heavily influenced...by the mobilisation of the population around conflicts over issues or sets of issues'; and that, as a result, 'the stability of the party system may be more apparent than real'.

Neither Jaensch nor Papadakis, however, provides much in the way of evidence. Jaensch is impressed by changes of government (1972, 1975, 1983) and 'a series of unprecedented', though undocumented, 'turnovers in seats' — evidence which ignores the fact that governments can change, as can seats, without an unusually large turnover in votes. Jaensch is also impressed by the rise of the Australian Democrats. But once he concedes that their support has never exceeded the level once enjoyed by the DLP, his point about the unprecedented nature of the phenomenon is already lost.

In arguing that the 'impression of stability may be misleading' Papadakis refers to evidence of a decline between 1967 and 1990 in the strength of 'party identification' (the idea that what anchors party support is electors' sense of themselves as Liberal, Labor, etc); increased vote switching (from election to election), and 'tactical voting' (voting one way in the House of Representatives, another in the Senate); and the way voting patterns reflect 'institutional constraints' (the electoral system) rather than 'enduring commitment' (the electorate's actual beliefs).

The decline in the strength of party identification to which Papadakis refers took place not between 1967 and 1990 but between 1979 and 1987; between 1967 and 1979 there was no change at all. Part of the explanation for the decline — the proportion in the surveys feeling 'very strongly' Liberal, Labor or whatever falling from 31 per cent to 19 per cent (recomputed from McAllister 1992a: 40) — may be methodological, having to do with differences (face-to-face, 1967–79, and mail thereafter) in how the surveys were conducted (cf. Esaiasson and Granberg 1993), their proximity to an election (cf. Miller *et al.* 1990: 4–5), and the questions asked. But in any event, increased preparedness to switch (if that is what weaker party identification means) is not in itself evidence of increased switching; in 1990, when the minor party vote jumped from 8.3 to 17.4 per cent, the strength of party identification remained unchanged.

The more direct evidence on vote switching to which Papadakis appeals is based on respondents' recall: 'Since you have been voting in federal elections, have you always voted for the same party or have you voted for different parties?'. The proportion saying they had voted for the same party was 65 per cent in 1967, and 52 per cent in 1979. A 'gradual change'? Not necessarily: most of it might have occurred in, say, 1969 or 1972 or 1975. And far from the vote becoming increasingly unstable, in the second half of the 1980s the instability was reversed. Life-time voting, as respondents reported it, was about as stable in 1990 as it had been in 1967 (McAllister and Bean 1990: 178).

Like most students of electoral behaviour, McAllister acknowledges the folly of asking respondents whether they changed their vote at the 'last election' (McAllister and Mughan 1987: 75–78); as the AES surveys confirm, questions of this kind (which conflate research questions with interview questions) produce a skewed result (cf. McAllister *et al.* 1987, 1990, Jones *et al.* 1993, and Table 7.4 below). An obvious inference is that asking respondents whether they have 'always voted for the same party' — especially when the question fails to distinguish between voting for the House and voting for the Senate — is even more likely to run up against the problem of selective recall. Similarly, to ask respondents about the party they first voted for — crucial to McAllister's (1992a: 158–61, Jones and McAllister 1989) and Aitkin's (1982: Chapter 6) attempts to reconstruct political profiles for particular eras — is likely also to produce a distorted result.

Has 'tactical voting' increased? The principal problem for Papadakis' argument is that the choice of candidates on the Senate ballot is almost always wider than the choice in the House. The main reason why, for example, the Nuclear Disarmament Party in 1984 won 0.2 per cent of the national vote in the House, while in the Senate it captured over 7 per cent, was that in the House it contested just 6 of 148 electorates, while in the Senate it stood candidates in every state. The dealignment in patterns of voting for House and Senate, which reached a post-war high in 1984, is largely explicable in terms of this structuring of opportunity. In 1990 and 1993 the dealignment was no greater that it had been in 1951 (Table 7.3).

Papadakis' real interest lies not in 'tactical voting' but in the idea that the Senate more truly mirrors the electorate's mind. In the House, single-member constituencies, even with preferential voting, may well discourage electors from voting for minor parties — they certainly discourage minor parties from nominating. Multi-member constituencies, especially with quota preferential or proportional voting, may well encourage a minor party vote. But even if the electoral system were the same, voters would not necessarily see the two chambers in the same light. Of those who choose to vote for a minor party in the Senate, but not in the House, a sizeable proportion may do so to keep 'the bastards honest', provide checks and balances, or allow minority voices to be heard (Chaples 1993: 324–27). To see the Senate as more truly the representative of the people's will begs a crucial question.

Volatility Measured
One way of thinking about volatility is in terms of the sum of the

TABLE 7.3 *Senate Voting at Elections held in conjunction with Elections to the House of Representatives, 1949–93*

Year	ALP	LC(N)P[a]	DLP/AD[b]	Other	Net inter-house difference[c]
1949	44.9	50.4	–	4.7	1.1
1951	45.9	49.7	–	4.4	2.3
1955	40.6	48.0	6.1	5.2	4.0
1958	42.8	44.1	8.4	4.8	3.3
1961	44.7	41.4	9.8	4.0	3.9
1974	47.3	42.6	3.6	6.6	4.4
1977	36.8	45.6	11.1	6.6	5.5
1980	42.3	43.3	9.3	4.9	5.9
1983	45.5	40.0	9.6	4.0	7.6
1984	42.2	39.5	7.6	10.7	11.9
1987	42.8	41.8	8.5	6.9	7.1
1990	38.4	41.9	12.6	7.0	2.3
1993	43.5	43.0	5.3	8.1	2.3

[a]LC(N)P includes parties in some states bearing variant names
[b]DLP (1955–74), AD (1977–93)
[c]Calculated by summing the differences in party support in House and Senate elections and dividing by two
Source: Macintyre 1991: 7–13, 18–24, Australian Electoral Commission, for 1993

movements from one party to another, during inter-election periods or from one election to the next. The only way of measuring this *gross* volatility, is through panel studies, where the same respondents are interviewed and re-interviewed at various points in the electoral cycle, or just before (or after) each of two (or more) consecutive elections.

In Australia such studies scarcely exist. Panel studies there are, but none covers changes in the inter-election period, and all rely on recalled vote. One study, relying on respondents' recall of their 1966 vote (in 1967), and of their 1969 vote (after the 1969 election), suggested that 24 per cent of the panel might have switched (Aitkin 1985: 82–83). A more recent study, based on interviews after the 1984 election and re-interviews after the 1987 election, claimed that 13 per cent of those with a party identification (and that was almost all the sample) changed their vote (Bean and Kelley 1988: 85). These figures, for what they are worth, certainly do not suggest that volatility has increased; volatility was twice as great in the earlier period, notwithstanding that the proportion of strong party identifiers was about half as great again (see McAllister 1992a: 40 for the data on party identification).

Another way of thinking about electoral volatility is in terms of the changing share of the vote going to each of the main parties, minor parties and Independents at consecutive elections. *Net* volatility, as it is usually called, can be measured (following Pedersen 1979) by adding up all the party gains, from one election to the next, and all the party losses — and dividing by two, since losses on one side of the ledger always show up on the other side as gains. This measure is inferior to the measure of gross change because it masks the movements to and fro that balance out. In addition, votes for very small parties and Independents are usually aggregated, thus adding to the masking effect. Nevertheless, as Aitkin (1985: 79–80) observes, with 'a large enough set of elections...we would expect the same trends', in net and gross terms, 'to appear'.

The most striking conclusion to be drawn from the figures for net change in House of Representatives elections from 1910 to 1993 (Table 7.4), is that volatility was much greater when voting was more closely related to social location or 'class' than it has been since 'class voting' began to decline. The high points are 1910, the election from which the modern party system is usually said to date; 1931, when a Labor group organised around Jack Lang took on the federal ALP; 1937, after the Lang push had been largely defeated; 1943, when the United Australia Party vote collapsed and support for minor parties reached a level not seen before (or since); and 1946, after the newly created Liberal Party reorientated non-Labor politics. The impact of each of these changes dwarfs the upheaval wrought by the split in the mid-1950s, changes of government in the 1970s and 80s, and even the emergence of the Democrats.

TABLE 7.4 *House of Representatives Vote, 1910–93*

Year	ALP	Main Non-Labor[a]	C(N)P	Minor[b]	Other	Net volatility[c]
1910	50.0	45.1	–	–	4.9	20.3
1913	48.5	48.9	–	–	2.6	3.8
1914	50.9	47.2	–	–	1.9	2.4
1917	43.9	54.2	–	–	1.9	6.5
1919	42.5	45.1	9.3	–	3.2	10.6
1922	42.3	35.2	12.6	–	9.9	10.1
1925	45.0	42.5	10.7	–	1.8	10.0
1928	44.6	39.1	10.5	–	5.8	4.0
1929	48.8	33.9	10.3	–	7.0	5.4
1931	27.1	36.1	12.3	10.6	14.0	21.8
1934	26.8	33.0	12.6	14.4	13.2	4.2
1937	43.2	33.7	15.6	–	7.6	20.1
1940	40.2	30.2	13.7	2.6	13.3	8.4
1943	49.9	16.1	12.5	0.7	20.8	17.2
1946	49.7	33.0	10.7	1.6	5.0	17.8
1949	46.0	39.4	10.9	0.7	3.1	6.6
1951	47.6	40.6	9.7	–	2.0	2.9
1954	50.0	38.6	8.5	–	2.9	3.3
1955	44.6	39.7	7.9	5.2	2.6	6.3
1958	42.8	37.2	9.3	9.4	1.2	5.7
1961	47.9	33.6	8.5	8.7	1.3	5.2
1963	45.5	37.1	8.9	7.4	1.1	3.9
1966	40.0	40.1	9.8	7.3	2.7	5.6
1969	47.0	34.8	8.6	6.0	3.6	7.9
1972	49.6	32.0	9.4	5.3	3.7	3.5
1974	49.3	35.0	10.0	1.4	4.4	4.3
1975	42.8	41.8	11.3	1.3	2.8	8.2
1977	39.7	38.1	10.0	9.4	2.8	9.7
1980	45.2	37.4	9.0	6.6	1.9	6.6
1983	49.5	34.4	9.2	5.0	1.9	4.6
1984	47.6	34.4	10.6	5.5	2.0	2.0
1987	45.8	34.3	11.5	6.0	2.3	1.8
1990	39.4	34.8	8.4	11.3	6.1	9.6
1993	44.9	36.8	7.2	3.8	7.4	8.8

Note: Votes may add to 99.9 or 100.1 due to rounding
[a]Liberal (1910–14), Nationalist (1917–29), UAP (1931–1943), Liberal (1946–93)
[b]Lang Labor (1931–49), DLP (1955–75), AD (1977–93)
[c]Calculated by summing the differences between consecutive elections, column by column, and dividing by two
Source: Macintyre 1991: 2–13, Australian Electoral Commission 1993

If we divide electoral history, post-1910, into four more or less equal parts, both the average change (mean) and the range (standard deviation) appear to have been greatest in the period 1926–46, and smallest through the post-war years of Liberal-Country Party rule (Table 7.5). As Aitkin (1985: 81) suggests, though his own figures barely show it, net volatility increased in the 1960s (a mean of 5.7 compared with 4.6 for the 1950s), and increased again in the 1970s (a mean of 6.4). The 1980s, however, saw a sharp decline, to 3.4. That changes over the last twenty years have ranged more widely (from 1.8 to 9.7 percentage points) than in the immediate post-war years, testifies less to any decline in the strength of party identification than to the very varied strengths of recent political winds.

Although Aitkin acknowledges that volatility was 'less pronounced' in the post-war period than before it, he vastly underestimates just how pronounced this difference was. This is partly because of some rather baffling errors in his measurement. In larger part, however, it reflects his broader view about the Australian party system's 'massive stability' — and not just in net but in gross terms. This was attributable to 'widespread, stable, partisan loyalty'; his belief that 'the penetration of party politics into the outlook of the electorate...already substantial by 1910...reached a point of stability in the 1940s'; and the idea that movements in electoral support since the 1920s have been 'tiny' (Aitkin 1982: 7, 12–14).

To maintain this view requires some remarkable glossing of electoral change. 'Tiny' is hardly the adjective that most would apply to the net shift (let alone the probable gross shift) in many of the elections since the 1920s. Nor is it easy to think of the 1940s as a high point of stability when the UAP dropped to a mere 16 per cent (1943) and their successors, the Liberals, soared to 39 (1949).

Aitkin denies — his commitment to the idea that party identification anchors the system forces him to deny — that Australia has experienced a succession of non-Labor parties (Liberal, National, UAP, Liberal) each with its own philosophy, personnel, relations with supporting interests, and so on. Instead, a single party, the Liberal Party has 'undergone

TABLE 7.5 *Net Volatility, House of Representatives Elections, 1910–93*

Years	Number of elections	Mean	s
1910–28	8	8.5	5.39
1929–46	7	13.6	6.79
1949–69	9	5.3	1.54
1972–93	10	5.8	2.89

Note: s = Standard deviation
Source: As for Table 7.4

three changes of name' (Aitkin 1982: 3; similarly, Rawson 1961: 3-4). The inter-war years, as Rydon (1979: 51) has observed, were marked by 'splits, divisions and realignments on all sides'. Again, however, Aitkin's position obliges him to see things differently. He lumps together the large vote secured by Lang Labor during the Depression with the vote won by Lang's bitter rivals, Federal Labor; the schism itself passes without mention. At the 1940 election, Communist, Labor and State Labor (New South Wales) are all treated as 'Labor' (Aitkin 1982: 4, 1985: 77). Nor is this sort of thing restricted to the inter-war years. Calculating net volatility in 1910, Aitkin compares Labor's 1910 vote, not with Labor's 1906 vote, but with Labor plus the Protectionist vote; instead of a net volatility figure of about 20, he comes up with a figure of 7.6. Similarly, in 1943, the UAP's collapse is partly masked by his adding to its tally of votes the support won by various other non-Labor groups. Such moves bolster the appearance of stability by making nonsense of the concept of party identification.

Like the more fashionable arguments which stress current levels of change, uncertainty and disaffection, Aitkin's arguments for continuity are undermined by a failure to come to terms with history.

Conclusion

That the statistical association between occupation and the vote is much less substantial now than it was fifty or even thirty years ago cannot be denied. But that is far from saying that occupational status, in the 1970s, was 'almost...useless' in predicting votes (Kemp 1988: 4), or that, in the 1980s, it threatened to become so because support for Labor among first-time voters was as high within 'white collar' ranks as it was among 'blue collar' (McAllister 1992a: 161). If one looks at those occupational groupings, recognised in the polls, whose class character is most marked — managers, executives, people in the professions compared with semi-and unskilled urban workers — there are clearly distinct voting patterns. Even on the standard, though much more problematic, distinction between manual and non-manual jobs there is a clear difference in voting patterns, one which has shown little sign of fading in the last twenty years.

The fact that these occupational groups are not 'at loggerheads' does not, as Aitkin (1985: 213) thinks, call into question 'the meaning of the "classes" themselves'. The difference between a state of class demobilisation and the end of class itself is not, contrary to Kemp (1979: 170), 'one of semantics'. To say that electoral politics has a class structure does not mean that the country is in a continuous state of class war. Open, large-scale, conscious class polarisation — a sign of crisis in class relations — is historically rare. Aitkin and Kemp practically require a state of crisis before they will admit to class forces being significant in mass politics at all.

Even in a condition of class demobilisation like the present, there remains a strong connection between occupational composition and party preference at the electorate level — most visibly of course in the parties' 'heartlands' (Jupp 1982: 100–2, Scott 1991: 55, 61). According to Kemp (1977: 4), this evidence of political geography will be transformed when the statistical association between occupation (manual/non-manual) and vote completely disappears. Aitkin (1982: 301–2), too, dismisses such evidence as an ecological fallacy — the mistake of inferring individual behaviour from the study of aggregates. But these views are themselves methodologically mistaken. In Britain, where there has been a clear relationship at the constituency level between the size of the Labour vote and the proportion of the electorate who are employers and managers, 1966 survey data indicate that the partisanship of individuals was informed more by where they lived than what they did (Miller 1977: 65).

That the decline in the relationship between occupation and vote has not been a smooth one, and that it needs to be understood in political terms rather than just sociological ones, may have taken many political scientists of the previous generation by surprise, much as it defies the prevailing wisdom of the present. In one of the best pieces written on Australian electoral behaviour — specifically, on changes in the voting behaviour of Catholics — Spann (1961: 123, 135) cast considerable doubt on the view that the 'decrease in the "Catholic" Labor vote' was 'due to more Catholics becoming middle class'. Instead, he argued, the rise of the DLP was 'clearly connected with the decay of Labor as a "Movement" and with the general weakening of solidarity inside the party'. True, the attraction of the DLP to some Catholics may have been explicable in social status terms. But what needed to be stressed, he argued, was the Party's attraction to those who saw in it the embodiment of traditions for which the ALP had once stood, and those who found in it 'new communal ties'. Needless to say, Spann's views — and, more importantly, the principles of political action which underpinned them — were largely ignored at the time and have not been widely appreciated since.

Whether issue voting has expanded as 'class voting' has declined must remain unclear. There is no reason, in principle, why occupation-based voting should be incompatible with voting on the basis of interests, issues or ideology. That this is so is acknowledged, in a back-handed way, by Aitkin (1982: 142, 1985: 14) who manages at various points to associate party identification with blind following of 'the tribe', the conscious pursuit of occupational (but not class) interests, and an attachment to party based on ideology. Even if it were true that much, even most, of the vote that correlates with occupation has a non-rational quality to it, the same may also be true of voting traditions *not* grounded in class.

As a platform from which to make historical comparisons, the data connecting issues to votes is much less plentiful, and of infinitely worse quality, than the data connecting occupation and vote. The importance now attached to issues owes nothing to long-term empirical evidence and everything to: the rise in Britain and the United States of models of voting behaviour which assume voter rationality; a bias in favour of certain data gathering techniques (forced-choice items and questionnaires distributed by mail) through which the unmediated voice of voters simply cannot be heard, and the ready availability of prestigious, computer-assisted, statistical routines (most notably, regression analysis) which tempt researchers to think in terms of a single dependent variable (the vote) and multiple independent variables (including 'issues'). It is surely no coincidence that the academic political scientist of electoral behaviour who sounds most like a student of the previous generation — 'airheads and drongos are the apoliticals of our society' (Chaples 1993: 326) — shows little interest in 'economic' theories of voting and does not go in for highly abstract forms of data analysis, but does have extensive experience in listening to what voters say and how they say it.

As for the relationship between 'class voting' and volatility, it is even more difficult to see that there is one. The high correlation between occupation and vote — and the strong attachment to party — said to have characterised Australian politics from the 1920s to the 1940s does not appear to have provided much of a bulwark against the considerable instability of the inter-war years. This bears out Connell's (1971: 84) view that 'party choice appears, in principle, far more mutable than the identification thesis would make it'. The relatively low correlation between occupation and vote, and the weakened attachment to party, characteristic of recent Australian elections, have yet to produce a movement of voters on anything like the scale witnessed in the days when class and party (as we are now told) were holding the system together.

8
Aborigines: Citizens and Colonial Subjects

TIM ROWSE*

Australia is a colonial nation-state. The continent and off-shore islands known as 'Australia' have been occupied for many thousands of years by people now known as 'Aborigines' and 'Islanders'. From 1788, the land mass was proclaimed a possession of the British crown and invaded by waves of immigrants. Some 228,709 Aboriginal and 28,624 Torres Strait Islanders were provisionally recorded in the 1991 Census, and together make up about 1.5 per cent of the 1991 total Australian population. They have been overwhelmed numerically, and in every other conceivable sense, by the immigrants and their descendants. The indigenous people of Australia, while sharing the status of 'citizen', remain as well the nation's colonial subjects.

Citizens and Colonial Subjects

Or do they? Is it possible to be both citizen and colonial subject? Opinions vary. On Australia Day 1992, the National Aboriginal Islander Legal Services Secretariat led an occupation of the old Parliament House in Canberra. Their leaflet proclaimed 'our right to self-government and self-determination in our lands and territories' (Leaflet, *Sydney Morning Herald*, 29 January 1992) — in short, a declaration of Aboriginal sovereignty. A similar perspective has been offered, since 16 July 1990, by the Aboriginal Provisional Government. The APG 'wants an Aboriginal State to be established, with all of the essential controls being vested back in Aboriginal communities', with 'oversee powers' for the APG itself. All Crown Land (and some other lands) would be conceded to the APG by Australian governments, and indigenous Australians would be able to choose whether or not they could live under the APG or 'under the jurisdiction of white Australia' (APG statements in author's possession).

The idea that indigenous Australians should be treated by the Commonwealth as if they were a 'nation' was first put forward in

---

*I would like to thank Jo Robertson for her archival assistance and the editors for their comments on earlier drafts. This chapter does not deal with events since 30 September 1993.

the Treaty proposal made by the National Aboriginal Conference (an elected advisory body) in 1979. 'Aboriginal sovereignty' has remained a controversial goal and strategy among Aboriginal and Islander people. Many Aborigines and Torres Strait Islanders value their hard-won Australian citizenship because they see it as conferring things more immediate and tangible — status, political potential and material benefits — which are mistakenly sacrificed by those with sovereignty as their objective and method. As the Director of the Cape York Land Council wrote in April 1993, 'Advocacy of the full-blown sovereignty agenda has led us [into] a condition of haplessness, where rhetorical flourishes at the next gathering of the faithful are the most that we can look forward to' (Pearson 1993: 16).

The case against basing indigenous political actions on an acceptance of 'citizenship' is that such status formally expresses the sovereignty of an Australian nation established by invasion and conquest. To accept Australian citizenship is inconsistent with proclaiming Aborigines' sovereignty over the continent. As well as this rather formal argument, an historical critique can be made, arguing that the options for redress which the Australian state provides to indigenous citizens don't work. 'With all domestic options exhausted', the press release of the 1992 Parliament House occupiers stated, 'a sovereign treaty is our only peaceful way to justice'(APG papers).

Since 1986, certain 'domestic options' appear to have been exhausted. That March, the Hawke government abandoned its proposed 'national land rights' legislation, unable to find agreement among indigenous spokespersons, and under severe pressure from the Western Australian government and the mining industry lobby. The Catholic Church's leading adviser on Aboriginal and Islander matters, Frank Brennan, has described this decision as 'the grossest breach of faith committed by any government towards Aboriginal people since white settlement' (Brennan 1991: 72). Certainly it was a major political defeat, for 'land rights' is by far the most important issue which indigenous Australians have raised in their search for social justice.

But is it strategically rational for Aboriginal people to conclude that 'all domestic options' are 'exhausted'? At least one observer, Colin Tatz, has long argued that indigenous people have not been in a position to expect much from the Australian political system (Tatz 1982a, 1982b). According to him, 'law and legal process are a more effective means of asserting and recovering rights than conventional politics' (Tatz 1982b: 207). His recommendation that indigenous Australians make use of legal process (and, by implication, that indigenous peoples accept empowerment as 'citizens' of Australia) has arguably been vindicated, in two ways. First, Tatz has long been confident that Aborigines could gain power by formally incorporating. In 1982, he wrote that 'the legal cocoon or umbrella of incorporation has now given Aborigines an organisational framework with which to meet other corporate men [sic], a vehicle of and for respect, an affiliation which can convey an outward sense of power, of security and continuity even if those attributes are lacking within'(1982b: 217). Recently, Mr Elliott Johnston QC, Royal Commissioner reviewing the issues underlying Aboriginal deaths in custody, agreed that such organisations (which now number some 2,000), had become a major means of indigenous empowerment; several of his recommendations (numbers 190, 191, 192, 193, 196 and 199, for example) were intended to further the autonomy of such corporations in their use of public subsidies (Johnston 1991).

Second, in June 1992, the High Court ruled on *Mabo* in such a way as to open up to indigenous people significant new avenues of legal redress against the colonial theft of their land. Ten years of legal research and argument culminated in a decision that Queensland's annexation of the islands of the Torres Strait in 1879 had not extinguished the Islanders' customary property rights in land. The 'common law' of Australia, while undoubtedly founded in the Crown's sovereignty over the entire continent, is henceforth to be understood to include protection of 'native' rights to land. The High Court ruled that such rights could be extinguished by Australian legislatures, but only if that were the stated intent of the legislators and as long as the statute did not contravene the Commonwealth's Racial Discrimination Act 1975. This decision, according to the High Court's Justice Brennan, upheld 'the equality of all Australian citizens before the law' (High Court of Australia 1992: 47).

But the value of such legal avenues of indigenous empowerment remains debatable. Elsewhere (Rowse 1992b, 1992c), I have shown that the Commonwealth government has been very cautious in its response to the Royal Commissioner's recommendations in favour of greater political autonomy for Aboriginal organisations. Seeking to guarantee that public money is expended according to Public Service principles of program accountability, the government has said that 'program management requires control. Control is contrary to self-determination' (quoted in Rowse 1992c: 171).

As for the *Mabo* decision, the High Court's concessions to indigenous land rights are also qualified. The APG's Michael Mansell commented that the High Court, while recognising 'native title', was still against (four judges out of seven) compensating the vast majority of indigenous people whose 'native title' has already been overridden. He estimated that 250,000 of Australia's estimated 300,000 indigenous people did not enjoy the continuity of occupation of land which qualified as 'native title' in the High Court judges' reasonings about indigenous land tenure. Their chances of successfully basing their own land claims on the *Mabo* decision were thus slim or nonexistent. He concluded that the decision offered comfort to some indigenous Australians, but denied justice to all (Mansell 1992).

While critics such as Mansell claim that Aborigines are not so much citizens as colonial subjects, a more common view asserts the opposite: that indigenous Australians are fooling themselves and everyone else if they see themselves as anything other than citizens. According to certain understandings of what a 'nation' is and what 'colonial' means, it is simply impossible — a confusion of categories — for Aborigines and Islanders to be both 'citizens' and colonial subjects of the same legal entity, the Australian state.

Culture and Nation

Two beliefs about the Australian nation and its history encourage such dismissals of the claims that Aborigines and Islanders remain a 'colonised' people. One is that the significance of being of Aboriginal or Islander descent must and should diminish, until it has no meaning or effects whatsoever on individuals or on policies of the state. This process, by which a majority culture absorbs and extinguishes a minority one, is commonly known as 'assimilation'. Belief in its inevitability and desirability inspired government policies in Australia, in different forms, from the 1930s until the 1970s. As official policy, 'assimilation' has fallen into disrepute under the weight of indigenous accusations of governments' 'cultural genocide'. 'Assimilation' remains a popular ideal for many Australians nonetheless, because it seems to guarantee that the nation will be culturally homogeneous.

Another belief about nationhood which denies the possibility that Aborigines and Islanders are both colonial subjects and citizens is the notion of multiculturalism. That is, it is possible to recognise the persistence of Aboriginal and Islander cultures, but to see them as only two additional ethnic identities. It is sometimes assumed that, because Australia is a 'multicultural' society, Aborigines and Islanders fit into it in much the same way as Vietnamese, Lebanese or Chinese do. Like many such people, many Aborigines and Islanders do not speak English as their first language; they also follow exotic, non-Christian religions; they eat foods other than those regarded as 'normal' by Anglo-Australians; they have difficulties finding employment; and they live in disadvantaged suburbs. The similarities of their conditions, as 'non-Anglo' Australians, are evidently confirmed by the fact that certain remedial measures in health, education and welfare, and labour market programs (e.g. interpreters, language training, the employment of public servants from the ethnic group targeted by the program) can be developed to correct or to compensate for the cultural handicaps they suffer through being 'different'. In short, Aborigines and Islanders are sometimes understood to be 'ethnic minorities' with remediable problems typical of all 'ethnic minorities'.

Multiculturalism is a powerful ideology of Australian nationhood because it accommodates so much cultural variation within Australia, whereas 'assimilation' wishes such variation away. But two considerations make it impossible to include indigenous people within the 'multicultural' conception of Australian society.

First, many Aborigines and Islanders vociferously reject the implication that they are 'ethnic groups'. They point out *and attach significance to* the undeniable historical fact that all 'ethnic minorities' migrated to Australia some time in the last 204 years. If Aborigines and Islanders can be seen as 'migrants' to this continent, their migration is ancient, not recent, so ancient that its details remain controversial among prehistorians: migration plays no part in their contemporary sense of cultural identity. For other ethnic groups (including the largest, those from Britain) a country of origin with its languages and customs beyond Australia is an essential symbol of ethnic identity. Aborigines and Islanders say they are 'indigenous' to the continent, not 'immigrant' to it: their identity, unlike those of other groups comes entirely from *this* land.

Second, the notion 'indigenous' now carries considerable force both in international and domestic law (Davies 1987). The Australian government is party to a number of international conventions which proclaim the rights of 'indigenous' people. The International Convention on the Elimination of All Forms of Racial Discrimination, for example, was ratified by Australia in 1975, its principles incorporated in the Racial Discrimination Act. In 1992, the High Court judges ruled that Section 10(1) of that Act protected indigenous property right ('native title') from processes of dispossesion by the Crown, other than those lawful exercises of the Crown's right in land to which all Australian property holders are subject.

Developments in other countries reinforce the distinct status of indigenous peoples. The possibility that Australia could have a 'treaty' with its own indigenous people is encouraged by the fact that New Zealand is bound by the Treaty of Waitangi to honour certain obligations to the Maori, and that Canadian Indians have had their rights to land embodied in revised constitutional arrangements. Such precedents in the domestic political life of these settler colonial nations is encouraging the United Nations Working Group on Indigenous Populations, established in 1982, to develop a Universal Declaration on Indigenous Rights. An Australian debate on whether to ratify such a Declaration (still in draft) would further focus attention on the distinct histories and rights of *indigenous* minorities.

The nature of these rights will remain controversial, as will the manner in which they could be embodied in the laws and policies of states. Nonetheless, such conventions clearly nominate a category of 'indigenous' citizens whose rights and welfare demand special consideration. Aborigines and Islanders have participated in international meetings to clarify 'indigenous rights' since 1980, putting pressure on

Australian governments to account for their policies to other nations and other indigenous peoples. Australia's dealings with such nations as South Africa and France on matters of human rights have been troubled by criticism that Australia's policies towards its indigenous people disqualify it as a critic of other nations.

If Australia's relations with its indigenous citizens are not to be understood within the frameworks of 'assimilation' or 'multiculturalism', what concept of 'nation-state' can we turn to? If we develop a theory of the *colonial* nation-state, are we also committing ourselves to the view that citizenship is no more than a sham status, a beguiling invitation which indigenous people must refuse? If they accept that they are citizens of the Australian nation, are they seizing political and legal instruments which are of any value to their ultimate cause — the restoration of significant portions of land to indigenous ownership and control? The rest of this chapter will pursue these issues by asking the following question: if Australia is a settler colonial society, are there limits to what the colonial state can do to meet the demands of indigenous people?

Theories of Australian Colonialism

Charles Rowley, a seminal critic of Aboriginal policies from the early 1960s, developed a multifaceted, historical account of the authority relations between Aboriginal and non-Aboriginal Australians. I will not try to do justice to that work here, apart from drawing attention to a significant remark in his final book *Recovery* (Rowley 1986), in which he emphasised that although the visibility of colonial relationships varies from region to region, *all* indigenous Australians remain subjects of a colonial order, not only those who live in remote regions. However:

> In the metropolis it is likely to be lost to the casual observer as the Aborigines once in central slums have moved out to better housing ... The further you go beyond the city boundary, the more obvious is the long-standing relation of town to fringe dwellers. In the final stages you go deep into areas marked by social relationships from the colonial past. (Rowley 1986: 14)

The contested authority of the police, as depicted in the recent Reports of the Royal Commission into Aboriginal Deaths in Custody, is a good illustration of Rowley's point that Australia's colonialism remains a pervasive structure of power. Both Commissioner Wootten and Commissioner Johnston saw the police as central to the processes of Australian colonialism. Wootten (1991: 275–76) argued that, as the invasion spread over the continent, 'issues that cried aloud for solution in a spirit of toleration and negotiation have been handed to police to resolve by the application of the force of law'. As in other settler colonial societies, the police were the front line agents of a dispossessing, invading society, having to confront and control the dispossessed. Police have probably been held responsible for more than could fairly be attributed to them, Johnston suggested (1991: v. 2, 206). However, that 'the police did not make the policies which they enforced would often not have been obvious, and in any event would have been irrelevant, for Aboriginal people who suffered under them'. Wootten commented that the corrupt 'police culture' noted in some recent inquiries is in part a legacy of the police having been the instrument of colonialism's brutal purposes.

Nowadays, the Aboriginal population remains demonstrably over-policed. In Chatswood, an affluent 'non-Aboriginal' Sydney suburb, the police/population ratio is 1 : 926; in 'Aboriginal' Redfern 1 : 353. In places where the Aboriginal population is larger, the ratio is strikingly different: for example, Bourke 1 : 142 and Wilcannia 1 : 77 (Wootten 1991: 301). Wootten (1991: 303) deplored the use of specialised 'para-military' police units against Aboriginal people, and ridiculed the interpretations placed on Aborigines' political assertiveness by 'police intelligence' (1991: 292–96).

Johnston drew attention to the cultural blindness of much policing practice. Many Aboriginal 'offences' are behaviours which are 'not so much unlawful but simply different to the proprieties observed, at least in public, by many non-Aboriginal people'(1991: v. 2, 196). He, too, discerned colonialism's continuities. 'The warfare for the control of the countryside has long since ceased, but in many towns in rural Australia another kind of warfare has continued for control and use of the open space in towns'(1991: v. 2, 206). The aspiration of the police to control the streets was actively destructive, he said, in that it worked 'against the very mechanisms for social control that continue to operate within Aboriginal societies'(1991: v. 2, 195).

Welfare Colonialism
Jeremy Beckett is an anthropologist who shares Rowley's respect for an historical understanding of the Aboriginal and Islander condition. Witness to more sophisticated techniques of government that most of those analysed by Rowley, his theoretical model of the colonial state seeks to understand an apparent liberalisation of political relations between indigenous and non-indigenous Australians. The following quotation indicates the terms in which Beckett sets up his basic definition of colonialism:

> A colonial order arises when the state has annexed a territory formally and *systematically discriminates* between the conquering invaders and the subject indigenes in such a way as to *entrench the dif-*

ferences between them and to foster their *economic, political and cultural inequality*. This discrimination is sustained by *some form of ideology* that justifies the domination of the indigenous population in terms of race, mentality, moral qualities, cultural advancement, religion, or historic destiny. (Beckett 1989: 120, emphasis added)

Three features of Beckett's model should be noted. First, he refers to the state's work as 'systematic discrimination', suggesting that the actions of the colonial state have a certain coherence; they are not haphazard. Second, the effects of the state's actions in perpetuating inequalities may be thought about under the headings 'economic', 'political' and 'cultural'. Third, while pointing to the importance of 'some form of ideology' to sustain what the state is doing, Beckett acknowledges that the substance of the ideology is quite open to variation across regions and countries, as well as through time. There is not one kind of 'colonial ideology'; history reveals that many have existed.

Beckett's recognition of the historical variations in colonial ideologies enables him to take into account an historical development of great importance — the colonial state's granting of citizenship to its colonial subjects. According to him, this step marks an epochal shift in the colonial state's logic, a shift to what he and others call 'welfare colonialism'. It is the state's strategy for managing the political problem posed by the presence of a 'depressed and disenfranchised indigenous population in an affluent and liberal democratic society'. Under welfare colonialism, he says:

Discrimination is systematically renounced and abandoned by the state (though some embarrassing residues of discrimination still may have to be dealt with). The inequalities sustained by colonialism are no longer ideologically defensible, but stand as a reproach to a renewed liberal and egalitarian ideology of the nation in which *all* citizens are equally entitled to the good life. (Beckett 1989: 123)

There is no particular date at which Aborigines and Islanders were 'granted citizenship'. In 1942, 'non-nomadic' Aborigines and Islanders were deemed eligible for social security benefits, on the same terms as other Australian citizens (Shaver 1987: 417–18). In 1948, the Nationality and Citizenship Act made it a legal fact that any person born in Australia was automatically a citizen of this country. However, certain categories of indigenous Australians continued to be denied some of the tangible benefits of citizenship for a generation after that. For example, only in 1960 were Aborigines and Islanders on Northern Territory missions and reserves entitled to the same social security benefits as other Australians, and unemployment benefits were withheld from many 'nomadic' Aborigines as late as 1974–75. Aborigines and Islanders could not vote in Commonwealth elections until 1962, and were not counted in the national Census until 1971. Some states were slower than the Commonwealth to grant the rights to vote and to drink alcohol. In Western Australia, Aborigines could not vote in local government elections until 1984!

The Australian state's transition from 'colonial' state to 'welfare colonial' state could therefore be argued to have taken place in the forty-two-year period from 1942 to 1984. It certainly did not happen as a particular, decisive event, although it is common to hear the 1967 referendum which gave the Commonwealth powers concurrent with the states, and put Aborigines into the national Census, recalled as the moment when 'citizenship' was granted.

Beckett describe the results of this transition to 'welfare colonialism' thus:

> At a practical level [the welfare colonial state] engages in economic expenditure well in excess of what the minority [Aborigines and Islanders] produces. At the political level, it sets up machinery for the articulation and manipulation of minority opinion. At the ideological level, the 'native' who once stood in opposition to the 'settler' and outside the pale of society undergoes an apotheosis to emerge as its original citizen. (Beckett 1989: 123)

Beckett differentiates the modes and the effects of the state's actions into 'economic', 'political', 'ideological' or 'cultural'. Where the state once worked to produce inequalities along these dimensions, under welfare colonialism if there is 'discrimination', it is discrimination which favours, at least nominally, the indigenous people. How helpful is this view in understanding the actions of the Australian state towards Aborigines and Torres Strait Islanders since the 1960s?

Economic: Generosity, Justice and Dependency
Aborigines and Islanders have been the beneficiaries of many government programs conceived since the 1960s to improve their housing, health, standards of education and living. When the Commonwealth government initiated national programs for Aboriginal people in 1968–69, the budget allocated was $10 million. In 1992–93, the Commonwealth's outlays on Aboriginal and Torres Strait Islander programs totalled $1,316 million — in real terms more than twelve times the initial Commonwealth commitment.

Increasing access to public funds, however, is judged by some to be of mixed value to indigenous people. The growth in Commonwealth expenditure has coincided with worsening unemployment for Aboriginal and Islander people, leading to what some call 'dependency'. In the early 1980s, Fisk calculated one measure of the trend in 'dependency': the contribution of social security payments to Aborigines' and Islanders' total income grew from 46 to 53 per cent (Fisk 1985: Table 8.1). It is possible to see such dependence on public sector provision as the basis of continuing indigenous political weakness. Some with this view advocate policies, including land rights, which would give indigenous people an income-generating resource base, and so bring 'dependency' to an end. The Aboriginal Development Commission was established in 1980 to purchase assets for Aboriginal people. Its first Director, Charles Perkins, sketched his aims for the ADC (1982: 165):

> A sound economic basis will help us to cut the welfare umbilical cord that binds us. Increasingly, we must become active producers, instead of passive users, in the context of the Australian economy. We must develop sound economic and social infrastructures...in order to take control of our own destiny. Unless these imperatives are achieved, Aborigines will continue to be gripped by a counter-productive 'hand-out mentality' and destined to be a race of economic cripples and perpetual dependants.

Perkins now sees 'Aboriginal enterprise' as the main path of Aboriginal advancement.

Politics: Representation or Manipulation?
The formation and expression of Aborigines' opinions and demands has been assisted by the Commonwealth government since the 1970s. In 1973, the first Minister for Aboriginal Affairs, Gordon Bryant, not only established the Department of Aboriginal Affairs, but set up the National Aboriginal Advisory Committee (NACC), an elected body of Aborigines, clothed only in advisory powers. In 1977, after a critical independent review (Hiatt 1976), it was replaced by the National Aboriginal Conference (NAC). The NAC was dissolved by the Hawke government in 1985 and replaced by ATSIC (the Aboriginal and Torres Strait Islander Commission) in 1990. Unlike its troubled predecessors, ATSIC has been given genuine executive powers; it took over the programs and functions of the Department of Aboriginal Affairs and the Aboriginal Development Commission.

However, despite these state-sponsored political gains, the scope of ATSIC's powers and its independence remain limited. First, there is a crucial implicit limitation on what ATSIC can propose as Commonwealth policy. At no stage in the Hawke government's presentation of the ATSIC Bill (first outlined in December 1987) was there any suggestion that the government might revive the 'national land rights legislation' which it had abandoned in 1986. Although indigenous people were being empowered, through ATSIC, to decide the details of certain programs, they were not being encouraged to re-open the larger and more troubling issue of indigenous land entitlement. In the political debate following the High Court's *Mabo* decision, ATSIC leaders were at first careful not publicly to criticise the Keating government's contentious proposals to legislate recognition of native title. However, when the draft Bill was tabled at the end of August 1993, ATSIC leaders were so alarmed that they began to lobby Labor backbenchers and minor party Senators to amend the Bill. In this, ATSIC leaders showed unprecedented independence from Cabinet.

Second, ATSIC is but one of many players. Just under 49 cents out of every dollar spent by the Commonwealth on 'Aboriginal affairs' in 1992–93 was put through departments other than ATSIC. State and Territory departments are not obliged to spend their Aboriginal program money in accordance with the wishes of the elected Commissioners and Regional Councillors of ATSIC.

Third, ATSIC's elected representatives have no formal control over ATSIC staff; all are Commonwealth public servants accountable to their senior professional peers. Confirming this lack of executive power in 1992, the Commonwealth rejected the recommendation of the Royal Commission into Aboriginal Deaths in Custody that ATSIC become an employing authority in its own right. The government's response assured us that ATSIC could achieve such control by recruiting indigenous people as staff — and it would be better for such recruits, the government argued, if they were able to continue to pursue careers across the many departments managed by the Public Service Commission (Rowse 1992b).

Fourth, the government's recruitment of indigenous public servants and its induction of elected Commissioners and Regional Councillors has threatened to blur the boundary between public servant and indigenous representative. Regional Councillors have been invited to observe codes of secrecy on government business, codes similar to those binding public servants (Rowse 1992b). As for the seventeen elected Commissioners, they have reportedly been warned that the efficiency of programs under their control will be subject to the severest of scrutiny by such central organs of state as the Department of Finance. This is in keeping with Minister Gerry Hand's promise to Parliament when defending the Bill to establish ATSIC: 'There is no other department or statutory authority in existence in the Commonwealth which will be as accountable as ATSIC' (cited by Brennan 1991: 93).

Ideology
At what Beckett calls 'the ideological level', there has undoubtedly been a re-evaluation of what is meant by 'Aboriginality'. Governments have abandoned previous genealogical definitions of 'Aboriginality' which allowed indigenous peoples' entitlements to be judged according to their percentage of 'European blood'. People can now choose whether to identify as Aborigines (or as Islanders). Such official enlightenment has not, however, eliminated 'racial' notions from popular understandings. It is still common to hear the indigenous identity of

(usually outspoken) individuals questioned as biologically implausible. In this ideology, the colour of Michael Mansell's eyes becomes a political issue.

Beckett's 'apotheosis' of the once-despised native into the first Australian is nowhere better displayed than in the arts. In 1973, the newly-formed Australia Council, the government's arts patronage body, included an Aboriginal Arts Board. Since then, the activities of the Board and of galleries and other art industry institutions have given rise to an unprecedented recognition of the 'value' of Aboriginal arts and crafts, both visual and performing arts. Indeed the Australia Council's logo is an Aboriginal rock art image. Other instances of this revaluation can be cited: the increasing appearance of Aborigines in the mass media, including their contributions as practitioners of media arts, and the pressure on those celebrating Australia's bicentenary to acknowledge in some way the problem of indigenous peoples' relationships with such festivities. Sally Morgan's *My Place* achieved enormous sales and there has been a proliferation of fiction, autobiography and verse by other indigenous Australians (Davis 1990). Perhaps the Australian government's most powerful symbolic affirmation of 'Aboriginality' was the incorporation into the forecourt of the new Parliament House of a giant mosaic, designed by Michael Nelson Tjakamara of Papunya, based on traditional Western Desert ceremonial ground paintings.

But what is the underlying logic of the welfare colonial state? Has the Australian state shrugged off its colonial formation in order to preside over a genuine decolonisation of indigenous people? These are the questions to which Beckett leads us with his ironic, critical and ambivalent term 'welfare colonialism'. The same questions are raised by the rhetoric of the APG and by those who occupied the old Parliament House in 1992, saying that all domestic options have been exhausted.

There is another body of theoretical work which seeks to disclose an underlying colonial logic within the Australian state: the Marxist tradition. Here, the key term is 'exploitation'.

Colonialism as Exploitation
The term 'exploitation' refers to two colonial processes: dispossession of land and subordination of labour to the needs of capital.

Australian colonialism has undoubtedly sought to control natural resources, both terrestrial and marine. Non-indigenous people now control nearly all of them. The movement for 'land rights' (which includes rights to marine resources long used by coastal peoples) has nonetheless enjoyed certain successes since the 1970s. A large proportion of the Northern Territory has passed, or could soon pass, back into Aboriginal control. A substantial part of South Australia is also under Aboriginal control. Smaller pockets of land have been given back to indigenous ownership in New South Wales, Victoria and Queensland. In Western Australia, indigenous people have been given long leases to some land (for a concise overview see McRae *et al.* 1991: 147–60).

But the brief flowering of land rights legislation (from South Australia's Aboriginal Land Trust Act of 1966, through the Commonwealth's Aboriginal Land Rights (NT) Act of 1977, to Queensland's flawed Aboriginal Land Act of 1991) has done no more than set certain broad limits to non-indigenous control. Until the High Court's *Mabo* judgment pointed the way to further litigation by some indigenous people, it seemed that these statutes were as much restitution of stolen land as the Australian state was ever going to allow. And, as noted, even the *Mabo* judgment does not hold promise of restitution for all descendants of indigenous people.

Those Aboriginal people apparently advantaged by the Court's decision have already faced formidable political opposition. In August 1993, the Commonwealth and Queensland governments agreed to complementary legislation which would extinguish (with promise of financial compensation) the 'native title' of the Wik people of western Cape York. The Wik had aspired to negotiate a commercial arrangement with Conzinc Riotinto Australia (CRA), a company permitted by Crown grants since 1957 to mine bauxite on Wik land. CRA pressure on both governments had raised the spectre of 'investor insecurity', and the Queensland Premier declared new jobs (occasioned by related CRA investments) to have priority over indigenous rights to land. The supposition that 'native title' amounts to a threat to future employment was challenged repeatedly by Wik representatives insisting that they did not wish to see mining cease. That the 'native title or jobs' choice defined government thinking and much public perception was a triumph for years of mining industry publicity.

When Hawke abandoned his government's commitment to land rights legislation in 1986, he argued that there had been a 'backlash' against Aborigines. Research shows, however, that this is a self-serving reading of available poll research (Rowse 1988, Goot and Rowse 1991), providing Australia's political élite with a spurious popular mandate to capitulate to the mining lobby's repeated warnings that Aboriginal land rights 'locks up' exportable resources, to the nation's detriment. Our reading of the data for the 1980s traces a persistently large minority (35 to 45 per cent) of polled people in favour of indigenous land rights — a large enough minority to encourage politicians to build up a land rights mandate over several years. In July 1993, 51 per cent polled by Saulwick thought that those enjoying native title should have the right to veto mining on their land (*Age*, 4 August 1993).

The High Court judgment on *Mabo* created sufficient uncertainty in Australia's system of land tenure to stimulate the Keating government to promise legislation — securing non-Aboriginal tenure and recognising 'native title' in certain circumstances — in the second half of

1993. Prime Minister Keating's promised legislation had been outlined but not enacted at the time of writing. He and his Ministers have consistently discouraged Aboriginal expectations that holders of 'native title' would enjoy strong consent/veto rights when negotiating with commercial developers. Substantial powers to determine the use of land held under native title will remain in the hands of state governments, which are all firmly in favour of giving 'economic development' priority over indigenous rights, should the two come into conflict.

The logic of the colonial state's approach to indigenous land rights therefore seems all too clear: restrict the possibility of 'land rights' to a certain minority of indigenous people who can prove continuing associations with lands once set aside as 'reserves'; circumscribe the powers of such landowners so that state and territory governments who wish to encourage 'development' are not hindered by what mining industry leaders call 'black tape'; treat all claims that land is spiritual or cultural property as convertible to sums of money, so that 'native title' becomes an asset or commodity purchased by a colonial state keen to show that it is now non-discriminatory in its procedures of dispossession (compensation for extinguishing native title).

So much for natural resources. What about labour? Here the underlying logic of colonialism is much less clear. The high rates of unemployment among Aboriginal and Islander people (three times the national average, according to the 1991 Census) imply that the capitalist economy has found comparatively little use for indigenous labour. Indeed, governments, urged on by indigenous leaders and by such advocates of indigenous interests as the Royal Commission into Aboriginal Deaths in Custody, now pursue labour market programs which aim to increase Aborigines' and Islanders' access to paid employment. Aboriginal unemployment is understood to be a 'social problem' which governments must tackle. In the typical terms of this understanding, no reference need be made to indigenous people as 'colonised'; rather they are understood as disadvantaged in the labour market and therefore 'unemployed', deficient in income and self-esteem and bored.

If we think about these high rates of unemployment in the context of colonialism, however, the desirable political prescription is not quite so clear, for to employ indigenous people may be to make them economically dependent on wages and salaries. Some indigenous people, now totally dependent on welfare benefits, aspire to this change. Others, living on a mixture of welfare payments, artefact sales and hunting and gathering, should not be assumed to share that aspiration. For them to have to work for an employer would reduce their autonomy in the disposal of their time; it might also require them to move to an urban centre, away from kin and country. Especially in remoter parts of Australia, where indigenous people retain use of land

and sea as sources of food, it is possible for indigenous people to support themselves with a combination of hunting and gathering, welfare cheques and occasional sales of artefacts. The application of the terms 'employment' and 'unemployment' to Aboriginal and Torres Strait Islander people is therefore not straightforward (Smith 1991). Their way of life, while materially poor, may be regarded as one way of putting into practice the stated wish of governments to let indigenous people determine for themselves the degree and the manner of their incorporation into the wider Australian society.

The Community Development Employment Projects (CDEP) scheme has been popular with Aboriginal and Torres Strait Islander people at least partly because it creates a niche for some of its clients within the welfare economy and labour market: it provides a more culturally autonomous mode of employment (Altman and Sanders 1991, Rowse 1993). Empowering local Aboriginal political élites, such as incorporated councils who administer CDEP, the scheme may turn out to be the prototype of larger and more complex arrangements for the public sector's underwriting of indigenous self-government. Executive Director of the Kimberley Land Council, Peter Yu, reports that his organisation wishes to negotiate with the Commonwealth and state governments 'on issues relating to self-government and Regional Agreements'. As he explains, the issues to be negotiated include: 'funding mechanisms to Aboriginal organisations, control over government service delivery, local Aboriginal employment, equitable participation for Aboriginal people in the regional economy and decision-making in the regional planning process' (Yu 1993: 17). Yu's perspective denies that public sector funding necessarily compels 'welfare dependence'.

The colonisation of the indigenous people of Australia has been very uneven in its impacts. In some regions natural resources (which are also sacred property) have not been fully alienated from indigenous use and, throughout the continent, a relatively small proportion of the available pool of Aboriginal labour has been drawn into the workplaces of private enterprise, public bureaucracy and Aboriginal organisations. In parts of Australia where indigenous people have both land rights and welfare benefits, they are not materially dependent on the capitalist economy's ability to provide them with a job; materially poor, they remain rich in their freedom to dispose of their own time in a mixture of traditional and non-traditional pursuits.

There are, however, considerable obstacles to extending this option to a greater number of indigenous people. Not only would it require more land to be handed back; it would also require recognition that Australians are not uniform in their material and cultural needs, and that people who are not employed are not necessarily 'bludgers' or 'social problems'. The effect of such recognition would be that the measurement and comparison of Aborigines' and Islanders' welfare with the welfare of all other Australians would become more complex, grounded less in numbers and more in cultural understanding (Young 1988). Defending and extending the decolonising options of indigenous people is thus not only a political but a cultural problem for Australians used to thinking of the 'good life' in material and measurable terms, and valuing 'national unity' as something underpinned by a common 'way of life'.

It has been argued that some of these modes of indigenous survival are exploitative, and that the conservation of Aboriginal 'backwardness' is in fact an underlying policy of the colonial state. As expounded by Drakakis–Smith (1983), this theory begins by pointing to a certain tension between the dynamics of the capitalist economy and the purposes and methods of the state. On the one hand, the economy's dynamic tends to undermine Aboriginal and Islander traditions, to absorb indigenous people into the roles of wage and salary earners and consumers of introduced commodities, until little, if anything, remains of the older indigenous ways. In the assimilationist scenario it was expected that indigenous people would prosper; they would become educated in the ways of the introduced culture as quickly as they lost their own, and so become effective citizens, politically and industrially. But the colonial state is no longer avowedly 'assimilationist'. In the new cultural pluralism of the contemporary welfare colonial state, government policies seek to 'conserve' aspects of indigenous tradition. By affirming and guaranteeing the survival of indigenous ways (a policy which may seem a very liberal improvement upon 'assimilation') the state in fact underwrites the persisting subordination of indigenous people. Preserved in their traditions, they lack the skills to cope with the modern world.

Without necessarily endorsing such a theory of the state, the educationist Kevin Keeffe (1992: 4) has recently evoked an illustrative dilemma now facing Aboriginal parents:

> What some Aboriginal people are beginning to question is whether putting human energy and institutional resources into separate cultural maintenance, at the expense of access to the dominant culture, involves making a negative choice for the future of Aboriginal Australia. Aborigines are concerned about being caught between what seems to be a 'culture trap' and an 'assimilation trap'.

History, Theory and Strategic Realism

I began this chapter by insisting that we commit ourselves to the view that Australia is a colonial state, and that indigenous Australians are therefore pursuing an anti-colonial political struggle, albeit as citizens of the colonial state. I have highlighted the issues of the extent and nature of indigenous land title and of the political terms on which indigenous groups receive Australian governments' services and financial aid. Citing one strand of indigenous political analysis, I posed an issue both theoretical and practical: is the Australian political system so stacked against the indigenous interest that Aborigines and Torres Strait Islanders should renounce, as colonial status and as delusory empowerment, their citizenship, and seek their own 'nation' through the forums of international politics? Is there an underlying colonial logic in the structures and processes of the Australian state, a logic which defeats indigenous attempts to win back control over land and to secure public finance for structures of self-government?

After reviewing the available theories of Australia as a colonial state, I conclude that the 'logic' of the colonial state is elusive. If I can discern a 'logic' it is this: having granted Aboriginal and Islander people citizenship (1942 to 1984), and having begun to invent new forms of political representation for them, the colonial state systematically produces ambiguous opportunities. It is the contemporary 'logic' of the colonial state that it generates political dilemmas for indigenous people: it courts them while confining them; it raises the possibility of 'reconciliation' while labouring against enormous economic and political pressures in any measure to heal the outstanding indigenous grievances — land theft and welfare dependency. It allows its own federal structure to demote 'national' issues by devolving key decisions about land use to the states and territories; it muddies the lines of responsibility between government department and Aboriginal organisation. Finally, when the High Court postulates 'native title' as essential to Australia's common law, the government of the day is persuaded that meeting the challenge to investor confidence must shape official understandings of 'justice' and 'reconciliation'.

Beckett's phrase, 'solicitous rather than exploitive', is appropriate in its equivocation. He is not saying that exploitation has ceased, and he recognises that a variety of indigenous identities and interests might be precipitated by the state's diverse and complex acts of solicitation. Within the range of processes to which 'solicitation' refers, we should include 'political development', because the opportunities for political mobilisation afforded by the contemporary colonial state demand indigenous peoples' continuing, difficult reassessments of their options, chances and interests.

In Australian politics, some interests have been able to stabilise their agendas and to achieve some continuity of ideological self-definition by attaching their cause to a particular party or bloc of parties. The labour movement's relationship with the Labor Party is the classic example. But the indigenous interest has no secure political affiliation. The Labor Party has been little better than the parties of the Coalition in helping to advance the cause of land rights. A Labor government formulated a politically acceptable Land Rights Bill in 1975, out of

Justice Woodward's radical recommendations in the previous year. A Coalition government, after diluting Woodward's prescription a little further, saw the Bill through Parliament in 1976. A Liberal government in South Australia legislated the Pitjantjatjara Land Rights Act in 1981, the only legislation to come close to matching the provisions of the laws giving land rights to Northern Territory Aborigines. In 1983, the Wran Labor government enacted a land rights law in New South Wales, while also validating almost a century of piecemeal reductions of the indigenous land-base in that state — the closure of 'reserves'. A Labor government sought to reduce Northern Territory Aboriginal landowners' powers to refuse mining in the mid-1980s, in the interests of finding a politically acceptable formula for national land rights legislation; the same government then abandoned the quest for national land rights partly in response to pressure from the Labor government in Western Australia. When Queensland's Labor government passed an Aboriginal Lands Act 1991, the result was in one very important respect less favourable to indigenous interests than the (non-Labor) South Australian legislation of 1981: Mr Goss's Act contained no legislative recognition of the need to establish and to fund indigenous land councils. Brennan has commented on the continuities between Labor and National Party views of land rights in Queensland:

> The ALP has not been prepared to recast the balance of rights between Aboriginal landholders and miners. The concessions won by Aborigines from the Nationals for timber, quarry and mining rights were all that the new Labor government was prepared to implement. (Brennan 1992: 169)

This lack of significant differences between the parties can be called 'bi-partisanship'; it has no stronger advocate than the current Minister for Aboriginal Affairs, Robert Tickner. On the twenty-fifth anniversary of the 1967 referendum, Tickner recalled the bipartisan support in that year for voting 'yes'. He rejoiced that, almost a quarter of a century later, in 1991, both Houses of Parliament had supported unanimously his own Council for Aboriginal Reconciliation Act (Tickner 1992). Tickner's very reasonable strategy appeared to be to lock both sides of Australian politics into an open-ended discussion of the possibilities for 'reconciliation'.

The strengths and weaknesses of such strategy can be seen, however, in the enormous plasticity of this term. On the one hand, Aboriginal critics of Keating's first native title law proposal (2 September 1993) could insist that land rights were essential to the reconciliation process. On the other, reconciliation can be endorsed as a very conservative doctrine. Lawyer and businesswoman Eve Mahlab has recently explained that, to her:

reconciliation means acceptance of a situation by an aggrieved party ... The process of reconciliation has to take place within the Aboriginal people. The Prime Minister can talk with the Premiers and mining companies but until Aborigines themselves become reconciled to the situation, to the fact that they had their land taken away from them, I don't think anything is possible. (Mahlab 1993: 31).

I began this chapter by suggesting that if Aborigines and Islanders are colonised subjects as well as citizens, they face a strategic choice about which of these statuses to emphasise in the rhetoric, tactics and demands which characterise their political mobilisation. The Aboriginal Provisional Government has sometimes seemed extreme in its pessimism about even such apparent breakthroughs as the High Court's recognition of 'native title', and perversely Utopian in its alternative vision — Aborigines' national sovereignty. Persuaded of the futility of the APG quest, Frank Brennan (Brennan and Crawford 1990, Brennan 1991) has cautioned Aborigines and Islanders such as Mansell to be realistic:

Ambit claims to separate nation status will gain nothing, except good press and hostility from vested interests. They will form no part even in the process, let alone the outcome, of an instrument of reconciliation...Aboriginal claims to sovereignty would be more assured of success and on firmer moral ground if the emphasis were on greater autonomy for local communities within the Australian nation state, accompanied by reciprocal rights and duties by all seeking the common good. (Brennan 1991: 155)

Responding to Brennan, historian Peter Read advised indigenous leaders not to 'lower their horizons effectively to ground level' in the interests of political realism. He suggested that, should a 'reconciliation' agreement eventuate, its concessions to indigenous people would be greater if indigenous advocates delay until the very last minute the acceptance of compromises.

The difference of opinion between Brennan and Read illustrates one of the themes of this chapter: that it is difficult for any two observers to agree in discerning a logic to the dynamics of welfare colonial statecraft. Lawyer and priest, Brennan writes as if he has discerned a logic, expressed in certain likely limits to what bi-partisan political opinion could encompass by way of a charter of recognition. For historian Read, no such predictive confidence is possible. Radical questioning of Australia's sovereignty, Read (1992: 9) argues, is not unrealistic in a world of such dynamic political arrangements as produced the sudden decline of the Soviet Union and its Communist imperium:

It is possible ... that circumstances may become less sympathetic to indigenous peoples than they are already ... Yet the western world is in a crisis of self-doubt which has by no means touched bottom ... I would advise Aborigines, for purposes of practicality as well as moral justice, to hang on and fight every inch of the way to the parliament. The future is simply not clear enough to warrant the abandonment of long-held, not to mention morally justified, positions, for dubious practicalities.

Whether, and how, Aborigines and Torres Strait Islanders should explore the sovereignty option has become a more sophisticated discussion in which the polarities between indigenous perspectives are beginning to disappear. In April 1993, Cape York Land Council Director Noel Pearson publicly invited Michael Mansell to step back from his advocacy of 'full blown sovereignty' and to join other Aboriginal leaders in exploring the potential of a post-*Mabo* political climate: 'to take part in negotiations where the validity of Australian sovereignty is not negotiable, but where land rights, self-determination and self-government are' (Pearson 1993: 17). In August 1993, Mansell joined other Aboriginal leaders meeting at Eva Valley in the Northern Territory to co-ordinate an Australia-wide indigenous effort to get the best 'social justice package' from the Commonwealth.

At the same time, Dr H.C. Coombs (1993: 40) urged Australians not to dismiss the idea of negotiating about institutional forms of Australian sovereignty. He pointed out that 'sovereignty' was something which the Commonwealth was well accustomed to conceding by measured agreements — with the states, with its various territories (notably Norfolk Island), and with such international bodies as the International Court of Justice and agencies supervising international covenants to which Australia is signatory. Australia's sovereignty is thus already 'significantly divided, limited and has been varied in its history by decisions of the [High] Court, by constitutional change and by acts of the Crown and the Commonwealth, often after negotiations and agreements with other authorities'.

So why not with Aborigines and Torres Strait Islanders?

9
Immigration and Immigrants

ULDIS OZOLINS

The issue of immigration was until recently a sleeper in Australian politics. Since World War II, Australia has committed itself to a process of nation building through immigration: over four million migrants since then represent half the total population growth for the period. The children of these immigrants constitute a second generation of substantial proportions. Despite occasional skirmishes over administration and detail, for most of this period the immigration program has enjoyed bipartisan support. Few deny that the post-war immigration program was both well-founded and in Australia's interests. During the 1980s, however, this changed, and immigration and its associated policy of multiculturalism became the focus of heated public debates. At stake in such debates was not only traditional political conflict over the distribution of resources among the population, but more fundamental questions about who should constitute that population, and who has rights to the benefits of citizenship.

In his classic work on class and citizenship, T.H. Marshall (1950) distinguished three levels of citizenship: civil, political and social. Taking Britain as a model, he argued that *civil* citizenship, the result of the slow accretion of common law and the independence of the judiciary which guaranteed equal legal treatment, was largely won by the eighteenth century. *Political* citizenship, the broadening of the franchise to ensure political representation for all classes, was largely achieved by the end of the nineteenth. *Social* citizenship, equal rights to well-being through access to social benefits such as health, education and income security, had only been secured to any extent in the twentieth.

In looking at issues raised by migration for Australian society, we can extend Marshall's concept of social citizenship to include access to cultural goods, such as the right to speak one's own language and to follow one's particular cultural traditions, which are now widely regarded as contributing substantially to well-being.

In colonial Australia, the overwhelming portion of the population was of English, Scottish or Irish background. This Australia was hostile to non-white, particularly Asian immigration, leading to the White Australia Policy which had as its most explicit expression the Immigration Restriction Act 1901, with its notorious Dictation Test. Non-whites who remained in Australia could only gain citizenship through often difficult legal proceedings. In contrast to its resistance to Asian migrants, Australia was keen to recruit white migrants, overwhelmingly from Britain, but in small numbers from Europe as well. Where British migrants were able to vote after six months permanent residence, and were not required to take out citizenship, non-British migrants had to apply for citizenship through the courts to be able to vote. Non-British settlers were also expected to assimilate. From the beginning of the century European migrants came under suspicion if they formed national concentrations: there was sporadic anti-Italian feeling in several incidents around the country (Price 1963), and profound anti-German attitudes during World War I, resulting in the closing of German language schools, publications and community activities. Despite attempts to keep alive migrant communities, culture and language, the fate of most migrant groups before World War II was, indeed, to assimilate. Issues of citizenship and membership of the nation were thus only of minor concern in a society overwhelmingly 'British' in make-up.

The Origins of Post-war Immigration to Australia

Substantial changes have been wrought in Australia throughout the past forty-five years. The contemporary observer may find it difficult to appreciate how different Australia was at the end of World War II: a population of only seven million; most important cultural institutions derived from, or subservient to, British values; a pervasive ignorance or even fear of its region; and a typically colonial economic relationship with Britain: exporting raw materials in exchange for value-added British manufactured goods. It must be noted, however, that this supposed monoculturalism in fact masked significant conflicts, which in part had an ethnic basis: the all-pervasive Protestant/Catholic division in society and politics, which reflected English/Irish ethnic divisions, was a feature of Australian life until after World War II.

The origins of Australia's post-war immigration program have been well covered in other studies (Borrie 1947, Markus 1984a, 1984b, Martin 1978, Jupp 1988). The main reasons for its establishment were defence fears arising from Japanese attacks in World War II, concern over a potentially declining population as a result of a dramatic dip in the birthrate during the 1930s Depression, and severe labour shortages for the tasks of post-war reconstruction. No departure was envisaged from the policies of a White Australia, and Labor's Immigration Minister, Arthur Calwell, anticipated that the majority of migrants would continue to come from Britain. But Britain's reluctance to provide shipping and its own reconstruction needs led Calwell to look for migrants from the large numbers of European Displaced Persons (DPs) under the care of the International Refugee Organisation. Calwell agreed to take these refugees to meet his own target of adding 1 per cent per annum to the Australian population through immigration (just over 70,000 migrants). To avoid recurrences of previous hostility to aliens, a policy of assimilation was strongly reasserted. As it was, the DPs arrived at a time of acute labour shortage, and had an immediately positive economic impact. From the early 1950s, Australia enthusiastically extended migrant recruitment to other European countries (Kunz 1988: 102–3).

In contrast to some Western European countries which saw migrants as 'guest-workers', essentially without political rights, who would eventually return to their homelands, Australia wished to encourage its immigrants to become permanent residents (Castles and Kosack 1973). Citizenship was thus made relatively easy: five years' residence (for white non-British migrants), a minimum (undefined) level of English, and no criminal record. British and other white Commonwealth migrants ('British subjects') continued to enjoy the privilege of voting rights after six months' residence. Citizenship among non-British migrants was also seen to encourage assimilation and acceptance of Australian values. Meanwhile, tight controls over non-citizens ('aliens') were maintained: all migrants who were brought out at government expense signed two-year work contracts, under which the government could assign them to meet labour shortages anywhere in Australia, scattering them over the country to discourage 'national concentrations', and controlling movement and residence.

The desire for 'aliens' to become Australian citizens captures well the peculiar mix of tolerance and intolerance that characterised the government's policy of assimilation towards immigrants in the 1950s and 60s. It also eventually undermined the policy of assimilation itself. Under the ideology of assimilation government-funded English learning programs for adult migrants were combined with institutional suspicion of migrant languages and cultures. War Precautions legislation dating back to the 1930s demanded that foreign language newspapers be licensed, that they publish 25 per cent of their content and any lead articles in English, and that they not oppose the government policy of assimilation. In the 1950s similar controls were extended to broadcasting in foreign languages. Yet as these settlers rapidly became citizens, the appropriateness of such restrictions being maintained on *citizens* came into question: it was one thing to ask that migrants who wanted to become Australian citizens be able to speak English, and quite another that, having become citizens, they could not express themselves, in any language, with the same freedom as other citizens. Restrictions on the foreign language press were the first area of assimilation policy to change. They were repealed in the mid-1950s (Gilson and Zubrzycki 1967).

From 1950 to 1970, the government ran an annual Citizenship Convention where aspects of immigration policy were explained to, and supported by representatives from a wide range of Australian institutions, and where important policy announcements were often made. These Conventions stressed the attractiveness of citizenship to new arrivals, and encouraged conformity to Australian values. Among the claimed success of the immigration policy was the relative ease of the absorption of migrants, lack of political antagonism to their coming, and the absence of any migrant activism or dissent of any note (Palbas 1988: 108–11).

Over the 1950s and 1960s, migrants seemed to make little use of their political citizenship, tending to be politically passive — indeed almost politically invisible. Davies (1966: 6) argued that we should expect passivity of this group because 'migrants are people whom politics has already failed: their distaste for it runs deep'. An extensive study in the early 1970s (Wilson 1973) reported low interest in politics, low political participation, and little interest in migrants on the part of mainstream Australian political institutions. Although the major political parties had sporadically established committees to recruit migrants, these had relatively little continuity or influence. Such political passivity should not be seen only in terms of a lack of interest in politics on the part of migrants, but also in terms of the constraints placed on migrant political activity by the policy of assimilation, according to which exercising political citizenship meant fitting in with Australian institutions, on terms dictated entirely by them.

Within their own groups, many migrants were far from passive, for despite the policy of assimilation, migrant groups *did* maintain their cultural, social and in some cases political organisations throughout the 1950s and 60s. The setting up of part-time schools teaching language and culture was almost universal among migrant groups, and there was a growing output of foreign language publications. Some groups were also active politically — for example refugees from Eastern Europe, who maintained a strongly anti-Communist presence, and were recruited at times by Right-wing forces in the industrial, party political or even espionage areas (Richards 1978, Aarons 1989). A few migrants also began to make an impression on the Left of politics, particularly in some unions, but only very slowly in political parties (Collins 1976, Allan 1978). And despite the government's explicit policy of discouraging national concentrations, by the end of the 1950s it was clear that many migrants were settling in inner city areas which provided a variety of social and cultural contacts to sustain their community lives.

Martin (1978: 27) characterised the prevailing view of migrants in the 1950s as being 'lucky to have found a home in Australia, away from the tensions and economic desolation of post-war Europe; they were essential to economic growth and they were assimilable'. By the mid-1960s, however, this view began to give way to the view of migrants as a problem; this was the dominant view of the late 1960s and early 70s. One sign of this was the clear division of labour that had developed in the Australian workforce, with migrants over-represented in the hardest, dirtiest, most dangerous occupations (Jupp 1966, Storer *et al.* 1976). Migrants were more likely to be living in poverty than the native-born, and their children experienced greater problems at school (Martin 1978: 104–5). In the 1960s the first critics of the immigration program began to appear. James Jupp, for example, in *Arrivals and Departures* (1966) argued that although the Department of Immigration was successful in attracting large numbers of migrants to Australia, it had little concern for their plight once they were here. The high rates of return of migrants — up to one-quarter in some years — posed questions about the seriousness with which the government took the task of attracting permanent settlers. And despite official pronouncements on the success of assimilation, many of the migrants who stayed were forming socially disadvantaged minorities in Australian cities.

These criticisms brought a response from government. Billy Snedden (Minister for Immigration, 1966–69) championed the end of assimilation as a government policy in favour of a policy of 'integration', where migrants would not be expected to forget or downplay their own culture and background. Snedden also set in place means to give adequate recognition to migrants' skills (lack of such recognition had been a deterrent to well-qualified migrants coming to Australia), and initiated welfare measures including welfare services targeted to specific ethnic groups, as well as English teaching for newly-arrived migrant children (Martin 1978: 106–9).

Although wanting to improve both skills levels and the new settlers' reception in Australia, Snedden still saw the immigration program in terms of its original aim of attracting large numbers of migrants to help build the Australian nation. Intakes reached as high as 180,000 per year. But, for the first time, the desirability of these numbers began to be challenged politically: the Labor opposition under Gough Whitlam condemned the continual bringing of large numbers of migrants to Australia to live in unsatisfactory social conditions. This was to be an important new perspective of the incoming Labor government in 1972.

The post-war decades also brought a major change to the White Australia Policy. Newly-independent Asian countries began to criticise Australia's immigration policy as racist, and Australia was keen to establish friendly relations with such countries. In 1950 it had been an enthusiastic founder of the Colombo Plan, which brought thousands of Asian students to study in Australia. Through these experiences, as well as through increased travel or in some cases wartime experience, many Australians began to see Asians as people for the first time. All these factors led the government to modify some aspects of the White Australia Policy. In 1956, Asians who had previously settled in Australia became eligible to apply for citizenship after 15 years residence (as against five years for other migrants); in 1958, the government abolished the much-criticised Dictation Test, and permitted 'highly qualified and skilled' migrants of non-white background to apply for temporary residence (Palfreeman 1967). By the late 1950s, overt domestic opposition to White Australia had developed: a vocal Immigration Reform Group, consisting largely of university intellectuals, religious leaders and other public figures, pressured the government to abandon the policy officially, and allow a small quota of Asian migrants (Immigration Reform Group 1960). In 1966, the Immigration Minister, Herbert Opperman, signalled the end of White Australia: citizenship requirements were made the same for migrants of any origin, and non-whites could be considered for settlement on the same basis as other migrants. This was a diplomatic gain, and a symbolic change that at first meant very little: there was no shift of immigration patterns from European and Mediterranean migrants to non-whites, and no Immigration Department activity in Asian offices. Although it was now theoretically possible for non-whites to migrate to Australia, relatively few were in fact to do so for the next decade.

The Politics of Immigration: the 1970s

The Whitlam government brought about two quite fundamental shifts in immigration policy. First, the post-war immigration program's assumed goal of assimilation was questioned by Immigration Minister, Al Grassby. He broke new ground in arguing that migrants should not be seen as aliens who had to be moulded to an Australian image, whether through the hard-line approach of assimilation, or the supposedly softer way of integration, but rather that Australia needed to appreciate the profound contribution that migrants were making to the country. Australia's own identity and self-image thus needed to change to reflect this new cultural contribution. Grassby championed multilingualism and the learning of migrant languages through the education system, government support for migrant communities, and a racial discrimination Act; he increased expenditure on interpreting, translation and other settlement services; and he encouraged migrants' own expression of their interests, which in his view had long been either ignored or discouraged.

Second, Grassby linked social justice for those migrants already in Australia to immigration numbers. He argued that there could be no improvement in the condition of migrants' lives while huge intakes constantly strained social resources. Immigration intakes were cut dramatically from 1973, and after economic recession added another imperative to reduce immigration numbers, the annual intake dropped to around 50,000 in 1975–76, a decline of two-thirds on the huge intakes of the late 1960s (Borrie 1988: 111–12).

Grassby's pluralism was not popular with everyone. In the 1974 elections he was defeated in his rural electorate, following a strong campaign by the extreme Right. The second Whitlam government amalgamated the old Department of Immigration (DI) to create a new Department of Labour and Immigration (DLI), to provide a sharper manpower planning focus, a move criticised by the Liberal Party. On coming to government in late 1975, the Fraser government re-established the old DI in a new guise, as the Department of Immigration and Ethnic Affairs (DIEA). This signified the mainstreaming of ethnic affairs in Australian politics.

The incoming Fraser government faced an immigration and ethnic affairs scene remarkably changed over the three years of the Whitlam government. For example, in contrast to the previous suspicious watchfulness towards broadcasts in foreign languages, such initiatives were encouraged. Ethnic radio stations 2EA and 3EA had been set up in Sydney and Melbourne, initially to give information in other languages about government programs, but gradually assuming a wider role. An 'access' station, 3ZZ, established by the ABC in Melbourne also attracted significant numbers of ethnic broadcasters (Patterson 1981). Elsewhere, schools had responded to Grassby's encouragement of multilingualism by enlarging the number of languages offered and attending more systematically to English learning needs. Government inquiries now recognised the contributions of part-time ethnic schools in teaching many languages day schools were not able to offer (Martin 1978: 127–32).

Immigrant political activism also developed during the Whitlam years. Writing in 1973, Aitkin argued that migrants appeared to have 'no need for political structures to help them gain employment, housing or social services — these functions have been carried out efficiently by the governmental bureaucracy and private enterprise' (1973: 29). Yet in this same year migrant workers forced a prolonged and bitter strike at the Melbourne Ford factory, defying their own union to win improved conditions and recognition of grievances. As a consequence, migrant worker organisations held the first of several Migrant Workers' Conferences. An off-shoot of the Conference formed a broadly-based Migrant Education Action Group, which engaged in extensive lobbying on migrant education issues. Migrants formed their own political organisations, such as the Italian Workers' Organisation, FILEF. Ethnic Communities Councils were also formed in 1974 and 1975 to provide a representative voice for migrants' interests. Migrants asserted themselves as active participants in political decisions rather than as the passive objects of government policy, and from this time the role of migrant communities became an integral aspect of debate on immigration and related matters. Migrants were now using their political citizenship to press their demands for social citizenship, for their particular social needs to be recognised and met by government policy (Collins 1988: 957–58).

With the improvement in economic conditions after 1975, the Fraser government was keen to incease immigration. This was not to be a return to 'the numbers game', with high intakes of generally low-skilled migrants, but a highly selective intake. In 1978, Immigration and Ethnic Affairs Minister Michael Mackellar announced a selection system based on three main categories: family reunion, skilled workers and refugees. The family reunion category allowed only immediate family members (Birrell and Birrell 1981: 221–22). For the skills-based category, a points system was devised to assess applicants' educational and occupational background. Australia clearly wanted to move away from an immigration system which attracted largely unskilled or semi-skilled workers, to one attracting only the most highly skilled and economically useful migrants.

The third category identified by Mackellar was humanitarian. Australia has had a substantial history of assisting refugees: from Hitler's Germany to Australia just before and during World War II; Eastern European refugees, who provided the basis of the massive post-war immigration program from 1947; others from Hungary in 1956, Czechoslovakia in 1968, Chile in 1973 and Lebanon from 1974 onwards. Yet Australian attitudes to refugees were put to the test when the Vietnam War ended, causing a flood of refugees to other countries in Southeast Asia, with some continuing on to make the dangerous journey to Australia in open boats. These 'boat people' forced the government to develop a clear refugee policy and an annual quota was assigned (Viviani 1984). In the late 1970s, refugees constituted about 20 per cent of the total immigration intake, reducing to around 10 per cent in the 1980s. It was hoped that making the refugee category a planned part of the immigration intake would enable an orderly response to queues of potential refugees, as well as discouraging refugees from coming to Australia without being invited.

Although Fraser overturned many policies of the Whitlam governments, he kept and if anything intensified the government's promotion of multiculturalism. He also improved settlement services. A major Report into post-arrival services for migrants, chaired by lawyer Frank Galbally, was tabled in Parliament by Fraser in 1978, in ten languages. The Report argued for the co-ordination of many previously disparate services, and urged a wider promotion of multiculturalism in Australia (Australia 1978). In broadcasting policy, Fraser closed 3ZZ (Dugdale 1979), but established the Special Broadcasting Service (SBS), which took over operation of the two EA stations in 1978, and which in 1980 introduced multicultural television, broadcasting much of its material in other languages with English subtitles. Elsewhere too, the government was keen to promote multicultural perspectives, urging migrants to take out citizenship, stressing support for the maintenance of migrant cultures and languages, and establishing the Australian Institute of Multicultural Affairs (AIMA).

The Politics of Immigration in Contemporary Australia

In their detailed survey of immigration policy during the Hawke government, Parkin and Hardcastle (1990: 315) point to the relatively uncontroversial nature of most aspects of immigration policy before the 1980s, noting that the massive post-war immigration program and its attendant changes 'took place with surprisingly little social tension and few significant disagreements between the major political parties. Yet controversy over immigration policy became much more pronounced following the election of the Hawke government in 1983. This controversy encompassed several distinct issues: the size and composition of intakes; the renewed issue of race and social cohesion; and the complex politics of multiculturalism.

The Size and Composition of the Immigration Intake
Since the mid-1970s immigration intakes have tended to follow the fortunes of the Australian economy: from the nadir of 1975–76, intakes increased steadily in the late 1970s, fluctuated in the early 1980s, then rose again under a confident Hawke administration to over 100,000 per annum, before being cut as a result of economic recession from 1990 onwards. Behind these trends, however, has been a quite furious battle over the desirability and the internal composition of this intake.

During the 1980s strong arguments began to be put for a massive reduction of immigration intakes on the basis of environmental costs, the spending needed for social infrastructure and macro-economic considerations. Bob Birrell of Monash University has been a long-standing critic along these lines of large immigration intakes, and his position gained some support in the 1980s from other academics (Birrell and Birrell 1981, 1987, Birrell, Hill and Nevill 1984, Day and Rowland 1988). This perspective, however, has generally had little influence on immigration policy; for example, the Hawke government's major report on immigration, the *FitzGerald Report* (Australia 1988) argued for a substantially *increased* (but better targeted) intake, specifically to boost skills and productivity.

There has also been disagreement over the distribution of the intake among the different categories, particularly over family reunion and independent migrants. The right of migrants to bring out immediate members of their family (spouse and dependent children) has been long established. However, more distant family — siblings, nieces and nephews, non-dependent parents and so on — do not have virtually automatic right of reunion. From the late 1970s, Ethnic Communities Councils mounted a strong campaign for a more generous definition of 'family' (FECCA 1984). Opponents pointed to the effect of such intakes upon skill levels: given the massive numbers of unskilled and semi-skilled migrants who came to Australia in the past, any more generous family reunion policy would bring many similarly low-skilled migrants (Birrell and Birrell 1987: 273–75). Trying to meet both sides of this argument, the Fraser government in 1981 introduced a new category, 'Concessional family'. Members of families who were siblings, parents of working age, nephews or nieces, would still have to pass the points test for skills and education, but would receive 'concessional' points for having relations in Australia; this category could thus enter with somewhat lower skill levels than independent migrants.

Many problems also attend the category of independent migrants. The points systems, successively refined since 1978, have sought to select young, highly-educated migrants with readily recognisable skills which are in demand. However, it has proved difficult to calibrate this category against actual labour demand. There has also been concern over using immigration to bring skilled workers to fill vacancies while training facilities in Australia for locals remain inadequate (Collins 1988). Attempts to bring business migrants with capital to invest in Australia have also faced considerable problems. On many fronts, it has been difficult to give a clear economic focus to immigration to Australia, a somewhat curious outcome given the heavy economic justification for immigration usually advanced.

Although refugees now form only around 10 per cent of planned immigration numbers, several specific refugee issues have also aroused concern. The Tiananmen Square Massacre of 1989 led the Hawke government to allow some 14,000 students and others from China temporarily in Australia to extend their stay, initially for four years, and later announcing they would be able to stay permanently. This blanket approval, in place of the case-by-case approach to determination of refugee status, caused considerable debate and vigorous protests from the Opposition. Small but undetected landings by boat people from Cambodia in 1991 led to an extended period of highly-publicised legal wrangling, against the dramatic backdrop of Cambodian peace initiatives, in which Australia played a significant role. The government's desire, as on previous occasions, to discourage refugees from coming under their own initiative was in this case matched by a desire to assert the growing normalisation of life in Cambodia itself. Australia's place in a region marked by political instability will continue to bring it face-to-face with refugee issues.

Race and Issues of Social Homogeneity

Although the White Australia Policy was officially buried and reburied by successive governments, Australia's actual confrontation with large numbers of non-white migrants occurred only after the end of the Vietnam War in 1975. While initial reactions varied somewhat at this time (Viviani 1984, Lewins and Ly 1985), the overall response to the sizeable Asian intake apparent by the early 1980s was on the whole positive, and certainly no more negative than that towards previous intakes of non-English-speaking migrants (Goot 1988). In their otherwise critical examination of immigration policy in 1981, Birrell and Birrell (1981: 246) noted this issue only briefly, concluding that: 'At present it seems far-fetched to imagine opposition to Asian migration could trigger off a major public issue.' Yet precisely this issue was to arise on two dramatic occasions in the 1980s.

The first, in 1984, came as a result of a series of public interventions by conservative historian Geoffrey Blainey (Blainey 1984). He argued that the intake of large numbers of Asian migrants had run ahead of public opinion, was bringing new cultural influences at odds with Australian norms, and that Australians — particularly working class Australians — felt that large numbers of Asian migrants were a threat both economically and culturally. Their feelings, he argued, were being ignored by political parties and ethnic lobbies. Blainey was roundly attacked by people ranging from academics (Markus and Ricklefs 1985) to politicians, but his intervention rekindled the issue of race that has since become an abiding subtext in debates over immigration.

Race and immigration also briefly became a party political issue, as a result of a deliberate but ill-fated strategy on the part of Opposition leader John Howard in 1988. Seeking to differentiate his stance on immigration from that of Hawke, Howard argued that 'balance' should be restored to immigration intakes and, in particular, that there should be an adjustment to the proportion of Asian immigrants. Again, his comments were immediately attacked by commentators and the government; they led also to schism within the Liberal Party, with bipartisanship on immigration only restored when Andrew Peacock replaced Howard as leader of the Opposition in 1989 (Parkin and Hardcastle 1990: 324–25).

The Complex Politics of Multiculturalism

Multiculturalism has also been a hotly-contested concept in recent years — much more so perhaps than any other immigration issue. The debate over multiculturalism clearly shows how important apparently 'symbolic' debate can be in our society. This is not a debate about symbols alone, however; at its heart it reveals important differences in understanding what membership of Australian society means, the status of different cultures and groups, and how Australian identity is to be defined.

Multiculturalism was promoted by the Fraser and early Hawke governments as an explicit policy welcoming the cultural contribution of migrants, guiding government policies on settlement services and such matters as anti-discrimination, and providing a basis for social harmony (e.g. Australian Council on Population and Ethnic Affairs 1982). Some on the Left have seen multiculturalism as a conservative state ideology that stresses the cultural aspects of migrants' position in Australian society in order to obscure wider class conflicts and mask the class position of migrants themselves. Jakubowicz (1981: 9), for example, argued that 'the implicit potential of multiculturalism to assert the priority of ethnicity over class, marked its transformation into a means of social control' (see also, de Lepervanche 1980, Foster and Stockley 1984, Collins 1988a). Such authors see immigration politics as largely concerned with the effective reproduction of a necessary labour force, and the ideology of multiculturalism as basically a conservative attempt to focus on apolitical cultural aspects of migrants' lives in order to deny the reality of exploitation.

In ironic counterpoint to this charge of conservatism by the Left, those on the Right have argued that multiculturalism is essentially a radical, subversive (or at least misguided) program of social engineering (Chipman 1980, Knopfelmacher 1982, Sestito 1982, Blainey 1984, Betts 1988). They have stressed Australia's need for a common culture, and attacked what has been seen as an entrenched multicultural lobby and its potential for social fragmentation. Knopfelmacher (1982: 48), for example, argued that promotion of multiculturalism would inevitably lead to 'separatism, divided loyalties, the emergence of rancorous minorities and, eventually, to disruption of the state by irredenta and civil war'. From a more straightforward political science approach, Sestito (1982) concentrated on the political manipulation and mobilisation of ethnicity by competing political parties and élites. He argued that the origin of the rise of multiculturalism as public policy and ideology was the desire of the parties to win ethnic votes, rather than any groundswell of articulated sentiment from migrant groups themselves. It was the political nature of this mobilisation that would lead to dangers of social division and ethnic conflict.

Multiculturalism has also had strong supporters. The Federation of Ethnic Communities Councils of Australia (FECCA) have strongly supported policies aimed at supporting cultural and linguistic diversity, while also asserting concerns about economic issues, rights of migrant workers and social justice. Such a perspective has also characterised those concerned with policy and social welfare provisions (Storer 1975, Australia 1986), who have asserted that cultural identity and socio-economic issues need to be addressed jointly.

While the Hawke government tended to support the Fraser/Galbally initiatives in this area, it signalled a decided shift in policy in the Budget of 1986, proposing to phase out Commonwealth support for continuing English as a Second Language (ESL) education, to abolish the Australian Institute of Multicultural Affairs and the Multicultural Education Program (which provided federal funds for multicultural initiatives in schools), and to merge SBS with the ABC. These cuts and changes were justified in the budget largely on the grounds of needing to cut government spending. They brought a furious reaction from ethnic communities and other commentators, which had the government on the back foot for the following six months. Under pressure, the government was forced to discard the amalgamation of SBS and the ABC, and agreed to review its ESL cuts. Hawke here showed particular political astuteness, reversing policies that were potentially damaging;

in 1987, with the Liberal opposition itself only lukewarm on many of these issues, Hawke was able to re-establish his credentials with ethnic communities in time for that year's election by announcing additional initiatives such as the adoption of a National Policy on Languages (Ozolins 1993). Hawke also established an Office of Multicultural Affairs (OMA) for policy advice within the Department of Prime Minister and Cabinet, as well as a Bureau of Immigration Research. Both these had much more economically focused briefs than the previous AIMA, as well as a renewed interest in equity issues for migrants. A similar perspective on this protean concept of multiculturalism has been maintained by both Hewson and Keating.

Ethnic Voting and Political Participation

While some overseas studies of migrant politics, such as Glazer and Moynihan's classic study of New York (1963), have identified ethnic voting blocs, Australian studies have not. Ethnic leaders in Australia cannot and do not try to 'deliver the vote' for a political party on any issue, and the heterogeneity of Australia's ethnic composition means there are rarely attempts to appeal to particular ethnic groups (Jupp 1984). There are wide disparities in how members of particular ethnic groups vote, and the psephologists have so far only been able to identify a very broad profile of migrant voting.

McAllister and his associates (McAllister 1981, 1988, McAllister and Kelley 1982, 1983, Salmons 1993) have traced changes in ethnic voting patterns from the late 1960s to the early 1990s. They split the migrants into three groups — Eastern European, Northern European and Southern European — and noticed significant changes to their voting, particularly through the 1970s. The Eastern European group, which at the beginning of the 1970s was marginally more likely to vote for the Coalition, became much more likely to do so by the 1970s; in 1993, however, the majority appears to have voted Labor. The Southern Europeans, who tended to favour Labor in the early 1980s, became much more likely to vote Labor over the next decade. The Northern European group was fractionally more likely to vote Labor than the electorate as a whole for most of this period, but fractionally less so in 1993. McAllister also argued that these trends in voting for the three groups were more pronounced than could be predicted from occupational position alone: birthplace or cultural factors did seem to be exercising some independent influence. However, explanations for these differences in voting patterns remain few.

Scanty evidence for the existence of an ethnic voter does not mean that ethnic communities have not attempted to influence policy or to defend the gains of particular policies, however. The strong reactions to the proposed 1986 Budget cuts are one such example. On particular policies (e.g. language services, SBS, support for teaching English, support of family reunion), they have lobbied all parties rather than tying their fortunes to one particular party. This tendency is one more force helping bi-partisanship to survive. One should not, however, see this as a situation in which the parties are hostage to ethnic pressures: while the amounts spent on post-arrival services and related areas such as SBS have increased steadily since the 1970s, in real terms these are still small and usually accounted for by one or two relatively uncontroversial programs. The teaching of English, which started as a component of assimilation policy, dwarfs every other multicultural educational initiative.

Migrants have also been politically involved in the industrial area. In the motor vehicle industry, for example, the 1973 Ford strike mentioned above was repeated in 1981, again with migrants at the forefront, and again resulting in shopfloor workers taking action not supported by their union hierarchy. The largely migrant Port Kembla ironworkers have been successful in gaining control of their union and using standard industrial relations methods to advance a number of issues, including those specifically affecting migrant workers (Lever-Tracy and Quinlan 1988). Across Australia in the 1980s there has been a more significant response on the part of unions to migrant issues, with an ACTU Migrant Workers' Conference in 1981, and migrant concerns receiving recognition in several industrial awards (for example, learning English on the job), although migrant involvement in unions and as union officials remains sporadic (Collins 1988, Nicolaou 1991). The position of migrant women, in industry as in other spheres, has also attracted attention (Storer *et al.* 1976, Bottomley and de Lepervanche 1984, Bottomley *et al.* 1991), and again has led to demands for social policy to accommodate migrant needs.

The other area of politics in which ethnic communities have been significant is in relation to international conflicts involving past homelands. One such incident occurred during the Whitlam government, when Whitlam reversed the long-standing policy of not recognising the incorporation of the Baltic states into the Soviet Union. This created a sizeable outcry from the relatively small but well-organised Baltic community, which was successful in persuading the Opposition to reverse the decision when it came to power in 1975 (Knight 1979). For most other conflicts, it is more difficult to trace government decisions to such internal pressures. On the Middle East, for example, while Australia in the 1950s and 60s was a strong supporter of Israel (and the number of Jews at that time in Australia far outnumbered Arabs), by the 1970s and 80s Australia had shifted to a more even-handed policy on the Middle East. Middle East immigration had also been strong in these decades, but it would be wrong to see this as determining this shift in outlook. Other international factors have been much more important for determining Australian policy towards the Middle East than the views of migrants (Bell 1983, Harris 1993: 36–38).

Homeland politics can, however, raise issues of conflicting loyalties, as was demonstrated by much media comment during the Gulf War in 1991 (Goot and Tiffen 1992) — although the Australian government strongly denied that this was an issue. Ethnic Communities Councils have also scrupulously avoided taking sides in such cases, and there has been little open conflict between ethnic groups over such issues. Where some degree of internal conflict has occurred — the Yugoslav groups being one of the few significant examples — the government has tended to distance itself from all conflicting parties, attempting to take an even-handed approach, and to follow international trends.

Conclusion

I have argued that while immigration can at times become an issue of considerable political importance, this is generally not so in terms of party politics. On crucial elements of policy, there has been a broadly sustained bi-partisan approach since the initiation of a large-scale immigration program after World War II. There is still considerable belief in the role of immigration in helping to build the Australian nation, and indeed immigration probably remains a rough litmus test of the state of the economy. Restoring the economy's health so that immigration can be increased again, and in turn contribute to more economic growth, is still the prevailing view of the links between immigration and the economy, reflecting the long post-war experience.

Just as we have generally seen bi-partisan accord, there has also been an absence of serious ethnic conflict. Despite the (at times) acrimonious debate over multiculturalism, and vigorous activity on the part of ethnic groups on a range of issues, there has been nothing in ethnic affairs similar to the dramatic politics of Aboriginal Australian's struggle for citizenship rights of every kind. Australia still sees as part of its future the continuation of immigration, and of policies that attempt to provide the basis of accommodation rather than conflict, after settlement in Australia.

10
Economic Policy

GREG WHITWELL

For those not trained in economics, discussions of economic policy can seem terribly complex, a journey into a mysterious world of confusing jargon and incomprehensible technicalities. The casual reader of newspaper articles on economic affairs is likely to experience intense frustration trying to comprehend sentences littered with phrases such as level playing fields, current account deficits, depreciating exchange rates, Reserve Bank intervention, goods and services taxes, zero-tariff proposals, auto industry plans, debt servicing ratios, deteriorating terms of trade, the public sector borrowing requirement, M3 — and a thousand other such terms. That there is something called micro-economic policy, and something else called macro-economic policy — but what exactly is the difference? The need to do something in Australia about unemployment, and the idea that the economy 'is in a mess' seem to be taken for granted. But what should — and can — be done? And is it true that the Australian economy's performance is fundamentally a reflection of what is happening in the international economy, and events over which we have very little control?

When pushed, a great many people are likely to admit to ignorance on economic matters and put questions of economic policy into the 'too-hard basket'. With some reluctance they are likely to come to the conclusion that informed debate on economic policy is best left to the 'experts'. For those who give up less easily, who acknowledge that economic matters are difficult to comprehend, but who sense they are nonetheless of critical importance, I want to suggest some ways in which we can pierce the veneer of jargon to begin to get a deeper understanding of economic policy. I have no intention of offering something along the lines of 'Everything you need to know about economics in order to understand economic policy debate'. Instead, I want to try to provide a 'behind-the-scenes' guide to economic policy. I intend doing this by considering the following three propositions, and the questions they yield :

- *Decisions on whether particular economic policies should be adopted, modified or abandoned are influenced by the relative power of a variety of competing interest groups.* Who are these interest groups?

How did the Hawke/Keating governments attempt to reconcile them?
- *Economic policy, because of its technical complexities, increases the dependence of politicians on those government departments and 'outside advisers' providing economic expertise.* If this is so, which departments have been the most powerful providers of economic advice? More generally, by what processes do economic ideas become the basis for policy?
- *The policy advice provided to governments by economists within and outside the federal bureaucracy reflects certain (often unstated and unconscious) preconceptions, ideas, philosophies, mental pictures and visions of how market economies can and should operate.* But what, you might ask, does all this mean? More especially, what do terms such as 'mental pictures' and 'visions' mean? How are these things formed, and are they subject to change? What exactly is the link between these 'philosophies' and 'preconceptions', and the formation of policy?

There is no suggestion, of course, that these propositions encapsulate all that is essential about economic policy. They do, however, provide a starting point for considering a complex topic. I should also point out that the focus of the chapter is on domestic economic management. The ways in which international economic forces affect the Australian economy and impinge on the policy options available to governments are not discussed. In any case, there are already good introductions to this topic (Viviani 1990). Nor is any attempt made here to provide a chronology of the various phases of economic conditions and policy during the Hawke/Keating years. Again, useful guides are available elsewhere (Stutchbury 1990). Moreover, I want to avoid getting bogged down in a blow-by-blow account of the economic policies of the last decade. The recent furore over economic rationalism suggests that questions of economic *philosophy* have again come to the fore. Attention is increasingly being paid not so much to individual policies but to the broad thrust of economic policy. We seem to be at something of a crossroads. Faith in the efficacy and beneficence of market forces has been greatly weakened, but it is not clear that governments are necessarily being seen again in a positive light.

Interest Groups and How to Deal with Them

The federal election of 1983 saw the demise of the Fraser government and its replacement by an ALP administration under Bob Hawke. The Hawke government came to power preaching the need for, and efficacy of, consensus and 'national reconciliation'. Emphasis was placed on the power of reasoned arguments and active consultation between governments, business and the union movement, as the means to a stronger and more stable economy. This attitude was given some substance by the holding of a National Economic Summit in April 1983, and by the introduction of a prices and incomes Accord between the government and the Australian Council of Trade Unions (ACTU). While much was made of the need for consensus, the Hawke government continued to use much of the rhetoric of its immediate predecessors, pointing, for instance, to the need for budgetary restraint and the evils of large Budget deficits. To the surprise of many commentators, the new government was willing to question some of the ALP's sacred economic nostrums and to entertain the idea that there might be some virtue in deregulating the financial sector. Even more surprisingly, it was prepared, unlike the Fraser government, to convert words into actions. In December 1983 it was decided to float the Australian dollar. so that its value relative to other currencies would not be determined administratively but by the forces of supply and demand. The Hawke government also removed virtually all foreign exchange controls. Soon after, in January 1984, the government announced it had accepted the principle that there would be advantages to the Australian economy if a limited number of foreign banks were allowed entry. In April 1984, Australian stock exchanges were deregulated.

In 1989, Michael Keating and Geoff Dixon, then respectively Secretary and Assistant Secretary in the Department of Finance, presented an insider's view of economic policy during the Hawke years. Their book sought to show that it is wrong to assume that consensual policies and market-oriented ones are mutually exclusive. Their argument was in effect that the Hawke years demonstrated the two could be pursued simultaneously, and to great effect. There were a number of important preconditions, however, for the two strategies to be blended successfully. Of key importance was the formation of peak 'encompassing' interest groups, particularly representing employees and employers. The former were represented by the ACTU and the latter by the Confederation of Australian Industry, the Business Council of Australia, and the Australian Chamber of Manufactures (Galligan and Singleton 1991, Matthews 1991). Under the Hawke government, the argument continued, these 'encompassing' groups engaged in 'bargained consensus', which in essence meant promoting the interests of the group as a whole, usually at the expense of the objectives of some of its constituent parts so that, for example, the ACTU might have agreed to proposals which were perceived to benefit workers as a whole but which might well prove prejudicial to certain individual unions and their members. Other preconditions for the blending of consensual and market-oriented policies included the 'learning experience' of the 1970s and 80s. The major lesson of this was the need for wage increases not to exceed the economy's capacity to pay them.

Another lesson was the growing realisation that Australia was living in a competitive world: the floating of the exchange rate was critical in emphasising this fact. Of importance also was increased sophistication in analysing the benefits and costs of policy options. Another precondition was the quality of the leadership of the tri-partite institutions engaged in 'bargained consensus'. This in turn reflected the intellectual ability of those charged with the task of leadership and the fact that they had strong mandates (Keating and Dixon 1989).

The Economist's Vision

Keating and Dixon argued that while the Hawke government's *style* in formulating economic policy may have been consensual, one of its main *objectives* was to make the negotiating parties, whether representatives of labour, business, welfare or environmental groups, more attuned to market realities. This objective has become the source of fierce debate in recent years. The buzz-phrase to describe the government's approach is 'economic rationalism'. Its *rhetoric* goes as follows: greater efficiency must be seen as a sacred goal. Increased competition and the unlocking of market forces are the key means to obtain it. The public sector is riddled with inefficiencies. The private sector, by contrast, is self-evidently superior. To the extent that the private sector often operates less than optimally, a major reason is the plethora of perverse governmental regulations which hamper its efficiency. Despite such problems, the public sector needs to model itself wherever possible on the private. And where public sector activities can be, or are being done in the private sector, the public sector should surrender them. The inevitable result will be an increase in net economic welfare: the economy will become more dynamic, and scarce resources will be allocated more efficiently.

The debate over economic rationalism intensified as the economy's performance deteriorated. With the economy in deep and protracted recession, with unemployment at historically high and intractable levels, and with the continued demise of the Australian manufacturing sector, economic rationalism came to be identified by its detractors as the villain of the piece. A recent book is entitled *The Trouble with Economic Rationalism* (Horne 1992); another is *Shutdown: The Failure of Economic Rationalism and How to Rescue Australia* (Carroll and Manne 1992). The argument is that economic rationalists do not really understand how economies function. Furthermore, in their zeal for liberating market forces and exposing the economy to much greater competition, the economic rationalists have inflicted great damage. Their predictions are false: the economy has not emerged leaner and meaner; instead it has become punch-drunk. It is now tottering; soon it will collapse. According to this view, the Hawke/Keating governments, and the economic rationalist zealots in the Canberra bureaucracy (most notably the Treasury), have much to answer for. As far as the critics are concerned, a change of government would only have made matters worse, for the Liberal Party under Dr Hewson has emerged as one of economic rationalism's great champions. The 1993 election was a competition between two versions of the same world view. Labor's only advantage was that it was more attuned to the fears of the electorate. Its economic rationalism was tempered by electoral opportunism.

I have no intention here of trying to adjudicate on the virtues and vices of economic rationalism. Instead I want to suggest that underpinning the debate are competing 'visions' of how market economies operate. By 'vision' I mean the interpretive framework by which people make sense of reality. In a 1978 study on structural change, the federal Treasury pointed to the importance of competing interpretive frameworks when it said that 'basically different mental pictures of how the Australian economy works underlie different policy prescriptions in this area'. What I want to make clear is the role of 'mental pictures' in underpinning economic policy debate. Further, I want to argue that these different pictures or visions have different implications for appropriate roles of governments.

Some examples will help to clarify what I have in mind. In considering examples, it needs to be stressed that the debate over economic rationalism is not new; it has emerged in different guises at various time in the Australian past. One such occasion was in the 1960s (Whitwell 1986, 163–68). The federal Treasury, fiercely protective of its position as the major source of economic advice to the government, became entangled in a continuing wrangle with the Department of Trade and Industry. What brought this dispute and rivalry to a head was the publication in 1965 of the Report of the so-called Committee of Economic Enquiry, headed by Sir James Vernon. The Committee's conclusions were informed in part by projections of what Gross National Product (total output), Gross National Expenditure (total spending), and imports and exports would be over the coming decade. On the basis of these projections, the Vernon Committee concluded that there would be a need for personal consumption expenditure to be reduced, or for savings to increase. This would probably have to take the form of 'forced' savings by governments, using Budget surpluses in which revenue exceeded expenditure. The Committee also suggested that investment would also have to be increased, which would probably require more generous investment allowances. Another suggestion was that exports would need to be increased, and imports might need to be reduced. These proposals were supported by Trade and Industry. Indeed, the former Secretary of the department, Sir John Crawford, was one of the Report's principal authors.

The Treasury reacted with rancour to the Committee's suggestions. It set out to demolish the proposals by insisting that policy recommendations should not be based on projections, for these were nothing more than guesses. Why, you might ask, was the Treasury so hostile to projections as a basis for prescriptive decisions? Part of the reason can be found in the views it expressed in a 1964 paper on economic growth. Treasury argued that 'particular rates of economic growth ... cannot be treated as ends in themselves'. The 'real question' which had to be asked was 'not how the growth rate compares internationally but whether, given the pattern of demand, the output required to meet that demand has failed to grow as fast as it might if all available resources had been used with the highest efficiency'. Such arguments implied that there was no need to achieve a particular target growth figure. The economy was simply a device for satisfying an ever-changing variety of needs. Thus, if community demands were such that resources were used in a particular combination or pattern that yielded a lower rate of growth than another combination would have yielded, then so be it. What mattered was not growth rates as such, but the satisfaction of ever-changing demands. Implicit in this view was a disdain for purposive action — that is, for government action designed to achieve particular goals. It was not difficult to take such arguments a step further and argue that what is 'natural' is best. Following this line of reasoning, it could easily be argued, for instance, that governments should not attempt to achieve an arbitrarily-defined level or zone of socially acceptable unemployment. The department could not accept the commonly accepted (though entirely arbitrary) view in the 1960s that 'full employment' meant keeping unemployment to no more than 1.5 per cent of the labour force. Instead, unemployment should be left to seek its own determined level.

The distinguishing characteristic of Treasury thought, as with that of all economic rationalists, was a basic confidence in the workings of the market mechanism. Underpinning this was its unquestioned conviction concerning the responsiveness of 'economic agents' to changes in relative prices. Treasury's confidence in market processes, it needs to be understood, implied a limited role for government. There was simply no need for the government to take the initiative in trying to direct the pace and pattern of economic change; in fact, it was likely to have harmful effects if it tried.

Those who wrote the *Vernon Report*, however, saw the world differently. In their view, people in business often tended to be sluggish in their responses to relative price changes and, concerned with possible risks, often anxious to avoid taking initiatives. It was perhaps not surprising therefore that the authors of the Report came to quite different conclusions from the Treasury on the role of government. As the academic economist Eric Russell described their view:

> To change the structure of the economy, a key role will be played by non-market government forces which break through special hind-

rances to change. The Vernon Report (and the enormous tradition it reflects) finds the market a weak instrument for securing coherent, overall objectives. Well-informed administrators can nudge, encourage, entice, coerce the economy onto a better path ... This is a view that extends naturally to making projections of the level and structure of output and demand, based on existing policy objectives which in total will provide a framework within which private enterprise will act confidently and vigorously and coherently. (Russell 1978: 198–99)

A very similar line is now being expressed by those who deplore economic rationalism. They want governments to be more interventionist, to provide guidance, incentives and rewards, as well as assistance in the form of maintaining existing tariff rates.

Consider another, and very much related example of the role of competing 'visions' (Whitwell 1986: 230–35). It was common practice by the mid-1970s to talk of 'the crisis of manufacturing' and to point with grave concern to the fact that manufacturing's share of Gross Domestic Product at constant prices had slipped from 25.4 per cent in 1972–73 to 22.4 per cent in 1977–78, and that its share of total employment had fallen from 24.7 per cent in 1971 to 19.8 per cent in 1978. Two committees, the Jackson and Crawford Committees, were established in the second half of the 1970s to investigate the malaise in manufacturing. Indicative too of mounting concern with the fate of the manufacturing sector was the publication in 1977 of the governmental *White Paper on Manufacturing Industry*.

The Treasury did not share this concern. Its response to the 'crisis' was simply to argue, in line with views put forward in the 1960s, that 'there can be no rational justification for aiming at any pre-determined economic structure, or seeking to defend the existing economic structure'. Changes in the economic structure were considered 'only the means through which the economy keeps pace with the changing demands the community makes of it'. 'Particular economic structures or directions for change', therefore, 'cannot sensibly be advanced as ends in themselves'.

In any case — and here the Treasury's underlying vision came to the fore — there was simply no need to fear the employment consequences of structural or technological change. Such fears were misplaced, it maintained, because they ignored the fact that the complex linkages, interrelationships and interdependencies between 'economic agents' were such that the economic system was able to cope with any domestic or international economic disturbances. Treasury could argue, for instance, that 'market economies embody complex linkages across markets, such that the very process of decline in some industries signals the opportunities for expansion in others'. It was the essence of technological change that it not only imposed costs but also provided opportunities. There was no reason, it argued in a 1979 paper, why economic difficulties should become cumulative:

> In a flexible, continually adjusting economy, along with specific employment losses there can be expected to be employment gains. Just as activity in some industries is necessarily deterred by the expansion of others, so job displacement in a particular industry can bring cost savings elsewhere in the economy with the consequent potential for new and additional demands and new employment opportunities.

Here was a positive view of the inherent forces in market economies. The idea was that market forces were somehow natural and therefore good and that, provided they were allowed to work, the economy would work more efficiently. Efficiency, in turn, was assumed to be the chief determinant of economic growth. And provided wages were sufficiently flexible, unemployment would not be a problem.

Such a view of the nature of structural change gave rise to a particular set of policy prescriptions. Some observers, such as the Jackson Committee, believed the government should take the lead in counteracting the apparent decline of manufacturing by the use of policies such as depreciation and other investment allowances, research grants, relocation grants, export incentives, retraining schemes and aid to particular industries. As we have seen, the Treasury line was that governments should not attempt to mould the nature of economic change. Those opposed to the Treasury insisted it was simply being unrealistic. To them, government intervention should not be seen as unnatural or a 'distortion' but as indispensable and very much a positive force. Not surprisingly, some of those opposed to the Treasury's economic rationalism pointed to the crucial role played by governments in the remarkably successful East Asian economies, such as Japan, South Korea and Taiwan.

The Political Power of Economic Ideas

Although it is true that the Treasury has long been a powerful source of economic advice, it should not be assumed that the federal government's economic policy in the post-war period closely reflected Treasury views. Governments are forced to rely heavily on institutions such as the Treasury, but as the section above indicated, within the bureaucracy there is the possibility of strongly divergent views on what are, and are not, appropriate economic policies. One of the characteristics of the Whitlam era — one that has persisted — was the proliferation of rivals to the Treasury within the federal bureaucracy, and the use of 'outside advisers'. This in turn increased the scope for the possibility of disagreement. (It should be said, though, that it has become popular to argue that disagreement has tended to be muted because so many of the key economic advising institutions share a basic acceptance of the major principles of economic rationalism.) In any case, the economic policies which are adopted by governments will inevitably be influenced not only by the competing advice of departments, but by the myriad of political pressures provided by competing factions within governmental parties, and by interest groups outside Parliament, each with different ideas on the proper objectives of economic policy, and of their implications for issues such as equity, efficiency and economic growth. They will be influenced, too, by the electoral cycle (the promise and consequences of policies designed to win votes), and by the complications of Australia's federal system. It may be, as I have suggested, that governments can and will try to impose their views on this myriad of pressure groups. Politics is all about the art of compromise.

This leads to a closely related issue. It is one thing to describe the competing 'visions' of government departments, but it is another to understand how one particular 'vision' triumphs over another and wins widespread acceptance. This is a complex matter. One way to begin to approach it is to note that economic policy, more especially the broad approach to policy embraced by governments and by the community, is subject over time to swings in fashion. Budgetary policy, the government's spending and revenue decisions, provide a good example of this.

Throughout the 1930s, the era of the Great Depression, the annual Budget continued to be seen by most parliamentarians as a mere financial statement rather than an instrument for stabilising the economy. This view was linked in turn with the belief that governments were essentially impotent in their ability to deal with unemployment. The Budget was seen by the Treasury in terms of 'mere money', governed by accounting, balance-sheet principles. Budgeting was simply a matter of estimating expenditure and then determining the ways in which the revenue to cover this could be raised. Balanced budgets (with expenditure matching expected revenue) were the inviolable ideal.

By the end of World War II, however, there had been a marked change in attitude. The war saw the Commonwealth explicitly accept the notion of economic management. In doing so, it embraced the ideas put forward by the English economist, John Maynard Keynes. The 1945 White Paper, *Full Employment in Australia*, was the great symbol of this change in attitude and of the adoption of Keynesian ideas. The White Paper opened with the declaration that the government considered full employment a 'fundamental aim'. Unemployment was branded an evil. The provision of 'the general framework of a full employment economy, within which the operation of individuals and businesses could be carried on' was deemed a responsibility and an obligation of federal and state governments. The White Paper involved a fundamental break with the past. It involved looking at the economy differently. Output levels, rather than cost and price levels, were now the main source of attention. Linked with this, the importance of aggregate demand (the total level of spending) was recognised and emphasised. Despite a certain haziness about just how the Budget would be used, it was now appreciated that it affected, and was affected by the rest of the economy. More importantly, the government was now proposing a form of intervention in the economy previously considered unwise and improper. Expenditure levels were to be regulated by altering public capital (investment) expenditure to maintain total expenditure at a level which would ensure the continuation of full employment, and which would remove the instability to which the economy seemed inevitably prone. Implicit in this view was the notion that governments could and should control the level of economic activity to achieve particular desired ends. There was confidence that the nation's destiny was in its own hands and that governments could be, with the insights provided by Keynesian economics, powerful and positive forces.

An essentially Keynesian approach to budgetary policy remained the norm for the 1950s and 60s. Gough Whitlam, Prime Minister from 1972 to 1975, recalls that:

> During the years of the post-war economic boom [1945–73], questions of economic management were scarcely deemed to require original answers. The broad principles, and indeed objectives, of Keynesian economics held sway over the major parties. If prices rose and the supply of labour grew short, then expenditure was tightened, taxes increased and credit squeezed to produce a decrease in inflation and employment. If prices fell and employment grew scarce then expenditure was expanded, taxation decreased and credit relaxed to produce an increase in prices and employment. The apparent clarity and certainty of economic management opened up new prospects and induced high hopes for social reform. (Whitlam 1985: 184)

All this was to change in the 1970s with the onset of a new and persistent era of economic instability in which growth faltered, unemployment increased, and inflation persisted at high levels. Gone were the economic buoyancy and remarkably low unemployment which had been achieved for almost thirty years during the long postwar boom, and which had come to be considered the normal state of affairs. The view came to be held, most especially by the federal Treasury, that what had also gone were the days when governments could hope to honour a pledge to maintain full employment. In fact, the Treasury came to see the actions of governments as often not the solution to the problems of unemployment and inflation but as a major source of them. Balanced Budgets were again seen as the most important budgetary goal. In trying to achieve this goal, governments would have to exercise expenditure restraint. This would help reduce the relative size of the public sector, leaving more resources for the private. It would also help reduce the rate of increase in the money supply. Another benefit was that governments would be forced to offer fewer handouts to business as well as to welfare recipients. This in turn would help discourage the socially unproductive habit of the private sector seeking maximum protection and assistance. Much of the Budget rhetoric of the Fraser government (1975–83) was along these lines.

The question then arises: what produces these swings in fashion? This brings us back to the broader issue of the political power of economic ideas. What, we might ask, were the circumstances that led to the adoption of Keynesian ideas as the basis for economic policy during and after World War II? Alternatively we might ask why the rhetoric of economic rationalism became so widely propagated in the 1980s. In seeking answers to such questions, we can draw on a stimulating recent analysis which concentrates on the spread of Keynesian ideas across nations, but which is of critical importance in understanding the more general issue of the link between economic ideas and their adoption or rejection as the basis for policy (Hall 1989: 8–13). Peter Hall, its editor, distinguishes between three broad approaches to the question of how and why Keynesian ideas and policies were accepted. The first is the *economist-centred approach*. The implicit assumption here is that the adoption of new economic policies — be they Keynesian, economic rationalist or whatever — occurs as a result of expert advice provided to politicians by economists. The task is then to explain two things. Why, to consider the Keynesian example, did professional economists decide to adopt Keynesian modes of analysis and theoretical precepts? And by what means, and through what institutional arrangements, do professional economists communicate with and influence policy makers? More precisely, how do institutional arrangements structure the nature of such communication?

Hall argues that the economist-centred approach has one great virtue and one great weakness as an explanation of why new economic ideas are adopted. Its chief virtue is that it draws attention to the qualities of the ideas themselves. 'It suggests that ideas may have a persuasiveness, and hence a political dynamism, of their own; and it forces us to ask which ideational qualities make for persuasiveness and which detract from it.' The main defect is that the influence of economists over policy is probably exaggerated.

Another approach to the adoption of new economic ideas is the *state-centred approach*. The argument here is that 'the reception accorded new economic ideas will be influenced by the institutional configuration of the state and its prior experience with related policies'. On the first point, the institutional configuration of the state, analysts who adopt this approach focus their attention on the capacity of bureaucracies to implement new ideas and programs. This capacity will be influenced by 'the relative openness of policy-making institutions to advice from outside economists ... and the administrative biases implicit in the institutional division of responsibility within the state'. On the second point, the importance of prior experience with related policies, one could contrast the way Sweden and Britain have reacted to Keynesian ideas. Prior experience with public works projects as a means of ameliorating unemployment made the Swedish state more receptive to Keynesian ideas, whereas in Britain, where prior experience was with unemployment insurance, the Labour Party and a great many policy makers fixed their attention on this rather than on proposals to boost public works expenditure. Hall suggests that the state-centred approach has certain merits:

> It draws our attention to the role that administrative, as opposed to purely economic, problems play in the process of economic policy making. It reminds us that the officials responsible for economic policy during the interwar period were usually not economists, and that even in the postwar period, they have had many concerns besides developments in economic theory. Most important, the state-centred approach provides us with a set of tools for explaining cross-national variation in the reception given Keynesian [or other new economic] ideas. (Hall 1989: 11–12)

The weakness of the approach is the overriding importance it attaches to the state apparatus and to officials. The implied suggestion is that politics and political leaders play a minor role in the determination of policy, and the adoption or rejection of new approaches.

This criticism cannot be levelled against the third approach, the *coalition-centred approach*. Here politics is of central importance. As Hall explains, this approach 'emphasises that politics must mobilise support among broad coalitions of economic groups on whose votes and goodwill elected politicians ultimately depend'. In terms of Keynesianism, he says that

> a nation's readiness to implement Keynesian policies may be said to turn on the ability of its politicians to forge a coalition of social groups that is large enough to sustain them in office and inclined to regard Keynesian measures as something that is in their interest. The feasibility of such a coalition, in turn, rests on the ingenuity of politicians and the constellation of preferences expressed by the relevant economic groups. (Hall 1989: 12)

What is valuable about this approach, Hall notes, is the 'renewed emphasis' given to the broader political context in which new economic ideas are considered. Furthermore, 'it reminds us that politics is ultimately about the conflict among groups with divergent interests for claims on scarce resources'. Its main weakness is that 'it leaves somewhat open the question of how these groups come to define their interests in a particular way'.

In summary, in explaining the influence of new economic ideas, each of the three approaches outlined above tends to see different actors as occupying centre stage: economists in the first, public servants and officials in the second, and politicians (and social groups) in the third. What the analysis also suggests is that the adoption of economic ideas as a basis of economic policy requires that these ideas be (seen to be) viable in economic, political and administrative terms.

The Historical Context of Contemporary Economic Policy

The discussion in the preceding section gives a taste of some of the great variety of ways in which we can analyse economic policy matters. Implicit in the discussion is the view that those ideas which inform economic policies evolve. I want here to pursue this suggestion further, and to argue that analysis of contemporary economic policy becomes much more fruitful when it is set in historical context.

There is more to this than simply an acknowledgment of swings in fashion (such as the swing to and away from Keynesianism, mentioned earlier). Debate on economic policy reflects the fact that we now live in an economic world whose 'mood' is fundamentally different from that which existed in the 1950s and 60s. Before the early 1970s, as I have already suggested, a mood of confidence and optimism pervaded post-war Australia. Eventually, however, optimism was to give way to pessimism, confidence to puzzlement. By the mid-1970s, mainstream economics was said to be in crisis, and began to be derided as an impotent collection of conflicting ideas and policy prescriptions. Economists struggled to come to grips with a confused and confusing world. While they did so, consensus vanished. This could be seen most clearly in the way budgetary policy was discussed. By the end of the 1970s, as Nevile (1983) points out, some economists had come to the conclusion that budgetary policy was dead. Most, however, continued to accord such policy a valuable role in economic management. But just what form this role should take was a source of great debate:

> The trouble is that different groups give diametrically opposed advice about appropriate fiscal policy to combat stagflation. On the one hand it is argued that fiscal policy should aim to balance the budget (or at least to reduce the deficit as much as possible) either in

order to reduce inflationary expectations and restore confidence or in order to reduce interest rates. An opposing view is that fiscal policy should fight inflation by cutting taxes either to reduce costs or to increase productivity. Another view is that fiscal policy should be used to increase output, at least moderately, with the strategy to reduce inflation built around prices and incomes policies. (Nevile 1983: 1–2)

A major cause of this disagreement was that the 1970s represented a sudden, then increasingly protracted, departure from what had come to be considered 'normality'. The 1970s saw the dissolution of a whole host of what were thought to be 'usual' or 'traditional' relationships, most notably the coexistence of rising inflation and rising unemployment, a phenomenon which was directly counter to the accepted wisdom that an increase in one led to a decline in the other. There was an altered relationship, too, in the wages and profits share of national income, and in the nature of wage increases relative to movements in productivity. Furthermore, such was the size of the movement in a number of key economic variables during the 1970s (most especially during the Whitlam years) that they provided something of a 'scale shock'. Unemployment was on a scale unprecedented in the post-war period. The rate at which prices and wages increased in 1973–74 had not been experienced since the early 1950s, and came to be described, quite appropriately, as a 'wages explosion'. Industrial disputation rose markedly, to reach record levels. The rate of increase in public sector outlays and receipts and, in particular, the scale of the budget deficit were, again, unprecedented in the post-war period. So too was the size of the public sector borrowing requirement. Tariffs were suddenly cut in 1973 by 25 per cent. In the early 1970s, official reserve assets leapt dramatically to reach record levels, and in 1972–73 the money supply (using the measure known as M3) jumped by almost 26 per cent. There were also marked fluctuations in the exchange rate, and sudden rises in interest rates.

The departure from 'normality' was significant in that it bred confusion. And confusion led not only to questioning of accepted wisdom, but encouraged a search for simplicities, 'basic truths', as the first stage in coping with the complex of new and altered relationships. Herein lay a key attraction of economic rationalism. For the central message of economic rationalism was remarkably simple: the path to economic efficiency and to the restoration of 'normal' relationships was to let the market rule. Another argument also grew in popularity. This was that in a world of confusion and 'distortions' to traditional relationships, and uncertainty resulting from inflation and sharp changes in the nature and purpose of governmental policies (the Whitlam era was noteworthy for inconsistency in the use of a number of economic policies), the way to restore business confidence was to pledge consistency and predicability in the use of policy tools. These sorts of ideas lay behind the Fraser government's insistence on the importance of a pledge to achieve balanced budgets. They also lay behind the government's initial support for the announcement of conditional projection ranges for growth in M3.

The Hawke/Keating Governments and Economic Rationalism

In an address given in 1987, Paul Keating pointed to what he considered was one of the principal lessons of the Whitlam years:

> The problem of the Whitlam Government was that the gap between ideals and outcomes grew to a chasm over that three-year period. The Party, at last hungry for government and in government had failed to mature as a government. The ideals and objectives were constant but the economic growth upon which the 'program' was based, was disappearing. The task became, not the distribution of wealth but its creation, but neither Whitlam nor his successor as Prime Minister seemed to recognise it. Over a decade later, as we rake through the embers of his period of office we are reminded of Gough's success in refurbishing Labor and returning it to relevance; but we must also be struck by the vulnerability of any party which maintains a static political or economic posture in rapidly changing times. (Keating 1987: 13)

He went on to say that although Labor's ideals had to 'remain true to its basic faith, the means of achieving its objectives must adapt in a changing world. The mismatch of ends and means was the fatal flaw in the makeup of the Whitlam Government. It is a flaw well understood by this Government.'

Four years after making this speech, Keating found himself presiding over a situation in which, to use his phrase, 'economic growth ... was disappearing'; indeed, it had temporarily vanished. He, too, faced the task not so much of distributing wealth but of creating it. In one of those lovely ironies of political and economic history, Keating launched in 1992 a series of initiatives under the rubric *One Nation*. This involved a package of spending measures applauded by Whitlam and, so he argued, very much in the spirit of his own government's approach to economic matters.

Others were less fulsome in their praise. The package, they said, was a case of too little, too late. Moreover, it was the ALP's determination to reduce tariffs and deregulate the financial system (initiatives which Keating as Treasurer had championed), which, by one means or another, had been the principal reason for the eventual emergence in Australia of economic stagnation, intractable balance-of-payments problems, and appallingly high unemployment. To make matters worse, Keating's critics were confronted by an Opposition promoting further deregulation, more privatisation, the introduction of radical taxation initiatives, and reduction in the size of the public sector. One thing was clear to all those who were voicing these complaints: economic rationalism was both pervasive and a disaster. It was a form of lunacy which had led to tragic results.

Economic rationalism, it needs to be said, has become a convenient mono-causal explanation for anything and everything that seems to have gone wrong in the Australian economy over recent years. This is unfortunate, because it is intellectually indefensible to provide such a narrowly simplistic 'explanation' of complex events. It is unfortunate for another reason. Economic rationalists ask certain questions of governments. For example, have the costs and benefits of a particular proposal been fully and explicitly analysed? What is the evidence that the public sector will be able to perform tasks better than the private? How can we nourish competitive industries and avoid the need for perpetual handouts? Those who label economic rationalism as the cause of all of our ills run the risk of implying that economic rationalism has absolutely nothing to commend it, and that the sorts of questions listed above need not be asked. Such a conclusion would mean a return to an antediluvian approach to economic policy.

Perhaps not surprisingly, economic rationalism is much discussed but rarely defined. A book that has attracted an enormous amount of attention, one around which much of the debate on economic rationalism has focused, is Michael Pusey's *Economic Rationalism in Canberra* (Pusey 1991). But look for a clear and concise definition of economic rationalism in the book, and you will not find it. The more one listens to those participating in the chorus of disapproval of, or approval for economic rationalism, the more ambiguous the term becomes. As Battin points out, the term 'might be used to describe any harsh cost cutting policy, to label any right-wing policy generally [and what is 'Right-wing'?], to identify the principle of user-pays, or to contrast it with other policies which are held to be, by implication, irrational' (Battin 1991: 295). Again, this ambiguity is unfortunate because debate will soon become meaningless unless there is some sort of agreement on just what is being debated. Furthermore, by using the term in such an all-embracing way, a misleading appearance of cohesion and of singularity of approach has been given to the way the Hawke/Keating governments' economic policies.

On this last point, it is appropriate to consider the Hawke government's steel, textiles and car plans, the subject of much complaint in daily news reports of plants closing and workers being laid off. The plans were certainly part of the mix of consensual policies (in this case through the use of sometimes protracted tri-partite negotiations between government and employers and trade unions in the industries concerned) and market-oriented ones. But there was more to the plans than just a decision to bring about phased reductions in protection and/or to encourage rationalisation within each industry. The plans were in fact contrary to the ideals of economic rationalism, in that they targeted selective industries, involved either government grants or the provision of temporary relief from import competition, and required that certain production, investment, employment, productivity and price targets be met.

Likewise, the prices and incomes Accord helped to achieve wage restraint, but was achieved not in response to market forces but, on the contrary, as part of a highly-centralised wage fixing process. Finally, one would be hard pressed to show how the Dawkins revolution in higher education, with its highly interventionist and centralising policies, and how so many of the Hawke government's environmental decisions, fit the 'economic rationalism' label. None of this is meant to deny the influence of economic rationalism as a force influencing economic policy, but it needs to be said that while the rhetoric seemed to triumph in the 1980s, it was not always converted into practice.

I return to the first proposition listed in this chapter. Decisions on whether particular economic policies should be adopted, modified or abandoned are influenced by the relative power of a variety of competing interest groups. To the extent that policies are a product of compromise, and that an economic rationalist policy approach provides benefits for some but distinct costs for others (witness the beleaguered manufacturing and public enterprise sectors), rhetoric will always be modified according to the relative power of those groups with something to win or lose as a result of a change to the status quo. Furthermore, it is always easier in a situation of economic buoyancy for governments to push new economic initiatives, and to win acceptance of the need for change. What the last few years have shown is that when instead the economy is plunged into deep recession, it becomes much harder, and politically more damaging, for governments to preach the virtues of policies involving more competition, less protection, and more self-reliance. These are likely to be seen no longer as a solution to, but as a cause of the nation's economic problems. The fate of the Coalition parties' *Fightback!* package provided a grim warning.

11
Industry Policy

WINTON HIGGINS*

Until the election of the Hawke government in 1983, 'industry assistance' was a familiar part of the Australian political tradition. The term referred mainly to a high and permanent tariff wall around our manufacturing industry, although it also covered bounties and the construction of roads, railways and ports for new industrial developments. Though the wisdom of this 'industry assistance' came under serious attack from the late 1960s, the term itself endured up to the publication of the ALP-ACTU Accord in February 1983.

The Accord promised something new, an industry *policy*. It was an international term that hinted at the abandonment of our native, single-instrument approach to industrial development in favour of something both more complex and more recognisable as a normal part of public economic management in other advanced capitalist countries, not least in those with enviable performances in international competition in traded industrial products. At least on the level of political rhetoric, the abandonment of traditional industry assistance was uncontroversial. But fundamental disagreement would ensue over the appropriate policy regime to replace it. The debate over industry policy plumbed basic issues about the meaning and uses of industrialisation in a society like ours, and about which conditions were likely to foster its development towards long-standing aspirations for an industrialised society. These issues reactivated the underlying and enduring conflicts in Western politics between economic liberals, who want all economic development to be determined by unregulated markets, and their collectivist critics, who advocate a role for public institutions in steering development.

This conflict originally explored the meaning of industrialisation, and it needs to be retrieved as the missing dimension in the present Australian debate. This I will attempt to do in the first section of this chapter. We can then move into the problems that industrialisation has posed in Australia from a political vantage point, and this we do in the

---

*I would like to thank Ian Hampson for sharing with me insights from his doctoral research on the politics of industry development in Australia. It would also like to thank the editors for their suggestions on earlier drafts.

second section. In the third section, we look at some of the more promising explanatory themes in the recent literature that seeks to identify the causes of competitive success and failure in manufacturing countries. As we shall discover, a nation's policy network emerges as a key variable in explaining success and failure. In the fourth section, as we follow the search for an Australian industry policy over the last decade, we will see how reform of our policy network became the central contested issue in the debate. The fifth section notes the failure to reform our policy network under the Labor government, and the consequent defeat of initiatives to introduce industry policy, a defeat that leaves intact a traditional and discredited approach to managing our manufacturing effort. In the sixth section I follow the line of retreat from industry policy adopted by a number of earlier proponents of reform in the wake of their political defeat. Finally, I will draw some not altogether optimistic conclusions.

The Politics of Industrialisation

In the classic account of the rise of economic liberalism in early nineteenth century England and of the consequences of its consolidation in Western countries, Polanyi (1957) characterises it as a highly interventionist political program to establish the Utopia of 'market society'. A common feature of human societies is the subordination of economic arrangements (including productive roles and how economic rewards are distributed) to social custom, which includes the clear ethical basis of community, as well as to accepted political authority. Economic liberals sought to reverse this relationship. Private property and unregulated markets, the operative elements of capitalist economy, were to become the sole legitimate constitutive influences on society. Economic liberal interventions sought to wipe out all existing political, ethical and communitarian institutions that infringed on rights of property, and to suppress any expression of collective interests that obstructed individualistic market behaviour. The creation and defence of this Utopia necessitated a 'nightwatchman state' whose manifold powers of coercion followed an exclusive and immutable agenda of enforcing individual property rights and contractual obligations.

Polanyi goes on to describe the 'social catastrophe' — pauperism, the brutality of the factory system and chaotic urbanisation — that this political program unleashed during the Industrial Revolution. Economic liberalism came under attack from a motley collection of sometimes reactionary, but increasingly radical enemies whose business was 'the self-protection of society': the reassertion of the ethical foundations of social life and of the state's role as a vehicle of elective and collective human purposes.

In Polanyi's presentation we see the origins of the perennial underlying polarity in Western politics. The clear and timeless political program of orthodox economic liberalism constitutes one pole. In *The Wealth of Nations*, Adam Smith (1776) had already conjured up a benign and omnipotent 'hidden hand' that underwrites the transcendent Reason behind the mundane discomforts of market society. On this basis an economics profession has grown up to legitimate economic liberal politics. At the counterpole gather diverse political currents of whom the most important for our purposes are various socialist currents and dissident collectivist liberals.

Economists and other economic liberals usually appeal to 'science' to justify their claims, but the conflict between economic liberalism and its opponents is fundamentally a political one between the proponents of 'market forces' on the one hand and advocates of conscious political guidance of economic development on the other (Esping-Andersen 1990). Should our political choices and processes shape our socio-economic destiny or should we abdicate the choice of both goals and means to the hidden hand?

The conflict has shown a remarkable propensity to surface in Western political life in all crucial areas of public policy, such as the management of the national manufacturing effort on which 'the wealth of nations' (apart from oil sheikhdoms) really depends. It does so for the obvious reason that manufacturing integrates the two greatest sources of wealth creation, large-scale human co-operation and labour-saving technology. At the same time it deploys the most powerful engine of wealth distribution, paid employment. But marked differences in the industrial fortunes of manufacturing nations alert us to the consequence of mismanaging the national manufacturing effort, as of course do the varying degrees of environmental degradation that it induces.

When economic liberals and their collectivist opponents bring their conflict into the realm of manufacturing politics, however, we become aware of a curious twist. The conceptual foundations of economic liberalism and of mainstream economic theory are both pre-industrial. Their analysis remains on a highly abstract level of allocating resources (land, labour and capital), and does not address the concrete issues of wealth creation in an industrialised society. In other words, the specificity of manufacturing, consisting of its organisational and technological issues, is lost in a highly abstract theory of economic action in general, one that abstracts in particular from historical and institutional settings and technological possibilities.

The analysis of specifically *industrial* development has thus fallen to the collectivist side of politics and the occasional dissident economist. Karl Marx criticised the incongruity between private forms of calculation holding sway over what were effectively interlocked society-wide industries. Less notorious, but in crucial ways more pointed, was the critique of the British collectivist liberals from the 1880s to the 1920s (Freeden 1978, 1986). Today's debate over industry policy owes more to them than to any other earlier intellectual influence. They can thus help us make the contemporary Australian debate intelligible.

Economic liberals have always celebrated (without specifically analysing) manufacturing precisely for its contribution to national wealth, or Gross Domestic Product (GDP) as we would say today. This is an abstract quantitative value, and also a measure of economic efficiency that admits of no enquiry into the product range it comprises or its social utility and distribution, still less the non-monetary (i.e., social, human and environmental) costs of its production. The 'new liberals' of the 1880s to World War I, by contrast, celebrated industrialisation for its potential to eliminate human drudgery and want (and so indirectly social and international conflict), to underpin social progress and to provide the working population with intellectually challenging employment. Tacitly, they were thus promoting an alternative measure of *industrial* efficiency based on social usefulness. Production was efficient to the extent that it targeted social need, served explicit priorities in social development and generated meaningful employment, provided benefits that were equitably distributed, and was consistent with an acceptable working and living environment.

Market-led industrialisation in Britain failed each of these criteria spectacularly (Tomlinson 1981: Chapters 1–3). The nineteenth century collectivist critics summed up its achievements as 'war, waste and unemployment'. Their successors in the 1920s had to confront the failure of *laissez-faire* industrialisation even on its own terms. Their inquiry into British industrial decline and recommendations for its reversal are contained in the famous Yellow Book (Liberal Industrial Inquiry 1928). Uninhibited by the assumptions and pre-industrial concepts of mainstream economics, its authors catalogued the backwardness, dislocation and disinvestment that unregulated market mechanisms and unfettered managerial prerogatives had led to. (After all, Britain was the birthplace, and remained the showpiece, of *laissez-faire* public economic management.) They proposed far-reaching, selective interventions whereby public authorities, working through new institutions, could take effective responsibility for Britain's manufacturing performance.

The Yellow Book remains the *locus classicus* of industry policy formation and the first blueprint for the institutional arrangements that could support it. But the ascendant Labour Party and the Conservatives stoutly defended their common stock-in-trade, orthodox economic liberalism, and consigned industry policy to political oblivion (Skidelsky 1967) — a scenario that essentially the same players would repeat a half-century later on the other side of the world.

The Original Sins of Australian Industrialisation

Two of the most striking features of Australia in the early 1990s are the supremacy of economic liberal politics (which both the major sides of federal politics espouse) and the real prospect of the country's late and fitful industrialisation being reversed. As I will suggest below, the one feature is implicated in the other. Less virulent strains of economic liberalism have accompanied our industrialisation since its inception in the 1910s, and have inhibited state and federal authorities (as well as organised capital and labour) from taking responsibility for the rational growth, integration and modernisation of our manufacturing base. Today's far more fundamentalist economic liberal revival (rebadged, but hardly revised, as 'economic rationalism') reveals its pre-industrial origins in an anti-manufacturing bias in public economic management. Indeed, we could borrow Margaret Thatcher's idiom to dub our patchy industrialisation a Wet liberal development, and its more recent doldrums a Dry liberal triumph.

But if we wish to analyse our industrial malaise more constructively we need to move on from the universal and abstract discourse of economic liberalism and look at the national institutions and policies that moulded our manufacturing sector. There are two compelling and interrelated reasons for doing so. First, as hinted before, there are winners and losers in industrial competition, and we have to identify those national influences that place us in the latter category. Second, as we shall see in the next section, the only analyses that seriously address our comparative industrial performance, and the question of how to salvage our industrial future, home in on the peculiarities of national institutional settings. But it is worth a brief look at Australian industry's historical emergence before returning to the conceptual issues that underpin today's industry policy debate.

By the end of the nineteenth century, Australia enjoyed the world's highest standard of living. It had a modern class structure in that around 76 per cent of the economically active population were wage earners (Castles 1988a: 110). The largely urban working population was poised to become the most unionised in the world (28 per cent in 1910: Kjellberg 1983: Table 3). In the early twentieth century Australia's maturing labour movement was well placed to take advantage of the tension between urban and rural capitalist interests by clinching an 'historical compromise' with the former. In this process Australian labourism crystallised around the three major points in the compromise — White Australia, protection and compulsory arbitration.

Castles (1985: 84–106) has characterised the thrust of this labourism as 'wage-earner security'. White Australia reinforced Australian labour's advantage in a high employment labour market, while trade protection secured its high wage levels. Arbitration shored up craft unionism (based on traditional skill classifications) and its fragmentation of organised labour into a large number of small, exclusive unions. So watertight did this security net appear for its white, male and employed beneficiaries that it distracted the labour movement from any ambitions towards a universalistic social policy, that is, one that would have directly addressed social insecurity in all its forms.

Labourism, together with the national prosperity based on primary industry that nurtured it, were all in place before mechanised production began in the years leading up to World War I. Secondary industry was a new area of expansion for urban capital (Connell and Irving 1992: 155–58), but given its permanent regime of protection and its narrow focus on the home market to the exclusion of any attempt to find export markets, secondary industry in Australia followed a quite different rationale from its modernising, prosperity-generating role elsewhere. Australian exports would remain overwhelmingly concentrated in the primary and mining sectors. Rather, industrial activity boosted redistribution of wealth from rural industries to urban centres. In particular, it became a mere support system for 'wage earner security', a generator of arbitration-regulated employment.

With the social usefulness of Australian industry so peculiarly limited, it grew up as the neglected child of pre-industrial labourism and a similarly pre-industrial liberal approach to economic management, pursued by both public authorities and capital. No interest group had a stake in the technical efficiency or rational integration of the manufacturing sector, and neither market pressures nor public authorities required it, since the sector could provide employment and redistribute income without producing goods efficiently as long as it was protected. For their part, the trade unions remained proudly aloof from managerial issues ('the boss's problems'). Obsolete plant was imported. State governments vied with each other in enticing new industrial establishments and, in their own tendering and procuring routines, favoured local state suppliers. The already small national market was thus further fragmented to spawn a disjointed mosaic of small-scale industrial facilities. Except during wartime emergencies, no public authority was charged with responsibility for national industrial performance. Public largesse was bestowed on corporate favourites, but no investment or efficiency requirements were enforced or even demanded in return (Ewer *et al.* 1987: Chapter 2). Behind the tariff wall, bi-partisan economic liberalism provided the alibi for this malign neglect.

During World War II, public authorities did intervene to rationalise industry, but the policy of neglect reasserted itself in the post-war reconstruction period. During this boom, which saw the expansion of industry to eclipse the primary and rural sectors' contribution to national income, tariffs and favouritism (now directed at foreign firms) exhausted the industry development agenda.

We have paid dearly for this policy stance. Small countries need to rely heavily on trade as a proportion of national product to maintain a high standard of living. Those small countries that have succeeded best have expanded manufactured exports in particular to take advantage of the fastest-growing category of post-war international trade — that with the most favourable movement in terms of trade. By contrast, Australia is the only small economy in the Organisation for Economic Co-operation and Development (OECD) area that is not a heavy trader. Indeed, it is the third most closed OECD economy after the United States and Japan, whose huge domestic markets obviate the need for heavy trade dependence. And the composition of our exports remained virtually static, with around 80 per cent comprising rural and mining commodities, which have suffered from fluctuating demand and declining terms of trade (Castles 1988a: Chapter 3).

The decay of the long boom in the late 1960s and early 70s revealed how unsustainable this model of economic development was for our standard of living — and for the traditional strategy of wage earner security. A spontaneous decline in investment in Australian manufacturing in the latter half of the 1960s began a vicious cycle of increasing backwardness, disorganisation and loss of domestic market shares to imports, while in the 10 years from 1974 manufacturing's share of total employment fell from 22.8 to 17.8 per cent (Ewer *et al.* 1987: Table 2.2, Chapter 3). From the mid-1970s, 'the lucky country', with the world's sixth highest standard of living, began its exceptional decline into a high unemployment, high inflation economy. By 1990 we had slipped to fourteenth place in terms of our GDP per capita, which was only 94 per cent of the OECD average (Dow 1993: Table 3.9). More recently, in the early 1990s, inflation has come under control in a recession at the expense of 11 per cent unemployment. Our traditional strategy of 'wage earner security' has left us with a stunted welfare state that has made the human misery attendant on this decline all the more palpable. In 1988 our social security transfers amounted to only 8.8 per cent of GDP, as against the OECD average of 13.2 per cent and even the United States' 10.6 per cent (Dow 1993: Table 3.13).

The rest, as they say, is (recent) history. Two successive economic liberal revivals (monetarism, then economic 'rationalism') in public policy fashions have accompanied our socio-economic decline. The accompaniment has commonly taken the form of tirades against the evils of dole bludging and tariff protection (with the latter label indiscriminately applied to any public policy stance other than deregulation). These have supposedly provoked the hidden hand into spanking mode.

How well has Australian industry performed under the new market discipline? The increased openness of the Australian economy has naturally led to a brisker trade in manufactured goods as we import manufactures we used to make ourselves and find export markets for some of our specialised manufactures which previously had none. But this development would only be a sign of industrial health and competitiveness if it were accompanied by a satisfactory rate of growth in our total industrial output and by signs that we were now moving towards balanced trade in manufactures. As it is, our industrial output rose only 40 per cent between 1975, when 'market forces' became the *leitmotif* of public economic management, and 1990. This is well below the OECD average of 60 per cent (Dow 1993: Table 3.3). In 1991–92 our manufactured trade deficit — spread over nine out of our twelve manufacturing industries — amounted to $17 billion, which is almost exactly the same deficit (in current prices) as that posted six years earlier (BIE 1993: 5).

Policy Networks and Industrial Fortunes

Some analysts of Australian manufacturing decline have fortunately rescued the discussion of policy options from the intellectual nadir described above, and particularly from the simplistic free trade versus protection debate. It is worth pausing again to take some conceptual bearings before plunging into the jungle of opinions about, and prescriptions for industrial health. This has sprung up in the decade since the term 'industry policy' began to circulate in Australian public policy debates, in the early 1980s.

The most important change in the international economy since World War II has been the growth in trade between, and in the trade dependency of the advanced capitalist countries of the OECD. In 1960, OECD countries on average traded 22.4 per cent of their GDP; by 1990 this proportion had risen to 38.1 per cent (Dow 1993: Table 3.11). As their economies have become increasingly interdependent, these countries have developed a range of policies and policy making institutions to manage this interdependence. Following Katzenstein (1978, 1985) we can locate four distinct groupings on a spectrum of policy responses to economic dependency. The liberal economies of the United States and Britain on the one hand, and the highly state-interventionist (or 'statist') Japanese economy on the other, constitute the two extremities of this spectrum. The larger continental European economies (France, Germany and Italy) occupy a position mid-way on the spectrum and exhibit both liberal and statist elements. Also located here is another group, industrially successful, small European countries, above all Sweden, Norway and Austria, which combine open economies with highly interventionist policies for industrial efficiency and smooth social adjustment to industrial change. These states are sometimes called 'democratic corporatist' ones, a reference to the way organised labour contributes directly to the policy process in these countries. One way to understand Australia's past and present policy choices is to contrast them with the strategy towards international competition this group has adopted.

Sweden, Norway and Austria have strong labour movements that have promoted generous welfare states and comprehensive economic policies to enhance the competitiveness of industrial exports. These arrangements support a strategy of 'domestic compensation' (Katzenstein

1985) whereby the national economy is left open to international economic impulses which trigger industrial development and restructuring, while people who directly bear the brunt of these changes (in the form of redundancy and regional decline) are compensated by welfare arrangements. The Australian tradition of 'wage earner security' reverses these principles. The Australian economy has been shielded from international influences in a strategy of 'domestic defence' (Castles 1988a: 92–93), which appeared to obviate the need for a comprehensive welfare state.

The different approaches to managing trade dependency and international vulnerability depend less on 'scientific' and public debate than on the kinds of political actors present in each country, their relationships and relative power. Once dominant political actors make their strategy choices and pursue them over time, the strategies so chosen tend to be institutionalised in policy making bodies which analyse problems within this perspective only. Each country thus exhibits not only a choice of strategy underlying its policy making in an area like the public management of the manufacturing sector, but also exhibits a 'policy network' (Katzenstein 1978: 19) which maintains the policy line. This network consists of the major interest organisations and social and public institutions, together with the coalitions, conflicts and relative power that permeate their interrelationships (Kenis and Schneider 1991).

Given the critical role manufacturing industry plays in each country's socio-economic destiny, the policy network's management of the national industrial effort is vital to a country's status as a winner or loser in international competition. Especially in the post-war period, the traditional economic liberal orientation of economic policy in Britain and the United States has placed them foremost among the losers in industrial competition, with large and growing deficits in trade in manufactured goods inflation (Ewer *et al.* 1987: Chapter 4, Audretsch 1991). They have suffered this discomfiture at the hands of the statist industrial powers (Japan, and more recently the newly industrialised 'tiger' economies of East Asia, especially South Korea), which operate huge trade surpluses. With statist industry policies, the larger continental economies (the third group) have held their own in international competition, while the fourth group, the small European economies, have not only held their own, but also produced the best long-term outcomes in terms of growth, employment levels, egalitarian distribution and low inflation (Schmidt 1982, Therborn 1986, ACTU/TDC 1987).

When we situate Australia in this international pattern, we come closer to appreciating the background to its dispiriting performance both as a manufacturer and as an equitable provider for its citizens. Its traditional policy stance of 'domestic defence', in contrast to the 'domestic compensation' of the successful small economies, has failed both to allow international impulses to constantly modernise and restructure our economy (especially our manufacturing sector), and to establish the policy institutions that would allow these processes to proceed with minimal human cost and political resistance. Behind the defensive shield we have maintained our Anglo-Saxon heritage of economic liberal public irresponsibility for industrial performance.

When the defensive shield began to fail in the 1970s, we compounded the problem by opting for the worst available option, managing our intensified interdependence by dogmatically abandoning what little leverage public authorities might have had on our industrial development. Instead of drawing lessons from the successful strategies of comparably-sized economies, we have aped the discredited deregulatory policies of Britain and the United States by dismantling (rather than re-shaping) co-ordinating mechanisms in the capital and labour markets, trade and currency. Labor in power not only colluded in this policy thrust, but led it, in a return to economic liberalism that invites comparison with Ramsay MacDonald's quixotry in Britain during the Great Depression (Skidelsky 1967, Higgins 1986). It has radically denied the state's 'deliberative capacity' and the industrial future it could have brought about. It has entrenched the politically partisan economics profession in the decisive policy organs as a prophylactic against both (Pusey 1991: Chapter 2, Ewer and Higgins 1986, Ewer *et al*. 1987: Chapter 5).

It is not hard to discern the historical influences at work in our national policy network that have converged in this choice. The coalition of Labor and urban capital referred to earlier continues (McEachern 1991: 103–4), but with internationalised finance capital displacing national manufacturing interests as the dominant voice in capital's political representation. Whatever the merits of the now unseated generations of 'nation building' labourist politicians and bureaucrats that Michael Pusey (1991: Chapter 5) extols, their liberal assumptions held them back from cultivating an interest — let alone a competence — in the art of production policy. At best, they championed the social utility of manufacturing as an employer and wealth distributor, while neglecting the technical and organisational preconditions to its becoming a sustainable generator of wealth.

But the past decade has also witnessed heroic attempts to reform and re-orient Australia's policy network. It remains for us to review the more salient of these efforts to identify the preconditions to industrial regeneration, and to write them into the policy agenda.

The Search for an Industry Policy

A common departure point for attempts to develop an industry policy in Australia has been the analysis of what statist and 'democratic corporatist' policy networks actually do when they foster successful industrial development. What specific needs of manufacturing can they meet, directly or indirectly? Answers to this question have come from correlating the preconditions to technological innovation and diffusion, rate of productivity growth and extending market share on the one hand, with the elements of industry policy that successful industrial states exhibit on the other. This was the approach adopted by the two major industry policy documents of the 1980s, one produced by the metal trades unions (MTU 1984) and one produced by the ACTU and the Trade Development Council (ACTU/TDC 1987) after a joint delegation visited Western Europe. Sympathetic academic analysts (e.g. Ewer *et al.* 1987: Chapter 4) also adopted this approach. Of the two union documents, the first focused on the Japanese variant, while the latter focused almost exclusively on the democratic corporatist models of Western Europe. A thematic summary may help us to appreciate the rationale of the reform agenda they proposed in the public management of Australia's manufacturing sector (see also Ewer *et al.* 1987: Chapter 4).

A considerable literature, particularly in economic history and management studies, points to a number of processes that are vital to sustained industrial expansion, but that market mechanisms fail to provide. First, infant industries require large amounts of seeding capital to develop their new processes and products, not least for research and development. But as their returns are particularly uncertain, and usually distant prospects at that, they do not attract the favour of financial markets in search of low risk, high yield, short-term placements. Invariably, they also require temporary protection, if not more positive forms of public assistance as well. Second, at the other end of the industrial life cycle 'mature' industries must undergo capital-intensive rationalisation and technological renewal if they are to survive. For similar reasons, finance is repelled from them as well. Third, industrial branches and technologies develop relations of mutual dependence; for example, steam and metallurgy, aluminium and power generation, machine tools and computers. Market mechanisms are poor guarantors that these vital linkages will be forged, let alone endure as new technologies develop. Fourth, certain industries occupy critical positions in a system of industrial linkages: basic inputs like steel, and producer goods (especially manufacturing equipment) which diffuse new technologies into the branches of manufacturing that use their products. Markets, oblivious to the importance of linkages, do not foster them and are prone to run them down. Fifth, new or expanding industries typically face formidable barriers to entry into markets already dominated by other suppliers. They may need to incur temporary heavy losses breaking into these markets and establishing distribution and service networks. Financial markets however, focus on short-term profitability.

Not least of the attractions of Japanese industry policy that the MTU (1984) took up was that it compensated for each of these market failures in its determination to take responsibility for national manufacturing performance. It has done so through an industry policy that is both overarching and highly selective, without coming anywhere near the pretensions or frailties of planned economies like those of the former Soviet bloc (Johnson 1992). Japan's post-war rise to international industrial dominance has been co-ordinated by public institutions that heavily protect potential export industries in their fledgling stages, forge links between interdependent industries, and underwrite heavy financial commitments in research and development and export facilitation schemes.

The Japanese policy network, however, included features that could not be reproduced in Australia or were abhorrent to the major advocate of an Australian industry policy, organised labour. The most important of the features that could not be reproduced are the *Keiretsu,* the 'industrial groups' which bring big industry and financial institutions together to meet industry's perennial need for external financing, while at the same time suppressing the anti-manufacturing forms of short-term calculation of unregulated financial systems. Without such a link, transplanting the Japanese model in Australia would require massive and politically unrealistic increases in public saving and investment.

Australian labour's resistance to the model however, had much more to do with its growing awareness of the dark side of the Japanese policy network: its resting on the suppression of organised labour in the 1950s and the latter's continuing exclusion from political and managerial processes. The consequent fragmentation and brutalisation of labour are integral to Japanese manufacturing systems as a whole (Williams *et al.* 1992). Moreover, the striking underdevelopment of social policy in Japan not only reflects the political exclusion of labour, but necessitates a permanent, massive trade surplus to maintain full employment and thus social stability. As the Australian union movement's creativity in industry policy intensified in the 1980s, its attention turned away from Japan to the 'democratic corporatist' industrial winners — Sweden, Norway and Austria. Like Australia (and unlike Japan), these small countries have had to seek their industrial fortunes in the wider world without the luxury of a huge domestic market in which to incubate potential export industries and provide a cushion against fluctuations in international demand. Moreover, each provided a positive example of organised labour's inclusion in the national policy network. Within it, labour movements (especially the unions) have acted as the bearers of economic rationality. They have taken the initiative in wage fixation, labour market policy, economic restructuring, the reform of work life, and in various mechanisms to steer investment into the key aspects of manufacturing development which financial markets invariably neglect (Higgins 1987).

Australia Reconstructed (ACTU/TDC 1987), the Report the ACTU delegation produced, may well rank as 'the most ambitious and sophisticated blueprint for economic and social policy ever produced in Australia' (Castles 1988a: 12). It argued for the socio-economic effectiveness of the policy regimes it had studied, and for their adaptability to conditions in Australia. As the title suggests, the Report outlines a major reconstruction of the national policy network to provide it with institutions charged with fostering industrial regeneration. An affront to the policy tradition shared by both government and Opposition, it advocated collective (and otherwise targeted) capital formation, state intervention to promote rationalisation and new industrial technologies, export facilitation, labour market programs and the reform of work life (including radical changes to job classifications and union structure that broke with craft unionism). In short, the Report appeared to be heralding the 'social democratisation' of the Australian union movement, an attempt to move on from an abstentionist, pre-industrial labourism to an industrial union movement capable of playing a leading role in public and private economic management (Higgins 1987).

But the attempt to graft social democratic forms of mobilisation on to the Australian labour movement failed. The message of *Australia Reconstructed* fell on the deaf 'rationalist' ears of the Labor government, except to the extent that the latter took up certain labour market proposals and reworked them to fit into its unfolding deregulatory mission. (We will return to these matters in the next section.) Within the union movement itself the policy proposals foundered under the historical weight of factionalism, the vested interests of craft union élites and labourist incomprehension of the new interventionist 'strategic unionism' (Ewer *et al.* 1991: 78–80).

In the wake of this Report, industry policy remained nailed to the ACTU mast (see ACTU 1987, 1990). But in practice, the ACTU has run dead on industry policy in recent years, choosing to manage its 'special relationship' with the federal government (symbolised by the close personal ties between ACTU secretary, Bill Kelty, and Paul Keating) on the basis of the uncontroversial remnants of the original vision (encapsulated in award restructuring) and on Accord renegotiations which hardly go beyond wage-tax trade offs.

The most recent attempt to revive the search for an Australian industry policy has come not directly from the labour movement but from the consultants Pappas Carter Evans and Coop. They undertook a major project on Australia's industrial future for the Australian Manufacturing Council (AMC), a tri-partite body on which unions, employers and government are represented. *The Global Challenge: Australian Manufacturing in the 1990s* (AMC 1990) is a far more conciliatory document than *Australia Reconstructed*. Its underlying model is not Scandinavian but Canadian, and thus technocratic to the exclusion of organised labour's participation in the policy process. It maintains a deferential tone towards neo-classical free trade nostrums (although without binding itself to them), and what it says about labour market reform (under the rubric 'new workplace culture') would certainly not jar the ear of the Business Council of Australia.

Nonetheless *Global Challenge* argues against the myth of the 'level playing field' and in favour of a strong tradeable manufacturing sector to restore Australia's prosperity. Its originality lies in its careful identification of the kinds of industries Australia could realistically include in a resurgent manufacturing sector, given the country's resources, size and distance from significant markets. It advocates further industrial refinement of our resource exports; this would generate added value and reduce shipping costs. It suggests we remedy our natural disadvantage in non-resource-based scale-intensive industries (such as cars, aerospace and information) by integrating local manufacture into the increasingly internationalised production process. It also suggests we use our skill base to develop industrial complementarities with Asian manufacturing, to sustain knowledge-intensive industries. Our overall aim, urges the Report, should be to increase the number of strong exporting firms.

The Report also develops some relatively inexpensive suggestions for realising these ideas. Public support could partially underwrite the financially risky processes of breaking into overseas markets, research and development and capitalising infant industries. With a little administrative creativity both federal and state authorities could co-ordinate public procurement to foster local manufacturing and forge linkages ('networking') between actually or potentially related industries.

Despite its authors insisting that *Global Challenge* is based on 'a new paradigm', one that transcends the stale protectionism versus free trade debate, the highly-placed holders of the hidden hand were not beguiled. 'Most of Canberra cleaves strongly to the neo-classical view,' was the rueful response of one of the Report's authors to its frosty reception there (Evans 1991: 40).

The Empire Strikes Back

As we have seen, Australian unions until recent times abstained from getting involved in production issues. The little they contributed to discussion on industry assistance before the late 1970s was restricted to support for manufacturers' interests that coincided with their own (Warhurst 1982: 124). In this field, as in economic policy in general, the 1983 ALP/ACTU Accord appeared to be a watershed. It heralded union inclusion in policy making, both in the ACTU being a signatory to this far-reaching policy document, and in the tri-partite institutions for which it provided — a tri-partism that promised the union movement's greater participation in the policy network.

But the Accord also appeared to herald a new era in the management of the manufacturing sector by committing the ALP and the union movement to a comprehensive industry policy. The Accord proclaimed a return to full employment as the 'paramount' objective of economic policy, and denounced 'the inappropriateness of general economic management policies and the *ad hoc*ery and uncertainty of specific policies'. The recession and dismal economic outlook, it argued, 'demonstrate the hopelessness of policies which seek to attain full employment by use of market forces alone'. The parties to the Accord committed themselves to 'interventionist policies which are closely monitored and comprehensive in nature'. They also committed themselves to establish new tri-partite institutions to perform this close monitoring, and to review the activities of the Industries Assistance Commission (IAC), the prominent institutional expression of the pure market approach against which the Accord set its face (ALP/ACTU 1983: 416–17).

With hindsight it seems that the ALP leadership entered into these commitments with the same cynical electoral calculus that its British counterpart demonstrated in the forlorn history of social contract politics in the 1960s and 70s (Panitch 1976). In neither case was there any indication that the political leadership intended to honour its promises. Deregulation set the tone of economic policy virtually from the start (Langmore 1991). The main tri-partite 'planning' body set up under the Accord, the Economic Planning Advisory Council (EPAC) was soon colonised by Treasury and its fellow travellers. It became a legitimator of 'rationalist' policies — with the added twist that the ACTU's participation locked it into complicity with them (Boreham 1990).

The IAC, formerly the Tariff Board, is an ancient part of the Australian policy network. In 1967 it was the entry point of a free trade approach to managing the manufacturing sector, by its then-chairman, G.A. Rattigan (Glezer 1982: 71, 91–94). When the Whitlam government revamped the Board in 1973 as the IAC, its hard line free trade approach earned it the nickname Industries Assassination Commission. It has steadfastly held to Ricardian trade theory which, applied to Australia, suggests that we enjoy no comparative advantage as a manufacturer, and that an 'efficient' allocation of resources — one arranged by the hidden hand — would see them invested in a post-industrial (that is, de-industrialised) future. In short, we would revert to our pre-industrial export mix, plus services. On the level playing field we make it as drink waiters in the tourist industry, but not as engineers.

Since the IAC was the government's major source of policy on the management of the manufacturing sector, the review of its workings promised in the Accord was obviously a precondition to the industry policy the latter outlined. The appointment of a prominent free trader and anti-unionist, John Uhrig (later chairman of the Westpac board), to chair the review, was a good measure of the government's 'commitment' to the promised reforms. Uhrig, predictably, found the IAC to be in no need of reform, and it continued to be an influential advocate of economic liberalism (Warhurst and Stewart 1989: 169–70). In 1989, the Treasurer, Paul Keating, returned it to its spiritual home in Treasury, having merged it with the Interstate Commission and renamed it the Industries Commission (IC). He appointed Tony Cole, his own former senior private secretary, to its chair. Keating affirmed the Commission's still 'greater role in industry policy...as the government's major review and inquiry body in industrial affairs' (*Australian Financial Review*, 16 August 1989).

At the same time, the government appointed Professor Ross Garnaut to write its keynote policy document on one of its major long-term ambitions, Australia's integration with the more 'dynamic' Asian economies. Garnaut was a well-known publicist for deregulatory policies and Australia's economic integration into Asia (see, for instance, Anderson and Garnaut 1986), and there was little doubt about the conclusions that his 'review' would turn up. In his much-promoted Report, Garnaut (1989) sought the abolition of all tariffs, anti-dumping provisions and other forms of protection (read intervention), by the year 2000. The IC (1991) then supported the Garnaut line with its own analysis of the industrial winners of East Asia. In this particular reckless flight of the neo-classical imagination, even the most statist of all countries, Japan and the Republic of Korea, find their way into the pantheon of 'market conforming' economic liberal heroes!

There has been no shortage of arguments that the government's deregulatory approach to managing the manufacturing sector amounts to (in the words of the most impressive of them) 'a quiet revolution' and a fundamental change from a 'protective' to a 'corrective' state (Capling and Galligan 1992: xi, Chapter 4). But this kind of argument rests on institutional changes alone, and neglects the historical and doctrinal, as well as the overriding deregulatory thrust of economic policy. When Labor's policies on manufacturing are seen in this context, they reveal their political traditionalism, and the failure of reform under the Accord becomes the more interesting question to study. A number of writers who have taken up this question (Stilwell 1986, Ewer *et al.* 1991, Bell 1991) have argued that the union movement was too weak and divided to hold the ALP leadership to its undertakings, and that the Accord's claim to have broken with the past has in any event been exaggerated. In fact, it preserved aspects of the labourist tradition, in its failure to break with the 'wage earner security' legacy that excluded the interests of women and welfare recipients; in its failure to espouse comprehensive welfare arrangements that might have addressed a broad spectrum of social inequalities; and in its not seeking to make inroads into capital's socio-economic power. Certainly, Labor's management of the manufacturing sector was marked far more by continuities: a commitment to liberal economic management laced with *ad hoc* interventions to assuage the pressing electoral demands of its constituency. The only real discontinuities were the tariff cuts, the new economic liberal slogans ('market freedoms', 'level playing field'), and the corresponding demotion of *ad ho*cery.

As I have indicated, the main obstacles to industry policy under Labor have been its emphasis on macro-economic policy and the precedence the government has given its deregulatory economic policy. Both of these were antithetical to the selective intervention that make up an industry policy. Labor's priorities have meant that the key economic ministries (Treasury, Finance, and Prime Minister and Cabinet) have overshadowed the Department of Industry, Technology and Commerce (DITAC), the Department of Trade and the Department of Employment and Industrial Relations (DEIR), the federal departments most concerned with the manufacturing sector. Of these three, only DITAC has had a direct role in the sector. For most of Labor's term Senator John Button the Minister responsible for DITAC. He generally supported the government's free market policies, and the advice he received from the Bureau of Industry Economics (BIE) within DITAC has closely followed the IC's reports. But he has also presided over a number of sectoral 'plans' which, while hardly adding up to an industry policy for the manufacturing sector as a whole, provided a glimpse of what such a policy might have achieved.

For the purposes of this chapter, the car plan is the least interesting of the sectoral plans. It was an inheritance from the Fraser Liberal government, and even under Labor it continued to rely mainly on the manipulation of tariffs to induce necessary rationalisation of the overabundant manufacturers and car models in the industry. DITAC's first sectoral initiative under Labor, however, was the steel plan of 1983–88, an intervention into a crisis-ridden basic industry that was greatly facilitated by the fact that it had to be negotiated with only one employer, BHP. This plan went well beyond the traditional manipulation of tariffs and bounties to include the novelties of a basic agreement between the government, unions and BHP on investment and productivity targets and industrial relations. An independent tri-partite body, the Steel Industry Authority, was set up to monitor progress. The plan allowed BHP to rationalise and so maintain its facilities in Newcastle, Wollongong and Whyalla, to recover its share of the domestic market and become a successful exporter (Capling and Galligan 1992: 184–92).

Under union pressure, DITAC agreed to follow this precedent with the Heavy Engineering Adjustment and Development Programme of 1986–89. It also gave private firms targeted assistance under a tri-partite agreement covering productivity gains through job reorganisation and increased managerial efficiency. The plan was implemented by a tri-partite Heavy Engineering Board within DITAC, which vetted the corporate plans that firms had to submit in order to participate in the assistance measures (Bell 1991: 123).

But even these sectoral plans were at risk of being overtaken by the government's short-term budgetary policy. The 1986 federal Budget cut the bounties promised by the steel plan by 20 per cent. The 1987 Budget sliced $17 million off the original commitment of $90 million to the heavy engineering plan (Higgins 1991: 112, Capling and Galligan 1992: 186). A similar fate overtook DITAC's fourth sectoral plan covering mature industries, the textile, clothing and footwear (TCF) plan. This was adopted in 1986 and was institutionally less creative, since its major mechanism was phased reductions in protection over the ensuing decade. Despite the plan's tri-partite origins, the government's March 1991 Industry Statement unilaterally accelerated the tariff reductions that had been negotiated (Capling and Galligan 1992: 248–49).

DITAC has also intervened (albeit with much more modest levels of assistance) in 'sunrise industries' such as aerospace, pharmaceuticals, information, food and mineral processing and forestry. But it made it clear that these sectoral interventions are exceptions to its preference for non-selective forms of industry development (Bell 1991: 123–24, DITAC 1986: 23).

The one body that might have had the potential to form a comprehensive industry policy was the tri-partite Australian Manufacturing Council (AMC), which came under the aegis of DITAC and in turn had a number of sectoral industry councils under it. The Accord provided for the reform of the AMC (originally set up in 1977), but the Labor government delayed re-establishment as it engaged the union movement in a long-drawn-out dispute over its charter and the appointment of a director of its secretariat. The industry councils were not set up until 1984, and were under-resourced, as was the AMC itself. All this helped to marginalise the AMC, which in any event had no authority to implement its proposals. Even within DITAC it had to contend with the ideological opposition of the BIE (Ewer *et al.* 1987: 123–25).

Some sections within the Department of Employment and Industrial Relations (DEIR, later DIR) and the Department of Trade defied the economic liberal orthodoxy in Canberra. These departments, however, had a much less direct impact than DITAC on the manufacturing sector. The DEIR promoted industrial democracy which could have facilitated productivity growth under an industry policy, even though it falls outside the conventional limits of that policy. The Department of Trade, on the other hand, could have contributed more to an industry policy because of the way trade policy influences the competitive pressures and market opportunities of industry. Lionel Bowen, the first Minister of Trade under Labor, set up a tri-partite Business Union Consultative Unit (BUCU) within the existing Trade Development Council (TDC) in his department. The BUCU had strong union links. Under Ted Wilshire's leadership it began to develop and propagate elements of industry policy — the only federal body to do so apart from the AMC. The BUCU initiated a number of union/TDC projects, the most important of which was the 1986 ACTU/TDC delegation to Western Europe that produced *Australia Reconstructed*. But as the government's attitude to industry policy hardened, the BUCU's influence declined. In 1989 it was reduced in size, renamed the Directorate of Industrial Relations Development, and moved to the DIR. Two years later it was abolished altogether (Higgins 1991: 109).

In Australia, federal authorities control the most important elements of public economic management that affect our manufacturing fortunes: monetary and fiscal policy, the revenue required for possible major interventions; exchange rate, tariff and trade policy; and significant labour market and financial regulation. The problem was not simply that Labor refused to adopt industry policy, but that its choices in other areas of policy tended to frustrate manufacturing enterprise (Dow 1992, Carroll 1992, Marceau 1992). This has left little room for state governments to pursue industry development policies, although some attempts in this direction have been made, the most ambitious of them in Victoria. Indeed the fate of Victoria's industry policy illustrates the difficulties of operating an industry policy in a deregulatory environment.

Industry policy was an integral part of the Cain government's economic strategy, which it developed in a series of policy documents over four years. The first of them, *The Next Step*, was released in 1984. The strategy recognised the inadequacy of the state's financial resources to intervene effectively in large-scale industry, and so concentrated on medium-to-small enterprise. It targeted two kinds of enterprise in particular — new 'hi-tech' firms and mature firms that were based on the exploitation of Victoria's natural resources. The State Department of Industry, Technology and Resources (DITR) was expanded to co-ordinate industry policy. The Victorian Investment Corporation (VIC) was established to provide 'seeding money' to new firms, and the existing Victorian Economic Development Corporation (VEDC) was upgraded to inject capital into mature industries. Victoria pioneered a successful Industrial Supply Office (ISO) to link local capital equipment makers to new projects and other equipment users in the state — an innovation which the New South Wales and federal governments later adopted. The Victorian government also introduced new training and export facilitation programs and stimulated industrial research (Hartnett 1991: 154–58, Ewer *et al.* 1987: 131–33).

The later spectacular financial collapses in Victoria politically discredited all forms of interventionism under the economic strategy, including industry policy. Both the VIC and VEDC had (under pressure from a deregulatory, 'easy money' environment) left themselves exposed to the stock market crash of 1987, and the subsequent collapse of property values. Although smaller than the other important Victorian financial institutions that failed (Tricontinental, the State Bank and the Pyramid Building Society), their fall obscured the gains of the strategy.

At all times between 1983 and 1989, Victoria's unemployment was the lowest of any state; its employment growth exceeded the national average (2.7 per cent against 2.5 per cent), and investment grew at an annual average of 7.9 per cent, well above the national average of 4.5 per cent. At the same time it had the lowest growth rate in government expenditure (Hartnett 1991: 159–60).

In sum, industry policy has disappeared once more from Labor's agenda. The old tradition of 'general economic management policies and the *ad ho*cery and uncertainty of specific policies', that the Accord so pointedly foreswore, have gained a new lease of life. And once again, it has bi-partisan support. In the Liberal and National Parties' program for the 1993 Federal Election, *Fightback!*, industrial development was reduced to familiar macro-economic headings (tariff policy and deregulation, especially in the labour market) and to 'infrastructure reform' (Hewson and Fischer 1991: 57–59).

Flexible Deckchair Arrangement: A Surrogate Industry Policy

A central argument in this chapter is that industrial success depends primarily on a policy network capable of managing the national industrial effort by meeting certain institutional, technical and financial preconditions that are peculiar to manufacturing activity. The failure of Australia's manufacturing effort — the root cause of our structural trade deficit, growing foreign indebtedness and declining relative prosperity — can be traced to the persistence of a pre-industrial policy network infused with an equally pre-industrial cocktail of economic liberalism and labourism.

That is not to say that the reform of our policy network and development of an appropriate industry policy could turn Australia into another 'Asian tiger'. In the British case, Cutler *et al.* (1986: Chapter 4) have dampened enthusiasm for Japanese-style industry policy by pointing out that its success rests on firms with efficient manufacturing systems capable of taking up the challenges and opportunities that the policy regime creates. British management being what it is, these authors are pessimistic about the outcome of even the most finely-tuned of hypothetical industry policies. Given the closeness of the Australian managerial tradition to its British counterpart, naïve optimism would be equally out of place here. In an earlier study of British industrial failure, the same group of analysts identified four factors that impinge on enterprise decision making and hence bear the seeds of industrial success or failure: the industrial firms' relationship to external sources of finance; government economic policies and operations (such as public procurement); market structure and composition of demand; and the industrial relations system, including job and skill classifications and managerial traditions (Williams *et al.* 1983: Introduction). Industry policy can help to rectify, but can hardly eradicate, all the obstacles to industrial progress that can lurk in these four broad areas.

An international managerial literature that tends to downplay or ignore the role policy reform must play has taken up the search for 'winning' manufacturing strategies and systems (e.g. Hayes and Wheelwright 1984). Some of this literature has its virtues as a complement to industry policy, but when it suggests manufacturing success can be conjured up in a policy vacuum it diverts us from an essential reform agenda. It also has a tendency, as Williams *et al.* (1983) point out, to narrow its search for manufacturing disorders to 'the labour problem'. Labour costs are among the few readily quantifiable factors in the analysis of comparative industrial performance, and empirical researchers are thus tempted to give them undue weight. More importantly, empirical findings can give credence to sloppy cultural stereotypes, such as the enthusiastic, loyal Japanese worker versus the slack, belligerent Australian one.

The Australian industrial relations system is, by common consent, badly in need of reform if the country is to retrieve its industrial fortunes. Narrow job and skill classifications, the Byzantine award structure and craft unionism obstruct the technological diffusion and job re-organisation necessary to introduce new processes and products and to win the productivity gains necessary for international competitiveness. Award restructuring, the most prominent item on this agenda, was heralded in *Australia Reconstructed* in the context (as we saw earlier) of a comprehensive industrial reform program. The union movement's line of political retreat from this ambitious project has been the line of least resistance into an exclusive focus on award restructuring. Presented in isolation, award restructuring does not ruffle a single Treasury or Business Council feather. On the contrary, it is the stuff of Labor's new world of consensus politics, the lion lying down with the lamb.

The music that so soothes the savage beast is contained in the word 'flexibility'. If a manufacturing system is imbued with flexibility — which is predominantly an attribute of labour — it can meet any contingency and rise to any challenge, without the need for politically divisive industry policy. In the mouths of employer lobbies, flexibility tends simply to recap the traditional Anglo-Saxon managerial mission to build a cheap, docile, expendable and above all non-unionised labour force. In the mouths of economists it refers to removing the 'rigidities' of labour market regulation to cheapen labour inputs (i.e., reduce real wage incomes and working conditions) and raise profits. But neither of these agendas could easily be smuggled undetected past an experienced shop steward. What has proved considerably more seductive is the account of flexibility contained in two overlapping grand narratives, 'post-Fordism' and 'flexible specialisation'.

The thrust of these narratives is that mass production, together with the assembly lines and narrow job classifications based on it, are becoming increasingly unviable as markets for standardised goods become saturated, and the pattern of demand turns towards a diverse range of customised commodities. Instead of the rigid, integrated assembly lines based on dedicated machinery and a highly fragmented labour process appropriate to long production runs ('Fordism'), today's successful manufacturer deploys flexible plant and a broadly skilled workforce that is capable of producing a range of products with minimal turnover times, making much shorter production series commercially viable. Relatively autonomous work teams replace assembly lines, as 'linear' processes give way to 'cellular' ones ('post-Fordism': see especially Piore and Sabel 1984, Mathews 1989a, 1989b, Hirst and Zeitlin 1989).

Even to this point, the tale is somewhat problematic, especially in the lack of clarity of the key terms 'mass production' and 'flexible specialisation', and in the lack of empirical support for the central historical assertion that the one is giving way to the other. But two important claims then add to the confusion. The first is the suggestion that cellular production works best if it is democratically organised. The second is the association of the new (invariably Japanese) manufacturing systems with 'lean production', by which term they are better known in Western managerial circles. 'Lean production' refers to a variety of techniques to greatly increase the tempo of work and the tasks of each worker, while reducing the firm's need to store components through just-in-time (JIT) techniques.

The concept of 'lean production' was launched in a management book with the suitably epic title *The Machine that Changed the World* (Womack *et al.* 1990), based on a study of the United States and Japanese car industries. As the Japanese (with Toyota in the lead) were pushing the major American car makers out of the American market, the authors chose a central issue in comparative manufacturing performance. They found that the American firms had clung to mass production techniques, with all their quality and productivity problems, while the Japanese had used a radically different 'lean' system which, among other things, halved the labour content in each car. Happily, the Japanese were found to be transplanting these systems to the United States, so that as the latter took hold in domestic production, balanced trade would be restored.

The methodology and findings of the MIT research project and the claims in the book have been seriously questioned. Williams *et al.* (1992) demonstrate that the contrast between lean and mass production is not empirically sustainable; the Japanese productivity gains are considerably exaggerated and are partly due to temporary historical factors quite different from those identified by the researchers, and partly to component manufacture in small firms that are in fact traditional sweatshops. Nor are the Japanese exporting their manufacturing systems. What they are transplanting is their approach to labour management. This is summed up in the Japanese term *kaizen* ('continuous improvement'), usually retranslated as 'management by stress'. This refers to such practices as deliberate understaffing and the use of 'andon boards' that identify the slower workers (so that their colleagues can rush to their assistance), with routine use of unpaid overtime, foregone holidays and so forth.

The ACTU has retreated from its commitments to a comprehensive industry policy in *Australia Reconstructed*, to award restructuring and thence to enterprise bargaining in a major concession to labour market deregulation. 'Flexibility' has been the ubiquitous slogan that has covered this retreat, and not coincidentally it has also covered employers' successful onslaught on both labour market regulation and the standing of unions as negotiators (Ewer *et al*. 1991: Chapters 6–8). Both sides have promoted 'flexibility' as the necessary and sufficient basis for an industrial renaissance in Australia. If the argument of this chapter is correct, this attempt to dispense with industry policy will leave today's mass unemployment and declining real incomes unaddressed. Labour market deregulation in pursuit of 'flexibility' will also marginalise unions and erode equity and solidarity within the workforce (with women and migrants the predictable victims). Beyond that, 'Japanolatry' and enterprise bargaining on a deregulated labour market leaves the door open to an Australian version of *kaizen*. 'Flexibility' comes down to 'management's right to manage' (another currently popular slogan in managerial circles), free from the 'rigidities' of regulation to secure workers' rights and of the obligation to negotiate change with them or their organisations.

Conclusion

Political debate over industry policy is still a relative novelty in Australian political life. But it rehearses in clear terms an older, broader conflict over the promises and purposes of industrialisation as such, a conflict that goes to the heart of Western political life. In this chapter I have attempted to situate the Australian debate in its proper doctrinal context so that the positions taken by the protagonists in the industry policy debate can find both their true relation and due proportion. These are not rarefied conversations between specialists on the merits of alternative technocratic models, though the technocrat (especially the economist) never ceases to try to spirit moral choices out of the public domain in this guise.

As I suggested in the first section of this chapter, the moral choices were built into the two contending notions of efficiency that industrialisation as a socio-economic phenomenon called forth over a century ago. The economic liberal notion emphasised market dominance and abstract national 'wealth'. In our times, these criteria translate into the outcomes that internationalised financial institutions applaud and reward: high (paper) profitability, low public expenditure and balance of payments equilibrium. Whatever advantages these conditions may bestow, they are hardly the uncontroversial *goals* of economic activity (as 'rationalists' assume) for which social injustice, insecurity and environmental degradation are self-evidently acceptable sacrifices.

Against the denial of moral issues endemic in economic liberalism, we can set the collectivist attempt to define moral aspirations for industrialisation and so define efficiency in terms of social and human outcomes: social equity, affluence and quality of life (including work life). Despite the formidable productivity gains in industrialised societies since these aspirations were formulated — gains that brought them within easy reach technically — few societies have approached their fulfilment. In Australia in the 1990s they are remote — and receding. No lack of resources or technical opportunities have led to this dispiriting outcome, but rather the absence of the political will to pursue sustainable industrialisation and mould it to coherent social priorities. Today, as Australia de-industrialises and degenerates into increasing social insecurity and injustice, the absence of that political will is more palpable than ever.

Herein lie two related ironies. First, the recent political breakthough of economic liberal fundamentalism in public economic management has gone hand in hand with Australia's economic failure in this tradition's own terms: massive Budget and balance of payments deficits and spiralling foreign indebtedness. As Polanyi (1957: Part 2) argued so long ago, 'market society' is an ultimately unachievable Utopia, but its pursuit is an enormously destructive undertaking. Second, while the native labourist tradition originally (if haphazardly) integrated liberal economy with some sense of the social usefulness of a manufacturing base, it has now resolved the tension between the two by being 'born again' in the new, purer economic liberal fold. Labourism marches on unreformed, but now as the gravedigger of Australian industry rather than as its neglectful guardian.

The origins of industry policy lie in the collectivist tradition. Attempts over the last decade of Labor government to promote an Australian industry policy have naturally gone hand in hand with an attempt to settle accounts with a pre-industrial, liberal-leaning labourism. The reformers have tried to do this by introducing into the labour movement some of the industrial and collectivist tenets of social democracy. This reforming thrust appeared particularly appropriate given the role of social democratic labour movements in the small successful industrialised economies of Europe. But the reformers worked from too narrow a base in a wider, factionalised union movement, much of which still reflected the traditionalism of the Labor leadership itself. In the hostile climate of the 'rationalist' ascendancy, the attempt to transplant both social democracy and industry policy failed.

For the first five years of Labor government, the ACTU and the manufacturing unions provided the only authoritative and coherent Left opposition to bi-partisan economic liberal economic policies. Industry policy was this Opposition's major stock-in-trade. But as it has been forced into retreat since the late 1980s, it has effectively abandoned industry policy and lapsed into the political incoherence of labour market 'flexibility' as a surrogate for industry policy, a political line that converges with the deregulatory enthusiasm of today's prophets of market society.

Whether Australia is ever to get an industry policy — and thus stand a chance of enjoying an industrial future — depends on some future Left opposition proving itself capable of conceiving and implementing the necessary institutional reform of our policy network. No such development is currently on the horizon. But when that opposition does emerge it will face some hard questions about the fate of both industry policy in Australia and of social democracy in the latter's home territories over the decade reviewed here. Why did it prove so difficult to mobilise around industry policy among the union rank and file and in Labor's wider constituency? Why has European social democracy itself failed to hold an ideological line against economic liberalism? How useful are any of the existing overseas policy models in harnessing viable manufacturing to defensible social priorities, including environmental sustainability?

It would be a fair guess that these questions will dissuade a new Left opposition from merely dusting off the industry policy canons reviewed here. But we can be confident that industry policy will be the lynchpin of its reform strategy. And if it is to prove adequate to the job of salvaging a morally sustainable society after the 'rationalist' deluge, the Left will need to go back to first principles. What, it must ask, is industrialisation for?

12
Unions, the Accord and Economic Restructuring

MARK BRAY*

Introduction

For most of the twentieth century the general public and many social commentators have perceived the trade union movement as a powerful force in Australian economic and political affairs. Until the 1920s, union membership as a proportion of the working population was the highest in the world: union density, as it is technically known, remained at around 50 per cent until the 1980s. This strength of membership, combined with the backing of a relatively successful political party, the Australian Labor Party, and significant institutional support from a compulsory arbitration system, seemed to indicate an Australian union movement of considerable importance.

Its position, however, was not as impressive as it seemed. Unions lacked genuine power, said some critics, because of their small size and fragmented structure, and because of their dependence on the arbitration system (Howard 1977, Martin 1980). Similarly, their close relationship with the Labor Party was said to weaken their industrial strength by diverting organisational effort away from their workplace base (Kuhn 1952). While unions exercised considerable political clout when Labor held office at state level, their influence was confined to traditional 'industrial' issues (like wages, hours of work and annual holidays). The political failures of Labor at federal level excluded unions from the 'real' corridors of power (Martin 1963–64). In recent times even union leaders have acknowledged the weakness of unions' traditional position in Australian society, attributing it to a 'relatively benign environment':

> Workers accepted unionism readily; governments were often willing to bargain with unions and pass supportive legislation; many employers, cushioned by tariffs or catering for non-competitive markets, struck up close relations with unions; industrial tribunals provided union recognition and award regulation of employment conditions; these

*I would like to thank John Buchanan, Pat Walsh and George Strauss for comments on earlier drafts of this chapter.

institutions tended to support centralised industrial relations policies. This was Australia's traditional system of industrial relations. (Crean and Rimmer 1990: 50)

The role of unions in economic restructuring provides a valuable case study in the limits of their power. The first section of this chapter argues that the Australian union movement's influence before 1983 over restructuring issues at both macro- and micro-levels was at best weak. It was confined to a relatively narrow range of objectives associated with the consequences of restructuring rather than its direction. Even in those instances where unions sought and achieved broader influence, their policies were defensive and unco-ordinated. The causes of this limited influence lay in the hands of the unions themselves, and in the environment in which they operated.

During the 1980s, the unions came to recognise the weaknesses of their traditional approach. In the context of economic crises, which threatened the jobs and incomes of their members, and in response to a series of political challenges, they adopted a new strategy. As the second section of this chapter reveals, Australian unions became less defensive and more accepting of the need for change. In fact, the union movement became a leading advocate of policies which encouraged greater economic efficiency and productivity. This new approach demonstrated a far broader range of policy interests, moving the union movement away from a preoccupation with questions of income distribution, to questions of the production and creation of wealth. Australian unions also sought more effectively to co-ordinate their activities, producing a more strategic approach.

The main instrument by which unions sought to implement their new strategy was the Accord between the ACTU and the Labor government. This had its origins in the late 1970s, but became a reality in February 1983, just before the election which brought the Labor government to power (Kelly 1992: 707–8). Under it, the Labor Party and the ACTU agreed to work towards a number of common policy objectives. These were initially set out in a written document, which with subsequent revisions has become more of an informal agreement. Nonetheless, the Accord has been at the heart of Australian politics and industrial relations since (Stilwell 1986, Carney 1988, Singleton 1990).

Few commentators have questioned the importance of the Accord, but considerable debate has emerged over how it (and the allied change in national union strategy which it represents) should be interpreted. In particular, differences have developed between those who have heralded the Accord as an experiment in 'corporatism' (Bray and Walsh 1993, Archer 1992), and others who reject this label (e.g. Gardner 1990). The latter argue that the Accord falls comfortably within the 'labourist' traditions of the Australian labour movement (Singleton 1990, Matthews

1991). Much of the debate revolves around ambiguities in the definitions of 'corporatism' and 'labourism'. The controversy is valuable, however, because it focuses attention more closely on at least two important aspects of the Accord experience: the nature of its *policy making processes* and its *consequences* for the balance of industrial power in Australian society. Some commentators argue that essential features of corporatism, as the term is commonly applied to countries like Sweden and Austria, are tri-partism and ideological consensus; the exclusion of employers from the Accord and the failure of the Liberal-National Party Coalition to support it, leads them to deny that it represents a form of corporatism (Singleton 1990, Matthews 1991). Other accounts insist that corporatist systems inevitably involve the subordination of labour to the benefit of capital; if the Accord benefits the union movement, then again it cannot be corporatist (Singleton 1990).

This chapter will not directly enter these debates, but is concerned nevertheless with similar issues. Its focus is on the substance and effect of changes in union strategy. It argues that Australian unions did adopt a new national strategy during the 1980s and 90s, illustrated by their policies towards economic restructuring, but that despite their new ambitions and despite some victories, they largely failed to achieve many of their policy objectives. Union power was limited by weaknesses within the union movement, by divisions within the Labor government and by the opposition they encountered from employers, conservative political parties and bureaucrats.

The Pre-Accord Period

The traditional approach of Australian unions towards economic restructuring can be seen at three levels: the national, where the main issues were wages policy and a plethora of economic and social policies; the industry level, where policies about industry planning and development have been determined; and at the level of the individual enterprise or workplace, where many of the struggles over issues like technological change, work organisation, incentive payments and industrial democracy have taken place.

National Economic Issues
The union movement's input into debate over national economic issues was by necessity channelled through its main national peak organisation, the Australian Council of Trade Unions. From its formation in 1927, but especially after World War II, ACTU Congresses regularly debated and formulated policies on a wide range of economic and social issues, including income distribution, immigration, taxation, foreign ownership and social welfare (cf. Hagan 1981: 334–39, 386). These union policies were communicated to governments in a variety of ways, from media

statements and informal discussions with government officials, to more formal delegations to government Ministers. The ACTU even came to be recognised in later years as the sole national representative of workers in institutionalised consultative committees and councils (Hagan 1981: 324–27, 430–32; Dabscheck 1984). Yet despite the existence of these policies and the many opportunites to communicate them, the ACTU's real influence on national economic or social policy was at best weak, and even then was largely confined to a narrow range of issues (Hagan 1981: 437–38).

It was during periods of Labor government that the unions had most influence. Yet even at these times, ACTU input into the policy process was limited. During the Chifley years (1945–49) the government's rigid approach to post-war reconstruction precluded many unions' industrial and social objectives, and led to major confrontations between the government and some unions (Sheridan 1989, Hagan 1981: 189–96). Under Whitlam (1972–75), there were marked policy differences, personality conflicts and a lack of effective co-operation between the two wings of the labour movement (Hagan 1981: 414–24, Singleton 1990: 10–49). These problems became particularly apparent when a brief attempt by the Whitlam government in 1974–75 to gain union co-operation in the implementation of an incomes policy based on wage indexation largely failed, because the unions insisted they retain the right to bargain for wage increases beyond those specified in the policy (Hagan 1981: 421–23, 436–37, Singleton 1990: 30–49).

For the most part, however, Labor was rarely in power at the federal level; in the important post-World War II period, Labor (until 1983) held office for only eight out of the thirty-eight years. Conservative governments occasionally sought to consult with the ACTU, but they were unsympathetic:

> What benefit either party derived from these discussions it is difficult to say. The ACTU put to the Government its general policies and applied them to the particular circumstances of the economy at the time. The Government's policy never accepted any of the ACTU's major arguments, and the few minor suggestions it did act on, it applied in a much weakened form. More than once, the ACTU's submissions formally queried the point of the discussions. (Hagan 1981: 338, also Singleton 1990: 50–55)

The issues over which the ACTU (and therefore the union movement) had greatest impact were 'industrial': wages and other employment standards, for instance. Here, the ACTU's influence was at times considerable. It came not through legislative change, but through the arbitration system, especially the National Wage Cases. These were used by the ACTU to advance the interests of weak unions, to protect general employment standards in bad economic times and, in good ones, to achieve rules which allowed stronger unions to bargain for additional improvements outside arbitration (Donn 1983).

In pursuing this broad strategy, the ACTU's objective was almost exclusively to gain wage increases which redistributed income towards workers rather than to influence the manner in which that income was created (Ewer *et al.* 1987). This preoccupation allowed the union movement to concentrate its activities on defending or improving wages and working conditions, while at the same time bearing little responsibility for the efficiency or productiveness of the economic system which produced these improvements:

> One [theme]... permeates every aspect of the ACTU economic philosophy and has since the beginning. It is that wages ought to be viewed primarily as incomes of workers, and only secondarily, if at all, as costs of production. This approach is a logical extension of thinking of workers primarily as people whose welfare is of the utmost concern, rather than as inputs into the production process. In economic jargon, when unions are talking about wages, they are thinking of workers as consumers. (Donn 1983: 172)

Thus, even though participation in the arbitration system forced the ACTU to present arguments before the tribunals couched in terms of national economic welfare, the ACTU was in fact more concerned with the 'needs of workers' than with the 'capacity of the economy to pay'. For this reason 'the unions objected strongly to [arbitration] judgments which subordinated equity and the settlement of industrial disputes to the pursuit of national economic policy' (Dufty 1968: 43). Even during the 1970s, when difficult economic times coincided with a Labor government, the ACTU largely denied any impact of wage increases on inflation and unemployment, and unions remained unsympathetic towards government appeals for wage restraint (Hagan 1981: 421–23, 436–37, Singleton 1990: 30–49).

The limited role of the ACTU in national economic decisions beyond wage determination reflected both the dominant labourist ideology of the Australian union movement and the unions' pragmatic perceptions of what was achievable in the circumstances, especially during the long years of non-Labor rule. The weakness of the unions' peak organisation itself was also important. Formed as late as 1927, the ACTU was dominated until the late 1950s by small unions, which held sway over the state Trades and Labour Councils, which, in turn, were divided along political, occupational (craft) and regional lines. These forces made internal consensus more difficult to achieve and reduced the commitment of the larger, more powerful unions to ACTU policy (Pilkington 1983). Until the 1970s, the resources allocated to the ACTU by its affiliates were meagre; this prevented it from independently developing research and policy proposals (Rawson 1982, Hagan 1981: 319). The capacity of the ACTU to speak with authority to governments as the voice of the union movement was also impaired by a lack of representativeness: the country's largest union (the Australian Workers' Union) did not affiliate with the ACTU until 1967, and rival peak organisations among white collar unions (the Council of Australian Government Employee Organisations and the Australian Council of Salaried and Professional Associations) continued to operate until the late 1970s (Griffin and Guica 1986). In the early 1980s, the ACTU was still not recognised as a strong peak organisation.

Industry Planning
Australian unions have a long history of support for tariffs and other forms of protection to encourage the development of domestic manufacturing industries; tariffs were one of the main planks of the labour movement's earliest political programs (Hagan 1981: Chapter 1). The protectionist stance of the union movement was motivated by concerns about job prospects (and union membership), and the maintenance of fair wages and employment conditions, both of which were threatened by the importation of cheap manufactured goods, especially from low-wage countries (Glezer 1982: 252–55). Although some disagreement emerged within the movement in the 1970s (Warhurst 1982: 123–24), neither the ACTU (Hagan 1981: 419) nor most unions in the manufacturing sector (Sheridan 1975: 52, 85–86, 109–10, Ellem 1990) really questioned their support for protection. The movement's narrow goals meant that their policies rarely went beyond generalised support for protection to raise questions about the shape of the industries created behind the tariff barrier or to challenge the 'non-industrial' decisions made by manufacturing employers (Ewer *et al.* 1987).

The development of protectionist policies, however, did not reflect the power of the unions as much as the coincidence of interests between manufacturing employers, unions and the major political parties (Glezer 1982); unions and employer groups frequently joined forces to lobby governments and regulatory authorities. The limits of union influence in this area became more obvious during the 1970s, when Labor began to move against protection. In 1973, the Whitlam Labor government implemented an across-the-board reduction in tariffs of 25 per cent, after virtually no consultation with the union movement. This action caused great resentment among manufacturing unions, but they were unable to change government policy or even force the ACTU leadership to mount significant criticism of the move (Singleton 1990: 15–26, Hagan 1981: 419–21).

Company and Workplace Issues
Union organisation at the company and workplace levels has generally been very weak in Australia. Union representatives in the workplace have

not been common; they have assumed few responsibilities; they have not been part of the official union hierarchy nor integrated into union decision making processes (Hince 1967, Benson 1988). Nor did full-time officials fill the gap by representing union members at the workplace level. As a result, in most workplaces unions rarely challenged the right of management to decide economic restructuring issues. According to one observer in the 1950s, Australian managers retained considerably more control over their workforce than their American counterparts, despite the system of arbitration (De Vyver 1958).

Despite this general picture of union weakness and failure at company and workplace levels, there were exceptional situations where union organisation was strong and union representatives were active. These exceptions disproportionately coloured the image of Australian unionism. Early examples of significant union workplace activity were in large public sector enterprises, like power stations and railway workshops, as well as in the mines, large print shops and on the waterfront. Later examples included establishments in the metals and engineering and building industries (Frenkel and Coolican 1984, Rimmer 1989). In these areas, union activity centred on job protection through defensive tactics like restrictive work practices (Cruise 1957), the policing of strict demarcation lines (Wright 1983), and opposition to the introduction of technological change (Markey 1987, Deery 1989) and incentive systems of pay (Hagan 1981: 84–85, 247–48, 323–24, Wright 1991). Through the threat of industrial action unions were able to exercise a virtual veto over economic restructuring. They also refused to support moves by employers towards more participative forms of management (Deery and Plowman 1991: Chapter 15).

The causes of the general weakness of Australian unions at workplace level, and their reactive approach in the few areas of strong union activity, may well be similar. Occupational (craft) unionism encouraged sectionalism within the workplace, while the traditional labourist ideology focused union resources on narrow 'industrial' objectives pursued through arbitration rather than by organisation and action at the workplace (Ewer *et al.* 1991). Other factors, including the small size of most enterprises, reinforced the unions' neglect of the workplace. Employers did not readily accept that unions had a legitimate role to play in workplace decisions, and often fought doggedly to protect their own prerogatives (Frenkel and Coolican 1984: Chapter 4, Plowman 1988). Even the arbitration system, which gave considerable support to the unions in other ways, discouraged union initiatives over workplace or company restructuring. By law, intervention by the tribunals was restricted to the settlement of 'industrial disputes' over 'industrial matters', terms which were narrowly construed to exclude union action which challenged managerial prerogatives (De Vyver 1958, Fisher 1983, Ludeke 1991).

Unions, the Accord and Economic Restructuring

The economic stagnation of the mid-1970s and early 1980s increased inflation and unemployment. The union movement suffered a significant decline in membership, with total union density falling from over 50 per cent to just over 40 per cent (Peetz 1990). The economic crisis and membership decline led union leaders to question their traditional methods of organisation and their conventional structures (ACTU 1987, Berry and Kitchener 1989). They also encouraged a new strategy:

> For unions, the decade coming to a close [i.e. the 1980s] has been characterised by acceptance, firstly, of the need to broaden objectives to encompass a concept of the social wage rather than simply chasing money wage rises; secondly, of the need for a strategic approach to achieving objectives; thirdly, of the need to bargain directly with governments; and fourthly — following from the above — of the need to act in a centrally co-ordinated, collective way in pursuit of major central objectives. (Kelty 1989: 176)

The Accord with the new Labor government provided the main mechanism by which unions sought to implement this strategy, and led the movement to adopt a different set of policies and strategies towards economic restructuring at national, industry and workplace levels. The unions' agenda thus widened beyond distributional questions to include the processes by which income was produced, and the union movement's approach to economic restructuring became more positive, co-ordinated and strategic. The novelty and many achievements of their new strategy, however, cannot hide a range of policy failures, which serve to emphasise the limitations of union power.

National Economic Issues
The foundation of the Accord's economic strategy was a voluntary prices and incomes policy, in which the ACTU co-operated with the government by abiding by the terms of a bargained wage system in return for government sponsorship of union-preferred economic and social goals. The process by which this policy was negotiated and administered remained much the same from 1983 until 1991, changing only slightly thereafter. The Accord partners first negotiated among themselves the procedural and substantive features of the future wages system, and then made similar submissions to National Wage Cases convened by the Industrial Relations Commission. Despite occasional attempts to draw them in, employers were rarely part of these proceedings: they were not sufficiently united to present a common front and, for both industrial and political reasons, few employer groups were prepared to be part of these incomes policy negotiations anyway (Plowman 1987, Frenkel 1988, Matthews 1991). Presented with such a display of unity

between two of the three major players, the Commission consistently felt compelled to accept the major terms of the new Accord, which were then implemented through the Commission's wage determination principles. Once their proposals were accepted by the Commission in this way, the ACTU undertook to ensure that all unions abided by the rules of the new wage system; the unions' peak organisation thus acted as both author and administrator of the incomes policy.

Not until the National Wage Case decision of April 1991 did the Commission substantially reject the submissions of the Accord partners, by postponing their planned moves towards enterprise bargaining (Mitchell 1992). Although this decision was reversed in October, it contributed to growing unease within the ACTU about the Commission. Evidence of this unease came in amendments to the Industrial Relations Act in 1992, which reduced Commission supervision of certified agreements; a dispute over the salaries to be paid to Commission members; and the wage agreement embodied in Accord Mark VII, which contained no recommendation as to maximum wage increases (Green 1993). Since then, the ACTU and the government have continued to negotiate new wage systems, but have relied less on the Commission to implement them.

Despite the broadly similar procedures by which each Accord has been negotiated and implemented, changing economic imperatives have forced the partners to be flexible in their choice of economic policy objectives and instruments. Under the terms of the first Accord (1983-85), the ACTU and the Labor Party agreed to pursue full employment, the maintenance of real wages, and improvements in the social wage. In the wages area, this led to the introduction in September 1983 of a new system of wage indexation, whereby all wages under federal awards were adjusted every six months according to changes in the Consumer Price Index. Additional wage increases beyond the indexation adjustments were strictly regulated by guidelines or 'principles' issued by the Commission, and individual unions were obliged to make statements promising to comply with these guidelines (Teicher 1989). The aim of this early version of the Accord was to exploit a highly centralised wages system which allowed the Labor government to pull the economy out of deep recession with expansionary fiscal and monetary policies, without the fear of a concomitant explosion of wages (Singleton 1990).

After 1985, in response to the rapidly declining value of the Australian dollar and the country's growing balance of payments problems, the policy emphasis shifted towards greater wage restraint and improved 'micro-economic efficiency'. Accord Mark II, announced in September 1985, produced an agreement to continue the centralised wage indexation system, but with wage increases discounted to accommodate the inflationary impact of the depreciation of the Australian dollar (Teicher 1989). However, subsequent revisions of the Accord (Mark III-VII) moved towards a combination of centralised wage controls and decentralised collective bargaining over productivity at industry and workplace levels (Willis 1988, Kyloh 1989, Gardner 1990): a system of 'managed decentralism' (McDonald and Rimmer 1989).

These later Accord agreements found expression in the 'two-tiered' (1987–88), 'award restructuring' (1988–91) and 'enterprise bargaining' (1991–93) wage systems introduced by the Commission. Although there were important differences between them, they were similar in two main ways. First, they made available to workers and unions specified maximum wage increases. Unions were expected to avoid making wage demands beyond these maxima, thus regulating aggregate wages in line with the Accord's macro-economic targets. Second, in order to be granted such increases, unions had to demonstrate to the Commission that collective bargaining with employers had resulted in changes to awards or workplace practices, encouraging greater efficiency and productivity. Wage determination principles issued by the Commission set out its perceptions of proper bargaining procedures and outcomes.

Throughout the various Accord negotiations and wage systems, the union movement maintained a remarkable discipline. Collective objectives were determined and final agreements with the government ratified through the ACTU Wages Committee and special ACTU congresses (Davis 1987, 1991). Union compliance with the national wage principles was strict and the incidence of strikes declined dramatically (Chapman and Gruen 1990). This compliance emerged not only because of effective mechanisms administered by the Commission, but also because of the role performed by the ACTU (Teicher 1989). The ACTU's authority within the union movement went far beyond its earlier standing.

There were a number of reasons for the ACTU's new authority. The economic crisis seems to have had an impact on the thinking of national union leaders; a new sense of urgency and a collective commitment to remedy the problems was the result. This economic imperative was reinforced by the rise in the mid-1980s of the New Right in Australia, and the shift to the Right of the federal Liberal-National Party Coalition in the early 1990s, demonstrated by its *Fightback!* and *Jobsback* policy programs. The ACTU also enjoyed a new representativeness (brought about through mergers with ACSPA and CAGEO) and better funding, allowing it to expand its research capacities. It developed structures which gave larger federal unions a greater say in policy, binding them more effectively to ACTU policy. And there was the role of individuals: the ACTU was led during the 1980s by a new and especially effective group who had close personal ties with senior Ministers (especially the Treasurer, Paul Keating) in the Labor government.

The union movement's internal discipline was all the more remarkable in the light of wage outcomes. The 1980s saw significant declines in real wages (Chapman and Gruen 1990, Lewis and Spiers 1990), the share of national income accruing to wages decreased, and there was a corresponding growth in profits (Eaton and Stilwell 1993).

There was also strong evidence of increasing inequality in the distribution of wage income (Raskall 1993). Under the Accord, the union movement was prepared to accept such declines, although at times reluctantly.

In return for such restraint the unions expected gains in other areas which were articulated for the first time in strategic plans. The early Accords, for example, contained detailed policy statements on employment, taxation, migration, social security, education, health, industry policy and prices (cf. Stilwell 1986: Appendix 1). Further debate within the union movement led to strategic documents like *Australia Reconstructed, Future Strategies for the Trade Union Movement* and *Can Unions Survive?*. *Australia Reconstructed*, in particular, contained a very broad program which sought to restructure the Australian economy through regulatory mechanisms bargained between the main social and economic groups (ACTU/TDC 1987, Castles 1988b).

The unions can point to some success in areas of economic and social policy. These were gained largely because of the importance of the Accord's incomes policy to the economic strategy of the government and the centrality of economic management to the government's electoral prospects. ACTU representatives became influential members of tripartite consultative bodies like the Economic Planning and Advisory Council (EPAC) and unions leaders were regularly consulted in more informal ways by senior government ministers. The ACTU President, Simon Crean, claimed that the Accord had given the ACTU 'legitimacy as a genuine partner in social and economic reform at all levels of the economy' (cited in Singleton 1990: 183). In the same speech, he also claimed more substantive achievements for the union movement through the Accord, in terms of:

> employment; household disposable income; labour market initiatives; education and training; superannuation; Medicare; taxation reform; housing assistance; improvements to pensions; increases in assistance to youth and Aboriginal and Torres Strait Islanders; national occupational health and safety legislation; and sex discrimination and affirmative action legislation. (Singleton 1990: 183)

Especially important was employment, which grew strongly through the years from 1983 to 1989. Unemployment, too, declined significantly (Lewis and Spiers 1990, Chapman and Gruen 1990). Despite falls in money wages, the social wage of Australian workers was said to have improved as a result of the government's reforms in taxation, superannuation, health and social welfare (Cook 1992). Similarly, it was claimed with some justification that government taxation and social welfare policies had ensured a measure of equality when *family income after the receipt of government transfers* was considered rather than the money wages of individuals (Harding 1993).

There were, however, at least as many failures as successes for the union movement. Advances in the social wage, for example, were contested, and the ambiguity of the concept makes definitive assessment difficult (Ewer *et al.* 1991, McHutchinson and Urquhart 1992). The rapid growth in unemployment after 1989 reversed previous gains and there was evidence of increasing segmentation of the labour market as part-time, casual and contract employment increased (Ewer *et al.* 1991). More generally, the propensity of the Labor government to pursue policies of deregulation and privatisation of the public sector went against the preferences of the union movement (Keating and Dixon 1989).

Perhaps the biggest factor preventing the unions from achieving greater policy influence was the strong support for economic rationalist ideas among business, the bureaucracy and significant sections of the Labor government, including the man closest to the ACTU, Paul Keating (Ewer *et al.* 1987: 120–26, Pusey 1991). The growing dominance of such ideas led to the rejection of (or at least unenthusiastic support for) union policy proposals:

> The Labor government's muted response in 1987 to the ACTU's document on strategy, *Australia Reconstructed*, showed that senior ministers were sceptical about systematic planning, welfare expansion, and industrial democracy. There was already evidence...that the Economic Planning and Advisory Council, the Australian Manufacturing Council and the Trade Development Council had been deprived of the resources necessary for providing forceful policy advice independent of [the economic rationalists in] Treasury, the Industries Assistance Commission and the Department of Industry, Commerce and Technology. (Head 1988: 476)

Industry Planning
The approach of Australian unions to industry planning also changed in the 1980s as they recognised the failure of previous policies. A new concern for production as well as distribution informed much of the unions' new strategy:

> There is an urgent need to develop in Australia a production consciousness and culture, both in industry and in the community... *The creation of wealth is a prerequisite of its distribution.* Without in any way diminishing the importance of equitable distribution, the current situation brings into sharp focus the need to develop widespread awareness of the fundamental importance of creating wealth and income. In essence the two are inseparable. (ACTU/TDC 1987: 154, emphasis in original)

The development of the new approach was most obvious in manufacturing, where unions accepted a need to reduce tariff protection and restructure industry in order to encourage greater efficiency and export production (Keating and Dixon 1989: 45–50). The leading advocate of this new approach was the metalworkers' union, whose membership had been very badly affected by both the long-term decline in manufacturing and the short-term impact of the 1982–83 recession. Metalworkers' officials persuaded the ACTU and the ALP to include extensive provisions on industry policy in the first Accord statement (Stilwell 1986: 96–102, Ewer *et al.* 1987: 97–99). Its main features were recognition that industry policy needs to be integrated with general macro-economic policy; rejection of market forces as the main instrument of change in favour of industry planning; insistence that unions play a prominent part in this at national, industry and company levels; and emphasis on the need for retraining and other adjustment mechanisms when industry restructuring occurred (Stilwell 1986: Appendix A).

The dramatic decline of the Australian dollar and the urgent balance of payments problems in 1984 and 1985 thrust industry policy into the political spotlight. In the renegotiation of the Accord in September 1985, the unions gave a prominent place to industry restructuring (Ewer *et al.* 1987: 102–3). The unions' position was further developed in *Australia Reconstructed*, where the experiences of Sweden, Norway, Austria and Germany were used to justify an integrated and interventionist policy backed by investment through a National Development Fund and expanded superannuation funds (ACTU/TDC 1987: Chapter 3). Subsequently, the ACTU supported a Report commissioned by the Australian Manufacturing Council which advocated an active role for government in fostering an export-oriented manufacturing sector (Pappas *et al.* 1990, ACTU 1990).

The unions' new approach met with only limited success, however. Certainly, the government was persuaded to establish a range of tripartite committees and councils to advise it on industry policy, bodies on which union representatives occupied important positions. As well, quite effective 'industry plans' were introduced in the early years of the Accord, to restructure the vehicle, steel, textile, clothing and footwear, and heavy engineering industries (Ewer *et al.* 1987, Kelly 1988). But these were exceptions rather than the rule. One problem was that many employers rejected the interference in managerial prerogatives inherent in such policies and preferred to emphasise deregulation and market forces as mechanisms for reform (Ewer *et al.* 1987: 109–11). More importantly, policy disputes within the federal government were largely won by economic rationalists, who favoured across-the-board reductions in protection and reliance on market forces (Ewer *et al.* 1987: 105–8, Stilwell 1986: Chapters 6 and 7). This trend became even more obvious in later years (ACTU 1990: 4–5). As recently as March 1991, the government's Industry Statement announced accelerated reductions in tariff protection and generalised, rather than selective, tax and other industry incentives (Department of the Prime Minister and Cabinet 1991, Jones 1991a):

In contrast to the government's previous role in providing protection, its involvement in the improvement of work practices and levels of training has been limited to sympathetic support, with many of the initiatives and associated detailed negotiations being the responsibility of representatives of employers and employees. The manner in which improvements in industry competitiveness are now achieved reverses a long standing philosophy of government assistance for industries in trouble and replaces it to a significant degree with one of employer-employee self-help, with the role of government being catalytic rather than providing all-pervading support. (Keating and Dixon 1989: 48)

This 'self-help' approach, however, was not always effective, because it required a co-operative relationship between employers and unions. Moreover, there was considerable disagreement between the parties over the type and level of bargaining most appropriate for this restructuring exercise. The ACTU and the federal government favoured a link between restructuring and the national wage system. Wage increases, they argued, should only be available to unions and workers who had engaged in productivity bargaining with employers, and this bargaining was to be conducted at an increasingly decentralised level. The unions also argued (until recently) that productivity bargaining at the enterprise level should operate within a strong centralised framework, negotiated through the Accord and administered by the Industrial Relations Commission. Some employers, such as the MTIA's Bert Evans (1989), accepted this approach, although they disputed some of the details. Others rejected centralised control outright, arguing instead for enterprise bargaining between union representatives and management or (excluding unions) between employees and management, without any external constraints (Business Council of Australia 1990, Howard 1990). Under Accord Mark VII, the unions accepted enterprise bargaining without significant supervision by the Commission, although an agreement between unions and the federal government negotiated in August-October 1993 ensured that unions would not be completely excluded from the bargaining process even in companies without union members.

This 'self-help' approach to industry planning and restructuring had mixed results (Rimmer and Verevis 1990, Curtain *et al.* 1992, Short *et al.* 1993). The most successful case was the metal and engineering industry, where the major employer association (the Metal Trades Industry Association) enthusiastically embraced the opportunities presented by the new union policies and emerging wage systems (Evans 1989). Although the parties in this industry continued to disagree over some issues, they generally worked together to negotiate significant reforms (Frenkel 1987, Plowman 1990). In many other industries, award restucturing and enterprise bargaining failed to achieve major reforms. In any event, there were significant limitations to the types of reforms possible under these restructuring systems. Changes to job design, work practices, training practices and payment systems could be encouraged, but union ambitions on broader issues like company structures, investment patterns and marketing arrangements could not be pursued realistically through such mechanisms.

Company and Workplace Issues
The new approach by Australian unions towards national economic issues and industry planning was accompanied by an acceptance by union leaders of the need for workplace change (Burgess and Macdonald 1990). The desire to improve efficiency and productivity was not, however, motivated purely by altruistic concerns for the state of the national economy. Unions leaders saw change as something forced on their movement by economic circumstances. Their task was to achieve reforms which accommodated these pressures but at the same time advantaged unions and union members. The ACTU portrayed award restructuring, for example, as a policy which allowed unions to retain some influence on workplace changes while offering workers the prospect of more interesting, more skilled, better-paid jobs and career paths:

> Put broadly [said the ACTU Secretary], there are two choices in terms of the so-called flexibility debate. The first choice is to say that what we really need is a wages system with a very low minimum rate of pay, where individuals negotiate with their employers on an individual basis and where flexibility will be based on some employers being able to force down a wage rate and some being able to force it up...The other option is to say this country has to grow, it has to develop training, has to be more productive, it has to confront the world economy but on our terms to whatever extent we can. Therefore we need increased training, we need fewer demarcation problems between unions, we need effective career structures for workers, we need a capacity to generate growth but a capacity to adapt, and adapt rapidly, because the key to success for this country is its capacity to adapt rapidly. All of those forces — forces of technological change, the forces of international competition, the forces of change in social attitude — are going to impinge upon us all. (Kelty 1988)

This interpretation of the need for workplace change and of the most desirable types of change, owes much to post-Fordist ideas (Campbell 1990, also Curtain and Mathews 1990). These emphasise the ways in which advanced technologies and more flexible forms of work organisation can to be accompanied by a more skilled workforce, and more democratic power relations at the point of production. The ACTU's interpretation can also be contrasted to that of many employers, whose demands for workplace change focuses on reductions in labour costs, the elimination of penalty rates, a rearrangement of working hours, and the introduction of part-time and contract labour (Curtain and Mathews 1990, Bray and Taylor 1991).

The unions also promoted procedures which stressed consultation by employers and participation by workers and unions in the planning and implementation of workplace change. Under award restructuring and enterprise bargaining employers were forced to negotiate with unions over workplace innovations. The unions also adopted a new approach towards industrial democracy, portraying it as vital to the success of the company and the economy:

> In Austria, Norway, Sweden... consultative processes, employee representation on company boards and involvement in structural change are all based on commitment and growing workforce capabilities. On the other hand, the needs of modern production virtually demand that such rights and responsibilities are not only desirable but *essential*. This is especially so with regard to quality control, innovation, delivery commitment, inventory control, and many other essential rapid flexible responses of production or service. (ACTU/TDC 1987: 154, emphasis in original)

Industrial democracy schemes provided the opportunity for unions to monitor the effectiveness of company management: 'the aim should be to ensure independent trade union input so that influence can be exerted on management to perform' (ACTU/TDC 1987: 154). This is a far cry from the suspicion with which unions viewed industrial democracy and worker participation during the 1970s (Deery and Plowman 1991: Chapter 15).

To buttress union influence in workplace change, the ACTU launched several test cases within the arbitration system to establish the rights of workers and unions when new technologies were introduced (Deery 1989) or when workers were made redundant or work reorganised. Victories in some of these cases led to a winding back of the legal protection previously given to managerial prerogatives (Ludeke 1991) and to new opportunities for unions.

Some unions exploited the opportunities created by these cases and by the various wage systems: they achieved improved wages, more training and new access to career ladders. However, such successes were far from universal (Rimmer and Verevis 1990, Ewer *et al.* 1991, Curtain *et al.* 1992, Short *et al.* 1993). Some unions simply failed to deliver wage increases to their members. Others were forced by employers to accept changes which cut labour costs by altering working hours or reducing penalty rates rather than contributing positively to improved productivity. All too often, union officials were either unable or unwilling to leave negotiations to shop stewards and other workplace representatives, which meant that negotiations over award restructuring were confined to an industry level with enterprise agreements never being consummated. Even when bargaining did occur at workplace level, strong shop stewards sometimes opposed the restructuring measures agreed to by union officials, thus hindering workplace change.

Further evidence of the lack of union influence at company and workplace levels can be gleaned from the 1989–90 Australian Workplace Industrial Relations Survey (AWIRS). Its data show that regular consultation and bargaining between management and union representatives were relatively rare:

> Management was also asked about consultation with unions in relation to the introduction of major organisational changes in the two years prior to the survey. These changes included the introduction of major new technology, change in product or service, restructuring of management, and change in senior personnel and workplace ownership. In nearly three-quarters of workplaces... unions were not consulted or even informed about organisational changes which would affect employees. (Callus *et al.* 1991: 135)

The findings showed that the role of unions in organisational change varied with the size of workplace and with industry type; unions were either 'consulted' or had 'significant input' in over 50 per cent of the largest unionised workplaces (with 500 employees or more), but in only 20 per cent of those with 20–49 employees (Appendix A72). Such evidence is hardly consistent with widespread union success in influencing management decisions at the company or workplace level (Green 1991).

Thus, despite a new approach by union leaders, changes to the role of unions at company and workplace levels have not been great. The explanation for this lies partly with employers, many of whom remain either unwilling to adopt more consultative techniques or unable to do so because they lack the necessary resources or expertise. These failures are apparent in the uneven development of participatory practices (Frenkel 1989, Frenkel and Weakliem 1989) and the disappointing results of award restructuring (Rimmer and Verevis 1990) and enterprise bargaining (Short *et al.* 1993). But the biggest problem may lie in the unions' own failures at company and workplace levels. Where unions have some organisational strength, shop stewards do not necessarily share their unions' enthusiasm for change. But the majority of workplaces are not unionised, and where they are they are largely ineffectual; the AWIRS survey found that 34 per cent of unionised workplaces did not even have union delegates representing the members (Callus *et al.* 1991: 48–53, 102). The continued weakness of unions and the lack of management expertise have led some commentators to doubt the capacity of either side to support any significant extension of collective bargaining at workplace or company levels (Callus 1991).

Conclusions

The limited success of the unions' new approach towards economic restructuring presents them with several dilemmas. How much should they co-operate with government in incomes policies if their main outcome is a continuing decline in real wages and questionable returns in wider areas like unemployment, social welfare and taxation? How far should unions promote the restructuring of industry if their policies of managed change are largely rejected in favour of unfettered market forces achieved through simple reductions in protection? Should unions support improved efficiency and productivity at a company level if they are excluded from the change process, and their members are either retrenched or forced to work harder for lower incomes?

These questions have generated conflict within the labour movement. Critics from the Left claim that the Accord has been used to manipulate unions to the benefit of employers, and to the disadvantage of union members (Stilwell 1986, Bramble 1989, Ewer *et al.* 1991), while those from the Right advocate a freeing-up of the labour market in contrast with the restrictions imposed by the Accord (Costa and Dufty 1991). The bulk of the union movement, however, has continued to support the Accord. Its supporters emphasise the gains which have been made through this new strategy. But just as important is the absence of a viable alternative. In a situation where Labor's conservative political opponents promise industrial and social reforms that are repugnant to most union activists, and where most employers seem inclined to avoid union consultation when given the opportunity, unions find themselves between a political 'rock' and an industrial 'hard place'. Flawed as it is, the Accord remains the only real policy option for Australian unions.

13
Social Policy

DEBORAH BRENNAN

Introduction

Social policy is a term which covers a range of overlapping concerns located at the crossroads of economic policy and social welfare. The boundaries of social policy are notoriously difficult to define. In this chapter the term is used to incorporate three broad areas of government activity: social welfare arrangements such as pensions and benefits (the traditional domain of 'welfare'); labour market policies concerning the availability and distribution of paid work; and policies concerning the provision of services such as child care and care for the elderly.

Social policy is a major function of governments in Australia and comparable societies. The provision of income support for particular groups of citizens (primarily those who are aged, unemployed, sole parents or disabled) now accounts, on average, for more than half the budget outlays of the Organisation for Economic Co-operation and Development nations, the group representing the world's major Western economies. Thus, in terms of public expenditure, income redistribution is 'the major activity of most OECD governments' (Saunders 1992b: 12). In addition to income support, governments provide, regulate and subsidise a large range of community services. The extent to which governments should be involved in this type of activity is highly controversial. There are vigorous debates about whether state intervention should be restricted to the alleviation of poverty, or whether social policies should assist citizens to maintain their previous standard of living when they are outside the workforce. Similarly, the question of whether it is desirable for governments to be involved in establishing child care centres and nursing homes (or whether these activities should be left to the market) is highly contentious. Such issues are at the heart of social policy debate and, even though by international standards Australia devotes a fairly small proportion of its resources to social welfare, variants of these debates are prominent in Australian politics. According to Bob Gregory, a labour market analyst from the Australian National University, the welfare state is likely to become 'the battleground of the 90s' (*Sydney Morning Herald*, 17 July, 1993).

Despite the centrality of social policy to modern government, it is frequently neglected by social scientists. The Swedish sociologist Göran Therborn makes the following caustic assessment of some major European writers:

> In general political theory, political science, sociology, and historiography, the welfare state has so far received scant attention, if any. A prominent sociological theorist...can write an almost 400-page long treatise on the modern state hardly touching the welfare state at all. A distinguished French political scientist publishes a series of studies on 'The Logic of the State', in which any social service logic is completely missing...A major collective work on western European state formation...bypasses the welfare state problematic altogether. (Therborn 1989: 63)

Therborn goes on to comment that, while many of the 'grand theorists' have ignored welfare, writers in the British empiricist tradition such as T.H. Marshall and Richard Titmuss have provided stimulating theories of the welfare state. To some extent, this situation is paralleled in Australia. Political scientists tend to ignore, or at best give only passing attention to, the welfare function of modern governments. In the main it has been historians and sociologists who have furthered debate about the politics of social policy in Australia.

Social policy arrangements provide valuable insights into power relationships within a society. Writers who have explored the distributional consequences of policy arrangements have traditionally focused upon the issue of class power, examining the extent to which welfare arrangements achieve (or fail to achieve) redistribution of income and social opportunities towards lower income groups. Contemporary theorists have developed new frameworks within which to analyse and compare welfare states, but these still focus on class power as the key issue. The Swedish writer Esping-Andersen (1990), for example, has developed a typology of welfare regimes in his book *Three Worlds of Welfare Capitalism*. He argues that the extent to which social policies allow labour to be de-commodified, or freed from dependence upon market incomes, is the crucial issue in distinguishing between welfare regimes. His analysis starts with the fact that, under capitalism, most people survive by selling their labour power in return for wages, or by depending on someone who does: labour is, in effect, a commodity. Social policy measures such as pensions and benefits qualify the power of capital by breaking the link between paid market work and economic survival. They 'de-commodity' labour. Feminists argue that Esping-Andersen's analysis is male-centred, and does not provide an adequate explanation of interconnections between the labour market, the welfare system and the home — especially for women. His focus on income transfers and his virtual neglect of service provision and of the crucial role of unpaid labour in the home, has also been criticised (Cass 1992, Pateman 1989, Lewis 1992, Gordon 1990).

Social policy arrangements have been in flux in Australia since the early 1970s. From 1945 until the election of the Whitlam government, a broad consensus existed between the major political parties concerning the general direction of social policy. Both the Liberal and Labor parties accepted the existence of a mixed economy, centralised wage fixing, full employment and the incremental growth of welfare. Social welfare itself was seen as subsidiary to the goal of full employment. Since the 1970s, however, this has changed. Demographic factors have included the gradual ageing of the population, changes in family patterns (notably the growth in sole parent families and the extraordinarily rapid increase in the labour force participation rates of women with young children). Together with the persistence of disturbing levels of unemployment, these have demonstrated the need for a fundamental re-assessment of basic approaches to social policy.

This chapter examines the development of social policies in Australia in the post-war period, especially under the Hawke and Keating governments. The merits of social assistance and social insurance models of welfare provision, the relationship of social policies to notions of citizenship, and the recognition and valuation of unpaid caring work within contemporary social policy are some of the themes explored. The chapter does not present a comprehensive analysis of developments in social policy but rather uses particular issues and historical periods as the basis for exploring broader debates.

Historical Context

Australia has a distinctive system of welfare provision. Although conservative critics complain of this country having a bloated welfare state, Australian expenditure on welfare is low by international standards. In the most recent Commonwealth Budget social, security and welfare accounted for 36 per cent of projected outlays (Commonwealth of Australia 1993), while among the OECD nations 54 per cent (on average) of national budgets is spent on income transfers alone (Saunders 1992b).

Unlike Britain and most Western European nations, Australian welfare is based on the principle of 'social assistance' rather than 'social insurance'. Funding for welfare comes from general revenue rather than from specific taxes or individual contributions, and benefit levels are geared towards poverty alleviation rather the replacement of previous income. Social welfare payments in Australia are strictly means-tested, usually on the basis of family or household income. This represents another major difference from insurance systems in which people's entitlement to benefit relates to them as individuals. Another feature of social welfare benefits in Australia is that they are paid at a flat rate, so that everyone in the same circumstances receives the same benefit. Social security in most comparable societies provides assistance which is linked to previous income or insurance contributions; a lower level of payment, sometimes carrying considerable stigma, is usually provided for those who do not have social insurance. The Australian system is thus one in which benefits are provided on a highly selective basis.

In one respect, however, the Australian system is more generous and inclusive than insurance models: the fundamental basis of entitlement is need, not prior workforce participation. This means that some groups who would be decidedly disadvantaged in European-style, insurance-based welfare systems (for example, school leavers, recent immigrants or women who have been outside the workforce caring for children or elderly relatives), are not denied benefits in Australia, although they may have to undergo waiting periods.

Both the Commonwealth and state governments play a major role in Australian social policy. Under the Constitution, the Commonwealth was originally given very limited powers in this area. Its only areas of defined power were over invalid and old age pensions. The broad division of responsibility which has developed since the 1940s is that the Commonwealth has responsibility for income support (pensions and benefits), while the states are the major providers of services such as child welfare, juvenile justice and social work services. This division, however, is by no means clear-cut. Over recent decades the Commonwealth has become a major provider of some types of services, notably child care and services for the elderly and disabled.

Economic and social policies have been closely intertwined in the development of income security arrangements in Australia. According to Frank Castles, one of the reasons that Australia has not developed a European-style welfare system is that the labour movement has placed full employment and reasonable wage standards ahead of welfare as political goals. Castles argues that this is part of a strategy of 'domestic defence' which Australia has adopted in order to cope with its extreme vulnerability to international economic forces. The other elements of this strategy have been institutionalised mechanisms of wage determination (arbitration courts), control of immigration, and the protection of manufacturing through tariffs and other trade restrictions (Castles 1985, 1988a). By contrast, small European nations, which have faced similar external pressures, have opted for greater exposure to international markets, combined with the development of quite elaborate compensatory welfare and labour market arrangements. Castles' description of Australia as a 'wage-earners' welfare state' is intended to convey the idea that the primary means of social protection in Australia has been full employment and wage protection, rather than the welfare system.

This description can be misleading, however, since it might be taken as suggesting that in Australia welfare benefits are tied to one's status as a wage earner, rather than as a citizen. Moreover, as feminists have pointed out, the very system which protected men's wages and (post-war until the 1970s) provided them with a virtual guarantee of full employment, consigned women to receiving only a fraction of men's pay and often contributed to their marginalisation in the labour market. Bryson argues that a more accurate description of the Australian system would be a 'white, male wage-earners welfare state' (Bryson 1992).

Despite these criticisms, Castles' account of how and why Australia has developed its distinctive approach to welfare is useful in thinking about the relationship between welfare and economic policy under Hawke and Keating. Since 1983 the government has attempted to make the Australian economy more internationally competitive by reducing tariffs, encouraging exports, deregulating the financial system, and lifting some of the controls over the labour market. The social and economic dislocation which has resulted from these efforts to make Australia less protected and more outward looking has also been fundamental to the restructuring of this country's welfare arrangements.

Early Debates
One of the central arguments in the history of Australian social policy concerns the relative merits of social insurance and social assistance approaches to income security. Although comparatively little debate took place on these prior to the introduction of the Commonwealth old age pension in 1908, a report on social insurance prepared a few years later by the Commonwealth statistician, G.H. Knibbs, generated considerable interest. In 1910 the Liberal Party advocated the establishment of a comprehensive scheme of social insurance. The possibility of introducing such insurance for unemployment and invalidity was briefly considered by the second Fisher Labor government in 1911, but the Labor Party quickly disassociated itself from the idea of compulsory contributions, arguing that social benefits should be provided on a universal basis from general revenue (Kewley 1973: 99–103). Debates concerning the possibility of introducing some form of social insurance surfaced again in the 1930s. The experience of the Depression showed clearly the need for more systematic and extensive provision of social welfare, but there were deep conflicts within the Australian community about the arrangements which ought to be adopted. The Lyons UAP-Country Party government advocated a system of social insurance, arguing that this would encourage individuals to take responsibility for themselves, minimise the burden on the state, and reward the thrifty. Another argument put forward to support the principle of social insurance was that it would remove the taint of stigma from the receipt

of benefits, since people would be seen to have earned, and indeed worked for, the assistance they received (Kewley 1973: 159–65).

Labor and the unions wanted to keep means-tested and non-contributory programs. They argued that the contributory principle would minimise redistribution and force workers to fund their own social security. A non-contributory system financed from general revenue was seen to be more in keeping with Labor ideals since, under the principles of progressive taxation, those on higher incomes would contribute proportionately more of their income to finance the welfare system. This was especially so since only a minority of the population paid income tax at this time. A range of other groups shared Labor's opposition to the notion of insurance-based social security: they included farmers and the self-employed (both excluded from the proposals for insurance), and employers who feared the additional burden of taxation. The vigorous opposition of these groups ensured that the National Insurance Act, although passed in 1938, was never implemented (Watts 1987: 18–24).

War and Post-war Reconstruction
The major components of the modern Australian welfare system were laid down in the 1940s, particularly in the period of post-war reconstruction. The 1940s were years of ferment in Australian society. The immense suffering and social upheaval caused by the Depression were still fresh in people's minds. At that time Australia had provided no systematic protection to the unemployed, and thousands had tramped the countryside in a vain search for work. The subsequent mobilisation of the population for war, together with the enhancement of the powers of the Commonwealth for the duration of the war, turned attention towards the creation of a more just and equitable society in the post-war period. In 1941, the Menzies government introduced child endowment — not so much for reasons of equity and justice but to put a brake on wage increases (Cass 1988). Labor followed, with widows' pensions (1942), new maternity allowances and funeral benefits (1943), and unemployment, sickness and special benefit (1944). It also introduced employment and rehabilitation services, signed a housing agreement with the states and began financial assistance to hospitals. These achievements were followed by the promise of free medicine (1944) and free hospital treatment in public wards (1945). During this period the Commonwealth took over income taxing powers and established a National Welfare Fund, financed by taxation, from which all social security benefits were to be paid.

Welfare itself was not the goal of the Curtin or Chifley governments. Underpinning the rapid development of Australian social security arrangements during the 1940s was a belief that full employment and sustained economic growth would largely obviate the need for welfare, except for residual categories such as widows and the elderly. Chifley expressly described social services as 'at best palliatives to the world's economic problems' and saw them as becoming less and less necessary as economic difficulties were overcome, full employment maintained, and national incomes raised (Waters 1975: 232).

Australia's welfare arrangements remained relatively static under the Liberal-Country Party Coalition which governed from the late 1940s to the early 1970s. Although there were minor incremental changes to particular benefits and programs, no major reassessment of the philosophical basis of welfare was considered necessary. The rapid population growth of the post-war period, brought about through immigration and the post-war 'baby boom', ensured that employment and housing were the nation's major social preoccupations (Coombs 1981: 48–55, 68–70). Welfare itself was not seen as a high priority. The assumption that economic growth and prosperity would, of themselves, reduce or eliminate poverty, engendered complacency. By the late 1960s, however, it was becoming clear that the national prosperity of the post-war decades had masked, rather than overcome, poverty (Castles 1989: 22, Henderson *et al.* 1970). A series of reports began to call attention to the plight of the poor, sometimes described as the 'hidden people' of Australia (Stubbs 1966, Appleyard 1965, Hollingworth 1972, Henderson *et al.* 1970). The Commonwealth rejected the possibility of extensive poverty and disadvantage in Australia, insisting that only small 'pockets' of poverty were likely to exist. The concerted research and lobbying of various researchers and journalists, however, forced a reconsideration. In 1972, the McMahon government commissioned Melbourne economist Ronald Henderson to investigate the extent of poverty in Australia, and the factors that contributed to it. The *Henderson Report*, published in 1975, demonstrated an alarmingly high incidence of poverty. Using rather cautious measures, it estimated that more than 10 per cent of households were 'very poor' while a further 7 per cent could be considered 'rather poor' (Australian Government Commission of Inquiry into Poverty 1975).

Whitlam: Expanding the Vision of Social Welfare
The short-lived Whitlam government breathed new life into Australian understandings of welfare. Soon after becoming leader of the Labor Party in 1967, Whitlam began the process of changing the party's thinking on welfare issues. His aim was to locate welfare and the provision of community services at the centre of Labor's program for *all* Australians — not to have them restricted to people who could be classified as poor and needy. Whitlam believed that the powers and financial resources of the national government ought to be harnessed to provide social services and urban amenities appropriate to a wealthy, modern nation. This proved a difficult task. Whitlam later commented that it was 'difficult to push ALP thinking beyond the basic concept of the provision of cash payments' (Whitlam 1985: 351). Nevertheless,

by the time it formed a government in 1972, Labor had adopted a broad program of reform which incorporated an expanded vision of welfare, going far beyond the alleviation of poverty (Hayden 1972). The new approach was intended to appeal directly to middle class urban dwellers to whom the Labor Party was pitching its electoral appeal.

Whitlam argued that the main causes of inequality in Australia were not those arising out of the ownership of wealth and property but were based on regional disparities in the provision of urban and social services, particularly education, health and community facilities. An individual's standard of living, according to Whitlam, was determined 'not so much by income but by the availability and accessibility of the services which the community alone can provide and ensure'. In a statement prefiguring the notion of the social wage he declared:

> The quality of life depends less and less on the things which individuals obtain for themselves and can purchase for themselves from their personal incomes and depends more and more on the things which the community provides for all its members from the combined resources of the community. (quoted in Freudenberg 1986: 134)

The approach to welfare adopted by the Whitlam government was akin to the European social democratic model in which services are seen as a right of all citizens:

> The overriding objective of my Government was the establishment of equality of opportunity and security for all Australians...My Government endeavoured to create an efficient system of welfare benefits and services which vigorously attacked the problem of financial and social deprivation in Australia. We wanted to establish a welfare apparatus which was devoid of class discrimination and could not be stigmatised as providing charitable concessions to the 'deserving poor'. (Whitlam 1985: 359–60)

Under Whitlam there was an explosion of activity in the field of social policy. Advisers were brought in from outside the bureaucracy and a new body, the Social Welfare Commission, was established to bring fresh ideas into welfare policy making. Part of the brief of the SWC was to put forward proposals that were not constrained by traditional policy and the views of welfare professionals. The SWC was responsible for launching an ambitious and controversial program known as the Australian Assistance Plan. Under the AAP, local communities were to be empowered to work out their own priorities for community and welfare services, and would receive funding on a per capita basis (plus additional funding for disadvantaged areas), to implement their goals. This was a reversal of the previous 'top down' approach to planning and was specifically intended to bypass the traditional welfare power brokers — state governments, local authorities and charitable organisations (Graycar 1981: 41).

Meanwhile, new benefits including the supporting mother's benefit, a special pension for orphans, and handicapped child's allowance, were introduced in quick succession. Rates of unemployment and sickness benefits were raised in order to bring them into line with other social security payments. The means test was abolished in 1973 for pensioners aged over 75, and in 1975 for those aged over 70. Funding was provided for community health programs, women's refuges and child care, and a new Department of Urban and Regional Development was established.

Despite (or perhaps partly because of) the pace and scale of activity in the social policy area, many of Labor's ambitions were unfulfilled. The SWC was later described by its Chairman, Marie Coleman, as a concept which was 'politically courageous but naïve...a good idea for an Opposition party but [one which] had problems for a Government' (Coleman 1978). The AAP, the subject of a challenge to its constitutional validity and under constant attack from state governments, is generally regarded as having failed in its key objective of redistributing power (Graycar 1981). Even Peter Wilenski, who was principal private secretary to Whitlam, has argued that 'to the very limited extent that there was a transfer of power, it was not to the powerless recipients of welfare but to the existing welfare establishment of persons already actively involved in voluntary organisations, local government or other welfare activities' (Wilenski 1986: 107).

Perhaps the most serious flaw in Labor's social policy program was its assumption that continuing economic growth would enable ever-increasing, and relatively painless, funding of its social programs. Social expenditures increased under Labor from 12.5 per cent to 17.6 per cent of Gross Domestic Product — though even with this level of social expenditure, Australia remained towards the bottom of the OECD in terms of welfare spending (Castles 1985). Labor, plagued from 1974 onwards by unemployment and inflation, had begun to expand welfare provision at an inauspicious period. Labor's last Budget, introduced in August 1975, recognised this. In Castles' words (1989: 22), 'the Australian labour movement began to pursue a European-type welfare strategy at just the point when the economic preconditions for such a policy were being called into question'.

Nonetheless, the Whitlam period was one of immense significance for Australian social policy. The initiatives of the period changed community perceptions of the possible role of welfare in society, showed the potential for national programs and invigorated community activists in a range of policy areas.

The Fraser Years
The Liberal-National Country Party government, headed by Malcolm

Fraser, came to power in December 1975. After three years of relentlessly criticising the Whitlam government for its alleged social and economic irresponsibility, profligate expenditure and spendthrift policies, the Coalition was committed to reining in government expenditure, especially in the area of social welfare. For both economic and ideological reasons the Fraser government wished to return responsibility for some functions to the states, and to promote the role of the unpaid care provided by family members as an alternative to state-provided services and income supports. Furthermore, the new administration was intent on bringing to an end what it saw as the 'excesses' of open government as practised by Labor. Procedures such as seeking advice from outside the Public Service, establishing independent policy making bodies, publishing reports for public discussion and giving citizens relatively easy access to Ministers were destined to come to an end (White and Kemp 1986: 143–52, 158–63, Ayres 1987: 303–27).

In the realm of social policy, Fraser saw the aim of a Coalition goverment as being the promotion of personal freedom and independence — goals which, he claimed, were threatened by big government. He also criticised the provision of 'universal services administered by a centralized government monopoly' on the grounds that they 'make everyone dependent on what the government chooses to provide'. In outlining the objectives of his party, Fraser declared that it would promote individual freedom, decision making and independence by cutting government expenditure and introducing significant incentives for private enterprise (Elliott 1982: 123).

A number of Whitlam government social policy initiatives were brought to an unceremonious conclusion. The Social Welfare Commission was disbanded, the AAP was handed to the states, the Department of Urban and Regional Development was abolished, and funding for a range of Aboriginal, community health and social welfare programs was reduced (Graycar 1983). However, not all the Fraser government's actions in social welfare involved winding back or dismantling the initiatives of the previous government. The persistence of certain lobby organisations, the efforts of key bureaucrats within the federal bureaucracy (especially in women's policy areas) and the efforts of Social Security Minister, Senator Margaret Guilfoyle ensured that some important programs were retained and others expanded (Cass and Whiteford 1989, Sawer 1990).

The Fraser government thus had a mixed record in relation to social policy. Overall, the policies of the period represented a retreat from the broader vision which had flourished under Whitlam. The emphasis on targeting services to the needy, the introduction of the 'user pays' principle and the freezing of benefits for certain groups of recipients were all part of the government's effort to distance itself from the expansive, social democratic philosophy of the previous government, and to restore the notion of welfare as a safety net for the poor. Despite such measures, the government proved unable to reduce Commonwealth expenditure on income support, as it had promised, or to reduce the proportion of the population dependent upon pensions and benefits: indeed, largely because of growing unemployment, both the number of people receiving the benefits and total outlays increased (Cass and Whiteford 1989, Saunders 1989). By the Coalition's last Budget, *total* government outlays as a proportion of Gross Domestic Product had declined only fractionally compared to the high point of the Whitlam years — 29.2 per cent in 1982, 30.1 per cent in 1975 (Ayres 1987: 405). The 'failure' of the Fraser government to achieve significant reductions in government expenditure, particularly in social outlays, together with its inability to reduce the numbers of people dependent upon welfare, caused some conservatives to view with it contempt. For them, a far more radical approach to cutting social welfare was called for. This strategy emerged full-blown in the policy document for the 1993 election, *Fightback!* (Hewson and Fisher 1991).

Social Policy Under Labor in the 1980s and 90s

Since 1983, Labor has instigated profound social policy changes. There is no agreement, however, as to how these changes should be assessed. As Gibson notes (1990: 180) the welfare policies of the Hawke government have been classified as 'reformist, reactionary and most things in between'. The weight of Left-wing commentary, however, is undoubtedly critical. Carter (1992), for example, characterises Labor's policies during this period as a 'failure'. Maddox (1989: 4) calls them a 'betrayal of Labor tradition'. Beilharz and others claim that New Right thinking has become pervasive within Labor ranks, and that 'social citizenship' has been abandoned in favour of 'market citizenship'. This, they explain, means 'citizenship provided by and through the market...as a result of property ownership' (Beilharz *et al.* 1992: 51, also Yeatman 1990). These assessments can be tested by looking at policy areas like unemployment, sole parents and retirement incomes.

The negotiation of the Accord between the trade union movement and the Labor Party in the lead-up to the 1983 election gave social policy issues a new place on the political agenda. The centrepiece of the Accord was the unions' acceptance of wage restraint in return for increases in the social wage (benefits and services such as child care, higher education and health care which augment the individual wage), the introduction of policies designed to assist growth and employment opportunities and efforts to improve the relative position of low-paid workers. Although it has been modified and re-negotiated several times, the Accord continues to provide the framework within which the union movement and the government operate.

Since 1983, some important social policy initiatives have been negotiated in this context. For services, the most significant have been the reintroduction of universal health insurance and the expansion of child care. Equally significant are changes to various income support arrangements.

Unemployment

Unemployment is the central issue in contemporary Australian welfare policy. During the post-war decades, characterised by rapid economic growth, unemployment was very low. Following a downturn in the world economy in 1973, exacerbated by domestic policies which led to an uncharacteristic increase in real wages, Australia's economic performance began to deteriorate, and both unemployment and inflation soared. Relatively high unemployment continued throughout the decade, peaking at just under 10 per cent in 1983. Following a period of sustained job growth between 1983 and 1989, unemployment fell to less than 6 per cent. Since then, growth in employment has fallen significantly, and in 1993 unemployment reached 11 per cent.

In addition to the officially recorded level of unemployment, it is now accepted that there are a considerable number of 'hidden unemployed' whose desire for work is not recorded in official statistics. The hidden unemployed include a large number of discouraged job seekers who, although they would like to have work, believe that the search for it is futile; older workers who have opted for the relative dignity of early retirement rather than face continual rejection from employers; women (and some men) who cite 'family reasons' as the main reason for not seeking work; and young people who are prolonging their education in order to postpone entry to the labour market. In addition, there are almost half a million people considered 'underemployed' because they are working shorter hours than they would like (ABS 1992).

Unemployment is far from equitably shared within the community. It bears most heavily upon men and women who have low levels of educational attainment, few job skills, and who receive low earnings when in employment. The highest rates of unemployment are borne by people previously employed in manufacturing and construction industries; the lowest rates are for those employed in finance, property and community services. There are marked differences between urban and rural areas, with lower rates of unemployment in capital cities compared with non-metropolitan areas. In general, people born outside Australia have only a slightly higher rate of unemployment than those born here. However, there are significant differences between migrant groups; recently-arrived migrants and those whose English is poor have high levels of joblessness. Aborigines and Torres Strait Islanders have the highest rates of unemployment — up to 50 per cent in some communities (Cass 1988: 53).

Since 1974 not only has the rate of unemployment risen, but more and more people who lose their jobs remain out of work for a long time. In the 1970s a person who had been out of work for more than six weeks was classified as 'long-term unemployed'. But the definition has been progressively extended, and now refers to those who have been without a job for twelve months or more. In 1993, around 350,000 of the one million unemployed had been without work for more than a year. Each successive wave of recession seems to have led to an even greater pool of long-term unemployed. New jobs go overwhelmingly to new entrants to the labour market, those switching jobs or those who have not been out of work for long.

Australia has experienced a radical restructuring of its economy and fundamental changes in the age, gender, industry and occupational composition of the labour force. Despite high unemployment, its employment base remains strong. The proportion of the population employed in the early 1990s is very similar to that at the height of the post-war boom. But the nature and distribution of paid work has changed enormously, with long-term decline in manufacturing and agricultural employment and a rapid rise in community, financial and leisure services. From 1971 to 1992, part-time and casual jobs increased from 10 to 24 per cent of all employment (Freeland 1993). There has also been an overall decline in male employment, while women have increased their share of the labour force from 30 to 42 per cent. But women remain clustered in low paid, low status jobs and are disproportionately likely to work part-time (Women's Bureau 1991: 12). Women continue to do a vastly disproportionate share of unpaid work.

There are enormous social and economic costs associated with unemployment, for the individuals concerned, their families, and the community as a whole. Unemployment is the major cause of poverty in Australia. Further, unemployed people tend to suffer from depression, poor health, reduced self-esteem and loss of social contact. The longer a person is unemployed, the more intense these effects become (Cass 1988: 133–38). The cost of unemployment to the community — measured in terms of social security payouts, additional services for the unemployed and their families and lost tax revenue — has been estimated to be around $18 billion per year (Dixon 1993).

In the face of these profound changes in the labour force, and in the rate and duration of unemployment, social security arrangements designed in 1945 are clearly inadequate. These were established in a time of great optimism, when full employment was the central goal of policy, and when reliance on benefits could be expected to be only a very temporary measure. In 1986 the government, spurred by the need to adapt social welfare policies to vastly changed social and economic conditions, launched a major review of the social security system. Bettina Cass, a prominent feminist sociologist and social policy analyst, was appointed to head the review. The Social Security Review was requested to focus on three major areas of policy: income support for families with children; social security and workforce issues; and income support for the aged. Six major reports (called Issues Papers) and thirty-one background and discussion papers were produced in the course of the review. This material provides a wealth of information on the Australian social security system.

The Social Security Review Discussion Paper on unemployment proposed a new system of income support and labour market programs geared more closely to assisting the unemployed back into the workforce (Cass 1988: Chapter 16). The idea was to move the unemployed away from passively receiving benefits towards more active job seeking, and to provide them with opportunities for appropriate training and education. As a result, the government abolished the old system of unemployment benefits in 1991, and introduced two new programs, Job Search Allowance (for those unemployed for less than twelve months), and Newstart for the long-term unemployed. Key welfare organisations supported the more active approach embodied in Job Search and Newstart, but were highly critical of the government for making the change at a time of recession and rising unemployment (Mitchell 1991: 2).

Although recipients of unemployment benefit were previously required to satisfy a 'work test', requirements under the new programs, especially Newstart, are far more onerous. Recipients of Newstart are required to enter into an agreement which sets out what is required of them in order to enhance their job prospects. The contract is far from one between equals. While the Commonwealth has power to withdraw benefits from anyone who fails to fulfil his or her side of the bargain, there is no corresponding obligation on its part to provide employment or even to guarantee a place in a training program. Clearly, the ground here has shifted. Entitlement to income support during unemployment now requires a contract between the unemployed person and the Commonwealth Employment Service.

Do the changes in unemployment policy represent a turn to the Right? In one sense, they do. But it is important to be aware that not only has Labor changed its approach to unemployment, the Coalition has also shifted. The differences between the parties are significant. In *Fightback!* the Coalition proposed much harsher treatment for the unemployed. It called, for example, for much longer waiting periods before benefits could be received, and advocated that receipt of benefits be limited to nine months (Hewson and Fisher 1991). In another sense, the changes to Australia's system of unemployment income support move us closer to the model employed in social democracies.

Further, the Australian system retains the principle that unemployment benefits are available to all those who meet the relevant criteria — not only to those who have a previous history of workforce participation or who have made contributions to an insurance fund. This means that school leavers, immigrants (after a waiting period), and women who have previously been engaged in child-rearing or other home-based activities, are not excluded. The entitlements of citizenship, in this instance, are not restricted to workers (which is what the principle of 'market citizenship' would imply). Obviously it would be better for such people to have employment, but the fact that they are eligible for assistance (and would not be in most insurance-based systems) ought not to be disregarded.

Sole Parents
Policies towards sole parents raise a different set of issues. In Australia sole parents are entitled to government support without having to meet a work or activity test: they are assumed to be fully occupied in caring for their children. Social policy (through the provision of a pension until the youngest child is sixteen) endorses this as a legitimate choice, worthy of public support. Not all societies provide such support. In Sweden, for example, parents, whether married or single, are expected to participate in the labour force and there is no equivalent to the sole parent pension. (Sweden does, however, provide extensive support to enable parents to combine child rearing and workforce participation. It has generous family allowances and housing subsidies, and an internationally-renowned system of paid parental leave, which provides either mother or father, or both in succession, with up to 90 per cent of normal wages until the child is eighteen months old.)

The treatment of sole parents raises complex and value-laden questions concerning the boundaries between family and government responsibilities, and the legitimacy of unpaid caring work. The key questions in public debates concern the responsibilities of non-custodial parents in providing financial support for their children, the timing of sole parents' re-entry to the workforce (whether this should occur when the youngest child is sixteen or twelve or some other age), and equity between single and married parents.

Assistance to sole parents has a relatively long history in Australian social security. Widows' pensions were introduced in New South Wales under Labor, by Jack Lang in 1928. These were superseded in 1942 when a Labor Commonwealth government introduced widows' pensions payable to *de jure* and *de facto* widows, deserted wives, divorcées and women whose husbands were in prison or mental hospitals. The implicit rationale here was that the loss of the male breadwinner was sufficient to entitle a woman to government support so long as she was either a mother (and could thus legitimately expect to remain outside the workforce to care for her children), or over fifty, in which case she could not reasonably be expected to seek employment (Kewley 1973: 214). Widows' pensions embodied clear assumptions about appropriate patterns of gender dependency: widowed men and deserted fathers were not entitled to these benefits (Colledge 1991: 40). The introduction in 1973 of the supporting mothers' benefit made Commonwealth income support available to women who had never been married (Cullen 1991: Chapter 5). The Fraser government's extension of this benefit to male sole parents, in 1978, represented a significant break with previous policy assumptions. It made the need to care for a child, rather than the gender of the parent, the essential criterion of entitlement.

By the 1980s, a number of concerns were emerging around the income support arrangements for widows and sole parents. These centred on the growth in the number of sole parents, their high rate of dependence upon income support, and their high levels of poverty. The low levels of maintenance provided by non-custodial parents (mainly fathers) was a further cause of concern. In addition, the system was complex and hierarchical, with four different categories of widows' pensions in addition to supporting parents' benefit. One category of pension, Class B, was particularly contentious. The Henderson Report had recommended its abolition, pointing out that 'it is difficult to find a consistent rationale for the pension to middle aged widows without dependent children' (Commission of Inquiry into Poverty 1975: 14). Feminists, too, had criticised its existence, claiming it embodied patriarchal assumptions about women's dependence (Bryson 1984: 155). In addition, as married mother's workforce participation rates climbed, some began to question the philosophy behind providing government assistance for sole parents to remain outside the workforce until their youngest child was twenty-four (if in full-time education). Some questioned whether enabling women to remain outside the workforce until this stage was in women's long-term interests; others regarded it as unduly favourable to sole, as distinct from married, parents. Still another line of criticism came from neo-conservatives such as Swan and Bernstam (1989), who argued that government policies, including the very existence of income support programs, had led to the creation of the problem of sole parents. They advocated consideration of 'workfare' programs, such as those operating in parts of the United States, the re-introduction of a six-month waiting period for benefits, and further deregulation of the labour market to enable beneficiaries to supplement their pensions with part-time employment.

In 1987, a number of changes were made to supporting parents' benefits, each of which signalled some change in government and community feeling about sole parents. One major change was the decision that eligibility for supporting parents' benefits would cease once the youngest (or only) child reached sixteen years. This indicated a revision in the government's thinking about how long a parent might legitimately expect to remain out of the workforce caring for a child. The Coalition proposed in *Fightback!* that benefits should come to an end once the youngest (or only) child turned twelve. Another important change was the decision to phase out the pension paid to widows, aged fifty or more, who did not have children. The assumption that the loss of a male partner in itself could qualify a woman for state support was regarded as anachronistic in the 1980s.

In addition to restricting access to income support for sole parents and widows, a number of other initiatives were taken. The Jobs, Education and Training Scheme was introduced in 1990, aimed at encouraging and facilitating workforce participation by sole parents. Participation in JET is entirely voluntary; those who become involved do so because of their own desire to join or rejoin the workforce, and not because of any coercion or threat of benefit withdrawal. JET advisers work closely with each client, providing access to training and education, assistance with child care, and support with job placement and workforce skills. One of the ideas behind the changes in sole parent policy is that clients ought to be able to combine part-time work with benefit recipiency. The proportion of sole parents with an earned income in addition to the pension more than doubled from 1983 to 1991; the average earnings of sole parents increased significantly; there was a substantial reduction in the proportion of sole parents who receive any form of pension (down from 79 per cent to 69 per cent), and the proportion receiving a part-pension almost trebled (Colledge 1991).

The introduction of child support legislation has been another aspect of policy change towards sole parents. This legislation attempts to ensure that non-custodial parents (mainly fathers) contribute financially to their children's support. Before the introduction of this legislation, only a minority of non-custodial parents provided financial support to their children after separation, despite court orders. A survey conducted in 1986 showed that less than 30 per cent of non-custodial parents paid any maintenance for their children and that the amounts paid were usually very small (Cabinet Subcommittee on Maintenance 1986). Since the legislation, both the proportion of parents paying maintenance and the amounts paid have increased substantially. Further, there have been real gains for sole parent pensioners from this initiative. In many overseas countries which operate similar schemes, receipt of private maintenance results in a sole parent's pension being reduced on a dollar-for-dollar basis. In Australia, the first $15 (plus $5 for each subsequent child) does not result in any pension reduction, and above these amounts, the pension is reduced by 50 cents for each dollar received. While the amount of child support which can be received without loss of pension is small, the existence of this 'disregard' amount is of great importance to sole parents operating on very tight budgets. According to Yeatman, this scheme represents an effort to shift sole supporting parents from public to private support (Yeatman 1990: 92). Yeatman describes the notion that children have a right to share in their parents' income as 'deeply regressive' (1990:

92). Beilharz and others (1992: 51) concur in this assessment, describing the system as 'the effective privatisation of child maintenance payments'. The assessment presented here, however, suggests the contrary: the child support scheme represents public enforcement of the rights of sole parents (typically women) and their children. There has been no reduction in the real value of sole parents' pension since the introduction of the child support legislation. Such parents have in fact received substantial boosts to their incomes. Between 1983 and 1992, sole parents with two children and renting privately have received a 37 per cent increase in real income, while those not renting privately have had an increase of 31 per cent (Keating and Howe 1992: 24).

It would be absurd to interpret these policies simply as a manifestation of New Right tendencies, even though some of them (such as lowering the age of the qualifying child), have also been advocated by neo-conservatives. The critical factors are the *total* context of policies, and the extent to which Labor's initiatives in the area of sole parent policy are in line with feminist arguments about the importance of workforce participation, and the risks attendant upon long-term workforce withdrawal.

Retirement Incomes
Most Australians can expect to receive the means-tested age pension, either in full or in part. It is the cornerstone of the social security system. Changes to the system of retirement incomes have a particular significance. The introduction of compulsory superannuation involves a fundamental shift in thinking about the basis of entitlement for support in old age. The age pension is a means-tested benefit, funded through (mildly) progressive income taxes. Entitlement is based on need. Superannuation is based on entirely different principles. Retirement benefits from superannuation are linked directly to labour force participation, with the highest benefits accruing to those with a history of continuous, full-time, paid employment. Workers with a pattern of intermittent, part-time, low-paid work will derive little benefit from superannuation. Further, large employers are required to pay higher contributions. Those with payrolls of over a million dollars contribute 5 per cent for their employees, and smaller employers only 3 per cent. Commonwealth assistance to superannuation (provided mainly through the concessional tax treatment of contributions and fund earnings) is regressive: the greatest benefits go to high income earners.

Since 1992 it has been compulsory for superannuation contributions to be made on behalf of all workers earning $450 or more per month. Labor has put forward four basic arguments to justify this move. The first is that, given the ageing of the population and the high rate of dependence in Australia on the pension, demographic pressures will push expenditure in this area to unsustainable levels. Superannuation is thus necessary in order to reduce expenditure on the age pension. A second argument is that community expectations are changing. The 'baby boomers' now moving towards retirement have higher aspirations than previous generations, and will not be willing to spend the last decades of their lives on a subsistence income. The third is that compulsory superannuation enhances equity and social justice. The claim here is that superannuation, which has long been the preserve of privileged executives and a select group of white collar workers, ought to be extended to the rest of the workforce. Finally it is argued that Australia needs to boost its savings in order to have capital for investment. Compelling workers to put aside some savings will, so the argument goes, ensure the provision of a domestic capital base.

Are these arguments valid? Australia's age structure is changing due to a combination of factors: a lower birthrate, increased life expectancy, and the movement of the post-war 'baby boom' generation towards retirement age. In 1989 there were approximately 1.9 million people over the age of 65; by 2021 this number will reach 3.9 million. Looked at another way, the proportion of the population aged 65 and over will increase from 11 to 18 per cent (Howe 1989: 19). However, the link between rates of ageing in the community and the pension bill is a complex one. In addition to the number of people in the relevant age group, expenditure on the pension is determined by other factors, including eligibility criteria (age, residency, means and assets testing) and the actual level of pension payment. The Social Security Review Discussion Paper on retirement incomes showed that expenditure on age and service pensions fell between 1983–84 and 1986–87, despite more people meeting the age criteria for the pension, because entitlement was restricted through tightening of income and assets tests (Foster 1988: 15). In any case, although in the long term occupational superannuation is likely to lead to fewer people being fully dependent upon the age pension, it will be many decades before this has a significant effect on pension outlays. In the meantime, reductions in direct pension outlays will to some extent be counterbalanced by revenue foregone in tax concessions for superannuation.

Will the extension of superannuation contribute to greater equity or fairness in retirement incomes? As the government claims, the push to extend superannuation has widened coverage of this benefit significantly. In 1983, only 40 per cent of employees had employer superannuation; in 1991, the proportion was 72 per cent (ABS 1992). Many low-paid workers and part-time employees (mainly women) who would never have been offered superannuation as a 'perk' by their employers, are now covered by compulsory superannuation. Nevertheless, the benefits to be gained will vary substantially, and it may well be that the overall impact of the new arrangements will be to create a more finely graded system of inequality. The compulsory system will be irrelevant to highly paid professionals and executives who will continue with their private superannuation arrangements (some subsidised by employers), generously underwritten by tax concessions. For the next level of workers, those in full-time continuous employment, there will be some substantial benefits. However, few will be fully reliant upon their superannuation. In order to accrue a retirement benefit equivalent to 60 per cent of average weekly earnings, a worker would need to put aside 12 per cent of salary for 45 years, working continuously, for example, from age 20 to age 65. Lower levels of benefit will be earned by those who have shorter, less continous work histories, but for some, superannuation benefits may simply lead to a small additional private income which will be offset against reduced pension entitlement. Given that the introduction of superannuation involves trading off current wage rises against future benefits, the overall effect may well be negative for some workers. Further, given the unequal pattern of paid work opportunities, the unequal division of responsibility for domestic work and child care, the lower pay received by women and their greater propensity for part-time work, the winners will overwhelmingly be male, the losers female (Cox and Leonard 1991).

The argument that superannuation will create a pool of savings which will be able to be used for investment in productive enterprises is not particularly compelling. The sums of capital involved in superannuation are very large and *could* have been used this way. However, despite calls from groups such as the Australian Council of Social Service, the government declined to introduce measures to ensure that a proportion of superannuation funds are used for productive investment in Australia, or the development of Australian infrastructure. There is no government control over the investment of these superannuation funds. Private companies control superannuation funds to maximise their profits, many of which are earned off-shore or in stoking the boom and bust cycles of property speculation.

The restructuring of retirement incomes under Labor has undoubtedly moved Australia towards greater reliance upon market-oriented criteria for citizenship. In the future, income in retirement will be tied closely to 'success' in the labour market during working life. The implicit principle of solidarity between citizens embedded in the previous old-age pension system has been abandoned in favour of a system in which the inequalities of the labour market will be reflected, and in some cases magnified, in old age.

Conclusion

Over the last two decades, social policy has moved to a central position in Australian politics. This new prominence has been brought about, in part, by changes which have occurred in the structure of the Australian economy and labour force, in demographic patterns and in family arrangements. Many of the assumptions upon which the post-war welfare state was built — particularly assumptions regarding full employment and the nature of family relationships — have been shown to be hopelessly outmoded. But the new prominence of social policy issues in Australian politics has not been due solely to structural changes. Since the early 1970s new ideas about the potential role of social policy in Australian society have been espoused by sections of the Labor Party, as well as by feminists, ethnic organisations, environmentalists and gay activists.

The division between the major parties on social issues is every bit as deep in the 1990s as it was in the 1970s; arguably it is even deeper. The Liberal Party under John Hewson has adopted far more radical policies regarding welfare than were ever considered under Fraser or Howard. The proposals put forward in *Fightback!* included the cessation of funding for some programs, reductions in benefit payments, increases in waiting periods, extra surveillance of beneficiaries and severe limitation on access to benefits such as the sole parents' pension and unemployment benefit. They would have resulted in a profound transformation of the role of social welfare in Australia. The *Fightback!* proposals contrasted strongly with Labor's record and proposed agenda in regard to social policy. Given this context, to characterise Labor's social policies as New Right is neither accurate nor illuminating.

There are strong continuities in the approach to social policy of the present government with previous post-war governments — both Labor and Liberal. In general, Labor's policies continue to embody the principle that economic security is best attained through participation in paid employment. Labor's efforts to make unemployment policies more 'active', and the changes it has introduced to retirement incomes, can be understood as an extension of this principle rather than evidence of any dramatic turn to the Right. Developments in relation to sole parents do not, however, fit easily into this model. Although there have been some policy initiatives designed to encourage sole parents to move into the workforce, and although eligibility for the sole parent pension is now limited to those with children below sixteen, the government continues to recognise that sole parents' care of young children is a legitimate activity, worthy of financial support. The recent decision to withdraw the dependent spouse rebate from couple relationships where there are young children, and pay an equivalent sum directly to the parent caring for the children as a 'home child care allowance' is another example of the public recognition of caring work outside the market. In both these instances, the model of Australia as a 'wage earners' welfare state' is undermined by policies which provide support for caring work (usually undertaken by women), regardless of previous, current or anticipated workforce participation. As these examples show, government policies are not always based on a single, coherent set of principles. Policies in regard to particular groups are developed by different people, within different political contexts and in response to different policy communities.

Most Australian social policy continues to be based on a social assistance model and there has been little discussion in recent times of the principles of social insurance. Although such assistance is sometimes presented as an inferior or less developed form of welfare than social insurance, it has been argued in this chapter that the Australian model has benefits for many vulnerable groups. In regard to unemployment benefits, for example, the Australian system compares favourably with overseas social insurance models in its treatment of school leavers, migrants and women moving into the labour market after a period of unpaid work in the home. Under the principles of social insurance, people in these categories would be ineligible for benefits, because they would have no history of contributions. The changes introduced by Labor to retirement incomes over time, creating a strong link between incomes during working life and post-retirement ones, will have an effect similar to an insurance-based system of provision for old age. The important exception will be that there will continue to be a basic level of assistance for those who have little or no market income.

Australia's social welfare system continues to rely on a 'categorical' approach, in which people are assisted only if they fit into predetermined categories of need. A more inclusive approach to welfare, such as would be involved in the provision of a basic minimum or 'citizen's income' has not gained the support of any party in Australia. Discussion of such a system has occurred in this country from time to time. Recently, Cass has described a citizenship income as one which would provide adequate support for 'all adults excluded from market work by unemployment, illness, disability, old age and by their responsibility to care for young, elderly or disabled dependants, and also provide additional support to those whose market incomes fall below a basic income' (Cass 1993: 87–88). Debate about such a proposal could prove an important way of gaining recognition of the many forms of community and household work which are currently unacknowledged, either in monetary or social terms. The foundation stone of the Australian welfare state — full (male) employment — has crumbled. Alongside the necessity to restructure our welfare arrangements, this presc , the opportunity to rethink our basic attitudes to the distribution of all kinds of work, both paid and unpaid, in our society.

14
Foreign Affairs and Trade

JOHN RAVENHILL

Australia's external environment has changed dramatically in the last ten years. The most remarkable of these changes was the demise of the Soviet bloc and the consequent ending of the Cold War. The declaration by the Conference on Security and Co-operation in Europe in November 1990 that NATO and Warsaw Pact members were 'no longer adversaries' marked the end of the bi-polar system that had dominated international politics since the end of World War II. Previous assumptions about the nature of global security and Australia's role within it, including the role of alliances and the relevance of particular force structures, had to be discarded. With the demise of the Soviet Union, the balance of power within the Asia-Pacific region changed fundamentally. The developments in the security sphere also inevitably spilled over to other dimensions of international relations. During the previous four decades, for instance, the United States had underwritten a relatively liberal international economic order because of its desire to maintain a strong Western bloc of allies against the Soviet Union. With the ending of the Cold War, Washington was less willing to tolerate the protectionist policies of the European Community and Japan, and more inclined to intervene in international markets to promote its own domestic economic interests.

The post-Cold War world generated new uncertainties in several dimensions of international affairs. International economic relations have become increasingly politically contentious, posing new challenges for Australian foreign policy makers. Australian exports suffered from the rise in protectionist policies; agricultural exporters were particularly adversely affected by the subsidy war between the European Community and the United States. The growth of economic interdependence and the increasing integration of markets (stimulated by the liberalisation of capital markets in the 1980s) ensured that even if Australian governments wished to, they would no longer be able to insulate the domestic economy and society from developments in the global economy (Castles 1988a). Environmental issues were added to an ever-lengthening international agenda. And, in the second half of the 1980s, a number of Australia's immediate neighbours, the island states of the South Pacific, including Australia's former colony and Trust Territory,

Papua New Guinea, were afflicted by political instability (Ravenhill 1989).

In many ways the Labor Party governments of Hawke and Keating met these challenges creatively. In a relatively short period, the government articulated a new approach to defence policy, presided over the amalgamation of the Departments of Foreign Affairs and Trade, arguably the most significant restructuring of the foreign policy apparatus since World War II, and launched important initiatives on such diverse topics as the Uruguay Round of talks within the General Agreement on Tariffs and Trade (GATT), the environment of Antarctica, chemical weapons, Asia Pacific Economic Co-operation (APEC), and the Cambodian conflict. Yet despite this unusual burst of foreign and defence policy activism, there was disquiet among many observers who feared that the government and its bureaucratic advisers had yet to come to terms with the implications for Australia of the post-Cold War order (particularly, but not exclusively, in the security field: see Fry 1991).

This chapter begins with a review of the foreign policy making process, and the constraints under which Australian foreign policy makers operate. It then examines the issues that have dominated the foreign policy agenda under Labor governments since 1983 — in particular, the development of a new defence policy of 'self-reliance within alliance', Australia's foreign economic diplomacy, and efforts to link the country more closely with the Asia-Pacific region. The chapter concludes by briefly reviewing some of the main contemporary foreign policy challenges faced by Australian governments.

Policy Formulation

International relations scholars have frequently been preoccupied with the constraints that the structure of the international system place on the autonomy enjoyed by governments in their formulation of foreign policies (the classic source is Waltz 1979). The options available to Australian governments appear to be particularly constrained by the country's location within the international system, and by its socio-economic characteristics. As a sparsely-populated country with small, albeit well-equipped armed forces, inhabited by a largely European population located in a region dominated by 'alien' cultures; and as a country dependent on an economy driven by primary products and thus particularly susceptible to the vicissitudes of world markets, Australia would not be expected to be a major actor in world affairs. This has been the case for most of the relatively brief period in which Australia has sought to establish its own identity in world politics. (Most commentators view World War II as the period when Australia began actively to play an independent role in international affairs; some, such as Meaney (1976) argue that governments had earlier succeeded in making an independent Australian voice heard on the world stage.) As Miller (1992: 117) noted: 'Australia is usually a quiet and hardly visible performer on the international stage.'

Yet while structures constrain they do not necessarily determine outcomes. Individual actors, even small states, can make a difference if they are persistent in putting forward a credible argument in international forums. In recent years international relations theorists have become particularly interested in the interaction between the constraining effects of structures and the latitude for foreign policy initiatives enjoyed by 'agents' (foreign policy decision makers and other actors in world politics; for a useful discussion see Wendt 1987). The essence of the argument is that structures alone do not determine outcomes: there is scope for decision makers, if they so choose, to respond creatively to the constraints and challenges they face. For much of the post-war period, one might plausibly argue that Australian leaders chose not to do so. Foreign policy was subject to self-imposed constraints, as decision makers eschewed independent thinking so as not to offend the perceived wishes of Australia's allies — in Menzies' phrase, its 'great and powerful friends'. Far too frequently Australia's foreign policy decision makers have displayed *excessive empathy*: they have been too willing to view matters from the perspective of their foreign policy partners rather than from those of Australia's national interests. Such a tendency has been evident in diverse issues of policy ranging from economic relations with Japan to the recognition of the People's Republic of China. And this habit has by no means disappeared. An eschewing of independent thinking on a number of important foreign policy issues caused leaders incorrectly to perceive an identity between Australian interests and those of other countries.

On occasion, however, Australian governments did seek to play an active independent role in international affairs. This was true of Prime Minister Billy Hughes at the Versailles conference; of Minister for External Affairs, H.V. Evatt, in the establishment of the United Nations and the design of the post-war international system; of Prime Minister Gough Whitlam on recognition of the People's Republic of China; of Prime Minister Malcolm Fraser against South African apartheid; and of Labor Governments since 1983 on the issues noted in the introduction to this chapter (useful sources on the history of Australia's international relations are Meaney 1985 and Millar 1991).

Australia's recent foreign policy activism has led it to be frequently categorised as a 'middle power'. This concept lacks analytical precision (for the same reasons as the equally ill-specified concept 'small state': see Thakur 1991). Middle powers are best characterised not so much by what they are, as by what they do. That is, such objective criteria as Gross National Product, or size of territory and population, are less helpful in defining middle powers than the activities that these countries undertake in the international arena. Middle powers are those states that have the capacity/expertise and credibility to put forward initiatives on various issues of international affairs, and the diplomatic capacity to follow these through. Their bureaucratic capacity and expertise distinguish them from small states; unlike the great powers, their relatively limited diplomatic resources require them to concentrate on a small number of initiatives (Evans and Grant 1991: 324 characterise this as 'niche diplomacy').

Middle powers are sometimes uniquely well placed to put forward initiatives on controversial issues where proposals from major powers might cause offence. An example is Australia's promotion of the Asia-Pacific Economic Co-operation group. Being a 'good international citizen' in this manner is one of the attributes that Evans and Grant identify as characteristic of a middle power, and one of the core factors, they argue, constituting Australia's national interest in international affairs. The idea of national interest, of course, extends beyond this. Most scholars would accept Foreign Minister Gareth Evans' (1989) characterisation of Australia's national interests as including geopolitical or strategic interests (especially the defence of Australian sovereignty), and economic and trade interests (especially the enhancement of economic welfare). But once one moves beyond these generalities, the concept of national interest becomes particularly contentious. The current leader of the Opposition, Dr John Hewson, has asserted in several speeches that a future Coalition government will not be beholden to special interests, but will pursue the 'national interest'. But how easy will it be to identify 'national' interests when there are numerous, competing, sectional interests? The question is often raised: 'In whose interest is the national interest?' Even if there is consensus about objectives, there is often profound disagreement about how such goals might best be pursued. Some means of achieving 'national' objectives clearly favour certain groups of the population and may adversely affect the interests of others. (For discussion of the concept of national interest in international relations, see Morgenthau 1952). How core national interests might best be realised often becomes a matter of partisan political debate.

How a government identifies the country's key national interests to be pursued through foreign policies depends in large part on the views of the Prime Minister and Foreign Minister of the day. Foreign policy, even more so than domestic policy, in virtually all political systems is primarily the domain of the executive branch. The reasons are straightforward. Much of foreign policy revolves around reactions to events overseas, reactions that, as Gareth Evans (1991: 45) notes, frequently have to be made 'on the run' under pressure from the media for instant responses. Furthermore, effective foreign policy requires a detailed knowledge of the issues and parties with which a country is dealing; few Members of Parliament have the time or inclination to keep abreast of the many issues on the foreign policy agenda. The requirement for confidentiality on such issues also limits the role the legislature can play. And in Australia, unlike the United States, Parliament is not required to ratify treaties that have been signed by the government of the day — a matter of increasing controversy since the Commonwealth government has used its obligations under international treaties to extend its influence into matters that constitutionally would otherwise be the sole competence of the states. (This is discussed in more detail later.) Nor is Parliamentary consent necessary before Australia goes to war, as was seen most recently in the government's decision to send vessels in support of the United Nations campaign against Iraq (the best discussion of the role of the various branches of government in Australian foreign policy decision making is Smith 1992; see also Evans and Grant 1991).

Prime Ministers have typically played a decisive role in shaping Australian foreign policy. The advent of telecommunications, enabling easy contact between heads of government, and the growth of 'summitry', reinforces the leading role of Prime Ministers on issues in which they have taken a particular interest. Foreign policy may also be used by Prime Ministers for domestic political purposes. They have often attempted to improve their domestic political stature by strutting the world stage, and endeavoured to gain legitimacy by being seen in the company of the leaders of the major world powers. Even visits by foreign leaders, in Australia traditionally those from Britain and the United States, have been perceived to confer substantial domestic political benefits. Hence the desperate manoeuvring of then-Prime Minister Bob Hawke, at a time when his leadership was under challenge from within his own party, to attempt to secure a visit from American President George Bush, in 1991. Yet, as Bush himself discovered, electorates are not so unsophisticated that they fail to recognise that politicians sometimes use a high profile in foreign policy to divert attention from their failure to resolve domestic problems.

As Evans and Grant (1991: 47) note, although the Foreign Minister is officially charged with the prime responsibility for external affairs, this responsibility 'is in fact subject to the role the prime minister himself chooses to play'. They record that there were three major foreign policy initiatives in recent years — the establishment of APEC, the regional initiative on chemical weapons, and the campaign to ban mining and oil drilling in Antarctica — where the Prime Minister was 'unequivocally the prime mover, with the Foreign Minister playing a subsequent implementation role'. The ability of Prime Ministers to launch such initiatives has been enhanced over the years by the strengthening of the Department of Prime Minister and Cabinet, and by the establishment in 1977 of the Office of National Assessments, a bureau that co-ordinates the analysis of intelligence information, and which reports to the Prime Minister. In the early 1990s, the International Division of the Department of Prime Minister and Cabinet had a staff establishment of thirty-one (Trood 1992: 168; for further discussion of the department, see Walter 1992).

The particular interests of the Prime Minister can shape the priorities established for Australia's diplomacy, and the consequent apportionment of departmental resources. Whitlam, for instance, who held the role of Foreign Minister as well as Prime Minister in his first year in office (1972–73), was pre-occupied with the recognition of China, with improving relations with the Soviet Union, and with promoting arms control. By contrast, Malcolm Fraser's antipathy towards the Soviet Union dominated his foreign policy initiatives. Fraser was, however, also particularly concerned with relations between less developed and industrialised countries, and especially with moving southern Africa towards black majority rule — a stance that placed him at odds with the British government which, however, shared his views on the Soviet Union. Hawke was particularly fascinated with China, and with maintaining good relations with, and access to the leaders of the United States and Britain. The concerns of his government to be a 'good international citizen' did not, however, lead him to share the determination of his predecessor to give Australia a prominent voice in international discussion of development issues. In his first year in office, Prime Minister Keating gave priority to Australia's relations with Asia.

The extent and limitations of Prime Ministerial influence in foreign affairs are illustrated by two incidents during the Hawke period. In 1984, Hawke decided without consultation to agree to provide assistance to American aircraft involved in the testing of MX missiles in the South Pacific. The government was eventually forced, to its embarrassment, to withdraw the offer of support, following protests from the Labor Party Caucus and the general public (for discussion of public response to the decision, see Goot 1986). In 1990, Hawke committed Australia to provide three warships in support of the enforcement of United Nations sanctions against Iraq, following its invasion of Kuwait. The commitment was made ostensibly in response to a telephone call from President Bush seeking Australian assistance, but it is now clear that the decision was taken before this call, which appears to have been requested by the Australian ambassador in Washington (Cockburn 1992, Leaver 1991). Before making this commitment, Hawke only consulted his Foreign and Defence Ministers (by phone); no discussions were held with senior members of the Department of Foreign Affairs and Trade, while Cabinet and Parliament were presented with a *fait accompli*. Clearly, the Prime Minister enjoys some considerable latitude for unilateral action in foreign affairs, but the MX decision shows that, if the Prime Minister's credibility within the party and Parliament is not to be placed at risk, ultimately the support of the Cabinet and party must be obtained (for further discussion of the role of the Prime Minister in foreign policy making, see Trood 1992).

Prime ministerial intervention in foreign affairs occasionally brings conflict with the Foreign Minister of the day. This was particularly evident during the early years of the Hawke government, when conflict arose on several occasions between Hawke and his Foreign Minister, Bill Hayden, over relations with the United States. Hayden's outspokenness on American policy towards Central America and on arms control caused resentment in Washington; Hawke's desire to maintain close relations with the American President led him to undermine the statements of his Foreign Minister. Although there were fewer conflicts of this type when Evans replaced Hayden, relations with the United States continued to generate occasional friction between the Prime Minister and his Foreign Minister. When Washington rejected Evans' call for a Conference on Security and Co-operation in Asia, along the lines of the Conference on Security and Co-operation in Europe (established in Helsinki in 1975) because it feared that this would offer the Soviet Union a platform to press for naval arms control in the region, Hawke spoke out against the Evans proposal (see 'Hawke Disowns CSCA', *Pacific Research,* November 1991: 32).

Just as the personal interests of Prime Ministers can shape the foreign policy agenda, so too can those of Foreign Ministers. For Hayden, arms control, multilateral diplomacy, and human rights were priority areas; he devoted relatively little attention, after his initiative for a Cambodian peace settlement was rebuffed by ASEAN, to relations with Australia's immediate neighbours. Evans, on the other hand, has given priority to regional relationships. A particularly energetic, if impetuous and abrasive Foreign Minister, Evans has presided over the launching of most of the foreign policy initiatives noted in the introduction to this chapter. He has also provided a great deal more explanation to the public of the formulation and implementation of foreign policy — a most welcome move. According to one commentator, Evans 'has an almost compulsive desire to erect intellectual frameworks' (Jenkins 1991: 57). This has been seen not only in his co-authored book (Evans and Grant 1991), but in his discussion of priorities in Australian foreign policy (Evans 1989), and in his ministerial statement on Australia's regional security (reprinted as an Appendix to Fry 1991).

The other significant ministerial actors in foreign policy formulation are the Ministers for Defence, and for Trade and Overseas Development. The latter position is a product of the merger of the Department of Foreign Affairs with the Department of Trade (to produce DFAT, the Department of Foreign Affairs and Trade). Although this Minister has Cabinet-level rank (with primary responsibility for trade policy and negotiations, and for Australia's foreign aid program), the occupant is the junior Minister within the overall Foreign Affairs and Trade portfolio, and clearly subordinate to the Foreign Minister in policy determination. The Ministry of Defence has been a traditional rival in Canberra to Foreign Affairs. Defence's primary responsibility, of course, lies with the maintenance of Australia's security, and includes policies relating to Australia's defence industry and arms exports. Not infrequently, the interests of Defence and DFAT come into conflict. For instance, the Defence Department's desire in recent years to build up Australia's arms exports, as part of its objective of making Australia more self-reliant in the provision of its own security, clashes on occasion with the efforts of Foreign Affairs to promote arms control. The Minister for Defence has to juggle often conflicting advice from civilian bureaucrats and from the defence forces — something further complicated by the pursuit by individual wings of the defence forces of their own bureaucratic objectives. The relationship between Defence and Foreign Affairs frequently depends on that between their respective Ministers. In the period when Kim Beazley was Minister for Defence, and Evans Minister for Foreign Affairs, a particularly good working relationship was formed. (Both came from the same Labor Party faction; both are former academics.)

There is an 'international' component to virtually all the other government departments, but usually they are very much junior players in the foreign policy area. Occasionally, however, there are issues that are significant and sensitive to both domestic and international constituencies — and thus to both DFAT and a 'domestic' ministry. Such occasions have tended to become more frequent as international economic relations have increasingly impinged on domestic constituencies.

Immigration is one of the best examples of an area of potential conflict between DFAT and domestic interests. The Department of Immigration, Local Government and Ethnic Affairs (DILGEA) has concerns that sometimes place it at odds with DFAT. For instance, DILGEA frequently comes under pressure from migrant lobbies in Australia to grant refugee status to particular groups. Yet foreign governments, with whom DFAT normally wishes to maintain good relations, often become offended if their citizens are considered to be refugees, since such action is taken as a negative assessment of these governments' domestic policies. A similar clash sometimes arises from DILGEA's policy of attempting to increase the proportion of skilled and business immigrants in the overall migrant intake. This action again may offend foreign governments which resent Australian actions that are perceived as contributing to a 'brain drain' (Harris 1993; for further discussion of the role of the bureaucracy in the formulation of foreign policy, see Viviani 1992, Evans and Grant 1991: Chapter 4).

Parliament plays a relatively minor role in the day-to-day formulation of foreign policy. Debates on it are relatively infrequent, and have become more so in recent years. The decision by the Hawke government to change Australia's policy to one of recognition of states rather than governments, removed one potential source of controversy from the foreign affairs agenda — whether or not recognition should be given to governments that have come to power by extra-constitutional means (Bergin 1988). Parliament has an important function in calling to account the policies of the government of the day, and in extracting information on details of foreign and defence policies. Question Time is the principal vehicle for the latter; parliamentary committees an important means for the former. The Joint Committee on Foreign Affairs and Defence, established in 1952, is the largest of all the Parliamentary committees; it has three sub-committees and a total membership of thirty drawn from both Senate and House of Representatives. All major parties have membership on it; the government usually has a majority and provides the chair. In addition there is an eight-member Senate Committee on Foreign Affairs and Defence. These committees, and Members of Parliament in general, are able to draw on the support of the Legislative Research Service of the Parliamentary Library (for further discussion of Parliament's role, see Knight and Hudson 1983).

One factor contributing to Parliament's relatively minor role is the considerable bi-partisanship that has existed on foreign affairs in recent years (Matthews and Ravenhill 1989). This was by no means always the case. Attitudes towards the Soviet Union in particular, and towards Communism in general, during the height of the Cold War, were at the heart of the split in the Labor Party in the mid-1950s, and the emergence of the strongly anti-Communist Democratic Labor Party. In the late 1960s, the parties were divided in their attitudes towards the Vietnam conflict and the recognition of the People's Republic of China. In the 1980s, however, there have been few issues on which the major parties have differed, other than on matters of detail and emphasis. Labor governments since 1983 have proved masters at occupying the middle ground on foreign policy, leaving their Coalition opponents with few grounds for criticism, and yet also succeeding in reining in their own troublesome Left faction. Hawke's obsession with maintaining excellent relations with the United States avoided a problem that had afflicted earlier Labor governments — the accusation from their Coalition opponents that Labor was undermining Australian security by weakening the country's most important alliance. Similarly, Hawke shared the Coalition's traditional antipathy towards the Soviet Union. The government's emphasis on a strong defence policy for Australia also left the Opposition with little to criticise. Foreign policy issues barely entered the 1993 election campaign.

The major party-political opposition to Labor governments' foreign and defence policies came not from the official Opposition but from fringe parties — those advocating nuclear disarmament and, more recently, the environmental movement. Yet even in dealing with concerns raised by these parties (whose policies often had the sympathy of Labor's Left faction), the Hawke governments proved to be masterful tacticians. In the middle of the Reagan years, when concern was at its height about the American administration's Star Wars program and its preoccupation with developing its nuclear war fighting capabilities, the Hawke government appointed an Ambassador for Disarmament and provided funding for a Peace Research Centre at the Australian National University. Similarly, when faced by a challenge from the anti-nuclear movement in his Perth constituency, spearheaded by the Nuclear Disarmament Party's West Australian Senator, Jo Vallentine, then-Education Minister John Dawkins used finance from his Department of Employment, Education and Training to establish a peace studies centre in Perth. As anti-nuclear concerns subsided and environmental issues gained ascendancy, an Ambassador for the Environment was appointed, in 1989. The lack of obvious achievements of these appointees (although the Ambassador for Disarmament did play a major role in promoting the government's chemical weapons initiative) was less important than the symbolism: the appointments enabled the Labor leadership to accommodate the concerns of its Left faction, and provide a sop to the fringe parties, while freeing the government to pursue what it regarded as the 'main game' in foreign affairs. This entailed the maintenance of good relations with the United States, and the improvement of relations with Asia.

Interest groups are another source of influence on policy making, although in most instances are less important in foreign policy than in domestic policy making. All manner of such groups attempt to influence the formulation of policy on foreign affairs and trade. These range from representatives of particular ethnic groups concerned about immigration policies or events in the lands from which they or their parents migrated, to aid organisations or business groups and trade unions. The success of such groups depends in part on their electoral clout (the major asset of the ethnic groups); whether they have expertise that is useful to the government (as is sometimes the case with the non-governmental aid organisations); and/or whether the groups have 'insider' status — that is, whether they are part of the regular consultation process in which governments engage. For instance, in the trade and development portfolio, representatives of interest groups sit on a number of advisory bodies consulted by the government, including the Trade Negotiations Advisory Group and the Consultative Development Committee.

Interest groups that lack insider status or whose policies are regarded as hostile to those of the government of the day must often rely on sympathetic coverage by the media if they are to exert some influence on policy making. Although foreign affairs have not normally been regarded as a major political issue by the Australian public, and therefore the impact of the media on foreign policy formulation would be expected to be limited, Maher (1992: 51) is undoubtedly correct in his assertion that 'in terms of agenda setting, commentary and general debate those sections of the media which take an interest in foreign policy clearly leave their mark'. Governments are always concerned about their public image and, in particular, whether they are regarded as performing their responsibilities competently. Adverse media comment on government handling of foreign affairs certainly does affect public perceptions and thus may feed into attitudes towards the government of the day.

The individual Australian states also attempt to influence foreign policy. State governments on various occasions have attempted to pursue foreign policies that were at odds with those of the Commonwealth government. This was particularly the case in Queensland during the populist conservative administration of Joh Bjelke-Petersen. The constitution has been interpreted by the High Court, however, as giving exclusive power over external relations to the Commonwealth. The occasional proclamations by state leaders on foreign policy issues have not been taken seriously by foreign governments. Perhaps the most significant impact that Australia's federal structure has had on foreign affairs is through state competition for overseas investment and markets — which has prevented Australia from speaking with one voice on these matters. Meanwhile, the Commonwealth government has used its external affairs power under Section 51 (xxix) of the Constitution to extend its authority into areas traditionally regarded as being within the exclusive competency of the states. In 1982, in the *Koowarta Case*, the High Court ruled that the Commonwealth government's signature on the 1965 International Convention on the Elimination of All Forms of Racial Discrimination legitimated the Commonwealth's Racial Discrimination Act 1975. In the following year in the *Tasmanian Dam Case*, the High Court held that a treaty obligation under the UNESCO Convention for the Protection of the World Cultural and Natural Heritage was a matter of 'external affairs' under the Constitution, thereby justifying the Commonwealth's intervention to prevent the construction of a dam on the Gordon-below-Franklin River in Tasmania. In neither matter, in the absence of its external treaty obligations, would the Commonwealth have had the constitutional power to intervene. (For further discussion of the impact of federalism on Australia's foreign relations, see Ravenhill 1990.)

The New Foreign Policy Agenda

Three developments in Australia's foreign policies stand out in the 1980s: the articulation of a new defence strategy, the efforts to cope with an increasingly uncertain external economic environment, and attempts to improve links with Asia.

'Self Reliance within Alliance'

For most of its existence, Australian foreign and defence policies have, as noted, been shaped by the desire to maintain the support of 'great and powerful friends' (Bell 1988, Matthews and Ravenhill 1991). The popular perception, shared by governments, was that Australia was geographically isolated, threatened by hostile neighbours, and incapable of defending itself. Australia's security was to be ensured through alliance relations with protectors — initially Britain and, after World War II, the United States. To stake a claim for such protection, Australian governments pursued a policy of 'forward defence' in support of the war efforts of the country's protectors. Forward defence refers to the deployment of forces outside Australia with the intention of thwarting potential enemies or defusing political instability before security risks reach Australia's coastline. (For further discussion, see Horner 1992.)

The strategy of forward defence dictated the structure of the defence forces. These were fashioned to meet the objectives, first, of being able to project Australian military power outside its boundaries and immediate geographical region. Second, Australian forces were to be able to integrate easily with the forces of more powerful allies, without whose participation such overseas projection of Australian forces would have been non-viable. But when, in 1970, American President Richard Nixon proclaimed, in what became known as the Guam Doctrine, that the United States in future would expect its allies to assume primary responsibility for their own defence, with the United States playing at most a supporting role, the logic that underlay the forward defence strategy evaporated. That era effectively ended with the withdrawal from Vietnam, and the scaling-back of Australia's commitment of forces to Malaysia. A new approach to defence began to be articulated in the 1976 White Paper, *Australian Defence* (Commonwealth of Australia 1976). Its emphasis on giving priority to the defence of Australian territory and maritime approaches, and to the acquisition of counter-offensive capacity was, however, undermined by the Fraser government's push for longer-range operational capabilities in response to the Soviet invasion of Afghanistan.

A more complete reformulation of Australia's defence strategy did not occur until 1986, when the government commissioned a review of Australia's defence capabilities from ANU academic Paul Dibb. The principal thrust of Dibb's Report was that it was possible for Australia to defend itself using its own resources. Australia, he asserted, faced no identifiable military threat to its overall security at that time and for the foreseeable future, although the country should be prepared to meet lesser contingencies such as disruption of sea lanes. Dibb proposed that the defence forces be equipped to pursue a strategy of 'denial'; they were to be confined to the Australia mainland and maritime approaches; priorities in the purchase of equipment were to be dictated by the strategy advocated in the Report, the expectation being that defence expenditure would be substantially increased. Criticisms that the Report was unduly complacent, and that the strategy of 'denial' was too isolationist, led to changes in emphasis in the 1987 Defence White Paper, which became the basis for implementing the recommendations of the Dibb Report. Greater emphasis was given to uncertainty over future security developments in the Asia-Pacific region and to the centrality of the American alliance to Australia's defence; the concept of 'defence in depth' was substituted for Dibb's strategy of 'denial'. (For further discussion, see Cheeseman 1992, Dibb 1986.)

Subsequently the government has appeared to retreat from some of the key elements of the Dibb Report. The contradictions of a self-reliant strategy, most importantly that a build-up of Australia's defence capabilities would actually increase its dependence on the United States for the supply of high-technology equipment, have been acknowledged in the reformulation of the strategy as one of 'self-reliance within alliance'. Perhaps more significantly, the government has shown increasing enthusiasm for the dispatch of military forces both within and outside the Asia-Pacific region, and for more extensive military co-operation with other states in the region. The government has displayed a great deal of disquiet about security developments in the region, particularly in the South Pacific. Then-Defence Minister Kim Beazley raised the possibility of Australian military intervention following the military coups in Fiji, earning him a variety of macho nicknames in the press, such as 'Bomber Beazley'. With the Foreign Minister of that period, Bill Hayden, not giving the region high priority, there was concern in DFAT that Australia's policies towards its immediate neighbours were being Defence-driven.

The concern to re-assert the primacy of DFAT in determining foreign policy towards the Asia-Pacific region was one of the factors behind the 1989 statement, *Australia's Regional Security*, by Hayden's successor, Evans. A product of collaboration between DFAT and the Department of Defence, the statement did little to reduce the concerns of those commentators who perceived the emergence of what they termed a New Australian Militarism (Cheeseman and Kettle 1990). Although Evans' statement carefully qualified the circumstances in which Australia might intervene, the press focused instead on its pronouncement that in 'unusual and extreme circumstances' the use of military force 'may conceivably be appropriate'. As had also occurred in previous statements from the Department of Defence, *Australia's Regional Security* expressed concern about the new threats to peace in the Asia-Pacific region following the demise of the Warsaw Pact. As Leaver (1991) noted, it was almost as if Australian foreign policy decision makers were nostalgic for the 'certainties' of the Cold War.

Although Evans' statement proclaimed the need to conceive of security as a multi-dimensional phenomenon, embracing economic and environmental issues as well as the military, it demonstrated little capacity to integrate these various dimensions. Indeed, economic and environmental issues were treated primarily within the context of the impact that they would have on the more traditional military dimension of security. (For further discussion, see Fry 1991, especially the chapters by Crawford, Cheeseman, Viviani and Camilleri.) Moreover, there is little recognition in Evans' statement that Australia's neighbours may not share its priorities in security, defined more broadly.

As was characteristic of other areas of foreign policy under the Hawke governments, symbolism was substituted for detailed analysis. The statement was replete with snappy phrases such as 'comprehensive engagement with South East Asia' and 'constructive commitment in the South Pacific', but the policy implications of these remained poorly defined. In short, the most recent comprehensive official discussion of Australia's security raised as many questions as it answered. There is little evidence that our foreign policy makers have yet grappled successfully with the international agenda of the post-Cold War world. The role of Australia's alliance relations in the New World Order has received little detailed attention. In his 1991 book, for instance, Foreign Minister Evans continued to refer to the *Western* alliance, hardly consonant with Australia's proclaimed desires to be perceived as part of Asia. Furthermore, there was no indication that the Foreign Minister anticipated that the Soviet Union would not survive beyond the end of the year in which the book was published. Events in the international arena appeared to have moved so quickly that Australia has not fashioned a coherent response.

For some critics of government policies, the end of the Cold War and the absence of any identifiable threat to Australia's security suggest that the government is spending too much on defence, especially on purchasing new aircraft and frigates. Others question the balance of government expenditure, suggesting that too much is allocated to weaponry and insufficient to personnel. Still others (most recently the Coalition in its October 1992 defence statement) have argued that the government should respond to the uncertainties in the region in the post-Cold War era by acquiring an extended strike capability, and by abandoning the strategy of 'denial'.

Energetic Economic Diplomacy
Economic issues have always been prominent on Australia's foreign policy agenda. With economic welfare heavily dependent on export earnings from primary commodities, Australian governments have always given high priority to maintaining access to existing markets and to seeking secure access to new ones, and for many years attempted to insulate the income of domestic producers from the worst fluctuations of world markets (Ravenhill 1992). As global markets have become increasingly integrated, and as Australia's major compe-

titors in agricultural trade, the United States and the European Community, have increasingly subsidised their exports, so it has become more difficult for governments to intervene to attempt to protect domestic producers. Labor governments since 1983 have decided that the optimal strategy for a small economy like Australia is to push for free trade, and especially to negotiate new international rules to end the subsidisation of agricultural production and exports. Australia remains a very efficient producer of many agricultural commodities, especially its major rural exports of wool and wheat. Yet it has lost overseas wheat sales to subsidised exports from the European Community and the United States (whose Export Enhancement Program was introduced in retaliation for the subsidising of exports by the European Community). Canberra lacks the resources to compete in a subsidy war with the economic superpowers.

Agricultural trade has never figured prominently on the agenda of the various rounds of tariff bargaining which have occurred since 1945 under the auspices of the General Agreement on Tariffs and Trade (GATT). Initially it was the United States that refused to include agriculture in negotiations on tariff reductions; from the late 1950s onwards the major obstacle to reform of agricultural trade has been the European Community's Common Agricultural Policy. Japan and Korea have also given heavy protection to their domestic agricultural producers. As Australia's major exports were ignored by GATT, governments up until the late 1970s were unenthusiastic about the Agreement. In the 1980s, however, a new series of talks on tariff reductions (the Uruguay Round, named after the country in which the initial negotiations took place), offered an opportunity to attempt to gain international agreement to limit the agricultural subsidies which were increasingly damaging the income of Australia's rural sector.

The Hawke government's response to this opportunity was innovative. The government took the initiative in building a coalition of countries that did not provide large subsidies to their agricultural producers, and which supported the liberalisation of world trade in agriculture. This coalition, which includes Argentina, Brazil, Canada, Chile, Colombia, Fiji, Hungary, Indonesia, Malaysia, New Zealand, Thailand, the Philippines, and Uruguay, became known as the Cairns Group. (For further discussion see Higgott and Cooper 1990.) The Group has helped to keep agricultural issues in a prominent position on the agenda for the Uruguay Round, and undoubtedly has given its members greater leverage than they would have enjoyed had they acted individually. The elevation of agriculture to a prominent position on the GATT agenda, however, owes as much to the new American concern with this sector as to the activities of the Cairns Group. And the final outcome of the GATT talks on this issue, as on others, was decided largely by negotiations between the 'Big Three' players in international trade: the European Community, Japan and the United States.

Beside agricultural trade, the other international economic concern that has dominated government activities in recent years has been growing fears that the world economy is in danger of fragmenting into closed regional trading blocs. Australian welfare would be particularly vulnerable to such a development. Over the last thirty years, the pattern of Australia's trade has changed dramatically. Unlike most small economies, trade is not heavily concentrated with a single partner, but diversified, with Japan, other East Asian countries, the United States, and the European Community all providing significant markets for Australian exports (Figure 14.1). Australia is not a natural member of any trading bloc. Clearly, despite the wishful thinking on this matter of some politicians and businesspeople, Australia would never be welcomed as part of a European trading group. Some commentators, and the leader of the Opposition, John Hewson, have suggested that the country should become a member of an expanded North American Free Trade Area. Again, such a move looks unpromising — it is unlikely that trade in agricultural products, an area of great concern to Australia, would benefit from such arrangements. (These are largely excluded from the free trade agreement between Canada and the United States; for further discussion, see Snape 1986, 1989.) The Department of Foreign Affairs and Trade has also been concerned that an application to join an expanded North American Free Trade Area would alienate Australia's trading partners in Asia, which collectively provide a larger market than North America does for Australian exports. As for the final alternative, a closed regional bloc of Asian countries, it would again probably not resolve problems of access for agricultural exports. Simultaneously, membership of such a bloc would place Australia's exports to other regions at risk.

The Hawke/Keating governments decided that a global trading system based on liberal principles is the optimal arrangement for Australia, and worked energetically to promote such an outcome during the Uruguay Round. In addition, through its creation of the Asia Pacific Economic Co-operation grouping (APEC), Australia has attempted to ensure that any trading group that emerges in the Asia-Pacific region will be based on 'open regionalism', that is, will act in accordance with the GATT principle of non-discrimination and will attempt to promote the liberalisation of world trade. The formation of a grouping along the lines of APEC has long been advocated by academics within Australia. (For a discussion of the history of such proposals by one of their principal proponents, see Drysdale 1988.) The establishment of APEC was the result of the Prime Minister's initiative on a visit to Seoul in 1989. The group has grown to include fifteen member states, including all the major countries of North and Southeast Asia (except North Korea, Cambodia and Vietnam), Australasia and North America. Various rounds of talks have been held with the objective of identifying and removing obstructions to regional trade. What can be expected

FIGURE 14.1
(a) Australia's Principal Export Markets (% of Total Exports)

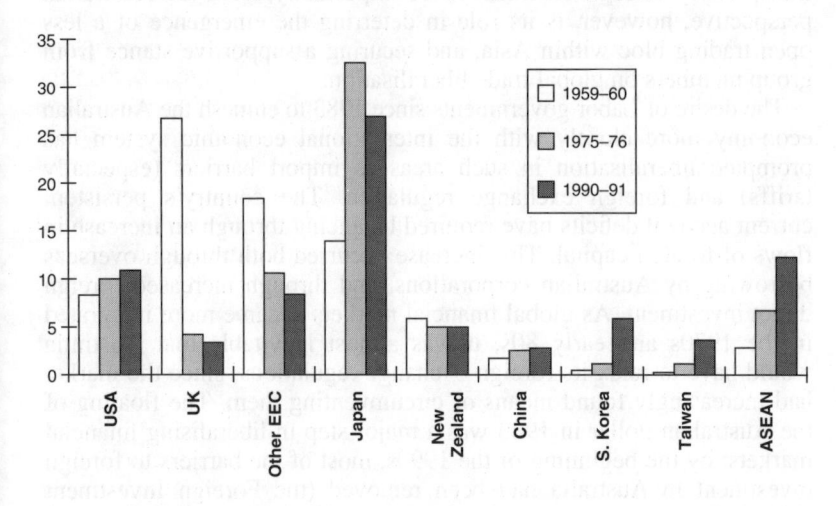

(b) Australia's Principal Sources of Imports (% of Total)

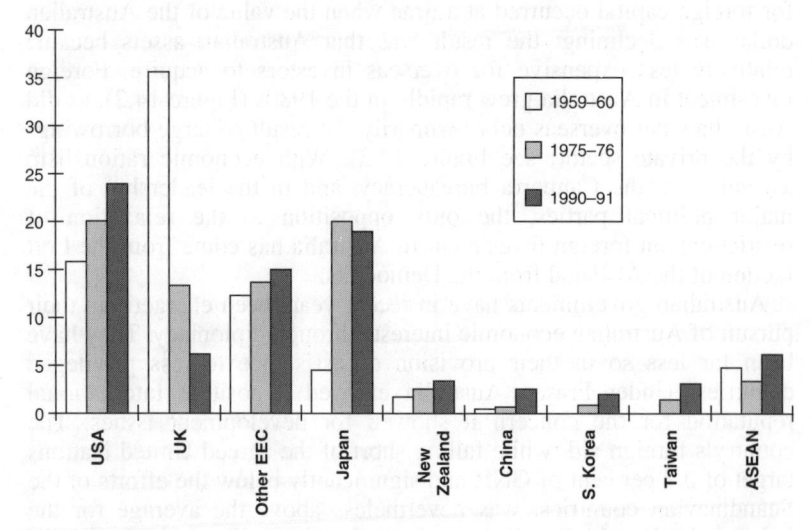

Source: Australian Bureau of Statistics

to emerge from APEC is substantially less than some of its Canberra-based supporters suggest: there is no reason to believe, for instance, that APEC will be more successful than bi-lateral negotiations in resolving the most significant trade problems in the region. The organisation may help in removing minor irritants and increasing the transparency of regional trade. More importantly, from the Australian perspective, however, is its role in deterring the emergence of a less open trading bloc within Asia, and securing a supportive stance from group members on global trade liberalisation.

The desire of Labor governments since 1983 to enmesh the Australian economy more closely with the international economic system has prompted liberalisation in such areas as import barriers (especially tariffs) and foreign exchange regulation. The country's persistent current account deficits have required balancing through an increase in flows of foreign capital. This increase occurred both through overseas borrowing by Australian corporations, and through increased foreign direct investment. As global financial markets became more integrated in the 1970s and early 80s, it was almost inevitable that Australia would have to relax its foreign exchange regulations, since the market had increasingly found means of circumventing them. The floating of the Australian dollar in 1983 was a major step in liberalising financial markets; by the beginning of the 1990s, most of the barriers to foreign investment in Australia had been removed (the Foreign Investment Review Board maintained a few residual powers of scrutiny over proposed foreign investments in a few specified industries). Easier access for foreign capital occurred at a time when the value of the Australian dollar was declining: the result was that Australian assets became relatively less expensive for overseas investors to acquire. Foreign investment in Australia grew rapidly in the 1980s (Figure 14.2), as did Australia's net overseas debt (primarily the result of large borrowings by the private sector; see Figure 14.3). With economic rationalism ascendant in the Canberra bureaucracy, and in the leadership of the major political parties, the only opposition to the relaxation of restrictions on foreign investment in Australia has come from the Left faction of the ALP and from the Democrats.

Australian governments have in recent years been energetic in their pursuit of Australian economic interests through diplomacy. They have been far less so in their provision of assistance to less privileged countries. Under Fraser, Australia enjoyed a positive international reputation for the concern it showed for development issues. The country's foreign aid, while falling short of the agreed United Nations target of 0.7 per cent of GNP, and significantly below the efforts of the Scandinavian countries, was nevertheless above the average for the industrialised world. But during Labor governments from 1983 onwards, both the aid ratio and Australia's reputation on development issues were allowed to slip. In part this resulted from Australia's own economic problems in the period, but it also reflected the influence of a hostile Treasury and largely indifferent Foreign Ministers. Neither was there pressure from the Opposition, which advocated even more severe cuts to the aid budgets). Not only did the ratio of aid to GNP and aid to

FIGURE 14.2 *Foreign Direct Investment in Australia and Australia's Investment Overseas*

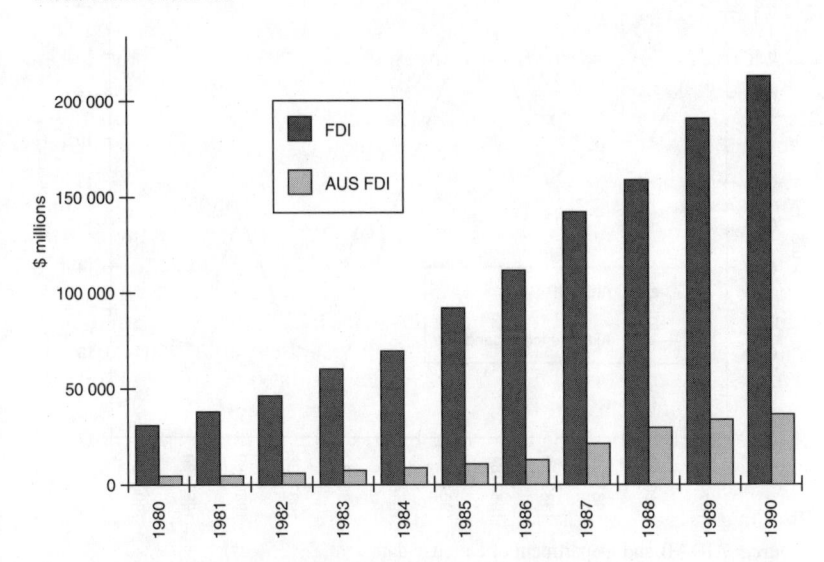

Source: R.A. Foster and S.E. Stewart (1991) *Australian Economic Statistics, 1949–50 to 1989–90*, Reserve Bank of Australia, Sydney, Occasional Paper 8

FIGURE 14.3 *Australia's Net Overseas Debt*

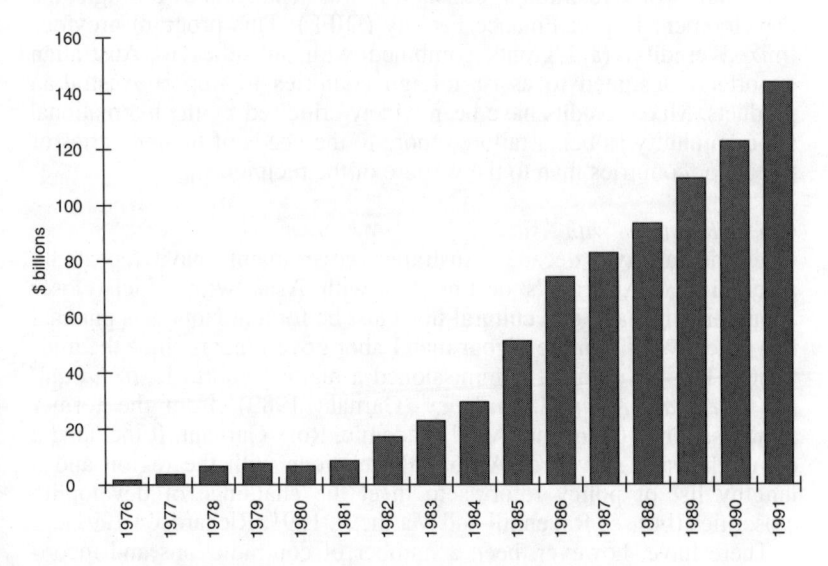

Source: As for Figure 14.2

FIGURE 14.4 Australian Aid and Defence Expenditures

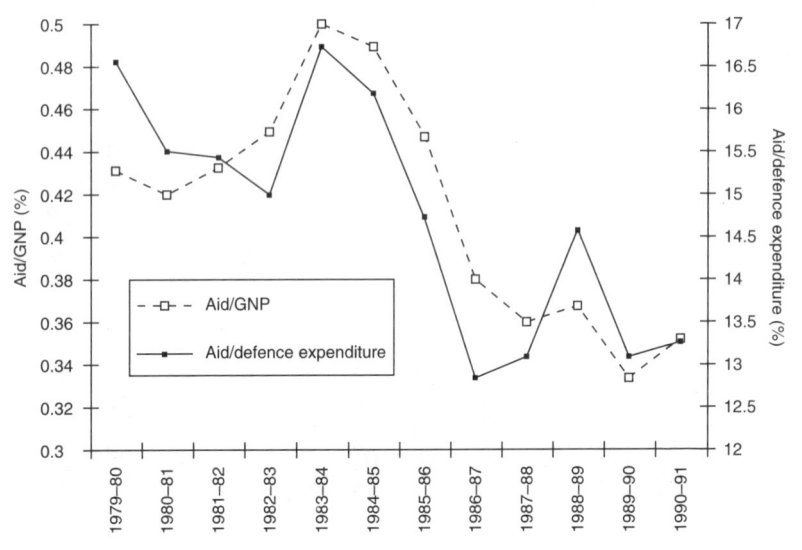

Source: AIDAB and Department of Defence data

defence expenditure decline significantly (Figure 14.4) but an increasing percentage of Australia's assistance was channelled through the Development Import Finance Facility (DIFF). This program provides 'mixed credits' (aid grants combined with subsidies to Australian exporters) designed to assist foreign countries to import Australian products. Mixed credits have been widely criticised by the international aid community as being tailored more to the needs of the industries of the donor countries than to the welfare of the recipients.

Closer Relations with Asia
Over the last two decades Australian governments have repeatedly asserted that Australia's destiny lies with Asia, with which closer economic, military, and cultural ties must be forged. None has pursued this objective with more vigour than Labor governments since the mid-1980s. The government commissioned a major Report, *Australia and the Northeast Asian Ascendancy* (Garnaut 1989), from the former Ambassador to China and ANU academic, Ross Garnaut. It included a comprehensive survey of Australia's relations with the region and a lengthy list of policy reforms to meet the challenge of developing closer ties (but see Ravenhill and Matthews 1991, Richardson 1991).

There have, however, been a number of contradictions and inconsistencies in the new approach to Asia. The government has not succeeded in convincing either the Australian people or Asian governments that Australia is part of the region. A Saulwick Poll conducted for the *Sydney Morning Herald* (21 April 1992) asked respondents whether they 'think of Australia basically as separate from Asia or as part of Asia'. More than two-thirds of respondents stated that they thought of Australia as separate from Asia; only 29 per cent thought Australia was part of Asia. A similar majority believed Asians saw Australia as separate from their region — an accurate perception, to judge from the comments made by leaders of Asian countries. (As Goot has frequently reminded us, however, care must be taken in interpreting opinion polls, since the answers obtained depend on the questions asked. An Australian Social Monitor poll, reported in the *Bulletin*, 28 July 1992, found that a majority of respondents thought that 'We have to realise we are part of Asia, not Europe.')

Inconsistencies within Australia's foreign policy in recent years have given Asian leaders good reason to doubt Australia's commitment to the region. Prime Minister Hawke, for instance, gave priority to visits to, and communications with Washington and London; he seldom visited Southeast Asia during his eight years in office. The maintenance of the alliance with the United States continued to receive pride of place in Australia's foreign policy. Hawke also made the commitment to send Australian warships to the Gulf without consulting any Asian leader, a move seen by some commentators as violating Australia's promise to consult its Asian neighbours on all military decisions (Malik 1991). Asian leaders have expressed irritation that they have not been consulted in advance on a number of Australia's foreign policy initiatives, including Foreign Minister Evans' proposal for a Conference on Security and Co-operation in Asia (Camilleri 1991).

Yet if on some issues Australian foreign policy makers could be criticised for failing to consult their Asian counterparts, on other issues they could equally be criticised for allowing the sensitivities of Asian countries to dictate policies. Nowhere has this been more obvious than in relations with China prior to the Tiananmen Square massacre. Australia's first Ambassador to the PRC, Stephen FitzGerald, criticised Canberra for its 'craven, even slavering' attitude to China, which enabled Beijing to exploit the relationship for its own ends. Australia had been overly generous in its financial support to Beijing, but received little in return. Furthermore, Canberra had allowed China to constrain Australian relations with Taiwan, thereby jeopardising substantial trade interests. (For further discussion see Fung 1992.)

In a similar manner, Australia at times appeared to permit China and ASEAN to dictate its policies on Cambodia and on the provision of aid to Vietnam, and the sensitivities of other Asian governments to mute its criticisms of their human rights practices. Australia's restraint in its criticisms of human rights abuses in its Southeast Asian neighbours stood in marked contrast to its outspokenness on such abuses in South Africa.

In its relations with Asia, Australia has had to navigate between, on the one hand, giving offence by failing to engage in consultation and, on the other, restricting itself by permitting the sensitivities of its neighbours to dictate its policies. Achieving such a balance is no easy matter for any government. On a number of important issues in the last decade the government has erred on one side or the other, as noted above. In its relations with Asia the government has yet to establish coherent and well-defined policies for the post-Cold War era. In particular, there is continuing imbalance between regional links and the emphasis given to the American alliance, with little conceptual integration of strategic elements and other dimensions, such as the economic or the environmental. Australia's engagement with Asia will depend heavily on economic relations, which in turn hinge on Australia's economic performance: there is little reason to believe that the textbook economics advocated by the Treasury and the *Garnaut Report* are themselves sufficient to provide foundations for the necessary structural transformation of the Australian economy.

Conclusion

Australia enters the era of the New World Order with more than a little uncertainty over the direction of its foreign policies. Although Labor governments since 1983 have won praise from commentators for their creative diplomacy in some areas, particularly in international economic relations, there were others where the dominant characteristics have been lack of careful analysis, of consultation and of foresight. For all governments these are unsettling times in which the conventional foreign policy wisdom of the last forty years provides few guides to the future. In particular, Australian foreign policy makers have to meet the following challenges:

- Determine what role the American alliance will play in an era in which there is no 'natural' enemy. There was more than a little irony in reports that the United States, without consulting Canberra, had offered Russia access to intelligence from the Joint Facilities, which Australia claims to be one of its most important contributions to the 'Western' alliance (see 'Evans in Dark on Soviet Nuclear Link', *Australian Financial Review,* 4 November 1991). If trade relations between the United States and Japan should deteriorate further, Australian governments may find it increasingly difficult to avoid becoming enmeshed in a dispute that pits the country's principal partner in the security realm against its principal trading partner;

- Fashion policies that support ecologically responsible and self-sustaining growth, when there are direct conflicts with Australian interests as a major exporter of fossil fuels. (For one of the few considerations of the environmental challenge for Australian foreign policy makers, see Harris 1992);
- Set relations with Asia on a new footing, in which Australian policy making autonomy and cultural values are preserved, yet appropriate consultations are undertaken with Asian governments on foreign policy initiatives.

Governments may not agree, of course, that these should be the major priorities on their foreign policy agendas. A future Coalition government, for instance, would be unlikely to give significant priority to environmental issues, probably preferring to take actions that would facilitate the development of further mining, mineral and timber processing activities to contribute to Australia's foreign exchange earnings.

As a peripheral state with limited military, economic and diplomatic resources, Australia has few opportunities to make a major impact on world politics. Its principal influence lies in its ability to make use of its foreign policy expertise to persuade others to move more rapidly in a direction to which they were already inclined. Yet even in these activities Australia has to proceed with caution: the spate of initiatives that were launched at the end of the 1980s not only caused some Asian neighbours to complain of 'initiative fatigue', but also threatened to produce what Mediansky (1992a: 21) terms 'leadership overstretch' — a situation characterised by an over-estimation of Australia's ability to influence events, and by an over-extension of Australia's limited diplomatic resources.

15
Media Policy

RODNEY TIFFEN

No area of Australian life has been transformed more dramatically during the period of the Hawke and Keating governments than the mass media. The changes were stimulated by government policy, but have borne little relation to the Labor Party's platform. Nor on the whole have they produced a more vibrant, diversified or higher-quality industry.

Two episodes tower over all else in the media developments of the last decade. The first was the change in media ownership laws, announced in late 1986. This set off the greatest frenzy in media transactions the country has ever seen. It was followed over the next several years by newspaper closures and unprecedented losses in the television industry. The second was the Broadcasting Services Act 1992, notable not only because it encapsulated many changed assumptions about media regulation, but because it foreshadowed the introduction of pay TV and revolutionary new delivery systems. These two episodes form the core of this chapter. First, however, introductions to the nature of media policy, and to media politics during the Labor decade, are necessary. The chapter will conclude with a consideration of the nature of media policy making.

The Characteristics of Media Politics

The mass media are central to a contemporary society's political and cultural life. This centrality gives media policy a peculiar passion. For many, decisions about media involve strong symbolic stakes. They are a statement about our national identity and cultural aspirations, and about the boundaries of social acceptability. Simultaneously, however, media policies involve big businesses with huge material stakes in preferred outcomes, and a variety of union, bureaucratic, legal and other vested interests.

Many areas of policy in a liberal democracy revolve around the scope and limits of the role of government. In media policy, the issues are particularly acute. They include: balancing the government's responsibilities as the guardian of society's common life, and its possibilities and limits as a source of cultural and educational enrichment, against the dangers of government as a dispenser of patronage for political favours, and its threat as a source of social control, a political 'big brother' or cultural commissar.

There have always been contrasting traditions in broadcasting and print media concerning the proper role of the state. Most obviously, the Australian federal system assigns them to different layers of government. The Constitution effectively gave the federal government power to legislate over broadcasting, while power over print remained with the states (Harding 1985, Armstrong 1982). More fundamentally, while government efforts to control the number or output of newspapers are seen as a threat to democracy, such efforts are seen as essential in broadcasting.

The original rationales for this distinction are now crumbling (Mayer 1979, 1980). Most Australian consumers have easier access to choice among radio and TV stations than they do among newspapers. The original basis for government's role in broadcasting (allowing commercial reliability and avoiding 'excessive' competition) required regulation of access to the broadcasting spectrum. While arguments about the cultural power of radio and TV have also been common, the bedrock justification of the state's role has been that the privilege of secure private access to the scarce public resource of the wavelength entailed public obligations, to be decided by government. Government policy has thus been a much more central factor in the development of broadcasting than in newspapers — or, indeed, magazines or films.

Government actions in media can be grouped under four headings:

Regulating Media Ownership
The first basic questions in media regulation concern who can own what. How many commercial TV and radio licences will there be, and what are the criteria for owning one? Who, if anyone, should be prevented from owning a licence — foreigners? 'unfit or improper' persons? newspaper owners in the same market? What limits should be placed on how many stations can be owned? How are licences to change hands? When TV began, access to the airwaves was granted first of all by government decision, with inquiries to discover the most suitable licensee. After the initial allocation, as long as the new licensees conformed to ownership regulations, licences have been traded like a property right, subject only to normal commercial provisions, with official approval following.

Supporting Government Media Enterprises
Australian governments, following British tradition, have long thought that there were some broadcasting activities which only governments could undertake. Although now of no political relevance, there has always been a strand within Labor thinking that the state should monopolise broadcasting — just as it should socialise other major sectors

of the economy. Except for the radical free market fringe of Australian political thinking, all important groups acknowledge that government institutions can achieve things in broadcasting which commercial organisations cannot. So the second aspect of policy involves enterprises which the government itself undertakes or supports financially, notably the ABC and SBS.

Controlling Media Infrastructure
Government plays the pivotal role, both as rule maker and financier, in determining the development of media infrastructures. As custodian of the broadcasting spectrum, it decides upon the number and types of services available, usually based on a murky mixture of technological and commercial considerations. It also decides when new services will be developed. It often supplies the infrastructure for undertakings too large or forward-looking for commercial enterprises, or where there are judged to be public interest reasons, perhaps as a common carrier or arbiter.

Regulating Media Content
Much more cumbersome than regulating media structures and deciding upon financial support is the effort to regulate media content: what programs will be made compulsory? which prohibited? which encouraged — and how? Although without any coherent overall rationale, this has traditionally focused on a number of recurrent concerns: specifying types of programs which must be shown (news, religious, children's, Australian); more problematically, specifying material which must not be shown (obscenity, some types of violence); and limiting the amount and nature of advertising.

In all four areas, significant movement has occurred during Labor's decade in power. This has raised basic questions about the rationales and purposes of government action, and the agendas of the Hawke and Keating governments.

Labor's record has differed sharply from the earlier pattern of partisan difference in media policy (see Edgar 1979, Evans 1983). After the Fraser government's harshness to the ABC and apparent beneficence towards commercial proprietors, many expected that the pendululm would swing again, with a major infusion of funds to the ABC and a clear message to the commercial networks that 'self-regulation would no longer suffice' (Harding 1985: 260). Rather, there has been increased concentration of media ownership, and overall movement towards deregulation of media markets and content. In an age of rapid technological development, the government have has adopted a cautious, patient approach. The Hawke and Keating governments have had much less supportive relations with the ABC than their Labor predecessors, both financially and ideologically (Harding 1979, Inglis 1982).

Media policy is a microcosm of a government's general political approach and of the climate in which most policy decisions are taken. Three more general political factors are a necessary prelude to understanding the dynamics of media policy under the Hawke and Keating governments.

Electoral Pragmatism
The Hawke government became the longest-ruling Labor government in Australian history partly because it was devoted, perhaps above all else, to ensuring its political longevity. Its electoral pragmatism was characterised not only by sensitivity to public opinion, but by a careful choice of which battles to fight, and when. The government was keen to avoid symbolic issues which aroused excitement and anxieties which could not be easily allayed. It consulted widely, especially with strategic groups who could command publicity and other political resources. It thus repainted the political landscape, so that many traditionally anti-Labor groups either became allies or at least remained neutral. They included major media proprietors. With extravagant gestures and close consultations, the government signalled its friendship towards particularly the two great deal makers of the Australian media, Murdoch and Packer.

The Priority of Macro-Economic Restraint
Unlike earlier Labor governments, which had enlarged the scope of the public sector within the economy, the Hawke-Keating governments reduced it. This overall economic direction — the need to internationalise the economy and so control government spending and the deficit, while obeying the electoral need to keep taxation low — was the context in which any proposals for increased spending occurred. Although the mixed model of Australian broadcasting survived intact, and although both the ABC and SBS expanded and diversified over the decade (cf. Patterson 1992), there were many conflicts, and both endured considerable financial stringency (Brown 1989).

The Deregulatory Ethos
Beyond these political and economic imperatives was a policy ethos, embraced by key sections of the government, and pervading the bureaucracy and opinion makers. This was the dominance of what has been labelled economic rationalism. In its most influential manifestations, this signalled a suspicion that government spending was ill-directed; that government intervention distorted markets; and that government enterprises and regulators generated priorities of their own, which not only produced inefficiency, but departed from larger considerations of the public interest. Such arguments jelled with the post-Nader awareness of how often regulation, by limiting competition, in fact benefited business at the expense of consumers. Differing dissatisfactions with existing regulatory arrangements produced a policy ethos an-

tagonistic to the extension of regulatory controls in media policy, as elsewhere.

A Certain Tackiness
The three preceding political factors explain much about media policy under the Labor government, but are not sufficient to capture its flavour. Key members of the Hawke/Keating governments had a strong rhetorical arsenal for attacking critics they saw as being too idealistic, especially those who invoked apparently Labor principles against them. They derided the 'politics of the warm inner glow', the affirmations in ideological rectitude which had little practical effect, and which needlessly alarmed interest groups and swinging voters. They paraded, by contrast, their self-proclaimed pragmatism and their sense of economic and political priorities, where the 'main game' would not be endangered by symbolic distractions. However, their interest in pragmatism often merged into patronage for the powerful. Considerations of 'rationality' were always informed by a keen sense of power and powerlessness, and of whom they considered friends and enemies. At the end of Labor's decade in power, the belief, corrosive to good democratic government, that policy on media was the outcome of secret deals and the trading of favours, was at least as strong as at any previous time in Australian history.

Rumours of special deals abounded. The years of Labor government have been marked by a large interchange of personnel, with government advisers becoming network employees. The most notable (accorrding to Carroll 1990: 63) was Peter Barron, the quintessential *apparatchik* of New South Wales Labor's Right-wing machine. After being Prime Minister Hawke's principal private secretary, he became a senior employee of Kerry Packer, closely involved in lobbying government on media policy.

Labor's attempts to placate major media proprietors were doubtless driven by its desire to obtain favourable coverage. Hawke said: 'I had, from the start, a Cabinet of considerable talent. I've always believed the best approach to people management is to recognise talent and allow that talent to exercise itself...Ministers didn't have me poking about and interfering in any continuous way' (Kelly 1992: 58). Perhaps the strongest exception to this Prime Ministerial approach occurred in media policy, where Hawke was a constant and active participant for the most basic of reasons: 'Hawke told some senior ministers in the week before the key Cabinet meeting [in late 1986] that if Cabinet approved the new 75 per cent ownership rule for the Packer and Murdoch groups, then his Government would win the next election' (Carroll 1990: 68). However, the favoured media proprietors' *quid* was far more obvious than the Labor Party's *quo*. While the benefits of government decisions to Packer, for example, have been obvious, it is less obvious what the government has received in return. No evidence has emerged of Channel

Nine, for instance, under direction from above, giving the government favourable treatment. The disproportion in the relationship suggests that these avowedly pragmatic politicians were sometimes seduced by the buzz of the deal.

The Politics of Media Ownership

The most dramatic changes and the most controversial issues under Labor involved ownership changes. Legislation, announced in late November 1986 and enacted just before the 1987 election, banned cross-media ownership, but allowed TV networks to extend their holdings beyond the old two station rule, in the end permitting any one company access to 60 per cent of the Australian market. This triggered the most dramatic upheaval in media ownership in Australian history. After the initial binge, the hangover of debt led to sharp decreases in employment and quality in the following years.

Preludes
In the first years of the Hawke government, its approach was cautious. The government was reluctant to offend the major media companies, which in turn adjusted to the presence of a Labor administration. In the 1984 election, all the major press groups supported the re-election of the Hawke government, by far the greatest editorial endorsement the Labor Party had ever received (House of Representatives Select Committee on the Print Media 1992).

The oligopoly which had long dominated Australian media seemed likely to continue for the foreseeable future. The four major companies, the Herald and Weekly Times, Packer's Australian Consolidated Press, the Fairfax company, and Rupert Murdoch's News Ltd, between them owned all Australia's metropolitan daily newspapers, all the crucial Sydney and Melbourne TV stations, dominated other media markets such as magazines and suburban and regional newspapers, and had extensive holdings in radio stations, book publishing and theatres.

In TV, nothing suggested imminent changes to the established order. The key to Australian TV continued to be the Sydney-Melbourne axis. These two cities accounted for 43 per cent of the national audience, and stations in other states and regional areas overwhelmingly took their programming from them. Since 1960, both Channel Nines had been controlled by the Packer company (McQueen 1977, Hall 1976). The Channel Sevens were shared between Fairfax (Sydney) and the Herald and Weekly Times (Melbourne), in a sometimes uneasy partnership (Souter 1991: 175, Fairfax 1991). Channel Ten, the newest and least successful of the three networks, was the only one whose Melbourne or Sydney stations had changed ownership in the previous twenty-five years. After considerable drama, Murdoch's company had acquired both by 1981 (Mayer 1982). There was increased activity by the fringe players — Bond, Parry, Skase, Stokes and Holmes à Court — but nothing likely to challenge the stranglehold of the four main companies.

A year after the 1984 election, there was still nothing to suggest the scale or nature of the coming changes. There were, however, three 'straws in the wind'. Soon after accepting an Order of Australia from the Hawke government, Rupert Murdoch renounced his Australian citizenship in order to advance into American TV ownership. Even though he now transgressed the nationality regulations for holding a TV licence, Murdoch sought to maintain his Australian TV interests through reshuffling company structures, so that although he still profited from them, he claimed he would no longer control them. No-one seemed in any hurry to force Murdoch to divest, but (especially as the Fraser government had changed the law from residency to citizenship, specifically to accommodate Murdoch), it seemed probable there would one day be a sale of Murdoch's Channel Tens.

Two other hints of future re-alignments stemmed from government policy. After several mis-steps (Brown 1989), the government had determined upon moves towards aggregation in licensing rural TV stations. This would have enlarged the area of each licensee, but instead of having a monopoly in their region, they would compete with two other operators. The intention was to give rural viewers the same degree of choice as city viewers. Unsurprisingly, many local licensees, especially the biggest ones who had most to lose, objected to the termination of their comfortably profitable monopolies. They were able to mobilise support among National Party MPs and among some Labor MPs, by arguing that it would mean a decline of localism and an effective extension of the powers of the big networks. Cabinet proposals about aggregation were twice rejected in 1986 by the Labor Caucus. The direction of government thinking was, however, clear.

The other policy movement was an attempt to change the two station rule, one of the pillars of TV licensing. This rule allowed a licensee to own two stations, irrespective of the size of the markets served. Thus owning licences in Cairns and Townsville counted the same as holding them in Melbourne and Sydney. In fact, of course, *de facto* networking prevailed in program purchasing and production. In the government, with increasing support from outsiders, there were moves to re-express limits on station ownership in terms of national audience share, with the aim of introducing more centres of initiative and diversity into the system.

These moves had stalled in Cabinet because of a deadlock between the Minister for Communications, Michael Duffy, who wanted a limit of 43 per cent of national audience share, equalling the Melbourne-Sydney combined market, and Prime Minister Hawke, who wanted 35 per cent, a figure with no apparent rationale except that it would ensure the continued dominance of Packer and Murdoch as the biggest single players. The stalemate continued for a year. It became public late in 1985, with Senator Button quoted as challenging the Prime Minister to 'tell us what you want for your media mates' (Chadwick 1989, 13-16).

Labor's New TV Networking/Cross-Media Policy

After another year, the deadlock was broken by Treasurer Keating, who proposed that TV networks should be allowed access to 100 per cent of the market. Cabinet subsequently reduced this to 75 per cent and the Senate to 60 per cent. A new policy principle was also introduced, a ban on cross-media ownership. In any future media acquisitions, a proprietor would not be able to own both a newspaper and a TV station in the one market. In Keating's colourful language, an owner could be either a prince of print or a queen of the screen, but not both.

The effect and possibly the intent of the new legislation was to advantage Packer and Murdoch, and disadvantage Fairfax and the Herald and Weekly Times. It later transpired that the first two but not the latter two had had significant forewarning and consultation on the coming changes (Souter 1991: 175-77, Carroll 1990: 92-93). Because Packer had no newspapers, his TV expansion was uninhibited by the law. Similarly, because Murdoch, as an American citizen, was likely to sell out of TV, he was free to expand in newspapers. It left both the Packer and Murdoch companies in control of the Melbourne-Sydney network axis, but made it impossible for either Fairfax or the Herald and Weekly Times group to acquire such a position without major divestment of their newspapers.

Cabinet approved the Keating 'compromise'. On a generous reading, but it realised Labor's traditional concern about cross-media ownership, with political pragmatism towards favoured media proprietors. On a more critical reading 'its motives were confused between the destructive one of paying off old scores and the constructive one of spreading media ownership' (Carroll 1990: 69). An immediate casualty was Duffy's aim of allowing more than three key players to co-exist in Australian commercial TV.

Announced by press release after Parliament rose for the summer recess, the proposals finally passed through the Senate the following May, in chaotic circumstances. The National Party, like their Liberal partners, at first opposed the legislation, but the Queensland Premier, then gearing up his 'Joh for Canberra' push, supported it. So the Nationals in the Senate gave way and their support was crucial in allowing the government to achieve what it wanted. Labor's victory in the July 1987 election ensured that the new policy would continue.

Restricting cross-media ownership had long been an ambition of Labor policy makers. Its rationale was easy to understand: when there were so few press owners in Australia, when most of the time they were anti-Labor, and when these major proprietors also owned TV stations, the result was not conducive to diversity. Oligopoly cushioned the large media proprietors from the need for market responsiveness. Between 1956 and 1972, Australian society changed much more than Australia's media. Its increased education, its greater cultural diversity and internationalisation were reflected only very partially in the media.

Similarly, the two station rule, and the monopolies given to commercial TV stations outside the capital cities, were meant to enshrine some ideal of localism, but this overlooked the *de facto* reality of networking. They ensured that regional TV stations made comfortable profits (Brown 1986), with a minimum of risk and with no commercial alternatives offered to dissatisfied viewers. Under the new system, there were no incentives towards localism.

The Media Ownership Revolution, 1986–87

The new policy triggered the biggest upheaval of media ownership in Australian history. Between December 1986 and August 1987, six major transactions (see Figure 15.1) transformed the face of Australia's media. In less than a year, 12 of the 19 metropolitan daily newspapers had changed owners, three of them twice, while one closed. Eleven of the 17 metropolitan TV stations had changed owners, two of them twice. None of the four companies which had dominated Australian

FIGURE 15.1 *The Binge: The Six Key Media Ownership Changes, 1986–87*

1 Murdoch's takeover of the Herald and Weekly Times launched early December 1986, consummated late January 1987: Murdoch acquired all assets except the *West Australian*, the *Daily News*, ADS7 and HSV7 and some radio stations. Divested himself of the *News* and *Sun*
2 Mid-January: Bond's acquisition of Packer's TV stations, TCN9 and GTV9, and some radio interests, for $1.05 billion
3 Late January: Lowi's acquisition of Murdoch's TV interests TEN10 and ATV10, for $842 million
4 July: Skase's acquisition of of three Fairfax TV stations (Channels 7 in Melbourne, Sydney and Brisbane), for approximately $700 million
5 July: Lowi's acquisition of Stokes' TV channels (ADS7, CTC7 and WA's yet-to-be-opened Channel 10)
6 Beginning in August, the Fairfax self-privatisation was essentially consummated by December: Warwick Fairfax bought out other family members and shareholders to gain 100 per cent of the newspaper company, incurring great debt and divesting Fairfax of the Macquarie radio network, the *Canberra Times* and many magazines and regional newspapers

Note: Here and in other transactions, attention is normally limited to metropolitan TV stations and metropolitan daily newspapers. To include radio, magazines, suburban and provincial newspapers and other media would drown the main outline of the changes in a welter of detail. Similarly, companies are usually identified by their principal owner, whereas the actual corporate structures were sometimes characterised by a complexity which said more about taxation and investment strategies than about control television in November 1986 were still involved a year later. (See Tables 15.1 and 15.2.)

News reporters were agog at the enormous prices being commanded for media assets. By the end of the year the major media companies had incurrred unprecedently high levels of debt — although Murdoch's were due to his overseas, not his Australian, operations. The nature of

TABLE 15.1 *Metropolitan Television Stations, Ownership, 1986–92 December of each year; entries in middle columns only made when change from previous year*

Station	1986	1987	1992
HSV7	HWT	Skase	Seven
GTV9	Packer	Bond	Packer
ATV10	Murdoch	Lowi[a]	Canwest
ATN7	Fairfax	Skase	Seven
TCN9	Packer	Bond	Packer
TEN10	Murdoch	Lowi	Canwest
BTQ7	Fairfax	Skase	Seven
QTQ9	Bond	Bond	Packer
TVQ0	Skase	Darling Downs	Canwest
ADS10	HWT	Lowi	Curran
NWS9	Lamb	Lamb	Lamb
SAS7	Holmes à Court	Holmes à Court[b]	Seven
TVW7	Holmes à Court	Holmes à Court[b]	Seven
STW9	Bond	Bond	Sunraysia
NEW10	(Stokes)	Lowi	Curran

Note:

[a] These channels also had intervening ownership changes: from Lowi to Cosser, and then Cosser to Westpac

[b] These channels had an intervening ownership change: from Holmes à Court to Skase. NEW10 had not opened at this time

Adelaide stations changed call signs: ADS was 7 and SAS was 10

The Seven Network Limited is owned 100 per cent by Television Holdings Ltd, the four directors of which own 15 per cent each; staff super fund 10 per cent; and banks (State Bank of NSW, ANZ, Chase Manhattan, Bank of America, Hong Kong Bank, Société Générale Aust Ltd) all 5 per cent each

Seven Network now owns 5 channels, with 64.63 per cent audience reach; Qintex had owned 66.76 per cent

Capital TV Holdings Ltd is owned 50 per cent by Curran investments, and 50 per cent by Westfield capital group

TABLE 15.2 *Metropolitan and National Daily Newspapers, Ownership and*

Newspaper	Location	Owners 1986
Sun News Pictorial	Melbourne AM	HWT
Herald	Melbourne PM	HWT
Age	Melbourne AM	Fairfax
Sydney Morning Herald	Sydney AM	Fairfax
Daily Telegraph	Sydney AM	Murdoch
Daily Mirror	Sydney PM	Murdoch
Sun	Sydney PM	Fairfax
Courier-Mail	Brisbane AM	HWT
Telegraph	Brisbane PM	HWT
Daily Sun	Brisbane AM	Murdoch
Advertiser	Adelaide AM	HWT
News	Adelaide PM	Murdoch
West Australian	Perth AM	HWT
Daily News	Perth PM	HWT
Mercury	Hobart AM	HWT
Canberra Times	Canberra AM	Fairfax
Australian	National AM	Murdoch
Australian Financial Review	National AM	Fairfax

	1967	1972	1977
Total circulation ('000)	3,781	3,935	4,047
% change in 5-year period	+4	+3	+2
Circulation as % of population	32.6	30.1	28.8

Proprietors' Share of Metropolitan and National Daily Circulation

	1982	1992
Murdoch	24	66
Fairfax	24	22
H&WT	52	–
Other	–	12

Notes: Circulation figures are for the six months April to November each year, taken from Audit Bureau of Circulation figures
Business Daily existed from November 1986 to February 1987, not long enough to show in any Audit Bureau of Circulation figures

Circulations 1972 to 1992 (by 5-yearly intervals)

		Circulation ('000)		
1987	1972	1982	1987	1992
Murdoch	648	612	559	584
Murdoch	498	385	213	..
Fairfax	206	245	235	240
Fairfax	274	258	259	269
Murdoch	316	310	275	459
Murdoch	312	364	284	–
Fairfax	309	330	232	–
Murdoch	260	258	214	258
Murdoch	159	160	113	–
Lowi	–	–	126	–
Murdoch	217	220	216	220
Lowi	133	180	156	–
H. à Court	218	249	238	263
United	123	122	91	–
Murdoch	53	56	54	53
Packer	34	44	43	47
Murdoch	136	119	139	150
Fairfax	39	63	78	75

1982	1987	1992
3,975	3,525	2,618
– 2	– 11	– 25
26.6	22.0	15.4

the prices paid was less widely commented upon: they constituted a drain on, not an investment in the media. The money was spent not as a means to use or develop resources, but to gain occupation of a strategic position, an entry fee and an exit bonus for media proprietors.

Only the first transaction, Murdoch's takeover and carve-up of the Herald and Weekly Times, provoked significant public controversy. This transaction was a saga in itself (Chadwick 1989, Bowman 1988). There were three regulatory avenues through which official action could have changed or prevented Murdoch's actions: the Foreign Investment Review Board, the Trade Practices Commission, and the Australian Broadcasting Tribunal (Chadwick 1989). Only the first involved direct decision by the government. The Act leaves considerable discretion to the government to block a foreign takeover it judges to be 'against the national interest'. Later, when the British press entrepreneur Robert Maxwell sought to buy the Melbourne daily, the *Age*, Treasurer Keating simply announced the government would not let him do so.

This political controversy crossed party lines. In the government, Hawke and Hayden took contrasting positions, as did Labor's Right and Left. In the Liberal Party, shadow Minister Ian McPhee clashed with Opposition leader John Howard. Even in the National Party, Federal leader Ian Sinclair took a different position from Queensland Premier Joh Bjelke-Petersen. Former Prime Minister Fraser, by contrast to his friendly actions towards Murdoch while in government, came out as a particularly strong critic of media concentration and the power wielded by Murdoch. The pattern seemed to be that those out of power decried media concentration, while those in power, or with immediate hope of gaining it, accommodated themselves to it.

After the policy changes, both Murdoch and Packer used the moment to sell out at enormous profits rather than to extend their TV empires. One stockbroker estimated that before the announced changes, the total for the combined sale would have been around $800 million, so that the combined selling price of nearly $1.9 billion (Packer $1.05 billion, Murdoch $842 million) constituted a government-generated windfall of $1.1 billion for the two companies (*Sydney Morning Herald*, 23 April 1987).

Fairfax was seen by the top levels of the government as hostile: some of its journalism was 'out of control and dangerous' (Carroll 1990: 61). As a result, the company did not receive advance briefings and consultation as Murdoch and Packer did (Souter 1991: 176–77). This probably damaged Fairfax's ability to respond to the takeover of the Herald and Weekly Times, but market factors and tactical skill during the takeovers were also important. Certainly no-one in the government could have foreseen the amazing saga of the Fairfax privatisation, in which the twenty-six-year-old Warwick Fairfax sought control by incurring enormous debt, selling off many company assets. This dramatic weakening of the Fairfax company further enhanced Murdoch's newspaper dominance.

Aftermath

The architect of the policy which prompted these spectacular and dramatic changes, Paul Keating, was apparently pleased with his work: 'I saw it as an opportunity to refashion the ownership structure of the media in a way which buttresses the democratic practices and norms of Australia and at the same time to guarantee that never again would we have such a hostile set of monopolies arrayed against the Labor Party ...[The result is] what I think is a beautiful position compared with what we did have' (Bowman and Grattan 1990: 154). By late 1987, Keating thought that the great shakeout was at an end: 'there's nothing left to shake out' (Carroll 1990: 222).

The long painful financial hangover was just beginning, however. The following five years saw a series of crises, bankruptcies and closures (see Figure 15.2). None of the three new network owners survived in TV. The industry reeled under the heaviest losses in its history. Fairfax

FIGURE 15.2 *The Hangover: Key Ownership Changes and Media Failures, 1987–92*

1. August 1987: Closing of *Business Daily*
2. December 1987: Closure of Holmes à Court's weekly *Western Mail*
3. February 1988: Closure of the afternoon Brisbane *Telegraph*; *Sun* switches to evening paper
4. March 1988: Sydney *Sun* and *Times on Sunday* closed
5. May 1988: Holmes à Court sells *West Australian* to Bond
6. June 1989: Packer sells *Canberra Times* to Kerry Stokes
7. September 1989: Frank Lowy departs from TV, making deal with Steve Cosser to take over Channel Ten, and in October sells Perth, Adelaide and Canberra Channel Tens to Curran
8. November 1989: Banks declare Qintex in receivership; Skase leaves country
9. June 1990: Packer regains control of Channel Nine, when Bond Media unable to make final payment to him
10. July 1990: Closure of *Daily News* in Perth after dispute when TPC refused to allow sale of it to Bond Media
11. September 1990: Westpac puts Channel Ten into receivership, forces Cosser out, and instals own team
12. October 1990: Murdoch merges morning and afternoon papers in Sydney and Melbourne into '24-hour papers'— widely viewed as effectively closing the two afternoon papers
13. Late 1991: Bond's Bell Group (*West Australian*) put into receivership; public float early 1992
14. December 1990: Banks move on Warwick Fairfax, put company into receivership; prolonged auction for the company begins
15. December 1991: Brisbane *Sun* closes
16. December 1991: Conrad Black's bid gains control of Fairfax company
17. April 1992: Adelaide *News* closes
18. November 1992: Consortium headed by Canwest gains control of Channel Ten

family control of their newspapers, which had lasted 149 years, ended when the company was forced into receivership. The 19 metropolitan daily newspapers of 1986 are now reduced to 11. Between March 1988 and April 1992, all the nation's afternoon newspapers disappeared, although in Melbourne and Sydney, they were replaced by multi-edition '24 hour newspapers'. There had been a long-term trend for the circulation of afternoon newspapers and, more importantly, their attractiveness to advertisers, to decline. Before the closures of the last two afternoon newspapers, the jounalists' union estimated that 1,200 journalistic jobs had been lost over the preceding three years, predominantly from newspaper closures — by far the biggest loss in the industry's history (AJA 1991). Commercial TV staff reached a peak of 7,745 in 1988, declining three years later to 6,316 (ABT 1992a: 55).

The most important reason for these losses was the intrinsic unsoundness of the original acquisitions. Over the following three years, TV revenue rose steadily, from $1,144.7 million in 1986–87 to $1,756.4 million in 1989-90, up a total of 53.4 per cent over 3 years. Only with the onset of recession in 1990-91 did it decline, by 2.5 per cent to 1,711.7m (ABT 1992a: 55). But by then indebtedness had brought the original TV deals unstuck.

None of the three new TV owners had had much experience in broadcasting. All had had some commercial success as developers. Television in the 1980s was not, however, well suited to developers' logic. TV penetration had already reached saturation levels, and there were indications that viewing was decreasing slightly. In 1979, 55.4 per cent of households were viewing TV in peak time, but this had dropped steadily by 1987, to 51.6 per cent (*Sydney Morning Herald*, 8 October 1987). The share of advertising expenditure going to TV had also levelled out, at 34.3 per cent of all advertising (ABT 1988: 126). A range of devices, such as the videocassette recorder, gave viewers easier control over just how much they watched TV advertisements and followed the programmers' schedules. Most fundamentally, it was only a matter of time before, via terrestrial services, satellite, cable, and various hybrids of the three, the central position of the traditional TV networks would be challenged.

All three networks were keen to improve their position relative to the other two, despite their heavy gearing. Some areas benefited from a spending spree. Most importantly, Ten set off a bidding war for high-rating American programs. The networks' total spending on foreign programs had declined to $126.0 million in 1987-88, but rose to $251.4m in 1988-89, peaking at a disastrous $283.9m in 1989-90 (ABT 1992a: 56). The outcome was less a competitive improvement for Channel Ten than a stalemate between the networks at a much more expensive level, with Ten's initiative effectively redistributing funds from the Australian industry to the American.

After making enormous losses, Channel Ten went first to Steve Cosser, and a year later, amid great controversy, was put into receivership by the Westpac Bank. Ten's share of the audience has subsequently declined: in Sydney, from 29 per cent in 1988 to 21 per cent in 1991, and from 30 to 20 per cent in Melbourne (ABT 1992b: 44). It has made economies across the board, and adopted a blatantly down-market programming strategy. This has achieved its bankers' aims. With expenditure and revenue more in balance, albeit at a much reduced level, the network was sold to Canwest, a Canadian TV company, which then sought Australian partners. For the first time, possession of a TV licence, the fabled 'licence to print money', had proved ineffective against the commercial incompetence of its owners. Not only did three TV licensees go out of business but, with the dual burdens of debt and recession, the industry itself made a loss for the first time in over thirty years.

Inevitably, production standards have suffered. Figures suggest the proportion spent on Australian programming has declined (ABT 1992a: 16–17). The amount spent on news and current affairs halved in two years: from $249 million in 1988–89 to $119.8 million in 1990–91 (ABT 1992a: 18–19). In 1986, most state capitals had state-based current affairs programs on commercial TV. Over the following few years, these all disappeared in favour of nationally-produced ones. There is a strong case to be made that Channel Ten, in particular, has fallen well below the standards of the full and comprehensive programming expected of a licensee. Channel Ten drastically reduced the number of journalists it employed, to the point where it was questionable whether it was providing an independent news service. In 1991 Channel Nine, employed 95 journalists in its Melbourne and Sydney stations, and Seven 54, but Ten had only 29 (ABT 1992a: 341–42). Nine spent $49.3m on news and current affairs, Seven $30.9m and Ten $15.1m.

The Politics of Inaction
The travails within the media industry have been greeted by political paralysis — an apparent unwillingness not only to take new initiatives, but to enforce existing regulatory provisions. The Parliamentary Inquiry into the Print Media illustrates the deflection of public concern into political inaction. There has been a considerable constituency concerned over the fate of the press since the Murdoch takeover of the Herald and Weekly Times. This was compounded by the series of newspaper closures, and climaxed with questions about the future of Australia's most prestigious newspapers when the Fairfax company was put into receivership. Despite earlier public statements by Hawke and Keating, opposing the idea, the 1991 ALP National Conference agreed to hold the inquiry into the print media. During its deliberations, the Brisbane *Sun* closed; within days of its Report being released, the Adelaide *News* did likewise. The committee, however, gave no attention to the fate of such afternoon papers.

The inquiry had been made a House of Representatives, rather than a Senate, inquiry so that Labor could keep control. It was also very short. Introducing it, the chairman, Michael Lee, contrasted its cheapness with the expensive ineffectiveness of British and Canadian Royal Commissions into the press. Indeed, economy was the inquiry's major virtue. It undertook no research of its own; rather it asked people for submissions, then treated any contentious aspect, or divergence in the evidence before it, as an invitation to inconclusiveness. Its Report was marked by strategic silences and deliberate ambiguities. Whenever it embraces high principles, there follow insipid or non-existent policy proposals. The acknowledgement of short-term impossibilities never inhibited the expression of long-term hopes (see Brown 1992, Chadwick 1992, Schultz 1992, Australia 1992).

The Broadcasting Services Act 1992

Over the decades, the Broadcasting Act of 1942 had become an unreadable, inchoate patchwork, as successive amendments were added to it. In 1989, the government announced an ambitious attempt to encapsulate the legislative requirements into a single, coherent Act, which would provide a basis for future developments in an increasingly dynamic area. This attempt was some years in the coming. Three years and four Ministers later, the new Act was introduced into Parliament by Senator Collins.

Most public attention focused on the framing of policies for the introduction of pay TV and the new media systems, and on what this meant for current proprietors. The Act also changed many crucial assumptions about Australian media policy. It introduced a new regulatory agency, the Australian Broadcasting Authority, with different functions and powers from its predecessor, the Australian Broadcasting Tribunal. It crystallised many current assumptions about what policy should and could achieve, reflecting not only the deregulatory policy ethos, but the lessened expectations of media resulting from the recent financial disasters. It was passed, minus its provisions for the introduction of pay TV, in May 1992. After a spectacular series of false starts and changed plans, a scheme for pay TV was passed by Parliament in late 1992 — although whether it survives as the legislative basis until this form of TV begins must be open to considerable doubt.

The Act was notable firstly for the close public scrutiny it received (e.g. Communications Law Centre 1991). Earlier major decisions about media policy, by contrast, had often passed with a minimum of public debate. The policy community for media issues in the 1990s includes the industry lobby groups, the Federation of Commercial Television Stations (FACTS) and the Federation of Radio Broadcasters (FARB); the major unions (now amalgamated into the Media and

Entertainment Alliance); small but vocal public interest groups (both general, like the Communications Law Centre, and specific, like the Children's Television Foundation); more active and vocal national broadcasters (ABC and SBS); community broadcasters; a large range of lawyers for whom media-related work is now a staple of their practices; some academics; a visible and accountable regulatory agency (formerly the Australian Broadcasting Tribunal); a more activist bureaucracy with more ambitious members (the Department of Transport and Communications); and parliamentary and Caucus committees on media matters. Increasingly, media issues overlap with other communications areas, so that Telecom, Aussat and the new company, Optus, are also involved. Moreover, all the other major political interests in society, ranging from the Festival of Light to gay pressure groups, from environmentalists to large corporations, are occasionally roused by media issues, when they feel their constituencies are affected.

One distinction within this diverse policy community is the difference between those groups whose interests are essentially symbolic, to do with endorsing values and affirming the boundaries of acceptability, and those whose interests are material, most notably the TV networks. The former tend to be spasmodically mobilised, while the latter have large permanent organisations. Each step by the government has been scrutinised, therefore, by a large and vigilant policy community.

Media issues rarely, nevertheless, become electorally crucial. They are reported regularly in the quality press, but rarely command headlines or prominent attention elsewhere. On those occasions when they do, quite different dynamics come into play, and the considerations of the policy community can be quickly superseded. In late 1992, for example, the Prime Minister suddenly raised the issue of TV violence and its effect on children. Opposition Leader Hewson immediately joined him in calling for new measures.

There were two key ironies in the sudden eruption of this issue. First, rules of the type which Keating wanted had largely been consigned to the networks under self-regulated industry codes, in the Act passed in May. Second, TV violence had already been subjected to considerable policy scrutiny over the previous few years. A major Tribunal inquiry, involving extensive participation and research, had developed new guidelines (e.g. ABT 1992b: 9). The political leaders' statements commanded more media attention than had any of the inquiry's extensive deliberations. Neither leader's statements suggested any knowledge of recent policy movements, and nor, by and large, did the reporting of the issue by the Canberra press gallery.

'State' and 'Market'
The essential tradeoff in TV regulation has been that in return for privileged access to a scarce public resource, the airwaves, the TV

licensee should meet various public obligations. The logic of the licensee's position, once in secure possession of the licence, has been to attempt to minimise these requirements. Their public arguments stress that any increase in obligations would be financially ruinous, or that the stations' interest coincides with the public interest anyway as manifested in the ratings. Market rhetoric centres on giving the public what it wants, with no acknowledgement that demand is anything other than autonomous.

The regulation of commercial television provides a classic illustration of conflict over the roles of the state and the market. Simple oppositions are, however, misleading. There are many types of state involvement and state enterprise (see e.g. Hood 1986, Chapter 4), and, more importantly for present purposes, the peculiar characteristics and limits of different types of markets.

The 'market', as it operates in Australian commercial TV, has at least three idiosyncratic features. First it involves a rigidly-circumscribed choice for the consumer, with the number of channels limited to three. In free market theory, one of the key guarantees of responsiveness to consumers and of product quality is the openness of the market to new competitors. The enforced oligopoly gives the channels considerable potential leverage in their dealings with advertisers, governments and program suppliers.

Second, while market rhetoric focuses on giving consumers choice, it de-emphasises the other side of market forces, securing the cheapest supply. If two stations both have programs attracting 30 per cent of the audience, but one costs three times as much to produce, the other will be more profitable. The problem with Australian programs on Australian TV has not been their lack of popularity, but rather the relative expense and risk of producing them compared with purchasing established overseas programs.

Third, the relationship of audiences to the programs they watch and the economic support for these is indirect. In Australia, commercial TV has been ostensibly free to the viewer. Its economic logic is that via the bait of attractive programming, it hooks audiences for advertisers. The implicit equation is that viewers pay for the TV programming by buying the products advertised. In normal consumer transactions, the buyer chooses a product on the basis of both price and quality. But when the implicit equation is that viewers pay for TV programming by buying the products advertised, there is no sensitivity regarding their relative satisfaction from, or involvement in the programs watched. They count merely as numbers in the ratings. There is thus no commercial incentive to show a program which comes third, with 18 per cent of the viewing audience, even if for those 18 per cent it is the highlight of their viewing week.

In sum, the 'market' which operates in commercial TV is much more partial and peculiar than market rhetoric would suggest. It cannot be assumed that any invisible hand produces a coincidence between network profitability and public satisfaction, nor that the cost considerations, limited three-way competition and subsidy of the industry by advertising, combine to give the public what it most wants.

The Scope and Limits of Content Regulation
Regulatory regimes on TV content have focused, first, on areas where a purely profit-driven licensee may not provide socially valued program types because of the expense of supply (e.g. news, children's TV, and Australian content); these have typically been included as requirements a TV licensee must meet. Second, they have focused on areas where market forces have not been trusted to be identical with 'community standards' (violence, obscenity); these have been the subject of prohibition or limitation. Third, there have been areas where the oligopoly of the networks may allow them to pursue their own interests in defiance of consumers, notably in not limiting the time allowed for advertising.

Under the Hawke government there was a move towards more consultative models in policy making about media content. On the three issues of program content which aroused the greatest public involvement — children's TV, Australian content, and violence — there were far-reaching inquiries. Each tested the ability of regulators to maintain a semblance of consensus, and in each some progress was made towards workable rules which partly satisfied all parties. Although in the process of compromise between the major participants, basic questions about media effects and the public purposes of entertainment media tended to be buried, the result was a generally more constructive policy approach than had prevailed earlier.

The Broadcasting Services Act 1992 implicitly reflected considerable disillusionment with all attempts to regulate media content. Effective public regulation involves well-defined rules, policed by a regulatory agency, and with clearly-stated and enforced penalties. In health regulations concerning food, for example, one presumes there is a clearly-stated rationale deriving from knowledge of hygiene considerations, a clear law following, and a range of penalties related to the seriousness of the offence. In regulating media content, however, none of these considerations operates unproblematically: there is no accepted scientific basis for regulation; the link between particular content and its presumed effects is contentious; there is frequent ambiguity over what a regulation means; and there is no established body of practice relating to the imposition of sanctions upon errant media organisations.

To take up the last point: only rarely have media organisations been penalised for breaching program standards. When this happens, there is a strong arsenal of rhetoric ready to be deployed against the regulators. In 1992, during disputes about the content of children's television, the networks launched a campaign blitz, the effect of which was to suggest the Tribunal was trying to 'ban' Skippy (Gilliard 1992). When Sydney talkback radio pundits John Laws and Ron Casey were criticised by the Tribunal for racist statements, they launched high-profile campaigns to portray themselves as martyrs, using the 'punishment' as a publicity boost.

This is not to suggest that the regulators are always, or even usually right. The symbolic concerns with TV content of many public interest groups could never be met. If implemented, many would be out of line with majority audience opinion. Similarly, bureaucrats are often bloody-minded or wrong. But the media enjoy a clear advantage in their capacity to command publicity, and to invoke strong rhetorical themes: 'big brother', thought police, wowserism, unreasonable bureaucrats, martyrdom — even if these bear little relation to the particularities of a case.

Regulating media content is usually a politically unrewarding enterprise, beset by contention and uncertainty. Regulators cannot achieve good TV; they can only construct quotas and impose penalties for 'bad' TV. Moreover, regulating content, unlike regulating structures, requires a constant and expensive monitoring apparatus, which has rarely proved cost-effective. The networks' immediate inclination will be to resist and oppose, something likely to result in protracted and expensive wrangles, whose impact on the quality of programming will be marginal at best.

The move in the Broadcasting Services Act towards industry codes, reached after public consultation but involving much more self-regulation, is certainly going to be cheaper and may be more productive. Questions must remain, however, about likely effectiveness. To what extent does the enlightened self-interest of the industry, and the public interest coincide? Is the industry capable of enlightened self-interest?

The Push for Deregulation
When the Hawke government came to power, the principal means of sanction against a TV station was the threat of revoking its licence. Starting in the late 1970s, under Bruce Gyngell as Chairman, the Tribunal had conducted a series of licence renewal hearings, which left most of the participants exhausted and embittered. The Tribunal had never failed to renew a licence, although it renewed some for a shortened period, and issued some moral rebukes. The only material punishment for a station was the equivalent of capital punishment, and one could confidently predict that the Tribunal would never impose it.

The movement in the 1992 Broadcasting Services Act towards deregulation owed more to dissatisfactions with regulatory arrangements than to any deep analysis of the peculiarities and limits of the Australian commercial TV market. It was rooted in ideological conviction, in the Department of Transport and Communications and elsewhere in the Canberra bureaucracy, rather than in any consideration of the recent achievements of the TV networks.

Total complaints to the Tribunal increased from 1,611 in 1988-89, to 2,836 in 1990-91, and to 6,813 in 1991–92 (ABT 1992a: 45–46). The new Act has stopped the central recording and processing of complaints, which are now referred back to the networks. Under the new system, it has become a more tortuous process for viewers to complain, with no reliable view of the pattern of complaints emerging. Similarly, the new Act makes the presumption that a licensee is a fit and proper person, unless confronted with evidence to the contrary, and liberalises the definition. This change follows a period when three TV licensees — Bond, Skase, and Rowse (owner of Tasmania's ENT company) — had criminal charges levelled against them.

The elimination of regulatory ritualism is to be welcomed, but it is less clear that its replacements will achieve more effective public accountability. In many areas, the new Act gives great discretion to the Australian Broadcasting Authority, also making it more subject to ministerial direction, thus increasing further the dangers of politicisation in the interpretation of policy. Many of the Australian Broadcasting Authority's processes and decisions will not routinely include public participation, or even be open to public scrutiny (Davies and Spurgeon 1992).

Regulation can be wrongly cast as pitting public interest groups against commercial operators. A great proportion of regulation in fact operates to protect licensees, especially in limiting the competition. A sub-theme in the moves towards deregulation, embraced most enthusiastically by economists working in the bureaucracy, has been to break the closed shop of media ownership (seen most clearly in Bureau of Transport and Economics 1990, and Department of Transport and Communications 1989). In an observation rich in ironies, there have been private complaints by industry representatives that the Department of Transport and Communication, now seen as a desirable career step for ambitious public servants, has been too full of free market zeal, and has not taken sufficient account of the peculiarities of the industry. The November 1991 draft Bill foreshadowed that free-to-air commercial TV's enforced oligopoly would end in 1997. By the time the Bill was presented to Parliament the following May, however, this had become merely a promise to review the situation in 1997. Nevertheless, while the oligopoly in free-to-air television remained, easier entry into narrowcasting services was introduced, and the introduction of pay TV services was signalled.

The Politics of New Media

The aspect of the Broadcasting Services Act which commanded most public attention was the apparently imminent introduction of pay TV. The Act for the first time recognised that change was a continuing feature of media, and facilitated the introduction of new services; in principle at least, the legislative bias towards inertia which has so far marked broadcasting policy, was eliminated.

The age of technologically-based scarcity in broadcasting media is over. The advent of more powerful delivery systems via satellite, cable, enhanced terrestial transmission and hybrids of the three, plus the advantages offered by digital technologies, will allow more messages to be transmitted, more cheaply, than ever before. Moreover, the traditional delineation of markets by geography is increasingly obsolete, with satellites in particular able to reach national, even international, audiences simultaneously with the same service.

It is impossible to envisage what the new media will look like a decade or two after their introduction. Traditionally, the main concern about mass media has been concentration, how their 'massness' permits a few senders to transmit their chosen messages to such vast audiences. Will a new concern about fragmentation arise? Or depending upon institutional arrangements, will the levers of control in the new system still be centralised, with a few major corporations monopolising key points in the system? How much will the public be prepared to pay for TV services? Under free-to-air television, consumption was spread across the whole socio-economic spectrum, with less educated and lower income groups being the heaviest viewers (Mayer 1980b). Under pay TV, will economically-based inequalities arise?

Policy making about new technologies and new media is a fraught process. Until recently there has been a bias against innovation. A positive decision to move into a new technology appears to need all significant groups' assent, while any one large interest can exercise a veto — or at least win long delays. The Australian approach was set early, when Sir Keith Murdoch prevailed upon the Lyons government not to allow ABC radio to broadcast any news until 7.50 pm, simply on the grounds that the sales of afternoon newspapers might be damaged (Inglis 1982: 34, 64). It was not until the Whitlam government that FM radio and colour TV were introduced, despite being available overseas long before this (Edgar 1979).

The free-to-air TV stations have a clear interest in delaying the introduction of any services which would undermine their monopoly, and in this they have been very successful. Every year that passes without their introduction is a victory for the existing networks.

Until recently, the pressure for the introduction of pay TV services has not been great. It has been on the policy agenda since the Fraser government. The Minister for Communications, Tony Staley, announced the government would be introducing cable TV. However, after the enthusiastic Staley's retirement, the government retreated, asking the Tribunal to inquire into whether cable TV and/or Radiated Subscription TV (RSTV) services should be introduced. Despite a positive recommendation, the government prevaricated. In 1982, there was a widespread expectation that Communications Minister, Neil Brown, would announce the introduction of cable TV at the end of a conference on that topic. Later a freedom of information search by Dr Kate Harrison revealed that the draft of the Minister's speech did indeed announce the introduction of cable TV. But at the last minute, for unknown reasons, this decision, which would have fundamentally altered the direction of Australia's media development, was not made.

Although the Hawke government endorsed the Fraser government's decision to proceed with the satellite (Brown 1989), it placed a low priority on deciding about new services. There were several inquiries, but only after the 1990 election was there any momentum towards a positive decision. The political environment then was more propitious. A new Minister, Kim Beazley, was supportive, and there was general urgency about micro-economic reform, focusing especially on telecommunications. Most importantly, soon after the election, the extent of Aussat's financial disaster emerged. In October 1991, Cabinet decided to introduce pay TV services. Soon after, it was announced that Optus had been given the contract to act as the competitor to Telecom, and would take over Aussat as part of this agreement. There was then the presumption that pay TV would begin as a service transmitted by satellite.

Over the next thirteen months, however, Labor went through several stages in its thinking about how pay TV should be introduced, changing its position on such sensitive issues as the number of services; whether one technology would be annointed as the favoured mode of delivery; the role of the free to air commercial networks; the role of the ABC; limits on foreign companies; prohibitions on advertising; and regulations of program content. After several policy somersaults, the government finally advocated 10 new services, with two commercial consortia controlling four each, and the ABC having two. Parliament passed this scheme in late 1992.

Over the summer, a new issue erupted. Because the same service could now be delivered by a variety of technologies (e.g. satellite, terrestrial and cable) the new Act sought to legislate types of service, rather than technologies. This proclaimed technological neutrality was, however, in some tension with the government's presumption that pay TV would begin as a satellite service. The new Act also imposed far less regulation on 'narrowcasting' than 'broadcasting' services, although no clear distinction was drawn between these. Steve Cosser, the businessman who had been ousted from control of Channel Ten by the Westpac Bank, sought to exploit these ambiguities by buying nearly all the microwave licences in Sydney and Melbourne, with the aim of introducing a pay TV service. Amid great controversy, the government sought to stop any such moves. The 'market' thinking of the Department was manifested in the decision to award the new satellite TV licences simply on the basis of the highest bid. So the high farce of the policy process put in train continued throughout 1993.

Making Media Policy

Media policy has become a central and volatile part of the political agenda, and attracts a large and diverse policy community. It is marked by intractable conflicts over large questions of principle, including the role of government itself; by confused debates using problematic evidence; and by policies producing unintended effects. Over and above the rights and wrongs of particular decisions, contemporary media policy is marked by the following characteristics:

Each step in the regulatory process, from values to rules to enforcement, is fraught with problems
Media policy has been characterised by a gap between rhetoric and legislation, between the proclamation of an ideal and the set of regulations to embody it. There are genuine difficulties in enshrining values in legislation, in moving from an ideal like diversity to framing an enforceable statute about media structures and content. Regulators do not directly produce programs, so how the rules they lay down will impinge on managements' programming strategies and programmers' creativity is far from clear. Moreover, even after rules are laid down, the capacity of regulators to police them has been limited. The step from rule to enforcement has often been as problematic as the step from principle to rule.

Policy making is surrounded by ambiguous effects
Underlying all media policy is a lack of certainty about the impact of the media upon their audiences and on society, conflicting ideals about cultural and political values, and ambiguity over what these might mean in practice. Such fundamental questions are always likely to remain unresolved, and policy formation soon becomes a search for acceptable tradeoffs — with acceptability defined by the relative power of different lobby groups. While much of the rhetoric about media policy is at the level of ideals, most of the bargaining is about numbers. As public controversies rage, particular numbers momentarily become invested with symbolic importance. For example, is Australia's cultural identity protected by an Australian TV content quota of 40 or 50 per cent? Is Australian independence endangered by allowing foreign ownership of 15 or 30 per cent? Concern about the power of the big networks is manifested by reducing their possible reach from 75 to 60 per cent of the national market. What difference in practice does the 15 per cent make? Debates about incommensurable principles are politically difficult, but numbers allow compromise.

The process of policy making is itself chaotic and problematic
The value conflicts, the effects and the difficulties of framing and enforcing legislation, all contribute to a high degree of discontinuity in policy movement. It is an area marked by 'transverse cleavages' (Tiffen 1989: Chapter 8), where the divisions within parties are often as great as the differences between them. Some of the most prolonged

and bitter battles *within* the Labor government occurred over media policy.

Policy movement has tended to be non-cumulative, subject to sharp changes in direction and style, not only when the government changes, but with each change of Minister. Beyond questions of personal performance, the important point is that only in an area with such uncertain foundations could a change of individuals have such impact. The same mixture of ideals has even allowed regulatory agencies sharply to diverge. The most dramatic contradiction came in 1980 when the Australian Broadcasting Tribunal rejected Murdoch's acquisition of Channel Ten, only to have this later overturned by Justice Morling of the Administrative Appeals Tribunal (Mayer 1982). In few other areas of policy or law could you find two verdicts offering such strikingly different rationales. This procedural uncertainty in some ways disadvantages all participants. However, to the extent that it involves ineffectual regulation, it assists those who benefit from prevailing conditions.

Universalist principles are always overlaid and undercut by particularist considerations

Considerations of power and patronage outweigh calculations of the public interest in many areas of policy. The problem is particularly acute, however, in the media, because politicians perceive media support itself as a crucial political resource. The key political operators in any government are particularly likely to be involved in media decision making.

Moreover, there are so few key players in Australian media that principles are often viewed merely as codewords for signalling winners and losers. The small number of players means that initial responses are tribal, that long-established loyalties and antagonisms are ready to come into play. Because media ownership is so concentrated, the possibility of backroom deals is much facilitated. The government's conduct over a number of years has fanned this perception.

After a decade of Labor rule, the media in Australia are a much less vibrant industry than they were. In media policy, unlike, say, unemployment, there have been few excuses to offer. Government policy has not always been the direct cause of the catastrophes that have occurred — but was often a central catalyst. The policy process has been typically unedifying, and the costs of policy have been far more apparent than its benefits.

16
Environmental Politics

PETER CHRISTOFF

Green Foundations

Australian politics has undergone a process of 'greening' over the past two decades. But how have ecological problems emerged as matters of public concern, and to what extent have they reshaped the Australian political agenda, its political culture and institutions? This chapter looks at the political impact of environmental issues during the 1980s and early 90s and at some of the questions facing the Australian state and the environmental movement as they grapple with the environmental problems of the new century.

Australian environmental politics draws strongly on two distinct traditions: resource conservation and nature preservation. Resource conservation is concerned to ensure the wise use of natural resources for maximum human benefit, whereas nature preservation increasingly aims to protect nature from the ravages of human use (Hay 1959). In Australia, as in the United States, both traditions emerged during the last decades of the nineteenth century and the first part of the twentieth. Until the 1970s, they shared the dominant utilitarian ideology which sought 'wise use' for future human benefit. As Lacey (1989) describes it for the United States, the first tradition was part of a history of production, and the second the history of consumption. In terms of political forms and modes of action, neither tradition was promoted by social movements as these are now commonly understood. Individuals and groups sought to refine the legislative and administrative functions of the state from within, in order to work against the unco-ordinated impacts of the market. They wanted to rationalise and facilitate (where private resources were insufficient) use of the environment for the general social good or, more usually, for the advantage of sectoral interests. It is wrong, therefore, to see environmental politics as a phenomenon of the 1980s. Conservation and environmental issues and politics both derive from the nineteenth century. However, their mode of expression and action was, until the emergence of the new social movements in the 1960s and 70s, constrained by traditional paternalistic and élitist political forms.

Until the late 1960s, conservation and environmental politics occurred through negotiation and planning, with the state as the arbiter. It encompassed those economic and social groups with resource conservation interests: the professional resource associations; parts of the scientific community; and agricultural, union and manufacturing industry organisations. These groups broadly constituted a lobby seeking administrative and legislative change. Their concerns were inscribed in the administrative structures of the state (in Departments of Agriculture, Mines and Rivers and Forestry Services). Their interests, however, were not automatically reflected in government policies or decisions. Nevertheless, matters such as a lack of infrastructure (like dams), water pollution or soil erosion, which limited productive capacities and industrial development, were recognised as legitimate matters for state involvement, and resolutions were negotiated without significant social conflict.

Since the late 1960s, environmental politics in Australia has become increasingly populist and conflictual, characterised by public confrontations over such issues as 'slum clearance' or the clearing of 'old growth' forests. The modes of action and political organisation adopted in recent decades by the emergent environment movement have much in common with those of other new social movements, in part because of commonly-held values about citizenship and participatory politics. However, the environment movement is additionally characterised by its reaction against the colonisation and regulation of Nature in the name of 'economic development'. At the heart of its struggles to preserve biodiversity lies a demand for political recognition of the rights and needs of other species and future generations of humans. This 'ecocentric' core represents a new political challenge, one which for the first time seeks to redefine human aspirations in an ecological context (Eckersley 1992). The demands of the new environment movement have also led to new pressures on the state and the emergence of competing and apparently contradictory functions within it, catering for resource exploitation and economic growth on the one hand and environmental protection and conservation on the other.

A detailed historical treatment of recent environmental issues would show that the language and modes of action of the new and the old politics often merge. The new politics, challenging the authority of the state with the demands of non-institutional political organisations, uses the forms and language of symbolic protest which has come to dominate public perceptions of what constitutes environmental politics. Nevertheless, the old politics, which uses conventional strategems such as lobbying, formal input into government policy and political party programs, and electoral politics, is still influential. In practice, both political modes are used interchangeably by the new proponents of environmentalism and, increasingly, by their opponents.

The new era in Australian environmental politics was provoked by international reaction to the ecological effects of industrialisation after World War II, to what Hardin (1968) called 'the tragedy of the commons', the contamination of 'free' environments such as air, rivers and oceans, and the near-extinction of exploited mammal species such as whales and elephants. Seminal studies such as Rachel Carson's *Silent Spring* (1962) and, locally, *The Great Extermination* (Marshall 1966) and *The Last of Lands* (Webb et al. 1969), helped make these impacts into 'quality of life' issues. The predominant focus, however, was still on human health and well-being. In the 1970s, new emphases emerged. The 1973 oil crisis, the Limits to Growth debate (Meadows et al. 1972) and the Ehrlichs' neo-Malthusian *Population, Resources, Environment* (1970), focused popular attention on the potential outcomes of exponential resource use and population growth. This new environmental awareness was marked by a deep, scientifically-informed pessimism about the benefits of progress, where this was defined as unrestrained technological change and growth in material output, fuelled by dispute over the social, economic and ecological costs of oil and nuclear power, and by widely-reported accounts of disasters such as the Torrey Canyon oil tanker spill, Minamata and Love Canal. By the 1980s, disasters like Bhopal and Chernobyl, acid rain and climate change had strengthened this concern, leading to the formation of Green parties throughout Europe, the global debate over sustainable development (WCED 1987), and the United Nations' Earth Summit in Rio in 1992.

In Australia, the surge in environmental policy and legislative innovation at first broadened the definition of natural resource management to place greater emphasis on the impacts of environmental mismanagement upon human health. During the early to mid-1970s, a wave of landmark administrative reforms and legislative change at both state and federal levels enhanced pollution regulation. These reforms were often modelled on solutions developed overseas, mainly in the United States, responding to pressure from administrators and scientific leaders alarmed at the mounting evidence of the human and economic costs of air and water pollution (Gilpin 1980). Compared with later conflicts, there was little sustained public pressure from local protest groups, and reform predominantly occurred in response to the lobbying of élites.

In Australia's federal system, political responsibility for land use and resource management primarily lies with state and local governments. The most significant reforms took place first at state level. During the early 1970s, most states established environment protection agencies and related bodies, with powers to regulate industrial pollution and define environmental standards. They reformed their planning laws to incorporate environmental factors. At the same time, most states created separate departments of conservation, responsible for environmental management, including the protection of native flora and fauna. In a pattern which still persists, policy precedents were set in those states with innovative administrative or legislative cultures. Victoria, which in 1958 was the first Australian state to enact air pollution laws, followed Californian environmental standards and the United States

National Environmental Protection Agency (NEPA) model in developing the first EPA-style body in the country. This approach was followed in other states shortly afterwards. Considerable differences in environmental practices and standards emerged between states. This became a persistent source of later problems.

Environmental issues also began to influence the federal sphere. The Gorton government established an Office for the Environment in 1971; this became the portfolio of neglected issues: Environment, Aborigines and the Arts. In the following year, the Whitlam government created a separate Department of the Environment and Conservation, as well as two Commonwealth/state ministerial councils, the Australian Environment Council and the Council of Nature Conservation Ministers, and passed key enabling legislation. It also signed international conventions which were to provide important assistance to conservation groups over the next decade. Here, as elsewhere in its reformist agenda, the Whitlam government was intent on defining, expanding and fortifying the federal government's constitutional rights to enable or require national policy implementation, in the face of hostility from conservative states (Whitlam 1985: 534). In 1974, Australia became the seventh nation to ratify the World Heritage Convention, which came into force in 1975. It subsequently signed the Convention on Wetlands of International Importance, and joined the International Union for Conservation of Nature and Natural Resources (IUCN), the International Centre for the Study of the Preservation and Restoration of Cultural Property (ICCROM) and the International Council of Monuments and Sites (ICOMOS). The Australian Heritage Commission and the Australian National Parks and Wildlife Service were established on the basis of these commitments (Whitlam 1985: 547). By October 1981, the Great Barrier Reef, Kakadu National Park and the Willandra Lakes Region had been included in the World Heritage list.

There have been two major periods of federal environmental legislative innovation: 1974–75 and 1983–90. Each coincides with a federal Labor government. Key Commonwealth Acts were passed during the period 1974–75, and precedents set which enabled further reforms during the 1980s. The Racial Discrimination Act 1975, and Australia's ratification of the Covenant on Civil and Political Rights (also in that year) set the scene for the use of external affairs powers by the federal government to override states resistant to its preferred environmental policy outcomes. In 1982, in the *Koowarta Case*, the High Court upheld the Commonwealth's capacity to use international obligations to extend its powers, and so established a precedent which led directly to the successful High Court defence of the Hawke government's use of the World Heritage Properties Conservation Act 1983 to save the Franklin River, against the wishes of the Tasmanian government.

Perhaps the most important Commonwealth legislative development during this time was the Environment Protection (Impact of Proposals)

Act 1974. This sought comprehensive Environment Impact Statements (EISs) for all major projects. It was specifically to be used to establish inquiries into sand mining on Fraser Island and uranium mining in the Northern Territory. The Whitlam government had hoped to establish through this 'a parallel process, a marrying of the economics and the effects on the total environment of the proposed development' (*CPD*, H of R 1974: 4569). As was the case for the Commonwealth's Endangered Species legislation twenty years later, environmental considerations would not occasion the use of a veto. Even so, the legislation was strongly opposed by the states (Whitlam 1985: 538). Upheld by the High Court in the *Murphyores Case* in 1976, the Act provided the first indication of the reinterpretation and expansion of environmental powers under the Constitution which would continue over the next decade.

The late 1960s and early 70s were also a transitional period for conservation groups. Most states can point to key disputes during this time, in which the state-managed politics of conservation was challenged by the new politics of environmental protest. These disputes included, in Queensland, the campaigns to preserve Fraser Island from sand mining and logging, and to save the Great Barrier Reef from threats associated with oil drilling (Wright 1977). In Victoria, there were campaigns to block agricultural settlement in the Little Desert (Robin 1993), and to halt the industrialisation of Westernport Bay (Timlin 1974). In New South Wales, Green Bans stopped speculative redevelopment of the inner Sydney working class suburb of Woolloomooloo (Roddewig 1978). In each case, local communities and individuals opposed to proposed developments at first failed to receive recognition and satisfaction from powerful politicians or intransigent governments. They were then able, with the assistance of media attention (and in the case of the Green Bans, union movement muscle), to convert local concerns into broad public pressure for political change, including changes to autocratic decision making procedures. The Fraser Island, Barrier Reef and Little Desert campaigns were also notable for their promotion of environmental preservation for non-anthropocentric reasons, and for the emergent role of scientists and ecologists as sources of authoritative information, and as public advocates for nature preservation policy decisions.

Perhaps the most influential single campaign for nature protection during this time was against the flooding of 'that exquisite alpine lake', Lake Pedder, in the rugged Tasmanian south-west. By August 1972, the lake had disappeared under the waters of the Serpentine Dam. However, the campaign and the process of political lock-out which accompanied it, catalysed the development of 'preservationist' environmentalism in Australia. The power and impenetrability of the Tasmanian Hydro-electric Commission, the responsiveness of the Tasmanian Labor Government to the HEC's advice, but not to the concerns of conservation petitioners, and the absence of effective arenas for public participation in decision making, became concerns as strong as those for Pedder itself (Jones 1971). Backroom negotiations between élites were ultimately rejected as ineffectual by environmentalists — especially as the flooding proceeded. Here was a typical confrontation between a state government and its agencies representing industrial development, arguing that the new Lake Pedder would be as beautiful, if not more so, than the old, and recreationally valuable. The new politics of the environment movement defend the spiritual and ecological authenticity of unspoiled Nature.

Although Lake Pedder was drowned, the conflict had a number of long-term outcomes. One was the involvement, for the first time, of the Commonwealth government in a state environmental issue. Fifteen days after his election in 1972, Whitlam wrote to Tasmanian Premier Eric Reece proposing a joint Commonwealth-Tasmanian committee of inquiry to report on feasible alternatives to the flooding of the Lake. The newly-formed National Estate Committee also promoted the preservation of the Lake as 'the focal point of the unique South West Tasmanian Wilderness region'. However, both the committee of inquiry and the request for a moratorium were rejected by Reece. Although federal involvement had been cautious and reluctant, and federal Cabinet had voted to reject action on the moratorium proposal (Cass 1981: 72), Whitlam later claimed that this loss added to the impetus to list significant heritage sites under the recently-developed World Heritage Convention (Whitlam 1985: 530). Another outcome was the 'palace coup' within the Australian Conservation Foundation (ACF), with the initial council and the senior staff resigning in the face of members' criticism that ACF's weak and compromised stance had contributed to the loss of the Lake. These resignations opened the organisation to more activist and populist politics. The loss of the Lake also provoked a core of Tasmanian activists to form the world's first Green Party, the United Tasmania Group (UTG 1974, Rainbow 1992), which became the forerunner of successful Tasmanian campaigns to save the Franklin River and the South-West Wilderness, preserve the Southern forests and halt the Wesley Vale pulp mill. It also became the predecessor of the Tasmanian Green Independents.

The Australian Environment Movement in the 1980s

Popular and media perceptions of environmental issues during the 1980s were dominated by a series of spectacular conflicts over the fate of remote, beautiful, near-pristine sites. These are well documented in Mercer 1991, Harding 1992, Kelly 1992, Walker 1992 and Bonyhady 1993. The 1980s were also dominated by the electoral activities of the environment movement, which sought to resolve these conflicts in its favour by influencing the outcomes of federal elections between 1983 and 1993 (Papadakis 1990a, 1993). In turn, the responses of Labor governments to environmental issues at federal and state levels were shaped by the need to both manage conflict, and retain slender electoral margins.

The fight to stop the damming of the Franklin River catalysed the emergence of a national environment movement. In January 1983, 14 major conservation groups, including the ACF, the Wilderness Society and state conservation councils, joined in a coalition to rally support from among more than 800 grassroots groups and their members to campaign against the dam and the Fraser government (Milliken 1983: 3). The debate captured the imagination of middle Australia and commanded a response from both major parties. The *Bulletin* in February 1983 featured 'Tasmania's Dam Busters' on its front cover, as its lead story. It carried photographs of the spectacular scenery of south-west Tasmania and of 'greenie guerillas on the Franklin Front', a term which understated the degree of national support for this campaign. A nationwide survey in January showed 48 per cent of Australians (including 62 per cent of Democrat voters and 55 per cent of Labor ones) were opposed to the Dam's construction, with only 25 per cent in favour. The same poll also suggested that only 37 per cent favoured federal intervention ('passing a law to stop the damming'), while 47 per cent were opposed to it (Nicklin 1983: 21).

The Australian environment movement changed dramatically during the decade. It grew rapidly. Its focus shifted from 'brown' issues, such as energy conservation and pollution, to 'Green' or nature preservation issues. Hostility between sections of the union movement and the environment movement increased, as environmental claims were increasingly seen to threaten jobs in the timber and mining industries. The larger national organisations became increasingly professional and bureaucratised, and consultation between government and the movement was increasingly channelled through these major groups.

Between 1970 and 1990, the movement grew to include some 2,500 environment groups and organisations. They included five prominent national environment organisations: the ACF, the Wilderness Society, World Wide Fund for Nature (Australia) (WWF), Greenpeace (Australia) and the National Trust. Since the 1970s, Conservation Councils in most states have represented small community-based groups. In 1990, the movement included more than 500,000 members, from a base of approximately 50,000 in 1970 (Grinlinton 1990, Mercer 1991). Differing considerably in their size, organisational forms and political approach, the persistent diversity of environment groups reflects not only the different issues around which they have formed but also their wide range of ideological positions which, at their extremes, are diametrically opposed.

The growth in the Australian environment movement was spurred by its concentration on Green issues. Already in 1983, Milliken could include rainforests, wood chipping, softwood plantations, conservation of mallee country, sand mining, the Great Barrier Reef and endangered species among eleven nationally recognised environmental battlegrounds, with uranium mining and pollution appearing almost as afterthoughts on his list. There were several reasons for this focus becoming sharper during the 1980s. By the start of the decade almost all major mainland rivers had been dammed or significantly altered, over half the continent's 'old growth' forests cleared, virtually all temperate grasslands converted to pasture, and many species either becoming rare or threatened with extinction. The frontiers for 'land breaking' resource use had been reached, and the last remaining areas of relatively pristine landscape were threatened. Increasingly, productive technologies, such as those used to harvest and mill timber from 'old growth' forests were accentuating the capacity to exploit a diminishing resource (Christoff and Blakers 1986, Watson 1990). The use of nature as a cultural icon, and its economic value for recreational and leisure pursuits had grown, as had the related popularity of the concept of wilderness as a spiritual antidote to urbanisation. These cultural factors were enhanced by media interest in the global environmental crisis — particularly climate change and the Greenhouse Effect — and ozone depletion, and in the scientific aspects of Australia as the unique continent. Environmental groups also discovered that skilled use of the media to focus on the physical beauty of threatened remote areas, the emotional attraction of certain vulnerable species, and the spectacle of bodies in front of the bulldozers mobilised activists and donors to support well-crafted campaigns. The works of photographers such as Truchanas, Dombrovski and Tatnall 'sold' the image of the Wild: Dombrovski's picture of Rock Island Bend on the Franklin remains one of the most widely recognised images of Australian landscape.

Increases in membership and donations brought tangible benefits. These were delivered mainly to the larger organisations, which were best placed to generate and capitalise on the momentum. Their budgets grew significantly during the late 1980s. Able to pay higher salaries, these organisations began to professionalise their research and lobbying skills. By offering career paths for activists, they ensured the retention of campaign skills and 'organisational memory'. For example, the Australian Conservation Foundation, whose influence depended initially on its connections with industry bodies and ruling élites, came to depend more on its size and its increasing sophistication as a campaigning and lobby organisation. Membership grew from 1,200 in 1967 to 7,500 in 1979, and from 13,470 in 1985 to 22,185 in 1990 (including a 15 per cent increase in 1989–90); another 35,000 were listed as supporters. Budget turnover similarly grew from $600,000 in 1983 to over $2.6 million in 1991 (ACF 1988, 1989a, 1991). This burst of growth had much to do with the changing public image of the organisation, represented by the selection of Phillip Toyne as its director, and the election in 1989 of the rock group Midnight Oil's lead singer and former NDP candidate,

Peter Garrett, as its president. Toyne, an accomplished lobbyist, was able to establish effective access to Hawke and successive Environment Ministers. This relationship, and the related successes of the Foundation's campaigns, confirmed the ACF's status as Australia's pre-eminent conservation body.

By the late 1980s, the Australian environment movement had effectively developed two tiers. The few well-resourced, professionalised national bodies were increasingly separated by their sophistication and size from the many small voluntary groups. Labor governments chose to focus on, and further elevate the public status of these large organisations through preferential consultation, much as the ACTU was elevated through the Accord. As state and federal Labor governments sought to consult with the larger, more 'stable' and 'predictable' groups, environmentalists in small groups had decreasing influence on government policy other than through the activities of the larger organisations.

Despite these developments, the breadth of community-based environmental interests and the absence of the organisational discipline and coherent representational politics common to the old social movements meant that stable outcomes based on decisions by 'peak' environment organisations were hard to achieve. For example, the ACF was unable to guarantee the support of local communities for a high-temperature incinerator. When Corowa was chosen as a potential site, Greenpeace and local groups successfully opposed the decision. Similarly, the ACF and WWF participated in the Ecologically Sustainable Development (ESD) process which the Wilderness Society and Greenpeace boycotted. Differences within the movement also manifested themselves in the simultaneous and often unco-ordinated use of a variety of tactics to fight on several fronts, such as occurred during the battles for preservation of 'old growth' forests in New South Wales and Victoria. Blockading the bulldozers, petitioning the federal government, encouraging the Australian Heritage Commission to classify disputed areas as being of National Heritage quality, and negotiating with the state government and its agencies to delay timber harvesting occurred simultaneously, with occasional disagreement within the movement about the validity, respectability and usefulness of various tactics. This unpredictability is a continuing source of confusion for government, industry and unions.

Electoral Interventions

Directing Preferences
By the early 1980s, environmental issues had also generated a 'third political force' in federal and state politics. In both state and federal elections since 1983, national organisations such as the ACF and Wilderness Society, and state-based bodies such as the National Parks Associations and Conservation Councils, have attempted to influence

party politics and shape voter intentions by publishing evaluations of candidates' and parties' policies. In several instances they have gone further, explicitly endorsing Australian Democrats and Green candidates, and campaigning actively for them. The two clearest examples were the 1983 and 1990 federal elections.

The environment movement intervened in the national electoral process for the first time in the 1983 federal election, when the Franklin was a major issue. A coalition of conservation groups identified thirteen key marginal electorates and targeted these vigorously. They recommended a vote for Labor (which was unequivocal in its intention to halt the dam), and the placing of the now-famous triangular 'No Dams' sticker on the ballot paper. Green (1984: 283) comments that 'opinion polls taken within a week of the election showed that an average of 2 per cent of Australians voted the way they did because of the Tasmanian dam'. The Hawke government came to power promising to stop the dam. When the new Parliament opened, the Minister for the Environment, Barry Cohen, secured the suspension of standing orders to introduce the World Heritage Properties Conservation Bill 1983 as its first piece of legislation.

The 1990 Federal election is regarded as the strongest moment to date in Green electoral politics (Bean *et al.* 1990). Because of the fall in its primary vote in the 1987 election, the federal Labor government knew it depended on secondary preferences for its return to office, and set about wooing the Green vote. With its strategy for re-election directed by the Environment Minister, Graham Richardson, it produced a series of decisions regarded by the environment movement as 'Green victories'. Queensland's wet tropical rainforests were nominated for World Heritage listing, as were Tasmania's Southern and Lemonthyne Forests. In 1989, Prime Minister Hawke's Statement on the Environment, *Our Country, Our Future* (DPMC 1989) heralded a Decade of Land Care. It contained a raft of strategies and programs on biodiversity and endangered species, wilderness, and the Greenhouse Effect. The government also promised to declare Stage 3 of Kakadu National Park, delay the decision over mining at Coronation Hill, and effectively block development of a chlorine-bleach pulp mill at Wesley Vale. In return, the major environment groups campaigned for the Democrats and Green Independents, directing their preferences to Labor.

Approximately 15.9 per cent of the primary vote in the Senate went to Green candidates (Green Independents and Australian Democrats). Australian Electoral Commission results indicate that the Vote for the Environment campaign influenced 2 to 3 per cent of the vote in targeted seats. Analysis of the vote by Simon Balderstone, former adviser to Minister Richardson, indicates that the direction of Green preferences, including through the Democrat vote, secured ten seats for Labor and significantly influenced the resulting margin of eight seats which the ALP enjoyed in its fourth term (Dunn 1992). The 1990 Australian

Election Study (AES) indicated that 'new political issues' had played a key role in shaping the election, and that the percentage of voters who regarded 'the environment' as important in determining their vote had risen from 31 per cent in 1987 to 51 per cent (Papadakis 1990b).

Green Parties
Environmental issues also made their way on to the political agenda through the policies of the minor parties. The Australian Democrats, formed in 1977, have long maintained strong environmental and anti-nuclear policies. While the party has identified itself as Green since the late 1980s, it is regarded as 'pale Green' by most commentators, and has remained detached from the social movements it purports to represent. Nevertheless, with seven Senators in 1993, the Democrats still represent a significant force for environmental reform. More interesting in terms of Green politics, because of their social movement origins, have been the Nuclear Disarmament Party (NDP), the Tasmanian Green Independents and the Australian Greens.

The Nuclear Disarmament Party
As well as Green issues, the early 1980s saw the rise of a strong international anti-nuclear movement. In 1983, the Hawke government comprehensively rejected the Australian movement's demands to stop uranium mining, close military bases servicing America's nuclear forces, ban nuclear-armed ship visits to Australia, and redefine the ANZUS treaty. These demands for an independent foreign policy for Australia challenged the government to assert a form of national sovereignty prominently represented by the Left within the ALP. Repeated resounding defeats on the uranium vote in Caucus and at the Party's National Conferences sent a practical and symbolic message to all within and beyond the ALP about the character of the new government. The failure of the anti-nuclear movement to achieve any of its goals led to a partial exodus from the ALP and contributed to the formation of the NDP in 1984.

The 1984 federal elections became a forum for these issues, accentuated by media fascination with the NDP's highest-profile candidate, Peter Garrett. The NDP and Democrats together polled 16.9 per cent of the Senate vote in New South Wales, 15.8 per cent in South Australia and 14.2 per cent in Victoria. Yet, despite the election of six 'anti-nuclear' Senators (including the Western Australian NDP candidate, Jo Vallentine), the government's policies remained unchanged. Labor proclaimed its re-election a vindication of its conservative pragmatism (Christoff 1985). The NDP was a precursor of the Australian Greens and one determinant of their delayed emergence. In 1985 it fragmented over whether minor Left party involvement in its forums constituted a 'takeover'. The repercussions of its demise, alongside the successes the environment movement enjoyed through its relationship with the Hawke government, helped retard the evolution of Green parties on the mainland for almost a decade after their formation in Europe.

Tasmanian Green Independents

Strong economic reliance on its forest and hydro-electric resources, the extent and beauty of its natural environment, and the proportional Hare-Clark electoral system which favours small parties and individual candidates, have all made Tasmania one of the most innovative arenas for environmental politics in Australia. The Pedder campaign, as noted, led to the establishment of one of the first Green parties in the world. In 1989, following the Wesley Vale dispute, five Green Independents, led by anti-Franklin Dam campaigner Bob Brown captured the balance of power in the Tasmanian Parliament, with a vote of 17.1 per cent. They subsequently entered into the Labor-Green Accord to ensure the viability of the minority Field Labor government (Hay and Eckersley 1993).

The success of the Greens emphasised the polarisation of the electorate, and entrenched resentment and opposition to them within Labor ranks. In October 1991, the Tasmanian Labor government, under pressure from its traditional constituency in the resource industries, broke with the Accord by increasing the export woodchip quota and indicating its intention to introduce resource security legislation. The Greens rejected the legislation, only to see it passed in another guise in November (Copas 1991). The Accord came to an end. The Field government was resoundingly defeated in the subsequent election, and the Green vote reduced.

The Australian Greens and the 1993 Elections

Despite the support of the major environmental organisations and the importance of Green preferences for Labor in its 1987 and 1990 federal election victories, the environment movement gained little from the federal government after 1990. Frustration with the environmental performance and economic rationalism of the Keating government led to discussions in 1991 about the formation of a national Green party. A series of meetings, initiated by Bob Brown, developed a ten-point charter based around the principles of ecological sustainability, democracy and grassroots participation, social justice and non-violence. A national constitution was adopted in August 1992. This did not, however, result in a union of the then-sixteen state-based or regional Green parties. While seven — including the Tasmanian and Queensland Greens — joined in the federation which became the Australian Greens, some refused: the Greens (WA) declined to join an organisation they perceived to be overly hierarchical and centralised. Others were excluded. The Australian Democrats were not involved in the later stages of negotiations and the Green Alliance/Democratic Socialist Party and other Left or socialist groups were proscribed in an attempt to avoid the infiltration which had destroyed the NDP almost a decade earlier. Nevertheless the outcome was Australia's first (almost) national Green party. It went on to contest federal elections eight months after it was formed.

In March 1993, fifty-nine House of Representatives seats were contested by Green candidates. The 1993 election results suggest a strong decline in electoral support for environmental issues. It may also be argued that this election displayed the 'hard core' of the Green vote in Australia. The total Green Senate vote (for Democrats, Australian Greens and Green Independents) fell from 15.9 per cent in 1990 to 8.4 per cent in 1993. Bob Brown, having resigned from his Tasmanian parliamentary seat, unsuccessfully contested the lower house seat of Denison. His vote, 13.9 per cent, was lower than expected, and in no other seat did the Green vote exceed 10 per cent. No Green candidates were elected to lower house seats. Results were generally below 5 per cent for both lower house and Senate seats — although the Greens (WA) averaged 5.8 per cent for the 14 lower house seats they contested. The unevenness of the results across the nation reflects the variable strengths and organisational and electoral immaturity of the different state Green parties and regional Green groups. Nevertheless, a second Green Senator was elected from Western Australia and the Greens (WA), together with the Democrats, now potentially control the balance of power in the Senate. According to the Greens, Australian Greens' preferences played a significant role in determining the outcome of 12 closely contested eastern states' seats (five in Queensland, four in NSW and three in Tasmania), adding on average around three per cent to the Labor vote through directed preferences and contributing to the government's 14 seat final majority (Lambert 1993, unpublished analysis of the election results for Australian Green Party).

Environmental Conflict, Corporatism and Changing Policy Cultures

The decade from 1983 to 1993 may be interpreted as a three-phase contest between successive federal Labor governments and the environment movement for control of the environmental agenda. From its election in 1983 until 1989, federal Labor under Hawke tried to manage conflict by providing sufficient (usually symbolic) victories to ensure the environment movement's continuing electoral support. Between 1989 and 1991, it sought to limit conflict by constructing new agencies and instruments for consensual policy making. Shifting the strong advocate of the environment, Richardson, from his portfolio in 1990, signalled that 'balance' would now be restored in the conservation-development debate. Since 1991, in a recessionary climate and under Keating, Labor has paid diminishing attention to the environment and the environment movement, and dismantled several of the key instruments created for conflict resolution.

Papadakis (1990a) has claimed that the Franklin decision raised expectations among environmentalists and exerted a decisive influence on the pattern and public projection of environmental policy under Labor. While several of the flagship victories of the 1980s — especially the Franklin and the Daintree — achieved a demonstrably high degree of popular support before government intervention, other issues were won or lost through a combination of factors which have not promoted stable or long-term environmental policy outcomes. In the absence of policies and decision making processes which integrate ecological issues with social and economic demands, it is inevitable that these demands will be seen to compete ever more fiercely against each other for priority, and that particular conflicts will be seen as tests of strength between them. The government will then be perceived as merely responding to crises and pressure, rather than enabling stable decisions to be made. Several contests display the government's loss of control over the environmental agenda during the period 1983 to 1990, including Wesley Vale, Coronation Hill, Daintree and Tasmania's Southern Forests. In each instance, although genuine environmental and economic factors were at stake, the symbolic content of the decision was of overriding importance. Successive decisions were constructed as public tests of the government's will either as a champion of conservation or of resource development, by their respective lobby groups.

In such a climate of contestation, decisions which have only a marginal bearing on national economic performance, domestic or foreign investment patterns, or the future of the mining sector, are inflated into vast symbols. For instance, in 1989, the fate of Stage 3 of Kakadu National Park became a public issue at a time when the Hawke government was becoming increasingly sensitive to the importance of Green preferences for its prospects in the 1990 election. The debate over the pristine Alligator River catchment area, and over the fate of gold, palladium and platinum deposits at Coronation Hill, within Stage 3, became a ferocious propaganda battle between the environmental and mining lobbies. Four Ministers with industry and resource development-related portfolios — Kerin, Walsh, Button and Dawkins — and the Environment Minister Richardson, ran strong campaigns both in and outside the Cabinet room, while the environment movement and the mining lobby conducted their contest through the media. Cabinet, deeply divided, decided to defer the inevitably politically damaging decision until after the 1990 election by using the newly-established Resource Assessment Commission (RAC) to investigate social, environmental and economic impacts of the proposal. In 1991, the RAC delivered its Report, sanctioning development with qualifications on environmental grounds, but also raising serious concerns about the likely violation of Aboriginal spiritual claims to the land (RAC 1991). On the basis of these concerns, Prime Minister Hawke determined the Cabinet decision not to proceed.

The conflict, during 1988–89, over the proposal by Noranda-North Broken Hill to invest $1.2 billion to establish a kraft-pulp mill at Wesley Vale in north-eastern Tasmania, led to more permanent outcomes. While the Tasmanian government sought to weaken existing environmental regulations to facilitate this significant investment, the federal government, acting pursuant to its Environmental Protection (Impact of Proposals) Act and responding to pressure from the environmental movement, demanded a revised and tougher set of environmental standards as a condition for permitting the development to occur. Following delays, during which standards were discussed and revised, and federal intervention threatening to block exports from the mill if it proceeded with less than world-best technologies, the investment proposal was withdrawn and the development lapsed. The outcome, portrayed as a victory by an alliance of local industry, farming community and conservation interests, was important as a catalyst for the establishment of the Resource Assessment Commission. It was also instrumental in the election of the local activist Christine Milne to the Tasmanian Parliament as one of five Green Independents. It is depicted by the industry lobby as another indication of Labor being hostage to Green political pressure.

Despite the symbolic importance of the Franklin in establishing the environmental credentials of the Hawke government, during the 1980s environmental policy was still not seen as a significant part of the national political agenda. Successive resource-use conflicts continued to be seen by government as peripheral and anomalous to 'normal government'. After the Wesley Vale and Coronation Hill disputes, however, the cost to government of such repeated, intense conflicts and its *ad hoc* reactions were clearly apparent. They distorted the potential for predictable policy formation, challenged the government's authority as a political manager and contributed to the view in Cabinet that 'balance' needed to be restored to decision making about resource use. A range of administrative solutions was proposed in Prime Minister Hawke's Environment Statement (DPMC 1989). These were intended to 'rationalise' the environmental policy process, to better organise inputs to decision making forums and to integrate economic and environmental objectives. They were to resolve conflict over resource use by extending the corporatist cast of policy formation used in other sectors to environmental policy, and intended to imbue its outcomes with a similar degree of stability, legitimacy and predictability for both government and industry. These solutions included the Resource Assessment Commission, the Ecologically Sustainable Development (ESD) process and, later, the Commonwealth EPA, a series of national strategies covering a variety of environmental sectors and concerns, and the Intergovernmental Agreement on the Environment (IGAE) between the federal and state governments. Central to these mechanisms was the belief that differences between industry and conservation lobbies can be reconciled — or conflict at least deferred — by managing public, scientific and industry participation in policy formation. State Labor governments also preferred such participatory planning and corporatist decision making — for instance, in negotiating timber industry strategies in Victoria and Western

Australia between 1984 and 1987 — to the environmental politics of confrontation and belligerence which characterised non-Labor governments in Tasmania and Queensland.

Elevation of groups into a privileged relationship with the state is a central feature of the corporatist political style. Access to policy arenas which promise influence over fundamental environmental, social and industrial change is attractive to major conservation organisations seeking to engage with policy instruments subtler than blockades. Such access comes, however, at a price. In such arenas, environment bodies must confront and compete with other interests, such as those of state and federal government bureaucracies, industry and the labour movement. For example, the elevation of 'ecologically sustainable development' to the political agenda (Commonwealth of Australia 1992) has introduced a greater level of complexity to the environmental debate and heightened attention to new and old concerns such as energy policy, manufacturing sector reform and trade and aid issues. But it has also blurred the uniqueness and urgency of ecological demands, which seem to become merely one component in negotiations over equally urgent demands from other lobbies for social welfare support, employment and industrial development. The participating groups are thus under pressure to reach and defend consensus over 'a package of workable measures' generated by mutual compromise. While the attractions of corporatist decision making for government and, to a lesser extent for other participant groups, are clear, this political mode is often inadequate for resolving complex and far-reaching environmental problems.

In general terms, since Keating's ascent to the leadership in 1991, the environmental policy style has reverted to the conflictual mode of the early 1980s, and several institutions of consensual policy making have been disbanded or allowed to fall into disrepair. In the 1993 budget, it was announced that the RAC would be dismantled upon completion of its Coastal Inquiry. The ESD process is moribund (the final strategy contains no firm commitments or timetable for implementation), and the Commonwealth EPA is floundering. Environmental organisations — particularly the ACF — have been retained in policy forums, yet simultaneously publicly castigated by the media, industry, unions and, especially, government. Irrespective of the actual breadth of their own policy interests and activities, the major groups are repeatedly represented in public as single interest groups bearing only narrow and occasionally extreme sectoral claims on the broader, legitimate concerns of government.

A good example of this new style of environmental political management is the Keating Environment Statement (DPMC 1992). The Statement, its public presentation and its subsequent defence by the Prime Minister, sought to drive a wedge between key environment groups and the public, by appealing directly to the public, rather than the movement with its focus on co-operative action on rural issues, such as land and river degradation in the Murray-Darling Basin, urban pollution and 'clean industries'. 'Our war with the environment is well and truly over...The old war with the environment will be replaced by a partnership in the national interest' (DPMC 1992: 2). When the Statement was given a lukewarm reception by the major environment organisations (Johnston 1992a), they were accused by the Prime Minister of lacking courage and leadership. He claimed that the Green movement was extremist, and not listened to any more. 'Bob Brown and people like him say the same thing no matter what the government does. The environmental lobbies have no moral lien over the environment. This issue belongs to the Government, to the nation,' he claimed (Johnston 1992b).

Silent Reforms

The overwhelming focus of media and academic attention on environmental conflicts has led to an underestimation of the importance of the environmental gains made during the 1980s, through co-operative negotiations between traditional resource conservation bodies, government departments and local communities, as well as environmentalists. These developments, including institutional and legislative reforms, have mainly, although not uniformly, concentrated on combating land and water degradation, and have for the most part occurred without significant public debate.

Major programs have developed co-operatively between Commonwealth and state governments, farmers' lobby organisations, rural communities and major environment organisations. The National Soil Conservation Program (NSCP), created in 1983, and the national Landcare program (which resulted from a joint submission in 1989 by the National Farmers' Federation (NFF) and the ACF, and a separate but similar proposal from the Cattlemen's Union in 1989), are cases in point. It is estimated that land degradation affects over half of Australia's agricultural land and costs over $2.5 billion each year in lost productivity. These programs aim to restore the productive capacities of farmland by promoting and funding a new 'land ethic'. By 1991, over 1,000 local Landcare committees, based on landholders representing farmers as well as public land user groups, had been formed nationwide. Revegetation through the One Billion Trees Program is also a major focus of the activities of such groups.

Another instance is the attempt to manage salinity. In Victoria, over 2.5 per cent of farmland is now affected, with the prospect of major increases over the next thirty years. Salinity management plans have evolved with a high degree of rural community involvement and interest which extends beyond agricultural to ecological concerns. They have been part of a wave of administrative innovation. For example, the Victorian Salinity Program depends on the involvement of ten government agencies and departments, and co-ordinates the development of the regional plans. These management plans are in turn co-ordinated with the Salinity and Drainage Strategy aimed at reducing salt inflows to the Murray River, agreed by the four states responsible for, or suffering salinity problems in the Murray Darling Basin. The negotiation of the interstate salt-reduction strategy occurred through the Murray Darling Basin Commission (MDBC). This includes the Commonwealth and the four states which share the Murray-Darling drainage basin, and itself represents a successfully institutionalised process of co-operative resource use based on shared ecological, rather than purely administrative boundaries. Similarly, incorporation of Greenhouse gas reductions into energy sector planning, although modest and inadequate to the problem, has been achieved through pressure from international obligations, consensus between industry and energy utilities, federal and state governments and conservationists, with public debate primarily fostered by the media rather than the environment movement (ANZECC 1991).

In evaluating such reforms, Kellow (1990: 205) asserts that the environment movement's propensity for conflict explains why its values have not been incorporated more fully into the policy process. He overstates his case, ignoring both the extent to which environment organisations have been involved in negotiations over a range of 'non-preservation' issues and the forces operating to ensure their exclusion from these arenas. Kellow also fails to comment on the highly variable outcomes where consensual involvement *has* occurred. He diminishes the problem of the limits to compromise on issues where values are held as fundamental, such as species' extinction or the loss of wilderness. But he correctly identifies the problem of the continuing marginality of ecological values in mainstream policy formation.

Greening Australia?

Several brief generalisations can now be made about the recent impact of environmental issues on Australian politics. The Green Decade (1983–93) produced undeniable gains for ecological protection in Australia. For instance, the total area of land nationally protected for conservation increased from 3.3 per cent (250,700 square km) in 1980 to over 5 per cent (364,800 square km) in 1989 (OECD 1991). The state's responsibility extended from resource conservation to nature preservation, a trend which began well before the 1980s but received a significant boost during the last decade. In general, the state's role as mediator between environmental and developmental concerns also became more pronounced and more complex, particularly at Commonwealth level. Environmental issues and policy formation increasingly became a matter of federal concern, through a process of political and administrative elevation — the raising of state-based issues to national level — either to achieve a new level of uniformity in environmental standards and industrial processes, or to meet evolving international obligations.

These gains, however, have failed to provide a significant challenge to the existing political or economic order. Most existing administrative boundaries, such as state and local government divisions, remain inappropriate to managing ecosystems. In addition, the integration of environmental concerns in all aspects of policy formation and implementation has occurred to only a slight degree. Despite the ESD process, the traditional compartmentalisation of economic, social and environmental issues between government departments and agencies survives largely intact. Institutional reforms adequate to meet ecological needs have been minimal. At all levels of government administration, adversarial relationships still predominate between departments and agencies established to further economic growth through resource exploitation, and those newly developed to protect the environment. These conflicts have become increasingly intense and public since 1980. Significant differences between the Commonwealth and the states (and among the states) continue to manifest themselves in environmental conflicts, despite the Intergovernmental Agreement on the Environment (IGAE), which is widely perceived to be a failure.

The costs of conflict resolution and environmental restoration place an increasing strain on federal and state government finances. Competition between states for economic investment, and a political climate which has placed overwhelming importance on economic growth, have limited the scope for innovative environmental policies at both state and federal levels. For a decade, the environment movement's predominant concentration on nature preservation issues has drawn attention from urban development, energy policy, and transport issues. Consequently, major transformations which are not necessarily beneficial to the environment have occurred largely unchallenged in these areas. In addition, economic policies which have made national and state economies more susceptible to international market forces have been ignored by the environment movement. The Australian state's capacity to deal with future ecological problems has, as a result, been weakened.

Emerging from the 'Green Decade', the environmental movement has now reached a second watershed. The 'environment issue' remains one of considerable public concern. In December 1990, the demands of the environmental movement were regarded as 'reasonable' by 63 per cent of people interviewed nationwide, and 79 per cent believed that 'the threat to the environment is real and must be treated seriously' (Mercer 1991: 5). Nevertheless, 'post-materialist' concerns are being seen by Labor as secondary to 'materialist' ones such as traditional economic growth. Despite significant growth in its membership in the late 1980s, the corporatist structure of the environment movement did little to activate these new members, and has left itself vulnerable to economic downturn. Major environmental organisations, such as the ACF and Greenpeace, are now concerned to marry 'brown' environmental issues with economic and social concerns such as job creation, environmentally sound investment, clean production and the promotion of ecologically sustainable industries. Such issues provide a more difficult political terrain for environmentalists than did the 'Green' issues of the 1980s (Weale 1992).

Australia's environmentalists have nevertheless highlighted the increasing severity of the global and continental ecological crisis. The threat posed by human activities to life on this planet has reached critical levels and promises ecological catastrophes of proportions unprecedented in the earth's history. Current evidence suggests that, globally, as a result of human activity, some 60,000 plant species — about one in six — may be extinct by the middle of the next century. At a minimum, several hundred vertebrates (higher order animals) and over a million species of insects will disappear in the next three to five decades. Some 10 per cent of Australia's native mammals and 15 per cent of its vascular plants are currently threatened with extinction. Political compromise is unlikely to deflect growing public concern over the extent and severity of this crisis, particularly where irreversible ecological losses are likely.

17
Censorship, Pornography and Sexual Politics: New Issues, New Conflicts

BARBARA SULLIVAN

Sexual politics is today a visible and highly-contested area of mainstream Australian politics. Issues like homosexuality, prostitution, pornography and censorship, abortion, rape, sexual harassment and sex discrimination are raised daily in the media, and are frequently the object of intense political debate. In recent years, for example, politicians have engaged in heated exchanges about whether prostitution should be legal, whether homosexuals should have the right to join the armed forces, whether abortion should be freely available and eligible for a Medicare rebate, and whether the law and judicial system adequately address the issue of sexual violence against women. Following feminist writers like Kate Millett (1970) and gay theorists like Denis Altman (1987), conflicts around such issues can be conceptualised as 'sexual politics' — about the social, political and economic relationships between power, sexuality and gender. Sexual politics focuses explicitly on the connections between public and private, between the intimate lives and sexual practices of individuals, and broader structures of public power.

Both levels of government in Australia are concerned with the regulation of sexuality. For example, state governments have prime responsibility for laws concerned with rape and domestic violence, prostitution, abortion and homosexuality, while the Commonwealth government determines the level of Medicare rebates for abortion, and sets conditions of service in the Australian armed forces. There are also many areas of joint Commonwealth-state responsibility. In relation to pornography, for example, Commonwealth Customs regulations determine which overseas publications or films will be permitted to enter Australia, while state obscenity laws apply to locally-produced publications and films. Similarly, Commonwealth and state governments over the last decade have been concerned with ending sexual violence and discrimination against women.

Sexual politics is not new. In the last decades of the nineteenth century and into the early twentieth century, Australian women mobilised in large numbers around the issues of temperance and votes for women. Allen argues (1988: 161) that underlying these political campaigns was an explicit concern with domestic violence, the sexual abuse of women and girls, and prostitution. Women wanted the vote in part to ensure that the social problems attached to men's private behaviour were addressed in the public sphere.

This chapter begins with an examination of the ideological basis of conflict over sexual politics issues over the last thirty years. The main ideological divide has not been between Labor and Liberal or National Party supporters as much as between conservatives and liberals. Regardless of their political party affiliation, both groups have fundamentally different approaches to the 'privacy' of sexuality, and to gender relations generally. Since the 1960s, there has been a shift in the ideological status quo towards liberal positions. So, for example, Australian parliaments have experienced increasing pressure for freer access to sexually explicit publications, and for the decriminalisation of abortion, homosexuality and prostitution. These demands have had an important impact on law and public policy. The second part of the chapter shows how social and politico-legal changes in both Britain and the United States haved influenced Australian liberalism. To illustrate some of the issues and trends in Australian debates, the third part examines the debate on pornography and censorship. It traces the emergence of anti-censorship movements in Australia during the 1960s and 70s, and looks at some important regional variations. By the mid-1970s, laws which prohibited pornography had been largely superseded by those which regulated its distribution and consumption. In the late 1970s, new political conflicts emerged over the issue of pornography, which challenged the limits of liberal reforms. Child pornography and material depicting explicit sexual violence against women generated both conservative and feminist opposition.

Ideology and Sexual Politics

Conservatives argue that a society is partly constituted by its traditional code of morality. This, they suggest, should be reflected in the laws which govern society, because laws constitute a public acknowledgement of virtue and vice, of right and wrong ways for human beings to live. It is thus proper for government to protect this moral code by punishing those who engage in what it regards as 'vicious' acts, such as homosexuality, prostitution and the production and consumption of pornography. If governments did not act in this way, then the health and well-being of society would be damaged, perhaps irretrievably. Conservatives emphasise the connections between the public and the private: virtuous private lives are integral to the maintenance of a strong and healthy public sphere (Devlin 1965, Coleman in Turner 1975).

Liberals do not see the same connection between the private lives of individuals and the public well-being of society. They stress the rights of individuals to pursue their own goals in life, and argue that privately conducted sexual acts which do not harm other people, even when these are considered disgusting or degrading by most members of society, should *not* be punishable by law. Consequently, liberals favour the repeal of laws which prohibit homosexuality, the consumption of pornography, prostitution and abortion (Hart 1963, Bacon in Turner 1975).

Since the late 1960s, liberal approaches have been adopted by large sections of the Liberal and Labor Parties; conservative approaches are associated with the National Party, sections of the Liberal Party and traditional Catholics within the Labor Party. Politicians, however, do not always adopt clear or consistent positions on issues of sexual politics. Most liberal politicians have clear limits to their liberalism: for example, they are usually prepared to maintain laws against 'extreme' pornography (although what is regarded as 'extreme' has clearly changed over the last twenty years), and to endorse some limitations on the legal availability of abortion, and prostitution. Similarly, many conservative parliamentarians are vehemently opposed to abortion, but are ambivalent about increasing the legal sanctions on prostitution, especially if they see it as an inevitable consequence of male sexual 'drives' (see Sullivan 1991).

Until the mid-1960s, there were few significant differences among politicians or political parties about how issues such as homosexuality, pornography or prostitution should be addressed in law and public policy. Regardless of how these matters were *actually* dealt with — by Customs, the police and the courts — there was substantial agreement among parliamentarians that strong laws prohibiting obscene and indecent literature, and penalising male homosexuality, as well as most prostitution-related activities, were a necessity.

From the 1960s onwards, this conservative consensus was increasingly called into question. The 'sexual revolution' changed people's sexual attitudes and practices. Younger people set aside taboos on pre-marital sexual intercourse and — to a lesser extent — on homosexuality (D'Emilio and Freedman 1988). Sexual activity outside marriage became more common with the increased availability of barrier contraceptives and, after 1961, of the oral contraceptive Pill (Gilding 1991, Siedlecky and Wyndham 1990, Bell 1975). There was also a significant increase in the production and distribution of sexually explicit publications. The New Left, counter-cultural politics and sexual liberation movements, such as gay liberation and the women's movement, played important parts in the widespread questioning of traditional sexual mores (Altman 1987: 77).

The sexual revolution was a consequence of profound changes in the the economic and social organisation of post-war Australia. Increasing contraceptive practices, the decline in the power of organised religion, and an increasing number of married women entering the paid workforce led to a dramatic shift in patterns of marriage and family formation which undermined the traditional material underpinnings of marriage and men's power in relation to women. Marriage came to be regarded less as an economic institution and more as a basis of companionship, sexual fulfilment and personal growth (Gilding 1991: 116–20).

One consequence of these changes was increasing public and political support for the idea that governments should not interfere in the private sexual behaviour of individuals. From the 1960s there were increasing demands for the repeal of laws designed to control sexual behaviour, and for public policy which more adequately reflected the sexual lives of ordinary Australians (Wilson 1972, Dutton and Harris 1970). A number of new pressure groups pressed for the repeal of laws against abortion, male homosexuality (female homosexuality was not illegal), prostitution and pornography.

As such laws fell into disrepute and became more difficult to enforce, politicians of various stripes in state and federal parliaments began to articulate more liberal positions. In the Commonwealth Parliament there were demands for relaxed censorship and votes in favour of the decriminalisation of homosexual acts between consenting adults. In South Australia the Dunstan Labor government pioneered a plethora of reforms, and over the next two decades reforms occurred throughout Australia. Abortion laws were liberalised in South Australia in 1970 and in the Northern Territory in 1974. In other states changes in the legal status of abortion came through case law rather than by legislation (that is, by judges interpreting existing laws in relation to particular cases): in Victoria in 1969, New South Wales in 1972 and Queensland in 1986. From 1975, abortion also attracted a rebate from Medibank (the precursor of today's Medicare), significantly extending women's access.

In the 1970s, most states also introduced new laws significantly extending the range of what adults could legally purchase, read and view. Since 1975, all states and territories (with the notable exception of Tasmania) have also decriminalised private homosexual acts between consenting adults. South Australia was the first state to do so (in 1975), followed by the ACT (1976), Victoria (1980), the Northern Territory (1983), New South Wales (1984), Western Australia (1989) and Queensland (1991). Since the late 1970s, several jurisdictions (most notably New South Wales, Victoria and the ACT) have partially decriminalised prostitution-related activities. With few exceptions (the decriminalisation of male homosexuality in Victoria being one), these reforms were instigated by Labor governments, although they often depended on the votes of liberal members of Opposition parties.

International Trends: Sexuality, Privacy and Decriminalisation

The trend towards the decriminalisation of private sexual behaviour in Australia was critically influenced by social and legal trends in Britain and the United States. Perhaps the single most important legal influence was the publication in Britain during 1957 of the *Report of the Committee on Homosexual Offences and Prostitution*, chaired by Lord Wolfenden. The Wolfenden Report was commissioned by the British government as a direct response to rising public concern in the immediate post-war period at an apparently increasing incidence of homosexuality and prostitution (Weeks 1981: 239). It argued that the law was *not* an appropriate or effective means of controlling 'sexual deviance', and thus that private sexual behaviour between consenting adults should not be a criminal offence. It recommended a decriminalisation of private, homosexual acts between consenting adults, as well as of privately conducted prostitution. It also, however, recommended stronger penalties for public manifestations of sexuality which were likely to cause public offence (for example, street soliciting for the purposes of prostitution).

The Wolfenden Report sought, and largely established, a new, liberal separation of law and morality in Britain. Over the next decade the conservative idea that the law should advance and defend a common, public morality was increasingly displaced by the liberal idea that individuals should be as free as possible to determine their own moral code and sexual behaviour. As Weeks (1981: 252) argues, this signalled a crucial shift in the balance of decision making. Decisions about the rightness or wrongness of sexual behaviour were to be shifted from the public to the private sphere, from public institutions to the individual. In this process a new set of boundaries between the public and the private aspects of citizens' lives was established, with sexual behaviour marked out as an innately private sphere of human activity. Over the next decade, legislation was enacted in Britain which liberalised the laws pertaining to abortion (1967), decriminalised private consensual homosexual acts (1967), and significantly increased access to obscene and indecent publications (1959). Not that changes in the law necessarily changed sexual behaviour. As Foucault (1976) has argued, Western culture has increasingly been 'governed' by the dissemination of new norms of personal and, in particular, sexual conduct. From this perspective, power is deployed less by the application of laws designed to punish aberrant sexual behaviour and more by the spread of ideas and 'discourses' about what is 'normal' and 'appropriate' sexual conduct. This latter sort of power may constitute a more efficient 'discipline' than any edict of law.

In Australia, the Wolfenden Report had an immediate impact upon public and parliamentary debates about censorship and sexually explicit publications. By the late 1960s the view that the law should allow sexual acts between consenting adults in private was gaining currency, especially among Labor parliamentarians (Sullivan 1991: 8–9). But this liberal contruction of the law did not have a significant impact on homosexual and prostitution law reform until the mid to late 1970s.

Pornography and Anti-censorship Movements in Australia

Political debate in Australia about the censorship of books, films and magazines began in the 1930s (Coleman 1974, Bertrand 1978). It was not until the 1950s, however, that censorship began to provoke significant political conflict, triggered by the arrival of American comics and cheap pulp novels with lurid representations of sex and violence on their covers. New laws, seeking to ban or more rigorously control these publications, were enacted right around Australia. In Queensland, for example, the Labor government established a Literature Review Board, which was not disbanded until 1990. The main concern was that children and teenagers would be corrupted by exposure to scenes of explicit sex and violence. At the same time liberal reformers — chiefly middle class pressure groups, societies of authors and civil liberties organisations — argued that adults should be free to read works of literary merit and should not be prevented from reading 'modern', 'socially realistic' novels which contained explicit scenes of sex and violence.

By the 1960s, there was increasing pressure on the Australian market, particularly from popular American publications designed for 'adult male' readers. Australians, like Americans, were becoming more interested in reading and talking about sex. In 1953 Hugh Hefner launched *Playboy*, and within two years it had achieved wide circulation (Talese 1980: 38). While *Playboy* was not available in Australia until 1963 (and was subject to repeated Customs bans until 1967), a range of somewhat less explicit men's magazines circulated widely during the 1950s (White 1979).

In Britain, the Obscene and Indecent Publications Act 1959, introduced in the wake of the Wolfenden Report, significantly enlarged public access to 'modern, adult novels', such as James Joyce's *Ulysses* and D.H. Lawrence's *Lady Chatterley's Lover*. It also brought about an increase in the production and distribution of commercial pornography (Sutherland 1982: 9). In the United States, laws which inhibited the distribution of pornography were liberalised as a result of the Supreme Court decision in the case of Roth (1957). Both developments had an impact on the Australian market, because the vast majority of books and magazines were imported here from Britain and the United States.

In 1957, the Liberal-Country Party government introduced administrative changes which significantly liberalised censorship controls on imported publications, particularly novels, although strict controls were maintained on popular magazines and commercial pornography

(Coleman 1974: 22–23). Some of the states objected to this liberalisation. In Victoria, for example, police directly supported the Liberal state government, seizing several novels which had been passed by the Commonwealth Literature Censorship Board (including Erskine Caldwell's *God's Little Acre* (1959) and Mary McCarthy's *The Group* (1964)), and commenced legal proceedings against various publishers and booksellers. Such actions provoked intense opposition from pressure groups like the Freedom to Read Association, as well as from some Labor members in the Victorian Parliament, who argued that 'the State's intrusion into their private affairs' was an abuse of power (*VPD* 1967–68, Vol. 289: 3,333). In Queensland, on the other hand, there was little public or political opposition to the activities of the Literature Board of Review, even though a large range of novels, children's comics and popular magazines were the object of its prohibition orders (Sullivan 1993: 116–20).

In New South Wales, decisions of the Commonwealth censor were largely accepted by the Labor government and there were few prosecutions. The state government and police adopted a relatively tolerant attitude to literary censorship. In the mid-1960s, however, influenced by the work of New Left theorists and Freudian Marxists such as Herbert Marcuse, a group of libertarians, anarchists and 'non-authoritarian socialists' attempted to use obscenity and pornography to challenge the status quo (Bacon 1972). Wendy Bacon, a prominent member of the group, explicitly argued the connections between sexual, economic and political 'repression'. In her view, sexuality needed to be 'de-repressed' in order for a broad cultural freedom to be achieved. In relation to censorship this meant that the main focus of concern was 'freedom, not literary merit' (Bacon 1972: 48). In 1964, prosecutions were launched, under the New South Wales Indecent and Obscene Publications Act, against two publications produced by members of this group' — *Oz* and the University of New South Wales student newspaper, *Tharunka*.

Modernising Censorship and Regulating Pornography

By the mid-1960s, the conservative argument that obscenity laws and censorship practices should protect public morality was under serious challenge in various parts of Australia. Some Members of Parliament, typically Labor MPs in states where the Labor Party was in Opposition, were now arguing that censorship was authoritarian, undemocratic, and indicative of prudish, outdated attitudes towards sex. In 1969 the ALP adopted a new party platform on censorship. It proclaimed that, as a general principle, adults should be entitled to 'read, hear or view what they wish in private or public', although no-one was to be exposed to unsolicited material offensive to them, and children were to be protected (Whitlam 1969).

Similar views were held by some members of the Liberal Party. In 1970, Don Chipp, Minister for Customs and Excise, instigated the Commonwealth Parliament's first debate on censorship for more than thirty years. He argued that a complete overhaul of Australia's censorship policies and practices was necessary because 'the pace of social change had quickened' and existing laws and regulations were inadequate to cope with the demands of a modern society (*CPD* 1970 ,Vol. 68: 3,372). He instigated administrative changes which led to the release of a number of previously banned books (not hard-core pornography) as well as to the introduction of the 'R' classification for 'adult' films. He also nominated a gender-biased standard for his administrative reforms, setting *Playboy* magazine as 'the benchmark beyond which we will not go in permissiveness as far as sex is concerned' (*CPD* 1971, Vol. 71: 500–11). New limitations, however, were placed on children; those under the age of eighteen, for example, were now prohibited from attending films with an 'R' classification.

This approach won widespread, but not universal support. Some Liberal and Country Party parliamentarians, for example, argued that such 'permissiveness' would 'sow the seeds of [social] destruction'; liberalising censorship laws would lead to the perpetration of more crimes of sex and violence (*CPD* 1971, Vol. 171: 449-51). On the other hand, parliamentarians who were more liberally inclined argued in favour of more profound changes. Several Labor parliamentarians advocated the complete abolition of censorship. Some, like Dick Klugman, argued that the ready availability of pornography (and its 'cathartic' effect) helped prevent crime. In his view, the consumption of pornography was a sign of sexual health and a positive adjunct to the acquisition of a healthy heterosexual orientation (*CPD* 1970, Vol. 68: 3,380, *CPD*, Vol. 71: 451–53, see also Sullivan 1991: 11). Others, including Bill Hayden, argued for a complete removal of censorship controls on sexual material (at least for adults), but wanted to maintain controls on material which depicted violence (*CPD* 1970, Vol. 68: 3,376–82). In this latter view, the consumption of sexually explicit material, including pornography, was a relatively harmless activity, although viewing and reading about violence could lead to the perpetration of real violence. Both sides used the findings of social scientists to support their views.

Between 1969 and 1972 the Australian debate over censorship shifted ground. The focus changed from literature to pornography, from novels which contained sexually explicit scenes and claimed some 'literary merit', to popular publications clearly designed to arouse the sexual feelings of their readers. This shift occurred for two main reasons. First, by the late 1960s, the *legal* distinction between literature and pornography was becoming impossible to draw; many novels now portrayed sexual activity in a way that previously had been confined to pornography. Consequently, magistrates, juries and governments became increasingly inconsistent in their judgments about what was and was not legally obscene, and thus what citizens were, or were not, entitled to read. An obvious example was Philip Roth's novel *Portnoy's Complaint*, which, in 1969, was classified as a prohibited import. In 1970, it was published in Australia, thus evading customs laws, and immediately became the subject of various prosecutions under state obscenity laws. In New South Wales, legal proceedings initiated by the Liberal-Country Party government failed on two occasions, because the jury could not agree on a verdict. In Western Australia, *Portnoy's Complaint* was found to be an obscene publication, but its literary merit was also established, and so all charges were dropped. In South Australia the Labor government refused to allow prosecution to proceed because it was considered inappropriate for 'the Government or anyone else to tell people what they may read' (*SAPD* 1970-71: 1,140). Prosecutions of varying sorts succeeded in Victoria, Tasmania and Queensland (Coleman 1974: 47). The very inconsistency of these responses, reflecting intense ideological differences between conservatives and liberals, as well as differences about the social consequences of pornography, generated further controversy about the appropriate role of law and government in relation to the circulation of sexually explicit publications.

A second reason for the shift in focus was the expansion of the pornography industry. In 1972, 'sex shops', selling imported pornographic magazines and 'sex aids' opened in several Australian capital cities. Their appearance generated a public furore. Political responses varied. In Victoria, new legislation enabled the Liberal government to close down the shops. In Western Australia, the Labor government indicated its intention to close the sex shop in Perth, but the parliamentary Caucus and Trades Hall argued that this was contrary to party policy; adults were to be free to read and view whatever they wished as long as children were protected and there was no overt and public display of offensive material (*WAPD* 1972: 508, 650). In South Australia, the Labor government also declined to intervene in the sex businesses. Premier Dunstan argued that if people made 'the unfortunate choice' of patronising sex shops and consuming pornography, it was not the government's role to intervene, as long as children were protected and there was no public offence caused by the display of 'unseemly' material (*SAPD* 1971-72: 4,121).

New Laws, New Freedoms

Censorship laws surfaced again as a political issue after the election of the Whitlam Labor government in 1972, especially once the Commonwealth moved to implement Labor policies on censorship. In 1973, Attorney-General Lionel Murphy announced that there would be no further prosecutions under Section 4A of the Customs and Excise Act, which pertained to the importation of obscene and indecent publications *(JSCVM*, Vol. 2: 332). This amounted to a virtual abandonment of 'point of entry' controls over pornography and forced the states to seek alternative approaches to its 'control'. Subsequently, state and Commonwealth Ministers responsible for censorship matters met to forge an agreement about laws on obscene and indecent literature. All states except Queensland agreed that pornographic publications which would normally be subject to state obscenity laws should in future be subject to classification, and a new system of regulatory controls. If sexually explicit material were distributed in accordance with classification guidelines, it was to be exempt from laws relating to obscene and indecent publications. The aim was to increase the freedoms which adults might exercise in relation to reading and viewing. Strict controls over children's access to pornography and over the public display of potentially offensive material were to be maintained.

Between 1973 and 1975, all states except Queensland passed legislation designed to establish regulatory schemes for the classification and control of pornographic material. This represented a substantial shift from traditional politico-legal approaches, which emphasised the need to prohibit pornography. While the legislation passed in each state was remarkably similar, there were some important differences, particularly in the way the proposals were debated in Parliament. In South Australia, for example, the Dunstan Labor government adopted a pragmatic administrative response to the issue, and emphasised that it was not the government's job to circumscribe citizens' private decisions about sexual behaviour and the consumption of pornography. Of course, Dunstan argued, citizens were entitled to be protected from the 'public flaunting' of material which was personally offensive to them, as were children, whose judgments were immature (*SAPD* 1973–74: 1,688). In New South Wales, where the Labor Party was in opposition, an extreme liberalism was manifested in the Parliament, an effect perhaps of the intense legal and political activism which still surrounded the issue of obscenity in that state. As in the Commonwealth Parliament during 1970, some Labor members argued that adults should have complete freedom to purchase and read whatever they wanted, even if it was pornography (*NSWPD* 1974–75, Vol. 117: 4,585). This argument was premissed on several grounds: that all government constraints on the freedom to read, as well as on private, consensual sexual activity, were illegitimate; that sex was an essentially good and healthy activity and that its representation in pornography was harmless (if not positively beneficial); and that the liberalisation of Australia's anti-pornography laws was a reflection of national maturity. From this perspective, the dismantling of censorship barriers was conducive to the formation of a more open and less authoritarian society (*VPD* 1972–73: 5,400). The consumers of pornography were now represented as 'ordinary decent people' (*NSWPD* 1972–73, Vol. 103: 3,856), who had rights which needed to be protected (*NSWPD* 1974–75, Vol. 116: 4,579). The use of pornography, it was argued, was becoming an integral part of 'normal' sexual relations and of marriage (*NSWPD* 1974–75, Vol. 116: 4,396). Queensland was the only state which did not adopt a classificatory approach to pornography in this period. Because of the dominance of conservative approaches among members of all political parties in Queensland, the state's Literature Board of Review, Film Board of Review (established in 1974), and its obscenity laws maintained a regime of prohibition. In the face of significant commercial pressures and changes in the type of publications available in Australia, the number of prohibition orders issued by the Literature Board of Review increased from an average of less than four per year in the 1960s, to an average of 46 in the 1970s. Most of these were issued against hard-core sex magazines, freely available to adults in other states. The upmarket and (at that time) soft-core *Australian Penthouse* was, however, also subject to prohibition in Queensland during the 1970s, as were several nudist, horror, crime/detective and martial arts publications (Sullivan 1993: 165–71).

New Conflicts

In the late 1970s and early 80s, new conflicts began to emerge around the issue of pornography in Australia. This occurred for several quite disparate reasons. First, some real changes became apparent in the type of pornography available on the Australian market: child pornography and material which depicted sexual violence (predominantly against women) had entered the market. Technological change introduced new methods of viewing and distributing pornography. Second, in the late 1970s, a conservative 'backlash' emerged against many of the recent reforms, particularly after the formation of the ultra-conservative and religious fundamentalist group, the Festival of Light. Third, by the late 1970s and early 80s, feminists were making a significant impact on mainstream politics. Feminist anti-pornography arguments were widely deployed in state and federal parliaments during the early 1980s.

These developments forced significant adjustments to exisiting schemes for regulating the classification and distribution of pornography. Public concerns about child pornography first forced their way on to the parliamentary agenda in New South Wales in 1976. Concern centred on material which depicted children naked and/or in explicit sexual activity with other children or adults. Designed for use by adults, such material was freely available if distributed under the appropriate classification guidelines. In 1977, concerns about the effects of child pornography were given wide press coverage when two visiting American experts claimed that there was a larger range of child pornography available in Sydney than anywhere else in the world. They also specifically linked the consumption of such material to what was perceived to be a rising incidence of child sexual abuse. A public outcry ensued, and new laws prohibiting child pornography were enacted in most states. This marked a clear departure from the principle established in public policy during 1973-75 that the state had no legitimate right to interfere with the freedom of adults to buy and read whatever they wished.

A further challenge to liberal regulatory approaches took place in 1983, when the Hawke Labor government sought to regulate video pornography. At the time, about 25 per cent of households had videos, and 25 per cent of the videotape market was said to consist of pornographic imports (*NSWPD* 1983–84, Vol. 178: 4,576). Many of these tapes contained explicit scenes of sexual violence, predominantly against women. Film censorship laws, however, did not specifically address videos designed for private home use, so the Australian market was virtually uncontrolled (Commonwealth of Australia 1988: 332–35).

In 1983, a meeting of Commonwealth and state Ministers agreed that a new 'X' classification for home use, hard-core pornographic videotapes should be introduced; only Queensland dissented. As with publications in the early 1970s, 'control' of the videotape market was to be achieved through a 'point of sale' scheme which specified how various categories of material were to be distributed. The new 'X' classification was to cover material more explicit than allowable under the existing 'R' classification. This scheme immediately, however, became the object of intense political conflict in both Commonwealth and state parliaments, and between members of the main political parties. To the traditional argument between conservatives and liberals were added feminist arguments about pornography. Indeed, feminist arguments became the main focus of the debate.

By the early 1980s, feminists had entered mainstream political institutions in Australia, such as Parliament, the bureaucracy and political parties, in significant numbers (see Sawer and Simms 1993). Consequently, when the issue of video pornography arose, feminists were well placed to participate in the debate. Although there was no unified feminist perspective on pornography, in Australia or elsewhere, many Australian feminists argued that pornography harmed women both directly and indirectly, by forcing them to participate in its production, by causing sexual violence and/or by promoting a general disrespect for women (see Jones 1984). This approach was strongly influenced by American anti-pornography feminism (see Dworkin 1979, Mackinnon 1987). Some Australian feminists, however, also argued that pornography was harmless, irrelevant or a less than central issue for feminism (Faust 1980). Others thought that it might have a positive role to play in the liberation of women and women's sexuality.

Australian feminists have taken a similarly diverse range of approaches to the issue of state censorship. Most anti-pornography feminists have called for tighter state controls over it. Others, however, have argued against censorship. Some simply argue against an extension of existing censorship controls on the grounds that these are sufficient, or the best that can be achieved. Some suggest that even if pornography does harm women, censorship laws and practices cannot be used to advance their interests because they are applied by a state which acts to preserve and defend the interests of men. Libertarian feminists argue that all censorship laws are, by their nature, repressive, and detrimental to individuals' (including women's) freedom.

During the public debate on video classification in 1983-84, most of these different feminist positions on pornography and censorship were aired. However, feminist anti-pornography arguments made in support of tighter censorship laws were the most influential. Such arguments were deployed by both male and female members of the ALP, the Australian Democrats and the Liberal Party. Senator Mason (Australian Democrats) argued that pornographic videos used 'the humiliation, the degradation and even the torture of women' as their central theme and, as such, were likely to incite rape and violence towards them (*CPD* 1984, Vol. 102: 1,164–65). Others voiced their concerns about the exploitation of women in the production of pornographic videos (*NSWPD* 1983–84, Vol. 178: 4,571–73). While an emphasis on the dangers posed to the community by pornography had been a traditional conservative theme, the self-conscious identification with feminist concerns, with the exploitation and degradation of women in pornography and, in particular, with the association of sex and violence, was new (Sullivan 1991).

Feminist anti-pornography discourse offered a substantial challenge to the liberal regulatory framework. It also made visible new conflicts in the Labor Party between liberals and feminists. The federal Attorney-General, Senator Gareth Evans, for example, attempted to deal with the feminist challenge by reiterating the basis of a liberal, reforming approach. He argued that while 'X' rated videos would not be allowed public screening, their home use was an 'appropriate' extension of a citizen's privacy (*CPD*, Senate 1984, Vol. 102: 1,179). As a result of continuing political pressure, the government eventually agreed to exclude from the 'X' category material which depicted sexual violence against non-consenting persons. Thus videos portraying rape and other sexual violence were to be classified as prohibited imports and excluded from the Australian market. Several Labor women parliamentarians expressed their support for the new regulations (including the reformulated 'X' classification). Senator Susan Ryan, a well known feminist and Minister Assisting the Prime Minister on the Status of Women, argued that all the major problems had been addressed. Others voiced a feminist opposition to censorship, arguing that it could be used to the detriment of women (Senate 1984, Vol. 102: 1,224–25). When the new proposals were debated in the Queensland Parliament, Ann Warner, also a well known feminist, argued that pornography was 'not a problem in itself; it is a manifestation of distortions in sexual relations'. In her view, pornography reflected rather than created this distortion, and censorship was an added evil (*QPD* 1984–85, Vol. 296: 3,033).

While the 'X' classification became, in 1984, a new legal category for videotapes in the ACT and Northern Territory, it has not to date been accepted by any state parliament, mainly because of the strength of feminist and conservative opposition. This situation has generated a substantial mail-order business for operators in the ACT.

Conclusion

An examination of the debates on pornography and censorship highlights some of the main issues and arguments associated with sexual politics debates generally. Over the last three decades, new liberal and feminist positions have ended any political consensus there might have been, and introduced a new dimension of conflict into mainstream Australian politics — one fought out within, as much as between the political parties, between different levels of government (state/Commonwealth) and between different arms of government (legislative, judicial, administrative).

A central issue in these debates is the 'appropriate' relationship between public and private, between the Australian state and the intimate lives of its citizens. All liberals (although to different degrees) claim private life as a realm of individual freedom which should be regarded as relatively separate from public life. Both feminists and conservatives, on the other hand, emphasise the connections between public and private. For conservatives, the state has a right to regulate in both spheres, in order to enforce traditional 'virtues' and modes of living. For feminists, the situation is somewhat more complicated. Most feminists do not share with conservatives a respect for the traditional structures of either public or private life; for example, they are critical of both the traditional family and the existing sex-based distribution of power in public institutions. Nor, however, do they always support the separation of the two spheres, which is at the basis of the liberal position, and which can easily be used to relegate issues of concern to women in the private realm.

Over the last fifteen years, Australian feminists have attempted to use the power of state institutions, such as Parliament, to challenge the power which men wield in both public and private spheres. In relation to abortion, this has meant that they have supported liberal reforms which seek to extend new freedoms to women by ensuring access to legal abortion. In relation to pornography and prostitution, however, most feminists have been less supportive of liberal reforms. Where liberals want to widen the realm of sexual freedom in relation to both prostitution and pornography, many feminists argue that such changes only increase the power of men.

Given the range of ideological positions within recent sexual politics debates it is hardly surprising that these issues are both widely discussed and hotly contested. Sexual politics involves issues of power, between women and men, and over life itself in issues surrounding procreation. Such issues are difficult to contain within mainstream politics. While important sexual politics debates do occur within public institutions, these are often only the surface manifestations of the power being negotiated in the private sphere, in daily pleasures and conflicts, and in intimate relationships between self and others.

Bibliography

Aarons, M. (1989) *Sanctuary: Nazi Fugitives in Australia*. Melbourne: William Heinemann Australia
Abel-Smith, B. and Titmuss, K. (eds) (1992) *The Philosophy of Welfare: Selected Writing of Richard M. Titmuss*. London: Allen and Unwin
Aboriginal Provisional Government (1990–92) Assorted, unsigned public statements in Tim Rowse's possession
ABT, Australian Broadcasting Tribunal (1988) *Broadcasting in Australia*, Sydney
— (1992a) *Broadcasting Financial Yearbook 1990–91*, Sydney
— (1992b) *Broadcasting in Australia*, Sydney
ACTU, Australian Council of Trade Unions (1987) *Future Strategies for the Trade Union Movement*. Melbourne: ACTU
— (1990a) Document Prepared by ACTU Industry Committee for Executive Consideration. Melbourne: ACTU
— (1990b) *Australian Manufacturing and Industry Development: Policies and Prospects for the 1990s and into the 21st Century*. Melbourne: ACTU
— (1993) *Putting Jobs First: Accord Agreement 1993–1996*. Melbourne: ACTU
— /TDC, Australian Council of Trade Unions/Trade Development Council (1987) *Australia Reconstructed*. Canberra: AGPS
Administrative Review Council (1992) *Rule Making by Commonwealth Agencies*, Report to the Attorney-General, Canberra: AGPS
Aitkin, D. (1972) *The Country Party in New South Wales*. Canberra: ANU Press
— (1973a) 'Electoral Behaviour', in H. Mayer (ed.), *Australia's Political Patterns*. Melbourne: Cheshire
— (1973b) 'Electoral Behaviour', in H. Mayer and H. Nelson (eds), *Australian Politics: A Third Reader*. Melbourne: Cheshire
— (1982) [1977] *Stability and Change in Australian Politics*. Canberra: ANU Press
— (1985a) 'Australia', in I. Crewe and D. Denver (eds), *Electoral Change in Western Democracies*. New York: St. Martin's Press
— (1985b) 'The New Electorate', in D. Woodward, A. Parkin and J. Summers (eds), *Government, Politics and Power in Australia*. Melbourne: Longman Cheshire
Aldons, M. (1986) 'Promise and Performance: An Analysis of Time Taken for Commonwealth Governments to Respond to Reports from Parliamentary Committees', *Legislative Studies* 1 (2), Spring: 20–23
— (1991) 'The Growth of Parliamentary Committees of the House of Representatives and Joint Committees', *Legislative Studies* 6 (1): 6–8
Alford, R. R. (1963) *Party and Society*. London: John Murray

— (1967) 'Class Voting in the Anglo-American Political Systems', in S. M. Lipset and S. Rokkan (eds), *Party Systems and Voter Alignments*. New York: Free Press

Allan, L. (1978) 'Ethnic Politics — Migrant Organization and the Victorian ALP', *Ethnic Studies* 2 (2): 21–31

Allen, J. (1988) 'Rose Scott's Vision: Feminism and Masculinity 1880–1925', in B. Caine, E. A. Grosz and M. de Lepervanche (eds), *Crossing Boundaries. Feminisms and the Critique of Knowledges*. Sydney: Allen and Unwin

ALP (1990) *Draft Report: Review and Recommendations on the Reform of the Party's Organisation*. Canberra: Organisational Review Committee

ALP/ACTU (1983) *Statement of Accord Regarding Economic Policy*. Melbourne

Altman, D. (1980) *Rehearsals for Change: Politics and Culture in Australia*. Sydney: Fontana/Collins

— (1987) 'The Creation of Sexual Politics in Australia', *Journal of Australian Studies* 20: 76–82

— (1988) 'The Personal is Political', in Head and Walter

Altman, J. C. (1989) *The Aboriginal Arts and Crafts Industry*, Report of the Review Committee, Chair: J. C. Altman. Canberra: AGPS

— and Sanders, W. (1991) *The CDEP Scheme: Administrative and Policy Issues*, CAEPR (ANU) Discussion Paper 5

AMC, Australian Manufacturing Council (1990) *Global Challenge: Australian Manufacturing in the 1990s*. Melbourne: AMC

Anderson, K. and Garnaut, R. (1986) *Australian Protectionism: Extent, Causes and Effects*. Sydney: Allen and Unwin

Appleyard, R. T. (1965) 'Pockets of Poverty in Australia', *Social Service* 17 (1)

Archer, R. (1992) 'The Unexpected Rise of Australian Corporatism', in J. Pekkarinen, M. Pohjola and B. Rowthorn (eds), *Social Corporatism: A Superior Economic System?*. Oxford: Clarendon Press

Argument, S. (1991) 'Annual Reporting by Commonwealth Departments and Statutory Authorities – The Cornerstone of Executive Accountability to the Parliament', *Legislative Studies* 6 (1) Winter: 16–24

— (1992) *Parliamentary Scrutiny of Quasi-Legislation*, Papers on Parliament 15. Canberra: Department of the Senate

Armstrong, M. (1974) 'Obstacles to Sensible Regulation of Australian Broadcasting', *Australian Quarterly* 46 (4): 7–21

— (1982) *Broadcasting Law and Policy in Australia*. Sydney: Butterworths

Audretsch, D. (1991) 'Industrial Policy in the 1990s: An International Comparison', Wissenschaftszentrum Berlin für Sozialforschung, Research Paper FX IV: 9–3

ANZECC, Australia and New Zealand Environment and Conservation Council (1991) 'Report of Programs Implemented and Policies Adopted since 1988 that Contribute to Reducing Greenhouse Gas Emissions in Australia', October

Australia (1978) *Migrant Services and Programs*, Review of Post-arrival Programs and Services to Migrants, Chair: F. Galbally. Canberra: AGPS

— (1986) *Don't Settle for Less!* Review of Migrant and Multicultural Programs and Services, Chair: J. Jupp. Canberra: AGPS

Bibliography 385

Australia (1988) *Immigration. A Commitment to Australia*, Chair, S. FitzGerald. Canberra: AGPS
Australian Bureau of Immigration Research (1991) *Immigrants and Australian Politics. An Annotated Bibliography*. Canberra: AGPS
ABS, Australian Bureau of Statistics (1992) *Social Indicators*, Cat. No. 4101.0
Australian Conservation Foundation (ACF) (1988) *Annual Report 1988–89*, Melbourne
— (1989a) *Annual Report 1989–90*, Melbourne
— (1989b) *Forward Plan*, Melbourne
— (1991) *Conservation News*, 23 (8)
Australian Council on Population and Ethnic Affairs (1982) *Multiculturalism for All Australians*. Canberra: AGPS
Australian Electoral Commission (1992–93) *Electoral Newsfile* 24, 36
Australian Fabian Society (1986) *The Whitlam Phenomenon*. Melbourne: McPhee Gribble
Australian Government Commission of Inquiry into Poverty (1975) *Poverty in Australia, First Main Report*. Canberra: AGPS
Australian Journalists Association (1991) Submission to the House of Representatives Select Committee on Print Media
Ayres, P. (1987) *Malcolm Fraser. A Biography*. Richmond, Victoria: William Heinemann
Bacon, W. (1972) *Uni Sex: A Study of Sexual Attitudes and Behaviour at Australian Universities*. Netley: Eclipse
Barbalet, J. M. (1975) 'Tri-partism in Australia: The Role of the Australian Country Party', *Politics* 10 (1): 1–14
Barwick, G. (1981) 'Retirement of Chief Justice Sir Garfield Barwick', *Commonwealth Law Reports* V
Battin, T. (1991) 'What is This Thing Called Economic Rationalism?', *Australian Journal of Social Issues* 26 (4): 294–307
Baxter, J., Emmison, M., Western, J. and Western, M. (eds) (1991) *Class Analysis and Contemporary Australia*. Melbourne: Macmillan
— and McAllister, I. (1990) 'The Electoral Performance of Parliamentary Candidates', in Bean, McAllister and Warhurst
Bean, C and Kelley, J. (1988) 'Partisan Stability and Short-Term Change in the 1987 Federal Election: Evidence from the NSSS Panel Survey', *Politics* 23 (2): 80–94
— and Mughan, A. (1988) 'The Changing Pattern of Party Competition, 1949–1987', in McAllister and Warhurst
—, McAllister, I. and Warhurst, J. (eds) (1990) *The Greening of Australian Politics: The 1990 Federal Election*. Melbourne: Longman Cheshire
Beckett, J. (1988) 'Aboriginality, Citizenship and Nation State', *Social Analysis*, Special Issue 24, December: 3–18
— (1989) 'Aboriginality in a Nation-State: The Australian Case', in M. C. Howard (ed.), *Ethnicity and Nation-Building in the Pacific*. Tokyo: United Nations University
Beilharz, P., Considine, M. and Watts, R. (1992) *Arguing about the Welfare State: The Australian Experience*. Sydney: Allen and Unwin
Bell, C. (ed.) (1983) *Ethnic Minorities and Australian Foreign Policy*. Canberra: Department of International Relations, Australian National University

— (1988) *Dependent Ally: A Study in Australian Foreign Policy*, second edition, Melbourne: Oxford University Press
Bell, D. (1960) *The End of Ideology: On the Exhaustion of Political Ideas in the Fifties*. New York: The Free Press
Bell, S. (1991) 'Unequal Partner: Trade Unions and Industry Policy under the Hawke Government', *Labour and Industry* 4 (1): 119–37
Bennett, S. (1983) 'The Fall of a Labor Government: Tasmania 1979–82', *Labour History* 45: 80–93
— (1989) 'The 1989 ACT Election', *Politics* 24 (2): 134–46
— (1992) *Affairs of State: Politics in the Australian States and Territories*. Sydney: Allen and Unwin
Benson, J. (1988) 'Workplace Union Organisation in Australia', *Labour and Industry* 1 (3): 407–30
Bergin, A. (1988) 'The New Australian Policy on Recognition of States Only', *Australian Outlook* 42 (3): 150–54
Berry, P. and Kitchener, G. (1989) *Can Unions Survive?* Canberra, Building Workers' Industrial Union, ACT Branch
Bertrand, I. (1978) *Film Censorship in Australia*. St Lucia: University of Queensland Press
Betts, K. (1988) *Ideology and Immigration*. Melbourne: Melbourne University Press
BIE, Bureau of Industry Economics (1993) *Industry Brief*. Canberra.
Birrell, R. and Birrell, T. (1987) [1981] *An Issue of People: Population and Australian Society*. Melbourne: Longman Cheshire
— Hill, D., Nevill, J. (eds) (1984) *Populate and Perish? The Stresses of Population Growth in Australia*. Sydney: Fontana/Australian Conservation Foundation
Black, D. (1991a) 'Factionalism and Stability, 1911–1947', in Black (1991b)
— (ed.) (1991b) *The House on the Hill; A History of the Parliament of Western Australia 1832–1990*. Perth: Parliament of Western Australia
Blainey, G. (1984) *All for Australia*. North Ryde: Methuen Haynes
Blewett, N. (1982) 'The Challenge of the New Conservatism' in Evans and Reeves
Bolton, G. (1991) 'The Good Name of Parliament, 1890–1990', in Black (1991b)
Bonyhady, T. (1993) *Places Worth Keeping: Conservationists, Politics and the Law*. Allen and Unwin, Sydney.
Boreham, P. (1990) 'Corporatism', in Jennett and Stewart
Borrie, W. (1947) *A White Australia?* Sydney: Australasian Publishing Co
— (1988) 'Changes in Immigration Patterns since 1971' in Jupp
Bottomley, G. and de Lepervanche, M. (eds) (1984) *Ethnicity, Class and Gender in Australia*. Sydney: Allen and Unwin
— and Martin, J. (eds) (1991) *Intersexions. Gender/Class/Culture/ Ethnicity*. Sydney: Allen and Unwin
Bowman, D. (1988) *The Captive Press*. Melbourne: Penguin
Bowman, M. and Grattan, M. (1989) *Reformers*. Melbourne: Collins Dove
Boyce, P. J. and Angel, J. R. (eds) (1992) *Diplomacy in the Market Place: Australia in World Affairs 1981–90*. Melbourne: Longman Cheshire
Bramble, T. (1989) 'Award Restructuring and the Australian Trade Union Movement: A Critique', *Labour and Industry* 2 (3), October: 372–98

Bray, M. and Taylor, V. (1991) 'Introduction: Flexibility, Marginal Workers and Trade Unions', in M. Bray and V. Taylor (eds), *The Other Side of Flexibility*, ACIRRT Monograph 3. Sydney: University of Sydney
— and Walsh, P. (1993) 'Accord and Discord: The Differing Fates of Corporatism under Labour Governments in Australia and New Zealand'. Sydney: mimeo
Brennan, D. and O'Donnell, C. (1986) *Caring for Australia's Children*. Sydney: Allen and Unwin
Brennan, F. (1991) *Sharing the Country*. Ringwood: Penguin.
— (1992) *Land Rights Queensland Style*. St Lucia: University of Queensland Press
— and Crawford, J. (1990) 'Aboriginality, Recognition and Australian Law: the Need for a Bipartisan Approach', *Australian Quarterly* 62 (2), Winter: 145–69
Brennan, G. and Buchanan, J. (1980) *The Power to Tax: Analytical Foundations of the Fiscal Constitution*. Cambridge: Cambridge University Press
Brett, J. (1989) 'Future Direction: New Conservatism's Manifesto', *Current Affairs Bulletin* 66 (1) June: 11–17
— (1992a) *Robert Menzies' Forgotten People*. Melbourne: Macmillan
— (1992b) 'The End of the Parties', *Arena Magazine*, September: 10–13
— (1993) 'Liberal Philosophy from Menzies to Hewson', *Australian Quarterly* 65(3): 45–56
Broom, L. and Jones, F. L. (1976) *Opportunity and Attainment in Australia*. Canberra: ANU Press
Brown, A. (1986) *Commercial Media in Australia: Economics, Ownership, Technology and Regulation*. St Lucia: University of Queensland Press
— (1989) 'Media Regulation' in Head and Patience
— (1992) 'Newspaper Ownership and the Australian Print Media Inquiry. Bad News and Some Spurious Facts', *Current Affairs Bulletin* 69 (7), December
Bryson, L. (1984) 'The Australian Patriarchal Family' in S. Encel and L. Bryson (eds), *Australian Society*. Melbourne: Longman Cheshire
— (1992) *Welfare and the State*. Melbourne: Macmillan
Buchanan, J. and Tullock, G. (1962) *The Calculus of Consent: Logical Foundations of Constitutional Democracy*. Ann Arbor: University of Michigan Press
Burchell, D. and Mathews, R. (eds) (1991) *Labor's Troubled Times*. Sydney: Pluto Press
Bureau of Transport and Communications Economics (1991) *Economic Aspects of Broadcasting Regulation*, Report 71. Canberra: AGPS
Burgess, J. and Macdonald, D. (1990) 'The Labour Flexibility Imperative', *Journal of Australian Political Economy* 27: 16–35
Burgman, V. (1993) *Power and Protest: Movements for Change in Australian Society*. Sydney: Allen and Unwin
Burns, C. (1961) *Parties and People*. Parkville: Melbourne University Press.
— (1964) 'Labor Traumas', *Dissent* 4 (1): 5–9
Burrow, J. W. (1988) *Whigs and Liberals: Continuity and Change in English Political Thought*. Oxford: Clarendon Press
Burton, T. (1992) 'Administration...the Power Within', *Sydney Morning Herald*, 4 July

Business Council of Australia (1990) *Enterprise-Based Bargaining Units: A Better Way of Working*. Melbourne
— (1991a) 'Government in the 1990s — Challenges and Reforms', *Business Council Bulletin* 75: 8–15
— (1991b) 'Paying for the New Federalism', *Business Council Bulletin* 81: 6–9
Butler, D. (1973) *The Canberra Model*. Melbourne: Cheshire
Butlin, N, Barnard, A. and Pincus, J. (1982) *Government and Capitalism*. Sydney: Allen and Unwin
Button, J. (1979) 'Decision Making in a Bizarre Working Environment', in *Working Papers on Parliament*. Canberra: Canberra College of Advanced Education
Caiden G. E. (1967) *The Commonwealth Bureaucracy*. Melbourne, Melbourne University Press
Callus, R. (1991) 'The Australian Workplace Industrial Relations Survey and the Prospects for Enterprise Bargaining', *Economic and Labour Relations Review* 2 (1): 42–56
— et al. (1991) *Industrial Relations at Work*. Canberra: AGPS
Calwell, A. (1945) *How Many Australians Tomorrow?* Melbourne: Reed and Harris
Camilleri, J. A. (1991) 'Problems in Australian Foreign Policy, January-June 1991', *Australian Journal of Politics and History* 37 (3): 375–95
Campbell, I. (1990) 'The Australian Trade Union Movement and Post-Fordism', *Journal of Australian Political Economy* 26, April: 1–26
Campbell, S. J. and Halligan, J. (1992) *Political Leadership in an Age of Constraint: Bureaucratic Politics under Hawke and Keating*. Sydney: Allen and Unwin
Capling, A. and Galligan, B. (1992) *Beyond the Protective State: The Political Economy of Australia's Manufacturing Industry Policy*. Melbourne: Cambridge University Press
Carney, S. (1988) *Australia in Accord*. Melbourne: Sun Books
Carroll, J. (1992) 'Economic Rationalism and its Consequences', in Carroll and Manne
— and Manne, R. (1992) *Shutdown: The Failure of Economic Rationalism and How to Rescue Australia*. Melbourne: Text
Carroll, V. J. (1990) *The Man Who Could Not Wait: Warwick Fairfax's Folly and the Bankers who Backed Him*. Melbourne: Heinemann
Carson, R. (1962) *Silent Spring*. Boston: Houghton Mifflin
Carter, J. (1993) 'Dealing with Policy Failure: A Social Policy Perspective', in Marsh
Cass, B. (1986) *Income Support for Families with Children*, Social Security Review Issues Paper 1. Canberra: Department of Social Security
— (1988) *Income Support for the Unemployed in Australia: Towards a More Active System*, Social Security Review Issues Paper 4. Canberra: Department of Social Security
— (1992) 'The State and Economy in Australia: An Overview of Work, Welfare and the Position of Women', Paper presented at Academy of Social Sciences Workshop, Women in a Restructuring Australia, Canberra
— and Whiteford, P. (1989) 'Social Security Policies', in Head and Patience
Cass, M. (1981) 'Gough said, "Stay out of Tassie",' in Green

Castles, F. G. (1982) (ed.) *The Impact of Parties: Politics and Policies in Democratic Capitalist States*. London: Sage
— (1985) *The Working Class and Welfare*. Sydney: Allen and Unwin
— (1988a) *Australian Public Policy and Economic Vulnerability*. Sydney: Allen and Unwin
— (1988b) 'Realism and Reality: The Australian Trade Union Movement Seeks a New Policy Stance', *Australian Quarterly* 60 (3): 308–16
— (1989) 'Social Protection by Other Means. Australia's Strategy of Coping with External Vulnerability', in F. G. Castles (ed.), *The Comparative History of Public Policy*. Cambridge: Polity Press
— (ed.) (1991) *Australia Compared*. Sydney: Allen and Unwin
Castles, S. and Kosack, G. (1973) *Immigrant Workers and Class Structure in Western Europe*. London: Pluto Press
Chadwick, P. (1989) *Media Mates*. Melbourne: Sun Books
— (1992) 'Print Media Inquiry Treads So Lightly It Makes No Impression' *Media Information Australia* 65, August: 44–52
Chaples, E. (1980) 'Political Ideas and Party Preferences among Working Class Australians', in Mayer and Nelson
— (1985) 'Softly Committed Voters and the 1984 Election', in D. Jaensch and N. Bierbaum, *The Hawke Government — Past, Present, Future*, Proceedings of the 27th Annual Conference, Australian Political Studies Association, Adelaide
— (1989) 'Public Funding of Elections in Australia', in H. A. Alexander (ed.), *Comparative Political Finance in the 1980s*. New York: Cambridge University Press
— (1992) 'Independents in Decline?', *Current Affairs Bulletin* 69 (3), March: 27–30
— (1993) 'The Australian Voters' in Smith
Chapman, B. and Gruen, F. (1990) 'An Analysis of the Australian Consensual Incomes Policy: The Prices and Incomes Accord', *Discussion Paper* 221, Canberra: Centre for Economic Policy Research, Australian National University
Cheeseman, G. (1992) 'Defence Policy and Organisation: The Search for Self-Reliance', in Boyce and Angel
— and Kettle, S. J. (eds) (1990) *The New Australian Militarism*. Sydney: Pluto
Child Support Evaluation Advisory Group (1992) *Child Support in Australia*, Vols. 1 and 2. Canberra: Commonwealth Government Printer
Chipman, L. (1980) 'The Menace of Multiculturalism', *Quadrant* 24 (10): 3–6
— (1982) 'The Children of Cynicism', in Manne
Christoff, P. (1985) 'The Nuclear Disarmament Party', *Arena* 70: 9–20
Clark, C. (1952) 'Principles of Decentralisation', in Sawer (1952a)
Coaldrake, P. (1985) 'Parliament and the Executive', in A. Patience (ed.), *The Bjelke-Petersen Premiership 1968–1983*. Melbourne: Longman Cheshire
— (1989) *Working the System: Government in Queensland*. St Lucia: University of Queensland Press
Cockburn, M. (1992) 'The Politics of Australian Involvement', in M. Goot and R. Tiffen (eds), *Australia's Gulf War*. Melbourne: Melbourne University Press

Coghill, K. (1987a) 'Regrouping to Win Hearts and Minds', in Coghill (1987b)
— (ed.) (1987b) *The New Right's Australian Fantasy*. Melbourne: McPhee/Gribble
Colebatch, H. K. (1992) 'Theory and the Analysis of Australian Politics', *Australian Journal of Political Science* 27: 1–11
Coleman, M. (1978) 'An Idea Before its Time', in A. Graycar (ed.), *Perspectives in Australian Social Policy*. Melbourne: Macmillan
Coleman, P. (1974) *Obscenity, Blasphemy, Sedition. Censorship in Australia*. Brisbane: Jacaranda
Colledge, M. (1991) 'Workforce Barriers for Sole Mothers in Australia', in P. Whiteford (ed.), *Sole Parents and Public Policy*, Proceedings of a Conference held in Sydney, August 1990, SPRC Reports and Proceedings 89. Kensington, NSW: Social Policy Research Centre
Collins, H. (1985) 'Political Ideology in Australia', in S. R. Graubard (ed.), *Australia: the Daedalus Symposium*. Sydney: Angus and Robertson
Collins, J. (1976) 'Migrants: the Political Void', in H. Mayer and H. Nelson (eds), *Australian Politics: A Fourth Reader*. Melbourne: Longman Cheshire
— (1988a) *Migrant Hands in a Distant Land: Australia's Post-War Immigration*. Sydney: Pluto Press
— (1988b) 'Trade Unions and Immigrants' in Jupp
Committee of Review of the Australian Broadcasting Commission (1981) *The ABC in Review: National Broadcasting in the 1980s*, Chair: A. Dix. Canberra
Commonwealth Grants Commision (1936) *Third Annual Report*. Canberra: AGPS
— (1983) *Equality in Diversity*. Canberra: AGPS
Commonwealth of Australia (1929) *Royal Commission on the Constitution, Report*. Canberra: Australian Government Printer
— (1976) *Australian Defence*. Canberra: AGPS
— (1983) *Reforming the Australian Public Service: A Statement of the Government's Intentions*. Canberra: AGPS
— (1988) *Report of the Joint Select Committee on Video Material*. Canberra: AGPS
— (1992) *National Strategy for Ecologically Sustainable Development*. Canberra: AGPS
Commonwealth Parliament (1983) *Joint Select Committee on Electoral Reform, First Report*. Canberra: AGPS
Commonwealth Parliamentary Library (1972) *Parliamentary Handbook of the Commonwealth of Australia*. Canberra: AGPS
Communications Law Centre (ed.) (1991) *The New Broadcasting Services Bill. Conference Papers*. Sydney: University of New South Wales
— (1992) 'Pay TV: A Chronology', *Communications Update* 82, October
Connell, R.W. (1971) *The Child's Construction of Politics*. Clayton: Melbourne University Press
— and Goot, M. (1979) 'The End of Class, Re-Run', *Meanjin* 38 (1): 3–25
— and Irving, T. H. (1992) *Class Structure in Australian History*, second edition Melbourne: Longman Cheshire
Considine, M. (1990) 'Managerialism Strikes Out', *Australian Journal of Public Administration* 49: 166–78
—and Costar, B. (1992) 'Conclusion: Federalism, Social Democracy and the Trials of State Reform', in M. Considine and B. Costar (eds), *Trials in*

Power: Cain, Kirner and Victoria 1982–1992. Melbourne: Melbourne University Press

Constitutional Centenary Foundation (1993) 'Representing the People: the Role of Parliament in Australian Democracy', Discussion Paper. Carlton: Constitutional Centenary Foundation Inc.

Conway, R. (1982) 'The Level Vision: the Religious and Ethical Basis of Conservatism', in Manne

Cook, P. (1992) 'The Labor Government's Industrial Relations Policy: Flexibility with Equity', *Economic and Labour Relations Review* 3 (1), June: 103–11

Coombs, H. C. (1981) *Trial Balance*. Melbourne: Macmillan

— (1993) 'Grasping the Mabo Opportunity', *Australian Business Monthly*, August: 38–41

Cooray, L. J. M. (1979) *Conventions, the Australian Constitution and the Future*. Sydney: Legal Books

Copas, C. (1991) 'New legislation for $1.2bn Tas. pulp mill angers Greens', *Australian Financial Review*, 11 November

Coper, M. (1988) *Encounters with the Australian Constitution*. Sydney: CCH Australia

— (1992) 'The Economic Framework of the Australian Federation: A Question of Balance', in Craven (1992b)

Costa, M. and Dufty, M. (1991) *Labor, Prosperity and the Nineties*. Sydney: Federation Press

— and Easson, M. (eds) (1991) *Australian Industry — What Policy?* Leichhardt, NSW: Pluto Press

Costar, B. and Woodward, D. (eds) (1988) *Country to National: Australian Rural Politics and Beyond*. Sydney: Allen and Unwin

Cox, E. and Leonard, H. (1992) *Superfudge or Subterfuge? Do Women Need Superannuation?* Glebe: Women's Economic Think Tank

Craven, G. (1992a) 'The States', in Craven (1992b)

Craven, G. (ed.) (1992b) *Australian Federalism: Towards the Second Century*. Melbourne: Melbourne University Press

Crean, S. and Rimmer, M. (1989) *Australian Unions — Adjustment to Change*. Melbourne: National Key Centre in Industrial Relations, Monash University

Crisp, L. F. (1961) [1949] *The Parliamentary Government of the Commonwealth of Australia*. London: Longmans

— (1983) [1965] *Australian National Government*. Melbourne: Longman Cheshire

Crommelin, M. (1992) 'The Federal Model', in Craven (1992b)

Crough, G. (1992) 'Towards the Public Sector Financing of Aboriginal Self-government'. Darwin: North Australia Research Unit Discussion Paper 8

— (1991) 'Aboriginal Australia and the "New Federalism" Initiative'. Darwin: North Australia Research Unit Discussion Paper 2

Cruise, H. (1957) 'Some Restrictive Practices in Australia: Their Extent, Effect and Origin', in J. Wilkes (ed.), *Productivity and Progress*. Sydney: Angus and Robertson

Cullen, P. (1991) *No is Not an Answer*. Sydney: Allen and Unwin

Cumes, J. W. C. (1988) *A Bunch of Amateurs: The Tragedy of Government and Administration in Australia*. Melbourne: Macmillan

Curtin, R., Gough, R. and Rimmer, M. (eds) (1992) *Workplace Reform and Award Restructuring*. Canberra: AGPS

Curtin, R. and Mathews, J. (1990) 'Two Models of Award Restructuring in Australia', *Labour and Industry* 3 (1), March: 58–75

Curthoys, A. (1988) *For and Against Feminism: A Personal Journey into Feminist Theory and History*. Sydney: Allen and Unwin

— (1991) 'Television before Television', *Continuum* 4 (2): 152–70

Cutler, T., Williams K. and Williams J. (1986) *Keynes, Beveridge and Beyond*. London: Routledge and Kegan Paul

Dabscheck, B. (1984) 'Menzies' Unforgettable 1951 National Economic Summit', *Journal of Industrial Relations* 26 (3), September: 405–12

Davidson, A. (1969) *The Communist Party of Australia: A Short History*. Stanford: California: Hoover Institute Press

Davies, A. and Spurgeon, C. (1992) 'The Broadcasting Services Act: A Reconciliation of Public Interest and Market Principles of Regulation?', *Media Information Australia* 66, November: 85–92

Davies, A. F. (1960) 'The Government of Victoria', in Davis

— (1961) 'Social Class in the New Suburb', *Westerly* 3: 15–18

— (1964) *Australian Democracy*. Croydon: Longmans Green

— (1966) 'Migrants in Politics', *Dissent* 17, Winter: 6–12

— (1967) *Images of Class*. Sydney: Sydney University Press

— (1972) *Essays in Political Sociology*. Melbourne: Cheshire

— and Encel, S. (1965a) 'Class and Status', in Davies and Encel (1965c)

Davies, A. F. and Encel, S. (eds) (1965b) 'Politics' in Davies and Encel (1965c)

— and — (eds) (1965c) *Australian Society: A Sociological Introduction*. Melbourne: F.W. Cheshire

Davies, M. (1987) 'International Development in Indigenous Rights', *Law and Anthropology* 2: 29–40

Davis, E. (1987) 'Unions and Wages: ACTU Federal Unions Conference November 1986', *Australian Quarterly* 59 (1): 4–14

— (1991) 'Throwing Down the Gauntlet: ACTU Special Unions Conference, May 1991', *Economic and Labour Relations Review* 2 (1), June: 31–41

Davis, G., Wanna, J., Warhurst, J. and Weller, P. (1993) *Public Policy in Australia*, second edition. Sydney: Allen and Unwin

Davis, J. (1990) *Paperbark: A Collection of Aboriginal Writings*. St Lucia: University of Queensland Press

Davis, S. R. (1960a) 'Diversity in Unity' in Davis (1990b)

— (ed.) (1960b) *The Government of the Australian States*. London: Longmans Green

Day, L. and Rowland, D. (eds) (1988) *How Many More Australians? The Resource and Environmental Conflicts*. Melbourne: Longman Cheshire

de Lepervanche M. (1980) 'From Race to Ethnicity', *Australian and New Zealand Journal of Sociology* 16 (1): 24–37

Deakin, A. (1902) 'Chariot Wheels of Central Government', in J. A. La Nauze (ed.) (1968) *Federated Australia: Selections from Letters to the Morning Post 1900 to 1910*. Melbourne: Melbourne University Press

Deery, S. (1989) 'Unions and Technological Change' in Ford and Plowman

— and Plowman, D. (1991) *Australian Industrial Relations*. Sydney: McGraw-Hill

D'Emilio, J. and Freedman, E.B. (1988) *Intimate Matters. A History of Sexuality in America*. New York: Harper and Row

Denning, W. (1930) *Unification*. Sydney: Labor Daily

Department of Primary Industry and Energy (1992) *National Electricity Strategy: A Discussion Paper*. Canberra: AGPS

Department of Prime Minister and Cabinet (1989) *Our Future, Our Country: Statement on the Environment*, The Hon. R. J. Hawke, Prime Minister of Australia, July. Canberra: AGPS

— (1990) *Ecologically Sustainable Development: A Commonwealth Discussion Paper*, June. Canberra: AGPS

— (1991) *Building a Competitive Australia: Statements by Prime Minister, Bob Hawke, Treasurer, Paul Keating, and Industry Minister, John Button*. Canberra: AGPS

— (1992) *Australia's Environment: A National Asset. Statement on the Environment*, Paul Keating, Prime Minister of Australia, 21 December, Adelaide. Canberra: AGPS

Department of the Parliamentary Library (1991) *Parliamentary Handbook of the Commonwealth of Australia*. Canberra: AGPS

Department of the Senate (1990a) *Senate Legislative and General Purpose Committees: The First 20 Years, 1970–1990*. Canberra: Senate Committee Office

— (1990b) *Senate Estimates Scrutiny of Government Finance and Expenditure*, Papers on Parliament 6. Canberra: Department of the Senate

— (1991) *Senate Committees and Responsible Government*, Papers on Parliament 12. Canberra: Department of the Senate

Department of Transport and Communications (1989) *Future Directions for Pay Television in Australia*, 2 Vols. Canberra: AGPS

Devlin, P. (1965) *The Enforcement of Morals*. London: Oxford University Press

De Vyver, F. (1958) 'The Weakening of Management Rights', *Business Horizons* 2: 38–48

Dibb, P. (1986) *Review of Australia's Defence Capabilities*. Canberra: AGPS

Dicey, A. V. (1959) [1885] *Introduction to the Study of the Law of the Constitution*. London: Macmillan

DITAC (1986) *Annual Report 1985–86*. Canberra: AGPS

Dixon, D. (1993) *Superannuation. The Costs and Benefits*. Fitzroy: Brotherhood of St Laurence

Dixon, Sir Owen (1957) 'The Common Law as an Ultimate Constitutional Foundation', *Australian Law Journal* 240, reprinted in Sir Owen Dixon (1965), *Jesting Pilate*. Melbourne: Law Book Co.

Docker, J. (1993) 'The Origins of Paddy McGuinness', *Arena Magazine* 3, February-March: 21–24

Dodd, T. (1988) 'Power Barons and Lowly Serfs Separate', *Australian Financial Review*, 9 May

Donn, C. (1983) *The Australian Council of Trade Unions: History and Economic Policy*. Lanham, Maryland: University Press of America

Douglas, R. (1978) 'Occupation, Economic Fluctuations and Support for the Government', *Politics* XII (2): 311–19

Dow, G. (1992) 'The Economic Consequences of Economists', *Australian Journal of Political Science* 27: 258–81

— (1993) 'The Transition from Markets to Politics: A Comparative Study of Conflict and Economic Policy since 1974'. University of Queensland: unpublished PhD Thesis

Downs, A. (1957) *An Economic Theory of Democracy*. New York: Harper and Row

Drakakis-Smith, D. (1983) 'Advance Australia Fair: Internal Colonialism in the Antipodes', in D. Drakakis-Smith and S. W. Williams (eds), *Internal Colonialism: Essays Around a Theme*, Developing Areas Research Group Monograph 3. Edinburgh: Institute of British Geographers

Drysdale, P. (1988) *International Economic Pluralism: Economic Policy in East Asia and the Pacific*. Sydney: Allen and Unwin

Dufty, N. (1968) 'Unions in Action: Aims and Methods', in P.W.D. Matthews and G.W. Ford (eds), *Australian Trade Unions*. Melbourne: Sun Books

Dugdale, J. (1979) *Radio Power: A History of 3ZZ Access Radio*. Melbourne: Hyland House

Duncan, G. (1978a) 'The ALP: Socialism in a Bourgeois Society?', in Duncan 1978b

— (ed.) (1978b) *Critical Essays in Australian Politics*. Melbourne: Edward Arnold

Dunn, I. (1992) 'Darwinian Struggle in the Political Ecosystem: Politics and the Environment in Australia', in Harding

Dutton, G. and Harris, M. (1970) *Australia's Censorship Crisis*. Melbourne: Sun Books

Dworkin, A. (1979) *Pornography. Men Possessing Women*. London: Women's Press

Eaton, M. and Stilwell, F. (1993) 'Economic Notes: Ten Years of Hard Labor', *Journal of Australian Political Economy* 31, June: 89–105

Eckersley, R. (1992) *Environmentalism and Political Theory: Towards and Ecocentric Approach*. Albany: State University of New York Press

Edgar, P. (1979) 'Radio and Television', in Patience and Head

Ehrlich, P. H. and Ehrlich, A. H. (1970) *Population, Resources, Environment*. San Francisco: W. H. Freeman

Ellem, B. (1990) *In Women's Hands: A History of Clothing Trades Unionism in Australia*. Sydney: New South Wales University Press

Elliott, G. (1982) 'The Social Policy of the New Right', in Sawer (1982b)

Ellis, U. (1963) *A History of the Australian Country Party*. Melbourne: Melbourne University Press

Emmison, M. (1991) 'Conceptualising Class Consciousness', in Baxter, Emmison, Western and Western

Emy, H. V. (1978) *The Politics of Australian Democracy: Fundamentals in Dispute*, second edition. Melbourne: Macmillan

Emy, Hugh (1991) 'From Liberalism to Conservatism', *Quadrant* xxxv (12): 10–20

— and Hughes, O. E. (1991) [1988] *Australian Politics: Realities in Conflict*. Melbourne: Macmillan

Encel, S. (1970) *Equality and Authority*. London: Tavistock

— and Campbell, D. (1991) *Out of the Doll's House: Women in the Public Sphere*. Melbourne, Longman Cheshire

Epstein, L. D. (1980) 'A Comparative Study of Australian Parties', *British Journal of Political Science* 21: 1–21

Esaiasson, P. and Granberg, D. (1993) 'Hidden Negativism: Evaluation of Swedish Parties and their Leaders Under Different Survey Methods', *International Journal of Public Opinion Research* 5 (3): 265–77

Esping-Andersen G. (1990) *Three Worlds of Welfare Capitalism*. Cambridge: Polity Press

Evans, B. (1989) 'Managed Decentralism in Australia's Industrial Relations', Eleventh Sir Richard Kirby Lecture, University of Wollongong

Evans, Gareth (1976) 'The Most Dangerous Branch? The High Court and the Constitution in a Changing Society', in D. Hambly and J. Goldring (eds), *Australian Lawyers and Social Change*. Sydney: Law Book Co.

—— (1989) 'Australian Foreign Policy: Priorities in a Changing World', *Australian Outlook* 43 (2): 1–15

—— and Grant, B. (1991) *Australia's Foreign Relations*. Melbourne: Melbourne University Press

——and Reeves, J. (eds) (1982) *Labor Essays 1980*. Melbourne: Drummond

——, —— and Malbon, J. (eds) (1981) *Labor Essays 1981*. Melbourne: Drummond

Evans, Geoff (1983) 'Communication Policy in Australia: Pragmatic Planning and *Ad Hoc* Decision Making', in P. Edgar and S. A. Rahim (eds), *Communication Policy in Developed Countries*. Melbourne: Kegan Paul International

Evans, H. (1991) 'Towards Closer Scrutiny of Legislation: New Procedures for Examination of Bills by Senate Committees', *Canberra Bulletin of Public Administration* 66, October: 13–20

Evans, R. (1991) 'The *Global Challenge* Report and the Clash of Paradigms', in Costa and Easson

Evatt Research Centre (1989) *State of Siege: Renewal or Privatisation of Australian State Public Services?* Sydney: Pluto

Ewer, P., Hampson, I., Lloyd, C. Rainford, J. Rix, S. and Smith, M. (1991) *Politics and the Accord*. Sydney: Pluto

—— and Higgins, W. (1986) 'Industry Policy under the Accord', *Politics* 21 (1): 28–39

——, —— and Stevens, A. (1987) *Unions and the Future of Australian Manufacturing*. Sydney: Allen and Unwin

Fairfax, J. (1991) *My Regards to Broadway. A Memoir*. Sydney: Angus and Robertson

Faust, B. (1980) *Women, Sex and Pornography*. Melbourne: Penguin

Fisher, C. (1983) *Innovation and Australian Industrial Relations*. Canberra: Croom Helm

Fisher, H. A. L. (1911) *Political Unions*. Oxford: Clarendon Press

Fisk, E. K. (1985) *The Aboriginal Economy in Town and Country*. Sydney: Allen and Unwin

Fletcher, C. (1992) *Aboriginal Politics: Intergovernmental Relations*. Melbourne: Melbourne University Press

Ford, B. and Plowman, D. (eds) (1989) [1983] *Australian Unions*. Melbourne: Macmillan

Foster, C. (1988) *Towards a National Retirement Incomes Policy*, Social Security Review Issues Paper 6, Canberra

Foster, L. and D. Stockley (1984) *Multiculturalism: The Changing Australian Paradigm*. Clevedon. Avon: Multilingual Matters

Foucault, M. (1981) *The History of Sexuality. Volume 1. An Introduction*, translated by R. Harley. Penguin: Harmondsworth
Freeden, M. (1978) *The New Liberalism*. Oxford: Clarendon Press
— (1986) *Liberalism Divided*. Oxford: Clarendon Press
Freeland, J. (1993) 'Reconceptualising Work, Full Employment and Incomes Policies', in *The Future of Work*. Sydney: ACOSS
Free University, Sydney (1969) 'Class and Politics in Australia' in Mayer
Frenkel, S. (1987) 'Management and Labour Relations in the Metal Industry: Towards Joint Regulation?', in S. Frenkel (ed.), *Union Strategy and Industrial Change*. Sydney: New South Wales University Press
— (1988) 'Australian Employers in the Shadow of the Labor Accords', *Industrial Relations* 27 (2), Spring: 166–79
— (1989) 'Explaining the Incidence of Worker Participation in Management: Evidence from the Australian Metal Industry', *Australian Journal of Management* 14 (2): 127–50
— and Coolican, A. (1984) *Unions Against Capitalism*. Sydney: Allen and Unwin
— and Weakliem, D. (1989) 'Worker Participation in Management in the Printing Industry', *Journal of Industrial Relations* 31 (4): 478–99
Freudenberg, G. (1977) *A Certain Grandeur. Gough Whitlam in Politics*. Melbourne: Macmillan
— (1986) 'The Program', in Australian Fabian Society. Melbourne: McPhee Gribble
Friedman, M. (1962) *Capitalism and Freedom*. Chicago: University of Chicago Press
Fry, G. (ed.) (1991) *Australia's Regional Security*. Sydney: Allen and Unwin
Fung, E. S. K. (1992) 'Australia and China', in Boyce and Angel
Gageler, S. (1987) 'Foundations of Australian Federalism and the Role of Judicial Review', 17 *Federal Law Review* 162
Galligan, B. (ed.) (1986) *Australian State Politics*. Melbourne: Longman Cheshire
— (1987) *Politics of the High Court*. St Lucia: University of Queensland Press
— (ed.) (1988) *Comparative State Politics*. Melbourne: Longman Cheshire
— (1989a) 'Federal Theory and Australian Federalism', in Galligan (1989b)
— (ed.) (1989b) *Australian Federalism*. Melbourne, Longman Cheshire
— (1989c) *Utah and Queensland Coal*. Brisbane, University of Queensland Press
— (1991) 'Senate Committees — Can They Halt the Decline of Parliament', in Department of the Senate, *Senate Committees and Responsible Government*, Papers on Parliament 12. Canberra: Department of the Senate
— (1992) 'Parliamentary Responsible Government and the Protection of Rights', in *Parliament: Achievements and Challenges*, Papers on Parliament 18, December. Canberra
—, Knopff, R. and Uhr, J. (1990) 'Australian Federalism and the Debate over a Bill of Rights', *Publius* 20 (4): 53–67
— and Mardiste, D. (1992) 'Labor's Reconciliation with Federalism', *Australian Journal of Political Science* 27: 71–86
— and Singleton, G. (eds) (1991) *Business and Government Under Labor*. Melbourne: Longman Cheshire

— Hughes, O. and Walsh, C. (1991) 'Perspectives and Issues' in B. Galligan, — and — (eds), *Intergovernmental Relations and Public Policy*. Sydney: Allen and Unwin
Gallop, G. and Layman, L. (1985) 'Western Australia', in Costar and Woodward
Gardner, M. (1990) 'Wage Policy' in Jennett and Stewart
Garnaut, R. (1989) *Australia and the Northeast Asia Ascendancy*. Canberra: AGPS
Garran, R.R. (1897) *The Coming Commonwealth*. Sydney: Angus and Robertson
Gibson, D. (1990) 'Social Policy', in Jennett and Stewart
Gilding, M. (1991) *The Making and Breaking of the Australian Family*. Sydney: Allen and Unwin
Gilliard, P. (1992) 'The Demise of the CPC, Children's Program Committee', *Media Information Australia* 65, August: 63–65
Gilpin, A. (1980) *Environment Policy in Australia*. St Lucia: University of Queensland Press
Gilson, M. and Zubrzycki, J. (1967) *The Foreign Language Press in Australia*. Canberra: ANU Press
Glazer, N. and Moynihan, D. P. (1963) *Beyond the Melting Pot*. Cambridge: MIT and Harvard University Press
Glezer, G. (1982) *Tariff Politics: Australian Policy-making, 1960–1980*. Melbourne: Melbourne University Press
Goot, M. (1973) 'Uniform Swings and the Meaning of the Class Vote', *Australian and New Zealand Journal of Sociology* 9 (2): 73–75
— (1986) 'Saying "No" to MX: The Electoral Fallout', *Australian Journal of Social Issues* 21 (4): 271–84
— (1988) 'Public Opinion on Immigration' in Jupp
— (1990) 'The Forests, the Trees and the Polls', in Bean, McAllister and Warhurst
— and Rowse, T. (1991) 'The Backlash Hypothesis and the Land Rights Option', *Australian Aboriginal Studies* 1: 3–12
— and Tiffen, R. (1983) 'Public Opinion and the Politics of the Polls', in P. King (ed.), *Australia's Vietnam*. Sydney: Allen and Unwin
— and — (eds) (1992) *Australia's Gulf War*. Melbourne: Melbourne University Press
Gordon, L. (1990) *Women, the State and Welfare*. Madison, Wisconsin: University of Wisconsin Press
Graetz, B. (1987) *Images of Class in Australia*. Canberra: Department of Sociology, NSSS, ANU
— and McAllister, I. (1988) *Dimensions of Australian Society*. Melbourne: Macmillan
Graham, B. D. (1966) *The Formation of the Australian Country Parties*. Canberra: ANU Press
Graycar, A. (1981) 'The Australian Assistance Plan', in S. Encel and P. Wilenski (eds), *Decisions: Case Studies in Public Policy*. Melbourne: Longman Cheshire
— (ed.) (1983) *Retreat from the Welfare State*. Sydney: Allen and Unwin
Great Britain (1957) *Report of the Committee on Homosexual Offences and Prostitution*, Chair: Lord Wolfenden, UK Cmnd. 247. London: HMSO

Green, F. (1969) *Servant of the House*. Melbourne: Heinemann
Green, Roger (ed.) (1981) *Battle for the Franklin*. Sydney: ACF/Fontana
Green, Roy (1991) 'Change and Involvement at the Workplace: Evidence from the AWIRS', *Economic and Labour Relations Review* 2 (1), June: 72–88
— (1993) 'Wages Policy and Wage Determination', *Journal of Industrial Relations* 35 (1), March: 142–56
Greenleaf, W. H. (1983) *The British Political Tradition*, London: Methuen
Griffin, G. and Guica, V. (1986) 'One Union Peak Council: The Merger of ACSPA and CAGEO with the ACTU', *Journal of Industrial Relations* 28 (4), December: 511–32
Grinlinton, D. (1990) 'The "Environmental Era" and the Emergence of "Environmental Law" in Australia — A Survey of Environmental Legislation and Litigation 1967–1987', *Environmental and Planning Law Journal*, June: 74–105
Groenewegen, P. (1979) 'Federalism', in Patience and Head
— (1989) 'Federalism', in Head and Patience
— (1993) 'Taxation Issues', in Marsh
Grossman, P. J. (1989) *Fiscal Federalism: Constraining Governments with Competition*. Perth: Australian Institute for Public Policy
— (1990) 'Fiscal Federalism Amongst States in Australia: The Demise of Death Duties', *Publius* 20 (4): 145–59
Gruen, F. and Grattan, M. (1993) *Managing Government: Labor's Achievements and Failures*. Melbourne: Longman Cheshire
Gusfield, J. (1966), 'The Study of Social Movements', *International Encyclopedia of Social Sciences* 14: 445–52
Hagan, J. (1981) *The History of the ACTU*. Melbourne: Longman Cheshire
Hall, P. A. (ed.) (1989) *The Political Power of Economic Ideas*. Princeton: Princeton University Press
Hall, S. (1976) *Supertoy. Twenty Years of Australian Television*. Melbourne: Sun Books
Hall, Stuart (1982) 'The Rediscovery of Ideology: The Return of the Repressed in Media Studies' in M. Gurvitch, T. Bennett, J. Curran and J. Woollacot (eds), *Culture, Society and the Media*. London: Methuen
Halligan, J. and Power, J. (1992) *Political Management in the 1990s*. Melbourne: Oxford University Press
Hamburger, P. (1991) 'Pusey on the Bureaucracy: Two Perspectives', *Australian Journal of Public Administration* 50: 569–70
Hampson, I. (1991), 'Post-Fordism, the French Regulation School and the Work of John Mathews', *Journal of Australian Political Economy* 28: 92–130
— (forthcoming) 'Post-Fordism and the Politics of Industry Development in Australia'. University of Wollongong: PhD thesis
Hancock, W. K. (1930) *Australia*. London: Ernest Benn
Hardin, G. (1968) 'The Tragedy of the Commons', *Science* 162, December 13: 243–48
Harding, Richard (1979) *Outside Interference. The Politics of Australian Broadcasting*. Melbourne: Sun Books
— (1985) 'Australia: Broadcasting in the Political Battle', in R. Kuhn (ed.), *The Politics of Broadcasting*. London: Croom Helm

Harding, Ronnie (ed.) (1992) *Ecopolitics V, Proceedings*. University of New South Wales: Centre for Liberal and General Studies
Harris, S. (1992) 'Implementing Foreign Policy: The Environmental Challenge', in Mediansky (1992b)
— (1993) 'Immigration and Australian Foreign Policy' in J. Jupp and M. Kabala (eds), *The Politics of Australian Immigration*. Canberra: AGPS
Hart, H. L. A. (1963) *Law, Liberty and Morality*. London: Oxford University Press
Hartnett, B. (1991) 'Victoria's Economic Strategy — Industrial Policy Pursued by a State Government', in Costa and Easson
Hasluck, P. (1986) 'Politics in the Public Service: The New Corruption', *Quadrant* xxx (3) March: 11–18
Haupt, R. with Grattan, M. (1983) *31 Days to Power: Hawke's Victory*. Sydney: Allen and Unwin
Haward, M. and Smith, G. (1990) 'The 1989 Tasmanian Election: The Green Independents Consolidate', *Australian Journal of Political Science* 25 (2), November: 196–217
Hawke, R. J. L. (1979) *The Resolution of Conflict*. Sydney: Australian Broadcasting Commission
— (1989) 'Challenges in Public Administration', *Australian Journal of Public Administration* 48 (1): 15–16
Hawker, G. (1971), *The Parliament of New South Wales 1856–1965*. Ultimo: New South Wales Government Printer
— Smith, R.F.I. and Weller, P. (1979) *Politics and Policy in Australia*. St Lucia: University of Queensland Press
Hay, P.R. and Haward, M.G. (1988) 'Comparative Green Politics: Beyond the European Context?', *Political Studies* 26: 433–48
— and Eckersley, R. (1993) 'Green Politics: Lessons from Tasmania's Labor-Green Accord', *Current Affairs Bulletin* 69 (11): 10–15
Hayden, B. (1972) 'New Horizons in Health and Welfare Services', in J. McLaren (ed.), *Towards a New Australia*. Melbourne: Cheshire
— (1982) 'The Contemporary Implications of Democratic Socialism', in Evans and Reeves
Hayek, F. (1944) *The Road to Serfdom*. London: Routledge and Kegan Paul
— (1960) *The Constitution of Liberty*. London: Routledge and Kegan Paul
Hayes, R. and Wheelwright, S. (1984) *Restoring our Competitive Edge: Competing Though Manufacturing*. New York: John Wiley and Sons
Hays, S. P. (1959) *Conservation and the Gospel of Efficiency*. Cambridge, MA: Harvard University Press
Head, B. (1982) 'The Social Policy of the New Right', in Sawer (1982b)
— (1988) 'The Labor Government and Economic Rationalism', *Australian Quarterly* 60 (4), Summer: 466–77
— (1989) 'Parties and Policy Agenda', in Head and Patience
— and Patience, A. (eds) (1989) *From Fraser to Hawke. Australian Public Policy in the 1980s*. Melbourne: Longman Cheshire
— and Walter, J. (eds) (1988) *Intellectual Movements and Australian Society*. Melbourne: Oxford
Heads of Government Meeting (1992) *Communiqué*, 11 May, Canberra
Healy, M. (1989) *That's It — I'm Leaving; Ministerial Resignations and Dismissals 1901–89*. Canberra: Department of the Parliamentary Library

Heath, A., Jowell, R. and Curtice, J. (1985) *How Britain Votes*. Oxford: Pergamon
Heatley, A. (1979) *The Government of the Northern Territory*. St Lucia: University of Queensland Press
Heberle, R. (1966) 'Types and Functions of Social Movements', *International Encyclopedia of the Social Sciences*, Vol. 14: 438–44
Henderson, R., Harcourt, A. and Harper, R.J.A. (1970) *People in Poverty*. Melbourne: Cheshire, for Institute of Applied Economic and Social Research
Hewson, J. and Fischer, T. (1991), *Fightback! It's Your Australia: The Way to Rebuild and Reward Australia*. Canberra: Liberal and National Parties
Hiatt, L. R. (1976) *The Role of the National Aboriginal Consultative Committee*, Report of the Committee of Inquiry, Chair: L. R. Hiatt. Canberra: AGPS
Higgins, W. (1985) 'Political Unionism and the Corporatism Thesis', *Economic and Industrial Democracy* 6 (3): 349–81
— (1987) 'Unions as Bearers of Industrial Regeneration: The Australian Case', *Economic and Industrial Democracy* 8 (2): 213–36
— (1991) 'Missing the Boat: Labor and Industry in the Eighties', in Galligan and Singleton
Higgott, R. and Cooper, A. F. (1990), 'Middlepower Leadership and Coalition Building: Australia, the Cairns Group and the Uruguay Round of Trade Negotiations', *International Organization* 44 (4): 589–632
High Court of Australia (1992) 'Eddie Mabo and Ors versus the State of Queensland', Court's Reasons for Judgment, No 2, 175 CLR1
Hill, R. (1993) 'The Australian Public Service: A Coalition View', Address to the Executive Development Scheme, Canberra
Hince, K. (1967) 'Unions on the Shopfloor', *Journal of Industrial Relations* 9 (3): 214–23
Hirschman, A. (1991) *The Rhetoric of Reaction: Perversity, Futility, Jeopardy*. Cambridge, Mass.: Harvard University Press
Hirst, J. (1988) *The Strange Birth of Colonial Democracy: New South Wales 1848–1884*. Sydney: Allen and Unwin
Hirst, P. and Zeitlin, J. (eds) (1991) *Reversing Industrial Decline?* London: Berg
Hollander, R. (1992) 'Negotiating Housing Policy: the Queensland Housing Commission and Federal, State and Local Governments, 1945–64', *Australian Journal of Public Administration* 51: 342–53
Hollingworth, P. (1972) *The Powerless Poor*. Melbourne: Stockland Press
Holmes, J. (1976) *The Government of Victoria*. St Lucia: University of Queensland Press
— and Sharman, C. (1977) *The Australian Federal System*. Sydney: Allen and Unwin
Hood, C. (1986) *Administrative Analysis. An Introduction to Rules, Enforcement and Organisations*. Brighton, UK: Wheatsheaf Books
— (1990) 'De-Humphreying the Westminster Model of Bureaucracy: A New Style of Governance?', *Governance* iii: 205–14
Horne, D. (1980) *Time of Hope: Australia 1966–72*. Sydney: Angus and Robertson
— (ed.) (1992) *The Trouble with Economic Rationalism*. Newham: Scribe

Horner, D. (1992) 'The Security Dimension of Australian Foreign Policy', in Mediansky (1992b)
House of Representatives (1986–90) *Work of the Session*. Canberra: AGPS
House of Representatives Select Committee on Televising (1991) *The Eyes Have It!*, Inquiry into the Televising of the House of Representatives and its Committees. Canberra: AGPS
House of Representatives Select Committee on the Print Media (1992) *News and Fair Facts: The Australian Print Media Industry*. Canberra: AGPS
House of Representatives Standing Committee on Finance and Public Administration (1990) *Not Dollars Alone: Review of the Financial Management Improvement Program*. Canberra: AGPS
House of Representatives Standing Committee on Procedure (1986) *Days and Hours of Sitting Time and the Effective Use of the Time of the House*. Canberra: AGPS
— (1990) *Greater Opportunities for Debate on Reports from Parliamentary Committees*. Canberra: AGPS
Howard, W. (1977) 'Australian Trade Unions in the Context of Union Theory', *Journal of Industrial Relations* 19 (3), September: 255–73
Howard, J. (1990) 'The Liberal/National Parties' Industrial Relations Policy: Deregulation by Providing an Enterprise Focus', *Economic and Labour Relations Review* 1 (2), December: 34–47
Howe, B. (1989) *Better Income: Retirement Income Policy into the Next Century*. Canberra: AGPS
Hughes, C. A. (1966) 'Electoral Behaviour' in H. Mayer (ed.), *Australian Politics: A Reader*. Melbourne: F. W. Cheshire
— (ed.) (1968) *Readings in Australian Government*. St Lucia: University of Queensland Press
— (1969) 'Electoral Behaviour' in Mayer
— (1986) *A Handbook of Australian Politics and Government 1975–1984*. Sydney: ANU
Hyde, J. (1982) *The Year 2000: A Radical Liberal Alternative*. Perth, mimeograph
IC, Industrial Commission (1991) *Strategic Trade Theory: The East Asian Experience*. Canberra: AGPS
Immigration Reform Group (1960) *Immigration: Control or Colour Bar?* Melbourne: The Immigration Reform Group
Inglis, K. S. (1983) *This is the ABC*. Melbourne: Melbourne University Press
Jaensch, D. (1977a) *The Government of South Australia*. St Lucia: University of Queensland Press
— (ed.) (1977b) *The Politics of New Federalism*. Adelaide: Australian Political Science Association
— (1985) 'South Australia and the Northern Territory' in Costar and Woodward
— (ed.) (1986a) *The Flinders History of South Australia: Political History*. Adelaide: Wakefield Press
— (1986b) *Getting Our Houses in Order: Australia's Parliament: How it Works and the Need for Reform*. Penguin: Ringwood
— (1989a) *The Hawke/Keating Hijack: The ALP in Transition*. Sydney: Allen and Unwin
— (1989b) *Power Politics: Australia's Party System*. Sydney: Allen and Unwin

402 Bibliography

— (1990) 'The 1989 South Australian Election', *Australian Journal of Political Science* 25 (2), November: 333–38
— (1991) *Parliament, Parties and People: Australian Politics Today*. Melbourne: Longman Cheshire
— and Loveday, P. (eds) (1987) *Challenge from the Nationals: The Territory Election 1987*. Darwin: North Australia Research Unit, Australian National University
Jakubowicz, A. (1981) 'State and Ethnicity: Multiculturalism as Ideology', *Australian and New Zealand Journal of Sociology* 17 (3): 4–13
Jarman, A. M. G. and Kouzmin, A. (1993) 'Australian Metropolitan Government: Local Government Reform and Urban Growth into the 1990s', *Government and Policy* xi: 143–60
Jenkins, D. (1991) 'The Southeast Asia Dimension', in Fry
Jennett, C. and Stewart, R. (eds) (1990) Hawke *and Australian Public Policy*. Melbourne: Macmillan
Johnson, C. (1989) *The Labor Legacy: Curtin, Chifley Whitlam, Hawke*. Sydney: Allen and Unwin.
— (1992) *MITI and the Japanese Miracle: The Growth of Industry Policy*. Stanford: Stanford University Press
Johnston, C. and Johnston, R. (1988) 'The Making of Homosexual Men', in J. Lee and V. Burgmann (eds), *Staining the Wattle*. Melbourne: Penguin/ McPhee Gribble
Johnston, E. (1991) *National Report of the Royal Commission into Aboriginal Deaths in Custody*. Canberra: AGPS
Johnston, N. (1992a) 'Greens unsure about PM's plan', the *Age*, Tuesday 22 December
— (1992b) 'Keating rebukes green groups', the *Age*, Wednesday 23 December
Jones, E. (1991a) 'The March Industry Statement', *Current Affairs Bulletin* 67 (11), April: 29–31
— (1991b) 'Economics, the State and the Capitalist Dynamic', Sydney University Political Economy Department Discussion Papers
Jones, F. L. (1989) 'Changing Attitudes and Values in Post-war Australia', in K. Hancock (ed.), *Australian Society*. Melbourne: Cambridge University Press
— and McAllister, I. (1989) 'The Changing Structural Base of Australian Politics since 1946', *Politics* 24 (1): 7–17
Jones, L. (1984) 'Some Thoughts on Pornography with Particular Reference to Video Pornography and its Effects on Women in Australia', *Fourth Women and Labor Conference Papers*, Brisbane
Jones, M. A. (1990) *The Australian Welfare State*. Sydney: Allen and Unwin
— (1993) *Transforming Australian Local Government*. Sydney: Allen and Unwin
Jones, R. (1971) *Damania: The Hydro-electric Commission, the Environment and Government in Tasmania*. Hobart: Fullers Bookshop
Jones, R. G. *et al.* (1993) *Australian Election Study, 1993*, computer file. Canberra: Social Science Data Archives, ANU
Jupp, J. (1966) *Arrivals and Departures*. Melbourne: Cheshire Landsdowne
— (1982) *Party Politics: Australia 1966–81*. Sydney: Allen and Unwin
— (ed.) (1984) *Ethnic Politics in Australia*. Sydney: Allen and Unwin
— (ed.) (1988) *The Australian People*. North Ryde: Angus and Robertson

Kasper, W., Blandy, R., Freebairn, J., Hocking, D. and O'Neil, R. (1980) *Australia at the Crossroads: Our Choices to the Year 2000*. Sydney: Harcourt Brace

Katzenstein, Peter (1978) *Between Power and Plenty*. Madison: University of Wisconsin Press

— (1985) *Small States in World Markets*. Ithaca: Cornell University Press

Keating, M. and Dixon, G. (1989) *Making Economic Policy in Australia 1983–1988*. Melbourne: Longman Cheshire

Keating, P. (1987) 'Address to the Victorian Fabian Society', 11 November 1987, *Fabian Newsletter*, December

— (1993a) 'Redfern Park Speech', *Aboriginal Law Bulletin* 3 (61), April: 4–5

— (1993b) 'Statement by the Prime Minister', Canberra, 24 March

— and Howe, B. (1992) *Towards a Fairer Australia Social Justice Strategy 1992–93*. Canberra: AGPS

Keeffe, K. (1992) *From the Centre to the City*. Canberra: Aboriginal Studies Press

Kelley, J. (1988) 'Political Ideology in Australia', in J. Kelley and C. Bean (eds), *Australian Attitudes*. Sydney: Allen and Unwin

— Cushing, R. G. and Headey, B. (1984) *Australian National Social Science Survey, 1984*, User's guide and data file. Canberra: Social Science Data Archives, ANU

Kellow, A. (1990) 'Spoiling for a Fight or Fighting for the Spoils? Resource and Environmental Politics in Australia towards 2000', in B. Hocking (ed.), *Australia Towards 2000*. London: Macmillan

Kelly, D. (1988) 'Towards Tripartism: Changing Industrial Relations in the Australian Steel Industry, 1978–1987', *Journal of Industrial Relations* 30 (4), December: 511–32

Kelly, P. (1984) *The Hawke Ascendancy: A Definitive Account of its Origins and Climax 1975–1983*. Sydney: Angus and Robertson

— (1992) *The End of Certainty: The Story of the 1980s*. Sydney: Allen and Unwin

Kelty, B. (1988) 'Bill Kelty's Vision for the New Australia', *Australian Financial Review*, 8 April

— (1989) 'Looking Beyond Wage Rises', the *Bulletin*, January 31–February 7

Kemp, D. A. (1975) 'Social Change and the Future of Political Parties', in L. Maisel and P. Sacks (eds), *The Future of Political Parties: Sage Electoral Studies Yearbook*, Vol. 1. Beverly Hills, CA: Sage

— (1977) 'Political Parties and Australian Culture', *Quadrant* xxi (12): 3–13

— (1978) *Society and Electoral Behaviour in Australia*. St Lucia: University of Queensland Press.

— (1979) 'Class, Culture and Parties', *Meanjin* 38 (2): 166–71

— (1988a) *Foundations for Australian Political Analysis*. Melbourne: Oxford University Press

— (1988b) 'Liberalism and Conservatism in Australia since 1944', in Head and Walter

— (1993) 'Defeated by fear, smear and cynicism', the *Australian*, 18 March

Kenis, P. and Volker Schneider, (1991) 'Policy Networks and Policy Analysis: Scrutinising a New Analytical Toolbox', in Marin and Mayntz

Kewley, T. (1973) *Social Security in Australia 1900–1972*. Sydney: Sydney University Press
Kjellberg, A. (1983) *Facklig organisering i tolv länder*. Lund: Arkiv
Knight, J. (1979) 'The Baltic States: Foreign Policy and Domestic Response', *Australian Journal of Politics and History* 25 (1): 18–28
— and Hudson, W. J. 1983, *Parliament and Foreign Policy*. Canberra Studies in World Affairs 13. Canberra: Department of International Relations, Australian National University
Knopfelmacher, F. (1982) 'The Case Against Multi-culturalism', in Manne
Kuhn, R. (1952) 'Why Pressure-Group Action by Australian Unions?', *Australian Quarterly* xxiv (3): 61–68
Kunz, E. F. (1988) 'Post-war Non-British Immigration' in Jupp
Kyloh, R. (1989) 'Flexibility and Structural Adjustment Through Consensus: Some Lessons From Australia', *International Labour Review* 128 (1): 103–24
Lacey, M. J. (1989) 'Three Decades of Environmental Politics', in M. J. Lacey (ed.), *Government and Environmental Politics — Essays on Historical Developments since World War Two*. Baltimore: Johns Hopkins
Lane, R. (1992) 'The Rationale for Fiscal Equalisation', *Australian Quarterly* 64: 262–74
Lang, J. (1962), *The Great Bust: The Depression of the Thirties*. Sydney: Angus and Robertson
Langmore, J. (1991) 'The Labor Government in a Deregulatory Era', in Galligan and Singleton
Laski, H. J. (1917) 'Sovereignty and Federalism', in *Studies in the Problem of Sovereignty*. New Haven: Yale University Press
Layman, L. (1982–83) 'Development Ideology in Western Australia', *Historical Studies* 20: 234–60.
— (1991) 'Continuity and Change, 1947–1965', in Black (1991b)
Leaver, R. (1991) 'Australia's Gulf Commitment: The End of Self-Reliance', *Pacific Review* 4 (3): 233–40
Lence, R. M. (ed.) (1992) *Union and Liberty: The Political Philosophy of John C. Calhoun*. Indianapolis: Liberty Press
Lever-Tracy, C. and Quinlan, M. (1988) *A Divided Working Class: Ethnic Segmentation and Industrial Conflict in Australia*. London: Routledge and Kegan Paul
Lewins, F. and Ly, J. (1985) *The First Wave: The Settlement of Australia's First Vietnamese Refugees*. Sydney: Allen and Unwin
Lewis, J. (1992) 'Gender and the Development of Welfare Regimes', *Journal of European Social Policy* 2 (3): 159–73
Lewis, P. and Spiers, D. (1990) 'Six Years of the Accord: An Assessment', *Journal of Industrial Relations* 32 (1), March: 53–68
Liberal Industrial Inquiry (1928) *Britain's Industrial Future*. London: Liberal Party of Great Britain
Liberal Party of Australia (1983) *Facing the Facts*, Report of the Committee of Review, Chair: J. Valder. Canberra
Lijphart, A (1984) *Democracies: Patterns of Majoritarian and Consensus Government in Twenty-One Countries*. New Haven: Yale University Press
— (1989) 'Democratic Political Systems: Types, Cases, Causes and Consequences', *Journal of Theoretical Politics* 1: 33–48

Lindell, G. J. (1986) 'Why Is Australia's Constitution Binding?', 16 *Federal Law Review* 29

Lloyd, C. (1983) 'The Federal ALP: Supreme of Secondary?' in A. Parkin and J. Warhurst (eds), *Machine Politics in the Australian Labor Party*. Sydney: Allen and Unwin

— (1990) 'The 1990 Media Campaign' in Bean *et al.*

— (1992) 'Prime Ministers and the Media' in P. Weller (ed.), *Menzies to Keating: The Development of the Australian Prime Ministership*. Melbourne: University of Melbourne Press

— and Reid, G. S. (1974) *Out of the Wilderness*. Melbourne: Cassell

— and Swan, W. (1987a) 'National Factions and the ALP', *Politics* 22 (1): 100–10

— and — (1987b) 'ALP Factions: An Explanatory Note', Politics 22 (2): 103–04

— and Troy, P. (1983) 'Duck Creek Revisited? The Case for National Urban and Regional Policies', in J. Halligan and C. Paris, *Australian Urban Politics*. Melbourne: Longman Cheshire

Loney, J. and Playford, J. (1973) 'Parliamentary Cretinism?', in H. Mayer (ed.), *Labor to Power*. Sydney: Angus and Robertson

Loveday, P., Martin, A. and Parker, R. (eds) (1977) *The Emergence of the Australian Party System*. Sydney: Hale and Iremonger

Lucy, R. (1985) *The Australian Form of Government*. Melbourne: Macmillan

Ludeke, Justice T. (1991) 'What Ever Happened to the Prerogatives of Management?', *Journal of Industrial Relations* 33 (3), September: 395–411

Lynch, A. (1988) *Legislation by Proclamation — Parliamentary Nightmare, Bureaucratic Dream*, Papers on Parliament 2. Canberra: Department of the Senate

Macintyre, C. (1989) *Rounding Up the Flock? Executive Dominance in the New Parliament House*,Canberra: Department of the Parliamentary Library/Australasian Political Studies Association

— (1991) *Political Australia: A Handbook of Facts*. Melbourne: Oxford University Press

Macintyre, S. (1984) 'The Short History of Social Democracy in Australia', in D. Rawson (ed.), *Blast, Budge or Bypass: Towards a Social Democratic Australia*. Canberra: Academy of the Social Sciences in Australia

— (1986a) 'The Short History of Australian Social Democracy', *Thesis Eleven* (15): 3–14

— (1986b) *The Oxford History of Australia, Vol. 4, 1901–1942*. Melbourne: Oxford University Press

— (1989) *Winners and Losers*. Sydney: Allen and Unwin

— (1991) *A Colonial Liberalism: The Lost World of Three Victorian Visionaries*. Melbourne: Oxford University Press

Mackay, H. (1993) *Reinventing Australia: The Mind and Mood of Australia in the 90s*. Sydney: Angus and Robertson

Mackerras, M. (1989) 'Fair Elections and Stable Government: Two Australian Cases Considered', Paper presented to the 1989 APSA Conference. Kensington: University of New South Wales

MacKinnon, C. A. (1987) *Feminism Unmodified. Discourses on Life and Law*. Cambridge: Harvard University Press.

Maddox, G. (1985) *Australian Democracy in Theory and Practice*. Melbourne: Longman Cheshire
— (1989) *The Hawke Government and Labor Tradition*. Melbourne: Penguin
— (1991) *Australian Democracy in Theory and Practice*, second edition. Melbourne: Longman Cheshire
— (1992), 'Political Stability, Independents and the Two-Party System', *Current Affairs Bulletin* 69 (6), June: 20–27
— and Battin, T. (1991) 'Australian Labor and the Socialist Tradition', *Australian Journal of Political Science* 26: 181–96
Maher, M. (1992) 'The Media and Foreign Policy', in Boyce and Angel
Mahlab, E. (1993) *Good Weekend*, August 21
Malik, J. M. (1991) 'Asian Reactions to Australia's Role in the Gulf Crisis', *Current Affairs Bulletin* 67 (11), April: 19–24
Manne, R. (ed.) (1982) *The New Conservatism in Australia*. Melbourne: Oxford University Press
Manning, H. (1992) 'The ALP and the Union Movement: "Catch-All" Party or Maintaining Tradition?', *Australian Journal of Political Science* 27: 12–30
Mansell, M. (1992) 'The Court Gives An Inch But Takes Another Mile: The Aboriginal Provisional Government Assessment of the Mabo Case', *Aboriginal Law Bulletin* 2 (57), August
Marceau, J. (1992), 'Industry Policy', in P. Vilinta, J. Phillimore and P. Newman (eds), *Markets, Morals and Manifestos*. Murdoch University: Institute for Science and Technology Policy
Marin, Bernd and Mayntz, Renate (eds) (1991) *Policy Networks: Empirical Evidence and Theoretical Considerations*. Frankfurt am Main: Campus Verlag
Markey, R. (1987) 'Technological Change, Unions and Industrial Relations' in G.W. Ford, J. Hearn and R. Lansbury (eds), *Australian Labour Relations*. Melbourne: Macmillan
Marks, G. N. (1993) 'Partisanship and the Vote in Australia: Changes Over Time [sic] 1969–1990', *Political Behaviour* 15 (2): 137–67
Markus, A. (1984a) 'Labor and Immigration: Policy Formation 1943–45', *Labour History* 46: 21–33
— (1984b) 'Labor and Immigration 1946–49: The Displaced Persons Program', *Labour History* 47: 73–90
— and Ricklefs M.C. (eds) (1985) *Surrender Australia?* Sydney: Allen and Unwin
Marsh, I. (1991) *The Committee System of the UK House of Commons: Recent Developments and their Implications for Australia*. Canberra: Senate Publishing Unit, Department of the Senate
— (ed.) (1993) *Governing in the 1990s: An Agenda for the Decade*. Melbourne: Longman Professional
Marshall, A. J. (ed.) (1966) *The Great Extermination: A Guide to Anglo-Australian Cupidity, Wickedness and Waste*. Melbourne: Heinemann
Marshall, T. H. (1950) 'Citizenship and Social Class', reprinted in *Sociology at the Crossroads* (1963). London: Heinemann
Martin, J. (1978) *The Migrant Presence*. Sydney: Allen and Unwin

Martin, R. (1963–64) 'Trade Unions and Labour Governments in Australia: A Study of the Relations Between Supporting Interests and Party Policy', in Hughes (ed.)
— (1980) *Trade Unions in Australia*. Ringwood: Penguin
Maskell, C. (1988) 'Federal Financial Relations, 1983–86', in R. Wettenhall and J. Nethercote (eds), *Hawke's Second Government: Australian Commonwealth Administration 1984–1987*. Canberra: Canberra College of Advanced Education
Mathews, J. (1989a) *Tools of Change*. Sydney: Pluto
— (1989b) *The Age of Democracy*. Melbourne: Oxford University Press
Matthews, T. (1991) 'Interest Group Politics: Corporatism Without Business?', in Castles
— and Ravenhill, J. (1989) 'Bipartisanship in the Australian Foreign Policy Elite', *Australian Outlook* 42 (1): 9–20
— and — (1991) 'Adrift in an Alien Sea? Australian Attitudes Towards the World', *Australia, New Zealand and the United States: Internal Change and Alliance Relations in the ANZUS States*, R. Baker (ed.) in New York: Praeger
Mayer, H. (1955) 'Why Parties?', *Current Affairs Bulletin* 16 (6): 83–96
— (1980a) 'Big Party Chauvinism and Minor Party Romanticism', in Mayer and Nelson
— (ed.) (1969) *Australian Politics: A Second Reader*. Melbourne: F. W. Cheshire
— (1979) *Dilemmas in Mass Media Policies*, Seventh Annual Lecture, The Academy of the Social Sciences in Australia, Canberra
— (1980) 'Broadcasting Regulation: The Eroding Bases', in Turbayne
— and Nelson, H. (eds) (1980) *Australian Politics: A Fifth Reader*. Melbourne: Longman Cheshire
— (1982) 'Murdoch wins the final round', *Media Information Australia* 24, May: 53–54
McAllister, I. (1981) 'Migrants and Australian Politics: Review Article', *Journal of Intercultural Studies* 2 (3)
— (1982a) 'Class, Ethnicity and Voting Behaviour in Australia', *Politics* 17 (2): 96–107
— (1982b) 'The Australian Democrats: Protest Vote or Portent of Realignment', *Politics* 17: 68–73
— (1988) 'Political Attitudes and Electoral Behaviour', in Jupp
— (1990) 'Political Behaviour', in Summers *et al.*
— (1992a) *Political Behaviour: Citizens, Parties and Elites in Australia*. Melbourne: Longman Cheshire
— (1992b) 'Australia', in M. N. Franklin *et al.*, *Electoral Change*. Cambridge: Cambridge University Press
— and Ascui, A. (1988) 'Voting Patterns' in McAllister and Warhurst
— and Bean, C. (1990) 'Explaining Labor's Victory', in Bean *et al.*
— and Jones, R. and Gow, D. (1990) *Australian Election Study 1990*, computer file. Canberra: Social Science Data Archives, ANU
— and Kelly, J. (1983) 'Changes in the Ethnic Vote in Australia', *Politics* 18 (1): 98–107

— and Mughan, A. (1987a) 'Party Commitment, Vote Switching and Liberal Decline in Australia', *Politics* 22 (1): 75–83
— and — (1987b) *Australian Election Study*, machine-readable data file. Canberra: Social Science Data Archives, ANU
— and Warhurst, J. (eds) (1988) *Australia Votes*. Melbourne: Longman Cheshire
McClelland, J. (1986) 'Where MPs go to Waste Their Time', *Sydney Morning Herald*, 29 September
McDonald, P. and Rimmer, M. (1989) 'Award Restructuring and Wages Policy', *Growth* 37, September: 111–34
McEachern, D. (1991) *Business Mates: The Power of Politics in the Hawke Era*. Sydney: Prentice Hall
McGregor, C. (1983) *Time of Testing: The Bob Hawke Victory* Ringwood, Vic.: Penguin
McGuinness, P.P. (1990) *McGuinness: Collected Thoughts*. Melbourne: Schwartz and Wilkinson
McHutchinson, J. and Urquhart, R. (1992) 'Trends in the Social Wage: The Social Wage Project', in P. Raskall and P. Saunders (eds), *Economic Inequality in Australia: Volume 1*, SSEI Monograph 1. Sydney: University of New South Wales
McKnight, D. (1986) *Moving Left: The Future of Socialism in Australia*. Sydney: Pluto
McNaughton, B. (1991) 'Referring Bills to Senate Committees: More Heat than Light?', *Legislative Studies* 6 (1), Winter: 34–45
McQueen, H. (1977) *Australia's Media Monopolies*. Melbourne: Widescope
McRae, H., Nettheim, G. and Beacroft, L. (1991) *Aboriginal Legal Issues*. Sydney: The Law Book Company
Meadows, D. H. Meadows, D. L., Randers, J. and Behrens, W. W. (1972) *The Limits to Growth* London: Pan
Meaney, N. (1976) *The Search for Security in the Pacific*. Sydney: Sydney University Press
— (ed.) (1985) *Australia and the World: A Documentary History from the 1870s to the 1970s*. Melbourne: Longman Cheshire
Mediansky, F. A. (1992) 'The Development of Australian Foreign Policy', in Boyce and Angel
— (ed.) (1992b) *Australia in a Changing World*. Sydney: Maxwell Macmillan
Melville, L.G. and Wainwright, J.W. (1929) *The Economic Effects of Federation*. Adelaide: South Australian Government Printer
Mercer, D. (1991) *A Question of Balance*. Sydney: The Federation Press
Millar, T.B. (1991) *Australia in Peace and War*. Canberra: Australian National University Press
Miller, J. D. B. (1954) *Australian Government and Politics*. London, Gerald Duckworth
— (1992) 'Reflections on Australian Foreign Policy', in Boyce and Angel
Miller, J. (1985) *Koori: A Will to Win*. Sydney: Angus and Robertson
Miller, T. (1986) 'Quis Custodies Ipsos Custodet?' A Review Article on the Committee System of the Australian Senate', *Legislative Studies* 1 (2), Spring: 5–19
Miller, W. L. (1977) *Electoral Dynamics in Britain since 1918*. New York: St Martin's Press
— et al. (1990) *How Voters Change: The 1987 British Election Campaign in Perspective*. Oxford: Oxford University Press

Millett, K. (1970) *Sexual Politics*. Garden City: Doubleday
Milliken, R. (1983) 'The Greenies Sharpen their Political Teeth', the *National Times*, January 16–22
Mills, R. C. (1928) 'The Financial Relations of the Commonwealth and the States', in W. Prest and R. Mathews (1980) *The Development of Australian Fiscal Federalism*. Canberra: Centre for Research on Federal Financial Relations, Australian National University
Mills, S. (1986) *The New Machine Men: Polls and Persuasion in Australian Politics*. Ringwood Penguin
Missen, A. (1982) 'Senate Committees and the Legislative Process', in J. Nethercote (ed.), *Parliament and Bureaucracy: Parliamentary Scrutiny of Administration: Prospects and Problems in the 1980s*. Sydney: Hale and Iremonger
Mitchell, M. (1991) 'Don't Punish the Victims', *ACOSS Impact* 21 (5)
Mitchell, W. (1992) 'Wages Policy and Wage Determination in 1991', *Journal of Industrial Relations* 34 (1), March: 153–61
Moore, B. and Carpenter, G. (1987) in Coghill (1987b)
Morgan, S. (1986) *My Place*. Fremantle: Fremantle Arts Centre Press
Morgenthau, H. J. (1952) 'Another "Great Debate": The National Interest of the U.S.', *American Political Science Review* XLVI (4): 971–78
MTU, Metal Trade Unions (1984) *Policy for Industry Development and More Jobs*. Melbourne: MTU
National Food Authority (1993) *Final Report of the Policy Review*. Canberra: AGPS
Nelson, H. (1988) 'Legislative Outputs', in Galligan
— (1992) 'Recipes for Uniformity: The Case of Food Standards', *Australian Journal of Political Science* 27, Special Federalism Issue: 78–90
— (1993) 'State Politics', in Smith
Nethercote, J. (1987) 'The Senate, The House of Representatives and the Condition of the Commonwealth Parliament', *Legislative Studies* 2 (2), Spring: 3–7
Nevile, J. W. (1983) 'The Role of Fiscal Policy in the Eighties', *Economic Record* 59, March
Nevitte, N. and Gibbins, R. (1990) *New Elites in Old States: Ideologies in the Anglo-American Democracies*. Toronto: Oxford University Press
New South Wales Cabinet Office (1990) 'Micro Economic Reform of Commonwealth State Relations', Discussion Paper Prepared for the Premiers Conference, 25 June
Nicklin, L. (1983) 'Poll shows most oppose Franklin Dam', the *Bulletin*, February 1
Nicolaou, L. (1991) *Australian Unions and Immigrant Workers*. Sydney: Allen and Unwin
Nurick, J. (ed.) (1987) *Mandate to Govern*. Perth, Australian Institute of Public Policy
O'Brien, P. (1985) *The Liberals: Factions, Feuds and Fancies*. Ringwood: Penguin
O'Keefe, P. (1988) *Deregulation, Merits Review and the Withering of Parliamentary Sovereignty*, Papers on Parliament 3. Canberra: Department of the Senate
— (1990), 'Towards Better Parliamentary Education', *Legislative Studies* 5 (1), Autumn: 18–24

O'Meagher, B. (ed.) (1983) *The Socialist Objective: Labor and Socialism*. Sydney: Hale and Iremonger

Olson, M. (1982) *The Rise and Decline of Nations*. New Haven: Yale University Press

OECD, Organisation for European Co-operation and Development (1991) *Environmental Indicators 1991*. Paris: OECD

Osterfeld, D. (1989) 'Radical Federalism: Responsiveness, Conflict and Efficiency', in G. Brennan and L. Lomasky (eds), *Politics and Process: New Essays in Democratic Thought*. Cambridge: Cambridge University Press

Ostrom, V. (1976) 'The American Experiment in Constitutional Choice', *Public Choice* 27: 1–12

— (1987) *The Political Theory of a Compound Republic*. Lincoln: University of Nebraska Press

Overacker, L. (1952) *The Australian Party System*. London: Oxford University Press

— (1968) *Australian Parties in a Changing Society: 1945–67*. Melbourne: F. W. Cheshire

Ozolins, U. (1993) *The Politics of Language in Australia*. Sydney: Cambridge University Press

Page, B. (1989) 'Cabinet', in Smith and Watson

— (1990a) 'Ministerial Resignation and Individual Ministerial Responsibility in Australia, 1976–89', *Journal of Comparative and Commonwealth Politics* 28 (2), July

— (1990b) *The Legislative Council of New South Wales: Past, Present and Future*. Sydney: New South Wales Parliamentary Library

Painter, M. (1986) 'Administrative Change and Reform', in Galligan

— (1987) *Steering the Modern State: Changes in Central Coordination in Three Australian State Governments*. Sydney: Sydney University Press

Palbas, T. (1988) 'Citizenship Conventions 1950–1963, in Jupp

Palfreeman, A. C. (1967) *The Administration of the White Australia Policy*. Melbourne: Melbourne University Press

Panitch, L. (1976) *Social Democracy and Industrial Militancy*. Cambridge: Cambridge University Press

Papadakis, E. (1990a) 'Environmental Policy', in Jennett and Stewart (1990)

— (1990b) 'Minor Parties, the Environment and the New Politics' in Bean et al.

— (1993) *Politics and the Environment*. Sydney: Allen and Unwin

Pappas, Carter, Evans and Koop (1990) *The Global Challenge: Australian Manufacturing in the 1990s*. Melbourne: Australian Manufacturing Council

Parker, D. (1990) *The Courtesans: The Press Gallery in the Hawke Era*. Sydney: Allen and Unwin

Parker, R. (1978) *The Government of New South Wales*. St Lucia: University of Queensland Press

Parkin, and Hardcastle, L. (1990) 'Immigration Policy' in Jennett and Stewart

— and Marshall, V. (1992) 'Federal Relations', in A. Parkin, and A. Patience (eds), *The Bannon Decade*. Sydney: Allen and Unwin

— and Warhurst, J. (eds) (1983) *Machine Politics in the Australian Labor Party*. Sydney: Allen and Unwin

Parliamentary Library (1982) *Parliamentary Handbook of the Commonwealth of Australia*. Canberra: AGPS
Parsler, R. (1970) 'Some Economic Aspects of Embourgeoisement in Australia', *Sociology* 4 (2): 165–79
Partridge, P. H. (1952) 'The Politics of Federalism', in Sawer (1952a)
Pateman, C. (1989) 'The Patriarchal Welfare State', in *The Disorder of Women*. Chicago: Polity Press
Patience, A. (1982) 'The Liberal Party and the Failure of Australian Conservatism', in Sawer (1982b)
— and Head, B. (eds) (1979) *From Whitlam to Fraser. Reform and Reaction in Australian Politics*. Melbourne: Oxford University Press
Patterson, R. (1981) 'The Origins of Ethnic Broadcasting: Turning the Dial in Australia', *Journal of Intercultural Studies* 2 (1)
— (1992) 'SBS-TV: Forerunner of the Future', *Media Information Australia* 66, November: 43–52
Pearce, D. (1977) *Delegated Legislation in Australia and New Zealand*. Sydney: Butterworths
Peachment, A. and Reid, G. S. (1977) *New Federalism in Australia: Rhetoric or Reality?*, APSA Monograph 18. Bedford Park, South Australia
Pearson, N. (1993) 'Reconciliation: to be or not to be — nationhood, self-determination or self-government', *Aboriginal Law Bulletin* 3 (61), April: 14–17
Pedersen, M. N. (1979) 'The Dynamics of European Party Systems: Changing Patterns of Electoral Volatility', *European Journal of Political Research* 7: 1–27
Peele, G. (1993) 'The Coalition' in P. Dunleavy *et al.*, *Developments in British Politics* 4. London: Macmillan
Peetz D. (1990) 'Declining Union Density', *Journal of Industrial Relations* 32 (2): 197–223
Penguin/Macquarie (1988) *The Penguin Macquarie Dictionary of Australian Politics*. Ringwood: Penguin
Perkins, C. (1982) 'Economic imperatives as far as Aborigines are concerned', in R. M. Berndt (ed.), *Aboriginal Sites, Rights and Resource Development*. Canberra: Academy of the Social Sciences in Australia
Peters, B. G. (1989) *The Politics of Bureaucracy: A Comparative Perspective*, third edition. New York: Longman
Phillips, H. (1991) 'The Modern Parliament, 1965–1989', in Black
Piesse, E. L. (1935) 'The Constitution under Strain', in W.G.K. Duncan (ed.), *Trends in Australian Politics*. Sydney: Angus and Robertson
Piore, M and C. Sabel (1984) *The Second Industrial Divide*. New York: Basic Books
Pilkington, G. (1983) 'ACTU Authority 1927–1957: From State Branch to Federal Union Legitimation', in Ford and Plowman
Plowman, D. (1987) 'Economic Forces and the New Right: Employer Matters in 1986', *Journal of Industrial Relations* 29 (1), March: 84–91
— (1988) 'Employer Associations and Bargaining Structures: An Australian Perspective', *British Journal of Industrial Relations* 26 (3), November: 371–96
— (1990) 'Administered Flexibility: Restructuring the Metal Industry Award', *Economic and Labour Relations Review* 1 (2), December: 48–70

Polanyi, K. (1957) *The Great Transformation*. Boston: Beacon Press
Portus, G. V. (ed.) (1933) *Studies in the Australian Constitution*. Sydney: Angus and Robertson
— (1948) *The Concept of Sovereignty*. Melbourne: Melbourne University Press
Power, J. (ed.) (1990) *Public Administration in Australia: A Watershed*. Sydney: Hale and Iremonger
Prest, W. (1963) 'The Economics of Federal-State Finance', in H. W. Arndt and W. M. Corden (eds), *The Australian Economy*. Melbourne: F. W. Cheshire
Price, C. A. (1963) *Southern Europeans in Australia*. Melbourne: Oxford University Press
Purdon, C. and Burke, T. (1991) *Local Government and Housing*, National Housing Strategy Background Paper 6. Canberra: AGPS
Pusey, M. (1991) *Economic Rationalism in Canberra: A Nation Building State Changes its Mind*. Melbourne, Cambridge University Press
Queensland (1989) Commission of Inquiry into Possible Illegal Activities and Associated Police Misconduct, Brisbane (the *FitzGerald Report*)
Radbone, I. and Robbins, J. (1986) 'The History of the South Australian Public Service', in Jaensch (1986a)
Rainbow, S. (1992) 'Why did New Zealand and Tasmania spawn the world's first Green parties?', *Environmental Politics* 1 (3): 321–46
Raskall, P. (1993) 'Widening Income Disparities in Australia' in S. Rees, G. Rodley and F. Stilwell (eds), *Beyond the Market*. Sydney: Pluto
Ravenhill, J. (ed.) (1989) *No Longer an American Lake? Alliance Problems in the South Pacific*. Sydney: Allen and Unwin
— (1990) 'Australia', in H. J. Michelman and P. Soldatos (eds), *Federated States in International Relations*. Oxford: Oxford University Press
— (1992) 'Economic Objectives', in Mediansky (1992b)
— and Matthews, T. (1991) 'Australia's Economic Malaise: A Northeast Asian Solution?', *Pacific Review* 4 (1): 45–55
Rawson, D. W. (1961) *Australia Votes*. Parkville: Melbourne University Press
— (1966) *Labor in Vain? A Survey of the Australian Labor Party*. Melbourne: Longmans
— (1982) 'The ACTU — Growth Yes, Power No', in K. Cole (ed.), *Power, Conflict and Control in Australian Trade Unions*. Melbourne: Penguin
— (1986) *Unions and Unionists in Australia*, second edition. Sydney: Allen and Unwin
— (1991) 'Has the Old Politics Reached an Impasse?' in Castles
Read, P. (1992) Review of F. Brennan, *Sharing the Country*, in *Australian Book Review* 143, August: 8–9
Reid, G. (1982) 'Parliament and Delegated Legislation', in J. Nethercote (ed.), *Parliament and Bureaucracy. Parliamentary Scrutiny of Administration: Prospects and Problems in the 1980s*. Sydney: Hale and Iremonger
— (ed.) (1983) *The Role of Upper Houses Today:* Proceedings of the Fourth Annual Workshop of the Australasian Study of Parliament Group. Hobart: University of Tasmania
— and Forrest, M. (1989) *Australia's Commonwealth Parliament 1901–1988, Ten Perspectives*. Melbourne: Melbourne University Press

Renouf, A.P. (1979) *The Frightened Country*. Melbourne: Macmillan
Resource Assessment Commission (1991) *Kakadu Conservation Zone: Final Report*, Volume 1, April. Canberra: AGPS
Reynolds, P. (1974) *The Democratic Labor Party*. Milton, Qld: Jacaranda
— (1979) 'The Australian Democrats' in H. R. Penniman (ed.), *The Australian National Elections of 1977*. Washington, DC: American Enterprise Institute
Richards, L. (1978) 'Displaced Politics: Refugee Migrants in the Australian Political Context.' Melbourne: La Trobe University Sociology Paper 45
Richardson, J. L. (ed.) (1991) *Northeast Asian Challenge: Debating the Garnaut Report*, Canberra Studies in World Affairs. Canberra: Department of International Relations, Australian National University
Richmond, K. (1978) 'The National Country Party', in Starr *et al.*
Rimmer, M. (1989) 'Work Place Unionism', in Ford and Plowman
— and Verevis, C. (1990) *Award Restructuring: Progress at the Workplace*, IRRC Monograph 28. Sydney: University of New South Wales
Robin, L. (1993) 'Of Desert and Watershed: The Rise of Ecological Consciousness in Victoria, Australia,' in P. Weindling (ed.), *Science and Nature*, Monograph of the British Society for the History of Science. Cambridge: Cambridge University Press
Rodan, P. (1983) 'The Liberals in Opposition', in B. Costar and C. Hughes (eds), *Labor to Office*. Blackburn: Drummond
Roddewig, R. J. (1978) *The Green Bans: The Birth of Australian Environmental Politics*. New York: Allanheld, Osmun and Co
Rose, R. and I. McAllister, (1986) *Voters Begin to Choose*. London: Sage
Rowley, C. D. (1986) *Recovery*. Ringwood: Penguin
— (1988) 'Middle Australia and the Noble Savage: A Political Romance' in J. Beckett (ed.), *Past and Present: the Construction of Aboriginality*. Canberra: Aboriginal Studies Press
Rowse, T. (1980) 'The Regulation of Children's Television — Prohibition and Pluralism', in K. Boehringer *et al.* (eds), *Media in Crisis*. Sydney: New South Wales Institute of Technology
— (1991) 'ATSIC's Heritage: the Problems of Leadership and Unity in Aboriginal Political Culture', *Current Affairs Bulletin* 67 (8): 4–12
— (1992a) *Remote Possibilities: The Aboriginal Domain and the Administrative Imagination*. Darwin: North Australia Research Unit, Australian National University
— (1992b) 'Top down tensions', *Modern Times*, June
— (1992c) 'The Royal Commission, ATSIC and Self-Determination', *Australian Journal of Social Issues* 27 (3), August: 153–72
— (1993a) 'Rethinking Aboriginal "Resistance": the Community Development Employment Program (CDEP)', *Oceania* 63: 268–86
— (1993b) *After Mabo: Interpreting Indigenous Traditions*. Carlton: Melbourne University Press
Russell, E. A. (1978), 'Foreign Investment Policy What Role for the Economist?', *Australian Economic Papers* 17, December.
Rydon, J. (1963) 'The Electorate' in J. Wilkes (ed.), *Forces in Australian Politics* Sydney: Angus and Robertson
— (1979) 'The Conservative Electoral Ascendancy Between the Wars', in C. Hazlehurst (ed.), *Australian Conservatism*. Canberra: ANU Press

— (1986) *A Federal Legislature; The Australian Commonwealth Parliament 1901–1980*, Melbourne: Oxford University Press.
— (1987) 'The Federal Elections of 1987 and Their Absurdities', *Australian Quarterly* 59 (2–3), Spring/Summer: 357–65
— (1988) 'The Federal Structure of Australian Political Parties', *Publius: The Journal of Federalism* 18 (1), Winter: 159–72
Ryle, G. (1949) *The Concept of Mind*. London: Hutchinson
Salmons, B. (1993) 'Ethnic Votes Desert Libs — Survey', *Australian Financial Review* 18, October
Sartori, G. (1976) *Parties and Party Systems: A Framework for Analysis*. Cambridge: Cambridge University Press
Saunders, C. (1992) 'Fiscal Federalism: A General and Unholy Scramble', in Craven
Saunders, P. (1989) *Towards an Understanding of Commonwealth Social Expenditure Trends*, Discussion Paper 11, Social Welfare Research Centre, University of New South Wales
— (1992a) 'Recent Trends in Welfare: Some Reflections on the Search for Equity', reprinted in Abel-Smith and Titmuss (eds)
— (1992b) *Recent Trends in the Size and Growth of Government in OECD Countries*, SPRC Discussion Paper 34. Kensington, NSW: Social Policy Research Centre
Sawer, G. (ed.) (1952a) *Federalism: An Australian Jubilee Study*. Melbourne: F.W. Cheshire
— (1952b) *Australian Government Today*. Carlton: Melbourne University Press
— (1956) 'Councils, Ministers and Cabinets in Australia', in Hughes (1968)
— (1967) *Australian Federalism in the Courts*. Melbourne: Melbourne University Press
Sawer, M. (1982a) 'Political Manifestations of Australian Libertarianism' in Sawer (1982b)
— (ed.) (1982b) *Australia and the New Right*. Sydney: Allen and Unwin
— (1983) 'From the Ethical State to the Minimal State: State Ideology in Australia', *Politics* 18 (1): 26–35
— (1990) *Sisters in Suits: Women and Public Policy in Australia*. Sydney: Allen and Unwin
— and Simms, M. (1993) [1984] *A Woman's Place: Women and Politics in Australia*. Sydney: Allen and Unwin
Schaffer, B. B. (1977) 'Spatial Factors and Institutional Performance', Paper to 7th IPSA Conference, Edinburgh
Scheiber, H. (1980) 'Federalism and Legal Process: Historical and Contemporary Analysis of the American System', *Law and Society Review* 14: 663–722
Schmidt, M. (1982) 'The Role of the Parties in Shaping Macro-Economic Policy', in Castles
Schott, K. (1991) 'Economic Rationalism in Canberra', *Current Affairs Bulletin* 68 (7), December: 30–31
Schultz, J. (1992) 'Encouraging Competition and Diversity without Offending the Monopolists', *Media Information Australia* 65, August: 53–62
Scott, A. (1991) *Fading Loyalties: The Australian Labor Party and the Working Class*. Sydney: Pluto

Senate Select Committee on Matters Arising From Pay Television Tendering Process (1993) *First Report*, September
Senate Standing Committee on Regulations and Ordinances (1990a) *Eighty-Sixty Report*. Canberra: AGPS
— (1990b) *Special Report on the Subdelegation of Powers*. Canberra: AGPS
Sestito, R. (1982) *The Politics of Multiculturalism*. Sydney: Centre for Independent Studies
Shamsullah, A. (1990) 'The Australian Democrats' in Summers *et al*.
Sharman, C. (1983) 'Calhoun: A New Perspective on Theories of Australian Federalism', Strathclyde Paper on Government and Politics 22. Glasgow: University of Strathclyde
— (1986) 'The Senate, Small Parties and the Balance of Power', *Politics* 21 (2): 20–31
— (1987a) 'Second Chambers', in H. Bakvis and W. H. Chandler (eds) *Federalism and the Role of the State*. Toronto: University of Toronto Press
— (1987b) 'Coping with the Future: The Political Apparatus of the States', in M. Birrell (ed.), *The Australian States: Towards a Renaissance*. Melbourne: Longman Cheshire
— (1990a) 'Australia as a Compound Republic', *Politics* 25 (1): 1–5
— (1990b) 'The Party Systems of the Australian States: Patterns of Partisan Competition, 1945–1986', *Publius: The Journal of Federalism* 20 (4): 85–104
— (1990c) 'Parliamentary Federations and Limited Government: Constitutional Design and Redesign in Australia and Canada', *Journal of Theoretical Politics* 2: 205–30
— (1991) 'Forward to the Past: A Reply to Bean and Butler', *Australian Journal of Political Science* 26: 342–47
— (1992) 'Ideas and Change in the Australian Federal System', *Australian Journal of Political Science* 27, Special Federalism Issue: 7–18
— Smith, G. and Moon, J. (1991) 'The Party System and Change of Regime: The Structure of Partisan Choice in Tasmania and Western Australia', *Australian Journal of Political Science* 26 (3), November: 409–28
Shaver, S. (1987) 'Design for a Welfare State', *Australian Historical Studies* 88: 411–31
— (1992) 'From Difference to Equality', Paper presented at the Academy of Social Sciences in Australia Workshop, Canberra, November
— (ed.) (1993) *Gender, Citizenship and the Labour Market: The Australian and Canadian Welfare States*, SPRC Reports and Proceedings 109
Sheridan, T. (1975) *Mindful Militants: The Amalgamated Engineering Union in Australia, 1920–1972*. Melbourne: Cambridge University Press
— (1989) *Division of Labour: Industrial Relations in the Chifley Years, 1945–49*. Melbourne: Oxford University Press
Shils, E. (1989) 'Totalitarianism and Antinomians: Remembering the '30s and the '60s', *Quadrant*, xxxiii (4): 8–17 April
Short, M., Preston, A. and Peetz, D. (1993) *The Spread and Impact of Workplace Bargaining: Evidence from the Workplace Bargaining Research Project*. Canberra: AGPS
Siedlecky, S. and Wyndham, D. (1990) *Populate and Perish. Australian Women's Fight for Birth Control*. Sydney: Allen and Unwin
Simms, M. (1982) *A Liberal Nation: The Liberal Party and Australian Politics*. Sydney: Hale and Iremonger

Singleton, G. (1990) *The Accord and the Australian Labour Movement*. Melbourne: Melbourne University Press

Skidelsky, R. (1967) *Politicians and the Slump*. London: Macmillan

Smith, A. ([1776] (facsimile reprint 1966) *An Enquiry into the Nature and Causes of the Wealth of Nations*. London: Strahan Catell

Smith, D. (1991) *Aboriginal Unemployment Statistics: Policy Implications of the Divergence between Official and Case Study Data*, Centre for Aboriginal Economic Policy Research/ANU Discussion Paper 13

Smith, E. (1989) *The Australia Card: The Story of its Defeat*. Melbourne: Sun Books

Smith, G. (1991a) 'Political Chronicle: Tasmania', *Australian Journal of Politics and History* 37 (2): 333–37

— (1991b) 'Political Chronicle: Tasmania', *Australian Journal of Politics and History* 37 (3): 505–9

— and Hopper, J. (1979) 'On the Partisan Component of the Informal Vote', *Politics* 14 (2): 287

Smith, H. (1992) 'Internal Politics and Foreign Policy', in Mediansky (1992b)

Smith, R. (1992a) 'Independents and Australian Political Behaviour', Paper presented at the APSA Conference, Australian National University, Canberra

— (1992b) 'Political Chronicle: New South Wales', *Australian Journal of Politics and History* 38 (2): 222–27

— (1992c) 'Political Chronicle: New South Wales', *Australian Journal of Politics and History* 38 (3): 419–25

— (ed.) (1993) *Politics in Australia*, second edition. Sydney: Allen and Unwin

— and Watson, L. (eds) (1989) *Politics in Australia*. Sydney: Allen and Unwin

Snape, R. H. (1986) 'Should Australia Seek a Trade Agreement with the United States?', Economic Planning Advisory Council, EPAC Discussion Paper 86/1, Canberra

— (1989) 'A Free Trade Agreement with Australia?', in J. J. Schott (ed.), *Free Trade Areas and US Trade Policy*. Washington, DC: Institute for International Economics

Solomon, D. (1979) 'Committees in the Commonwealth Parliament: A Research Note', in *Working Papers on Parliament*. Canberra: Canberra College of Advanced Education

— (1986) *The People's Palace: Parliament in Modern Australia*. Melbourne: Melbourne University Press

— (1988) 'Parliament's Stirrers', *Australian Society* 7 (3), March: 36–38

— (1992) *The Political Impact of the High Court*. Sydney, Allen and Unwin

Souter, G. (1991) *Heralds and Angels. The House of Fairfax 1841–1991*. Melbourne: Melbourne University Press

Spann, R. N. (1961) 'The Catholic Vote in Australia' in H. Mayer (ed.), *Catholics and the Free Society*. Melbourne: F.W. Cheshire

Stanford, J. (1988) 'The Long-term Effects of Federation on the Queensland Economy', *Working Papers in Australian Studies*. London: Sir Robert Menzies Centre for Australian Studies

Starr, G. (1977) 'The Party Roots of the New Federalism', in Jaensch (1977b)

— (1978) 'The Liberal Party of Australia' in Starr *et al*. (1978)

— (1980) *The Liberal Party of Australia: A Documentary History*. Richmond, Vic.: Drummond/Heinemann

— Richmond, K. and Maddox, G. (1978) *Political Parties in Australia*. Richmond, Victoria Heinemann
Stephen, Sir Leslie (1882) *The Science of Ethics*. London: Smith, Elder and Co
Stilwell, F. (1986) *The Accord...and Beyond: The Political Economy of the Labor Government*. Sydney: Pluto
Stone, Deborah (1988) *Policy Paradox and Political Reason*. Glenview, Illinois: HarperCollins
Stone, Diane (1991) 'Old Guard Versus New Partisans: Think Tanks in Transition', *Australian Journal of Political Science* 26: 197–215
Storer, D. (1975) *Ethnic Rights, Power and Participation*. Melbourne: Clearing House on Migrant Issues, Ecumenical Migration Centre and Centre for Urban Research and Action
— et al. (1976) *But I wouldn't want my wife to work here*. Melbourne: Centre for Urban Research and Action
Stretton, H. (1987) *Political Essays*. Melbourne: Georgian House.
Stubbs, J. (1966) *The Hidden People* Melbourne: Lansdowne
Stutchbury, M. (1990) 'Macroeconomic Policy', in Jennett and Stewart
Suich, Max (1990) 'The Trashing of a TV Network', *Independent Monthly*, November
Sullivan, B. (1991) 'The Business of Sex: Australian Government and the Sex Industry', *Australian and New Zealand Journal of Sociology* 27 (1): 3–18
— (1993) 'Australian Politics and the Sex Industry,' Unpublished PhD Thesis, Department of Government, University of Queensland
Summers, A. (1983) *Gamble for Power: How Bob Hawke Beat Malcolm Fraser: The 1983 Federal Election*. Melbourne: Nelson
Summers, J. (1986) 'The Salisbury Affair', in Jaensch (1986a)
—, Woodward, D. and Parkin, A. (eds) (1990) *Government, Politics and Power in Australia*. Melbourne: Longman Cheshire
Sutherland, J. (1982) *Offensive Literature. Decensorship in Britain 1960–1982*. London: Junction
Swan, P. and Bernstam, M.S. (1989) 'Support for Single Parents', in M. James (ed.), *The Welfare State: Foundations and Alternatives*, Centre for Independent Studies and New Zealand Centre for Independent Studies
Talese, G. (1980) *Thy Neighbour's Wife*. Dell.
Task Force on Management Improvement (1993) *The Australian Public Service Reformed: An Evaluation of a Decade of Management Reform*. Canberra: AGPS
Tatz, C. (1982a) 'Aborigines, Law and Race Relations', in *Aborigines and Uranium and Other Essays*. Melbourne: Heinemann Educational, Australia
— (1992b) 'The Recovery and Discovery of Rights: An Overview of Aborigines, Politics and Law', in R.M. Berndt (ed.), *Aboriginal Sites, Rights and Resource Development*. Canberra: Academy of the Social Sciences in Australia
Teicher, J. (1989) 'Unions and Wages Policy', in Ford and Plowman
Thakur, R. (1991) 'The Elusive Essence of Size: Australia, New Zealand and Small States in International Relations', in R. Higgott and J. L. Richardson (eds), *International Relations: Global and Australian Perspectives on an Emerging Discipline*, Canberra Studies in World Affairs 30. Canberra:

418 Bibliography

Department of International Relations, Australian National University
Therborn, G. (1986) *Why Some People Are More Unemployed than Others.* London: Verso
— (1989) 'States, Populations and Productivity: Towards a Political Theory of Welfare States', in P. Lassman (ed.), *Politics and Social Theory.* London: Routledge
Thompson, E. and Painter, M. (1986) 'New South Wales', in Galligan
Tickner, R. (1992) Speech to House of Representatives, 27 May 1992, reprinted in *25 Years On.* Canberra: ATSIC
Tiffen, R. (1988) 'The Revolution in Australian Media Ownership 1986–87', *Working Papers in Australian Studies* 36, Sir Robert Menzies Centre for Australian Studies, University of London
— (1989) *News and Power.* Sydney: Allen and Unwin
Timlin, J. (1974) 'Megacorp and Westernport Bay', in R. Dempsey (ed.), *The Politics of Finding Out: Environmental Problems in Australia.* Melbourne: Cheshire
Titmuss, R. (1956) 'The Social Division of Welfare: Some Reflections on the Search for Equity', reprinted in Abel-Smith and Titmuss
Tiver, P. G. (1978) *The Liberal Party: Principles and Performance.* Milton, Qld: Jacaranda
Tomlinson, J. (1981) *Problems of British Economic Policy 1870–1945.* London: Methuen
Toohey, J. (1993) 'A Government of Laws, and Not of Men?', 4 *Public Law Review* 158, and Paper delivered at Darwin, Conference on *Constitutional Change in the 1990s*, 6 October
Trood, R. (1992) 'Prime Ministers and Foreign Policy' in Weller
Troy, P. (ed.) (1978) *Federal Power in Australian Cities.* Sydney: Hale and Iremonger
Tsokhas, K. (1984) *A Class Apart? Businessmen and Australian Politics 1960–1980.* Melbourne: Oxford University Press
Turner, A. (1975) *Censorship. Wendy Bacon versus Peter Coleman.* Melbourne: Heinemann
Turner, K. (1973) 'The Liberal "Iceberg"', in H. Mayer and H. Nelson (eds), *Australian Politics: A Third Reader.* Melbourne: Cheshire
— (1985) 'The New Rules of the Game', in E. Chaples, H. Nelson and K. Turner (eds), *The Wran Model: Electoral Politics in New South Wales 1981 and 1984.* Melbourne: Oxford University Press
— (1989) 'Parliament', in Smith and Watson
Turbayne, D. (ed.) (1980) *The Media and Politics in Australia*, Public Policy Monograph, Department of Political Science, University of Tasmania
UTG, United Tasmania Group (1974) 'The New Ethic', in C. Pybus and R. Flanagan (eds), *The Rest of the World is Watching: Tasmania and the Greens.* Sydney: Sun Books
Viviani, N. (1984) *The Long Journey. Vietnamese Migration and Settlement in Australia.* Melbourne: Melbourne University Press
— (1990) 'Foreign Economic Policy', in Jennett and Stewart
— (1992) 'The Bureaucratic Context', in Mediansky (1992b)
Walker, K. (ed.) (1992) *Australian Environmental Policy.* Kensington: University of New South Wales Press

Walsh, C. (1989) 'State Decision Making: the Economic Framework and the Institutional Environment', in R. Blandy and C. Walsh (eds), *Budgetary Stress: the South Australian Experience*. Sydney: Allen and Unwin
— (1990) 'State Taxation and Vertical Fiscal Imbalance: the Radical Reform Options', in C. Walsh (ed.), *Issues in State Taxation*. Canberra: Federalism Research Centre, Australian National University
Walter, J. (1986) *The Ministers' Minders: Personal Advisers in National Government*. Melbourne: Oxford University Press
— (1992) 'Prime Ministers and their Staff', in Weller
Waltz, K. N. (1979) *Theory of International Politics*. Reading, Mass.: Addison-Wesley
Wanna, J. (1992) 'No Minister', *Australian Left Review* 136 February: 43–44
Ward, I. (1989) 'Two Faces of the ALP in the 1980s', *Australian and New Zealand Journal of Sociology* 25: 165–86
— (1991) 'The Changing Organisational Nature of Australia's Political Parties', *Journal of Commonwealth and Comparative Politics* 29 (2): 153–74
Warhurst, J. (1982) *Jobs or Dogma? The Industries Assistance Commission and Australian Politics*. St Lucia: University of Queensland Press
— (1983) 'One Party or Eight? The State and Territory Labor Parties', in Parkin and Warhurst
— (1990) 'Australian Politics: July 1987–February 1990' in Bean (1990)
— and Stewart, J. (1989) 'Manufacturing Industry Policies', in Head and Patience
Warner, K. O. (1933) *An Introduction to Some Problems of Australian Federalism*. Seattle: University of Washington Publications in the Social Sciences 9
Waterford, J. (1993) 'Keating's Quiet Power Shift', *Independent Monthly*, June
Waters, W. J. (1976) 'Australian Labor's Full Employment Objective, 1942–45', in J. Roe (ed.), *Social Policy in Australia: Some Perspectives 1901–1975*. Stanmore, NSW: Cassell Australia
Watson, I. (1990) *The Fight for the Forests*. Sydney: Allen and Unwin
Watts, R. (1987) *Foundations of the National Welfare State*. Sydney: Allen and Unwin
— (1989) '"In Fractured Times": The Accord and Social Policy under Hawke, 1983–87', in R. Kennedy (ed.), *Australian Welfare. Historical Sociology*. Melbourne: Macmillan
Weale, A. (1992) *The New Politics of Pollution*. Manchester: University of Manchester Press
Webb, L. C. (1954) 'The Australian Party System', in S. R. Davis *et al.*, *The Australian Political Party System*. Sydney: Angus and Robertson
Webb, L.J, Whitelock, D. and Le G. Brereton, J. (1969) *The Last of Lands*. Brisbane: Jacaranda
Weeks, J. (1981) *Sex, Politics and Society. The Regulation of Sexuality Since 1800*. London: Longmans
Weller, P. (1979) 'By Their Works...Parliamentary Committees and Their Reports', in *Working Papers on Parliament*. Canberra: Canberra College of Advanced Education
— (1982) 'Reforming Parliament', in Evans and Reeves
— (1989) *Malcolm Fraser PM: A Study in Prime Ministerial Power in Australia*. Ringwood: Penguin

— (1991) 'Prime Ministers, Political Leadership and Cabinet Government', *Australian Journal of Public Administration* 50: 131–44
— (ed.) (1992) *Menzies to Keating: The Development of the Australian Prime Ministership.* Carlton: Melbourne University Press
— Gardner, M., Ryan, N. and Stevens, B. (1993) 'The Role of the Public Sector: Implications for the Australian Public Service', *Canberra Bulletin of Public Administration* 72: 1–23
Wendt, A. E. (1987) 'The Agent-Structure Problem', *International Organization* 41 (3): 335–70
West, K. (1984) *The Revolution in Australian Politics.* Ringwood: Penguin
Western Australia (1992) Royal Commission into Commercial Activities of Government and Other Matters, WA Inc. Report. Part II, Perth
Western, J. Western, M., Emmison, M. and Baxter, J. (1991) 'Class Analysis and Politics', in Baxter *et al.*
Wettenhall, R. (1990) 'Australia's Daring Experiment with Public Enterprise', in A. Kouzmin and N. Scott (eds), *Dynamics in Australian Public Management: Selected Essays.* Melbourne: Macmillan
Whalan, D. (1991) 'Scrutiny of Delegated Legislation by the Australian Senate', *Statute Law Review* 12 (2), Autumn: 87–108
White, D. M. and D. A. Kemp (eds), *Malcolm Fraser on Australia.* Melbourne: Hill of Content
White, R. (1979) 'The Importance of being MAN', in P. Spearritt and D. Walker (eds), *Australian Popular Culture.* Sydney: Allen and Unwin
Whitlam, G. (1969) *Into the Seventies with Labor: 1969 Policy Speech.* Sydney: Australian Labor Party
— (1974) 'Australian Public Administration and the Labor Government', The Garran Oration, Canberra
— (1977) *E. G. Whitlam on the Australian Constitution.* Melbourne: Widescope International
— (1985) *The Whitlam Government 1972–1975.* Ringwood, Vic: Penguin
Whitton, E. (1980) 'White Hope of Parliamentary Democracy in Australia — Senate Committees, Televised', the *National Times*, 26 October–1 November
Whitwell, G. (1986) *The Treasury Line.* Sydney: Allen and Unwin
Wilenski, P. (1978) 'Labor and the Bureaucracy', in Duncan (1978b)
— (1986) *Public Power and Public Administration.* Sydney: Hale and Iremonger
— (1987) 'Can Governments Achieve Fairness? Two Views of Government and Society', in Coghill
Williams, K., Williams, J. and Thomas, D. (1983) *Why Are the British Bad at Manufacturing?* London: Routledge and Kegan Paul
—, Haslam, C., Williams, J., and Cutler, T. with Adcraft, A., and Johal, S. (1992) 'Against Lean Production', *Economy and Society*, 21 (3): 321–54
Willis, R., Minister for Industrial Relations (1988) *Labour Market Reform: The Industrial Relations Agenda,* Budget Paper 9. Canberra: AGPS
Wilson, P. (1972) *The Sexual Dilemma: Abortion, Homosexuality and the Criminal Threshold.* St Lucia: University of Queensland Press
— (1973) *Immigrants and Politics.* Canberra: ANU Press
Wiltshire, K. (1977) '"New Federalisms" the State Perspective', in Jaensch (1977b)

Womack, J, Jones D. and Roos, D. (1990) *The Machine that Changed the World*. New York: Rawson Associates.

Women's Bureau (1991) *Women and Work*, Spring. Canberra: DEET

Woodward, D. and Costar B., (1988) 'The National Party Campaign', in McAllister and Warhurst

Wootten, H. (1991) *New South Wales, Victoria and Tasmania*, Report of the Royal Commission into Aboriginal Deaths in Custody. Canberra: AGPS

World Commission on Environment and Development (1987) *Our Common Future*, the Brundtland Report. London: Oxford

Wright, C. (1991) 'Incentive Payment Systems in Australia', *Labour and Industry* 4 (1), March: 95–118

Wright, J. (1977) *The Coral Battleground*. Melbourne: Nelson

Wright, K. (1983) 'Union Demarcation Disputes: The Construction Industry' in Ford and Plowman

Yeatman, A. (1990) *Bureaucrats, Technocrats, Femocrats*. Sydney: Allen and Unwin

Young, E. (1988) 'Striving for Equity: Aboriginal Socio-economic Transformations and Development in the 1980s', *Geoforum* 19 (3): 295–306

Yu, P. (1993) 'Mabo: its Meaning for Aboriginal Australia', *Horizons* 2 (1): 16–17

Zines, Leslie (1991) *Constitutional Change in the Commonwealth*. Cambridge: Cambridge University Press

— (1992) 'The Commonwealth', in Craven

Subject Index*

Aboriginal Affairs, Department of 191
Aboriginal and Torres Strait Islander
   Commission (ATSIC) 191, 192
Aboriginal and Torres Strait Islander
   people 5, 182–201
   Australian Labor Party 14, 15–16
   Census 190, 195
   citizenship 182–201
   Coalition governments 199
   employment 193, 195–6, 288
   Eva Valley 201
   federalism 71, 72, 86
   Keating government 22
   police 187–8
   public sector recruitment and training 95
   reconciliation 199–200
   social movement politics 15–17
   social policy 188–93, 286
   social security 189, 195–6
   unemployment 288
   voting 189–90
   see also land rights, *Mabo* case, native common law title
Aboriginal Arts Board 193
Aboriginal Development Commission 191
Aboriginal Provisional Government 183, 184, 185, 193, 200
Aboriginal sovereignty 182–3, 200–1
Aboriginality 192–3
abortion 368, 370–2
Accord 14, 40, 99, 140–1, 171, 233, 287
   industry policy 234, 247–51, 260–1, 266–76
ACTU 14, 171, 219, 261–4
   ALP 139–40, 246, 270
   Accord 260, 266–7, 268
   formation and functions 261, 263
   industry policy 244–6, 252, 256, 258
   Migrant Workers' Conference 215
Administrative Appeals Tribunal 95, 124, 347
affirmative action, war veterans 90
age pension 281, 294
   see also retirement income

agencies, quasi-autonomous 73
agricultural trade 313–14
aid, overseas 305–6, 316, 318
air pollution 350
Alligator River 361
Antarctica 300, 303
ANZUS 358
apathy 154
arbitration 10, 73, 75, 76, 238, 259, 262–3, 274, 280
   see also industrial relations, trade unions
Arbitration Commission 10
arms
   control 306, 308
   exports 306
   see also chemical weapons, disarmament, Nuclear Disarmament Party
ASEAN 305, 319–20
Asia Pacific Economic Co-operation (APEC) 300, 302, 303, 314–16
Asia-Pacific region
   Dibb Report 311–12
   economic policy 224
   foreign affairs and trade 299, 300, 304–5, 309, 314–16, 318–21
   immigration 202–3, 206–7, 211–12
AUSSAT 339, 345
Australia Act 1986 (UK) 26, 28, 74
Australia Card legislation 127
Australia Council 193
Australia Day 182
Australian Assistance Plan 284, 285
Australian Broadcasting Authority (ABA) 338, 343
Australian Broadcasting Corporation (ABC) 213, 323–5, 345
Australian Broadcasting Tribunal (ABT) 334, 338–9, 341–3, 347, 383
Australian Capital Television v. *The Commonwealth* 23, 27–8, 37, 51, 53, 54, 55, 56–7

---

*Prepared by Patricia Holt

Australian Chamber of Manufactures 219
Australian Communist Party 6, 157
Australian Conservation Foundation 17,
    353–7, 363–4, 366–7
Australian Consolidated Press 327
    see also Packer media group
Australian Council of Social Service 85,
    296
Australian Democrats 148–50, 357–9
    electoral support 175–7, 179
    foreign policy 316
    legislation 116–18
    party politics 119
    veterans' hospitals 127
    see also class voting
Australian Environment Council 352
Australian Financial Review, New Right
    ideas 9
Australian Greens 358
Australian Heritage Commission 351,
    356
Australian Institute for Public Policy 9
Australian Institute of Multicultural Affairs
    209, 213, 214
Australian Labor Party (ALP) 3, 5, 6, 7,
    12–15, 84, 135, 136–41, 316, 334,
    337, 370
    Caucus 138, 304
    censorship 374, 375, 380
    environmental politics 357, 358
    industry policy 247–8
    land rights 198–9
    social democratic tradition 12–15,
        140–1
    social policy 12, 279, 283
    trade unions 259, 260
    see also class voting, foreign affairs and
        trade, industry policy, Labor
        governments, labour movements,
        labourism and labourist tradition,
        media policy, names of government
        leaders
Australian Manufacturing Council 246,
    251, 252, 270
Australian National Parks and Wildlife
    Service 351
Australian Penthouse 378
authoritarianism 6
aviation 64
award restructuring 246, 254, 256, 268,
    274–5

BHP 250
banks 108, 331
    nationalisation 166
    see also Westpac
Bank Nationalisation Case (1948) 35, 39
Barnard, Michael 18
Barron, Peter 326
Barwick, Sir Garfield 25, 43
Beazley, Kim 306, 311
Bell group 335
Bicentennial Authority 36
Bill of Rights 46–9, 51–2, 70
Bishop, Bronwyn 130
Bjelke-Petersen, Joh 146, 148
    foreign policy 309
    media policy 334
Black, Conrad 335
Black Power movement 16
Boilermakers' Case (1956) 43
Bond, Alan 328, 335, 343
bourgeoisie 4, 6
Bowen, Lionel 251
Brennan, Justice 34, 35, 38, 44, 46, 50, 52,
    53, 57, 184
British Colonial Office 74
British cultural and constitutional
    inheritance 64, 72–3, 182
    foreign affairs and trade 304, 310, 319
    immigration 202–4
    industry policy 241–3, 253
    liberal tradition 69–70
    New Right 18
    see also Imperial government,
        Westminster conventions
broadcasting 51, 117, 323–4
    assimilation policy 204
    ethnic 208–9
    FM 344
    Lyons government 44
    political broadcasting 51, 54–5
    SBS 209, 323–5
    see also media policy
Broadcasting Act 1942 338
Broadcasting Services Act 1992 117, 322,
    338–45
Brown, Bob 359, 360, 364
Brown, John 121–2
Bryant, Gordon 191
budgets 219, 225–7, 229, 231, 251, 257
Bureau of Immigration Research 214, 301
Bureau of Industry Economics 250

Burke, Edmund 5
Bush, George 303, 304
Business Council of Australia 86, 219, 247, 254
business interests, Liberal Party 143–5
Business Union Consultative Unit 251–2
Button, John 250
by-elections, 1992 151

Cabinet 89, 90, 93–4
   committees 93–5, 96
   foreign policy 304–5
   Hawke government and mega-departments 100–1
   see also Department of the Prime Minister and Cabinet, names of government leaders
Cain government, industry policy 252–3
Cairns, Jim 121, 122
Call to Australia Party 110, 151
Calwell, Arthur 203–4
Cambodia 300, 305, 319–20
Canada, industry policy 246–7
Canwest 331, 332, 335, 337
Capital TV Holdings 331
capitalism 3–8, 12
capital punishment 169
car industry 232–3, 250, 255
   Ford factory strike 208, 215
Car Plan 250
Casey, Ron 342
Cattlemen's Union 364
censorship 18, 368–82
Centre for Independent Studies 9
Chalk, Sir Gordon 91
chemical weapons 300, 303, 308
Chifley government 35, 262, 282
   impact on class voting 166
child care 11, 277, 280, 287, 291
   home child care allowance 297
child endowment 282
child support legislation 293
children
   censorship 374, 375, 378–9
   juvenile justice 280
   sexual abuse 378–9
   social policy 284–5, 291–4
   television 339, 341
   welfare 280
China, policy towards 301, 304, 307, 319–20

Chipp, Don 148, 375
citizenship 3–6, 70, 182–201, 202–8, 209
   social policy 279, 280, 287, 290, 296, 298
civil liberties 69–73
class 1–2, 18, 238, 278
   self-placement 153, 155, 158, 159
class voting 153–69, 171–2, 176, 179–81
   index of odds ratio 157, 162–7
Cleary, Phil 151
Codd, Michael 82
Cohen, Barry 357
Cold War 299, 307
   see also Soviet Union
Cole, Tony 249
Collins, Bob 130
colonialism, Australian 193–8
comics 373
Commonwealth Employment Service, 290
Commonwealth Grants Commission 75
Commonwealth of Australia Constitution Act 1900 24, 25, 26
Commonwealth-State Housing Agreement 85
Communist Party of Australia 6, 157, 179
Communist Party Case (1951) 41
Community Development Employment Projects 196
Community Services and Health, Department of 85
community services 85–6, 277, 283, 284, 286
competition 4, 12
   see also economic liberalism, economic rationalism
concurrent majorities, theory of 71–2
Confederation of Australian Industry 219
Connor, Rex 121, 122
consciousness raising 16
Conservation Councils 354
conservatism 2, 5, 17–20
   home ownership 158–9
   homosexuality 369–70
   new conservatives 8–12
   New Right 8–9
   sexual morality 2, 369–70
   theory of concurrent majorities 71–2
   see also Country Party, Liberal Party, National Party
Constitution 23–59, 62–4

see also federalism, Parliament
Constitution, Royal Commission on the (1929) 61
Consultative Development Committee 308
contraceptives 370, 371
Convention for the Protection of the World Cultural and Natural Heritage 309
Convention on Wetlands of International Importance 351
Conway, Ronald 5–6
Conzinc Riotinto Australia (CRA) 194
Coombs, H.C. 91, 95, 201
Coronation Hill 357, 361, 362
Corowa 356
corporatism 219, 241, 243–5, 260, 261
Cosser, Steve 331, 335, 337, 345
Costello, Peter 10
Council for Aboriginal Reconciliation Act 199
Council of Australian Governments 87
Council of Nature Conservation Ministers 352
Country Party 3, 7, 147
   see also National Party
Covenant on Civil and Political Rights 351
Crawford, Sir John 221, 223
Crean, Simon 269
'cultural location', and vote 170–1
cultural pluralism 197
cultural values 15–17
Curran investments 331, 335
Curtin government 74
   social policy 282
customs and excise 61
   pornography and censorship 368, 373
Customs and Excise Act 376–7

Daintree 361
Dawkins, John 308
Dawson, Justice 23, 36, 40, 41, 45–6, 51
Deakin, Alfred 5, 61
Deane, Justice 23, 34, 35, 37, 43, 44, 45, 46, 47, 52
decentralisation, administrative 77–8, 83–4
defence, expenditure 312, 318
   High Court 41
   intelligence information 303–4
   new Australian militarism 311–12
Defence, Department of 305–6, 310–11
democracies, capitalist state 3–8
democracy 50–1

Public Service 97
see also sovereignty
Democratic Labor Party
   foreign policy 307
   electoral support 159, 161, 163, 165, 177, 180
   Parliament 110
Democratic Socialist Party 359
dependent spouse rebate 297
deregulation 11
   finance 81, 219, 281, 316
   foreign exchange 316
   industry policy 240, 243, 245–6, 248–50, 252–3, 256
   labour market 11
   media 325–6
   stock exchanges 219
   see also economic liberalism, economic rationalism, free trade, regulation
development cooperation, overseas 305–6, 316, 318
Development Import Finance Facility 318
Dibb Report 310–11
Dictation Test 202, 206
Directorate of Industrial Relations Development 252
disabilities, people with
   public sector recruitment and training 95
   social policy 277, 280
disarmament 304, 305, 306, 308
   see also arms, chemical weapons, Nuclear Disarmament Party
Disarmament, Ambassador for 308
displaced persons 203–4
dole bludging 240
Dominion status 74
Dries 11, 143–4, 238
dumping 249
Dunstan government 92, 94, 371, 376, 377

Earth Summit 350
ecologically sustainable development 362, 363
economic diplomacy 312–18
economic liberalism 4, 8–12, 21–22
   Industries Assistance Commission 248–9
   industry policy 235–7, 242–3, 253
   new conservatism 17–19
Economic Planning Advisory Council 248, 269, 270

economic rationalism 1, 19–20, 218, 220–2, 224–5, 227, 230, 232, 233, 245–6, 249
  foreign investment 316, 317
  labour movements 245–6, 270
  Senior Executive Service 98–100
  see also industry policy
education 7, 19, 64, 83, 139, 284, 287
  migrants 204, 206, 207, 208
  see also English language education, skills
elections, federal 164, 166, 175, 176, 177, 178, 179
  1940s: 163
  1949: 166
  1950s: 145, 163
  1960s: 145, 163
  1972: 3, 143, 163–4, 165
  1974: 165
  1975: 13, 79, 96, 137, 143, 148
  1977: 13, 96, 148
  1980s: 137
  1983: 14, 141–2, 148, 171, 218, 253, 260, 287, 357, 359–60
  1984: 142, 165, 174, 327, 358
  1987: 142, 145, 146
  1990: 137, 150, 357, 359
  1993: 12, 20, 21, 87, 137, 142, 150–1, 151, 221, 287
  New South Wales 1988 141–2, 151
  Queensland 1989 137, 148, 151
  Victoria 1992 142
  see also by-elections, free speech, voting
Elliot, John 145
employment
  Aboriginal and Torres Strait Islander people 193, 195–6, 288
  Accord 14, 267
  Australian Labor Party 13
  class 238
  economic policy 222, 223, 225–7
  industry policy 245, 248, 253
  Keynes, John Maynard 7
  labour market programs 195–6
  media industry 336, 337
  social policy 279–82, 288–90, 298
  Victoria 253
  see also unemployment
endangered species 354–5, 357, 367
Engineers' Case (1920) 32, 33, 35, 55, 63, 64

English language education 204, 206, 208, 213, 215
enterprise bargaining 256, 268, 272–3, 275
Environment and Conservation, Department of the 352
Environment Protection (Impact of Proposals) Act 1974 352, 362
Environment Protection Agency 362, 363
environmental politics 17, 150–1
  Coalition governments 321
  devolution of power 86
  election issues 353–4, 356–60
  international law 351
  policy 233
equal employment opportunity 17, 95, 96, 97–8
equality of opportunity 13, 48, 284
Ethnic Communities Councils 208, 210, 213
Evatt, H.V. 47, 301
export markets 239, 315
  see also trade
external affairs power 34–5, 64, 74, 280, 309, 351–2, 365–6

factions
  ALP 137–9
  Liberal Party 144
Fairfax group 327, 329–37
family-centred values
  New Right 10–11
  social movement politics 15–17
farmland, environmental politics 363–4
fascism 1
federal institutions 67–8
federalism
  civil liberties 69–73
  definition and critiques 60–9
  dual 82–3
  fiscal 64–7, 74–5, 83–7
  liberty 69–73
Federation 24–7
Federation of Australian Commercial Television Stations 338–9
Federation of Australian Radio Broadcasters 338–9
feminism
  anti-pornography 378–81
  Australian Labor Party 14
  censorship 378–81

Index 427

social policy 15–17, 280–1
Festival of Light 339, 378
Field government 130, 359
Fightback! 12, 144, 146, 233, 253, 268, 287, 290, 292, 297
Fiji 311
film censorship 368, 373, 375, 379
Finance, Department of 96, 100–1, 192, 219, 250
FitzGerald, Stephen 319
'flexible specialisation' 254–5
food products 83, 87
Ford factory strike 208, 215
'Fordism' 254–5
foreign affairs and trade 299–321
   Department of 300, 304–6, 311
   environmental issues 299, 348–67
   policy 300–9
   overseas aid program 305–6, 316, 318
   see also external affairs powers
foreign debt 257
foreign exchange regulations 316
foreign investment 243, 317
Foreign Investment Review Board 316, 334
forests 353, 354, 355, 357
   see also World Heritage
Franklin Dam Case (1983) 30, 34–5, 36
Fraser, Malcolm 143
   economic rationalism 1–2, 20
   federal policies 78
   media policy 334
   'sentimental traditionalism' 20
Fraser government 142, 218
   Car Plan 250
   economic policy 143, 227, 231
   environment 354
   executive government 96–7
   foreign policy 304, 310
   immigration 208–12
   media policy 328, 334, 344, 345
   ministerial responsibility 121–2
   new federalism 79–80, 84
   New Right 11
   social policy 285–7, 291
   South Africa 301, 304
Fraser Island 352, 354–5
free trade 3, 241, 246, 250, 313
freedom of information legislation 95, 124
Freedom to Read Association 374

freedom of speech 23–4, 27–8, 36–40, 46, 49–57
   see also civil liberties, 'free speech' cases, censorship
Fullagar, Sir Wilfred 41, 42
funeral benefits 283

Garland, Vic. 121
Garrett, Peter 355, 358
Gaudron, Justice 37–8, 45, 46, 49–50, 52–7
gay liberation 370
   see also homosexuality, sexual morality
gender, social policy 15–17, 278
   see also feminism, women
General Agreement on Tariffs and Trade (GATT) 300, 313–14
   Cairns Group 313
Gordon Dam 80
Gorton government 76, 93–4
   environment 351
Goss, Wayne, land rights 199
Governor-General 24
Grassby, Al 207, 208
Great Barrier Reef 351, 352, 354–5
Green Alliance 359
Green Bans 352
Green Independents 353, 357–9, 362
Green parties 110, 119, 150–1, 353, 350, 356–60, 364
Greenhouse Effect 355, 357
Greenpeace 354, 356, 366–7
Greiner, Nick 130
Greiner government 81–4
Gross Domestic Product 237
Guam Doctrine 310
Guilfoyle, Margaret 286
Gulf War 303, 304, 319
Gyngell, Bruce 342

H.R. Nicholls Society 10
handicapped child's allowance 284–5
Hare-Clark electoral system 359
Harrison, Kate 344–5
Hawke government
   Aboriginal and Torres Strait Islander affairs 191
   Australia Card legislation 127
   censorship 379
   class voting effect 167
   economic policy 217–33

environment 351, 357–8, 361–3
executive government 97–8, 100–1
federalism 80–87
foreign affairs and trade 300, 304–8, 313–16, 318–19
immigration 209–10, 212–13
industry policy 235, 245–6, 257–8
land rights 183, 191, 194, 199
media policy 322, 324–30, 334–5, 337–9, 341–3, 345
ministerial responsibility 121–2
social policy 281, 287–98
Hayden, Bill
 class voting effect 167
 foreign policy 305, 311
 media policy 334
Hay, Andrew 10
Heads of Governments (HOGs) meetings 84
health 7, 81, 83, 85
 Aboriginal and Torres Strait Islander people 190
 Liberal government 7
 social policy 282, 284, 287
Hewson, John 11–12, 144
 Accord 261
 class voting effect 167
 economic liberalism 11–12, 20, 221
 foreign policy 302
 social policy 296–7
 see also Fightback!
Hielscher, Sir Leo 91
High Court of Australia 24, 30
 Constitution and Commonwealth powers 62–4
 legislation and judiciary 31–42
 see also external affairs power, *Mabo*
Holmes à Court, Robert 328, 331–3, 335
home ownership, effect on voting 158–9, 168
homosexuality 16, 368–70
 legislation on 371–3
 public sector recruitment and training 95
hospitals 78, 80, 127, 282
Houlihan, Paul 10
housing 7, 81, 83, 85, 283
 Aboriginal and Torres Strait Islander people 190
Howard, John 2, 144
 immigration 212
 media policy 334

New Right 11
Hughes, Billy 301
human rights
 Asia region 320
 Constitution 43–4, 46–7
 Covenant on Civil and Political Rights 351
Hyde, John 9

ideology 1–3, 140
 Aboriginality 192–3
 Liberal Party 142–4
 sexual politics 369–71
immigration 5, 202–16
 assimilation 15, 16
 citizenship 202–8, 204–7
 foreign policy 306
 intakes 7, 73, 210–11
 see also migrants
Immigration (and Ethnic Affairs), Department of 206–8
Immigration, Local Government and Ethnic Affairs, Department of 306
Immigration Restriction Act 1901 202
Independents 130, 133, 151–2
 see also Green Independents
industrial democracy 12, 251, 274
 Public Service 97–8
industrial issues 259, 262
industrial relations 254, 259, 260
 disputation 1970s 208, 215, 230
 see also Accord, arbitration, labour movements, trade unions
Industrial Relations Commission 38–9, 266–8, 272
Industries Assistance Commission 248, 270
Industries Commission 249
industry policy 8, 76, 223, 234–58, 264, 270–3
 seeding capital 244, 247, 252
 Victoria 252–3
 Yellow Book 237
 see also Accord, deregulation, economic policy, tariffs
Industry, Technology and Commerce, Department of 250–1
inflation 8, 240
Institute of Public Affairs 7
interest groups 73
 economic policy 218–20, 225
 environment 349, 364

Index 429

foreign policy 308–9
media policy 338–9
see also names of peak bodies
Intergovernmental Agreement on the Environment 366
International Centre for the Study of the Preservation and Restoration of Cultural Property 351
International Convention on the Elimination of All Forms of Racial Discrimination 186, 309
International Council of Monuments and Sites 351
International Union for Conservation of Nature and Natural Resources 351
Interstate Commission 249
invalidity insurance 281
Iraq 303, 304, 319
Irish immigrants 202, 203
Isaacs, Sir Isaac 32, 48
issue voting 154–5, 163, 167–73
Italian Workers' Organisation 208

Jackson Committee 223, 224
Japan
 foreign affairs and trade 301, 313–14
 industry policy 240, 241, 242, 244–5, 249, 253, 255–6
 social policy 245
Jensen, Jens 121
Job Search Allowance 290
Jobs, Education and Training Scheme (JETS) 292
Johnston, Elliott 184
Joint Committee on Foreign Affairs and Defence 307
journalists 2, 9, 18
jobs 336, 337
jury, trial by 46, 47
juvenile justice 280

Kakadu National Park 351, 357, 361
Keating, Michael 219
Keating, Paul
 ACTU 246, 268, 270
 Asia, relations with 304
 expenditure restraint 81
 industry policy 249
 leadership ambitions 82, 86, 87
 tax devolution 86
Keating government 22

class voting effect 167
economic policy 20, 217–33
environment 359–60, 363–4
foreign affairs and trade 300, 304
legislation and parliamentary politics 117, 119
media policy 322–47
native title legislation 191–2, 194–5, 199–200
One Nation 231
social policy 281
Kelty, Bill 1, 246
Keynesianism 7, 8, 225–6, 227–9
Koowarta Case 309, 351
Korea
 industry policy 242, 249
 trade 313
Kroger, Michael 145

Labor-Green Accord 359
Labour and Immigration, Department of 207–8
labour movements 5, 6, 138, 238–46
labourism and labourist tradition 12–14, 140–1, 238–9, 253, 257–8, 260–1, 263
laissez-faire 4, 7
Lake Pedder 352, 353, 359
Land Councils 183, 196, 201
land degradation 364
land distribution 5
land rights 15, 22, 183–5, 191, 193–6, 198–9
land use 350
Lang, Jack 291
Lang Labor 176, 177, 179
law and order 4
Laws, John 342
Leeth v. *The Commonwealth* (1992) 33, 45–6, 49, 52
Left 1, 2, 18, 19, 157
 multiculturalism 212–13
 see also class voting, names of Left parties
legislation 114–19
 Acts Interpretation Act 1901 126
 delegated 125–8
 judiciary 34–42
 see also Parliament, Senate
Liberal Party 141–6
 identity 178–9
 see also class voting, Coalition,

430 Index

conservatism, Fightback!, names of Liberal Party leaders and politicians
liberalism 370
   British tradition 69–70
   censorship 375–7, 380
   developmental 5
   Liberal Party 80
   see also economic liberalism, social liberalism
libertarianism 2
   censorship 374–6, 380
   federalism 69–73, 85
   social liberalism 22
Lindsay, Greg 9
Literature Board of Review (Qld) 378
Literature Censorship Board 374
Literature Review Board (Qld) 373
Little Desert 352
living standards 238–40, 253
Loan Council 65, 81
local government
   devolution 84
   relations with Commonwealth 78, 81
   untied grants 78–9
Lowy, Frank 335
Lynch, Phillip 121, 122
Lyons government 94
   media policy 344
   social policy 281

Mabo 22, 184, 186, 194, 200
McMahon government 283
Mack, Ted 151
MacKellar, Michael 121, 208–9
McLachlan, Alexander 121
McLachlan, Ian 10
McPhee, Ian 334
majoritarian politics 134–5, 146–7
majorities, concurrent 71–2
Malaysia 310
Management Improvement, Task Force on 88
managerialism 76, 82, 83, 87
   executive government 97–101
   industry policy 254
Mansell, Michael 193, 200, 201
manufacturing industries, *see* industry policy
marriage bar 90, 92
Marxism 1–2, 5, 6, 236
   colonialism 193–7

maternity allowances 282
Media and Entertainment Alliance 338–9
media, ministerial resignations 122
media policy 322–47
   cultural identity 346
   foreign language publications 204–5
   inquiry into print media 337–8
   interest groups 338–9
   ownership 322, 327–8
   regulation of content 324–5
   television ownership 327–37
   two station rule 328, 330
media releases, legislation by 114–15
Medibank 371
Medicare 139
   abortion 368
Melbourne Corporation v. *The Commonwealth* (1947) 32–3
Menzies, Sir Robert 7, 92, 142, 144, 145
Menzies government 163
   executive government 91–2, 94
   social welfare 282
Metal Trades Industry Association 272
metal trades unions 244, 245, 271
Metherell, Terry 130
microwave licences 345
Middle East
   migrant politics 215–16
Migrant Education Action Group 208
migrants
   guardianship of children 48
   industrial relations 208, 215
   political activism 205, 208, 213, 214–16
   voting 214–16
   see also English language education, immigration, multiculturalism
military bases 358
Miller v. *TCN Channel Nine* (1986) 48, 49, 51–2
Milne, Christine 362
mining industry
   environmental politics 354
   exports 239
   land rights 183, 194, 199
   see also Coronation Hill, sand mining, uranium mining
ministerial code of conduct 124
ministerial councils 64
ministerial power and responsibility 92–4, 96–7, 102–5, 119–24

Hawke government 97–101
monarchy 4, 169
Moore, Tim 130
morality, moral and cultural values debate 15–19
   see also homosexuality, sexual morality, social morality
Morling, Justice 347
motor vehicle industry 250, 255
   economic policy 232–3
   Ford factory strike 208, 215
multiculturalism 16, 202, 209, 212–14
   Aboriginal and Torres Strait Islander people 185–6
   Quadrant 18
Murdoch, Sir Keith 344
Murdoch media group 325–37, 347
Murphy, Lionel 51
   Bill of Rights 47–9
   censorship 376–7
   Senate standing committee system 116
Murphyores Case 352
Murray-Darling Basin 363–5
MX missile testing 304

NATO 299
National Aboriginal Advisory Committee 191
National Aboriginal Conference 191
National Aboriginal Islander Legal Services Secretariat 182
National Development Fund 271
National Economic Summit 219
National Environment Protection Agency (NEPA) 350–1
National Estate Committee 353
National Farmers' Federation 364
National Food Authority 83, 87
national interests 302–3
National Party 20, 146, 147–8, 178
   conservatism 370
   media policy 328, 329, 334
   see also Country Party
National Rail Corporation 83, 86, 87
National Soil Conservation Program 364
National Trust 354
National Wage Cases 262–3, 266–7
National Welfare Fund 282
nationalisation 7, 35, 166
Nationalists 142, 177–8
Nationality and Citizenship Act 189

Nationwide News Pty Ltd v. *Wills* 23, 28, 38–40, 52, 57
Nelson Tjakamara, Michael 193
New Administrative Law 95
New Class 18
New Right 8–12, 17–19
   economic policy 268
   federalism 66
   social policy 287, 297
   see also conservatism, Right
newspapers
   Commonwealth powers 328
   Inquiry into the Print Media 337–8
   Murdoch, Sir Keith 344
   ownership 327, 330–8
   see also media policy, names of newspaper magnates, publications
Newstart 290
'nightwatchman state' 4
Nile, Rev. Fred 151
Nixon, Richard 310
nuclear disarmament 306, 308
   see also disarmament
Nuclear Disarmament Party 174, 308, 355, 358, 359

OECD 241
   industry policy 240
   social welfare 277, 279, 285
obscenity laws 377
   see also censorship
Office for the Environment 351
Office of Multicultural Affairs 214
Office of National Assessments 303–4
Ombudsman 95, 124
Opperman, Sir Herbert 207
Optus 339
orphans' pensions 284–5
overseas aid 316, 318
Oz 374
ozone depletion 355

Pacific Islanders 5
Packer media group 325–35
Page, Sir Earle 65
Papua New Guinea 300
Parliament
   bi-cameralism 136
   censure motions 123
   committees 307
   foreign policy 304–7

gong 114–5
Public Service scrutiny 124–9
Question Time 122, 307
ratification of treaties 303
reform 106, 108–9
sitting time 115
see also democracy, legislation, Senate
Parliamentary Secretaries Act 1980 96
party identification 156, 170, 173–4, 178, 180–1
party system 2–3, 134–6
effect on Parliament 107–13, 119
minor parties 146–51, 175
Patmore, Peter 130
Payroll Tax Case (1971) 25
Peace Research Centre 308
Peacock, Andrew 144
Penthouse 378
Playboy 373, 375
Playford, Sir John 90
pluralism
cultural 197
federalism 70
protected pluralism 73, 76, 79
see also multiculturalism
police, and Aborigines 187–8
political activism 1, 3–6, 15–17
environment 349
migrants 213, 214–16
political broadcasting 51, 54–5
see also freedom of press, freedom of speech
political socialisation 154, 172
see also Liberal Party, National Party
pollution 350, 363–4
Polyukhovich v. *The Commonwealth* (1991) 44, 46, 49
pornography 368, 371, 375, 377–81
anti-censorship 373–6
censorship and regulation 18, 374–7
child sexual abuse 378–9
conservatism 369–70
feminism 378–81
liberalism 370
Portnoy's Complaint 376
Porter, Michael 9
'post-Fordism' 254–5
post-war reconstruction
industry policy 239
social policy 282–3
trade unions 262

Post-war Reconstruction, Department of 91
poverty 289
Henderson Report 283, 292
Marxism 6
migrants 206
social policy 277, 279
sole parents 292
see also social liberalism, unemployment
pragmatism 1
ALP 137, 139
Liberal Party 20, 142–3
new federalism 76
Premiers' Conference 84
pressure groups
see interest groups
Prime Minister and Cabinet, Department of the 82, 85, 100–2, 104–5, 214, 250
Prime Ministers, foreign policy 303–5
Priorites Review Staff 95
prisons, privatisation of 10
privatisation 10, 220
Privy Council 33, 74
productivity 268, 272
proletariat 6
prostitution 368–73
protectionism 3, 35–6
industry policy 8, 75, 76, 244, 264
trade 241, 244, 245, 249, 270
see also tariffs
Protectionist Party 5, 179
public choice theory 9, 66–7
Public Service 88–105
'Americanisation' 101, 105
Aboriginal and Torres Strait Islander people 184, 191–2
Commissions of Inquiry 93
economic ideas 224–9
economic policy 218
equity 95, 97–8
Fraser government 286
marriage bar 90
mega-departments 99–101
NESB recruitment and training 95
parliamentary scrutiny 124–9
reform 82, 93–4, 97–101
Whitlam government and economic policy 224–5
see also names of Departments, Senior Executive Service
Public Service Board 100, 102, 105
Public Service Reform Act 1984 97–8

Quintex 328, 331, 335, 343
Quadrant
 multiculturalism 18
 New Right ideas 9, 18
 'sentimental traditionalism' 20
quality of life, Whitlam government 284

Racial Discrimination Act 1975 184
racism
 social movement politics 15–17
 television 342
rape 368
Reagan, Ronald 8
reconciliation
 Aboriginal 199–200
 national 218–19
referenda 26–8
refugees 203–4, 205, 209, 211, 306
regulation 7
 media 345–6
 television 323–6, 339–43
 wages 14
 welfare state 8
 see also censorship, economic policy, deregulation
rehabilitation services 282
Reid Inquiry 97
Resource Assessment Commission 361–3
resource conservation 348
 see also environmental politics
Resource Security Bill 119
resources 247
retirement income 281, 294–6
Review of Commonwealth Government Administration 97
Ricardian trade theory 248
Richardson, Graham 121–2, 123, 124, 357, 360
Right 2, 8
 multiculturalism 213
 New Right 8–9
rights, implied 46–9
 see also civil citizenship, liberties, freedom of speech, human rights
Royal Commission into Aboriginal Deaths in Custody 187, 192, 195
Royal Commission on Australian Government Administration 95–6

salinity 363–5
sand mining 352, 354–5

Scandinavian countries, labour movements 241–2
Security and Co-operation in Asia, Conference on 319
Senate 109
 adult suffrage 109
 committee system 115–19, 125–9
 elections 173–5
 Estimates Committees 125
 Green parties 360
 Joint Committee on Foreign Affairs and Defence 307
 powers 111
 Queensland 108
 Standing Committee on Regulations and Ordinances 125–9
 states 109–10
 Supply Bills, 1975 111
 voting systems 113
Senior Executive Service 97–8, 101
 economic rationalism 98–100
 Metherell, Terry 130
separation of powers 24, 42–6
sex shops 376
sexual abuse 378–80
sexual behaviour, decriminalisation 371, 372
sexual harassment 368
sexual liberation movements 370
sexual morality 2, 370
 conservatism 369–70
 social movement politics 15–17
sexual violence, censorship and pornography 375, 378–80
sickness benefit 282, 285
Sinclair, Ian 121, 122, 123, 334
Skase, Christopher 328, 330–1, 343
skills
 immigration 206, 210
 see also education
slavery 46, 48, 71
Snedden, Billy 206
Snowy Mountains Hydro-electric Scheme 7
social democratic tradition 258
 Australian Labor Party 12–13, 14, 140–1
social insurance 279–80, 281, 287
social justice, competition 12
social liberalism 4–5, 22
 economic liberalism 8–15
 post-war consensus 6–8

Wets 11
Wilenski, Peter 14
social movement politics 3–6, 15–17
social policy 277–98
   Accord 99
   Coalition views 279, 281, 283, 285–7, 290–2, 296–7
   Japan 245
   local communities 284
   social insurance 279–80
   trade protection 238–9
   'wage earner security' 242, 249
social protection 280–1
social security 282
   Aboriginal and Torres Strait Islander people 189, 190–1, 195–6
   aged care 277, 280, 282
   economic policy 227
   income support 277, 280–1
   Liberal governments 7, 282, 286–7
   sole parents 291–4
   see also child support, retirement income, unemployment, welfare, welfare state
Social Security Review Discussion Paper 289–90, 295
social work services 280
socialism 6
sole parents 291–4
South Africa, Fraser government 301, 304
South Pacific, foreign affairs and trade 299–300, 311
South-West (Tasmanian) Wilderness 353
Southeast Asia
   human rights and foreign policy 319–20
   see also Asia-Pacific region
sovereignty
   Aborigines 182–3, 200–1
   federalism 62–4, 67, 69–70
   popular 23–33, 42, 60, 66–7
Soviet Union 299, 304, 305, 307, 312, 320
special benefit 282
Special Broadcasting Service (SBS) 209, 213, 323–4
stagflation 8
standard of living 238, 253
   trade 239–40
State, the 2, 3–8
   economic liberalism 8–15, 19–20
   post-war consensus 7
state governments

foreign policy 309
   industry 238, 239
   power of Premiers 92–3
   regulation of sexuality 368, 371
   social policy 280
   see also executive government, federalism, Federation, names of Premiers
State Labor 179
state upper houses 109–13
'states' rights' 61–2, 79, 81
   see also Constitution, federalism, sovereignty
Statute of Westminster 1931 26, 74
Steel Industry Authority 250
Steel Plan 250, 251, 271
stock exchanges 219
Stokes, Kerry 328, 330, 331, 335
Street, Sir Laurence 49
strikes
   Ford factory 208, 215
suburbanisation, and voting 158–9
Sunraysia 331
superannuation 139, 294–5
Supply Bills 1975 111
supporting mother's benefit 284–5, 291
   see also social security

Taiwan 319
Tariff Board 248
tariffs 8, 19–20, 75–6, 82, 139, 143–4, 230, 238–40, 249–53, 264, 270, 271, 300, 313–14
   see also industry policy
Task Force on Management Improvement 88, 104
Tasmanian Dam Case 309
Tasmanian Green Independents
   see Green Independents
taxation
   Commonwealth power 61, 64, 65, 80
   devolution of power 86
   federalism 61, 75, 80, 87
   income tax 65, 79
   National Welfare Fund 282
   wages 246
   see also Accord, *Fightback!*
Telecom 339
telecommunications
   Commonwealth power 64
   micro-economic reform 345

Index 435

privatisation 10
'summitry' and, 303
television 51
    advertising 336, 340–1, 345
    cable 336, 344, 345
    children and violence 339, 341
    colour 344
    content regulation 341–2, 345
    media policy 322–47
    ownership 327–37
    pay TV 117, 322, 323, 338, 343–5
    regulation 323–6, 341–2
    see also names of media organisations
Textile, Clothing and Footwear Plan 251, 271
textile industry 232–3
Tharunka 374
Thatcher, Margaret 8
Theodore, Ted 121
Tiananmen Square massacre 211, 319
tied grants 64, 77–9
Tjakamara, Michael Nelson 193
Toyne, Phillip 355–6
trade 251, 252, 312–18
    Asia-Pacific region 318–20
    dominion status and powers 74
    European 313–4
    exports 239
    interstate 35–6
    protection 73, 238, 241, 244, 245, 249, 270
    standard of living 239–40
    see also foreign affairs and trade
Trade, Department of 280–1
Trade and Industry, Department of 221
Trade Development Council 244, 251–2, 270
Trade Negotiations Advisory Group 308
Trade Practices Commission 334, 335
trade unions 259–76
    Australian Labor Party, 11–12, 139–40
    company and workplace issues 264–5, 273–5
    economic policy 232–3
    environment 354
    industry policy 238–9, 245–8, 251
    issue voting 169, 170–3
    job protection 265
    membership 259
    migrant issues 215
    New Right 10

power 171, 263–5, 274–5
response to New Right 14
socialism 6
see also ACTU, labour movements, industrial relations
transport 75
    privatisation 10
    rail services 83, 86, 87
Transport and Communications, Department of 339, 342, 343
Treasury 85, 96, 270
    economic policy 221–4, 225, 226
    EPAC 248
    IAC 248–9
    industry policy 250, 254

Uhrig, John 248–9
unemployment 19, 220, 269
    Aboriginal and Torres Strait Islander people 190, 195–6
    Depression, 1930s 7
    economic policy 222, 223, 225–7, 227, 231, 232
    industrialisation 237
    industry policy 240, 253
    social insurance 281
    social policy 277, 282, 286, 288–90
    stagflation 8
    trade unions 266
    Victoria 253
unemployment benefit 282, 285, 289
United Australia Party 142, 144, 176, 178, 179, 281
United media group 332, 333
United Nations 301
    Earth Summit 350
    environment conventions 309, 352
    Iraq 303, 304
United Nations Working Group on Indigenous Populations 186
United States of America
    Bill of Rights 46–7
    foreign affairs and trade 299, 300–5, 307, 310–11, 313–14, 319, 320–1
    industry policy 240, 241–3, 255
United Tasmania Group 353
united grants, local government 78–9
uranium mining 352, 358
Urban and Regional Development, Department of 286
urban planning 77, 78, 79

urban pollution 363–4, 366
'user pays' 286

Valentine, Jo 150, 308, 358
Victorian Economic Development Corporation 252
Victorian Investment Corporation, 252
Victorian Salinity Program 364–5
videocassette recorders 336
videos, censorship of 380
Vietnam
    foreign policy 319–20
    immigration 209, 211
Vietnam War 307, 310
    electoral politics 163, 165, 167, 169
violence
    domestic 368, 369
    pornography and censorship 375, 378, 380
    television 339, 341
voting 28
    Aboriginal and Torres Strait Islander people 189–90
    adult suffrage (upper houses) 109
    car ownership 168
    Catholics 180
    class 153–67
    geography 180
    home ownership 158–9, 168
    migrants 203, 205, 208, 214–16
    preferences 149, 356–7
    public choice theory 66–7
    Senate vs. House of Representatives, 156, 173–75
    'two-party preferred', 135
    upper houses 113
    volatility 153, 155–6, 173–9
    women, 368, 369
    see also elections, issue voting, referendums

'wage earner security' 242, 249
wages 20, 259, 268–9, 272
    Accord 14, 99
    Australian Labor Party 13
    economic policy 230
    industry policy 238–9, 246
    regulation 10
    social policy 280–1
    tariff reductions 20
    see also Accord, award restructuring, National Wage Cases

Wainwright, J. W. 90
war, power to declare 74
war crimes legislation 44
war veterans
    affirmative action 90
    hospitals, 127
Warsaw Pact 299
wartime government, Curtin 74
wealth creation 236–7
    economic liberalism 236
welfare
    colonialism 188–93, 195–6, 200
    'domestic compensation' 241–2
    economic policy 227, 249
    Liberal Party 142
    migrants 206
    new federalism 85
    New Right 10
    state 2, 7, 8, 277–80
    trade unions 14
    see also social policy, social security
Wesley Vale pulp mill 353, 359, 361–2
Western Port Bay 352
Westminster conventions 64, 72–3, 89, 90, 91–2
Westpac 331, 335, 337, 345
Wets 11, 238
Wheeler, Sir Frederick 91–2
White Australia policy 75, 202, 203–4, 207, 238
Whitlam government
    censorship 375–7
    class voting effect 163, 165, 173
    economic policy 224–5, 230–1
    environment 351–3
    executive government 94–6
    foreign policy 301, 304
    immigration 206–8
    industry 248–9, 264
    land rights 15, 198
    media policy 344
    ministerial responsibility 121–2
    new federalism 76–9, 84
    reform 8, 12–15
    social policy 279, 283–5
    Supply Bills, 1975 111
    trade unions, 262
    urban policies 78, 79
widow's pensions 282, 291–2
Wik people 194
Wilderness Society 354, 356–7

Wilshire, Ted 251
Withers, Reg 121
women 370
  anti-pornography 378–81
  Australian Labor Party 15–17
  discrimination 48, 368
  division of labour 11
  domestic violence 368, 369
  employment 289
  homosexuality 371
  Liberal Party 145
  public sector recruitment and training 95
  marriage bar 90, 92
  sexual abuse 369
  social liberalism 5
  sexual violence 378, 379
  social policy 249, 289, 291, 297
  sole parents 291–4
  temperance 369
  voting 368, 369
  see also child care; feminism
Women's Electoral Lobby 17
women's movement 370
  consciousness raising 16
  Whitlam government 3, 15–17
Woolloomooloo 352
working class
  labourist tradition 12–13
  Marxism 6
  see also Australian Labor Party, class, class voting, labour movement
World Heritage Convention 352, 353
World Heritage List 351, 357
World War II, ALP government 7
World Wide Fund for Nature 354, 356
Wran government
  land rights, 199

Young, Mick 121, 122

Author Index*

Aarons, M. 205, 383
Aboriginal Provisional Government 182–3, 193, 383
Administrative Review Council, 129, 383
Aitkin, D. 108, 147, 155, 157, 159, 161, 165, 169–72, 174, 176, 178–80, 208, 383
Aldons, M 108, 116, 118, 383
Alford, R.R. 156–7, 160–1, 163, 383
Allan, L. 205, 384
Allen, J. 369, 384
Altman, D. 15–16, 368, 370, 384
Altman, J. C. 196, 384
Anderson, K. 249, 384
Appleyard, R. T. 283, 384
Archer, R. 260, 384
Argument, S. 125–6, 128-9, 384
Armstrong, M. 323, 384
Ascui, A. 171, 408
Audretsch, D. 242, 384
Australia and New Zealand Environment and Conservation Council 365, 384
Australian Conservation Foundation 355, 383
Australian Council of Trade Unions 234, 246, 266, 271, 273, 383
Australian Council of Trade Unions/Trade Development Council 242, 244–5, 254, 256, 269–71, 383
Australian Council on Population and Ethnic Affairs 212, 385
Australian Journalists Association 336, 385
Australian Labor Party/Australian Council of Trade Unions 234, 246–7, 267–8, 384
Australian Manufacturing Council, 246–7, 385
Ayres, P. 286–7, 385

Bacon, W. 370, 374, 385
Barbalet, J. M. 147, 385
Barnard, A. 67, 388
Barnard, M. 18
Barwick, G. 25, 31, 43, 385

Battin, T. 140, 232, 385, 407
Beacroft, L. 194, 409
Bean, C. 136, 150, 174, 176, 357, 385, 408
Beckett, J. 188–90, 193, 385
Behrens, W. W. 350, 409
Beilharz, P. 4–6, 287, 293, 385
Bell, C. 216, 310, 385
Bell, D. 1, 386
Bell, S. 249–51, 386
Bennett, S. 107, 109, 112, 136, 386
Benson, J. 265, 386
Bergin, A. 307, 386
Bernstam, M. S. 292, 419
Berry, P. 266, 386
Bertrand, I. 373, 386
Betts, K. 213, 386
Birrell, R. 209–11, 386
Birrell, T. 209–11, 386
Black, D. 108, 111, 386
Blainey, G. 212–13, 386
Blandy, R. 143, 403
Blewett, N. 14, 386
Bolton, G. 108, 386
Bonyhady, T. 353, 386
Boreham, P. 248, 386
Borrie, W. 202, 207, 386
Bottomley, G. 215, 386
Bowman, D. 344, 386
Bowman, M. 335, 386
Bramble, T. 276, 387
Bray, M. 260, 274, 387
Brennan, D. 287, 387
Brennan, F. 183, 192, 199, 200, 387
Brennan, Geoffrey 9, 66, 70, 76, 387
Brennan Gerald 23, 34–5, 38, 44–6, 50, 52–3, 57, 184
Brereton, J. 350, 421
Brett, J. 11–12, 20, 22, 143, 387
Broom, L. 159, 387
Brown, A. 325, 328, 330, 338, 345, 387
Brown, N. 344
Bryson, L. 281, 292, 387

---
*Prepared by Judy Cole

Index 439

Buchanan, J. 8, 9, 66–7, 70, 76, 387
Burchell, D. 141, 387
Bureau of Industry Economics 241, 386
Bureau of Transport and Communication Economics 343, 387
Burgess, J. 273, 387
Burgmann, V. 16, 387
Burke, T. 84, 413
Burns, C. 155, 167, 388
Burrow, J. W. 70, 388
Burton, T. 127, 388
Business Council of Australia 86, 272, 387
Butler, D. 155, 387
Butlin, N. 67, 387
Button, J. 107, 388, 393

Caiden, G. E. 92, 388
Calhoun, J. C. 71–2
Callus, R. 275, 388
Camilleri, J. A. 312, 319, 388
Campbell, D. 92, 395
Campbell, I. 273, 388
Campbell, S. J. 92, 388
Capling, A. 144, 249–51, 388
Carney, S. 260, 388
Carpenter, G. 9–10, 410
Carroll, J. 1, 18–20, 220, 252, 388
Carroll, V. J. 326, 329, 334–5, 388
Carson, R. 350, 388
Carter, J. 287, 388
Cass, B. 278, 282, 286–9, 298, 353, 388
Castles, F. G. 73, 133, 238, 240, 242, 246, 269, 280, 283, 285, 299, 389
Castles, S. 204, 389
Chadwick, P. 329, 334, 338, 389
Chaples, E. 113, 130, 137, 161, 175, 181, 389
Chapman, B. 268–9, 389
Cheeseman, G. 311–12, 389
Chipman, L. 18, 213, 389
Christoff, P. 355, 358, 390
Clark, C. 66, 390
Coaldrake, P. 108, 119, 148, 390
Cockburn, M. 304, 390
Coghill, K. 10, 390
Coke, E. 29
Colebatch, H. K. 73, 390
Coleman, M. 285, 390
Coleman, P. 370, 373–4, 376, 390
Colledge, M. 291, 293, 390

Collins, H. 60–1, 390
Collins, J. 205, 208, 211, 213, 215, 390
Commonwealth Grants Commission 75, 390
Communications Law Centre 338, 391
Connell, R. W. 153, 161, 181, 239, 391
Considine, M. 4–6, 82, 98, 287, 293, 385, 391
Constitutional Centenary Foundation 64, 391
Conway, R. 5, 391
Cook, P. 269, 391
Coolican, A. 265, 396
Coombs, H. C. 91, 201, 283, 391
Cooper, A. F. 313, 401
Cooray, L. J. M. 25, 391
Copas, C. 359, 391
Coper, M. 63–4, 391
Costa, M. 276, 391
Costar, B. 82, 146–8, 391, 423
Cox, E. 296, 391
Craven, G. 63, 391
Crawford, J. 200, 221, 387
Crawford, Joanne 312
Crean, S. 259–60, 391
Crisp, L. F. 107–8, 111, 135, 154, 158, 170, 391
Crommelin, M. 63, 392
Crough, G. 86, 392
Cruise, H. 265, 392
Cullen, P. 291, 392
Cumes, J. W. C. 89, 392
Curtain, R. 272–4, 392
Curthoys, A. 16, 392
Curtice, J. 159, 162–3, 400
Cushing, R. G. 404
Cutler, T. 245, 253, 392, 423

Dabscheck, B. 262, 392
Davidson, A. 6, 392
Davidson, K. 19
Davies, A. 343, 392
Davies, A. F. 73, 90, 153–5, 158–9, 170, 205, 392
Davies, M. 186, 392
Davis, E. 268, 392
Davis, G. 99, 392
Davis, J. 193, 392
Davis, S. R. 153, 392
Dawson, D. 23, 36, 40–1, 45, 51
Day, L. 210, 393

440 *Index*

de Beauvoir, S. 16
de Lepervanche, M. 213, 215, 386, 393
Deakin, A. 61, 393
Deane, W. 23, 28, 33–5, 37, 43–7, 52, 54, 57
Deery, S. 265, 393
D'Emilio, J. 370, 393
Denning, W. 62, 77, 393
Devlin, P. 370, 393
De Vyver, F. 265, 393
Dibb, P. 310–11, 393
Dicey, A. V. 29, 63, 393
Dix, A. 390
Dixon, D. 289, 393
Dixon, G. 220, 270–1, 404
Dixon, O. 25, 32, 36, 39, 40–3, 47, 52, 55, 393
Docker, J. 2, 394
Dodd, T. 107, 394
Donn, C. 262, 394
Douglas, R. 155, 161, 394
Dow, G. 240–1, 252, 394
Downs, A. 170, 394
Drakakis-Smith, D. 197, 394
Drysdale, P. 314, 394
Dufty, N. 263, 276, 391, 394
Dugdale, J. 209, 394
Duncan, G. 12, 394
Dunn, I. 357, 394
Dunstan. P. 376
Dutton, G. 371, 394
Dworkin, A. 379, 394

Eaton, M. 268, 394
Eckersley, R. 349, 359, 394, 400
Edgar, P. 324, 344, 394
Ehrlich, A. H. 350, 394
Ehrlich, P. H. 350, 394
Ellem, B. 264, 394
Elliot, G. 286, 395
Ellis, U. 147, 395
Emmison, M. 159, 395
Emy, H. V. 8, 12–13, 22, 98, 107, 111, 114, 120–3, 138, 142–4, 153–4, 395
Encel, S. 92, 153–4, 159, 392, 395
Epstein, L. D. 135, 395
Esaiasson, P. 174, 395
Esping-Anderson, G. 236, 278, 395
Evans, B. 272, 395
Evans, Gareth 33, 272, 302–3, 305–6, 311–12, 380, 395

Evans, Geoff 324, 395
Evans, H. 117–18, 395
Evans, Ralph 247, 395
Evans, Ray 415
Evatt Research Centre 82, 395
Ewer, P. 140, 239–40, 242–4, 246, 249, 251–2, 256, 263–4, 265, 270–1, 276, 395, 396

Fairfax, J. 327, 396
Faust, B. 379, 396
Federation of Ethnic Communities Councils of Australia 210, 213
Fischer, T. 12, 253, 287, 290, 400
Fisher, C. 265, 396
Fisher, H. A. L. 61, 396
Fisk, E. K. 190, 396
FitzGerald, S. 210, 384
Fletcher, C. 69, 396
Forrest, M. 108, 116, 118, 414
Foster, C. 295, 396
Foster, L. 213, 396
Foster, R.A. 317
Foucault, M. 372, 396
Fraser, M. 1, 20
Freebairn, J. 143, 403
Freeden, M. 236, 396
Freedman, E. B. 370, 392
Free University, Sydney, 154–5, 396
Frenkel, S. 265–6, 272, 275, 396
Freudenberg, G. 284, 396
Friedan, B. 16
Friedman, M. 8, 396
Fry, G. 300, 305, 312, 396
Fullagar W. 41–42
Fung, E. S. K. 319, 396

Gageler, S. 31, 397
Galbally, F. 209
Galligan, B. 33, 68, 70, 84, 91, 109, 111, 140, 144, 219, 249–51, 388, 397
Gallop, G. 148, 397
Gardner, M. 101, 260, 268, 397, 422
Garnaut, R. xi, 249, 318–20, 384, 397
Garran R. R. 74, 397
Gaudron, M. 36–7, 45–6, 49–50, 52–7
Gibbin, R. 1
Gibson, D. 287, 397
Gilding, M. 370–1, 397
Gilliard, P. 342, 397
Gilpin, A. 350, 397

Gilson, M. 204, 397
Glazer, N. 214, 397
Glezer, G. 248, 264, 398
Goot, M. 153, 155, 169, 194, 211, 216, 304, 319, 391, 398
Gordon, L. 278, 398
Gough, R. 272, 392
Gow, D. 408
Graetz, B. 159, 162, 170–1, 398
Graham, B. D. 147, 398
Granberg, D. 174, 395
Grant, B. 302, 305, 395
Grattan, M. 94, 101–2, 139, 335, 386, 399, 400
Graycar, A. 284–6, 398
Green, F. 108, 398
Green, R. 267, 275, 357, 398
Greer, G. 16
Gregory, R. 277
Greiner, N. 83
Griffin, G. 264, 398
Grinlinton, D. 354, 398
Groenewegen, P. 66, 78, 80, 86, 398
Grossman, P. J. 67, 399
Gruen, F. 94, 101–2, 139, 268–9, 389, 399
Guica, V. 264, 398
Gusfield, J. 15, 398

Hagan, J. 262–3, 399
Hall, P. A. 227–9, 262, 264, 399
Hall, Sandra 327, 399
Hall, Stuart 1, 399
Halligan, J. 73, 76, 82, 89, 92, 101, 388, 399, 413
Hamburger, P. 99, 399
Hampson, I. 140, 395, 399
Hancock, W. K. 73, 90, 399
Harcourt, A. 283, 400
Hardcastle, L. 209, 212, 412
Hardin, G. 349, 399
Harding, A. 269
Harding, Ronnie 353, 399
Harding, Richard 323–4
Harper, R. J. A. 283, 400
Harris, M. 371, 394
Harris, S. 216, 306, 321, 399
Hart, H. L. A. 370, 399
Hartnett, B. 252–3, 399
Haslam, C. 245, 423
Hasluck, P. 92, 97, 101, 400

Haupt, R. 142, 400
Haward, M. 130, 150, 400
Hawke, R. J. L. 81, 100, 305, 326, 357, 393, 400
Hawker, G. 95, 108, 400
Hay, P. R. 150, 359, 400
Hay, S. P. 348
Hayden, W. 283, 375, 400
Hayek, F. von 8, 400
Hayes, R. 254, 400
Head, B. 11, 270, 400
Headey, B. 404
Heads of Government Meeting 87, 400
Healey, M. 121, 400
Heath, A. 159, 162–3, 400
Heberle, R. 15, 400
Henderson, R. 283, 292, 400
Hewson, J. 12, 144, 253, 287, 290, 292, 297, 302, 400
Hiatt, L. 191, 401
Higgins, W. 243, 245–6, 251–2, 396, 401
Higgott, R. 313, 401
Hill, D. 210, 386
Hill, R. 104, 401
Hince, K. 265, 401
Hirschman, A. 5, 401
Hirst, J. 108, 401
Hirst, P. 255, 401
Hocking, D. 143, 403
Hollander, R. 69, 401
Holling, L. 9
Hollingworth, P. 283, 401
Holmes, J. 112–13, 136, 401
Hood, C. 100, 340, 401
Hopper, J. 137, 418
Horne, D. 15, 19, 220, 401
Horner, D. 310, 401
Howard, J. 2, 11–12, 144, 272, 402
Howard, W. 259, 402
Howe, B. 293, 295, 404
Hudson, W. J. 307, 405
Hughes, C. A. 148, 154, 155, 157, 159, 402
Hughes, O. E. 8, 12–13, 69, 98, 107, 111, 114, 120, 138, 143–4, 395, 397
Hyde, J. 143, 402

Immigration Reform Group 207, 402
Industrial Commission 249, 402
Inglis, K. S. 324, 344, 402
Institute of Public Affairs 7

442 Index

Irving, T. 161, 239, 391
Isaacs, I. 31–2, 48

Jackson, G. 224
Jaensch, D. 12, 107, 109, 111–12, 132, 135–6, 138–40, 142, 147, 173, 402
Jakubowicz, A. 212, 402
Jarman, A. M. G. 84, 403
Jenkins, D. 305, 403
Johal, S. 423
Johnson, Carol 12, 403
Johnson, Chalmers 245, 403
Johnston, C. 16, 403
Johnston, E. 184, 187–8, 364, 403
Johnston, R. 16, 403
Jones, D. 255, 423
Jones, E. 271, 403
Jones, F. L. 157, 159–61, 168–9, 174, 387, 403
Jones, L. 379, 403
Jones, M. A. 84, 403
Jones, R. 353, 403, 408
Jones, R. G. 171, 174
Jowell, R. 159, 162–3, 400
Jupp, J. 142, 180, 203, 206, 214, 403

Kasper, W. 143, 403
Katzenstein, P. 241–2, 403
Keating, M. 220, 270–2, 404
Keating, P. 86, 102, 231, 293, 363–4, 393, 404
Keeffe, K. 197, 404
Kelley, J. 170–1, 176, 214, 271, 385, 395, 404, 408
Kellow, A. 365, 404
Kelly, D. 271, 404
Kelly, P. xi, 11, 20–1, 80, 142–4, 146, 260, 326, 353, 404
Kelty, B. 1, 266, 273, 404
Kemp, D. 7, 9, 11–12, 149, 153, 155, 157–61, 165, 167, 170–3, 179–80, 286, 404, 422
Kenis, P. 242, 404
Kettle, S. J. 311, 389
Kewley, T. 281, 291, 404
Keynes, J. M. 7, 8, 225
Kitchener, G. 266, 386
Kjellberg, A. 238, 404
Klugman, R. 375
Knibbs, G. H. 281
Knight, J. 215, 307, 405

Knopfelmacher, F. 18, 213, 405
Knopff, R. 70, 397
Kosack, G. 204, 389
Kouzmin, A. 84, 403
Kuhn, R. 259, 405
Kunz, E. F. 204, 405
Kyloh, R. 268, 405

Lacey, M. J. 348, 405
Lambert, G. 360, 405
Lane, R. 83, 405
Lang, J. 108, 405
Langmore, J. 248, 405
Laski, H. J. 70, 405
Latham, J. 41
Layman, L. 73, 111, 148, 397, 405
Leaver, R. 304, 311, 405
Lence, R. M. 71, 405
Leonard, H. 296, 391
Lever-Tracy, C. 215, 405
Lewins, F. 211, 405
Lewis, J. 278, 405
Lewis, P. 269, 405
Liberal Industrial Inquiry 237, 405
Lijphart, A. 132–3, 147, 405
Lindell, G. J. 25–6, 406
Lloyd, C. 78, 94, 138, 140, 150, 256, 265, 270, 395, 406
Loney, J. 107, 406
Loveday, P. 108, 136, 147, 402, 406
Lucy, R. 120, 406
Ludeke, T. 265
Ly, J. 211, 405
Lynch, A. 114, 406

Macdonald, D. 273, 387
Macintyre, C. 175, 177–8, 406
Macintyre, S. 5, 7, 13, 75, 112, 140, 142, 406
Mackay, H. xi–xii, 406
Mackerras, M. 112–13, 406
MacKinnon, C. A. 379, 406
Maddox, G. 61, 111, 130, 132–3, 135, 140, 146, 150, 287, 406
Maher, M. 309, 407
Mahlab, E. 199–200, 407
Malik, J. M. 318, 407
Manne, R. 1, 18–19, 20, 220, 388, 407
Manning, H. 141, 407
Mansell, M. 184–5, 407
Marceau, J. 252, 407

Index 443

Mardiste, D. 84, 397
Markey, R. 265, 407
Marks, G. N. 169, 407
Markus, A. 202, 213, 407
Marsh, I. 108, 407
Marshall, A. J. 350, 407
Marshall, T. H. 202, 278, 407
Marshall, V. 83–4, 412
Martin, A. 108, 406
Martin, J. 203, 205–6, 208, 215, 286, 407
Martin, R. 259, 407
Marx, K. 6, 236
Maskell, C. 81–2, 407
Mason, A. F. 27–8, 34, 37–40, 45, 49, 51, 54
Mathews, J. 255, 273–4, 392, 408
Mathews, R. 141, 387
Matthews, T. 219, 260–1, 266, 307, 310, 318, 408, 413
Mayer, H. 135, 146–7, 153, 323, 344, 347, 408
McAllister, I. 140, 149, 150, 152, 157, 160–2, 167–74, 176, 179, 214, 357, 385, 398, 403, 408, 414
McDonald, P. 268, 409
McClelland, J. 107, 108, 409
McCrann, T. 9
McEachern, D. 140, 243, 409
McGregor, C. 142, 409
McGuinness, P. P. 2, 9, 409
McHugh, M. H. 28, 37, 40, 45, 50, 52
McHutchinson, J. 270, 409
McNaughton, B. 116–18, 409
McQueen, H. 327, 409
McRae, H. 194, 409
Meadows, D. H. 350, 409
Meadows, D. L. 350, 409
Meaney, N. 301, 409
Mediansky, F. A. 321, 409
Melville, L. G. 75, 409
Mercer, D. 353, 354, 366, 398, 409
Metal Trade Unions 244, 410
Millar, T. B. 301, 409
Miller, James 16, 409
Miller, J. D. B. 153, 409
Miller, T. 116–18, 127–9, 409
Miller, W. L. 174, 180, 409
Millett, K. 368, 409
Milliken, R. 354, 410
Mills, R. C. 65, 410
Mills, S. 137, 410

Missen, A. 118, 410
Mitchell, M. 290, 410
Mitchell, W. 267, 410
Moon, J. 109, 417
Moore, B. 9–10, 410
Morgan, R. 162–3, 410
Morgan, S. 193, 410
Morgenthau, H. J. 302, 410
Moynihan, D. P. 214, 397
Mughan, A. 108, 385, 408
Murphy, L. 47–9, 51

National Aboriginal Islander Legal Services Secretariat 182
National Food Authority 83, 410
Nelson, H. 68, 83, 107, 410
Nethercote, J. 111, 410
Nettheim, G. 194, 409
Nevile, J. W. 229–30, 410
Nevill, J. 210, 386
Nevitte, N. 1, 410
Nicklin, L. 354, 410
Nicolaou, L. 215, 410

O'Brien, P. 11, 143, 411
O'Donnell, C. 287, 387
O'Keefe, P. 126, 128, 129, 411
O'Heil, R. 143, 403
O'Meagher, B. 6, 411
Olson, M. 133, 411
Organisation for European Co-operation and Development, 365, 411
Osterfeld, D. 67, 411
Ostrom, V. 66, 411
Overacker, L. 155, 158, 411
Ozolins, U. 214, 411

Page, B. 109, 112, 120–4, 411
Painter, M. 93–4, 124, 411, 419
Palbas, T. 205, 411
Palfreeman, A. C. 207, 411
Panitch, L. 248, 411
Papadakis, E. 150, 173–4, 353, 358, 360, 411
Pappas Carter, Evans and Koop 246, 412
Parker, D. 137, 411
Parker, R. 108, 111, 406, 411
Parkin, A. 82, 84, 138, 209, 212, 411, 419
Parsler, R. 161, 412
Partridge, P. H. 67, 412
Pateman, C. 278, 412

444 Index

Patience, A. 11, 400, 412
Patterson, R. 208, 325, 412
Peachment, A. 78, 80, 412
Pearce, D. 125, 412
Pearson, N. 183, 201, 412
Pedersen, M. N. 176, 412
Peetz, D. 139, 266, 272, 275, 412, 417
Perkins, C. 190, 412
Peters, G. 133, 412
Phillips, H. 112, 412
Piesse, E. C. 76, 413
Piore, M. 255, 413
Pilkington, G. 263, 413
Pincus, J. 67, 388
Playford, J. 107, 406
Plowman, D. 265–6, 272, 392, 413
Polanyi, K. 235, 257, 413
Portus, G. V. 65, 70, 413
Power, J. 73, 76, 82, 89, 92, 101, 399, 413
Prest, W. 66, 413
Preston, A. 272, 275, 417
Price, C. A. 203, 413
Purdon, C. 84, 413
Pusey, M. 19, 98–9, 232, 243, 270, 413

Quinlan, M. 215, 405

Radbone, I. 90, 413
Rainbow, S. 353, 413
Rainford, J. 140, 246, 256, 265, 270, 395
Randers, D. L. 350, 409
Raskall, P. 269, 413
Ravenhill, J. 300, 307, 309–10, 312, 318, 408, 413
Rawson, D. 139, 152–4, 158, 161, 170–1, 179, 263, 413
Read. P. 200, 414
Reid, G. S. 78, 80, 94, 107–8, 114, 116, 118, 125, 128–9, 136, 406, 412, 414
Reid, J. B. 97
Renouf, A. P. 101, 414
Resource Assessment Commission 361, 414
Reynolds, P. 147–8, 414
Richards, L. 205, 414
Richardson, J. L. 318, 414
Richmond, K. 147, 414
Ricklefs, M. C. 212, 407
Rimmer, M. 260, 265, 268, 272, 275, 391, 392, 409, 414
Rix, S. 140, 246, 256, 265, 270, 395
Robbins, J. 90, 413

Robin, L. 352, 414
Rodan, P. 111–12, 414
Roddewig, R. J. 352, 414
Roos, D. 255, 423
Rose, R. 172–3, 414
Ross, H. 414
Rowland, D. 210, 393
Rowley, C. D. 187, 414
Rowse, T. 71, 184, 192, 194, 196, 398, 415
Russell, E. A. 222–3, 415
Rydon, J. 108, 137–8, 154, 179, 415
Ryle, G. 172, 415
Ryan, N. 101, 422
Ryan, S. 380

Sabel, C. 255, 413
Salmons, B. 214, 415
Sanders, W. 196
Santamaria, B. A. 18
Sartori, G. 135, 415
Saunders, C. 64, 279, 415
Saunders, P. 277, 279, 415
Sawer, G. 63, 69, 94, 153, 415
Sawer, M. 11, 143, 145, 286, 379, 415–16
Schaffer, B. B. 92, 416
Scheiber, H. 69, 416
Schmidt, M. 242, 416
Schneider, V. 242, 404
Schott, K. 99, 416
Schultz, J. 338, 416
Scott, A. 141, 159, 180, 416
Sestito, R. 213, 416
Shamsullah, A. 148–50, 416
Sharman, C. 68, 72–3, 79, 109, 111, 113, 120, 133, 135–7, 141, 147, 149, 401, 416–7
Shaver, S. 189, 417
Sheridan, T. 262, 264, 417
Short, M. 272, 275, 417
Siedlecky, S. 370, 417
Simms, M. 7, 145, 379, 416, 417
Singleton, G. 139–41, 219, 260–4, 267, 269, 397, 417
Skidelsky, R. 237, 243, 417
Smith, A. 236, 417
Smith, D. 196, 417
Smith, E. 127, 417
Smith, G. 109, 130, 137, 400, 417
Smith, H. 303, 418
Smith, M. 140, 246, 256, 265, 270, 395
Smith, R. 113, 130, 418

Smith, R. F. I. 95, 400
Snape, R. H. 314, 418
Solomon, D. 63, 74, 116, 118, 418
Souter, G. 327, 329, 334, 418
Spann, R. N. 154, 180, 418
Spiers, D. 269, 405
Spurgeon, C. 343, 392
Stanford, J. 76, 418
Starr, G. 7, 79, 142, 144–5, 418
Stephen, L. 29, 418
Stevens, A. 396, 240, 242, 244, 251–2, 263–4, 271, 396
Stevens, B. 101, 422
Stewart, J. 249, 421
Stewart, S. E. 317
Stilwell, F. 14, 249, 260, 268–9, 271, 276, 394, 418
Stockley, D. 213, 396
Stone, D. 72, 143, 418
Storer, D. 206, 213, 215, 418
Street, L. 49
Stubbs, J. 283, 419
Stutchbury, M. 218, 419
Sullivan, B. 370, 373–4, 419
Summers, A. 142, 419
Summers, J. 92, 419
Sutherland, J. 373, 419
Swan, P. 292, 419
Swan, W. 138, 406, 419

Talese, G. 373, 419
Task Force on Management Improvement 88, 104, 419
Tatz, C. 183–4, 419
Taylor, V. 274, 387
Teicher, J. 267–8, 419
Thakur, R. 301, 419
Therborn, G. 242, 419
Thomas, D. 422, 422
Thompson, E. 124, 419
Tickner, R. 199, 419
Tiffen, R. 137, 169, 216, 346, 398, 419
Timlin, J. 352, 420
Titmuss, R. 278, 420
Tiver, P. G. 7, 142–3, 420
Tomlinson, J. 237, 420
Toohey, J. 33, 420
Toohey, J. L. 23, 28, 33, 36–7, 45–6, 52, 54, 57
Trood, R. 304, 305, 420
Troy, P. 78, 406, 420

Tsokhas, K. 144, 420
Tulloch, G. 8, 66–7, 387
Turner, A. 370, 420
Turner, K. 112, 118, 142, 420

Uhr, J. 70, 397
United Tasmania Group 353, 420
Urquart, R. 270, 409

Valder, J. 405
Verevis, C. 272, 275, 414
Vernon, J. 221–3
Viviani, N. 209, 211, 218, 306, 312, 420

Wainwright, J. W. 75, 409
Walker, K. 353, 420
Walsh, C. 66, 69, 397, 421
Walsh, P. 260, 387
Walter, J. 94, 96, 102, 304, 421
Waltz, K. N. 300, 421
Wanna, J. 99, 392, 421
Ward, I. 133, 141, 150, 421
Warhurst, J. 138, 145, 247, 249, 264, 357, 285, 392, 411, 421
Warner, A. 380
Warner, K. O. 65, 99, 421
Waterford, J. 101, 421
Waters, W. J. 282
Watson, I. 355, 421
Watts, R. 4–6, 282, 287, 293, 385, 421
Weakliem, D. 275, 396
Weale, A. 367, 421
Webb, L. C. 153, 421
Webb, L. J. 350, 421
Weeks, J. 117–18, 372, 421
Weller, P. 79–80, 94–5, 99, 101, 107, 118, 128–9, 143, 392, 400, 421–2
West, K. 14, 422
Western, J. 161, 170, 422
Wettenhall, R. 90, 422
Whalan, D. 124–9, 422
Wheelwright, S. 254, 400
White, D. M. 286, 422
White, R. 373, 422
Whiteford, P. 286–7, 389
Whitelock, D. 350, 421
Whitlam, E. G. 13, 76, 94–5, 226, 284, 351–3, 374, 422
Whitton, E. 107, 283, 422
Whitwell, G. 221, 223, 422
Wilenski, P. 14, 93, 95–6, 253, 286, 422

Williams, J. 245, 253–4, 392, 422
Williams, K. 245, 254–5, 392, 422
Willis, R. 268, 423
Wilson, I. B. C. 36
Wilson, P. 205, 371, 423
Wiltshire, K. 78, 423
Wolfenden, Lord 372, 398
Womack, J. 255, 423
Women's Bureau, 289
Woodward, A. E. 199
Woodward, D. 146–8, 391, 419, 423
Wootten, H. 187–8, 423

Wright, C. 265, 423
Wright, J. 352, 423
Wright, K. 265, 423
Wyndham, D. 370, 417

Yeatman, A. 287, 293, 423
Young, E. 197, 423
Yu, P. 196, 423

Zeitlin. J. 255, 401
Zines, L. 26, 74, 423
Zubrzycki, J. 204, 397